Citadel of

Although a novelist and author of several best-selling biographies, including lives of Edward VII and Ian Fleming, John Pearson's fascination is with families.

The first in his series of family biographies, *The Profession of Violence*, is a study of the Krays. It has become an underground classic and was awarded the Edgar Allan Poe special award by the Mystery Writers of America. He followed this with *Façades*, a major biography of a family of eccentric aesthetes, the Sitwells, which A. L. Rowse described as 'an important contribution to the intellectual history of our times'. Then came a study of an aristocratic English family, the Devonshires, *Stags and Serpents*. His most recent book, on the royal house of Windsor, he entitled *The Ultimate Family*.

John Pearson's own family consists of six children and step-children and he lives with his wife, Lynette, in Sussex.

Citadel of the Heart

Winston and the Churchill Dynasty

John Pearson

PAN BOOKS
IN ASSOCIATION WITH MACMILLAN LONDON

First published 1991 by Macmillan London Limited

This revised edition published 1993 by
Pan Books Ltd a division of
Pan Macmillan Publishers Limited
Cavaye Place London SW10 9PG
and Basingstoke
in association with Macmillan London Limited

Associated companies throughout the world

ISBN 0 330 32768 2

2 4 6 8 9 7 5 3 1

A CIP catalogue record for this book is available from
the British Library

Typeset by Pan Macmillan Ltd
Printed and bound in Great Britain by
Cox & Wyman Ltd, Reading, Berkshire

For my wife, Lynette

Contents

List of Illustrations ix
Family Tree xii
Introduction xv

1 Fathers, Sons and Others 1
2 The Ancestor 9
3 Two Brothers 16
4 The Jeromes 21
5 'A Victorian Tragedy' 26
6 Family Troubles 39
7 Death in the Family 50
8 Ambition 63
9 'Faithful but Unfortunate' 76
10 Power and Glory 83
11 Politics 96
12 Love and the Pursuit of Power 105
13 Light Fades from the Picture 119
14 Admiralty 129
15 God Bless the Dardanelles 136
16 Lullenden 154
17 To Russia with Love 167
18 The Chartwell Dream 186
19 'Paradise on Earth' 197
20 The Happy Family 207
21 Wilderness 216
22 Psychic Dynamite 233
23 Distant Friends 243
24 Two Love-Affairs 256
25 The Return of the Prophet 272
26 Family at War 284
27 'Poor Randolph!' 296

28 Master of Alliances   313
29 'The Shadows of Victory'   328
30 Opposition   342
31 'The Secret Battle': 1950–55   362
32 Pausaland   377
33 The Dark Angel Beckons   402
34 Aftermath   425

    Notes   437
    Select Bibliography   461
    Index   465

List of Illustrations

John Winston, 7th Duke of Marlborough, with his second son, Lord Randolph Spencer-Churchill (*Hulton Picture Company*)

George Charles Spencer-Churchill, 8th Duke of Marlborough (*Hulton Picture Company*)

Blenheim Palace (*British Library, London*)

Lord Randolph Churchill (*National Portrait Gallery, London*)

Lady Randolph Churchill (*Hulton Picture Company*)

Consuelo, Duchess of Marlborough, with her sons (*Country Life*)

Captain W. G. (Bay) Middleton (*National Portrait Gallery, London*)

Winston Churchill, Lieutenant with the 4th Hussars (*courtesy of Chas J. Sawyer, National Portrait Gallery, London*)

Winston Churchill, Lieutenant Colonel with the Royal Scots Fusiliers (*Hulton Picture Company*)

Winston Churchill at Durban, after his escape from Boer captivity (*Hulton Picture Company*)

Sunny, 9th Duke of Marlborough (*Hulton Picture Company*)

Winston and Clementine Churchill, 1923 (*Syndication International Ltd*)

Portrait of Randolph Churchill by Sir Philip László (*Courtauld Institute of Art*)

Diana Churchill with her first husband, John Milner Bailey (*Associated Press*)

Clare Sheridan with her children (*courtesy of the Gilbert Adams Collection, National Portrait Gallery, London*)

Sarah Churchill with her first husband, Vic Oliver, and Phyllis Luckett (*Hulton Picture Company*)

Photograph of Clementine Churchill by Cecil Beaton (*courtesy of Sotheby's, London*)

Pamela Churchill with Winston Churchill junior, 1943 (*Hulton Picture Company*)

Averell Harriman, Anthony Eden and John 'Gil' Winant (*Hulton Picture Company*)

Mary Churchill with Captain Christopher Soames on their wedding day (*Hulton Picture Company*)

Sarah Churchill with her second husband, Anthony Beauchamp (*Hulton Picture Company*)

Winston Churchill at Chartwell, surrounded by his family (*Popperfoto*)

Winston Churchill with Aristotle Onassis (*Popperfoto*)

Sarah Churchill in Rome in the 1960s (*Camera Press*)

The young Winston Churchill with his wife, Minnie, and their son, Randolph (*Hulton Picture Company*)

His friendship was a stronghold against which the gates of Hell could not prevail. There was an absolute quality in his loyalty, known only to those safe within its walls . . . This inner citadel of the heart held first and foremost his relations – in their widest sense. His strong family feeling embraced not only his mother and his brother Jack, but cousins, uncles, aunts – the whole Guest tribe and 'Sunny' Duke of Marlborough.

Violet Bonham Carter   *Winston As I Knew Him*

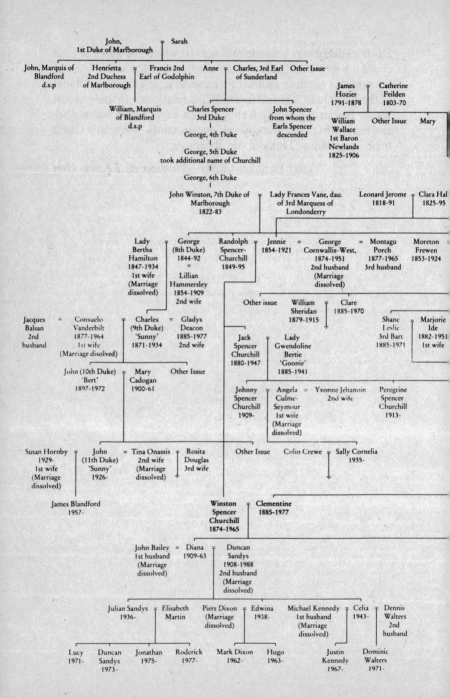

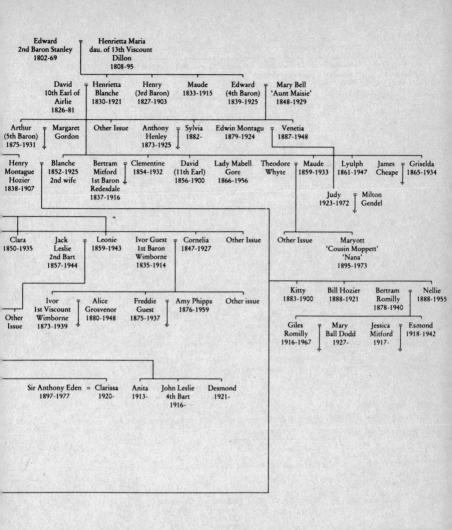

Edward
2nd Baron Stanley
1802-69
= Henrietta Maria
dau. of 13th Viscount
Dillon
1808-95

David
10th Earl of
Airlie
1826-81
= Henrietta
Blanche
1830-1921

Henry
(3rd Baron)
1827-1903

Maude
1833-1915

Edward
(4th Baron)
1839-1925

Mary Bell
'Aunt Maisie'
1848-1929

Arthur
(5th Baron)
1875-1931
= Margaret
Gordon

Other Issue

Anthony
Henley
1873-1925
= Sylvia
1882-

Edwin Montagu
1879-1924
= Venetia
1887-1948

Henry
Montague
Hozier
1838-1907
= Blanche
1852-1925
2nd wife

Bertram
Mitford
1st Baron
Redesdale
1837-1916

Clementine
1854-1932

David
(11th Earl)
1856-1900

Lady Mabell
Gore
1866-1956

Theodore
Whyte
= Maude
1859-1933

Lyulph
1861-1947

James
Cheape
= Griselda
1865-1934

Judy
1923-1972
= Milton
Gendel

Clara
1850-1935

Jack
Leslie
2nd Bart
1857-1944
= Leonie
1859-1943

Ivor Guest
1st Baron
Wimborne
1835-1914
= Cornelia
1847-1927

Other Issue

Other Issue

Maryott
'Cousin Moppett'
'Nana'
1895-1973

Kitty
1883-1900

Bill Hozier
1888-1921

Bertram
Romilly
1878-1940
= Nellie
1888-1955

Ivor
1st Viscount
Wimborne
1873-1939
= Alice
Grosvenor
1880-1948

Freddie
Guest
1875-1937
= Amy Phipps
1876-1959

Other issue

Other
Issue

Giles
Romilly
1916-1967
= Mary
Ball Dodd
1927-

Jessica
Mitford
1917-
= Esmond
1918-1942

Sir Anthony Eden
1897-1977
= Clarissa
1920-

Anita
1913-

John Leslie
4th Bart
1916-

Desmond
1921-

Pamela
Digby
1920-
1st wife
(Marriage
dissolved)
= Randolph
Spencer
Churchill
1911-68

June Osborne
1922-1980
2nd wife
(Marriage
dissolved)

Vic Oliver
1898-1964
1st husband
(Marriage
dissolved)
= Sarah =
1914-82

Antony
Beauchamp
Died 1957
2nd husband

Henry
23rd Baron
Audley
1913-63
3rd husband
= Marigold
1918-21

Christopher
Soames
created Baron
Soames 1978
1920-1987
= Mary
1922-

Winston
Spencer
Churchill
1940-
= 'Minnie'
d'Erlanger

Arabella
1949-
= James
Barton

Nicholas Soames
1948-

Emma
1949-

Jeremy
1952-
= Susanna
Keith

Richard
Hambro
= Charlotte
1954-

Rupert
1959-

Randolph
Spencer
Churchill
1965-

Jennie
1966-

Marina
1967-

Jack
1975-

Jake Barton
1973-

Clementine Sylvia
1976-

Introduction

This book really started many years ago when as a young reporter I first came in contact with Randolph Churchill. This was in 1966, and he helped me with a book I was writing on Ian Fleming, who had been an old antagonist of his. In Fleet Street, Randolph had a reputation as a drunk, a dangerous litigant, a brawler and a sort of establishment buffoon. But when I saw him in his house in Suffolk he was charm itself and very helpful. I recall an afternoon of fascinating talk which ended with my helping him dead-head roses in the garden.

This was two years before he died. He was clearly unhappy and unwell, and I drove back to London puzzled by this sad old monster and by the surrounding mystery of the Churchill family.

Diana, Randolph's eldest sister, had killed herself by then, but from time to time I used to see his once beautiful younger sister, the actress Sarah Churchill, in Chelsea. Sober she was as charming as her brother, but drunk she was a nightmare. And Sarah's situation seemed the more alarming in contrast with her exemplary younger sister, Mary, who appeared to be everything that Sarah was not. Happily married to the politician Christopher Soames, she was responsible and utterly respectable, with a large family, countless friends and the unfeigned affection of all who knew her.

So why this appalling difference in the lives of the offspring of the man so often hailed as the greatest Briton of his generation, if not of the whole century? In 1982 when Sarah, like Randolph before her, died of drink, the question raised itself again. Why should three out of four of Winston Churchill's adult children have effectively destroyed themselves?

There seemed no easy answer. It might have been sheer coincidence, or presumably there could have been a deep genetic flaw within the family. Perhaps some fault resided in the Churchill marriage, or had Churchill's larger-than-life personality contributed to his children's troubles?

It was tempting to see these three doomed Churchill children as victims of their father's 'genius'. There are various romantic theories which regard 'genius' as the final flowering of a family line, fatal to all who follow. Or perhaps it was something simpler. 'Great men are almost always bad men,' said the great Lord Acton, who also held well-known views about the corrupting nature of power. In his day, Churchill had been extremely powerful, and possibly this had caused the trouble. It was hard to know the truth, and the only answer to the problem lay within the Churchill family itself.

This was to be the starting-point from which I wrote this book. But, as I soon discovered, any attempt to understand the relationship between Churchill and his children had wider implications. There was the whole background of the family to be considered. There was the story of the Churchill marriage. There were the lives of the children and their friends and relations. And at the centre of it all, gigantic key to the whole immense conundrum, stood Winston Churchill. It was a series of extraordinary events within his family which helped to make him what he was. And he in turn totally transformed the lives of all around him.

In describing how this happened, I have tried to write a rather different book from other works on Winston Churchill. And, while attempting to avoid the pitfalls of hagiography and psychobiography, I have done my best to explain something of the nature of this clever, driven, powerful, courageous, infinitely baffling Englishman.

To do so I have drawn upon the immense wealth of published material on Winston Churchill, whose stature has been matched by the vastness of the literature about him. Foremost, however, is the eight-volume official biography, started by Randolph, and completed by Dr Martin Gilbert. Equally valuable has been the admirable series of companion volumes of documents and letters covering Churchill's life and political career up to the Second World War. I am most grateful to the trustees of the Churchill collections at Churchill College, Cambridge, for the opportunity to consult various additional documents.

I would also like to thank the following for their information and advice: Mr Michael Alexander, Mrs Nuala Allason, Mr Julian

Amery, Lady Avon, Mrs Natalie Barclay, Mr Andrew Bareau, Lady Baring, Mrs David Birkin, Mrs Virginia Barrington, Mr Alan Brien, Mrs Pauline Bretherton, Lord Charles Spencer Churchill, Mr John S. Churchill, Mr and Mrs Winston Churchill, Mr Peter Coats, Mrs Angela Culme-Seymour, Sir William Deakin, Mr Hugo Dixon, Mr Piers Dixon, Lady Mary Dunn, Mr Idris Evans, Mrs Farelly, Mrs Flor, Mr Michael Foot, Mr Alastair Forbes, Mr Roy Foster, Sir Nigel Fisher, Mrs Elizabeth Furze, Lady Gladwyn, Dr Martin Gilbert, Mr Francis Goodman, Mrs Susan Gough, Mrs Kay Halle, Miss Grace Hamblin, Mrs Pamela Harriman, Mr Tom Hartman, Miss Joan Haslip, Mrs Mary Huizinga, Mr David Irving, Mrs Edwina Kaplan, Lord Lambton, Lord Longford, Mrs Arabella Macleod, The Duke and Duchess of Marlborough, Laura Duchess of Marlborough, Mr Paul Medlicott, Mr Anthony Montague Browne, Lady Mosley, Mrs Maggie Parker, Mrs Tanis Phillips, Miss Ellen Pollock, General and Mrs Kenneth Perkins, Mr Patrick Proktor, Mrs Wendy Reeves, Miss Emma Soames, Dr John Seale, Mrs Graham Sutherland, Lady Carolyn Townshend, Mr Michael Tree, Mr Hugo Vickers, Mr Ralph Vickers, Mr Alan Watkins, Lady Christine West, Mr Peter Willes.

In addition I must thank my editors, Alice Mayhew, Susanna Wadeson and Hazel Orme, for their patience and unfailing competence. My friend and agent, Ed Victor, as usual made the whole book possible. Ann Hoffman, Jacqueline Williams, and Joyce Quarrie all gave invaluable help with research, as did Mathew Frankland with the illustrations and Air France with transport. Edda Tasiemka of the remarkable Hans Tasiemka Archive was a tower of information and support and Grace Hartley was, as ever, the perfect secretary. My debt to my friend, Peter Evans is greater than he probably realises, and only my family will know how much I have depended yet again on the calming presence of Ted Green. Finally I must thank my wife, whose patience and intelligence played so great a part in the writing of this book and who did not fail me.

1

Fathers, Sons and Others

May 28, 1932 was a red-letter day in the private life of Winston Churchill – it was the day his son Randolph came of age. And, since nothing was too good for his golden son and heir, the great man had made elaborate preparations, which he could ill afford, to place proper emphasis upon this important rite of passage.

Churchill was particularly proud of his handsome son's appearance, and the birthday portrait he had already commissioned from the most accomplished – and expensive – royal portrait-painter of the day, Sir Philip László, bears melancholy witness to the brief beauty of Churchill's dauphin. The profile is flawless, the brow regal, and the gaze from the bright blue eyes remarkably assured. László specialised in painting princes, and this is the portrait of a modern prince taking his inheritance for granted.

But the real celebration Churchill was planning in Randolph's honour consisted of an elaborate – and unusual – dinner-party to be held two weeks after Randolph's actual birthday at Claridge's Hotel, London's most famous home-away-from-home for royalty and visiting celebrities. In Churchill's eyes young Randolph was no ordinary twenty-one-year-old, but heir to a great tradition, of whom still greater things might be expected; and to express this fervent hope Churchill himself devised the evening's theme.

With over seventy invitations sent out, it was to be an all-male evening; and apart from a few close friends like Robert Boothby, Sir Oswald Mosley (soon busily leading the British Union of Fascists) and Churchill's own scientific guru, Professor Lindemann, the guests were to consist of great men and their sons – Max Lord Beaverbrook with 'Little Max' Aitken, Lord Rothermere with the urbane Esmond Harmsworth, Lord Camrose with Seymour Berry, Lord Hailsham with Quintin Hogg, and Lord Reading with young Lord Erleigh.

(One noted absentee was the former and future Conservative

Prime Minister, Stanley Baldwin, who had been invited with
his left-wing son, Oliver. Relations between Churchill and the
elder Baldwin had become strained since Baldwin had joined
the Labour Prime Minister, Ramsay MacDonald, in a 'national
government' the year before, leaving Churchill in the political
wilderness. The Baldwins had declined the invitation.)

The Churchills, being Churchills, made the most of the advance
publicity – which the presence of three famous press-lords and
their sons in no way diminished – and Randolph, acting like
the brashest sort of self-promoter, personally telephoned the
'Londoner's Diary' of Lord Beaverbrook's *Evening Standard* with
advance details of his birthday.

The 'Diary' at the time was edited by the dissolute but
well-connected former spy and flunkey of the rich, Sir Robert
Bruce Lockhart. Having composed an appropriately servile piece
about the party, based on Randolph's information, good Sir
Robert then pondered the event in his private journal that
evening: 'What an amazing thing privilege and position still are
in England. Here is a boy who, born in a less privileged circle,
would have had to work hard and make his own way. As it is,
he is lazy, lascivious, impudent, and beyond a certain rollicking
bumptiousness, untalented, and everything is open to him.'

In fact the tragedy – or farce, depending on one's point of
view – of Randolph Churchill's life was that everything was
not open to him. And it is interesting to note that, of all the
sons of that 'privileged circle' who sat down to roast duck and
champagne at Claridge's on that evening of 16 June 1932, one
only, Quintin Hogg – lawyer, Tory politician and future Lord
Chancellor himself – would in any way approach his famous
father's reputation and achievement.

In varying degrees, the rest were doomed to be overshadowed
by paternal 'greatness' – but none would fail so painfully and
variously as Randolph Churchill. An old Calvinist like Bruce
Lockhart might have known that there is celestial rough justice
which exacts a price for the excesses powerful indulgent parents
heap upon their children. But few great men in recent history
could have created such a scourge for themselves as doting
Winston did with his beloved son; and few great men's sons, as
loyal and loving as Randolph would remain towards his father,
could have endured such desperate disappointments from their
situation.

Luckily for all those confident young men and famous fathers sitting so convivially together on that June night in their private room at Claridge's (one day he would buy up all available stocks of 1928 Pol Roger champagne in London), all this lay hidden in the future. Reassured by the general bonhomie and a generous supply of Churchill's favourite beverage, no one seemed particularly concerned that they might possibly be tempting fate.

Churchill himself, always at his best in congenial male company, was as sparkling as his favourite drink as he enlarged upon the evening's theme – 'passing on the lamp' from one generation to the next, with the privileged, the powerful, the rich helping their sons achieve the greatness of their own position. Political success was Randolph's goal in life and, referring to his precious son's prospects as a politician, Churchill spoke proudly of his verbal fluency, comparing it, in vintage Churchill style, with a machine-gun.

'Gentlemen, let us only hope that he accumulates a large dump of ammunition, and – er – that he learns to hit the target.' (Laughter and applause.)

Churchill's theme was also expounded by an Etonian contemporary of Randolph's, the 2nd Lord Birkenhead (who was there alone, his father, the 1st Lord Birkenhead, former Lord Chancellor and Randolph's godfather and great exemplar, having died of drink some two years earlier). The young lord then proposed a toast to Randolph's health and to his 'rise to fame'.

In its way this rise had already been spectacular. Randolph seemed established as journalist, social figure and celebrity: he had written for Lord Beaverbrook, lectured across America and could not wait to enter Parliament.

His 'rollicking bumptiousness' held carefully in check, Randolph replied with unaccustomed but becoming modesty – yet, like most of the guests gathered in his honour, he nevertheless took it for granted that his aim in life was automatically directed to the great pursuit of power and political success. Referring to the evening many years later, he ruefully admitted: '. . . had anyone told me I wouldn't soon be in the House of Commons by the time I was twenty-one or soon afterwards, I would have thought them absolutely too ridiculous for words.' Pitt the Younger held office at twenty-three and was Prime Minister at twenty-five, 'and I saw no reason why I shouldn't do the same.'

Self-confidence of such extraordinary dimensions can only have had its origins in one place – Churchill himself. He had been grooming and preparing Randolph for politics from childhood, like a thoroughbred for the Derby. 'Politics is like prostitution and piano-playing,' he once remarked. 'The earlier you start the better.'

Throughout his adult life Churchill himself had been obsessed with the pursuit and exercise of political power, and the thought of this power magically passing from certain fathers to their sons was an idea which touched on one of the profoundest – and in many ways the most mysterious – elements within his extremely complex nature.

If ghosts could dine, the place of honour at the long oval table at Claridge's that night would have been set aside for a small dynamic man with prominent blue eyes and a very large moustache – Churchill's own father, Lord Randolph Churchill, after whom he named his son, and whose life and turbulent career could still produce extraordinary echoes in his own.

Lord Randolph's life was one of the great cautionary tales of Victorian politics. After a charmed ascent to the Chancellorship of the Exchequer by the age of thirty-six, the great orator, as arrogantly power-mad as only the son of a Victorian duke could be, had resigned from Lord Salisbury's government in 1886 in an ill-judged bid for the succession. He died, embittered and insane, some nine years later at the age of forty-five.

It was a fearful parable, pointing up such truisms as the hollowness of ambition, the lack of gratitude in politics, and the misery of failure – quite enough, one might have thought, to scare off any son from politics for ever. Yet Winston had inherited his father's grand obsession.

There were also some worrying coincidences in their joint careers. By that evening Churchill had recently occupied in succession the same two offices of state – Secretary of State for the Colonies and Chancellorship of the Exchequer – which his father held before his fall; and by the night of the party Churchill, too, was at the start of the most prolonged crisis of his life, which would keep him firmly out of office until war began in 1939.

To most of his fellow-politicians he seemed politically played out. (One of his favourite guests that night, his friend Lord Beaverbrook, would soon describe him as 'a busted flush'.) And, with an uncomfortable repetition of Lord Randolph's situation on leaving the Exchequer, Churchill was left out of power (relatively) hard up, and at odds with the Conservative hierarchy. He was still feared, still potent in debate, but he was also haunted by the possibility that some unseen destiny had trapped him in the very pattern that had destroyed his father.

Although a firm agnostic to the day he died, Churchill had long believed in destiny. This belief gave purpose to his existence, had saved him from death (so he claimed) in countless times of danger, and had kept his unrelenting ego high above the dross of hopeless doomed humanity. There were rare moments when he felt his destiny as an actual presence – 'over me beat unseen wings' was how he would describe the all-important stroke of luck that kept him out of Stanley Baldwin's government three years later.

Churchill's sense of personal destiny encompassed all the members of his family, dead as well as living, and linked him strongly with his father and his son. Asquith's daughter, Lady Violet Bonham Carter, who knew him well, and who had been in love with him many years before, wrote resignedly of his obsession with his family, and also how its members 'held pride of place within the citadel of his heart', to the exclusion of all others.

For his closest family his sense of destiny was a fact of life, and created problems to be coped with as best they could. This applied particularly to stylish Clementine, who at forty-seven still managed to appear considerably more than ten years younger than her bald and portly husband.

It is unlikely she was deeply hurt at missing out on her son's twenty-first-birthday dinner. Down-to-earth by nature, she must have felt the evening's theme a touch absurd – and probably a little vulgar. She would also almost certainly have agreed with most of what Bruce Lockhart wrote about Randolph in his diary; but her disapproval had never had much effect upon her husband's princeling.

The covert understanding between her husband and her son was one of many oddities within a most unusual marriage, and she was forced to build a personal survival route against her husband's dominating presence. Since she had married Churchill twenty-four years earlier she had frequently had to sacrifice herself upon the altar of his greatness. She had loved him, mothered him (with the children firmly taking second place), shared in his triumphs and seen him through his bouts of deep depression and his aggressive rage when thwarted.

She had accepted his belief that destiny had marked him out for greatness; and against her own somewhat puritanical nature had endured his compulsive taste for extravagance and luxury – armies of servants, silk underwear, cigars, extremely good champagne and the company of the very rich. She had learned to live with his elephantine ego, tolerate his more outlandish friends, accept his limitless capacity for work and understand his passionate desire for power. If Clementine became neurotic, and felt the need for prolonged periods apart from him, it was not surprising.

More seriously at risk were those two elder daughters, twenty-two-year-old Diana and her seventeen-year-old sister Sarah, who, as females, were also excluded from their brother's party, and from the sacred bond between son and father. (The baby of the family, nine-year-old Mary, safely home in bed, was to be protected by her youth from many of the influences which were to dislocate the lives of her siblings in the years ahead.)

All the Churchill girls were pretty, with the auburn hair and blue eyes of their mother. But Diana had inherited nothing of her father's toughness. She was nervous and petite – 'like a fairy', Sarah said – and her extreme self-consciousness made her particularly vulnerable amid the powerful vibrations emanating from within her family.

Sarah was altogether tougher than her sister, with a touch of glamour which her sister lacked. She was charming, extrovert and, like her father and her brother, tended to be intensely obstinate once she had her mind made up – hence her family nickname, 'Mule'. Outwardly this gave her all the signs of a born survivor, but she shared in Randolph's self-destructive streak; she, too, would finally fall victim to whatever force it was that drove their father forward, leaving such havoc in his wake.

Some of the extended family appeared immune to this. Winston's younger brother, Jack, was present at the party, together with his eldest son, Randolph's cousin Johnny. A tall good-looking man with a moustache, Jack was a City stockbroker; kind, unintellectual, easy-going, he worshipped his elder brother for qualities he notably lacked himself. Like his son Johnny, whose chief interests lay in acrobatics, pretty girls and fresco-painting, Jack was essentially a private person. Whatever demons brother Winston had inherited had passed him by entirely, leaving him immune to the magnetic pull of politics.

There was another guest at Claridge's that night who once enjoyed an elder-brother role to Winston Churchill. He was a small man with a thin moustache, a drooping eye, and the mark of worldly disappointment on his sallow face. Churchill treated him with notable respect, placing him directly opposite him at table. This was his noble cousin, Charles Richard John Spencer Churchill, 'Sunny' to his intimates, and 9th Duke of Marlborough to the world at large. Churchill revered him as the head of his all-important family. He also loved him, warts and all, and would describe him as 'my oldest, dearest friend'. Both had inherited their share of the depressive Churchill temperament, and both, in their early years, had shared a series of catastrophes and scandals that shook the family. But all those influences and far-off family disasters which played their part in shaping Churchill's destiny had acted differently on Cousin Sunny. Churchill had emerged strengthened for the pursuit of power and inspired for a life of action, but Sunny Marlborough had been left profoundly scarred. He was introverted, bitter, and suspicious of anyone outside the family. Winston he loved, but he was not the sort of man to warm to Randolph.

With the speeches and the port and the after-dinner conversation, midnight struck before Randolph's birthday-party ended; and as father and son stood in the foyer of that grand hotel, bidding their guests good night, they could congratulate themselves upon a most successful evening.

Neither could have possibly suspected that nothing would turn out as the party had suggested – and that the complex tale of Churchill's life was not drawing to its close. Far from 'handing on the lamp' to Randolph, his years of glory lay ahead of him, while Randolph's were already over. For that destiny which Churchill believed in was mysterious. It would bring him fame beyond the dreams of immortality, but it would also bring him secret anguish and destroy the lives of several who were closest to him. Contrary to his dearest wishes, it would leave him no successors.

Behind this monolithic figure lies a hidden story. It is a stranger story than the legends and the history-books admit – and it ends, as it begins, within that 'citadel' of Churchill's heart, his family.

2
The Ancestor

The dominating presence of the dynasty that meant so much to Churchill stands today surveying his possessions from a grandiose stone pillar set in the Oxford countryside, close to the palace named after his most famous victory. Cast in lead, with eagles at his feet, and attired like a conquering Roman emperor, John Churchill, first and greatest of the Dukes of Marlborough, continues to proclaim his triumphs over the armies of the French. So does the palace which he built, and which was paid for – in part – by a grateful nation after his victory near the village of Blindheim in Austria in 1704. He called the palace Blenheim, and it was here that, more by luck than by judgement, Churchill himself was born on 30 November 1874.

One cannot over-emphasise the influence which the Duke and his extraordinary palace had on Winston Churchill. Blenheim today is still immensely, almost absurdly grand – with a stone-paved courtyard big enough to hold a regiment, state apartments built for the exclusive purpose of receiving royalty, four elaborate stone towers, and a great external staircase leading to a pillared entrance-hall which rather overwhelms than welcomes any visitor. It is like a mirage which has floated from the high Italianate baroque, and which seems curiously at odds with the gentle landscape where it landed, seven miles north-west of Oxford.

It is also quite unlike any other English stately home. From the moment it was built it has remained an uncomfortably ill-omened house, hated or admired but rarely loved, the scene of much noble gloom and melancholy.

The splendours and miseries have largely stemmed from its uniqueness. Almost without exception, great English houses traditionally reflect the settled wealth and gradually accumulated power of their owners. Not so Blenheim, which was thrown up in eight ruinously expensive, frantic years. Its principal architect, John Vanbrugh (who also came to hate it), originally found fame in the theatre, and he made Blenheim first and foremost a theatrical triumph set in stone – or, as Sacheverell Sitwell put it less politely, 'a private monument that is a Roman triumph and a public pantomime'. Its hero was, and is, John Churchill, Duke of Marlborough.

Just as Blenheim is unique among ducal houses, so John Churchill stands unique among his peers. Like Wellington, he is that rarity, a self-made English duke – and unlike even Wellington he reached the apex of the aristocracy without an inherited title to begin with. Late in life, and against extraordinary odds, he made himself the greatest soldier of his age.

The Churchills had been undistinguished Dorset gentry, and the Duke's father was the first to bear the name Sir Winston Churchill. A disappointed Cavalier, who never regained the fortune he lost in the sacred cause of Charles I, he was also an original and an amateur historian, whose life work, entitled *Divi Britannici*, was an impenetrable volume on the kings of England. Macaulay dismissed Sir Winston as 'a poor Cavalier knight, who haunted Whitehall and made himself ridiculous by publishing a dull and affected folio, long forgotten, in praise of monarchy and monarchs'.

Neglected by his king, Sir Winston put his feelings into the family motto he invented in Spanish, *Fiel pero desdichado*, or 'Faithful but unfortunate'. It would prove a shade too apt for his descendants who adopted it; but his son, John Churchill, who became the Duke, was neither. He was a handsome man who used both battlefield and bed to promote his remarkable career in Restoration England. Macaulay says he cuckolded his king – the amiable Charles II – with the royal mistress, Lady Castlemaine, and was sharp enough to extract £5,000 from her for his services. Carefully invested, this was reputedly the start of what became the greatest private fortune in the land.

He fought in Holland and Tangier with some distinction, but more important than this early campaigning was his marriage in 1677 to Sarah Jennings, bosom friend of the Princess Anne who would ascend the throne of England as Queen in 1705. When Anne succeeded to the throne, she appointed her friend's husband to command her forces then fighting on the Continent against the French. This war was the dynastic conflict for

the mastery of Europe known as the War of the Spanish
Succession.

In 1705, John Churchill was fifty-three. He had fought, intrigued, plotted and betrayed ('ratting and re-ratting' as his
descendant Winston called it) to reach the top. He was time-
serving, ruthlessly ambitious and the most mercenary of men.
He was also, by an unexpected twist of fate, a military genius.

He earned his fortune, dukedom and immortality with a stag-
gering succession of victories over the greatest military presence
of his day – the united armies of France, Bavaria and Spain
led by the proudest king on earth, the Sun King, Louis XIV of
France.

The first and most spectacular of all these victories came
rapidly, after John Churchill had marched his men from Holland
to the Danube in a masterly campaign. The armies met thirty
miles from Vienna, and his bloody and unexpected victory saved
that city and the Holy Roman Empire from the French.

It was an extraordinary achievement and was treated accordingly. Honours and gifts were showered upon the victor – the
Dukedom of Marlborough, a princedom of the Holy Roman
Empire, the Order of the Garter, and the former royal estate at
Woodstock in Oxfordshire. A grateful Parliament voted £6,000
to build a palace there to celebrate his victory – and it was then
that Marlborough decided he would name it after the site of his
victory.

For the remainder of the war, while the Duke continued
battering the French – at Ramillies in 1706, Oudenarde in
1708 and Malplaquet in 1709 – Duchess Sarah battled on in
Oxfordshire with an army of her own: the horde of workmen
under Vanbrugh who were rapidly creating her husband's greatest
monument, the strange and all-consuming Blenheim Palace.

In the end Marlborough was defeated – not by the French
in battle, but by his Tory enemies at home, who played upon
the fact that Anne was tiring of the domination of her old
favourite, Duchess Sarah, and that the populace at large was
tiring of the war. The Peace of Utrecht, signed in defiance of
the Duke, returned to France almost everything that he had won
in battle.

At the end of 1711 his enemies publicly accused him of
illicitly receiving large sums of money from army contractors;
and, although he could show that this had been an accepted

perquisite from which he had actually financed his secret service on the Continent, this did not prevent his dismissal from all public offices, and gave credence to Macaulay's verdict on the Duke; he called him one 'who in the bloom of youth loved lucre more than wine and women, and at the height of greatness loved lucre more than power or fame'.

Instead of the triumph he expected, Marlborough's final years were passed in disgrace, and he 'lingered on in surly decrepitude'. His palace, started at his greatest moment of success, and to begin with paid for by the Crown, was finished while Duchess Sarah anxiously watched her husband's fortune being poured into its completion. Before it was completed she, too, had come to hate it. She called it 'that wild, unmerciful house'.

The pundits of ordered eighteenth-century taste unanimously labelled Blenheim a monstrosity. Pope would compare it with a stone quarry, and Horace Walpole found it so overloaded with decoration and crammed with the old Duke's trophies that he remarked 'it looks like the palace of an auctioneer who has been chosen King of Poland'. Even its architect, who had had endless arguments with the Marlboroughs about the house, casually remarked that he had always 'looked upon it much more as an intended monument to the Queen's glory, than a private habitation for the Duke of Marlborough'.

The Duke profoundly disagreed. Ignoring his critics and his enemies, the proud old gentleman lived obstinately on at Blenheim into his dotage until his death in 1722. He became more avaricious with the years, and was understandably embittered and given to long bouts of melancholy; but Blenheim was, his Duchess said, 'His greatest weakness'. He spent on it lavishly and loved it jealously, both as his 'private habitation' and as a demonstration to the world of all he had achieved.

Blenheim was the Duke's, and his alone, hung with vast Brussels tapestries depicting in detail all his greatest battles, adorned with the insignia of his countless titles, and crammed with the riches garnered from his victories. It was a treasure-house of one man's war – an expression, too, of one man's overweening ego.

This has made Blenheim, for all its magnificence, a forbidding place to live in. The old Duke craved not merely transient but immortal glory, which would outlive the obloquy surrounding him; Blenheim, with its dramatic towers, its treasures and its massive walls, would guarantee him this for ever.

Winston Churchill, who was not entirely unlike him and came to be obsessed with him, understood this perfectly, and compared his ancestor's building mania at Blenheim with the pharaohs' construction of the pyramids – both being a search for 'a physical monument which would certainly stand, if only as a ruin, for a thousand years'.

But the pharaohs built the pyramids as tombs. The first Duke of Marlborough intended Blenheim as the birthplace for a dynasty which would bear his titles through the centuries ahead. His descendants would perpetually renew his wealth, his honours and his grand position in society.

Such was the theory that enabled the decaying Duke to forget the politicians who had attempted to destroy him, and to spend his final years within this echoing great house in the assurance that his fame would long outlast them all – as indeed it has. But despite the honours and the wealth there was something debilitating in the way the old man also thrust his own remorseless ego on to his descendants.

Shortly before attending Randolph Churchill's birthday-party at Claridge's, the hapless Sunny, 9th Duke of Marlborough, had been sitting for the bust one sees today at Blenheim by the sculptor Jacob Epstein. Sunny had shown Epstein round his stately home, and the sculptor had been distinctly puzzled by the Blenheim chapel. Instead of any sign of Christ above the altar, there is a vast memorial in marble by another famous sculptor, Michael Rysbrack, showing the figure of John Churchill.

'What about God?' enquired Epstein.

'Here at Blenheim we worship John, First Duke of Marlborough,' Sunny answered.

As if condemned to the worship of a god whose expectations they could never possibly fulfil, the dukes who succeeded John have been unhappy lesser men. At Blenheim they cohabited with a greatness they never earned and never matched, and somehow the gloom of the old Duke's final years lingered on around them. Of all the members of the family who were infected by the fatal touch of Blenheim, only Winston Churchill truly overcame it, and rose to the challenge of his overwhelming ancestor.

*

The Churchill depression – 'Black Dog' as Winston called it when it started to affect him – is one of the recurrent mysteries of the family. Churchill himself was well aware of its dangers all his life.

John was himself the victim of a markedly depressive temperament. As well as the gloom that assailed his later years, he also suffered from attacks of migraine both before and after all his battles, and it is said that at least five subsequent dukes suffered from melancholia.

It is tempting to believe that the troubles of the Churchills were passed on genetically as a hidden part of John Churchill's legacy, but this is hard to prove. In the first place the Marlborough Churchills failed to descend in a direct male line from the first Duke. His son died in infancy, and it was only thanks to a special Act of Parliament that the dukedom travelled to his eldest daughter, Henrietta, on her father's death in 1722. Henrietta's only son also predeceased her, so that on her death the dukedom then passed, somewhat shakily, to the son of Henrietta's second sister, Anne, who had married Charles Spencer, Earl of Sunderland. It was this son – called Charles Spencer like his father – who became 3rd Duke of Marlborough, and subsequent dukes all bore the name of Spencer until 1817, when the name Churchill was tacked on to it in an effort to revive the memory of great Duke John when Wellington received his dukedom.

The Spencer stock was anything but melancholy. The eighteenth and nineteenth Spencer Earls of Althorp proved to be one of the most ebullient dynasties of the British upper aristocracy, and in our own time it has produced the powerfully assertive Diana, Princess of Wales. But somehow the Marlborough Spencers were infected by the gloom of Blenheim, which suggests that it was the old Duke's palace rather than his genes that caused the trouble.

For more than a century, the dukes who lived there were to prove themselves a resolutely sad and self-destructive lot.

The long-lived 4th Duke reigned at Blenheim more than sixty years from the middle of the eighteenth century. He was a great collector and outwardly had everything to make him happy – title, children, wealth and a supremely honoured position in society – but gradually the curse of Blenheim overwhelmed him. By his fifties he was already something of a hermit, locking himself

away at Blenheim to study astronomy. Soon he was dreading
any outside contact with humanity.

Not long before he died in 1817, the formidable Madame
de Staël, best-known for her famous salon frequented by the
French romantic writers of the period, tried to gain entrance
to the palace. Hearing that he had a visitor, the Duke cried to
his footman: 'Take me away! Take me away!' This was his last
recorded utterance.

After the hermit duke, the title passed to his son George,
one of the greatest spendthrifts of a spendthrift age, who did
his best, through lunatic extravagance, to empty the 1st Duke's
treasure-chest to pay his debts. This was none too easy since most
of the fabled books and gems and paintings were still guarded
by trustees. Even before succeeding to the dukedom George
could gaily lose £30,000 in an afternoon at Doncaster races;
and, although this was one of many debts that he refused to
pay, he remained chronically and wretchedly in debt throughout
his dukedom.

The early nineteenth century was a time when a duke could
get away with almost anything – even hoodwinking the Blenheim
trustees by melting down the solid gold state dinner service
presented to the 1st Duke by the Elector of Bavaria and replacing
it with a cheap pinchbeck replica. But, no matter what he melted
down, the desperate 5th Duke could never hope to pay his debts;
and, according to one visitor to Blenheim in the 1820s, all the
servants in the palace were in fact *bailiffs*.

Bankrupt, and deserted by his wife (who understandably
preferred a flat at Hampton Court to all the splendours of her
husband's house), the 5th Duke of Marlborough, according to the
Annual Register, ended up like his father, passing 'the latter years
of his life . . . in utter retirement at one corner of his magnificent
palace; a melancholy instance of the results of extravagance'.

The unhappy reign of the 5th Duke of Marlborough ended with
his death in 1840; and the seventeen years in which his son, the
6th Duke, filled the great position were not much brighter.
Money remained a chronic problem since the Marlboroughs, for
all the outward splendour of the house, lacked the sort of income
from their mere 15 000 acres to rival the seriously rich Victorian
grandees and Blenheim and the dukedom were expensive to
maintain. No coal was found beneath the Blenheim meadows, no

rich London leases buttressed the future of the line, and none of these dukes netted himself an heiress, either.

Hardly surprisingly, the Marlborough women seem as gloomy as their gloomy spouses. Two of the 6th Duke's duchesses expired in swift succession in the palace; and the third, who long outlived him in her house in London, was not mentioned in his will.

The situation brightened with the appearance on the scene of Winston Churchill's paternal grandfather, John Winston Spencer-Churchill, who succeeded to the title as 7th Duke in 1857. He was very different from his predecessors – a firm-jawed, rather solid character and a dedicated Christian, and neither a spendthrift nor a rake. His biographer has called him 'a full-blown Victorian prig', but at least he was not a victim of the family depression or of the desire to insulate himself at Blenheim from the world outside. Quite the contrary.

In 1843 he had married the equally strong-willed daughter of Lord Londonderry, by whom he swiftly had six daughters and two sons. The new Duchess's uncle had been the famous Lord Castlereagh, who as British Foreign Secretary had dominated European politics in the crucial period after the fall of Napoleon. Afflicted with bouts of melancholy – and rumoured to have been simultaneously blackmailed for homosexuality – Lord Castlereagh had cut his throat in 1822.

The Londonderrys were also close friends of Disraeli and at the centre of Tory high society and politics, having a pronounced streak of political ability themselves.

Thanks to Duchess Frances, Winston Churchill would have considerably more Castlereagh blood flowing in his veins than of his proudly claimed but very distant kinsman, John, 1st Duke of Marlborough. And, thanks to its new ducal family, Blenheim suddenly emerged from its century-long slumbers.

3

Two Brothers

'I cannot be grateful enough to God for all the goodness He has shown me,' John Winston piously remarked at dinner to a visiting Oxford don shortly after succeeding to the dukedom. Looking round him at his well-fed family, his liveried servants and his splendid dining room with its frescoes by Louis Laguerre, the Duke continued: 'My position here is really, of its kind, quite perfect, and if only I keep well I am thoroughly satisfied.'

The ducal satisfaction was forgivable; and for a brief period after his accession it seemed as if the arrival on the scene of this good man with his quiverful of children had finally repulsed whatever furies had been preying on the Marlboroughs for a century and a half.

Britain was at the zenith of the great Victorian stability; there were no death duties to encroach upon the dominant position of the landed interest, and a duke enjoyed the prestige of a prince within society. Supported by Disraeli's friendship, the Duke's political career was also flourishing, and he reached the Cabinet as Lord President of the Council in 1862. Most gratifying of all was the amity of Queen Victoria herself, for whom the Marlboroughs had become 'my dearest, dearest friends'.

Though still no pleasure-dome, Blenheim had become the home of a large and tightly knit Victorian family: George Lord Blandford (born 1844 and always addressed as 'Blandford'), the ducal son and heir, Lord Randolph, his younger brother (born in 1849), and their six adoring sisters, Lady Cornelia, Lady Rosamond, Lady Fanny, Lady Anne, Lady Georgiana and Lady Sarah. Each day they gathered in the chapel for morning and evening prayers, and for a while it seemed that God was listening. Then came the rumblings of disaster as if to tell John Winston that nothing could remain 'quite perfect' even for a duke.

In 1861 his picture-gallery ignited on a truly ducal scale – the whole of John Winston's great collection of Rubenses and Titians went up in smoke before anyone could save them. This was a loss the Duke could bear, he and his wife both having long had doubts about the propriety of many of the pictures, particularly Rubens's large canvas of 'The Rape of Proserpine'. More worrying was the chronic lack of money that pursued the family as the disasters of the 1870s hit the English landed classes.

Falling rents, the effect of the repeal of the Corn Laws in 1846 (which allowed foreign corn to undercut the produce of the Duke's own broad acres) and a succession of appalling harvests in the 1870s all made the situation worse. The Lord Chief Justice, after dining at Blenheim, said he was 'prepared to share almost anything in life, but drew the line at half a snipe for dinner'.

Economy was in the air. The 1st Duke's great white elephant of Blenheim Palace was consuming more than it provided; and the only answer was to strip the beast of its grandiose regalia. Thanks to the precedent of other noblemen hit by the troubles of their time, the Duke was able to do what none of his predecessors had managed – to break the legal trust controlling all the contents of his palace. The saleroom beckoned, and the rape of Blenheim started.

It would continue unabated after he was dead, although John Winston squandered the greatest splendours of the Churchill patrimony – the magnificent Blenheim Library (known as the Sunderland Library, it was one of the finest private collections in the land, but fetched a paltry £28,000 at auction), the fabled Marlborough gems (including the famous Roman sardonyx intaglio portrait of the Emperor Hadrian's lover, Antinous) and a number of the 1st Duke's pictures which had been spared the fire of 1861.

The Duke's faith enabled him to bear these losses with equanimity. 'Lay not up treasures on earth,' the Bible said. But, as with the Prophet Job, John Winston's faith would soon be tested by far worse afflictions, and the bitterest would come from within the bosom of his family. Both his sons were beginning to reveal disturbing aspects to their character – particularly the future duke, Lord Blandford, who seemed to be reverting to the Spencer-Churchill type with a vengeance. Winston Churchill's wicked Uncle George, who became 8th Duke of Marlborough in 1883, and would be remembered as the family's legendary 'Bad

Duke', was, like many villains, a fascinating character. Expelled from Eton at sixteen, he drank, gambled, hunted and womanised with such abandon that even worldly old Disraeli would dismiss him as 'a thorough-going blackguard'.

He was both irreligious and immoral, but since he was immutably heir to the dukedom, and the future of Blenheim rested on his slim unworthy shoulders, there was not a great deal anyone could do about it.

His one redeeming feature was his high intelligence. He was a self-taught scientist whose mouldering laboratory could still be seen at Blenheim in the 1920s, and he seems to have possessed a touch of genius, wiring up the palace for electric light, building his own dynamos and inventing an early form of telephone.

In 1869 he did make one concession to his parents' fears about the future. He agreed to marry, cynically accepting the first young woman they suggested, twenty-year-old Lady Albertha Hamilton, daughter of the Duke of Abercorn. Known to her intimates as 'Goosey', Lady Albertha was not considered over-bright, but she was an uncomplicated cheerful girl with a reputation as a sport and something of a practical joker; so that the old Duke must have felt that she, if anyone, could cope with his unpleasant son. She could not.

After the birth of the necessary son and heir in 1871 (the future 9th Duke, Churchill's cousin 'Sunny', who was christened Charles John Richard Spencer-Churchill), Lord Blandford paid her scant attention, and continued his experiments in adultery and electricity. By a twist of fate the former were to prove of considerable importance to the early years of his nephew Winston.

Because of the Bad Duke's terrible behaviour, his younger brother, Randolph, was guaranteed the role of favoured son from the beginning – and made the most of it. An unhealthy child – he almost died of glandular fever at the age of ten – he was doted on by the Duchess and pampered by his sisters.

He followed his brother more successfully to Eton and then to Oxford, where he enjoyed the social life and considerable privileges of a young aristocrat in the unreformed university; he dressed smartly, drank excessively, and sowed the customary upper-class wild oats. Although still 'delicate', he had a touch of wildness which would reappear at intervals throughout his life.

He drank, broke windows, and pursued the women of the town. 'I don't like ladies at all,' he said. 'I like rough women who dance and sing and drink – the rougher the better.'

Randolph was also known for his biting wit; like his brother he possessed a quick original intelligence and unusual powers of memory. One of his party tricks was to memorise at sight a page of his favourite author, Gibbon, then parrot it verbatim to his friends. Thanks to his memory and powers of concentration, he pulled himself together in the weeks before examinations, taking a respectable degree in history and law – something considered so extraordinary for the son of a duke that great things were predicted for him.

What they were, no one – least of all Lord Randolph – was very sure. It was unheard-of for a duke's son to pursue a commonplace career or earn himself a living. He might have joined the Church or the Army, or gone into politics, but none appealed to him. So, after leaving Oxford, he travelled on the Continent, learned perfect French, entered smart society, got to know the Prince of Wales, and lived at Blenheim with nothing very much to do, an aristocratic second son afflicted by the English malady of primogeniture.

His nerves were bad, his health remained 'uncertain'; and, since he, too, had inherited more than a fair share of the Marlborough melancholy, boredom made him subject to moods of black depression during which he kept apart from everybody, read French novels and chain-smoked Turkish cigarettes 'until his tongue was sore'. He could exhibit charm and wit with those he liked but could also turn to instant upper-class *hauteur* when bored or with those he did not know or disapproved of. Then, in August 1873, at a ball in honour of Nicholas, the son of Tsar Alexander III of Russia, during Cowes Week on the Isle of Wight, this difficult young nobleman met Jennie – or, as she liked'to style herself, 'Jeanette' – Jerome, fell in love and decided to marry her.

Like almost everything Lord Randolph did, this was an impulsive decision. Equally impulsive, Jennie instantly agreed.

Back at Blenheim, the news brought consternation from the family, and outright opposition from the Duke – on whom Lord Randolph was financially dependent.

Not that Lord Randolph allowed this to affect him in the least. Decision made, he stuck to it as he invariably did when he decided anything. It was as if some instinct urged him on towards the ideal partner to correct the inherited deficiencies of his line.

4
The Jeromes

Photographs of Jennie and Lord Randolph at around the time they met reveal a striking contrast between the two young lovers. Lord Randolph, a short slender figure like his brother Blandford, would always be a credit to his jeweller and his tailor, but at twenty-four he was already looking old beyond his years. With thinning hair, a serious moustache, and the 'poppy' Marlborough eyes, as Jennie called them, he had the haggard air of one who lived too much by his nerves – and smoked too many Turkish cigarettes.

Twenty-year-old Miss Jerome could not have been more different. Firm-browed, doe-eyed and ample-figured, she displayed more confidence and sensuality than ladylike refinement; hers was the sort of beauty that owed more to health and energy than to gentle breeding. Her mother, rich Mrs Leonard Jerome, late of Brooklyn, USA, and Paris, France, had taken a small villa on the Isle of Wight for the summer season, and Jennie was staying there with two unmarried sisters – Clara, then aged twenty-two, and Leonie, who was seventeen. Since the girls were presentable and pretty, they had enjoyed considerable success, but the Jeromes were not the sort of people the Marlboroughs would normally consort with. Leonard Jerome, Jennie's father – who at the time was suspiciously absent in New York – was, as the worried Duke discovered, three things no proper gentleman could be: a self-made man, a financier and an American.

'From what I have heard,' John Winston wrote anxiously to his son, 'this Mr J seems to be a sporting, and I should think vulgar kind of man. I hear he drives about six and eight horses in New York (one may take this as a kind of indication of what the man is).'

The Duke also made it clear that 'under any circumstances, an American connection is not one that we would like'. It would be a considerable 'coming down in pride for us to contemplate'. One thing, and one alone, might still permit the Duke to forget his pride – a fortune of such magnitude that even a Duke of Marlborough would welcome the 'connection'. But did this vulgar Mr J possess it?

Lord Randolph, who to his credit thought the subject more or less irrelevant, was not sure; and the Duke made businesslike enquiries which did little to reassure him. It appeared that this mysterious American was not as rich as Lord Randolph had assumed.

True, he had been a millionaire on a number of occasions, but he had also lost vast sums of money. As for the family, they were very ordinary indeed.

But Leonard Jerome was far from ordinary. Born in 1819, one of seven brothers from a farming family in Syracuse, New York, he had worked his way through Princeton, entered a firm of Wall Street brokers, and in the boom years of the 1840s made himself rich enough to spend two years in Italy, from 1851 to 1853, as American consul in Trieste, with his young wife, Clara, and their infant daughter, also christened Clara.

His wife loved Europe, but Jerome was bored and in 1853 brought his family back to their simple red-brick house in Henry Street, Brooklyn, where Jennie was born in 1854. Jerome was determined to make a great fortune – which he did with extraordinary despatch.

He was a handsome man whose nerves, like his physique, seemed made of steel (a quality his daughter inherited). He was a natural gambler, a still more natural self-promoter, and had the successful gambler's flair. This showed itself repeatedly in what he called 'that Wall Street Jungle' of the 1850s as he pitted his wits and money in the roughest financial trade of all – company promotion in the new railways and trusts of the rapidly expanding United States of America.

He needed nerve. In 1855 he lost everything he owned in the crash of the Cleveland and Toledo Railway, but within a year he bounced back. In association with the 'robber baron' Commodore Vanderbilt and the Rothschild representative in New York, August Belmont, he rode the wave of massive speculation that was only briefly interrupted by the Civil War, and became one of the richest speculators on the Street.

It was then that the uniqueness of Leonard Jerome's flamboyant character revealed itself. Unlike most Wall Street millionaires, he was an enjoyer as well as an acquirer, who believed that money should be spent, not saved: before he inevitably came unstuck in 1869 he had disposed of a reputed $10 million with more style and enjoyment than any comparable millionaire on Wall Street.

He was a many-sided hedonist. A talented amateur musician, he had a habit of adopting opera singers as his mistresses. Some were melodically exceptional and they included 'the Swedish nightingale', Jennie Lind (after whom he named his second daughter), and the formidable Adelina Patti. The first home-grown American prima donna, Minnie Hauk, was reputedly his natural child.

Moving from Brooklyn, in 1860 he built himself a mansion on the corner of 26th Street overlooking Madison Square, complete with stables and a private theatre. By now he had made himself a genuine celebrity. He owned an ocean-going yacht, he fished for shark, he drove a four-in-hand, and laid out Jerome Park, New York's first racecourse. In association with the even richer August Belmont he became the Founding Father of the American Turf by establishing the American Jockey Club. He also found the time and money to enjoy a summer house in newly fashionable Newport, Rhode Island, and to acquire a quarter share in the *New York Times*, in which he took an active interest.

In the time left over he managed to maintain a happy marriage by the old American expedient of making sure his strong-willed wife was never short of cash and letting her do exactly as she wanted. Clara Jerome, née Hall, who claimed both genuine Iroquois Indian blood and direct descent from a lieutenant in Washington's army, was clearly a romantic snob who had never quite got over those two years in Italy as Mrs Consul-General in Trieste. Having given birth to a third daughter, Leonie, in 1859, she decided New York society was not for her – or for her daughters – and again embarked for Europe where she spent her happiest, most determined years.

Paris was the city that delighted her, for in Paris rich Americans could find a *douceur de la vie* that did not exist in brash New York, with brand-new boulevards by Baron Haussmann, operas by Offenbach and Meyerbeer, and the most fashionable dresses in the world by Monsieur Worth. But, best of all, Paris offered

Mrs Leonard what she really loved – an Emperor and Empress whose court was ever open to rich foreigners.

By the 1860s Napoleon III (son of the great Napoleon's brother Louis, King of Holland) had established his gimcrack Second Empire, with its rebuilt Palace of the Tuileries and cheerfully absurd revival of the protocol and splendour of the Empire of Napoleon I. 'I have found the Court I want,' murmured Mrs Jerome, hoping that with proper finishing all her daughters might marry into the French aristocracy.

With a true snob's singlemindedness, she made sure that she and her girls were invited not only to Their Majesties' formal receptions at the Tuileries, but also to the more intimate parties of the Empress – the so-called 'Little Mondays' at the Palace of Compiègne. It was here that fashionable Paris watched his Majesty despatch the hunted stag and the 'beautiful Americans' had their chance to make another sort of killing.

Meanwhile, in New York, Leonard Jerome was engaging in a lethal struggle of his own as the boom years of the 1860s ended. By now his luck had turned for good. There was a simultaneous default on Indiana bonds and failure in Georgia stock, while his greatest speculation, in Pacific Mail, was on the point of failing, too. The final crash occurred in the financial panic of the early 1870s.

Jerome was giving a dinner-party in New York when a telegram arrived. He read it in silence; and not until the food was cleared away did he apologise for not speaking of it to his guests. 'But gentlemen . . . the bottom has fallen out of stocks and I am a ruined man. But your dinner is paid for and I did not want to disturb you while you were eating it.'

He would henceforth be most grateful for the $2 million he had signed over to his wife.

By a coincidence which would be of great importance to the future Winston Churchill, the golden years of Napoleon III and his Second Empire were also numbered. The hollowness of all that imperial splendour was revealed on the battlefields of Weisenberg and Metz, when the glittering French army was crushed by the greater one of Bismarck's Prussia. The mob sacked Paris, and the Emperor fled to England, closely followed by the beautiful Jeromes.

During these days when Paris was in flames, the image that persists of Mrs Jerome, before she stepped aboard the final train to London, is of her watching the auction of his Majesty's belongings while the Tuileries were still in flames. Practical as ever, even in disaster, Mrs Jerome purchased part of the Emperor's dinner service, then persuaded somebody to bring it back to her apartment in a wheelbarrow. She brought it to England with her, and was using it on the Isle of Wight when her daughter met Lord Randolph during Cowes Week.

5

'A Victorian Tragedy'

Faced with Lord Randolph's powerful determination to marry fresh-faced Miss Jerome, everyone involved began to weaken.

Mrs Jerome felt the second son of an English duke a pallid substitute for the romantic French aristocrat she had dreamed of having as a son-in-law, but since the France she loved had gone for good she bowed to the force of history. And Leonard Jerome, who as a former racehorse-owner had long had doubts about the over-breeding of the British aristocracy, but who could deny his favourite daughter nothing, also bowed to the inevitable.

Even John Winston recognised the steely nature of his son's unfortunate resolve, and suggested 'putting the idea of marriage to the test of time'. 'If this time next year', he told his son, 'you come and tell me that you are both of the same mind, we will receive Miss Jerome as a daughter, and I need not say, with the affection you could require of a wife.'

A year is a long time when you're in love, and the effete Lord Randolph exhibited a startling degree of ruthlessness to get his way. There was some inelegant but effective haggling with the amiable Mr Jerome on the subject of a dowry for his daughter. As an American, Mr Jerome felt a husband should support his wife. Lord Randolph felt otherwise, and not for the first time – or the last – an English aristocrat proved more than a financial match for a tough New York financier. Jennie was persuaded to put pressure on Papa, and after some huffing and puffing Lord Randolph got the promise of a settlement for his future wife of £50,000.

The groom-to-be also managed to exploit his father's political anxieties. For some time John Winston had been counting on his son Lord Randolph (who as the owner of a courtesy title could enter the House of Commons) to take the local parliamentary seat at Woodstock, which the Marlboroughs liked to think they controlled. With an election in the offing – and a despised Radical showing signs of winning – Lord Randolph pressed his father to accept an earlier date for his marriage. Otherwise, he made it clear, he would refuse to enter Parliament. The Duke was most upset at the thought of forfeiting the Marlborough interest to a Radical, and he agreed. Lord Randolph won the seat by a small majority, and the marriage was allowed to go ahead.

It took place in the British embassy in Paris on 15 April 1874 with all the signs of a somewhat hushed and rushed affair instead of the splendour which an international society wedding of such wealth and standing would normally receive. There was no public ceremony, little mention in the press, and the Duke and Duchess were conspicuously absent.

It was typical of the bride not to have let this faze her in the least – and of her father to have made the best of things. She had a mountainous trousseau – 'twenty-three French-made dresses, seven Paris bonnets, piles of delicately embroidered white underlinen' – and a splendid dinner for the guests the night before the wedding. Unlike the bridegroom's parents, the Prince of Wales's secretary, Francis Knollys, found time to attend – as Lord Randolph's best man and personal representative of His Royal Highness. And Jennie drove to the embassy from the family apartment on the Boulevard Malsherbes in resplendent style – white satin wedding dress trimmed with Alençon lace and several yards of billowing train, white malmaisons at her breast, and a 'simple' veil of tulle that covered her from head to toe. She wore her father's wedding gift, a rope of unadorned but perfect pearls; and if the Marlboroughs sent her anything it was not recorded.

Was she already pregnant? Piety says no, but the evidence suggests she might have been. Why else the rush, the discreet ceremony at the embassy, and the pointed absence of the Marlboroughs – followed by a notably uncomplicated birth at Blenheim seven months later? It would have been in character for both participants not to have allowed mere chaperones or dull convention to impede passion – and it would certainly explain much of what happened later. At the time the premature birth was accounted for by Jennie's falling while out shooting, followed by 'a rather imprudent and rough drive in a pony carriage', which brought on the pains of labour. A small downstairs room at Blenheim was improvised for the confinement, after which the lusty seven-month baby named Winston was consigned to the bosom of a wet-nurse.

Although they clearly disapproved of Jennie, Lord Randolph's family maintained appearances and tried to make the best of things, but they never reconciled themselves to this fast American – nor she to them – and much of their antipathy inevitably rubbed off on her child.

Lord Randolph was intensely proud of Blenheim. 'The finest view in England!' he cried out to Jennie as their carriage, pulled by loyal servants all the way from Woodstock station, brought the honeymooners in sight of the palace. But Jennie never liked it. As good as his word, the honest Duke did his best to demonstrate that 'affection' that his favourite son 'could require of a wife'; not so the others. The Duchess, who would always worship Randolph, could not forgive this brazen daughter-in-law for displacing her in his affections. Her six daughters found Jennie almost everything they were not – pretty, highly talented (she was a fine pianist and spoke excellent French and German) and, thanks to that trousseau, dressed in the height of Paris fashion.

Jennie, in return, found her sisters-in-law, like Blenheim, desperately dull. 'The fact is', she complained later to her mother after a few weeks at Blenheim, 'I *loathe* living here . . . and the Duchess simply hates me for what I am.'

Not that she needed to endure such tedium and disapproval long. The Duke had decently paid Lord Randolph's debts, and given him £1,200 on top of the annual £3,000 he was drawing in interest on Jennie's marriage settlement. He had his seat in Parliament, his friends among the cream of metropolitan society, and now that he was married he was offered by the Duke the lease on a house he owned in Mayfair.

The short life and political career of Lord Randolph Churchill were so spectacular and so awesomely disastrous that one of his biographers has described it as 'the most tragic career in 19th century British politics'. It does possess the elements of a high Victorian gothic horror tale, and it forms a sort of climax to the troubles of a troubled family.

But to begin with the marriage was a happy one. Baby Winston was entrusted to one of the most loved women in his life – his widowed nanny, forty-one-year-old Mrs Everest. Describing his parents at this period, he would later write that 'with very little money on either side . . . they could only live in the smallest way possible to people in London society'. But this did nothing to prevent this 'poor but honest' pair from making a considerable splash in fast fashionable society – particularly that part of it that had as its corpulent and bearded centre Lord Randolph's friend, His Royal Highness Albert Edward, Prince of Wales.

With her quick wit and cosmopolitan good looks, Jennie was very much the sort of fashionable young matron to appeal to the priapic Prince, but just how far their friendship went one will never know. Certainly within a year of marriage there were signs of a cooling-off in Lord Randolph's ardour – and one theory of his behaviour a year later ascribes it to jealous anger at the Prince. Certainly something most unusual must have made his Lordship act with the swift decision of a lunatic early in 1876.

To make Lord Randolph's actions stranger still, the overt cause of what occurred was the honour of that most dishonourable man, his brother Blandford. Between electrical experiments Blandford had been conducting one of his affairs with dark-haired and passionate Lady Aylesford, mother of three young daughters, and the much put-upon wife of Lord 'Sporting Joe' Aylesford, sportsman, gambler and crony of the Prince of Wales.

Sporting Joe had been in India tiger-shooting with the Prince when he got wind of what was happening at home. Gallumphing back, and finding his wife already bearing Blandford's child, he threatened divorce proceedings, citing Blandford. The Prince, though still in India, supported him, suggesting Blandford should divorce his unfortunate Albertha and do the proper thing by Lady Aylesford.

This was the point at which Lord Randolph angrily became involved. It seems that Blandford had not been the first to cuckold Sporting Joe. Joe's friend the Prince of Wales had been there before him – and had written the lady highly compromising letters which she passed to Blandford, who in turn, not having the faintest wish to marry pregnant Lady Aylesford, and still less to be involved in a divorce, showed them to his brother. Lord Randolph decided he would use the letters to persuade the Prince to stop supporting the aggrieved Lord Aylesford.

Blackmailing royalty is a risky business, even for the son of a duke, and Lord Randolph's behaviour bears out the verdict of Lord Derby on him some years later – 'thoroughly untrustworthy; scarcely a gentleman, and probably more or less mad'.

Mad or not, his mind made up, Lord Randolph acted with

his customary impetuosity, getting a warning to the Prince that, should he continue to agitate against Lord Blandford, the letters he had written to Lady Aylesford would be given to the press. He even tried a personal appeal to the Princess of Wales, who seems not to have understood what he was talking about. It was this attempt to involve his wife that particularly aroused Prince Albert Edward's wrath, and the next step in this regal farce was a challenge to Lord Randolph from the Prince to a duel in Amsterdam. To which, in turn, Lord Randolph answered that he would not think of fighting with his future king, but would willingly take on a substitute.

It was at this point that the Prince's friends decided they must intervene to stop what threatened to become a full-scale scandal. The Queen was informed, the Cabinet involved, and Lord Hartington – the future Duke of Devonshire and the discreetest man in English politics – finally made Lord Randolph see a little sense. The Prince's letters to Lady Aylesford were burned, Blandford was not compelled to marry her, and the whole unfortunate affair was more or less hushed up.

Lady Aylesford's life, of course, was ruined. A hearing before a House of Lords Committee proclaimed her son by Blandford illegitimate, and therefore incapable of succeeding to the Aylesford title. Blandford had nothing more to do with her – although she weakly permitted him to adopt their son. (Known as Guy Spencer-Churchill, he would live on at Blenheim until his death in 1923, the shadowiest of skeletons in the capacious ducal cupboard.) And Lady Aylesford lived out her days in Farnham Royal, short of money, deserted by her family, and never ceasing to lament the whole affair.

Blandford, sterling villain that he was, was the one person not to be affected by the trouble he had caused. For the rest of the family the repercussions were far from over. Good John Winston, deeply embarrassed with his friend her Majesty over all the trouble his sons had caused the heir apparent, felt it best to leave the country for a period. Disraeli, with his customary tact, arranged for his Grace to be appointed Viceroy of Ireland. It was an expense the Duke could ill afford – a minimum of £20,000 a year apart from the inconvenience of closing Blenheim and transporting all the silver, plate and servants off to Dublin Castle – but it meant that Lord Randolph, who was appointed as his father's secretary, would also have a spell away from the scene of his disgrace.

The Prince of Wales, despite his fat man's geniality, could be implacable with any who offended him – and his former friend Lord Randolph had offended heinously. Not for nothing was the Prince the head of smart society. He banned him from his circle, and it was as if the Pope had spoken. The doors of every fashionable house in London closed against Lord Randolph and his wife. As Winston Churchill put it when he came to write his father's biography: 'Powerful enemies were anxious to humiliate him. His own sensitiveness and pride magnified every coldness into an affront. London became odious to him.' One wonders what 'sensitive' Lord Randolph had expected.

There is no evidence that the Duke his father ever reproached him for the trouble he had caused. Another well-developed quality among the Churchills was an unusual sense of family loyalty; and Lord Randolph's actions could be seen as a misguided effort to protect the honour of the family.

Once in Ireland, where the Prince's ban could hardly affect them, the Randolph Churchills did not repine for long. During the Irish famine of 1879 they worked closely with the Duchess's relief fund, visiting the most afflicted parts of the country, and witnessing the poverty and suffering at first hand. And while Lord Randolph started to enjoy the company and conversation of Irish politicians Jennie found other diversions.

Like her father, she was a natural rider and, fashionable as ever, soon became one of the most outstanding fox-hunting females in the country. Jennie was very much her father's daughter, and in this period enjoyed a succession of admirers who would ride with her to hounds – men like handsome Colonel Forster, her father-in-law's Master of Horse, the womanising 'Star' Boscowen, Viscount Falmouth, who was the Duke's assistant military secretary and young Lord d'Abernon, whose memories reveal something of the effect she made on her admirers: 'a dark, lithe figure . . . a diamond star in her hair, her favourite ornament – its lustre dimmed by the flashing glory of her eyes. More of the panther than of the woman in her look, but with a cultivation unknown in the jungle.'

Clearly Jennie was already a dedicated flirt, and it has been suggested that her husband was not the father of the second son which she presented to Lord Randolph in 1880. That honour has been credited to the child's godfather, Colonel John Strange Jocelyn, who became 5th Earl of Roden shortly after, and gave the infant both his own christian names when he was christened John Strange Spencer Churchill.

Paternity is always more or less unprovable, but, despite the rumours, Colonel Jocelyn's role as father to Winston Churchill's younger brother is utterly impossible. Few seducers, having done the deed, would then publicly bestow both their names – and one of them such a recognisable one – on the result. And Jennie's notably unstuffy great niece, Anita Leslie, who investigated the Jocelyn story at length, was firmly unconvinced by it. As grand-daughter of Jennie's closest confidante, her sister Leonie, Anita knew much of the secret history of the family, but had heard nothing of the doings of the 5th Lord Roden. What she did discover was that Colonel Jocelyn, as he was at the time when Jennie's second child was conceived, was in fact a middle-aged Crimean veteran in poor health, who was firmly domiciled in England. It was as a friend of his near contemporary, the Duke of Marlborough, that he had been invited to stand godfather to the Duke's latest grandson, and it is inconceivable that Jennie would have taken someone like the ageing colonel as her lover.

However the birth of this second child did mark a most decisive change within the Churchill marriage. Shortly after, the 7th Duke's Irish exile ended, and he gratefully returned to Blenheim. The Randolph Churchills with their two young children also returned to London, with a house in fashionable St James's Place – and it was now that Lord Randolph's political career began in earnest.

His unenthusiastic start in Parliament – 'the speech of a foolish young man who will never come to any good' was the verdict of the influential Master of Balliol, Benjamin Jowett – gave little hint of what was to come. In the 1880 general election the Conservatives were resoundingly defeated by the Liberals. Disraeli was old and ailing. In the midst of this somewhat sorry scene, Lord Randolph saw his chance – and took it.

His was in many ways a strange ascent, for he was the odd man out in politics – erratic, often ill, scornful of his elders. But he vaulted from political obscurity to the position of one of the most famous – and controversial – politicians in the country. One theory has it that he was driven by the bitterness he felt against society for his treatment during the Aylesford affair. He was certainly ruthless – and often very funny – as he lampooned his many enemies in the political establishment, flailing his arms to make a point, jumping with anger on an official paper in the Chamber, and showing an unerring instinct for aiming at the jugular.

He was a natural showman, riding a bicycle across the terrace of the House of Commons or wearing extraordinary shoes in a debate. There was something of the guttersnipe about him, and something of the music-hall performer. Known as 'the Yahoo' and 'Cheeky Randy', he had an instinct for publicity and revelled in it. His advent on the scene of the gentlemanly world of Victorian politics marked the introduction of a new political species – the upper-class demagogue, the great statesmanlike celebrity with the common touch.

Paying immense attention to the details of his dress and the delivery of his speeches, he rapidly became a star performer in Parliament, and still more on his speaking tours through the country, where mass audiences revelled in his witty repartee and fiery invective.

'Give it 'em hot and strong, Randy!' his audiences shouted – and he did. For an important part of his appeal – and his strength – was that he could wound. Drawing on some underlying source of bitterness and anger, he had discovered in the political situation of his day the perfect outlet for his remarkable but uncomfortable talents.

'I have tried all forms of excitement', he explained, 'from tip-cat to tiger-shooting; all degrees of gambling from beggar-my-neighbour to Monte Carlo; but have found no gambling like politics, and no excitement like a big division.'

Swiftly exploiting any situation, changing opinion as it suited him, and mocking the worn-out policies and leadership of his fellow-Tories, he founded the so-called 'Fourth Party' of Tory dissidents, free-booting critics of the Government, who were soon the liveliest and most effective element of the opposition.

With political success came Lord Randolph's restoration to the London social scene. Relations were patched up then totally restored with his former friend the Prince of Wales and it was now that the Randolph Churchills' marriage changed abruptly. Once in the fast set round the Prince of Wales, both were soon living highly liberated lives, but their love-affairs posed no threat to their marriage. It was a period when divorce was inadmissible in smart society, and with the ambitious political and social life they were pursuing, Jennie and her husband were as important to each other as they had ever been and understood each other perfectly. She could provide this highly nervous, moody man with what he needed – an elegant and well-run home in London where he could work and receive his friends and allies. And he could give this extrovert dynamic woman what she wanted in return – a position of influence and status in society.

As for their private lives, they were sophisticated enough to face reality. When not travelling abroad with friends as he often was, Lord Randolph's energies and emotions were absorbed in the 'great game' – politics. Jennie had her freedom but was always careful that her friends and lovers followed the rules dictated by her situation. There must be no scandal, nothing to alert the press, and arouse Lord Randolph's quick irascibility.

But there was no essential conflict in their interests now – and there were many ways in which a clever and attractive woman could assist a husband with her love-affairs. The Prince of Wales had always been a great admirer, and she could easily ensure that he forgot that silly business with the Aylesfords, so that the Randolph Churchills were soon dining with their Royal Highnesses at Marlborough House as happily as in the past.

She could enslave financiers like Baron Hirsch and Ernest Cassel or rising politicians such as pompous but besotted young Lord Curzon or languid handsome Arthur Balfour. George Moore the novelist, who called her 'Black Jane', claimed to know the names of two hundred of her lovers. But Moore was Irish and a great exaggerator.

Sex and politics tend to go together, and Jennie was that particular American phenomenon, the politically ambitious married woman who is equally at ease with either. But her underlying interest was power and money. She was a lion-hunter and a snob, but she was not a fool. She talked well, knew exactly what she wanted, and her favourite dinner-guests were not necessarily her lovers. One was that great receptacle of rectitude, her husband's chief, and the future Conservative Prime Minister, Lord Salisbury. Another was the man for whom Lord Randolph showed consistent and outrageous enmity in debate, that 'Old Man in a Hurry' as he called him, William Ewart Gladstone.

'Dear Lady Randolph,' that urbane old gentleman remarked one evening after enduring a torrential drubbing from an enraged Lord Randolph in the Commons, 'I do trust that dear Lord

Randolph is not wearied by his *splendid* effort in the House this afternoon.'

In fact he often was – and one of Jennie's most important roles was to sustain him through his frequent periods of despondency and physical relapse. There was a particularly bad one in the summer of 1882 when for four months Lord Randolph was completely out of action with some mysterious malady. She loyally supported him and served as his information service and constant source of sound advice, on one occasion even delivering his election speech to the electorate in Woodstock.

Jennie was also a driving force in the Primrose League, the important nationwide campaign-group her husband founded to channel social and political support for the Conservatives throughout the country. Another sign of the underlying shrewdness of Lord Randolph's political awareness was that he sensed, as his parents' friend Disraeli had before him, the Conservatives' all-important need to attract the apparently unlikely vote of that growing and imponderable new force in politics, the working classes.

With his natural arrogance, his studied dress, the privilege and glitter of his very ducal way of life, no one was more the quintessential Victorian aristocrat than Lord Randolph, and many of his most polished insults were snobbishly directed at the members of the rising middle class among the Liberals. As a nobleman he was immensely arrogant and genuinely despised the middle classes, those smug inhabitants of suburban 'pineries and vineries' as he called them. But he also had that invaluable *alter ego* of 'Cheeky Randy', the hero of the public meeting and the great political performer for the common people.

Like many aristocrats, he sentimentalised the lower orders and believed that with his common touch he could create a union of interests between the highest and lowest in the land. 'The aristocracy and the working class are united in the indissoluble bonds of a common immorality,' was one of his more candid theories, and he invented something new in politics which he airily entitled 'Tory Democracy'. Like most of his policies, it was never very clear exactly what it was, beyond his own brisk definition: 'Tory Democracy is democracy which supports the Tories.'

However vague, Tory Democracy was an invaluable slogan, just as the Primrose League had now become a source of real influence throughout the country; Lord Randolph was beginning to emerge from the exuberance of opposition towards the settled aim of politics – power. Within five years of his return from Ireland he had made himself what his son Winston would proudly call 'a great elemental force in British politics'. He was barely thirty-five when Gladstone's Liberal government proposed Home Rule for Ireland, and largely thanks to Lord Randolph's powerful attacks the measure was decisively defeated by the Conservatives in the election of 1885. This despite the fact that, characteristically, Lord Randolph had previously seemed to support some form of Irish Home Rule himself.

When the Queen asked Lord Salisbury to form a new government in 1885, the time had come for Lord Randolph to enter into his political inheritance. He began with a typical show of resolution. Being appointed Secretary of State for India, he gained an instant place in history by swiftly annexing the troubled state of Burma to the British Crown.

Then, after fresh elections in July 1886, Lord Randolph found himself almost at the top of what Disraeli called 'the greasy pole of politics', when Salisbury made him Chancellor of the Exchequer and Leader of the Commons in this new administration.

It had been a meteoric rise. Despite uncertain health, despite his past disgrace, his countless enemies, his maverick reputation and his innumerable changes of direction, he had made himself at thirty-six the youngest Chancellor of the Exchequer since William Pitt – and an inevitable candidate for premiership.

'There is only one place, that is the prime minister. I like to be the boss,' he was to tell his friend Lord Rosebery.

Unlike Salisbury, who was nine years older and seated in that far less potent assembly, the House of Lords, Lord Randolph had his power-base in the country and within the House of Commons. He was passionately ambitious, a surprisingly good administrator as well as an orator, and the only man in his party who was a match for Gladstone. Now that he had the Chancellorship, all he needed was a little patience to achieve the greatest prize of all.

Inexplicably, patience seemed to be the one thing Lord Randolph suddenly lacked. Shrewd old Queen Victoria, who had known him all his life, had serious doubts about his appointment from the start – 'he is so mad and odd and also he has bad health', she noted ominously in her diary – and it was in these months of victory late in 1886 that Lord Randolph suddenly began to put at risk everything that he and Jennie had worked and fought together to achieve.

He did not consult her now, and for reasons of his own seemed set upon a trial of strength with Salisbury. Several times that autumn he threatened to resign to get his way within the Cabinet – and on each occasion he was mollified. Salisbury was a slow, strong, careful politician, and the last thing he wanted was a split within his government. But there were limits to Lord Salisbury's patience; and in December 1886 Lord Randolph – hell-bent, it seemed, on self-destruction – overstepped them.

As with the Aylesford affair, it seemed another of Lord Randolph's acts of lunacy. Choosing an absurdly minor matter on which to stake his whole career, he suddenly objected to a War Office request to the Treasury for an additional £560,000 for the Army, and delivered one more ultimatum to Lord Salisbury. His Lordship failed to support him, and on 20 December, after dining with the Queen at Windsor Castle, Lord Randolph wrote Lord Salisbury his famous letter of resignation – which Lord Salisbury calmly and implacably accepted.

According to Lord Randolph's muddled explanation, he had been hoping that Salisbury would again agree to his demands. Alternatively, he may have thought that Salisbury would destroy himself by accepting the resignation of so powerful a fellow-politician. Either way, Lord Randolph blundered.

He had made sure his resignation letter was published in *The Times*. He had also failed to inform her Majesty of his intentions over dinner, and the Queen was most offended. 'The want of respect shown to me and to his colleagues have added to the bad effect which it produced,' she wrote. He even failed to inform Jennie, who learned of his decision from *The Times*. In her memoirs, she described the scene that followed.

When I came down to breakfast, the fatal paper in my hand, I found him calm and smiling. 'Quite a surprise for you,' he said. He went into no explanation, and I felt too utterly crushed and miserable to ask for any, or even to remonstrate.

Mr Moore (his secretary at the Treasury), who was devoted to Randolph, rushed in, pale and anxious, and with a faltering voice said to me, 'He has thrown himself from the top of the ladder and will never reach it again!'

'Alas! he proved too true a prophet,' Jennie added – but it was worse than that. The true tragedy of Lord Randolph Churchill's tragic life was only just beginning. He was thirty-seven and still had nine tormented years to live, haunted by a sense of failure, shunned by the former colleagues who had hailed him, yet painfully intent on picking up the power he had squandered.

6

Family Troubles

There are conflicting views within the Churchill family about the nature of the illness which began afflicting Lord Randolph in his mid-thirties and resulted in his death at the age of forty-six.

The whole distressing subject was totally ignored in his grandson Randolph's early volume of the official biography of Sir Winston Churchill. And another grandson, Churchill's nephew Peregrine, maintains that Lord Randolph's troubles stemmed essentially from excessive medication – principally digitalis and belladonna – which were prescribed for nervous stress on a constitution weakened by the ravages of glandular fever caught in childhood. But other members of the family accept that Lord Randolph was in fact suffering from syphilis. His grand-daughter, Mary Soames, stated this unequivocally in her fascinating *Churchill Family Album*, remarking later that this was part of the received wisdom of the family; and Churchill himself undoubtedly believed this, too. (Among other sources, Lord Lambton told the author that as a young Member of Parliament he clearly remembers Churchill referring quite openly in conversation to his father's syphilis. The author similarly recalls hearing Randolph speak of 'my grandfather's distressing malady'.)

It is, of course, impossible to prove conclusively that somebody who died in 1895 was suffering from a particular disease – and especially syphilis for which the Wasserman test was not invented until ten years later. It has also been suggested that Lord Randolph was afflicted with a brain tumour. Medically this seems unlikely. The symptoms fail to match the case, his doctors never mentioned a tumour as a possibility, and a tumour would probably have killed him earlier.

What is incontestable is that, from around his mid-thirties, Lord Randolph was exhibiting symptoms suggesting the onset of an attack of secondary syphilis, that he almost certainly believed that he was suffering from it, and that those closest to him believed this, too, going to considerable lengths to hide this desperate and shameful situation.

Despite the conspiracy of silence which built up around his illness, there have been accounts of how Lord Randolph actually contracted what, in the days before antibiotics, amounted to a sentence to a slow humiliating death. The most colourful comes from the author and one-time editor of the influential *Fortnightly Magazine*, Frank Harris. Harris had known both Lord Randolph and his son Winston well, and he was to act as Winston's unofficial literary agent for a period. He is not the most reliable of sources, but since the story he included in his book *My Life and Loves* came originally from Louis Jennings, one of Lord Randolph's closest Oxford friends, political associates and his literary executor, it is worth repeating.

According to Jennings, Lord Randolph, while at Oxford, got drunk one night at an undergraduate party, and woke next morning in a filthy lodging-house to find an old woman lying in the bed beside him.

She had one long yellow tooth in her top jaw that waggled as she spoke. Speechless with horror, I put my hand in my pocket, and threw all the money I had loose on the bed. I could not say a word. She was still smiling at me; I put on my waistcoat and coat and fled the room. 'Lovie, you're not kind!' I heard her say as I closed the door after me. Downstairs I fled in livid terror.

Afterwards Lord Randolph, horrified by perhaps having contracted syphilis, was treated by an Oxford doctor and was finally assured that he was safe. He may not have been and an Oxford prostitute may have been the source of Lord Randolph's later troubles.

A more likely source, however, is that suggested by Jennie's great-niece, her sister, Leonie Leslie's granddaughter, Anita. Drawing on family knowledge, she insists Lord Randolph contracted the disease not at Oxford but from a mistress he was keeping in Paris in the early 1880s.

Again, this cannot be proved, but ultimately it is immaterial. In its non-ulcerous phase, syphilis is not infectious, and is not passed on to the mother or the child through semen. Even if Lord Randolph did contract it before his marriage, there was no particular danger to his wife and sons. The likelihood is that Lord Randolph would have regarded it for what it was, a youthful indiscretion, and have dismissed it from his mind, genuinely thinking he was cured.

But, for the victim who was unlucky, syphilis, like AIDS, could be a time-bomb of appalling consequences. Until antibiotic drugs there was no certain way of destroying the bacillus in the blood. Years of trouble-free remission could ensue, and then the microbes would begin a slow attack upon the central nervous system and the brain. Once this started there was no known cure. The symptoms were well known, and there was no escape from a slow and terrible decline which would often end with madness as the sufferer fell victim to GPI – general paralysis of the insane – the condition Lord Randolph was to die of.

From the early 1880s he was already being treated by a Dr Robson Roose, an expert in neurological disorders and author of a popular book called *Waste and Repair in Modern Life*. Lord Randolph must have been a text-book case for Dr Roose to study; and, to begin with, all his symptoms – sleeplessness, chronic irritability, and bouts of lethargy and deep depression – could be medically ascribed to the patient's nervous disposition and the gruelling pace at which he lived his life. But by 1885, the year Lord Randolph first entered Salisbury's government, it would seem that Dr Roose was having his suspicions that his famous patient could be suffering from something more serious. Later he would call in the famous London specialist in nervous diseases, Dr Thomas Buzzard, who in the final stages of Lord Randolph's illness would increasingly take care of him.

There is no record of Dr Buzzard's diagnosis, but the patient's state of health must have been causing serious concern for a doctor as eminent as Robson Roose to bring in a specialist like Buzzard. Much of Lord Randolph's behaviour at this crucial period in his career was clearly giving rise to grave anxiety.

Queen Victoria was not the only one to be worrying about his health and state of mind: so were Jennie and his mother. He was increasingly obsessional and irascible in his judgements, and suspicious of his friends. By now he was taking large amounts of digitalis as a sedative, and suffering attacks of dizziness and insomnia. The strain of late-night parliamentary sittings was becoming intolerable for this man of only thirty-five.

Lord Randolph was an educated man whose knowledge of French literature, if of nothing else, would have made him all too well aware of the dire fate that syphilitic madness brought to writers such as Verlaine, Maupassant and Jules Goncourt. He must have known Dr Buzzard's medical speciality when he saw him, and he was not the sort of man doctors lie to.

All the evidence suggests that by that summer of 1886 when Lord Randolph was appointed Chancellor of the Exchequer, and seemed to have the highest post in government within his grasp, he suspected what was wrong with him. His faculties were threatened. Time was running out.

'How long will your leadership last?' his friend Lord Rosebery asked.

'Oh, about six months,' Lord Randolph answered with uncanny accuracy.

'And then?'

'Why, Westminster Abbey,' he replied.

There was a certain irony to his situation. At the very moment when prodigious effort had been crowned with extraordinary success, everything was starting to collapse around him. He was heavily in debt. He and Jennie had been living increasingly beyond their means, having moved from St James's to a larger establishment in Connaught Place where they entertained in style. Lord Randolph had another house at Newmarket where he raced flamboyantly but ultimately at a loss. He lost still more dramatically at another of his expensive pastimes, baccarat, which he indulged in during frequent trips to Monte Carlo. He fared no better with financial speculations, his debts with the Rothschilds reaching £11,000 by the beginning of the 1890s.

Simultaneously there was an unexplained drama in his marriage, giving rise to exaggerated rumours about his private life. That October when his battle with Salisbury in the Cabinet was intensifying, he departed hurriedly on a mysterious trip around the capitals of Europe with his friend Tom Trafford. Although he used the pseudonym of 'Mr Spencer', he deceived nobody, and his every move was reported in the press. Further gossip followed. His mother seems to have suspected an affair with another woman, probably the notorious Lady Warwick, the former mistress of the Prince of Wales. This seems unlikely, and Lord Randolph's hurried journey remains unexplained. What is clear, however, is that he was going through some sort of crisis in the autumn of 1886, and that the responsibility for holding the family together fell on Jennie.

The Duchess's attitude towards her daughter-in-law changed abruptly. Ancient animosity forgotten, the jealous Duchess suddenly became her confidante and friend, and was begging Jennie to be 'patient' with Lord Randolph. She told her to forget her 'jealousy'; she must also bid farewell to her own past giddy life of 'flirting, gambling and fast friends'; above all, the Duchess urged her to be 'responsible and wise' and try to save her marriage. Jennie must have done as she was told, for the marriage did not break, but she was dealing with a husband in a highly nervous state and was powerless to prevent Lord Randolph's resignation that December.

One explanation for Randolph's action is that he had simply had enough of politics; he was tired and he was sick, and when he tendered Salisbury his resignation he irrevocably meant it. This is possible, but unlikely. Lord Randolph's life was centred entirely around politics. He was intensely ambitious and had nearly reached the top; and after his resignation he remained in Parliament, making serious efforts to re-enter Salisbury's government.

A more likely explanation is that Lord Randolph's resignation was actually a bungled bid for power, an attempt to precipitate a crisis which he believed he could win. He had always had that great ambition for the 'boss man's' role, and in a trial of strength with Lord Salisbury he still possessed a number of distinct advantages.

Lord Salisbury was in the House of Lords, but Lord Randolph had his power-base in that more crucial assembly, the House of Commons. Lord Salisbury lacked Lord Randolph's formidable charisma – and at this point still needed to establish full control over the Conservative Party throughout the country. Lord Randolph, with the fame of his public meetings and the Primrose League behind him, was a formidable opponent.

With his advancing illness these advantages would not last for ever. This sudden and dramatic resignation might have seemed to him his final chance of rallying his own supporters, toppling Lord Salisbury and reaching that longed-for goal of Prime Minister himself.

It was a forlorn venture, and as a gambling man Lord Randolph must have known the price of failure. It was also slightly mad, but so was he. It was him or Salisbury; and it was only when Lord Salisbury failed to topple – or even quiver on his perch – that the full extent of Lord Randolph's blunder was apparent.

His debts were mounting – and the loss of his ministerial salary of £5,000 a year made the situation worse. His party turned against him, as political parties always do against a loser, and he was bitterly attacked for his disloyalty.

This left Lord Randolph nervously prostrated – lying in a darkened room, smoking more Turkish cigarettes than ever and muttering of comeback and revenge. Rumours of the break-up of his marriage began to reach the press. The *New York Sun* carried details of the Randolph Churchills' separation. Lord Randolph reacted angrily, and the shipwreck of his life began in earnest.

His eldest son, twelve-year-old Winston, was at a small private boarding school in Brighton when Lord Randolph's resignation was announced, and he took it badly. He was an emotional small boy, passionate, possessive, and had been intensely proud of his father's rise to fame. As a schoolboy he had noticed proudly the way strangers in the street took off their hats when Lord Randolph passed, and he had heard grown-ups refer to him as 'Gladstone's great adversary'.

Now all that had changed abruptly, and something of the effect this had on Winston is revealed in a letter Jennie wrote to her husband early in 1887. 'Winston was taken to a pantomime at Brighton where they hissed a sketch of you. He burst into tears and then turned furiously on the man who was hissing behind him and said, "Stop that noise you snub-nosed radical!"'

This was very much in character for Winston had already shown himself a violent, uncontrollable small boy, who at the age of nine had already been removed from his first school, St George's, Asot, for terrible behaviour. The future novelist, Maurice Baring, who arrived at St George's soon afterwards, wrote that Winston's 'naughtiness appeared to have surpassed anything. He had been flogged for taking sugar from the pantry, and so far from being penitent, he had taken the headmaster's sacred straw hat from where it hung over the door and kicked it to pieces. His sojourn at this school had been one long feud with authority.' His behaviour at his next school was similar. 'The naughtiest little boy in the world' was how one of his female teachers in Brighton remembered him. Where his younger brother, Jack, was easy and affectionate, Winston was very much the opposite, as first sons who are jealous of more popular younger brothers often are.

It has been suggested that he was showing all the symptoms of a child neglected by his parents, and the blame is frequently placed on the flighty never-present figure of his mother. This is almost certainly unfair to Jennie, and the usual picture of the doleful sandy-headed son of the famous statesman being starved of childhood affection by neglectful parents is distinctly doubtful.

By upper-class standards of the day, Winston had been treated rather well, and until he went to boarding school he had enjoyed unusually close contact with his parents and relations. He also had the absolute devotion of an extraordinary woman – his nanny, the indomitable Mrs Everest. 'Woomie', as he called her (the nickname actually short for 'Woman'), was a sterling character. Self-educated, intelligent, warm and wise, Mrs Everest mothered Winston and Jack obsessively, and even when they went away to boarding school she was always urging Jack and 'dearest Winnie' to be sure to change their socks, repeat their prayers and eat their vegetables.

Had Churchill been deprived of mother-love in childhood, stout Mrs Everest was clearly the ideal mother-surrogate. But there is evidence that, far from being starved of Jennie's affection and attention, Winston's childhood owed much to Jennie's presence.

Some of this evidence is contained in a small appointments-diary Jennie kept for the first half of 1882 when her London social life was at its height.

Throughout this period, Jennie was involved with a passionate love-affair, an ailing husband and an energetic social life, but the most frequent references in her diary are to seven-year-old Winston.

'Gave Winston his lessons.' 'Winston rather ill. Thought he was going to have croup.' And on 24 February comes a fascinating reference for the future: 'Took Winston and had tea with Blanche Hozier in her lodgings.'

The headlong Lady Blanche Hozier, daughter of the Earl of Airlie, was one of Jennie's closest friends. They had much in common. Both were fashionable beauties, both were uncomfortably married, and both were unfaithful to their husbands.

Hozier was unhealthy, irascible and old, and Lady Blanche was currently involved with one of Jennie's former hunting friends from Ireland, a passionate pursuer of both fox and female named Bay Middleton.

By a coincidence, Jennie, too, had just begun the most romantic of her various romances with another great Victorian equestrian, Lord Randolph's friend, the handsome and elegant Hungarian Count Charles Rudolph Ferdinand Andreas Kinsky. Kinsky became the hero of London society by winning the Grand National in 1886, and unlike Lord Randolph was a man of great physical strength and easy charm. The combination of horsemanship, a European title and great high spirits made the Count irresistible to Jennie, and their love-affair became the great obsession of their lives. But, as always, Jennie had her family and her position in society to consider, and her diary gives only the most guarded references to Count Kinsky.

What it does give are frequent reminders of the parlous state of Lord Randolph's health. Jennie notes that he was 'ill' for most of February 1882, and in early March 'R nearly fainted after a hot bath'.

During childhood Winston also had a close relationship with his father. Lord Randolph's periods of illness must have interfered with this at times, and as with any dedicated politician he was frequently away from home and frequently distracted. But this had not prevented him taking Winston on holidays to France and Germany. On one occasion he took him to Barnum's Circus (where the concerned father refused to let him see the terrifying 'Boneless Wonder', considering that 'the spectacle would be too revolting and demoralising to my youthful eyes'). Later, knowing how much Winston loved tales of adventure, Lord Randolph introduced him to his friend the famous writer Bram Stoker, author of *Dracula*.

But for Winston all these happy times ended with his father's resignation and the family troubles that ensued. His idol had collapsed, and from then on everything began to change within the family – including his father's previous concern for him. Distracted and increasingly withdrawn, Lord Randolph was already turning from his family during the marital crisis which accompanied his fall. 'You never came to see me on Sunday when you were in Brighton,' Winston wrote to him accusingly just before his father's resignation.

During the months that followed, Winston's childhood ended. He was having to work hard for the examinations for Harrow School, which he would enter the following September, and simultaneously accept the loss of all that high ambition he had shared with his father.

Instead of the hero of the hour, set to become the most powerful man in Britain, with all that this could mean for his sons, Lord Randolph was increasingly revealed as a failure – unpopular and sick, rejected by his party and dependent on his strong-willed but unfaithful wife.

More than ever, Lord Randolph would be travelling abroad – but never again with Winston. Early that spring he was off to Russia, accompanied by Jennie; and more and longer foreign trips would follow in the wretched years ahead – to India, to southern Africa and to the East. In travel he found distraction and relief from all his troubles, while back at home was little but disaster.

He was still in Parliament, but his pathetic efforts at a come-back brought indifference or derision from those who used to fear him. He was soon a caricature of the man he had been. Lord Salisbury never answered his requests for the viceroyship of India or the ambassadorship to France. The debts with the Rothschilds mounted. The racehorses were sold; the stables followed, then the house in Connaught Place, after which the family moved in as lodgers with the Duchess in her house in Grosvenor Square. As Lord Rosebery put it, Lord Randolph became 'chief mourner at his own protracted funeral, a public pageant of gloomy years'.

Feeling abandoned, Winston was miserable at Harrow, and there were constant letters to his mother begging for visits, news and pocket-money, but she had other things beside a plangent son to worry over.

No matter how bad things became, she could not leave her husband. In her situation lovers were permissible, but the public scandal of divorce would have ruined her for ever. 'No public laundering of dirty linen' was the iron rule of upper-class society. Had she had money of her own, she would have had more independence; but Leonard Jerome, on whom she relied for additional financing earlier in the marriage, had become a burned-out one-time millionaire whose funds had gone, and whose schemes for a financial comeback failed before he died, another disappointed man, in 1891.

All she could do was wait for her husband's slow disease to take its course. Their relations were naturally erratic. He depended on her – as she had to do on him – and occasionally gave her signs of sad affection. Appearances were more or less maintained.

He seems to have tolerated her affairs – outwardly, at least, maintaining an old-world unconcern about her lovers. He continued his friendship with Count Kinsky almost to the last. It was rather stylish, this behaviour of a polished aristocrat who would not dream of letting anything as vulgar as his wife's liaisons colour relations with another nobleman. But behind the scenes Lord Randolph's self-control was less effective. According to his brother-in-law, Lord Tweedmouth, Jennie could irritate him unbearably, and there are references in contemporary diaries which show Lord Randolph angrily abusing her. In 1892, when Jennie herself was seriously ill with a rectal tumour, Lord Iddesleigh records him as 'inclined to abuse his wife although her life is still said to be in danger'.

Jennie made a full recovery, but Lord Randolph's tortured and tortuous decline continued as the bacillus steadily encroached upon his brain. One of the stranger side-effects of the onset of general paralysis of the insane is that the sufferer frequently fails to understand how much his faculties have been impaired. Isolated, with at best a fitful contact with reality, he is buoyed up with the belief that everything is normal. Lord Randolph had periods when he thought himself about to make his political comeback.

In 1893 he journeyed through southern Africa, believing he would make his fortune. His travels gave him even less time for Winston, who was continuing his own depressing school career at Harrow.

Although his home life was afflicted by parental misery and debt, Winston found a refuge with other members of his extended family. During these formative years of adolescence he developed a strong loyalty towards his kinsmen which continued all his life.

There was his gentle brother Jack, six years his junior. He was soon taller than Winston, placid, well behaved and rather dull. The family favourite, he was already being held up as an example to his brother, who was inclined to bully him but whom he seems to have adored. Almost from the start Winston dominated Jack, and when he allowed him to join in one of his favourite pastimes

– pitched campaigns with carefully assembled armies of toy soldiers – Jack was permitted no artillery and assigned the colonial infantry, so that Winston invariably won. Since Jack did not object, it was a situation that suited Winston perfectly.

Then there were the two Jerome aunts, Leonie and Clara, both of whom had followed their sister's example and married into the British upper classes. Neither made as grand a match as Jennie, but neither had to bear the strain and horror – and excitement – of their more powerful sister's life.

Leonie had married Colonel Jack Leslie, a dependable but easy-going Irish landlord with a large house, Castle Leslie, and 'about 44,500 acres' of County Monaghan. Members of Ireland's long-established 'Protestant Ascendancy', the Leslies were genially eccentric, and this eccentricity was passed on to Winston's cousin, Shane Leslie, born in 1885. Aunt Leonie had not inherited the looks or temperament of Jennie, but she was kind to Winston and increasingly became Jennie's confidante and principal adviser during the storms and trials of her marriage.

Jennie's other sister, Clara, was less dependable, having married one of the most spectacular young men of late-Victorian society, an immensely tall and unreliable adventurer called Moreton Frewen, who spent his life pursuing fortunes that eluded him. The Frewens inhabited a picturesque but mouldering ancestral home, Brede Place, near Rye in Sussex. Aunt Clara was prettier than Aunt Leonie, but less intelligent, and much of her life was occupied in a curious affair with the exiled King Milan of Serbia. The Frewens' daughter, christened Clare, inherited her mother's looks and her father's fecklessness, and would be a source of trouble and delight to her cousin Winston for many years to come.

But none of the Jerome relations could really hope to rival the Spencer-Churchills in the interest of the youthful Winston. In contrast with the constant strain of Lord Randolph's illness, and the anxieties of debt and of keeping up appearances, Blenheim, though having its own troubles, was a place of unassailable security. It beckoned this difficult and lonely child's imagination with historic splendour, compared with which the disappointments of Lord Randolph's life were almost insignificant. During this period Winston became preoccupied with heroic battles and conquering generals – and in particular with Blenheim's great creator, John, 1st Duke of Marlborough.

7

Death in the Family

It is significant that Winston's adolescence coincided with a
depressing period for all the Spencer-Churchills. Lord Randolph's
miseries were only part of the misfortunes now descending on his
blighted family.

John Winston, 7th Duke of Marlborough, former Viceroy and
bewhiskered pillar of the Church of England, had not lived to
see the triumph and disaster of his favourite son. The Duke had
died in 1883, and his palace had again relapsed into the gloomy
scandal it had known earlier in the century as the new duke, Lord
Randolph's elder brother, Blandford, cheerlessly embarked upon
his tenure of the dukedom.

'He was his own worst enemy,' *The Times* would write about
him at his death, but he picked up the nickname of 'the Bad
Duke' almost from the start, for at the time of his accession his
maltreated wife, poor Goosey, Lady Blandford, was divorcing
him with much scandalous publicity, which did little for what
was left of his public reputation.

She was so bitterly against him that she refused to be known
as his duchess. (For the rest of her life she would simply call
herself Lady Blandford.) His mother, the old Duchess, was so distressed at the thought of this reprobate son taking over Blenheim
in place of her worthy husband that she left the palace, never
to return there in his lifetime. But the member of the family
who suffered most from the changed regime was unquestionably
the new Duke's son and heir, Charles Richard John Spencer-
Churchill, who officially became Lord Blandford in his father's
place.

This title descended to the Duke of Marlborough's heir, but
since the Duke continued to be called 'Blandford' by all who
knew him, the new Lord Blandford would be known all his life
by his nickname, 'Sunny'. This was the diminutive of another of

the young lord's titles, Earl of Sunderland, but nothing could have been less sunny than the character and fate Charles Richard John had inherited from the Dukes of Marlborough.

Sunny was born in 1871 and was devoted to his mother, but he was sacrificed as part of the settlement of his parents' painfully fought divorce. Since he was now the heir to a famous dukedom, it was considered only right and proper for Sunny to be brought up at Blenheim. Thus at the age of ten he was unceremoniously bundled back to Blenheim and his father.

Sunny's aunt, Lady Lansdowne, always remembered him as having been one of the most 'charming and joyous' of small boys, but suddenly he changed, and she was alarmed to see that Sunny's good spirits seemed to have vanished. Having won his affection, his father almost instantly disliked him, and would either bully him or snub him. In his own words, Sunny was 'given no kindness and entirely crushed' during the years his father was alive.

His cousin Winston was three years his junior, and they had played together as small boys at Viceregal Lodge in Dublin during their grandfather's viceroyship of Ireland. Further contact between them ended shortly after Sunny's father succeeded to the dukedom, and Lord Randolph and his brother were involved in one final monumental feud.

As with most disagreements in the Churchill family, this had its origins in money – or the lack of it. John Winston had set a dangerous precedent when auctioning off the Marlborough gems and his famous library. Blandford was as short of money as his father, and on becoming Duke himself followed the paternal footsteps to the saleroom. He was not a sentimental man, and the palace was stripped of its remaining splendours, including Raphael's masterpiece, the Ansidei Madonna, and the magnificent Van Dyck portrait of King Charles I on horseback. Both ended up in the National Gallery in London; meanwhile Blandford built himself a new laboratory at Blenheim.

Lord Randolph had not objected to his father's depredations, but those of his brother must have struck him differently. He was violently opposed to what was happening, and attempted, unsuccessfully, to stop the sales. Communication ceased between the brothers, and the ban extended to Lord Randolph's family. From now until the Bad Duke's death, there was only one occasion when Winston and his brother Jack would visit Blenheim. During the diphtheria epidemic of 1888, Duchess Fanny arranged for them to spend a few nights at the palace to escape the danger of infection. Apart from this, romantic Blenheim, home of his ancestors and shrine of the greatest Churchill of them all, was forbidden territory to Winston while he was at Harrow.

Winston hated Harrow from the start, and since he got no further than the lower school and refused to concentrate on anything that bored him (this included classics, mathematics, science and all foreign languages) the legend grew around him (which he later did nothing to discourage) that he was something of a dunce. One of the habits of his form master was to place him in front of the class, saying: 'Look at the stupidest boy at Harrow who is the son of the cleverest man in England.'

In fact he was extremely clever at the things he liked. He had his father's powers of concentration and had inherited the Churchill memory, winning a prize for reeling off verbatim *1,200 lines* of Macaulay's 'Lays of Ancient Rome'. (The poem with its dramatic scenes of noble heroism, war and death in battle was a lifelong favourite: in 1947 he would recite large sections of it over lunch to the Italian film director Mario Soldati.) He also showed a most precocious gift for words and self-expression which the Harrow English master evidently appreciated; one of the few things Churchill admitted that his old school taught him was 'the construction of an English sentence, which is a noble thing'. As an old man, working on his Second World War memoirs, he told his assistant that it was then that he discovered, 'that I had this astonishing gift for writing'.

But Churchill insists that his schooldays were the unhappiest period of his life. He was undersized and seems to have been unpopular, with no close friends. Oswald Mosley remembered Churchill telling him, 'with some resentment, how certain little beasts used to flick him with wet towels'. With most of his school work, he was clearly behaving like many unhappy children and simply opting out.

Winston learned another tactic often used by unhappy and unpopular small boys at school – he became increasingly aggress-ive, and something of a bully when he got the chance. One of the famous stories of his Harrow days is of how he had the temerity to push another boy into the swimming pool, without realising that it was the tiny but formidable Leo Amery, athlete, captain of the school and future Tory politician. Winston gave himself away by his apology. 'I mistook you for a fourth form boy, you are so small,' he said, then added: 'My father too is small and he is also a great man.'

But the most revealing picture of Churchill then is provided by one of his contemporaries, the future pioneer and empire-builder Colonel Richard Meinertzhagen. According to Meinertzhagen, Winston was already 'precocious, bumptious and talkative'. 'He was', Meinertzhagen adds, 'a lonely boy, usually walking by himself, but everyone in the school knew him because he was out of the ordinary.' Meinertzhagen admits that, like several others, he 'thought he could take liberties' with Winston and on one occasion tried to push him off the pavement. 'I cannoned into an object like a brick wall and found myself in the gutter, for he was as hard as nails and even in those days was a fierce opponent of wilful aggression.' His look, we can assume, 'was not one of scorn or even of victory, but just a reminder that he was to be left alone'. Years later, when facing a wild boar in India, Meinertzhagen saw 'those same little beady eyes of warning', and as the boar prepared to charge he had a 'mental flash' of Winston Churchill.

At Harrow, Winston's developing powers of aggression were valuable in other ways. They helped him become a champion fencer – he was an unorthodox attacking fighter – and guaranteed his enjoyment of the warlike battles of the school army corps.

But his father found no joy in Winston's few accomplishments. During the rare periods when he was in London and not plunged in illness or despair, all Lord Randolph saw in Winston was a source of trouble and expense and a reminder of his own sense of failure.

Unlike his brother Jack, Winston always needed money and attention, and Lord Randolph came to regard him as ill-disciplined and lazy. He was also far too like Jennie, and it is interesting that the only person Lord Randolph could confide in now, his mother, Duchess Fanny, strongly disapproved of her bumptious unattractive grandson – and firmly agreed with her son about young Winston's character.

Father–son relations worsened steadily throughout Winston's later years at Harrow. There was a suggestion that Winston might enter the Church, but Lord Randolph agreed to his son's desire to be a soldier. Winston's childhood love of playing soldiers had developed into a great interest in military affairs. Even here however Winston failed his father, needing tuition with a special London crammer and three attempts to pass the entrance examination into Sandhurst Military Academy – all of which increased his father's debt with the Rothschilds. By the time Winston finally did pass, in the autumn of 1892, Lord Randolph seems to have frequently despaired of him.

But Winston, unlike his cousin Sunny, would not let his father's attitude destroy him. He found a substitute father-figure in his mother's lover, the glamorous Count Kinsky, who used to take him to Olympia and make a fuss of him on holidays from school in London. Winston purchased from his brother Jack a photograph of Kinsky winning the Grand National on his famous horse Zoedone, to hang on his study wall at Sandhurst. And he constantly appealed to his mother for support. He argued lucidly, cajoling his 'Dearest, Mummy' for attention and affection throughout the time he was at school. Then, at the moment when his schooldays ended, he found another world he needed.

On a November morning early in 1892, the ducal valet at Blenheim entered his master's bedroom with his customary pot of tea at the customary hour of eight o'clock, pulled the curtains, called the Duke, and took little notice of his failure to respond, for this frequently occurred. These days Blandford was increasingly moody and depressed; and, although he had complained of indigestion when he went to bed the night before, he otherwise appeared in perfect health for a man of forty-seven.

His Grace had little reason for his moods, for at last it seemed that he had come to terms with life. Having stripped his palace and dispersed the proceeds, he had resolved his financial problems by following the example of an increasing number of the British aristocracy of the period.

During a visit to New York, three years earlier, he had met the now ageing *bon viveur* Leonard Jerome, who had suggested a solution to his troubles – Lillian Hammersley, a widow with a heavy figure and a fortune of similar proportions. She had, explained Jerome, 'Plenty of tin', and nothing would make her happier than to share it with an English duke. It was a wish that Blandford was prepared to grant her.

Ugly, good-natured and extremely rich, Duchess Lily proved an admirable wife. She was thrilled to be a duchess, settled Blandford's debts and indulged him lovingly, buying him a brand-new boat-house for his lake and a massive Hammond organ for his empty picture-gallery. She even did her best with her introverted stepson, Sunny, who was not particularly responsive. Nor, sadly, was her husband, who had become increasingly afflicted with the Churchill melancholy.

Blandford never bothered to patent his electrical discoveries, still feuded with his brother, maintained a mistress, and was shunned by many of the local gentry, whose feelings he reciprocated. Like some miserable prisoner he had taken to expressing comments on his situation on the walls of his room. 'They say. What say they? Let them say,' he had scrawled. And 'Dust, ashes, nothing'.

This sentiment was curiously apt, for when the valet returned to help his master dress, he found the tea untouched beside the figure lying in the bed. At forty-seven, Blandford, eighth and most disreputable of the Dukes of Marlborough, had abruptly gone to meet his maker.

His brother was immediately informed, and that afternoon, for the first time for seven years, Lord Randolph entered his ancestral home to take charge of the situation. Despite his own illness, he behaved with admirable coolness. He reassured his nephew Sunny, who had hastened back from Oxford where he was now an undergraduate and who was somewhat dazed to find himself at twenty Duke of Marlborough. He comforted the Duchess with a cup of tea, then went to see the body of his brother.

He found him, as he reported in a letter to his mother, looking 'very peaceful'. 'His left hand', he wrote, 'lies easily on his waist, but his right hand is clenched tightly on his heart. There can be no doubt that the cause of death was sudden syncope, with no one near to offer any restorative, brought on by indigestion.'

He said the same, more briskly, to the reporter from the *Oxford Mail* who was soon upon the scene. There could be, he added, absolutely no question of foul play in the Duke's demise. And that was that.

When the Duke's will was read, it proved totally in character. He had left nothing to Randolph, nor to his bastard son, nor to his wife (not that she needed it), but there was a large bequest of £20,000 to his last mistress, the notorious 'sex goddess' of Victorian England, Lady Colin Campbell. He also made his feelings fairly clear about Blenheim: the only stipulation he insisted on about his funeral was that on no account were his remains to rest within its walls.

Instead, some four days later, and having lain in state and been accorded the ceremony and pomp which etiquette prescribes for even the most unsatisfactory of dukes, George Charles, 8th Duke of Marlborough was duly deposited in the spot that he had chosen – an anonymous corner in nearby Bladon churchyard. His duchess sensibly departed for her house in Brighton, where in the course of time she met and married the heroic soldier Lord Charles Beresford, VC. She enriched his life as she had previously enriched the Duke's; but, although legally Lady Beresford, the former Mrs Hammersley from Brooklyn insisted on retaining her title of Duchess of Marlborough. Presumably she felt that since she had paid for it she had a perfect right to keep it.

Blenheim was liberated by the 8th Duke's death, and so was Sunny, who from his miserable existence in his father's shadow had suddenly emerged as one of the most enviable and envied young men in England. He had the house and the title, and for the first time in his life could please himself entirely over what he did and whom he had to stay at Blenheim. One of the first to come was cousin Winston.

There is a somewhat grudging reference to this in a letter from Lord Randolph to his mother, written just after Winston passed into Sandhurst. 'Winston seems to have done well in his Sandhurst examination. . . . I don't mind him going to Blenheim as long as I don't go there myself. They seem to make a fuss of him, and of course he knows nothing of the past.'

'They' were Sunny and his mother, 'Goosey' Blandford, now happily installed at Blenheim as its chatelaine. As for knowing 'nothing of the past', Lord Randolph was clearly crediting his son with considerable naïvety and failed to understand the friendship developing between Winston and Sunny.

In some ways it was an unlikely friendship, for their characters could hardly have appeared more different. Sunny was as shy as Winston was assertive, Sunny was a duke and Winston a penniless cadet at Sandhurst, but there were a number of important things they had in common. Each had suffered from his father's disapproval and neglect, and both been deeply affected by traumas in the family. They were linked by blood; Winston was his cousin's heir should anything happen to Lord Randolph – as by now it seemed increasingly likely that it would. Above all, they shared in the extraordinary inheritance of Blenheim, and were free to enjoy it and to make the most of it together.

The vast house and its emotional legacy would affect both of them profoundly. As 9th Duke, Sunny would remain in thrall to Blenheim all his life; he would love it jealously and dedicate himself to making good the ravages inflicted by his grandfather and father, and to restoring the splendour and renown of the great 1st Duke of Marlborough. It was a pious cause to which he would sacrifice his happiness.

Winston's reaction to the house and all it represented was quite different. One can envisage the effect of sudden contact with an ancestral house like Blenheim on a highly imaginative eighteen-year-old at the tail end of a miserable adolescence. Blenheim represented the perfect contrast and escape from his own domestic chaos and depression; and in its overwhelming way it was the absolute embodiment of the sort of terrestrial greatness which Lord Randolph failed to achieve. Stripped of its treasures, it was still the living palace of a hero. With its multitudes of servants it remained inordinately grand. It was a living witness to the power of history; proof, if proof were needed, of the enduring splendour and uniqueness of the Spencer-Churchills. Here was the ducal life *par excellence*, a most compelling blend of pomp and power, feudal privilege, tradition, and great luxury for its chosen few.

Life was expanding fast, and for Winston as for Sunny freedom was at hand as Lord Randolph's illness entered its final, most distressing phase. Sandhurst Military Academy was more suited to Churchill's interests and abilities than Harrow School had been. He loved dressing up in uniform (a weakness that would continue almost all his life) and he was absorbed by the technicalities of battle. His fellow-cadets found him companionable, and for the first time in his life he began to work extremely hard. Military history – and in particular the lives of great military leaders – fascinated him. He scorned drills and team games but he loved riding and made himself a tough and skilful horseman.

There were several reasons for his enthusiasm for the horse. Riding was the gentleman's activity and Churchill was emphatically a gentleman. It was also a toughening activity. 'I am cursed with so feeble a body that I can hardly support the fatigues of the day,' he had written early on to Jennie. But by the exercise of willpower – particularly by forcing himself to spend long hours in the saddle – he could compel his undersized and undeveloped body to perform prodigies of strength and endurance.

There was also a subtler motive for his riding – rebellion against his father. Lord Randolph had firmly decided on the infantry for Winston – and had arranged with the Duke of Cambridge for a place in a rifle regiment. Winston, who would never see the point of walking anywhere when he could ride, entirely disagreed – in his stubborn way had set his heart upon the cavalry.

Lord Randolph's argument against the cavalry was that, with a horse alone costing £200 to buy, a son in a smart fast-living cavalry regiment would need considerably more than in the infantry. Lord Randolph's finances were desperate, and from the letters he wrote during Winston's time at Sandhurst it is clear that his disapproval of his elder son had reached obsessional proportions; along with Mr Gladstone and Lord Salisbury, Winston had become one of sick Lord Randolph's principal *bêtes noires*.

The docile Jack was emphatically his favourite now, and Lord Randolph rarely missed a chance of pointing out to Winston how much cleverer and more conscientious Jack was becoming. Winston was good for nothing, slovenly, extravagant, with 'little claim to cleverness, to knowledge, or any capacity for settled work', Lord Randolph wrote to Duchess Fanny. 'He has', he added, 'great talent for show-off exaggeration and make-believe.'

Lord Randolph was hard on Winston: 'You have demonstrated beyond refutation your slovenly, harum scarum style of work throughout your schooldays . . . always behind-hand, never advancing in your class, incessant complaints and total want of application. . . .'

He ended by warning him that, if his conduct did not improve, 'my responsibility for you is over'. Should he continue the 'idle, useless, unprofitable life' he led at school he would 'become a mere social wastrel and will degenerate into a shabby, unhappy and futile existence', with none but himself to blame for his misfortunes.

It was in June 1894, when Winston had left Sandhurst with the question of his future regiment unresolved, that Lord Randolph had a final consultation with those two harbingers of hopelessness, Dr Buzzard and Dr Roose. By now the family and the Duchess knew the truth and the sick man finally agreed to give up active life completely – for a period.

But Lord Randolph was still insisting that he *could* be cured, provided he was free from worry (which included worries over Winston). It was a wretched situation, with Lord Randolph caught between periods of inertia, terrible depression and outbursts of extraordinary rage. He had gone on too long, and from a victim to be pitied he had become a source of potential disaster to his family should the truth of his affliction ever reach the press. In moments of violence he was also dangerous.

The family closed ranks – as only Victorian upper-class families knew how to. There was no alternative. For years now Jennie had been waiting for her freedom and her chance to marry Kinsky; she would have to go on waiting. A few of the closest, most discreet of friends could tactfully be told something of the truth; this included 'old Tum' as Jennie irreverently called the Prince of Wales. The past forgiven and forgotten, His Royal Highness was to make concerned enquiries of Lord Randolph's medical condition through the unprincipled Dr Buzzard, who in turn conveyed 'such information' for the Prince 'about Lord R's condition as I think may be communicated *without indiscretion*'.

It was Dr Roose's task to do something rather similar with Winston. In November 1894 Winston wrote from Sandhurst. 'My Darling Mummy – you must not be cross with me for having persuaded Roose to keep me informed, as I shall never tell anyone, and it is only right that I should know.' Even had Roose put him off with generalities, he would have learned the truth from Jennie in the end.

She had the hardest task of all; everyone depended on Jennie to ensure that appearances were maintained and her husband's name and reputation were preserved untarnished for posterity. It was a sacrifice, but so much was at stake – including her children's name and future – that she had no alternative but to make it. Then in June 1894 her husband decided for himself the course events should take. 'I know instinctively what is for my good,' he told his mother, 'and that a year's quiet travelling with Jennie, and a change of air and complete repose of mind is what will really benefit me. I shall pursue my travels quietly, not tiring myself and travelling with all possible comfort.'

Once more, Lord Randolph was seeking diversion and escape in travel, but it must have seemed a daunting prospect for a wife to go off round the world with a husband in the throes of general paralysis of the insane. For the family, however, it was a way of

keeping him out of trouble and the public gaze. According to Dr
Buzzard's notes, his patient was now exhibiting marked symptoms
of his illness – 'tremor, faulty articulation, and successive loss
of power in various parts of the frame'. At times he suffered
'grandiose ideas' and could be 'violent of manner'; at other times
'dejection and apathy' were followed by 'unnatural bonhomie'.
As Buzzard told Sir Richard Quain, 'you will understand with the
uncertainty as regards the occurrence of the mental symptoms,
how important it was to get the patient away'.

Even on the eve of his departure Lord Randolph was still
worried that Winston might defy him and enter the cavalry.
'However, I will have none of it,' he told the Duchess, 'and
the Duke of Cambridge will be very angry if he did such things,
as he put his name down for the infantry three years ago.'

Lord Randolph's voyage around the world was the grim finale
to his life. He was forty-six, but with his staring eyes and thread-
bare beard he looked a hundred. His face had darkened with the
mercury treatment Buzzard had prescribed. Fortunately a young
physician, Dr Keith, was in constant and unenviable attendance,
together with a valet.

Travelling across America, 'with all possible comfort', Lord
Randolph seems to have improved, but once aboard a steamer
to Japan he became delusional. For a while he was sleepy and
confused, then at Yokohama tried to kill his valet. Dr Keith
managed to restrain him.

The journey continued to Burma – which in happier times he
had annexed for Britain – then to India, with his condition worsen-
ing all the time. That November, from Government House,
Madras, he managed to write in pencil to his mother – who
kept the missive in a black-edged envelope on which she wrote,
'My Darling's Last Letter'. It was in quivering hand and largely
incoherent, rambling on about the death of the Tsar of Russia,
his distaste for shipboard food, and ending with a final diatribe
against his old enemy, Gladstone, together with the prophecy
that Ireland would never get Home Rule. He made no mention of
either of his sons.

It was now that Dr Keith decided his condition was so serious
that he would have to get him back to London. Jennie must
have hoped that he would mercifully die. But there was a slight
remission, and the hurrying cortège accomplished their ghastly
journey up the Red Sea and the canal to Cairo, dragging Lord

Randolph with them. He could still stagger on his feet, but was almost totally insane.

In a lucid moment he expressed a wish to see Monte Carlo for the last time, so they took him there; but it meant little to him now, and Dr Keith, seeing he was dying, insisted they must leave for London. They reached the Duchess's house in Grosvenor Square on Christmas Eve. Unaware of what was happening, Winston and his brother Jack were spending Christmas with Sunny at Blenheim.

'Lord Randolph Churchill is suffering from General Paralysis, and lies in a semi-comatose and very critical condition.' This terse entry in Dr Buzzard's case-notes is dated Christmas Day, but by 1 January he had evidently rallied yet again, for the doctor then wrote that 'under regular feeding and rest his Lordship has greatly recuperated and can now converse'. He was feeble, but there seemed a chance of at least partial recovery.

This produced an anguished letter from Jennie to her sister Leonie showing something of the strain she had endured and what had been at stake throughout the final stages of her husband's illness.

Physically he is better, but mentally he is 1000 times worse. Even his mother wishes now that he had died the other day. What is going to happen I can't think or what we are going to do if he does get better. Up to now the General Public and even Society does not know the real truth, and after *all* my sacrifices and the misery of these six months it would be hard if it got out. It would do incalculable harm to his political reputation and memory and is a dreadful thing for all of us.

In the same letter, Jennie mentioned her old lover, Kinsky, whom she still longed for. He had grown tired of waiting and had married a twenty-three-year-old princess. It was the end of the great romance of Jennie's life, but she refused to feel sorry for herself. Nor did she want anybody's sympathy. 'I am not *quite* the meek creature I may seem to you,' she told her sister. As for Kinsky, 'He has not behaved particularly well and I can't find much to admire in him, but I care for him as some people like opium or strong drink although they would like not to. *N'en parlons plus.*'

Her real concern was with the task that she had set herself: ensuring the legend of her husband's greatness and playing the part expected of her. She had a bad cold, acute neuralgia, and had

eaten next to nothing since her return, but she was courageous
and had always had the dedication of a great actress to her role
in life. Nothing must be permitted to upset the grand finale of
her husband's deathbed.

He lingered on through most of January, but she rarely left his
room, alternating the bedside watch with Dr Keith. The house
already seemed in mourning with, as Jennie's sister Clara told
Leonie Leslie, 'masses of Churchills who sit with the old Duchess
and go one by one into Randolph's room'. A Victorian deathbed
was a serious family event, and both Jack and Winston were
among the constant visitors.

But, for Lord Randolph, fame and rank brought no ease
from his sufferings, and the horror mounted. He had taken so
much morphia that it was slow to work during the attacks of
inflammation of the brain, and his screams were clearly heard
throughout the house. But even then he had his lucid moments
and kept asking Jennie when they could go to Monte Carlo.

'We'll fetch your mother, and will all start tomorrow morning!'
she told him.

By 20 January the final crisis was beginning. According to the
case-notes of Dr Keith, 'Lord Randolph had a quiet night until
5 a.m. when his bowels moved in bed and continued moving for
three quarters of an hour, very watery and offensive. His pulse
began to rise until it reached 110.'

The next day he suffered delusion after delusion. 'At one time
his pulse ran up to 140 as he tried to make himself sick but it
soon fell.' By the next day he was comatose after two attacks
of violent mania in the night. His temperature rose, his lungs
began to be affected and, at 6.15 on the morning of 24 January,
Lord Randolph's agony was over.

Four days later he was buried in Bladon churchyard beside
the brother he had so disliked, and a memorial service was duly
held for him in Westminster Abbey.

8

Ambition

Lord Randolph Churchill's death brought long-overdue relief to everyone concerned. In later life his son would piously insist how much he missed him, how he regretted not having been closer to him, and what a cruel deprivation he sustained in this early death of his famous father. As he wrote later, 'All my dreams of comradeship with him, of entering parliament at his side and in his support were ended. There remained for me only to pursue his aims and vindicate his memory.'

But did it really? Deprived of a father he may have been, but one looks in vain through the mass of letters written at the time for any reference to Winston's grief. The dead man's mother, Duchess Fanny, was distracted, but if Winston wept for his father this was one occasion in his life when his tears came privately.

Far from having shown the faintest sign of wanting Winston 'at his side' in Parliament, Lord Randolph had been anxious to the end to ensure that his unruly son was assigned to oblivion in the infantry. And, on Winston's part, at the death of his father he did nothing to 'pursue' this 'aim'. On the contrary, and within a few days of Lord Randolph's death, he had his mother pen a deeply tactful letter to the grand old Duke of Cambridge asking for permission to rescind his posting so that he could enter the 4th Hussars, the smart and expensive cavalry regiment he had set his heart on.

His Grace gracefully agreed, so that at a stroke Churchill was relieved from the boring, foot-slogging, drill-dominated future Lord Randolph had tried so hard to condemn him to. Instead he could enjoy the fashionable, romantic, splendidly accoutred life of a Victorian hussar.

According to his own account in *My Early Life* – the most exuberant of all his books – 'from this moment', the future opened up 'like an Aladdin's Cave'. The story of his five ensuing years of soldiering and journalism reads like a happy tale of high adventure. But, strangely, his own version of events does rather less than justice to his real achievement, as this undersized young aristocrat, short of cash and walking over the constant opposition he encountered, set out to push the world in his direction.

Still less does it explain what drove him to these quite prodigious efforts. Instead, his account makes them sound remarkably straightforward, simply a time of high ambition, youthful spirits and patriotic love of action. But the more one learns of the circumstances behind these high endeavours, the less straightforward any of them seems. In an unguarded moment in old age Churchill would admit as much himself. In a letter to the widowed Lady Lytton, formerly Pamela Plowden with whom he had once been in love, he referred to himself in those early days as 'a freak – always that'.

Presumably, he failed to enlarge upon this odd admission because she knew the truth about those far-off years. But since it was then that his character was formed, and the whole pattern of his later life created, it is important to know more about this 'freakish' side of the adventurous young Winston Churchill.

Once freed from restraint and paternal criticism by Lord Randolph's death, he might have been expected to make the most of his good fortune and simply settle down to enjoy the happy life of a hussar in that 'slapdash, self-indulgent, extravagant' way his father had always feared he would.

Quite the reverse occurred. Barely was he posted to his regiment at Aldershot than he began to make it clear that he found little satisfaction in the gentlemanly life of a hussar. Not yet twenty-one, he was suddenly revealed by his father's death as a young man in an enormous hurry, with the most grandiose ambitions and a ruthless energy to make them work.

One of his heroes was inevitably Napoleon, and he had picked on the Emperor's famous maxim for success: '*l'art de fixer les objets longtemps sans être fatigué*'. Suddenly he seemed to have his own long-term objectives fixed with a tireless sense of purpose which startled everyone. Even that worldliest of politicians, Sir Charles Dilke, seemed over-awed by the young phenomenon, remarking later that he had always thought the future Prime Minister, Lord Rosebery, the most ambitious young man he had ever met – until he lunched with Winston Churchill.

Few careerists can have used connections and influence so

unashamedly or with such precocious flair as Winston. Instinctively he seemed to know the value of his father's name and his mother's beauty. 'This is a pushing age, and we must shove with the best,' he told her, as he enlisted her support in his search for glory and adventure. She had already given him her own golden rule for self-advancement – 'do business, darling, only at the top' – and, totally devoid of diffidence or shyness with the great, he was to leave no gilded string unpulled, no famous door unpushed to further his ambitions.

His first priority was to enjoy some real fighting. There was no prospect of this in the hussars, who in 1895 were tediously waiting to exchange the red-brick plains of Aldershot for the sun-baked plains of India. As a recently enlisted subaltern, Churchill was expected to conform to peacetime regimental duties. Impatient and insufferable, he saw no point in that at all.

These were still the palmy days when English cavalry officers (unlike the other ranks) enjoyed the enviable privilege of three months' summer leave. Since the Spaniards were suppressing a colonial revolt in Cuba, why not spend this leave seeing how such things were done? For an ordinary young officer this would have been impossible, but Lieutenant Churchill was no ordinary officer. He was Lord Randolph Churchill's son, and Lord Randolph always had enjoyed connections everywhere.

One of Lord Randolph's closest friends in politics had been Sir Drummond Wolfe, now British ambassador to Spain, and Jennie also knew the proprietor of the *Daily Graphic*. With some judicious nagging, she was persuaded to ask them for assistance. Churchill, meanwhile, used his father's name and friendship with the great Lord Roberts to gain *entrée* to the War Office, where he proposed to send back information on a new bullet being used by the Spanish forces in Cuba.

A few weeks later he was happily *en route* for Cuba, via a short stay in New York where he was briefly entertained and more lastingly inspired by one of his mother's lovers, the Tammany Hall politician and inspirational orator Bourke Cockrane.

Aged twenty, Churchill possessed a pronounced conviction of his own importance, which life was helping to confirm. Thanks to Drummond Wolfe, the Spanish Ministry of War had recommended him to their general in charge of operations, and the *Daily Graphic* had offered him five guineas a time for anything he cared to write about the fighting.

The Cuban war fulfilled his expectations. He saw his first rebels killed in battle, and the Spaniards awarded him a campaign medal which as a serving British officer he was not allowed to wear. He reported to the *Daily Graphic* and Whitehall, and he was even subject to a short but gratifying controversy in the London press which criticised the presence of a British officer in a war against oppressed colonials fighting for their freedom. He also acquired a lifelong taste for Havana cigars and a siesta in the afternoon.

This Cuban holiday was something of a dress-rehearsal for more serious activities in the next few years. It showed, if nothing else, what he could do through energy and sheer persistence. From then on there is a clear impression of this small impatient figure leaving no stone unturned, no log unrolled which could lead him swiftly on to fame and fortune.

But before this life of glory could begin there were frustrating months of home-based soldiering to be endured. During these boring months at Aldershot something of the hidden side of Churchill's nature revealed itself, showing a little of what lay behind that galloping ambition.

Like Lord Randolph, Churchill had inherited more than his share of the family depression, and even before he left for Cuba he was secretly complaining to his mother of the 'slough of despond' in which he was immersed at Aldershot. The success of his Cuban adventure changed all that – but not for long, and after his return to regimental life Churchill seemed sunk in misery and gloom as he waited for some rousing new activity to burst upon a grey horizon.

Although he had been deeply upset at the time of his father's resignation from the Treasury, and was miserable for periods at Harrow, this is the first recorded instance of Churchill being hit by deep depression, that near-suicidal affliction which he used to call 'Black Dog', which would plague him at intervals throughout his life.

Depression is an illness, but a most mysterious one; it can take many forms, and there is still no real understanding of its causes. In Winston's case, it seems to have been triggered off by his father's death. This was odd, remembering how little sign of grief he showed when Lord Randolph died. On the contrary, like Jennie, Winston reacted to his father's death with understandable relief. The shame and misery of Lord Randolph's final days were over. Mother and son were free at last from 'the hazard of concealing' and from the frightful strain of coping with the poor demented victim of those last appalling months. And both had finally achieved their longed-for independence – Jennie to live the life she wanted, and Churchill to seek fame and fortune in the cavalry.

But Lord Randolph's memory began to haunt him. He wrote of how he missed him, how he wished that he had known him better, and from now on his father's life, career and political beliefs would have an almost sacred significance for him.

A possible connection between Winston's unfilial reaction to his father's death and his subsequent depression is suggested by a recent 'memoir on madness' from the novelist William Styron entitled *Darkness Visible.* While emphasising the mysterious nature of depression, he puts forward a widely held hypothesis on the relationship between a certain type of chronic depression and what is termed 'incomplete mourning' following bereavement of the young.

There is apparently a high incidence of cases of acute depression following 'the traumatic death of a parent at around the time of puberty which are not entirely explained by grief. Indeed, serious depression sometimes follows cases where the young show little outward sign of sorrow, and it is suggested that emotional damage can actually be caused by failure to accept bereavement with 'the natural catharsis of accompanying grief '. Without this catharsis, everything is bottled up, and a young person who already has depressive tendencies can suffer 'irreparable emotional havoc' from his failure to come to proper terms with a parent's death.

Abraham Lincoln, who lost his mother during childhood, and exhibited symptoms of 'incomplete mourning' at the time, is cited as a classic case of this. Winston could well have been another.

It certainly seems likely that in Winston's 'incomplete mourning' for his father lay the root of much of his subsequent depression. His lifelong obsession with his father makes it clear how much he meant to him – and the truth was that his father's memory must have been a fearful burden. Not only had Winston gone against his father's wishes in his choice of regiment, but he also bore the knowledge of his dying father's deep and lasting disapproval. Worse still were sick Lord Randolph's fearsome prophecies of failure for his feckless son – 'the life of a wastrel', that 'shabby and futile existence' which the dying father had solemnly predicted.

Had Winston come to terms with his memories of his father through the natural processes of grief and mourning, he might have finally accepted what he said and been at peace. But for Winston such acceptance would have been difficult. There was no grief – there was no real mourning. What there was instead was guilt and subsequent despair, the prime ingredients of Churchill's enemy, Black Dog, which sometimes threatened him with self-destruction.

To understand this stage in Churchill's life, one must understand the power of depression and the agony endured by the true depressive. This is in a class removed from the normal person's feelings of unhappiness or 'feeling down'. It brings the constant pain of utter hopelessness. It causes total isolation and despair. For the true depressive in the grip of a serious attack there is an urge to self-destruction which no logic can relieve, no outside help or medication cause to go away. This was the situation which, at twenty-one, Churchill knew he had to cope with. The agony of his depressions was almost certainly the spur which drove young Winston on. The hyper-active depressive is a well-attested psychological phenomenon. As one psychologist puts it, 'many depressives deny themselves rest and relaxation because they cannot afford to stop. If they are forced by circumstances to do so, the black cloud comes down on them.'

There were in fact a number of activities he could turn to to avoid this, and the truly 'freakish' thing about him was the energy and sheer resourcefulness with which he used them all.

The most obvious, and easiest, was one he had already tried in Cuba: the sovereign anodyne of adventure and escape. He would soon turn to this again – and again, on countless occasions for the remainder of his life.

Another antidote against depression was to re-enter that favourite world of all imaginative unhappy adolescents – the world of fantasy and high adventure in which he shared a role with a favourite hero from the past. The way he picked Napoleon as a model for his own ambition was no accident; nor was the fact that he kept a small white bust of Bonaparte on his desk until the day he died. Inevitably Marlborough was an even more appealing source of inspiration, who offered Churchill a heroic model of permanent importance.

Thanks to those powers of 'imaginative make-believe' which he shared with Jennie (and which Lord Randolph had so strongly disapproved of), Churchill had little difficulty in adopting any grand heroic role he wanted.

But the inspiration of Marlborough and Napoleon was not enough to satisfy Churchill's vast ambition and keep Black Dog permanently at bay. In a letter he wrote to Jennie bewailing the misery of peacetime soldiering, Churchill also made a strange admission. The only way, he said, to rouse himself from the depths of depression was to read his father's political speeches, 'many of which I already know by heart'.

Churchill made no secret of what he was seeking when he memorised his father's words. His father was certainly the greatest man he had known, and his speeches held the magic formula for political success. 'I took my politics unquestioningly from him,' he wrote. 'He seemed to have possessed the key alike to popular oratory and political action.' What better 'long-term object' than to follow in his footsteps?

But Lord Randolph was an ambiguous example for a son to follow, his whole career a warning of the tragic awfulness of life. It would be tempting fate to copy him. Time was short, the end uncertain, but for his son there was no alternative.

It was one thing for Churchill to decide that in politics alone could he find true satisfaction for his driven nature; it was another to achieve this, particularly with his regiment due to leave for India for garrison duties in Bangalore in the autumn of 1896. But on the eve of embarkation news came that the Zulu War had started in South Africa.

Here was a chance of a repeat performance of the trip to Cuba, on a considerably greater scale. The situation demanded military action to defend the Empire and offered Churchill the chance to earn a medal he could wear as well as endless opportunities for lucrative and lively journalism. Where there was fighting there was fame and glory, which could lead directly to his ultimate ambition – the great career in British politics.

Once he had made his name, he told his mother, he would swiftly leave the Army for Westminster and, as he put it, 'beat my sabre into an iron despatch box'.

He was soon engaged in the same prodigies of push and pull that got him to Cuba, telling his mother 'he could not believe that with all the influential friends that you possess and all those who would do something for my father's sake, that I would not be allowed to go, were those influences properly exerted'.

This time influence was not enough. Jennie's friends were tiring of doing favours for her over-eager son, and in the end he sailed as planned for India and a bungalow in the hussars' base-camp at Bangalore. There, despite the heat and lack of real conversation, the *objets longtemps* stayed unwaveringly fixed within those very pale blue eyes which showed no sign at all of being *fatigué*.

From Calcutta he was soon writing to Jennie, saying that 'if only I can get hold of the right people, my stay here might be of value'. But the 'right people' failed to respond like their counterparts in England, and the pushing young careerist found himself consigned to spending fourteen months in virtual exile in boring Bangalore.

His duties were minimal, his fellow-officers unstimulating; so was southern India. He collected butterflies and grew roses, but Bangalore had even less than Aldershot to offset his frustration. For someone of Churchill's depressive temperament it could have been a recipe for suicide. Instead it proved the most formative time of his career.

For the first time in his life his extraordinary strength of will and powers of concentration helped him ward off a recurrence of depression as he embarked upon a strict regime of physical and mental self-improvement. Acutely aware of his deficiencies, he started to re-create himself in preparation for the life he wanted with a determination worthy of the young Napoleon himself.

In a fascinating analysis of Churchill's character, written in 1970, the psychologist Anthony Storr notices an apparent contradiction between Churchill's character and his physique. Physically, he seemed to be 'of endomorphic structure', small-boned and lightly muscled, a make-up which tends to go with qualities of carefulness, restraint and introversion. Churchill's 'love of risk', he writes, 'of physical adventure, his energy and assertiveness are traits which one would expect to find in the heavily muscled mesomorph'. This leads Storr to conclude that 'the more one examines Winston Churchill as a person, the more one is forced to the conclusion that his aggressiveness, his courage and his dominance were not rooted in his inheritance, but were the product of deliberate decision and iron will'.

This view is very much borne out by what we know about him at this period. Barely two years before, he was complaining to his mother about being 'cursed with so feeble a body' that he could 'hardly support the fatigues of the day' at Sandhurst. Since then he had forcibly endured the rigours of the riding school, but on landing at Bombay he had suffered a serious setback by dislocating his right shoulder, a weakness which tended to recur throughout his life. Despite this painful disability Churchill started playing polo with his right arm strapped against his side. Polo is not a game for weaklings, its principal ingredients being sheer aggression and the will to win. During his time in Bangalore, Churchill became one of the top polo-players with the Army in India.

While he was strengthening his body on the polo-field, the young lieutenant was doing something rather similar with his mind. Deeply conscious of his lack of the university education his father had enjoyed, during the long hot afternoon siestas he began a strenuous course of reading, which he pursued with much the same energy and willpower which he brought to the polo-field.

He read the two historians his father had approved of – Gibbon and Macaulay. History could be a source of lessons for the future, but for Churchill it was more important to use it as a model for his literary style. It was that rhetorical, measured eighteenth-century language which he consciously adopted in his speech, and which would resound through English politics for the next sixty years.

His reading was deliberate and wide. It included St-Simon's memoirs, Schopenhauer's pessimistic philosophy, biographies of heroes like Napoleon and Nelson, and 'that rich source of spurious erudition' Bartlett's *Familiar Quotations*, which he would recommend to Oswald Mosley and was still using for his speeches in the House of Commons in his fifties. He had no time for anything as frivolous as fiction; his studies were a highly functional, single-minded preparation for the 'great game of politics' he was determined he would play.

As further training he began working every day on copies of the *Annual Register* which Jennie started sending out to him. These leather-bound volumes faithfully record the great political speeches of the past, and Churchill set himself the daily task of writing out his own speech on a particular event, then carefully comparing it with what Peel or Gladstone or Disraeli had actually said in Parliament.

· But, as he wrote to Jennie, 'a good knowledge of the *Annual Register* is valuable only for its facts. . . . Macaulay, Gibbon and Plato etc. must train the muscles to wield that sword to greatest effect'.

Time was passing. He was nearly twenty-three, and sharp ambition had begun to goad him once again to hurry. Back on leave in England in the spring of 1897, he made his first attempt to test himself in active politics by speaking at a Conservative and Unionist rally near Bath. He was not a particular success – public speaking was one more accomplishment he would need to master through practice and through exercise of will – but he satisfied himself that the lisp inherited from Lord Randolph was no greater political impediment than it had been to his father.

His father's name and his mother's friends and influence remained his greatest assets, which he cultivated carefully. Jennie's friends could be useful sources of information, and it was at one of the houses of the rich and famous he would always love – Goodwood House, the Sussex stately home of the Duke of Richmond and Gordon – that he learned that war was brewing on the North-West Frontier. The imperial warrior, General Sir Bindon Blood, as warlike as his name, was already on the borders of Afghanistan, organising what he called 'a little pheasant shoot' with the Pathan tribesmen as his quarry.

Like the Cubans, these mountain people were attempting to assert their independence. The General's shooting party, the Malakand Field Force, was a retaliatory expedition to teach these 'lesser breeds' the power of the machine-gun. Churchill left Goodwood House desperate to join the General.

Having already met him socially, he had no difficulty with introductions. After sending a cable simply stating he was coming, he was on his way to the North-West Frontier, again with the double role of serving as commissioned officer and as correspondent for the *Daily Telegraph*.

This expedition marked another stage in Churchill's progress. Had he been simply a careerist, hell-bent on fame and fortune, he would have accompanied the troops as they burned the villages,

made copious notes on the background and the fighting, filed
his copy to the *Daily Telegraph* and prepared himself to write
a lively history of his experiences. All this he would do in his
first published book, *The Malakand Field Force*, but from the
letters Churchill wrote to Jennie from the field it is clear that
it was incidental to deeper purposes. He was seeking danger for
other reasons. In one letter he describes how on three separate
occasions he had ridden his conspicuous white pony in front of the
Pathans, 'all along the front of the skirmish line where everyone
else was lying down in cover. . . . Foolish perhaps', he added,
'but given an audience there is no act too daring or too noble.
Without the gallery things are different.'

Among other things Lord Randolph had criticised his son's
'great talent for show-off exaggeration and make-believe'; but on
a white horse in front of the Pathans make-believe could suddenly
become reality with 'an audience' to prove his bravery.

'Being in many ways a coward – and particularly at school –
there is no ambition I cherish so keenly as to gain a reputation
for personal courage,' he wrote to his mother. As it was, he had
to content himself with being mentioned several times in Blood's
despatches.

But there was more to Churchill's antics than flamboyant
medal-hunting. With the depressive's urge to self-destruction,
he was wagering his life against his great career, and detecting
destiny in his survival.

These were important moments in his personal theatre, and
until old age he would grimly relish standing in positions of exaggerated danger, like his hero Marlborough, on the battlefield.

Before the Malakand expedition, twenty-two-year-old Churchill
had written a large part of a novel which he called *Savrola*. It
would not be finished and published until 1899, but it reveals
much about his character during this period.

Savrola is an unexpected book to have come from the pen of
this bounding young careerist, and in later life Churchill would
generally advise his friends against reading it. This may have
been modesty, for as a novel this Ruritanian political romance
did little for his reputation. But at the height of his success he
may also have realised that *Savrola* gave away far more of his
inner self than he would wish.

The strangest thing about *Savrola* is that it was written at two quite separate levels. The plot is improbably romantic. It tells the story of a revolution in the mythical republic of Laurania led by the noble hero of the people, the young statesman Savrola, against the forces of its corrupt and aged president. After a battle in the capital, the revolution triumphs, the president is killed, but Savrola is rejected by the people he has saved and departs for exile with the only woman he loves, the distant beautiful Lucile, wife of the president he had helped to slay.

It is tempting to find echoes here of Churchill's own situation, with Savrola superseding the dead father-figure of the failed statesman, both in his political role and in the affections of the beautiful but motherly Lucile. The story has clear unconscious parallels to Churchill's own behaviour after Lord Randolph's death. But what is far more obvious is the extent to which the character of the romantic young Savrola is based upon the secret aims and great ambitions of the author. At this level *Savrola* becomes a highly polished exercise in the autobiography of dreams. Make-believe mingles with reality, and against the background of this painfully romantic schoolboy tale one can hear the unmistakable voice of young Lieutenant Churchill speaking out about philosophy and politics and, most of all, about himself.

His descriptions of the proud Savrola almost read like advertising copy for Lieutenant Churchill.

Vehement, high and daring was his cast of mind. The life he lived was the only one he could ever live; he must go on to the end. The end comes often early to such men, whose spirits are so wrought that they know rest only in action, contentment only in danger, and in confusion find their only peace.

There is more here than an ordinary description of Churchill's own driven nature. The idea of the need to hurry, spurred on by the likelihood of early death, was part of his clear identification with Lord Randolph's career – and a theme that persisted until his own robust old age disproved it. More interesting still are those words that he adopts as something of a motto for Savrola. At one point in the book, there is a sort of mirror-image as he describes Savrola reading Macaulay's *History of England*. 'Vehement, high and daring' are precisely the words Macaulay uses to describe John Churchill, Duke of Marlborough.

The mirror-images continue. Savrola, like Churchill, is a lonely aristocrat attracted irresistibly to the cause of politics. He is the idol of the people but despises the venal middle classes. He lives alone in high-minded studious seclusion, reading the classics, tended only by a devoted old nurse like Mrs Everest who cooks his food and tidies his bare apartment.

Why, Savrola muses, does he bother with the cares of politics?

The struggle, the labour, the constant rush of affairs, the sacrifice of so many things that make life easy or pleasant – for what? A people's good! That, he could not disguise from himself, was the direction rather than the cause of his efforts. Ambition was the motive force and he was powerless to resist it.

But behind ambition lies the true depressive's vision of the world and life itself: 'Life seemed unsatisfactory; something was lacking. When all deductions had been made on the scores of ambition, duty, excitement or fame, there remained an unabsorbed residuum of pure emptiness.'

Despite the fame and all the great achievements Churchill's ambition would lead to in the years ahead, that 'unabsorbed residuum' would haunt him for the remainder of his life.

9

'Faithful but Unfortunate'

While Churchill was abroad, his favourite cousin, Sunny, Duke of Marlborough, had struggles of his own at Blenheim.

True, this reserved and dignified young man possessed his dukedom and his palace; and outwardly, at least, his situation was easier than his cousin Winston's. In the 1880s a dukedom was still just one step down from royalty in public estimation. Resplendent at the apex of the aristocracy, dukes inhabited the world around them in much the same way as feudal princes; deference was automatic, Society was theirs, their whole position was almost too grandiose for comfort.

Sunny undoubtedly enjoyed his role and worshipped Blenheim. As well as the house, he inherited an assured income of £50,000 a year, a London mansion and fifteen and a half thousand acres of Oxfordshire. He had stables, carriages and servants, all in great profusion. Still only twenty-one, he, if anyone, should have been able to enjoy the winnings that the lottery of birth had dealt him. But there was, inevitably, a flaw in his great inheritance. Like Winston, Sunny had inherited the family depressiveness – without the lively genes of the Jeromes which were enabling Winston to control it. In addition there was Sunny's duty to his great inheritance, and the powerful dead hand of the greatest of the Marlboroughs weighed heavily upon him. Scarcely were the bonfires celebrating his accession cold than he was forced to understand his lifelong obligations to his overwhelming patrimony.

As always, Blenheim needed money – in abundance. Its acreage of roof was leaking, its farms required capital investment, the interior of the house was a disgrace and much of the famous gardens had become a wilderness. How was a conscientious duke of twenty-one to meet such an inordinate expense?

Even before his nephew succeeded to the title in 1892, Lord

Randolph's thoughts had turned to a sound financial marriage for the youthful Sunny. Lord Randolph had been meeting the young French duc de Breteuil, who had saved *his* family by marrying a very rich Miss Garner from America, and had discovered that she had a sister, 'neither pretty nor ugly, but of a good disposition and intelligent'. In addition she possessed an income of £20,000 a year. 'What a good business this would be for Sunny,' Lord Randolph had written to his mother. 'Where is that youth? I must see him. I think this might be cooked up.'

This was one more project Churchill's ailing father failed to 'cook up', but it shows the way the wind was blowing. Sunny's Uncle Randolph and his father had both married American heiresses. Why not Sunny, too?

The young man briefly fought against the notion, and for some months after succeeding to the dukedom was rumoured to have fallen in love with a bewitching but anonymous young woman. But dukes like Sunny could not afford the luxury of marrying for love. The debts at Blenheim were increasing, and after the depredations of his father and his grandfather, Sunny had little left to sell – except himself. So in the spring of 1893 he made himself forget the girl he was in love with, and placed himself firmly on the marriage market for the highest, most appreciative bidder.

In the 1890s the one spot on earth where an authentic English dukedom still conveyed as much prestige as it did in England was in the country where all titles were expressly forbidden by its founding fathers. In New York, English aristocrats, like old English furniture and pictures, conveyed immense if somewhat puzzling prestige, and much of the *nouveau riche* East Coast society was intent on acquiring its social hallmark in the form of European art and titles. An emotion similar to that which in the early seventies had impelled Mrs Leonard Jerome to Paris, now inspired Mrs Willie Kissim Vanderbilt to take a serious interest in Blenheim and the Duke of Marlborough.

Mrs Willie was wife of one of the two grandsons who had inherited the vast fortune of the rough-hewn Commodore Vanderbilt, the railway king of America. A monster of snobbish self-assertion, she was obsessed with using her husband's wealth to establish her position as queen of New York's superrich society against her principal rival, her even richer, equally assertive sister-in-law, Mrs Cornelius Vanderbilt II.

No holds were barred within the family as these two profoundly ugly women locked themselves like mastodons in a war of spectacularly conspicuous consumption that engaged the resources of the Vanderbilts throughout the 1880s. Steam-yacht was built to answer steam-yacht. A multi-million-dollar New York mansion was built and crammed with European works of art, only to be upstaged by an even larger New York mansion still more tightly crammed with European works of art.

Mrs Willie sensed victory when, in 1888, she commissioned Richard Morris Hunt, President of the American Institute of Architects, to design her a simple 'summer cottage' at fashionable Newport, Rhode Island. Her cottage cost $7 million, was modelled on Marie-Antoinette's Petit Trianon at Versailles, and decorated with the most ostentatious eighteenth-century French furnishings and works of art that the obedient Willie Kissim Vanderbilt could buy.

For ten brief weeks of that year's Newport summer season, the portly chatelaine of Marble House enjoyed her victory over her jealous rival. But Mrs Cornelius Vanderbilt II was not so easily put down. Barely had Marble House opened its regal doors than she, too, secured the services of Richard Morris Hunt – together with the self-same workmen who had built Marble House. And by 1892 Mrs Cornelius also had her simple 'summer cottage' on Bellevue Avenue, slap next door to Marble House. It was even bigger and more richly regal than its neighbour. With a touch of possibly unconscious irony it was called The Breakers.

The Breakers indirectly altered Sunny Marlborough's life. For it was in answer to her rival's house that Mrs Willie Kissim first began to plan a sensational marriage for her swan-necked seventeen-year-old daughter Consuelo.

Since earliest childhood Consuelo had been treated like the centrepiece of her parents' collection of precious works of art. Her future role in life was preordained when she was named after Consuelo Iznaga, a friend of Mrs Willie's who had married the Duke of Manchester.

Like her unassuming father, the young Consuelo was putty in her mother's hands and submitted to an education more fitting for a European princess than for the daughter of a simple New York multi-millionaire. She travelled extensively in Europe, was painted by the most fashionable French portrait-painters of the day and, even at home, conversed in French. When she occasionally rebelled or lapsed, her mother set about her with a riding crop.

Mrs Willie heard of the young Duke of Marlborough's situation from an important go-between in London society of the day, the lively Lady Paget, formerly Miss Minnie Stevens of New York. It was at Lady Paget's house in Cadogan Square that Consuelo Vanderbilt met Sunny Marlborough during her stay in London in the summer of 1893.

It must have been a most uncomfortable occasion. Consuelo, very tall and shy and overshadowed by her dreadful mother, was still only a teenager. Sunny was twenty-two and had been Duke for barely a year. They were placed next to one another, and one wonders what they found to talk about.

Probably not very much – for Sunny was still pining sentimentally for someone else and Consuelo, on her return to America, promptly fell in love with the rich and handsome sportsman Winthrop Rutherfurd.

None of this reached the ears of Mrs Willie, who was now intent upon her final coup. With Lady Paget as her London agent, all was proceeding with discreet efficiency. There was no unseemly rush, and with Lady Paget as a go-between she could complete her negotiations with Sunny.

In the spring of 1895, Consuelo and her mother made another trip to Europe, in the course of which they were invited for a long weekend at Blenheim. Consuelo, now besotted with Rutherfurd, did her best to make it clear that she was not interested in Blenheim or its duke; her mother made it clearer still that she was fascinated by them both. By now Lady Paget had completed her behind-the-scenes negotiations with Sunny, and Mrs Willie invited him to Newport for September. The Duke accepted.

That summer, Mrs Willie swept all before her. Rutherfurd was 'persuaded' to leave Newport in a hurry. Her husband was told that no expense could be too great to complete their daughter's happiness by making her a duchess. Consuelo herself was warned that no objections to her mother's plans would be tolerated. That September, when Sunny duly came to Marble House and unromantically proposed to Consuelo in the Gothic Room, she unromantically accepted.

The high spot of the autumn's Newport season was the coming-out ball at The Breakers for Consuelo's cousin Gertrude, much-loved daughter of the Cornelius Vanderbilt IIs. That same evening Mrs Willie arranged an informal dinner-party at Marble House before all proceeded to the ball. It was as dinner ended that she rose to give the news that made *her* happiness complete. Her daughter, Consuelo, would shortly be marrying *his Grace*, the Duke of Marlborough – and that evening it was Consuelo, not her cousin Gertrude, who was the star of Gertrude's ball.

With this final victory over her sister-in-law, Mrs Willie was preparing to bow out. In fact she was already starting divorce proceedings against her inoffensive husband, and would shortly marry her Newport neighbour, Oliver P. Belmont, who was almost as rich and rather more exciting than the ill-used Willie Kissim. But first there was Consuelo's wedding to be made the most of.

Having so carefully arranged the purchase of the Duke of Marlborough, Mrs Willie needed to ensure that Willie would meet the bill – which of course he did, like the fond father and honest businessman he was. It was not unlike the purchase of one of her prized European works of art; and Consuelo, something of a work of art herself, was guarded night and day.

Sunny arrived, together with his lawyers, although the Blenheim orchids, sent for Consuelo, failed to make it. The Vanderbilts had already fixed 5 November 1896 for the wedding day; but Sunny, remembering that this was Guy Fawkes Day, and that Guy Fawkes had once attempted to blow up the House of Lords, insisted on the sixth as 'more appropriate'.

'I spent the morning of my wedding day in tears and alone,' the bride recalled. This did not prevent her being punctually delivered to St Thomas's Anglican cathedral on Fifth Avenue, Manhattan, where the Bishops of New York and Long Island were awaiting her in the presence of a fashionable congregation. Sunny was also waiting – to receive both bride and a guaranteed annual income of $30,000.

So that there was absolutely no mistake, it had also been arranged that when Willie Kissim Vanderbilt entered the vestry for the signing of the wedding register he should also sign the marriage settlement.

It was here that the Marlborough lawyers proved their worth. That all-important document gave the Marlboroughs what their palace desperately needed – a capital lump sum of $2 1/2 million worth of shares in the Vanderbilt-owned Beech Creek Railroad, backed by a guarantee from the New York Central. As the

Washington Post observed, 'The roof of the Marlborough Castle [sic] will now receive some much needed repairs, and the family will be able to return to three good meals a day.'

There is a firm impression that, despite both bride and groom's lack of enthusiasm, Sunny's marriage might have had a chance, had it not been for Blenheim and his dukedom. The European honeymoon proceeded amicably enough, but once the couple finally arrived at Blenheim all the melancholy of that melancholy house assailed Consuelo as it had so many of her predecessors.

After the comfort and luxury of millionaires' New York, she found her palace positively spartan.

'How strange that in so great a house there should not be one really livable room,' she remarked to her husband. And she soon found the words of welcome left above the bedroom fireplace by her husband's father: 'Dust, ashes, nothing.' It might have been his verdict on her marriage.

Immediately, she and Sunny found themselves regretting the partners they might have married. Sunny felt Consuelo was failing to regard his great position in Society with sufficient reverence, and Consuelo felt that Sunny was a pompous bore.

Soon they were dining every night in ducal silence, waited on by footmen in livery but eating little and finding even less to say to one another. Consuelo describes how, in these silences, Sunny 'pushed his plate away . . . backed his chair away from the table, crossed one leg over the other, and endlessly twirled the ring on his little finger'. In retaliation, Consuelo started knitting during dinner, and the butler read detective-stories in the hall.

Somewhat surprisingly these frigid mealtimes did not prevent Consuelo performing her second most important task once Blenheim's roof had been repaired. It was a task which Duchess Fanny pointed out to her in no uncertain terms when they met in the dowager's drawing room in Grosvenor Square.

Duchess Fanny was still in mourning for Lord Randolph. Black lace cap on head, and ear-trumpet at the ready, she greeted Consuelo 'with a welcoming kiss in the manner of a deposed sovereign greeting her successor'.

'Your first duty', she told her, 'is to have a child, and it must be a son, because it would be intolerable if that little upstart Winston ever became Duke.'

This strange reference by the Duchess to the son of her beloved Randolph was a reminder of the fact that, since Lord Randolph's death, Winston was now directly in line for the dukedom. It also shows the hostility towards him in the family, and how its staider members were regarding his ambitious antics.

As for Consuelo's 'duty' – her husband romantically referred to it as 'providing the link in the chain' – she managed to oblige, giving birth to a ten-pound son in September 1897 who was duly christened John Albert Edward William. Taking the title of Marquess of Blandford, he was known henceforth as 'Bert'.

Consuelo was still in her early twenties; very elegant and tall and at last freed from her mother, she started to grow up. Her title allied with her own great private income gave her an element of independence which she began to make the most of; this further infuriated Sunny.

She started travelling abroad and forming friendships quite apart from Sunny. There was a second son, Lord Ivor, born in 1898, but the silences at dinner lengthened. She had lovers, and there were long estrangements. Sunny grew more miserable than ever and took lovers of his own.

But the link was firmly in the chain, the dukedom was secure for a further generation, and Blenheim, thanks to Willie Kissim Vanderbilt, was preserved.

If there were sacrifices demanded of a duke, Sunny was proud to make them; the marriage was maintained for much the same reasons as it was originally arranged. Blenheim demanded it.

10
Power and Glory

While Sunny was so consciously the martyr, and so painfully aware of having sacrificed his happiness to maintain the substance and the honours of the 1st Duke's earthly legacy, Churchill was acting not unlike the 1st Duke himself in the springtime of his own ambitious manhood.

In the 1660s young John Churchill was a brash careerist firmly on the make. In the 1890s Winston Churchill was not dissimilar. But times had changed from the colourful world of Carolean England – and it was Winston's very similarities with the first and greatest Duke of Marlborough which made the Duchess see him as an upstart and dread him succeeding to the dukedom.

A growing band of influential people were agreeing with her. Medal-hunting and blatant self-advertisement were bad form in late-Victorian upper-class society (such things, if done at all, were done discreetly, or by the rising middle classes), and what one biographer has called 'the rogue elements' in Churchill's character were generally ascribed to the unfortunate American influences in his heredity.

This was almost certainly correct. Without his mother's close support and the fresh genetic input from the Jeromes, it is hard to imagine Churchill breaking free from the doom-filled background of his father's family. But he had two great assets which made his drive and brashness always ultimately acceptable. The first was that, although socially a rebel and at odds with much of the settled social order, he remained at heart 'aboriginally' conservative and patriotic, with a romantic passion and obsession with the Empire. And the second was that, however angrily his enemies condemned him as a bounder, none could impugn his absolute credentials as a gentleman. These were important facts which, rightly used, conferred a sort of charmed invulnerability.

In conjunction with his frantic energy and ambition, Churchill employed them to extraordinary advantage.

The short period after the campaign with the Malakand Field Force on the North-West Frontier is a fascinating one in which the young careerist never missed a trick. His first requirements were fame and money. (His personal extravagance, combined with Jennie's, had brought the family closer than ever to disaster. Because of this, Brother Jack, instead of going on to university as he had wanted, would soon be entering a firm of stockbrokers with Jennie's friend Sir Ernest Cassel's backing.) He achieved both through the publication of his book on the Malakand campaign, which he wrote in five weeks flat.

The invaluable Jennie produced the publisher; Churchill's 'literary' uncle, Aunt Clara's wayward husband, Moreton Frewen, did a speedy and typically erratic job editing the manuscript; and the book was in the shops for the new year of 1898.

Churchill was anguished when he saw that, thanks to too much haste and Uncle Moreton's editing, the book was full of errors of typography and grammar. His reaction shows just how vulnerable he was to the disapproving judgement of the dead Lord Randolph. 'One more example of your slovenly shiftless habits,' he heard that unforgiving voice repeating. He added bitterly that awareness of his father's certain disapproval 'destroyed all the pleasure that I had hoped to get from the book', leaving only 'shame that such an impertinence should be presented to the public'.

Not that he need have worried, for despite the errors, this first published book was widely and favourably reviewed and earned him more than twice the annual salary of a subaltern. More important still, it brought its youthful author to the attention of those who mattered, in particular to the Prime Minister, Lord Salisbury, and to His Royal Highness the Prince of Wales. Again, this was largely thanks to Jennie, who ensured that advance copies reached them with an appropriate letter from her son.

'How do I address the Prince of Wales?' he asked her.

'Address him as "your Royal Highness", and start each fresh paragraph with "Sir",' she told him.

By 1898, Churchill had his heart impatiently set upon the next step in his great career; natural actor that he was, he was excited by the latest drama just about to start in the immense theatre of the British Empire.

Since General Gordon had been killed by the forces of the Mahdi and his Dervish army at Khartoum in 1885, and the British had lost influence throughout the Sudan. Now vengeance was at hand in the shape of gigantic General Sir Horatio Herbert Kitchener who, with an army twenty thousand strong, was advancing slowly up the Nile with all the new technology of military destruction. Churchill was determined to go too.

This was not easy for a cavalry lieutenant stationed in Bangalore. But by using his high-powered contacts and his dual role as journalist and soldier Churchill had perfected the technique of propelling himself as and where he wanted.

It should have been straightforward to get himself assigned to the expedition. Thanks to his book's success, newspapers were willing to employ him as a correspondent and, home on leave in the summer of 1898, he was graciously received by his father's ancient colleague/enemy Lord Salisbury (now in his third spell as Prime Minister), who wished to congratulate Lord Randolph's son upon his book.

'If there is anything at any time that I can do which would be of assistance to you, pray do not fail to let me know,' the man Churchill called 'the master of the British world' muttered as they parted. Taking instant advantage, he mentioned Kitchener and the Sudan. Lord Salisbury promised his assistance. So did another of the young man's famous readers – Albert Edward Prince of Wales.

But Kitchener was not impressed by journalists – nor was he having bright young officers with literary pretensions thrust upon him, even by prime ministers and future kings of England. Lieutenant Churchill, on the point of leaving for the Nile, received a most emphatic negative.

'No young man should ever take no for an answer,' Churchill remarked when no longer young himself – but it takes a young man of exceptional self-confidence to persist where a prime minister has been refused.

As always, he was in a hurry, knowing that the decisive battle for the whole Sudan was not far off. But he was also worldly-wise enough to sense that General Kitchener's high-handedness was brewing much resentment in Whitehall. Through family connections once again, he was able to exploit this. At a specially concocted dinner-party he persuaded the Adjutant-General to assert the authority of the War Office over General Kitchener by seconding Lieutenant Churchill to the Lancers on attachment to the expedition.

Having succeeded where Lord Salisbury had failed, he was swiftly on his way to Egypt with a profitable agreement to report on the expedition for the *Morning Post*.

'Life is very cheap, my dearest Mama,' he wrote to Jennie, echoing *Savrola*. 'I have a keen aboriginal desire to kill several of these odious Dervishes & drive the rest of the pestiferous breed to Orcus, and I anticipate enjoying the exercise very much.'

Before dawn on the morning of 2 September 1898, trumpeters awoke the British army bivouacked beside the Nile near the enemy city of Omdurman. Across the river Khartoum lay in ruins, and Churchill was to witness what he later called 'the most signal triumph ever gained by the arms of science over the barbarian', as General Kitchener, with heavy river-gunboats, Maxim guns and Krupp artillery, proceeded to eradicate the Dervish army.

Nine thousand enemy were killed at the cost of several hundred British and Egyptian casualties: Gordon was avenged and the *Pax Britannica* extended through the length and breadth of the Sudan. It was an emphatic reassertion of something that Lieutenant Churchill passionately believed in – the power of the Empire and the civilising mission of the British race over lesser breeds beneath them.

As sheer spectacle, Omdurman was clearly unforgettable; the two armies marched and counter-marched in the desert under the 'immense dome of the sky, dun to turquoise, turquoise to deepest blue, pierced by the flaming sun'. Despite the unequal nature of the conflict with the unromantic technical advantage of 'the British race', Churchill would remember Omdurman as a glimpse of fabled battles from the past, 'the last link in the long chain of those spectacular conflicts whose vivid and majestic splendour has done so much to invest war with glamour'.

He would never lose this sense of the beauty and excitement of the clash of arms, nor would he forget his vision of the warlike splendour of the Empire, and in extreme old age would fondly re-create the battle with ashtrays and cigar butts at the dinner-table.

Omdurman gave him what he longed for – glory in battle, and proof that the unseen hand of fate was still protecting him. Riding with the Lancers, he participated in one of the great nostalgic moments of the British army – the last full-scale charge of a regiment of British cavalry.

On the morning of the second, he was with the Lancers when they were ordered forward to engage the enemy's right wing. A massed Dervish force was unexpectedly encountered in a dried-up watercourse. The cavalry commander ordered his bugler to sound the charge. Seconds later, Churchill was spurring into the thick of the mêlée.

The charge proved a bungled but heroic business, producing three Victoria Crosses and the only heavy British casualties at Omdurman – almost a quarter of the cavalry were killed or wounded. Churchill was exalted by the danger. He had no consciousness of fear and, as he told his mother later, the charge passed 'like a dream'.

In fact he was practical enough to fulfil his 'aboriginal desire to kill several of these odious Dervishes'. In London he had bought himself the latest German Mauser automatic – what he cheerfully called 'a Ripper', on account of the hideous damage it inflicted with its heavy-calibre soft-nosed bullets. Excused from fighting with a sword because of his damaged shoulder, he employed the gun to powerful effect, 'despatching' several of the enemy. When the commander sounded the retreat, Churchill's instinct was to re-engage so that the killing could continue. That it didn't was his one regret. 'Another fifty or sixty casualties would have made the performance historic – and have made us all proud of our race and blood.'

He admitted later that the charge was strategically a 'futile' action, which did nothing to affect the outcome of the battle, but as a demonstration of the warlike genius of the British race it seemed to him a time of glory. It rapidly assumed an even more important inner meaning.

Writing to Jennie on the eve of battle he had said that, should he fail to return, she must calm her sorrow with what he called 'the consolations of philosophy and reflect the utter insignificance of all human beings'. His depressive's theme of the worthlessness of suffering humanity was back, but once he had survived the risks of battle he could feel himself exempted from this gloomy generality. He was truly 'chosen' for some higher purpose, just as he had been when he faced the bullets of the Afghan tribesmen.

'I do not accept the Christian or any other form of religious belief,' he solemnly informed his mother, but he was learning to create a personal religion from the miracles of his survival and the achievements of his dominating ego. Unseen forces were involved in his ambition, raising him above the 'utter insignificance' of humdrum unredeemed humanity. There was to him an obvious pattern linking that painful moment when he damaged his shoulder landing at Bombay with the way this made him choose the Mauser rather than the sword when riding into battle. That choice might well have saved his life.

His next priority was to write the story of the war as soon as possible. Already hard at work on the ship that brought him home to England, Churchill had learned the lesson of his rushed book on the Malakand campaign. He would not risk ridicule again. Instead he took his time, polishing his prose and checking all his sources. When *The River War* appeared in the late summer of 1899, it made his name as a military reporter.

Parts of *The River War* remain extremely readable. The background and the excitement of the story lighten the rhetoric which occasionally creaks with the influence of Gibbon. It is an extraordinarily assured book for an author not yet twenty-five. Judgements are made, policies applauded or denounced with the iron-clad confidence which became the hallmark of the public Winston Churchill.

There are two other interesting precursors of the author's future in *The River War*. One is the emphasis that Churchill places on that all-important charge of the British cavalry. Since it was the climax of his own experience, it has to be the climax of the book, and he uses all his literary skill to make an incidental military mistake appear the noblest of victories. This talent for slewing facts to suit his own perception of events would not desert him in the years ahead.

The second is his treatment of victorious General Kitchener. He had met him just before the battle and was snubbed by him. 'A great general he may be, but he is emphatically no gentleman,' he told his mother. Now he wanted his revenge. Kitchener became the first of a long sacrificial line of generals Churchill employed for literary target practice. Reading *The River War* one might conclude that General Kitchener had really very little part in that overwhelming victory he achieved at Omdurman; the charge of the heroic Lancers seems infinitely more important than the efforts of their distant and unsympathetic general. The most memorable descriptions of Kitchener come when Churchill accuses him of inhuman treatment of the Dervish prisoners, and of desecrating the grave of the Mahdi. Both accusations were denied, and neither appears in subsequent editions of the book.

After Omdurman, Churchill returned to his regiment in India, and it was there that, for the first time in his life, he turned his thoughts to marriage. He was twenty-five and suddenly believed himself in love. He was not a particularly successful suitor; love proved a difficult emotion for him to cope with, and sex an irrelevant diversion from more important matters which obsessed him. He was far from prudish, having grown up in the worldliest of male societies, and granted his enquiring mind and the romantic opportunities of cavalry officers it is hard to believe that he had remained sexually uninitiated. But it is possible. Seeing one's father die in agony of syphilis would deter all but the most determined from the delights of casual sex, and throughout his correspondence and the reminiscences of those who knew him there is no hint of any amorous adventure.

Until now, the young lieutenant's prime emotions had been directed to the pursuit of glory and his great ambitions. Sexual pleasure would have wasted precious time and energy: love for another would have made hiccups in the grand design.

When Churchill wrote *Savrola*, the best he could offer his hero was the chaste affection of ageing, motherly but still beautiful Lucile, widow of the president; in his own case, Jennie – ageing but still beautiful herself – remained the most important woman in his life. She provided him with all the female influence he required, and at the age of twenty-four he was still addressing her in letters as 'My Dearest' and 'My Darling Mama'.

Jennie was now preoccupied with her latest love-affair – an embarrassing passion for the boyish beauty of golden-haired George Cornwallis-West, son of her former friend and fellow 'society beauty' Patsy Cornwallis-West. When they met Jennie was forty-three and the unresisting George was twenty-four, sixteen days older than her doting and still dependent son Winston.

There are signs that Jennie was trying to pare down her son's dependence, and it was at her suggestion that Winston met some friends of hers in Hyderabad. It was here that he fell in love with the young woman he described as 'the most beautiful girl I have ever seen – bar none' – fresh-faced Pamela, the highly independent daughter of the British resident in Hyderabad, Sir Trevor Plowden.

Miss Plowden was intrigued by this difficult young officer. But although they rode an elephant together through the Hyderabad bazaar, and Churchill wrote in guarded terms of marriage, their relationship failed to progress.

Miss Plowden was used to having young officers in love with her and informed Churchill that she felt he was 'incapable of love'. He was certainly naïve about what appealed to frivolous young ladies. In the spring of 1899, when he and Pamela were both back in England, he was invited to stand as Conservative candidate for the Lancashire division of Oldham. Wishing Pamela to share in the fulfilment of his great ambition, he invited her to join him on the hustings.

In *Savrola* the beautiful Lucile had only to sense the power of the hero speaking from the platform, to fall totally beneath his spell; Churchill must have felt that Pamela would do the same. But Pamela was not enthusiastic: Oldham was so far from London and, since Winston had his mother with him, why did he need her there as well?

Politically he did extremely well – losing by a mere three hundred votes – and he was convinced that next time he would win. But romantically the by-election was a disappointment. By failing to appear at Oldham, Miss Plowden forfeited her place in the history of the twentieth century. There was no more talk of marriage. Churchill invited her to Blenheim later that summer, and they enjoyed each other's company, but then parted on the best of terms and rather gratefully – she to the calmer waters of an early marriage to the rich Lord Lytton, and he to the broad ocean of ambition and abiding glory.

Once more the great imperial stage was set for Winston Churchill to play a starring role. This time, with his books and war experience behind him, he had no need to push to get exactly what he wanted. Fighting was starting in South Africa between the Boers of the Transvaal and the British of the Cape. This involved the vast financial interests of the gold- and diamond-mining companies and was inspired by the dreams of the British High Commissioner, Lord Milner, to extend dominion from the Cape to the Transvaal. Churchill found no difficulty persuading the *Morning Post* to hire him as its correspondent at a record fee of £250 a month plus generous expenses.

He went to war in style, sailing first-class aboard the same ship as the British commander-in-chief, Sir Redvers Buller. He was also accompanied by letters of introduction from another of Lord Randolph's old admirers, Joseph Chamberlain, now Colonial Secretary – as well as with ample stocks of whisky and champagne.

J. B. Atkins of the *Manchester Guardian*, one of several other journalists aboard, was intrigued by the solitary figure he encountered:

He was slim, slightly reddish-haired, pale, lively, frequently plunging along the deck with neck out-thrust, as Browning fancied Napoleon; sometimes sitting in meditation folding and unfolding his hands, not nervously but as though he were helping himself to untie mental knots.

They talked, and Atkins soon discovered Churchill's conversation matched his bold Napoleonic stance.

When the prospects of a great career like that of his father, Lord Randolph, excited him, then such a gleam shot from him that he was almost transfigured. I had not before encountered this sort of ambition, unabashed, frankly egotistical, communicating its excitement and extorting sympathy. . . . It was as though a light was switched on inside him which suddenly shone out through his eyes.

The greatest actors are distinguished, not just by mastery of technique, but by some instinct which attracts them to the great dramatic roles that do them justice. Churchill possessed this instinct. He had shown it in Cuba, on the North-West Frontier and at Omdurman. Now he revealed it in polished form in his various adventures in South Africa.

He was after danger, self-advertisement and glory, and rapidly achieved all three, despite the deceptive lull in hostilities which he discovered when he landed. Hurrying to Natal, having heard that Ladysmith was under siege, he and Atkins were offered a trip aboard an improvised armoured train by Captain Aylmer Haldane, an officer he had known in India. Atkins refused, saying it was his duty to report the war rather than get killed or captured by the enemy. But, for Churchill, glory came before his duties to the *Morning Post*, and the risk and the adventure offered by this crazy train made it irresistible. As with the charge at Omdurman, this could provide the chance he needed. 'I have a feeling, a sort of intuition, that if I go something will come of it,' he wrote to Jennie. Something did.

The armoured train, as Atkins had foreseen, became an instant target for the Boer artillery. Enemy fire derailed the three front coaches, while the engine and the rear trucks crammed with troops remained on the tracks like a sitting duck. The hero's moment had arrived – and he was once more in his element.

While Haldane and his troops held off the Boers, Churchill took it upon himself to command the locomotive and, as the bullets whistled round his head, directed the wounded engine-driver in his efforts to free it from the wreckage of the front three coaches. This took time, but Churchill was stimulated by the danger, and he performed admirably. Thanks to his coolness and directions, the engine managed to break free; however, Haldane and the troops were left behind. Stopping the locomotive, Churchill ran back to join them, but the troops were now encircled by the Boers. Churchill attempted to escape on foot across the veld but, having left his trusty 'Ripper' on the train, was unarmed and finally had to submit to the ignominy of being taken prisoner.

At first, he was furious; but, calming in captivity, he realised how this could still enhance his reputation. He was soon thanking Haldane for allowing him what he called 'the star turn' of freeing the locomotive. His fellow-journalists were certain to describe it, and although this might cost him his position on the *Morning Post* the fame would certainly enhance his prospects when he stood for Parliament.

He was right, of course. As he knew quite well, his exploits made a perfect story for the British press, and while his audience at home was reading the heroic tale of his coolness under fire he was already planning the next enthralling episode.

He and Haldane were imprisoned in a temporary camp in Pretoria with a group of British prisoners, several of whom were thinking of escape. Churchill, chafing at inaction, begged to join them; but, according to Haldane's subsequent account, none was particularly keen to have him with them. He was considered too excitable and argumentative, and something of a glory-seeker. There were also worries over whether he was fit enough to make it, but he finally persuaded Haldane and a comrade to take him with them.

On the evening planned for the escape, Churchill went first, climbing through the window of an outside lavatory. But as he waited in the darkness for his friends to join him something alerted the Boer sentries, and Haldane whispered to him to return. Had Churchill been particularly concerned at the others' chances, he might have climbed back through the window and postponed his flight until he could go with them as planned, but such a course was hardly in his nature. He was on his own and at the start of yet another great adventure. Scruffy and unshaven, with a bar of chocolate and £75 sterling, he made his way through the outskirts of Pretoria, rode on a goods-train going east, trekked on by foot, and was finally assisted by a British coal-mine manager who hid him in his rat-infested mine and then helped him cross the frontier into Portuguese East Africa.

By this time the Boers were offering £25 for the British prisoner, Winston Churchill, dead or alive. From Lourenço Marques he telegraphed news of his escape, so that by the time he reached Durban he was guaranteed a hero's welcome. He made the most of it with a carefully prepared 'impromptu' speech, thanking the enthusiastic crowd who welcomed him outside Durban town hall. And, as he had foreseen, the press was eager for his story. After a series of humiliating victories by the Boers, Churchill's escape had much the British public longed to hear – human interest and excitement, great endurance, and this plucky grandson of an English duke outwitting a suddenly formidable opponent.

Churchill reached Durban just before Christmas 1899. By the time the century ended, he had made himself a national celebrity.

His strange capacity for making his fantasies a reality set him apart from all but the most accomplished politicians of the age. And this knack, combined with an actor's skill, caught the public eye, ensuring that anything he did was news. Lord Randolph had possessed something of the same ability – he was a natural actor, too – but he had built himself into a national celebrity over a long period in Parliament and at his public meetings.

Churchill managed this more swiftly before he even entered

Parliament; and in his case there were elements his father lacked. Foremost was his journalistic skill, which gave him access to the rapidly developing mass audience offered by the popular press he wrote for. But more important – and mysterious – was his all-consuming vision of himself, driven by some great Napoleonic purpose and protected by his sense of private destiny. This would be something he would never lose, and the South African experience gave him his first big opportunity to test it out in public.

During the course of this increasingly ferocious war, there would be countless acts of heroism and survival in comparison with which Churchill's 'star turn' would become almost irrelevant. But Churchill's exploits were secure in his personal mythology and would be remembered as great deeds in the hero's life. So would his subsequent adventures about which he wrote for the *Morning Post* while serving as unpaid lieutenant with the South African Light Horse.

His charmed life continued. He was excitedly present at several of the toughest battles of the war, including the disastrous engagement at Spion Kop, where he once more witnessed the results of British generalship – the massed slaughter of his compatriots by concealed Boer infantry. He entered Ladysmith, after the siege was broken, but his powerful imagination helped him write an entirely fictional 'eye-witness' account of the breaking of the siege, as if he had been present at the great event.

He even had his precious family around him. Jennie arrived in Durban with a hospital-ship paid for by the committee of Anglo-American wives she had organised in London. Brother Jack came too, and was wounded in the foot. Even Sunny managed to escape the cares of Blenheim, but all that his dukedom earned him was a humble place on Lord Roberts's staff.

In contrast, South Africa made his cousin Winston's name, but the true purpose of his life was still to be fulfilled. In the autumn of 1900 the Conservative government cashed in on the popularity of the war at home and called the so-called 'Khaki Election'. Churchill hurried back to Oldham for another try.

'Bronzed by African sunshine, close-knit by active service, and tempered by discipline and danger' – his description of his hero Marlborough, returning from *his* African adventures in Tangier at much the same age two hundred years earlier, applied just as well to Winston. He was welcomed as a hero, elected by a considerable majority, and before taking his seat at Westminster gave a lecture tour of the United States which netted him £1,200 – rather less than he expected.

In New York, where he lectured under the personal auspices of Mark Twain, the novelist not only presented him with a signed set of his collected works, but also generously introduced him as 'the hero of five wars, the author of six books [sic], and the future Prime Minister of Great Britain'.

11
Politics

Churchill was twenty-six. Max Beerbohm remembered him around this time as having 'dry hair like a wax-work, no wrinkles and the pallor of one who lived in the limelight. He also had hereditary bad manners and was courteous and brutal alternately.'

Wilfred Scawen-Blunt was kinder, describing him as 'a little, square-headed fellow of no very striking appearance, but of wit, intelligence and originality', when he took his seat in Parliament at the beginning of the new king's reign in February 1901.

The young MP was dedicated, hard-working and, if anything, a little too self-assured. As one of his biographers has put it, 'What was difficult to see in the young Churchill was any specific objective save that of an intense and somewhat alarming personal ambition.' But this was not entirely true. He did possess a clear but undisclosed objective, and he touched on it when referring to his father in his painfully rehearsed and memorised maiden speech to Parliament.

All the leading politicians of the day were there, including Balfour, Chamberlain and Asquith. They were attracted, not by Churchill, but by the eloquence of the greatest orator in Parliament, the young Welsh radical and future Liberal prime minister, David Lloyd George, who had just made a passionate denunciation of the war still dragging on against the Boers. Drawing on his own South African experience, Churchill made a clever speech, praising the bravery of the Boers, but also calling for greater efforts by the British government so as to make it 'easy for the Boers to surrender, and painful and perilous for them to continue'.

Pleading both for war and peace, he was applauded by both sides of the House, and the speech established him as something more than the son of a vividly remembered famous father. As he

sat down he thanked the House for the kindness and patience with
which it had listened to him – 'It has been extended to me, I know,
not on my own account, but because of a splendid memory which
many Honourable Members still preserve.'

It was modestly said; but, if it sounded like a formal tribute
to his father, there was more to it than that.

Since returning from South Africa, Churchill had been facing
a fresh crisis in the family. Despite the gossip of Society, and
bitter opposition from the young man's family, Jennie was set
on marrying her youthful lover, George Cornwallis-West.

Churchill and Jack were secretly appalled; but there was little
they could do to turn their mother's thoughts from marriage,
so they made the best of things. Their mother's marriage at St
Paul's Church, Knightsbridge, on 2 June 1900, was a potent
demonstration of the solidarity and sense of family of the
Spencer-Churchills.

Churchill persuaded cousin Sunny, as head of the family, to
give the eager bride away. The bridegroom's family was absent,
but the Churchills came in force to see Jennie change her name
from Lady Randolph Churchill to Mrs George Cornwallis-West.
And Churchill gave no sign of objecting to this step-father of his
own age in his father's place.

But Jennie's marriage did raise other problems. Until now, as a
journalist and serving soldier, Churchill had not required a settled
London base, and when in London always stayed with his mother
and his brother Jack at Jennie's house in Cumberland Place.

Since this was no longer possible – two grown sons around the
house would have cramped the style of the newly married lovers
– Sunny offered him the lease on a house he owned in Mount
Street, Mayfair, and Churchill and his brother moved in together.
A Mayfair house was grander than he could theoretically afford,
but it was just around the corner from the house in Curzon Street
which an earlier Duke of Marlborough had lent Lord Randolph
Churchill at the start of *his* political career. Nor did the similarities
stop there.

In *Savrola* Churchill had described his hero's study. 'A broad
writing-table occupied the place of honour . . . a large bronze
inkstand formed the centrepiece. It was the writing-table of a
public man.'

He was describing his father's old study as he remembered it
from the house in St James's Place – the scraps of paper littering
the floor, papers and telegrams lying unopened on the table and
'the room lit by electric light in portable shaded lamps'. (The
Churchills had once boasted one of the first houses in the city
to be lit by electricity.)

In Mount Street, he re-created the study for himself, complete
with his father's own impressive writing-table, big bronze inkstand
and carved oak chair, recently transferred from Cumberland Place
together with the portable shaded lamps and his father's precious
papers. Savrola had had the works of Plato and a marble statue
of the Capitoline Venus as his inspiration. Churchill had 'Spy'
cartoons of his father as a politician and bound volumes of his
speeches. The photograph of Jennie's lover Kinsky winning the
Grand National which had once held pride of place in his room at
Sandhurst had been discarded. In its place there was a photograph
of Lord Randolph's most successful horse, the Abbess of Jouarre
(commonly known as 'the Abscess on the Jaw'), carrying the
Churchill racing colours.

It was in this shrine to his father's memory that he started on
the book that would make his name in the literature of politics –
the official two-volume biography of Lord Randolph Churchill.
And it was here that he embarked upon the next great step in his
career – making himself a successful parliamentary politician.

He had long realised that there remained one all-important
weakness which he had to overcome if he was to scale the greatest
heights of politics – his serious deficiency as an orator. Until now
his skill had lain with the written, not the spoken word: he had
little talent for impromptu eloquence, he was uncomfortably
aware of his lack of commanding looks and stature, and he also
had a slight impediment of speech, a sort of lisp which made the
enunciation of *r* and *s* difficult.

But, for Churchill, life's difficulties were there to be overcome.
In the last five years he had trained himself to beat his weaknesses
of education and physique. Through prodigies of willpower he
had formed his mind and body to make himself a champion
polo-player, a man of action and a bestselling author. The skill
of oratory became a fresh accomplishment to master.

Part of the problem was simply one of practice, and during this
period he became a grim practitioner of tongue-twisters to offset
his lisp, and a great orator before his looking-glass. His speeches

were painstakingly prepared, like good dramatic dialogue, and as painstakingly committed to his actor's memory.

But, being Churchill, he could not stop there. He was absorbed in the subject, and composed his thoughts upon it in an essay which he wisely never published. He called it 'The Scaffolding of Rhetoric', and like *Savrola* it provides a powerfully subjective view, not just of oratory, but of his innermost ambitions as a politician. For him the orator stands as 'the embodiment of the passions of the multitude', which it is the orator's duty to reflect. 'Before he can inspire them with any emotion he must be swayed by it himself. . . . Before he can move to tears his own must flow. . . . He may often be inconsistent. He is never consciously insincere.'

By developing a 'striking presence' Churchill's ideal orator overcomes those personal deficiencies of which he was all too conscious in himself. 'Often small, ugly or deformed, the great orator becomes "invested with personal significance", and "a slight and not unpleasant stammer or impediment" can actually be of assistance in "securing the attention of the audience".'

Painstaking as ever, he was working out his theory of the art of rhetoric before he mastered it. Correctness of diction, the use of humour and analogy, argument and rhythm – all are carefully considered, and he offers a precise description of the pattern of the wartime speeches he would deliver forty years later. 'The sentences of the orator when he appeals to his art become long, rolling and sonorous', with 'a cadence which resembles blank verse rather than prose'.

More revealing still is the reason Churchill offers at the start of his political career for mastering the art of rhetoric.

'Of all the talents bestowed upon men,' he argues, 'none is so precious as the gift of oratory', for the unanswerable reason that it is the source of supreme power over all his fellow-men, a power he believes to be 'more durable than that of a great king'. Then he continues with a sentence showing exactly how his mind is working.

The great orator, he writes, is an independent force in the world: even the setbacks of party politics fail to destroy him. 'Abandoned by his party, betrayed by his friends, stripped of his offices, whoever can command this power is still formidable.'

This is a description which applies, of course, to one man only, his model and the source of all his thinking on the subject of politics and power – his father.

To write a biography is to conduct a voyage of discovery around one's subject. In Churchill's case it was a voyage which lasted three whole years – the time it took to research and to write the book – and in the course of it he got to know his father as never in Lord Randolph's lifetime.

Churchill was assiduous in his research, and never tired of hearing the reminiscences of his father's close associates – in particular those of Sir Francis Mowatt, now head of the Civil Service, who had served Lord Randolph at the Treasury; and even more those of his father's great admirer and loyalest friend, Gladstone's heir, Lord Rosebery, who was Liberal Prime Minister from 1894 to 1895. As he wrote, 'I loved to hear Lord Rosebery talk about my father. I had a feeling of getting closer to my father when I talked with his intimate and illustrious friend.'

Churchill was a sentimental man, and his was a sentimental age, so that it suited him to present himself as a devoted son, piously seeking out the tragic father-figure he had loved. In fact his quest bears all the signs of an attempt to propitiate – or, as he preferred to put it, 'vindicate' – his father's memory and make amends for his behaviour at his death.

But, if it was guilt that motivated these elaborate efforts by a son to resurrect his father, Churchill had other reasons for his three-year task. Almost from the moment of Lord Randolph's resignation, Jennie had been preparing her precocious son to recover the position her erratic husband had rejected. When he resigned she put aside Lord Randolph's robes of office for her son, saying that one day he would need them. It was a typically dramatic act of high maternal fantasy – but it was a fantasy her son eagerly adopted.

With Churchill, the essence of his fantasy lay in the re-creation of his father's great political abilities. By acquiring Lord Randolph's powers he could annul the failure his father had predicted for him; and it was in the details of Lord Randolph's political career that Churchill would discover what he needed for his own.

As well as the model for his oratory, here were the day-to-day political ideas he wanted. During his early months as a Conservative MP, Churchill loyally – and rarely unsuccessfully – echoed Lord Randolph Churchill's views.

Lord Randolph's nebulous but resonant invention, 'Tory Democracy', was one of these. 'I believe in the Tory working man,' Churchill insisted – this despite his almost total lack of contact with the working classes. And just as Lord Randolph had finally resigned over his government's additional expenditure on the armed forces, so Churchill was soon in angry opposition to *his* government's additional military expenditure.

On financial matters it was Sir Francis Mowatt who became his mentor, teaching him the essence of Lord Randolph's views on 'sound' – that is, highly economical – finance; for several years to come, Churchill would be the scourge of anything that even faintly smelt of military or naval profligacy.

In terms of parliamentary strategy, Churchill also used his father as his guide. Just as Lord Randolph made his name in Parliament with his breakaway 'Fourth Party', so Churchill tried to lead an iconoclastic splinter group of wild young Tories called the Hughligans (named after Churchill's more respectable but less dynamic parliamentary colleague, Lord Hugh Cecil).

He was soon talked about, distrusted, feared; and parliamentary journalists, recalling Lord Randolph in his fiery prime, could hardly help remarking on the quite uncanny similarities of his son in Parliament.

One described the 'startling' resemblances between 'the son of Lord Randolph and that brilliant statesman. . . . He has the square forehead, and the full bold eye of his father. . . . His hurried stride through the lobby is another point of resemblance; and when something amuses him he has his parent's trick of throwing back his head and laughing heartily.'

Another journalist was even more impressed by similarities of gesture:

When the young member for Oldham addresses the House, with hands on hips, head bent forward, right hand stretched forth, memories of days that are no more flood the brain. Like the father is the son in his habit of independent views on current topics, the unexpectedness of his conclusions, his disregard for authority, his contempt for conventions, and his perfect phrasing of disagreeable remarks.

Churchill would always need a role to play. Much of his genius lay in the way that he would take a part that suited him, work on it, build it in whatever way he needed, and act it out with absolute conviction. He had already been Savrola and the young Napoleon, the warrior of Omdurman and the literary recluse writing his books late into the night. But his most rewarding role of all, which he was now so busily rehearsing, was that of his father as a famous statesman.

Once he had mastered his 'scaffolding of rhetoric', it became easier. As long as he memorised his speeches he had no difficulty in Parliament (except when thrown by the demands of extemporaneous debate. On one occasion interrupters forced him to forget his words and he had to stop his speech entirely). But his dedication was absolute. Constant labour was the surest way of staving off depression, and according to his old friend J. B. Atkins 'he gave himself entirely to work. When he was not busy with politics, he was reading or writing. He did not lead the life of other young men in London. He may have visited political clubs, but I never met him walking in Pall Mall or Hyde Park where sooner or later one used to meet one's friends. I never met him at a dinner party that had not some public or some private purpose.'

With his belief in private destiny, Churchill could never be an over-awed backbencher, learning from his political superiors and patiently prepared to wait for time and merit to present him with his opportunities. His father's life had taught him all he needed, and as his self-appointed heir in Parliament, it was as if he had assumed his power already. The only question that remained was how to use it.

He was convinced that – like his father in so many other things – he was preordained to burn out young. Soon, with an effrontery that would have been preposterous had it not been totally sincere, he was planning his Savrola-style attempt to win the leadership of one or other of the major parties.

In 1901, when he had been in Parliament less than a year, he was staying with his parents' old friend Cecil Rhodes at his house in Scotland. He must have sensed the rustle of his father's mantle, having been visiting Lord Rosebery a few days earlier. The royal ex-mistress Lady Warwick – once rumoured to have also been Lord Randolph's *femme fatale* – was another of Cecil Rhodes's guests. Later she recalled the twenty-six-year-old Churchill discussing his own political position after dinner.

He was, he airily remarked, 'inclined to leave the Conservative leadership to Mr Balfour, and proclaim himself a Liberal. He wanted power and the Tory road to power was blocked by the Cecils and other brilliant Conservatives.' According to Lady Warwick, Cecil Rhodes was 'all in favour of his turning Liberal'.

One all-important portion of Lord Randolph Churchill's political legacy to his son was the memory of the way that he had been treated by the Tory Party. From an unbiased viewpoint, Lord Randolph's fatal resignation was an act of folly, verging on disloyalty, which more than justified the way Lord Salisbury subsequently kept him out of office. But Churchill was not unbiased where his father was concerned, and it was easy for him to conjure up a very different scenario. In his eyes, Lord Randolph had been cruelly betrayed by the ungrateful party he had resurrected by his genius and oratory. He had resigned on a point of all-important principle, and the villain of the piece had been the leading member of the Cecil family, good, reliable Lord Salisbury, 'the master of the English world', who, having sacrificed Lord Randolph, proceeded to enjoy his three unruffled terms as Prime Minister in his place. The Conservative leader in the Commons who, in 1902, followed his Lordship to become Prime Minister was himself another member of the Cecil family – the deceptively lethargic-seeming intellectual, Arthur Balfour. He had once enjoyed Lord Randolph's friendship as an ally in the great days of the Fourth Party, and then deserted him.

It was a scenario full of bitterness and high emotion which could absolve an ambitious young MP from ties of loyalty to a party – and a family – which had treated his own father with such scant regard.

Churchill would never be a wholly dedicated party politician – or an unconditional Conservative. In his greatest moments he would always strive to be above the petty cares of party machinations, and in his early years in politics he was more influenced by what his father might have done than by what his parliamentary leader wanted him to do. He was, as ever, overwhelmingly ambitious.

Even now, had Balfour had the sense to offer him a place in his government, Churchill would certainly have taken it. When he failed to, Churchill was finally convinced that he had no future in the Tory Party and prepared to make the move that his career required.

It took a little time to find a convincing reason for his exit. Early in 1903 it came. Another of his father's former allies, Joseph Chamberlain, proposed to defend the Empire and its precious trade by creating tariff barriers. Although Chamberlain, the great imperialist, planned to strengthen the Empire by his measures, Churchill was vehemently against them.

For a year he campaigned vigorously against his party, under the banner of free trade. Then in May 1904 he followed the logic of his interests and declared beliefs and crossed to the Liberal opposition.

It was a move which brought predictable and bitter enmity from the Conservative establishment for many years. But at the time he barely seemed to notice – even when his former allies christened him 'The Blenheim Rat'.

In terms of pure ambition, he had acted wisely. Riven by internal disagreements over tariffs, the Conservatives had reached the term of their long monopoly of power; Balfour had lost his touch as premier. Early in 1906, the Liberals, under Campbell-Bannerman, won an overwhelming victory in a general election. Churchill was returned for his Manchester constituency on a large majority, and was promoted to a junior ministry in the Liberal government. At thirty-one he had power at last.

As deputy to the Colonial Secretary, Lord Elgin, who was in the House of Lords, Churchill had full responsibility for presenting the Government's colonial policy to the Commons. And since Lord Elgin was a somewhat placid peer the new under-secretary was in the sort of situation that he loved. He had permission to range freely over any subject – if not in the universe, at least throughout the length and breadth of the great empire over which the sun still never set.

12

Love and the Pursuit of Power

Edwardian England made a cult of the moustachioed, immensely tall and silent god-like Englishman. Winston's mother had made her preferences in such matters clear by choosing the vapid George Cornwallis-West, an exaggerated version of the type to be her husband. And even Churchill's moustachioed brother, Jack, was proving an adornment to society. He was a splendid clothes-horse for the tailor's art which played so large a part in the image of the admired and sexually desirable Edwardian. Churchill – as he was all too well aware – could not have been more different. He was not a hairy man and, for all his efforts to imitate Lord Randolph, there was no sign of the exuberant moustache which formed so large a part of that statesman's personal appeal. What hair he did have was an unfortunate colour for a hero. Flaxen, black or even brown was currently in vogue, but sandy-coloured hair was not admired in the male.

It was now that he began to follow fashion, somewhat erratically but with a touch of the extravagance which was inseparable from his nature. Reluctantly, he gave up dallying with facial hair: better a naked upper lip than the downy fluff which was all that even the South African sunlight had managed to encourage on his upper lip. But he started dressing with determination.

Before this, the only clothes that appealed to him had been fancy dress or military uniform (especially the full-dress regalia of his beloved Oxfordshire Hussars: the gold-frogged tunic, cavalryman's shako, and broad-striped riding breeches). Too preoccupied to bother with his dress, in the past he had often seemed a sort of animated rag-bag.

Now this changed. His smooth unblemished skin called for the luxurious, pale pink, soft silk underwear he had made a habit of purchasing from the Army & Navy Stores. And, although no outer garment could make a dandy of him, his clothes took on a

hint of theatrical costume appropriate to whatever part it was that
he was playing. He had the astrakhan collar and black silk hat for
the young man about town, the morning coat and high wing-collar
for the politician, and the checked suits for his weekends in the
country. His most elaborate indulgence was the splendid hunting
pink he sported when he joined his cousin Sunny riding with the
local hunt, the Bicester.

In marked contrast with Churchill, Sunny Marlborough proved
a steadfast and determined womaniser almost all his days and
there are signs that Churchill envied his cousin's way with women.
Physically Sunny was even less favoured than his cousin but he
had notable success and, despite his status as a married man,
would shortly take as mistress one of the most spectacularly
ambitious beauties of the day – Consuelo Vanderbilt's former
friend and soulmate, the Bostonian Gladys Deacon, a liberated
and cosmopolitan lady who responded to the passion and position
of the Duke of Marlborough.

'He is quite different from me,' Churchill admitted, 'understanding women thoroughly, getting in touch with them at once
and absolutely dependent upon feminine influence of some kind
for the peace and harmony of his soul. Whereas I', he added,
with a stroke of rare self-revelation, 'am stupid and clumsy in that
relation, and naturally quite self-reliant and self-contained.'

Since his 'unofficial engagement' with Miss Plowden ended five
years earlier, Churchill had made at least two serious attempts to
find himself a wife – and both had failed.

He tried beauty in the form of the glamorous actress Ethel
Barrymore. He met her at the house of an older great dramatic
actress, Jennie's friend Maxine Elliot, rapidly proposed and was
as rapidly rejected.

He also considered marrying for money when introduced to
the shipping heiress Muriel Wilson. The summer parliamentary
recess of 1906 saw the thirty-one-year-old Under-Secretary for
the Colonies bumping at 40 miles per hour along the scenic
route from Bologna to Siena in a Panhard tourer with its
owner, wealthy Lionel Rothschild, at the wheel and the sturdy
Miss Wilson beside him. Miss Wilson was good-natured and
extremely rich, but neither she nor the beauty of Italy raised
him to romantic rapture. 'Nothing could exceed the tranquil
banalité of my relations with M, but I am glad I came,' he wrote
to Jennie. Hardly surprisingly, when he proposed marriage he

was once again rejected, and later he informed his mother that this was the last time he would think of marrying a fortune.

For a man who hated failure, Churchill's inability to find himself a wife was strange. Why was this self-created hero, man of action, paragon of will and figure of power so incompetent at such a relatively simple task?

It was at around this time that H. G. Wells compared him with another great volcanic man of action – his Italian contemporary, the poet–politician Gabriele d'Annunzio. Both had immense charisma, both were self-obsessed, and both were propelled by grand romantic visions of themselves. Compared with the tiny egg-like figure of d'Annunzio, Churchill was a young Adonis; yet it was d'Annunzio who had the most beautiful tragic actress in Italy dying for love of him, and the greatest ladies in society panting after him. No one showed signs of panting after Churchill.

There were several reasons for this prim and disappointing situation, all of which are more or less connected with crucial elements within his character.

With his thoughts so firmly focused on himself and his endeavours, he could not afford much attention to women. On rare occasions when he let himself be trapped beside an attractive female at a dinner-table, he tended either to ignore her or to lecture her about himself. Even the formidable but not unattractive social reformer Beatrice Webb had to endure the process and recorded her impressions in her diary.

Went into dinner with Winston Churchill. First impressions: restless, almost intolerably so . . . egotistical, bumptious, shallow-minded and reactionary, but with a certain personal magnetism. . . . More of the American speculator than the English aristocrat. Talked exclusively about himself and his electioneering plans. . . .

Rarely from such encounters are great romances born, but Churchill's relationships with women were made more difficult still by the mood-swings of his strange depressive temperament. On a manic up-swing he became all-powerful and needed no one, least of all a demanding and dependent woman, near him. On his depressive down-swings he was vulnerable and lonely, but on these occasions he had learned to keep his troubles to himself.

Lord Beaverbrook, who would experience at close quarters these two extremely different sides of Churchill's personality, remarked on the unexpected charm which Churchill could reveal when 'down'. The essence of this charm, he wrote, lay in 'the simplicity of a child which no contact with the world could ever spoil'. ('Churchill "up",' he added, was 'a quite different proposition . . . On top of the wave he has in him the stuff of which tyrants are made.')

Only two women had been permitted within this vulnerable depressive world of childhood – Jennie and his old nurse, Mrs Everest. Both were motherly relationships and both were naturally imbued with a certain innocence, which spilled over into Churchill's vision of his ideal woman.

One of the curiosities about Savrola is the contrast between his hero's lust for power and his total lack of lust towards his lovely heroine. Since the heroine, Lucile, is clearly based on Jennie, this is just as well, but it also helps explain the element of chaste romanticism which lay behind his concept of the other sex.

Asquith's daughter, Violet, shrewdly understood this. 'His approach to women', she would write,

was essentially romantic. He had a lively susceptibility to beauty, glamour, radiance, and those who possessed these qualities were not subjected to analysis. Their possession of all the cardinal virtues was assumed as a matter of course. I remember him taking umbrage when I once commented on the 'innocence' of his approach to women. He was affronted by this epithet as applied to himself; yet to me he would certainly have applied it as a term of praise.

Again, one is driven back upon the grim example of Lord Randolph's death. What better reason for a son to keep his sexual innocence than to avoid the trap that brought about his parent's downfall? What happier impulse than to stay instead with those 'innocent' memories which safely brought to mind his childhood vision of his mother – all that 'beauty, glamour, radiance' which the highly sexual Jennie had exuded in the presence of her schoolboy son.

Fortunately for Churchill's peace of mind, his first two years as junior minister in Campbell-Bannerman's Liberal government were busy and successful. The range of his activities was endless, his fortunes were ascending, Black Dog was safely kept at bay, and his energy and schoolboy zest for life were carrying the world before him. From his position of power he was soon poking at the dead wood in all corners of the colonial administration. 'He is most tiresome to deal with,' wrote the

Permanent Under-Secretary to Lord Elgin, 'and I fear will give trouble – as his father did – in any position to which he may be called. The restless energy, uncontrollable desire for notoriety and lack of moral perception make him an anxiety indeed.'

In other words, Churchill was in the sort of situation that he loved. Ironically, it was now, in the summer of 1907, that the woman problem suddenly erupted from a dangerous quarter in an unexpected shape.

At the beginning of that year his brother Jack had met Lady Gwendeline Bertie, the daughter of the Earl of Abingdon. Known as 'Goonie', she was twenty-one, dark-haired, vivacious and, judging from a portrait of her by Sargent, romantically attractive, with an expression of alert intelligence which that artist rarely noticed in the young English débutantes he depicted. She had led the customary sheltered life of English upper-class young ladies, and on meeting handsome young Jack Churchill decided she was suddenly in love.

Jack, at twenty-six, was only just beginning to get established as a stockbroker, but his manly looks and simple nature, coupled with his lack of means, must have made him seem romantically appealing to this strong-willed virgin. Flattered, he returned her love wholeheartedly, and before long brought her home to meet his mother at her country house, Salisbury Place, near St Albans. It was there that Goonie met his brother, Winston.

One can picture the ensuing situation – a tongue-tied and adoring younger brother, a clever and attractive girl-friend, the worldliest of mothers all too well aware of what was happening, and a hugely famous and successful elder brother down for the weekend to dominate the family with high spirits, a ceaseless flow of conversation and stories of great men and great events.

Throughout his life, Churchill had been scoring off his brother Jack, as if in retribution for the way Lord Randolph had made him so undisguisedly his favourite during their adolescence. One of the most admirable things about this admirable younger brother was his total lack of resentment. He seems to have accepted uncomplainingly the way his brother Winston had arranged himself an income from their joint inheritance while in the cavalry, but that no money was available for him to go to university. He took it for granted that his brother had inherited what brains there were in the family, and seemed to have escaped the family depression. An uncomplicated simple soul, he hero-worshipped Winston – but even Jack's powers of hero-worship would have been severely tested had he realised that something more than innocent affection was developing between his brother and the girl he loved.

It is hard to know how far or how consciously Churchill encouraged Goonie. One can imagine Churchill being so dominant and so exuberant that he failed to comprehend the obvious effect that he was having on this very bright and wilful girl. One can also see, from the few extant letters which she wrote to him, how it was she who played up to him, striking just that note of wittily flirtatious mockery which is unerringly appealing in relationships between clever younger women and older men.

In one letter she pretended to be concerned that his official duties would bring him in contact with Mohammedans; 'please don't become converted to Islam,' she implored him.

I have noticed in your disposition a tendency to orientalism, pasha-like tendencies, I really have: you are not cross with my writing this, so if you come in contact with Islam, your conversion might be effected with greater ease than you might have supposed, call of the blood, don't you know what I mean, do fight against it!

Jennie had her own suspicions of what was happening and that her elder son was responding too warmly to this warm young lady. She may well have warned him of the dangerous situation that was rapidly developing, for quite suddenly that August Winston fled.

He had been planning an official visit to East Africa, but his decision to depart was made so hurriedly that his new secretary, the socialite man of letters Eddie Marsh, had to join him later. Jennie only knew the details of his journey after he had left, and the first Goonie knew about the five-month expedition was the news of his departure. It produced an anguished letter of reproach: 'It is positively cruel of Fate to determine that we should not say goodbye', nor have the chance to 'wine and dine' in London as they had evidently planned. 'I cannot help rebelling against fate, for how entirely unreasonable it can be, considering what pleasure it should have given us.'

The next day, having heard that Churchill was *en route* to Paris, Goonie was writing him a second shameless letter:

Dear Mr Winston, I wish I could go with you to Paris on Sunday – I have not been there for two whole years, and I do love it so, but

I don't expect I know much of your Paris, it is the other Paris, the *jeune fille* Paris that I am acquainted with.

And a week later came her final *cri de coeur*: 'My Dear Mr Winston, Where are you? Where have you been? Where are you going to? What are you going to do? I have lost you for a whole week, I want to find you again – you have effaced yourself from my horizon.'

For the time being the effacement was complete, and Churchill's five-month absence in the British colonies of East Africa was one of those supremely happy periods in which the hero was able to submerge the cares of statesmanship and sex in the joys of travel, manly fellowship and big-game hunting. Writing to Jennie of rhinoceroses he had killed, he noted that 'the vitality of these brutes is so tremendous that they will come on like some large engine in spite of five or six heavy bullets thumping into them'. Aggressive as ever, he decided that rhino made the most satisfactory adversaries outside Parliament, and while he was busy 'thumping' bullets into them he heard from Jack. During the summer Goonie had been saying that she felt she could not promise to wait long enough for him to earn sufficient money to support a wife, but once Churchill left for Africa something had mysteriously made her change her mind. Now she had written to the patient Jack, saying that her love for him was even stronger than before.

As Jack put it in his letter to his brother, 'she said she would sacrifice anything for her love; that her ambition for riches and everything else had all vanished and that she would wait for me'.

Churchill had helped make Jack a happy man. In return, virtue brought rather more than its traditional reward. Refreshed and resolute, he was safely back in London in mid-January 1908 to discover that the Premier, seventy-two-year-old Campbell-Bannerman, was on the point of retiring through ill-health (he died in April). He was to be succeeded by the former Chancellor of the Exchequer, Herbert Asquith.

Asquith was a warm, if somewhat wary, admirer of Churchill (it was apropos of him that he coined the famous definition of genius as 'a zig-zag flash of lightning in the brain'), and it was thanks to him that at the age of thirty-three Churchill reached the next decisive level of power – his own ministry as President of the Board of Trade and a seat in Asquith's cabinet. But the marital problem remained to be solved.

With Jack eager to marry Goonie as soon as possible, and so break up their bachelor establishment, this was particularly urgent. Even so, the speed with which he acted was remarkable. So was the fact that he and the girl he fell in love with had met on a previous occasion when neither had shown the faintest interest in each other.

It was early March, less than eight weeks after his return from Africa, and Churchill was lying in his bath – his favourite form of relaxation – when his secretary, the epicene Eddie Marsh, reminded him in that high-pitched voice of his that he was due at a dinner-party at the home of Lady St Helier in Portland Place.

Churchill was disinclined to make the effort. He was already late and preferred the prospect of an evening on his own to a society gathering. But Marsh was a friend of Lady St Helier. Indeed, it had been through her that he had first been introduced to Churchill, and he insisted Churchill go.

Churchill was rarely punctual anyhow and, arriving very late, he was placed at the dinner table between Lady Lugard, wife of the great West African explorer, and a reserved and rather beautiful young lady named Clementine Hozier.

Lady Lugard was an interesting woman, and Churchill was particularly interested in Africa at the time. One might have expected him to spend the rest of dinner telling her his views, his plans and his experience of that fascinating continent. Instead, he turned the rays of his attention to Miss Hozier. Lady Lugard was ignored, Miss Hozier virtually 'monopolised' for the rest of the evening. With the same decision he had shown at Omdurman, Churchill's final marital campaign had started.

As they discovered, he and Miss Hozier had met and mutually ignored each other at a ball some four years earlier. But this time he employed his charm and knowledge of the world to powerful effect. Miss Hozier was captivated. So, it seemed, was Churchill, and the romance proceeded with much the same despatch and energy he brought to politics.

If Churchill was acting on the rebound from the all too eager Lady Gwendoline, he could not have picked a greater contrast in the person of the chaste Miss Hozier. Earnest, tall, vulnerable and shy, she had a classic beauty which was in a different class

from Goonie's brand of quick vivacious prettiness. Neither frivolous nor funny, she was an essentially serious person, largely
uneducated, highly unsophisticated, painfully short of money and
with a family background almost as turbulent as Churchill's.

Her father, the unfortunate Sir Henry Montague Hozier, had
died the year before. A largely self-made man who had ended up
as secretary of Lloyd's of London, he had married considerably
above himself – taking as second wife the beautiful and much
younger Lady Blanche, daughter of the Earl of Airlie – and
seems to have known little happiness thereafter.

There were four children of the marriage – Kitty, born in 1883,
Clementine, who followed two years later, and twins, Bill and
Nellie, who appeared in 1888 – but Sir Henry never managed to
convince himself that any child was his. This brought problems
to the marriage, and by the time Clementine was six, Blanche
Hozier was on her own with four young children to support.

While still with Hozier, Lady Blanche had been a friend of
Jennie's, and they had certain things in common. Both had been
great beauties in their day, both had endured disastrous marriages
and both had been promiscuous, offering discreet relief to many
members of the aristocracy, but there similarities between them
ended.

Jennie was a born survivor. As usual she was facing money
troubles of her own with her new husband – often referred to
in her letters as 'poor George' – floundering financially. But
Jennie, ever the American social entrepreneur, was finding ways
to keep them in the style of life which they demanded, writing
her memoirs, starting an up-market magazine, and finding houses
she could fashionably refurnish, redecorate and then resell at a
useful profit.

Had Lady Blanche been capable of such resourceful activities
– and she emphatically was not – she would have felt instinctively
that they were utterly beneath her. Born an aristocrat, she had
something of the headlong attitude towards life of the great Whig
ladies of a century earlier. She gambled, drank, spent money and
had love-affairs exactly as she pleased. Having married beneath
herself and without affection, she saw no reason to change
her habits. The results were disastrous, but Lady Blanche had
schooled herself to see disaster as something one dealt with by
ignoring it.

No one seemed to know the precise paternity of her children –
except that the father was almost certainly not Hozier and one of
her most dashing lovers was her brother-in-law, Bertram Mitford,
1st Lord Redesdale. He was married to Blanche's favourite sister,
Clementine, after whom she had named her second daughter, and
this fed the persistent rumours that blue-eyed Bertram Mitford
was Clementine Hozier's natural father.

For Clementine, life with such a mother who was supported
mainly by Lord Airlie was inevitably chaotic. There had been
enforced migrations and a running battle with a bitter and
revengeful Hozier, who tended to appear at awkward moments,
threatening to repossess the children. Partly to escape him, and
partly to enjoy the cheaper living and the nearby casino, Lady
Blanche had finally made her home across the Channel in Dieppe.
It was there that Clementine spent much of her adolescence.

Clementine reacted rather as one might expect, disliking almost
everything that Lady Blanche's way of life embodied. Hating
the mess and muddle they had lived in, she was obsessively
perfectionist in all she did; and, seeing the chaos that her
mother's love-affairs had brought her, she was something of
a puritan. Money worries could upset her deeply; gambling
and drunkenness depressed her. A strong character, she taught
herself to keep her locked-in feelings to herself, but beneath the
surface lay a tendency to uncontrollable hysteria which afflicted
her at intervals throughout her life.

By twenty-one she had already been engaged to a wealthy civil
servant nearly twice her age. Fearful, perhaps, of repeating Lady
Blanche's blunder of a loveless marriage with an older man, she
ended this with some recriminations and a nervous breakdown.
Yet she remained patently in need of certain things a husband ten
years older was likely to provide – stability, paternal authority,
social position and, above all, an overriding purpose to her
life. Clementine was custom-built to fall in love with Winston
Churchill.

Churchill's motives now were not so clear, and his behaviour
that evening at Lady St Helier's dinner table bears all the signs
of a determined act of will rather than of yielding to a sudden
rush of overwhelming ardour.

Clementine herself was always sensitive to suggestions that
Jennie had cleverly arranged things – which it is clear that
she had not. On the other hand, she certainly encouraged the

relationship. Once she realised that Clementine was the daughter
of her old friend Lady Blanche, there were certain sentimental
reasons which made it seem particularly appropriate. Clementine
was warmly invited up to Salisbury Lodge, where she met those
more established lovers, brother Jack and Lady Goonie, who
were making preparations for their marriage. The sight of his
younger brother, suddenly so happy with the girl he might have
wed himself, must have been a strong incentive to Churchill for
settling his own future now as soon as possible.

On 4 August 1908, Churchill, accompanied as ever by the
serviceable Eddie Marsh (but not by Clementine, who was
staying with the Barings on the Isle of Wight), attended Jack
and Goonie's marriage. Since the Berties were Catholic the
church marriage at Oxford was preceded by a civil ceremony
near their home in Abingdon. Churchill wrote to Clementine
about it: 'We all swooped down in motor-cars upon the town of
Abingdon and did the deed before the Registrar – for all the
world as if it was an elopement.' The bride and bridgroom, he
added, 'were entirely composed & the business was despatched
with a celerity & ease that was almost appalling'.

Seven days later, with an even more remarkable 'celerity',
Winston proposed to Clementine.

He did this, having carefully arranged the background as if
once more playing his own privately created part in history. It
had to be at Blenheim, where he was shortly due to spend a few
days' holiday. Cousin Sunny, as head of the family, also had to
play his own supporting role – so he persuaded him to send a
pressing invitation to the Isle of Wight.

Clementine had problems accepting at such short notice. She
had no maid, no chaperone, and later recalled that she was
'reduced to her last laundered and starched dress'. But Churchill
was insistent she should come. 'I want so much to show you that
beautiful place and in its gardens we shall find lots of places to
talk in and lots of things to talk about.'

Jennie, apprised of the situation, was hurriedly brought in to
act as chaperone; and Miss Hozier, with her one starched dress,
arrived at Blenheim on 10 August.

As good as his word, Churchill made arrangements to conduct
her round the gardens for their confidential talk next morning;
but even thoughts of marriage could not make him break the
habits of a late-rising lifetime. Clementine was left downstairs,

disconsolate, until Sunny Marlborough, seeing the situation and knowing his cousin's habits, sent him a message to his bedroom to bestir himself. He duly did, and later on a rainy Tuesday afternoon, beside the famous lake at Blenheim, Churchill proposed to Clementine – and was accepted. Never one to waste time once decisions had been taken, he insisted that the wedding should take place in London three weeks later.

In contrast to Jack and Goonie's wedding at the Abingdon register office, Churchill's was a considerable society event. St Margaret's, Westminster, was filled to overflowing with the politicians and the members of the aristocracy who formed so large a part of Churchill's life. Crowds of what the *Times* reporter called 'people of the better sort' filled Parliament Square and the adjoining roads to cheer the groom and bride on their arrival, and in church the families were on parade for this all-important tribal gathering.

Sunny Marlborough sat beside his Duchess and their infant heir, Lord Blandford. Behind them were the Tweedmouths and the Guests, the Wilsons and the Leslies and the Frewens, while on the bride's side were the Airlies and the Stanleys and the Mitfords. Directly behind the bridegroom sat the man he had succeeded at the Board of Trade, 'the Welsh Wizard' David Lloyd George, now Asquith's Chancellor of the Exchequer.

The bride wore ivory-coloured silk trimmed with *point de Venise* 'lent by Mrs George Cornwallis-West', and was given away by her sailor brother, Bill Hozier. The best man was not the bridegroom's brother Jack, but a reminder of Churchill's Tory past, Lord Hugh Cecil, the one-time leader of the Hughligans. Churchill made his marriage vows 'in a firm clear voice', while Clementine's were 'all but inaudible'. And when Lloyd George was invited to sign the marriage register in the vestry the bridegroom started talking politics to him rather than sweet nothings to his bride – thus proving the supremacy of habit over sentiment.

But the most spectacular attendants at the wedding must have been those two impressive ladies, once the toast and trophies of high Victorian male society and now the mothers of the bridegroom and the bride. Jennie was clearly out to steal the show as she took her front-pew seat beside 'poor George' who, whatever his failings as a husband, was still regularly described as 'the best-looking man in London'. As well as making sure that the newspapers had picked up the all-important point about the lace on the bride's dress, she had also dressed to kill – in purple silk with a large hat surmounted with a dahlia.

A somewhat blowsy fifty-six, Lady Blanche could not aspire to match her old friend's ample but still seductive figure – let alone her husband and her dahlia – but she did not entirely miss out. Dressed in mushroom-coloured satin, she had taken care to surround herself with a phalanx of her finest-looking, most distinguished lovers.

As a widow, she was suitably escorted by her brother-in-law, the ardent Bertram, 1st Lord Redesdale. Just behind sat Lord Elcho's son, the handsome Hugo Wemyss, who had also intermittently enjoyed her favours; and next to him was placed the remorseless seducer, Arabist, diarist and poet Wilfred Scawen-Blunt, who had been comforting her for many years.

To the gossip-riddled world of Society London, so many of whom were present, this must have seemed a notable riposte to Mrs George Cornwallis-West, particularly as those who were privileged to be in the know had long taken it for granted that Bertie Redesdale was the father of the lovely Clementine. Who better to be escorting his old mistress at their daughter's wedding?

But, not for the first time, gossip was inaccurate and missed the most intriguing point about the marriage. It was a point that united the mothers of the bride and the groom more closely than was realised.

Back in 1892, at the beginning of her long affair with Scawen-Blunt, Lady Blanche had confided in him the truth about the father of her daughters Kitty and Clementine. It was not Sir Henry Hozier – nor was it Lord Redesdale; Redesdale came later and was probably the father of the twins, Bill and Nellie. According to Scawen-Blunt's diary of the time, the father of the two elder girls was 'the gallant "Bay" Middleton, superb horseman and escort to the Empress Elizabeth of Austria in the shires'.

Far from being shocked or jealous, Blunt had approved of this on strict eugenic grounds. He was a great horse-lover, and it seemed sensible to him that the 'valiant Blanche', as he called her, should have chosen to improve the stock with a handsome and full-blooded sportsman such as Middleton, rather than spavined old Sir Henry, even if he was her husband.

Middleton, a regular army officer, was a member of a family of Shropshire gentry. His greatest claim to fame had come when he was chosen to accompany the horse-mad Empress Elizabeth on her hunting expeditions to England and to Southern Ireland in the 1870s. It was in Ireland that he had met Jennie, and there that they had first become close friends.

How close was anybody's guess. The empress was known to be frigid sexually, having contracted syphilis from her husband, the Emperor of Austria. Middleton had a reputation as a rampant womaniser, and Jennie was beginning to enjoy her freedom as a very liberated woman.

By the early 1880s, when Bay Middleton appears in the entries of Jennie's London diary, he is clearly Blanche's lover, and Blanche is Jennie's most frequently mentioned female friend. When Blanche gave birth to her two daughters shortly after, the worldly Jennie can have had no doubts about their true paternity.

So it was that this strange old tangle of forgotten love-affairs lay carefully concealed beneath the splendour of the wedding, and one wonders whether the two mothers-in-law discussed them. Probably not. Both were great believers in the *status quo* and keeping up appearances, and both had far too much to lose to allow such secrets to come out even within the family. This makes it even more unlikely that they allowed a hint of this to reach their children. Certainly Clementine's daughter Mary had no idea that Sir Henry Hozier was not her true grandfather until Elizabeth Longford published her biography of Scawen-Blunt in 1982.

But there remains a chance that Clementine suspected that Jennie did know something. She never liked or trusted her – any more than she really liked or trusted Lady Blanche – and the attitude with which she and her husband now embarked upon their marriage could not have been more different from that of the scandalous quartet to whom they owed their being.

13

Light Fades from the Picture

After the wedding night at ancestral Blenheim, and a simpler honeymoon in Venice, the couple embarked on marriage, first in Churchill's bachelor flat in Bolton Street, then moving to a more spacious house on a sixteen-year lease in Eccleston Square on the edge of Mayfair. Some were expecting Churchill, romantic man of action that he was, to lead a married life to match – sociable, extravagant, and full of high dramatic interest. Clementine, however, made it fairly clear in one of her earliest decisive acts of married womanhood that such was not to be the case.

Before departing on their honeymoon, Churchill had innocently asked his mother to redecorate the bedroom at Bolton Street as a surprise for their return, and Jennie had exercised her professional decorator's skill to some effect. The result sounds charming – but not for Clementine. 'To her simple and rather austere taste, the sateen and muslin covers trimmed with bows, which decked the chairs, dressing-table and bed, appeared cheap and tawdry,' writes her daughter Mary. According to the same source, Clementine regarded Jennie rather similarly – 'vain and frivolous' are the words she uses – and it is clear that Jennie's influence, like her taste in furnishing, would not impinge on Churchill's marriage. From the start, vanity and frivolity were out – simplicity and austerity would take their place, if Clementine had anything to do with it. By the standards of their group, the Winston Churchills were distinctly short of money, and it was on this note of high thinking and simple living that their marriage started.

It was to be a strangely sentimental marriage for a man of Churchill's warlike temper. Other people's whimsy is embarrassing, but here was the victor of Omdurman addressed as 'Mr Pug' by a strong-willed wife whom he called 'Mrs Kat'. Kat and

Pug inhabited a sentimental world with a private language full of furry animals.

In contrast with their fashionable friends and relations, they appear cosily middle-class to a degree, and some of their visitors expressed surprise at the scenes of almost childlike happiness they found in Eccleston Square. On Churchill's birthday, elegant Lord Esher discovered Kat and Pug purring lovingly together on the sofa in paper hats before a birthday cake with candles. This display of childlike affection was seen as touching and amusing, but it was also important for the future of their marriage. For both had been essentially lonely people, despite the great activity around them. 'I am a solitary creature in the midst of crowds. Be kind to me,' Churchill had begged Clementine, in a flash of candour, on the eve of marriage. And for Clementine, nothing could have been more solitary than the anxious straitened life she had led before she married.

Together they were now creating something of the happy childhood neither had enjoyed, and finding an exclusive private world which offered a defence against whatever threats they felt around them. There would always be a place in their relationship which no one else would enter. And it would be here, when needed, that Churchill would demand and find that total female love and understanding which he had longed for from his mother. Clementine in turn seemed eager to dedicate herself to him and his career. The arrival of their first 'Puppy-kitten' on 11 July 1909 – a red-haired daughter, christened Diana – seems to have delighted Churchill.

'Is she a pretty child?' Lloyd George asked him.

'The prettiest child ever seen,' the proud father answered.

'Like her mother, I suppose,' said Lloyd George.

'No,' said Churchill. 'She is the image of me.'

But whoever Diana actually resembled – and as a baby she *did* look rather like her father – she was not permitted to intrude upon her parents' private life together.

Clementine was not naturally maternal. 'Wife first and mother a very distant second' is how one of Clementine's friends described her. It was an attitude which suited the self-absorbed husband to perfection; but it is hard to tell what damage it inflicted on his daughter. It is also difficult to judge how far Churchill's demanding nature at this time was responsible for Clementine's decided lack of interest in all her children during infancy. It was as if he took the children's place, leaving his wife too little affection or emotion for the others.

One of Clementine's gravest disadvantages was a weakness in reserves of energy. Again, it is hard to know how much of this was due to a neurotic weakness already present when she married, and how much to the strains of coping with her dominating husband. Certainly an element of earnestness and somewhat humourless inflexibility on her part seems to have made the problem worse.

She could be jealous and extremely prickly, and some of her husband's colleagues found her tedious. 'She is, *au fond*, a thundering bore,' was Asquith's unforgiving verdict – and the worldly Jennie probably agreed. Jennie's friend, the royal mistress, Mrs Keppel, seems to have enjoyed pulling ingenuous Clementine's leg, on one occasion offering her an extravagant couturier dress – which Clementine indignantly refused – and on another seriously informing her that if she was truly dedicated to her husband's political career she should encourage him to have a mistress. Again Clementine was not amused, for she was not a rich sophisticate like Jennie, nor a natural wit like Goonie, but a simple, strong-willed young aristocrat, anxiously involved with her famous husband and his great career.

As for Churchill, marriage brought no change to his quest for power, nor to the rigid workaholic life which this demanded. As usual he worked late into the night, while Clementine was inclined to retire – and rise – early. They never breakfasted together and had separate rooms from the beginning.

During these early months of marriage it was as if Clementine had permanently banished Lord Randolph's gloomy ghost. To begin with, they went out little into smart society. As Churchill told Clementine, it was 'power and great business' that obsessed him, and as President of the Board of Trade he was already a key member of the most talented peacetime government of the century – while barely in his middle thirties.

It was now that Churchill showed a genuine interest in the underdog. He had been strongly influenced by reading Seebohm Rowntree's book on poverty – and by memories of his own experiences as a prisoner-of-war. Now he was in the vanguard of the great Liberal movement for social reform – one which Clementine, a Liberal herself, very much encouraged. He had been converted to this admirable cause some months before

they met through something of a 'divine' revelation, as his friend
C. F. Masterman makes clear in his eye-witness description of
the event.

It began tempestuously.

Winston swept me off to his cousin's house and I lay on the bed while
he dressed and marched around the room, gesticulating and impetuous,
pouring out all his hopes and plans and ambitions. He is full of the poor,
whom he has just discovered. He thinks he is called by providence to
do something for them. 'Why have I been kept safe to within a hair's
breadth of death,' he asked, 'except to do something like this?'

Guided by his rival, friend and mentor, the Welsh radical Lloyd
George, Churchill swiftly made his name as a social radical and
one of the founding fathers of the modern welfare state. During
his three years at the Board of Trade, he skilfully employed the
power he loved to establish labour exchanges, set minimum
standards and conditions in sweat-shops, prevent industrial ex-
ploitation of children, and begin a system of national insurance.

It was a formidable achievement which established him as
a great reformer – and also as Lloyd George's most obvious
competitor for the future Liberal leadership. It was an unlikely
situation for the grandson of a duke. Still more unlikely was his
role in the Liberal battle with the Conservative opposition when
the House of Lords rejected Lloyd George's so-called 'People's
Budget' in 1909.

Here for the first – and last – time Churchill spoke out against
his class and its privileges with gusto, wit and obvious enjoyment.
At one point he seemed perfectly prepared to abolish 'that feudal
assembly' the House of Lords, and ridiculed the peers, those
'heaven-born and God-granted legislators' in their 'prejudiced
chamber, hereditary, non-elected, irresponsible, and irremedi-
able'. As for the Conservatives, in one of his most memorable
phrases, he dismissed them all as 'old doddering peers, cute
financial magnates, clever wire-pullers, and big brewers with
bulbous noses'.

Some laughed, but others took predictable offence, and the
enmity of members of his own class deepened. 'I would rather
sweep the streets than be Winston Churchill,' said his one-time
friend George Wyndham.

'I would like to see him and Lloyd George in the middle of
twenty couple of dog-hounds,' said the Duke of Beaufort.

Churchill appeared impervious to unpopularity and stayed on sufficiently good terms with cousin Sunny to be invited to the customary ducal Christmas at Blenheim in 1909. It was not he, but Clementine who drew out the ducal wrath against the Liberals. A few months later, while on her own at Blenheim, she took great offence at Sunny's remarks on Premier Asquith's drinking habits; harsh words were spoken, and Clementine swept out of Blenheim, vowing never to return. But the incident did not affect her husband's friendship with his beloved Sunny.

It would seem that Churchill had everything he wanted out of life – a faithful and adoring wife, a comfortable home, a growing income from his writing, and glittering prospects. Even that 'supreme power' he had longed for seemed within his reach.

In February 1910 he became Home Secretary with a salary of £5,000 a year. It was an important post, responsible for police, for law and order, and day-to-day administration of the country. With this key appointment and a place in the Cabinet, everything was going as he had planned. But it was now that, unaccountably, he was hit by a mysterious crisis in his private life.

The novelist Henry James lunched with him around this time at Walmer Castle (Asquith's official residence as Lord Warden of the Cinque Ports), and that shrewd old specialist of human nature evidently spotted something in the young phenomenon which puzzled him. He did not say exactly what it was but, thinking about him later, he seems to have been uneasy about him. 'I confess', he wrote, 'that I am often struck at the limitations with which men of power pay the price for their domination over mankind.'

In Churchill's case the price was higher than Henry James suspected. For despite his 'domination over mankind', the young Home Secretary was finding himself tormented by his ancient enemy, 'Black Dog'.

Many years later Churchill talked about it to his doctor, Lord Moran, making it clear how serious it had been: 'For two or three years the light faded from the picture. I did my work. I sat in the House of Commons, but black depression settled on me.'

At times he was evidently suicidal. On railway stations he purposely avoided the edge of the platform when an express was passing. He kept clear of the sides of ships and of looking down at the water. 'A second's action would end everything. A few drops of desperation . . . ,' he told Moran.

All that seemed to help, he said, was to 'talk it over with Clementine'.

It must have been hard for this outwardly confident and brash young politician to maintain his everyday façade. For it is clear that behind the show of bounding self-assurance all the anxiety and sense of worthlessness associated with his father's judgement of him still persisted.

'Alas, I have no good opinion of myself,' he told Clementine. 'At times I think that I could conquer everything – and then again I know that I am only a weak fool.' To Moran he confessed how *angst* had chronically oppressed him. 'The mere thought that he might trip up filled him with apprehension,' says Lord Moran.

Further light was shed on the nature of this crisis forty years later, from an unlikely quarter. In 1952 the 'Puppy-kitten', Diana, was herself afflicted by a nervous breakdown. In the aftermath she told a friend how she had found her most sympathetic supporter in her now aged father; he said he understood exactly how she felt, having suffered a near breakdown of his own while Home Secretary. He also told her what he thought had caused it in his case – the anguish caused by his duty to study the cases of condemned murderers to decide whether to mitigate or confirm the sentence.

On the face of it this sounds hard to credit. This was the man who excitedly survived the slaughter on the North-West Frontier and in South Africa, and who purchased his 'Ripper' with its soft-nosed bullets for the charge at Omdurman. In later years, as war leader, he would make decisions which would affect the lives of thousands and then enjoy a good night's sleep.

How could such a man have been so grievously afflicted by the fate of a few hundred common criminals? The answer is of importance to understanding Churchill's psychology and subsequent career.

Even at Harrow there had been the contrast between his two opposed personalities. The sensitive schoolboy, miserable about his parents, could transform himself into the aggressive bully shoving Meinertzhagen off the pavement. Since then this tendency seems to have increased. Several people had noticed the uncanny difference between Churchill 'up' – confident, aggressive, carrying the world before him – and Churchill 'down' – vulnerable, hypersensitive and painfully aware of human suffering.

It was this second state which left him prey to the misery his congenital depression could inflict. Since 'discovering the poor', Churchill had been increasingly involved with something he had previously avoided – widespread human suffering and the misery beneath the surface of Edwardian England. This was the sort of nightmare world which he had always dreaded – that 'life in the gutter' which his father had predicted as the price of failure. But worse still was the fate of the most wretched group of all with whom, as Home Secretary, he found himself involved – murderers condemned to death. The misery of their fate preyed upon his mind; and it was then that, as he put it, 'the light faded from the picture'.

But always in his times of deep depression Churchill possessed an antidote which rarely seemed to fail – the sovereign remedy of aggression. His aggressive temperament had marked him out at Harrow, and brought excitement and success throughout his military career. Aggression was the great transformer, capable of changing the miserable depressive, with his fears and weakness, into the hero oblivious of danger. The astute journalist A. G. Gardiner had described him on a typical aggressive upswing: 'He is his own superman and is so absorbed in himself and in his fiery purposes that he does not pay others the compliment of even being aware of them.' This was his surest antidote to melancholy, and about this time he started to return to it.

Even in his period as social reformer, Churchill had not kept himself entirely from the joys of warfare. 'Do you know,' he had written to Clementine from his annual fortnight on manoeuvres at Camp Goring in May 1909, 'I would greatly like to have some practice in the handling of large forces. I have much confidence in my judgement on things, when I see clearly, but on nothing do I seem to *feel* the truth more than in tactical combinations. . . . I am sure I have the root of the matter in me – but never in this state of human existence will it have a chance of flowering – in bright red blossom.'

The chance was closer than he knew. Later in 1909 he got himself invited as observer to the German military manoeuvres where he met the Kaiser and witnessed his enormous forces. 'This army is a terrible engine. It sometimes marches 35 miles a day. It is in number as the sands of the sea . . . ,' he told Clementine.

This first sight of the power of German militarism made an indelible impression, clearly striking deep chords of powerful emotion in his nature. In the same letter, he admitted how much 'war attracts me & fascinates my mind with its tremendous situations'; at which point reason intervened, and he hurried to assure his wife that 'in the midst of arms' he also felt 'what vile and wicked folly and barbarism it all is'.

None knows better than the drunk the horrors of the demon drink, and Churchill would never lose a deep awareness of the horrors and the dreadfulness of modern war; but, like the drunk, his awareness of the consequences could not destroy its terrible attraction.

During the summer of 1910, his duties as Home Secretary made him responsible for law and order against the striking miners of South Wales. The ill-used miners and their unhappy families were the sort of people at the bottom of society to have aroused the sympathy of Churchill the reformer in the past. But once they went on strike and threatened violence, they were rapidly transformed into an enemy needing to be taught a lesson; and Churchill unhesitatingly ordered in the troops.

He did not order the use of bayonets against the strikers, any more than he deserved the blame for the so-called 'Tonypandy massacre' which ensued. But there is no mistaking the energy and relish he suddenly displayed with a conflict on his hands. There was no sign of the depressive in him now – nor of any sympathy for the unhappy miners.

Then, in the following year, the famous incident occurred which, while gaining him much notoriety, seemed to lift him completely from depression and signalled a decisive change of course in life and politics.

On 2 November 1911 two shadowy figures, one of them suspected (incorrectly) of being a Latvian anarchist code-named 'Peter the Painter', were cornered by police in a house in an East End slum called Sidney Street. Shots were fired, a policeman wounded, reinforcements summoned, and the so-called 'Siege of Sidney Street' started.

As Home Secretary, Churchill was swiftly on the scene where he transformed a fairly simple incident of law and order into a pitched battle on the streets of London. (Photographs taken at the time show Churchill on the scene in morning coat and smart top-hat, with a look of unmistakable excitement on his face.) The Guards were ordered in. Artillery arrived, and Churchill, warlike feelings thoroughly aroused, suggested an assault by troops with armour-plated shields. Before this could occur the house caught fire.

Churchill gave orders to prevent firemen from extinguishing the blaze, and the mysterious 'anarchists' were incinerated – thus marking the conclusion of the story. Sidney Street brought Churchill considerable criticism at home and outright ridicule abroad, none of which appeared to worry him. Depression and anxieties forgotten, he was happily embarked on yet another bold aggressive upswing. When his friend Masterman asked angrily, 'What the hell have you been doing now, Winston?', he lisped cheerfully in reply: 'Now, Charlie, don't be croth. It was such fun.'

With this regained zest for life in general, Churchill and his friend F. E. Smith, the future Lord Birkenhead – eminent lawyer, drinker, wit and Tory statesman – founded a private dining club, which would remain a source of happiness, conviviality and unrestrained discussion for almost the remainder of his life. Membership – by invitation only from the founders – was extended to politicians of all parties whose conversation they enjoyed. To make clear that they had no connection with a long-established gathering called 'The Club' which had recently had the temerity to blackball Churchill, they simply called the group the 'Other Club'.

The company of friends like Birkenhead was Churchill's favourite relaxation, and from now on he increasingly enjoyed it. What was also obvious about him during what proved to be his final months at the Home Office was a pronounced veering off from social questions – and from further conflict with the aristocracy – towards issues where his aggressive instincts could flourish unimpeded.

During that early summer, further labour troubles brought a clear revival of the spirit of Sidney Street as the Home Secretary soared to further heights of bellicose activity. There was no suggestion of conciliation as Churchill, like some great commander mustering his troops, prepared to smash the transport strike threatening the nation. ('Bloody hell!' he shouted when he heard Lloyd George had settled it by deft negotiation.)

The summer of 1911 proved a happy time for Churchill, for it was then that he became the father of a second child – the longed-for son and heir. He was a pretty infant with Clementine's forget-me-not blue eyes and flaxen hair. For Churchill with his sense of dynasty, this small blond version of himself was of almost mystical importance – giving a purpose to his great ambition, forging the 'link' in *his* dynastic chain, and also offering a chance of making further restitution to his father's memory. When it was time to christen the child at St Margaret's, Westminster, one name alone was possible – Randolph.

Just as his son was being born, the Imperial German Government was completing Churchill's happiness by sending a warship to the Moroccan port of Agadir. It was an arrogant exercise in power-politics against the French, and for a moment Europe seemed to hover on the brink of war. The crisis passed, but it revealed the danger of the Kaiser's Germany and the unpreparedness of the British fleet. In the aftermath of Agadir, Asquith decided on a new broom for the Royal Navy; in October 1911, despite his earlier impassioned opposition to more expenditure on the Fleet, an exultant Churchill was created First Lord of the Admiralty.

Even now he needed to believe that destiny was on his side, and he was reassured when Clementine, opening the Bible at random, hit on Psalm 107 and read: 'They that go down to the sea in ships, that do business in great waters. . . .'

14

Admiralty

Churchill was happier than he had ever been while at the Admiralty. The importance and excitement of his new role suited him, and in contrast with the first years of his marriage an exuberant Churchill was emerging – convivial, extravagant, and thoroughly enjoying rich and racy company.

This was hard on Clementine, who missed the closer, simpler existence of those first years in Eccleston Square. Against the infinitely grander background of their official residence at the Admiralty, Winston's extravagance disturbed her – as did his periods away. His propensity to gamble particularly upset her, and on at least one occasion she erupted jealously against one of the young women – probably Herbert Asquith's daughter, Violet – who were increasingly attracted by the new sociable Winston Churchill.

Her thirty-eight-year-old husband responded magisterially. Clementine should know better than to indulge in 'small emotions and wounding doubts'. 'Your sweetness and beauty have cast a glory on my life,' he told her. He was probably telling her the truth – and her fears about other women were unfounded. If nothing else, he was too busy to philander, and his truest pleasures lay in convivial male company. According to Colville, 'from 1911 onwards, Churchill's delight was to dine with F. E. Smith and sometimes Lloyd George. He would telephone to say that he was bringing them all back to dinner and it would be pleasant to have some lobsters and roast duck.'

It was lobsters and roast duck, rather than other women, which were to cause poor Clementine genuine anxiety. 'The problems of housekeeping on a comparatively small budget were something that Churchill never grasped,' says Colville. 'She would do her best, for she did not wish to jeopardise her husband's political career or snub his friends; but she resented the late nights, the excessive consumption of brandy, the noise and the rowdiness, which were inseparable from the garrulous evenings.'

Times had changed from the grim periods when he was plunged in deep despondency and Clementine had urged him to enjoy society. It was Clementine who was now increasingly depressed, especially after a miscarriage early in 1912 which left her weak and nervous. Churchill was solicitous, but did not change his habits. Nor did Clementine. Ultimately those who suffered most were the children, Diana and Randolph.

Clementine could barely cope with the household at the Admiralty, let alone with two extremely naughty children. In the absence of a firm reliable nanny-figure such as their father had had in the person of stalwart Mrs Everest, the children were consigned to a succession of underpaid and untrained nursery-maids. These were remarkable only for the frequency with which they came and went. Randolph's earliest memory was of himself and his sister rolling together down the steps of the Admiralty in smart white coats, followed at a distance by a frantic female who was incapable of stopping them.

Mrs Everest would never have permitted such behaviour – nor would Jennie – but in her weakened state Clementine seems to have had little influence. Indeed, she had little to do with either of her children until the evenings, when they were brought down from the nursery for their parents' brief approval. Already it was their father rather than their mother who was their source of genuine affection and excitement; but he had little time to spare, and what he did have went on radiant Randolph, rather than on reserved Diana. However much Diana may have resembled her proud father at birth, in personality she was taking after Clementine, and despite her naughtiness was a shy and somewhat nervous child.

Randolph could not have been more different. A happy, sociable small boy, with his blond good looks and easy nature, he had rapidly become the apple of his father's eye. Churchill was entranced with him, spoiling and indulging him, as if desperate to become the sort of father he had never had himself.

Churchill had found unexpected happiness in paternity, but behind his rediscovered zest for life his strange psychology remained unchanged, and he still sought an outlet for his aggression. Agadir had convinced him of what he first suspected when he saw the German army on manoeuvres: that a major

European war was coming. With uncanny accuracy, he actually predicted the course events would follow in a paper written for the Government shortly before moving to the Admiralty.

Foreseeing a major European war, it was his overriding duty to prepare his nation's sea-defences, and his work revitalising the Royal Navy also offered him the antidotes he still required against depression: a patriotic cause to inspire his sense of destiny, constant activity to keep his energies engaged, and a ruthless enemy to rouse his deepest instincts of aggression.

The Royal Navy also gripped his boyish imagination. Picturing the great ironclads as 'war castles foaming to their stations', he thrilled to the drama of their role, knowing that, if they sank, the British Empire would swiftly follow.

As First Lord of the Admiralty, he was at the centre of the greatest instrument of controlled aggression in existence, and he was awed and fascinated by the concentrated firepower of the Fleet. One of his key decisions was to introduce the latest fifteen-inch high-explosive naval gun. (Without it the Navy would have been fatally outgunned and outmanoeuvred in the First World War.) Another was to change the Fleet from coal to oil. This proved a crucial decision which improved the efficiency and speed of British warships in the war to come.

Technical problems always fascinated Churchill, and inevitably he was soon absorbed in the latest form of warfare – flying. He swiftly lost what he called his 'Aetherial virginity', and despite a curious lack of physical co-ordination which always made him such a menace on the road, Churchill doggedly persisted with his flying lessons. Only after one of his instructors had been killed did he agree to Clementine's entreaties to desist.

Fortunately, he had more important matters to attend to at the Admiralty – in particular updating the mentality and personnel of the naval high command. He found his admirals every bit as stupid as the generals he remembered from South Africa, and they were soon providing the rebellious *enfant terrible* of British politics with the sort of opportunity he loved – to range himself against the old, the father-figures, and the ingrained habits of a lifetime – all in the great cause of the British Empire.

He could be a fearful bully. Anyone he disagreed with rapidly became his enemy, and distinguished sailors quailed in his presence. One tried appealing to the great traditions of the Navy.

'Traditions! What traditions? Rum, sodomy and the lash,' the thirty-eight-year-old former lieutenant of hussars retorted.

Churchill's behaviour was soon bringing the naval establishment to a state of panic, but behind him lay a lot of false bravado. Shocked by Churchill's treatment of senior officers, Admiral Bridgeman – backed by the First Sea Lord, Prince Louis Battenberg – confronted him over his behaviour, 'and was stunned to see Churchill suddenly become so melancholy and weepy that he thought he must be ill'.

Churchill's meekness did not last – neither did Admiral Bridgeman. Once he was gone, there was little to detract from Churchill's frank enjoyment of the power he wielded and the splendours that accompanied his great position.

The Admiralty itself was like a ducal principality (far too ducal for Clementine with her continuing concern for marital economy), and the First Lord's residence was part of the impressive Admiralty establishment on the opposite side of Horse Guards Parade to Downing Street.

As First Lord, Churchill could begin to entertain in style. More important, he could now perfect the eccentric way of working which he followed in the years ahead. Each morning, after an ample breakfast he sat up in bed, with the counterpane littered with official memoranda and despatches. Framed by the baroque splendour of the historic Admiralty bed with its gilded dolphins, he would start work. He found that, with his secretary perched beside him, he could deal with business with remarkable efficiency. (It was now that a critic described him as 'ill-mannered, boastful, unprincipled, without any redeeming qualities except his amazing ability and industry'.)

Along with the splendour and comfort of the Admiralty itself went what Violet Asquith called 'the sweetest of the sweets of office' – his Admiralty yacht, appropriately named *Enchantress*. Recently constructed at great expense as the Navy's answer to the royal yacht, *Victoria and Albert*, this most elegant of ships was powered by the latest steam-turbines, had a complement of a hundred sailors and a displacement of four thousand tons. It was a potent symbol of the importance and prestige of Churchill's office, and it also offered him the sort of seaborne splendour only royalty or the richest of plutocrats could hope for in their private yachts.

Churchill made frequent and delighted use of *Enchantress*,

'using it not only to carry out official inspections, but also as a kind of floating hotel which he could place at the disposal of his family and friends'. September 1912 saw the Churchills playing host to the Lloyd Georges aboard *Enchantress*, and the following year it was the turn of the premier, Herbert Asquith, and *his* family – all at government expense.

Churchill was also able to give his mother a badly needed holiday at what was proving an awkward moment in her life. In 1913 her husband, George Cornwallis-West, finally deserted her, as everyone had always said he would, exchanging strong-willed Jennie for Bernard Shaw's great leading lady, the even stronger-willed Mrs Patrick Campbell. But while Shaw's favourite actress was enjoying what she called 'the comfort of the double bed after the hurly-burly of the chaise-longue', with Churchill's former step-father, Churchill himself could still offer his jilted mother a free Mediterranean cruise.

'Dearest Mama,' he wrote,

it would do you a great deal of good to get away from England, worry and expense for three weeks and bask a little in Mediterranean and Adriatic sunshine. . . . We start at Venice, and go round by the Dalmatian coast to Malta, Sicily, Ajaccio and Marseilles – The Asquiths are coming so you must make up your mind to get on with Margot and the PM.

Apart from the opportunity to give his wife and mother a holiday in considerable style at absolutely no expense, the three-week voyage also enabled him to exercise his charm on Herbert Asquith. It was during this cruise that the Prime Minister became particularly impressed by him. When Violet enquired whether he was like his father, Asquith replied: 'No, not really. He is like no one else. He derives from no one. He is an original and most extraordinary phenomenon.'

But it is Violet, clearly captivated herself, who provides the most revealing glimpse of Churchill on these halcyon voyages. Always incapable of relaxing on a holiday, he was impatient with the sight-seeing so enjoyed by the former classical scholar Asquith. 'Those Greeks and Romans, they are so overrated,' he exploded. 'They only said everything *first*. I've said just as good things myself. But they got in before me.'

He showed the same impatience with the pleasures of the simple tourist and delivered a still more irritated retort to the harmless gushing of devoted Violet. As they stood romantically together, she recalled, 'side by side against the taffrail, gliding past the lovely smiling coast-line of the Adriatic bathed in sun', she casually remarked: 'How perfect!'

'Yes,' he replied. 'Range perfect – visibility perfect – If we had six-inch guns aboard how easily we could bombard . . .' and details followed showing how effectively we could lay waste the landscape and blow the nestling towns sky-high.

These trips by Churchill and his friends did not escape notice of the opposition press. 'How much coal has been consumed by the *Enchantress* this year?' asked the *National Review*. 'How many lobsters have been eaten? How many magnums of champagne drunk?'

It is not likely that Churchill was remotely worried by what he must have considered petty carping at a time when war with Germany was imminent. He had a mission to ensure that Britain matched the German naval building programme. Three years earlier he had been angrily opposed to wasting money on the Fleet. Now he was even angrier that Lloyd George was seeking to restrict the naval budget.

'Winston is for 4 ships and George is for 2,' Max Aitken wrote excitedly to Rudyard Kipling.

I am told Winston will stand at 4. It is said that Northcliffe is backing him to bolt from the Liberal Party, and I presume form a new party. Cassel is reported to have promised him £5,000 a year. Winston's position will be rather amusing if he bolts from the Liberal party on the basis of £5,000 from Cassel.

It was a trial of strength, and Churchill got his battleships.

That August, while Europe waited for the inevitable war to follow the murder of Archduke Ferdinand in Sarajevo, Churchill took one of his very rare – and very brief – holidays with all his family, children included. He and his brother Jack rented two cottages on the Norfolk coast, and Churchill, with Jack and the children to support him, was soon revealing that mixture of the schoolboy and the military commander that was never far beneath the surface.

His nephew Johnny remembers how 'Excursions to the beach were organised with military thoroughness', and the sand on the beach marked out for a fort 'of colossal dimensions'.

He describes how Churchill, trouser-legs rolled up, supervised the battle with the sea: 'Taking on impossible odds, fighting a battle he could not hope to win, intrigued him. Not until the very last moment, when all was lost and our glorious castle had vanished, were we allowed to abandon our posts.'

With the Royal Navy already mobilised against the German Kaiser's fleet, Churchill would soon be leading his subordinates against still greater odds, into far more hopeless situations.

15

God Bless the Dardanelles

On the evening of 4 August 1914, as Britain awaited the German Kaiser's answer to her ultimatum against the invasion of Belgium, the Churchills, together with Jack, Goonie and Clementine's sister Nellie, were entertaining the editor of *The Times*. According to Nellie, Clementine – who was seven months' pregnant at the time – 'seemed crushed' by the occasion, 'but Winston was elated – Perhaps "elated" is the wrong word,' she added. 'Anyway, he was bursting with energy and excitement.'

While Churchill was enjoying his after-dinner brandy and a good cigar, Asquith and the rest of the Cabinet had already met, and were gravely sitting in the Cabinet Room at Downing Street, waiting for the Kaiser's answer. It never came. Through the open windows the politicians heard Big Ben toll eleven (midnight in Berlin), and as its echoes died away they sat in silence, trying to grasp the fact that Britain was at war with Germany. According to Lloyd George's secretary/mistress, Frances Stevenson, 'Upon this grave assembly burst Churchill, smiling, a cigar in his mouth and satisfaction on his face. "Well," he said, "the deed is done." The dream of his life had come to pass. Little he recked of the terrors of war, and the price that must be paid. His chance had come!'

This was the fateful moment for which he believed 'destiny' had been so carefully preserving him. All the other members of the Asquith government were pre-eminently men of peace, reforming Liberals unprepared for war and unacquainted with its grim reality. Churchill, on the contrary, was quintessentially a man of war. For three years he had thought of little else and, as he later said, 'nothing could equal the sheer drama' of the days that followed. He confounded his many enemies by having the fleet mobilised and ready as the war began; on his authority the signal 'Commence hostilities' was sent that night to every British warship at 11 p.m. sharp, and as shrewd a politician as Gladstone's old friend and biographer John Morley was predicting that if war came, Churchill would 'beat Lloyd George hollow', in any battle for the Liberal succession. The chance to lead his nation in the greatest war in history was finally in Churchill's grasp: all that insatiable ambition which he had nursed since his lamented father's lamentable death could be fulfilled at last.

Instead he failed – and his failure was so shattering and so extraordinary that it took its place among the greatest dramas of the war. It cost the lives of thousands; it precipitated the collapse of Asquith's government; and it presented Churchill and his family with a living nightmare.

What is fascinating about this great disaster is that, like its author's previous successes, it had its roots so firmly planted in his strange psychology. Granted what we know already of his personality, much of what happened now seems painfully predictable.

The outbreak of hostilities produced in Churchill the inevitable romantic stimulus which warfare always roused in him. He had shown this spirit at Malakand, at Omdurman and in South Africa. 'Everything tends towards catastrophe and collapse. I am interested, geared up and happy,' he confessed to Clementine, adding candidly: 'Is it not horrible to be built like this?' He was now in a unique position to 'direct those great formations' in the 'bright red blossom' of a major war, as he once dreamed of doing.

Savrola, his *alter ego* hero, proved himself by leaving politics to take command of his nation's forces in its time of danger. Faced by the sudden crisis of the enemy advance in Belgium, Churchill decided he would do the same. Early that October, Antwerp was about to fall to the Kaiser's armies; and, for Churchill the historian and would-be military hero, Antwerp lay at the centre of a sacred zone. Within a sixty-mile radius of the city, his exemplar and ancestor the 1st Duke of Marlborough had won his three great victories of Ramillies, Oudenarde and Malplaquet, fighting to defend this very land against the French. Now it was Churchill's chance to do the same against the Germans. And there were other motives for his decision to take charge on the battlefield. With his deep distrust of father-figures, and of aged generals in particular, he saw the British forces being led by what he cheerfully described to Asquith as 'dug-out trash' – a clear reference to his former enemy of Omdurman, the 'ungentlemanly' and unimaginative Field Marshal Kitchener.

With the confidence of youth, Churchill had long believed that, unlike such bemedalled incompetents, he had what he liked to call 'the root of the matter' in him. He longed to prove himself a new Napoleon, and genuinely believed that 'destiny' had saved him for the task.

As First Lord of the Admiralty, he had already thrown together what amounted to a private army of his own: six thousand untrained, untried members of the Naval Volunteer Reserve – the so-called 'Dunkirk Circus' – who had been uncomfortably transformed into a land-based force to defend the Channel ports. That October, in answer to Belgian calls for help, he sent these forces into Antwerp. Two days later he entered the historic city to take charge of them himself.

This was one of the very few mistakes he ever admitted to. After the war he wrote: 'I ought to have remained in London and endeavoured to force the Cabinet and Lord Kitchener to take more effective action than they did. . . . Instead I spent four or five vivid days amid the shells, excitement and tragedy of Antwerp's defence.'

The phrasing of this brief confession is significant. 'Excitement', 'tragedy', 'five vivid days': this is not the language of a soldier fighting a bitter battle to defend a stricken city, but of a natural actor excitedly immersed within the role of a heroic general and rising to the drama of the situation.

Churchill performed splendidly in the part. Arms outstretched, the tunic of his gold-trimmed uniform unbuttoned, he managed to harangue the citizens – in home-made French – presumably leaving them as puzzled by his eloquence as by his language. Photographers and war correspondents, equally intrigued by Churchill's garb, were told it was the full-dress uniform of an Elder of Trinity House, the historic organisation traditionally responsible for Britain's ports. ('Je suis un frère aîné de la Trinité,' he once told a Frenchman, who congratulated him on having such distinguished relations.)

As German field-guns intensified their barrage on the city, Churchill was so enlivened that he cabled Asquith asking to be relieved of his ministerial position in exchange for the rank of major-general. When Asquith relayed this to his Cabinet, it was greeted with what he called 'Homeric laughter'. Churchill was, of course, completely serious. 'His mouth waters at the thought of Kitchener's armies,' Asquith told his girl-friend, Clementine's cousin, young Venetia Stanley. 'He declared that his political career was as nothing in comparison with military glory.'

But the truth was that, whatever courage and panache the First Lord was displaying in beleaguered Antwerp, he was not a general but a politician. Role-player and natural actor that he was, he could act the general to perfection, but in military terms his role was farcical, for there was little he could do – except lose a quarter of his land-based sailors as prisoners-of-war and rapidly retreat from the city.

Clementine might have brought him to his senses, but she was out of action, having given birth to a second daughter, red-haired like her father, at the Admiralty on 7 October. It is some indication of the warlike and dynastic way his mind was working that he insisted that the child be named after Marlborough's indomitable wife, Sarah.

Beyond their 'Homeric laughter', Churchill earned angry criticism from colleagues in the Cabinet as well as from the press and opposition. According to Miss Stevenson, Lloyd George was 'rather disgusted with Winston' for 'having taken untrained men over there' and for having then 'left them in the lurch'. Privately he told Miss Stevenson, 'He would make a drum out of the skin of his own mother in order to sound his own praises.'

Asquith told Miss Stanley that they had gone 'like sheep to the shambles'; but Churchill seemed oblivious of the tragedy among so many other tragedies, as the slaughter of the great campaigns in northern France began in earnest. He was still all-powerful at the Admiralty, and more than ever now his energies were needed for the day-to-day direction of the Fleet.

In naval terms these early months of war were disappointing. Instead of the triumphs Churchill dreamed of, there was a fairly mediocre showing by the Royal Navy. It bungled the battle of the Dogger Bank; it allowed a German cruiser to shell the fashionable resort of Scarborough; and it was hoodwinked by the German warships *Goeben* and *Breslau* which passed beneath the very noses of the British fleet to hoist the Kaiser's flag in Constantinople.

The sailor king, King George V, was far from complimentary at the disappointing showing of his ships, and it was in answer to these near-disasters that Churchill took advantage of racist hysteria against his German monarch's German cousin, Prince Louis Battenberg, to accept the Prince's resignation from his post of First Sea Lord. In his place he reappointed the stormy petrel of the Royal Navy, seventy-three-year-old Admiral 'Jackie' Fisher.

Part mountebank, part naval genius, this monkey-like old sailor had been largely responsible for starting to reform the Navy during his earlier spell as First Sea Lord, when Churchill had been so vehement against the naval programme. Since then they had become good friends. With Fisher, very much a fighting admiral, beside him at the Admiralty, Churchill was happily convinced that the chance had come for naval power to break the stalemate in the trenches of northern France, where, as he put it, the Allied armies were 'chewing barbed wire'.

It was an irresistible temptation for someone of his temperament to discover how the Navy could be used to win the war.

'My God, this is living history!' Churchill exclaimed to Margot Asquith. 'Everything we are doing and saying is thrilling – it will be read by a thousand generations, think of that! Why, I would not be out of this glorious delicious war for anything the world could give me.'

Remembering himself – and Margot Asquith's reputation as a gossip – he drew up short.

'I say. Don't repeat that word, "delicious", but you know what I mean.'

Delicious or not, it is clear that Churchill was in love with what Keynes called 'the intense experiences of conducting warfare on the grand scale which [only] those can enjoy who make the decisions'. It is clearer still that he was now determined to attain his place in history, despite the recent setback at Antwerp.

It was just before the first Christmas of the war that the possibility of forcing the Dardanelles by naval power was broached at the Admiralty – reputedly by Captain William 'Blinker' Hall, famous as the founding father of British Naval Intelligence. These narrowest of straits between Europe and Asia Minor, linking the Black Sea and the Mediterranean, held a magical appeal for any strategist, Churchill included. But at the Admiralty he had already studied and dismissed the possibility of forcing them by sea. Without the help of land-based forces, 'no one could expose a fleet to such perils', he wrote in 1911; and he turned instead to ancient Admiral Fisher for his master-stroke of naval strategy.

Fisher had several bright ideas, including trying to establish British bases on Heligoland, and on the North Sea islands Sylt and Borkum. All had major disadvantages. Suddenly the Dardanelles began to beckon.

Britain's great erratic eastern ally, Russia, was calling for assistance because Turkey had joined forces with the Germans. Once the Dardanelles were forced, the Turkish capital, Constantinople, would fall, the Black Sea routes to Russia would open, and the Balkans would lie at the mercy of the Allied armies. Such was at any rate the strategist's scenario; it was the sort of grandiose master-stroke of war that Marlborough himself might have devised.

Churchill's friend C. F. Masterman graphically described how Churchill came to a decision. 'In nearly every case an *idea* enters his head from outside. It then rolls around the hollow of his brain, collecting strength like a snowball. Then after whirling winds of rhetoric, he becomes convinced that he is *right*; and denounces everyone who criticises it.'

This was very much the case with Churchill's swift conversion to the forcing of the Dardanelles. Once he was convinced that he was right, no one could unconvince him. 'Here', he told Violet Asquith, 'we can make our way to one of the great events in the history of the world.'

There was a technical attraction for him in the dream-like vision of attacking Turkey at Gallipoli: the vulnerability of land-based armies and defences to sudden overwhelming fire-power from the sea had long held an important place within his bellicose romantic fantasies.

When he wrote *Savrola*, nearly twenty years before, he ended it with a curiously prophetic scene in which the land-based forts defending the capital were shattered by the high-explosive shells of the Lauranian fleet steaming through the straits. (The fleet was commanded by an elderly no-nonsense admiral who might have been old Admiral Fisher.) The same theme reappears in *The River War*, with Churchill's graphic description of the effect of the fire-power of the Nile gunboats on the mullah's armies; and by the time he was telling Violet Asquith how to blast the Adriatic coast from the taffrail of *Enchantress*, it is clear that the destructive power of heavy naval guns against the land was genuinely obsessing him.

This obsession became clearer still early in 1914, when his answer to threatened Unionist rebellion in Belfast was to send his North Sea fleet to Belfast with a threat to shell the city at any sign of trouble.

Once convinced, no one in politics worked faster or more effectively than Churchill, but as this small excited man swept all before him one can see the dangers of his eloquence, the limitations of that strange intelligence, the perils lurking in that all-powerful imagination. Above all, one sees the havoc which could be created by a role-playing melancholic with a genius for politics, an obsession with war, a belief in destiny and a passionate desire to make his mark in history.

His inner need to prove that he was always right had made him impregnable in argument – especially on war, the subject where he really had great expertise. No one in the Cabinet was capable of arguing the very real case against the Dardanelles adventure: that it was immensely risky, that the fruits of its success were dubious, and that in terms of long-range strategy Britain's true advantage lay, not in chancy expeditions, but in keeping its naval power intact and maintaining a stranglehold on Germany. (It was this strategy which finally brought the German armies to a grinding halt in 1918 despite their territorial supremacy over the Western Allies.)

Churchill's nautical advisers faced the same stone wall. These were the men who should have raised the technical hazards of the operation, but they were even more easily overwhelmed in argument than members of the Cabinet. Admiral Fisher was dazed and dazzled by the infinitely swifter mind of this brilliant politician more than thirty years his junior. Temporarily suspending his instinctive disbelief about the Dardanelles proposals, he gave them his assent.

Even big slow-moving Field Marshal Kitchener was won over by Churchill's arguments, to the point of offering supporting troops when the Western Front could spare them. Churchill answered that the Navy did not need supporting troops, being quite prepared to force the Dardanelles alone.

But Churchill erred. His navy could not force the Dardanelles

unsupported. The first attempt, on 14 February, failed ignominiously. The Turks were alerted and prepared; their forts were
resistant to the broadsides of the Royal Navy; and Sackville
Carden, the commanding admiral, lost his nerve and called off
the attack.

The second great attack, on 18 March, though more determined, was an even worse disaster. No one had foreseen the
perils of the Turkish minefields in the straits, which disabled
six large Allied warships. Attempts to sweep the minefields
failed. The Turkish shore batteries proved even more effective
than before, and after a long day of concentrated carnage the
attempt to force the Narrows by the Royal Navy was again abandoned. It was not repeated.

But the Dardanelles campaign was far from over. Once
launched, it continued on like some great ill-fated ship with
its own terrible momentum. Kitchener, by now convinced by
Churchill of the strategic dividends of capturing the straits, found
the troops which he had promised. They included two divisions
of Australians and New Zealanders, as yet untarnished by the
heat of battle, waiting in reserve in Alexandria. On 25 April
Hamilton hurled them at the rocky beaches of the Gallipoli
peninsula, which commanded the Dardanelles. The Turks had not
been idle in the interval. Many hundreds of Allied soldiers were
slaughtered, machine-gunned by the boatload as they landed.

This was followed by a period of astounding incompetence
in the Allied high command, equalled only by the courage
of their troops. Opportunities were squandered; so were the
lives of countless soldiers lost to dysentery and Turkish bullets
under a scalding sun. Almost overnight, the master-stroke which
Churchill had intended as the answer to the impasse on the
Western Front became a by-word for insensate slaughter.

Back in London, an element of farce began to mingle with the
tragedy. Asquith's beloved Miss Stanley announced her surprise
engagement to his secretary, Edwin Montagu, leaving the Prime
Minister so distraught that he felt inadequate before the crisis of
the Dardanelles.

Churchill remained confident. Despite the losses, he believed
victory with all its benefits could still be snatched from the rocky
outcrops of Gallipoli. But, with the insulation of the egotist, he
had not appreciated the full extent of the problems.

On 12 May, Admiral Fisher suddenly resigned, saying he was

off to Scotland. In fact the old admiral sought refuge from his worries first in Westminster Abbey and then in the Charing Cross Hotel. Asquith invoked the King's name to order his return, and in the ensuing uproar Fisher aired his doubts about the wisdom of the whole campaign, and also his doubts about his friend and colleague, the First Lord of the Admiralty. By now the Tory press and opposition were in concerted clamour for the First Lord's blood.

The *Morning Post* was accusing him, among other things, of turning 'from melodrama to megalomania' in his conduct of the war. Simultaneously the Tory leader, Bonar Law, offered to join a crisis coalition, with one crucial stipulation – that Churchill leave the Admiralty. Isolated, and betrayed by Fisher, Churchill tried to cling to office with a desperation that showed where his true priorities resided.

'You don't care what becomes of me,' he told Lloyd George. 'You don't care whether I am trampled underfoot by my enemies. You don't care for my personal reputation.'

'No,' Lloyd George supposedly replied, 'I don't care for my own at the moment. The only thing I care about now is that we win this war.'

With the Tories now in the government, nothing could keep Churchill at the Admiralty. Asquith's leaden thunderbolt descended and, on 16 May, Churchill was translated from the power-house of the Admiralty to the still-room of the Duchy of Lancaster. (He remained in the Cabinet, and on the Dardanelles Committee, the small group of politicians and senior officers responsible for the day-to-day running of the campaign, but his prestige and power were fatally diminished.)

Violet Asquith met him in the Commons after the announcement. She found him 'silent, despairing – as I have never seen him. He seemed to have no rebellion or even anger left. He did not even abuse Fisher, but simply said, "I'm finished." I poured out contradictions, protestations – but he waved them aside. "No, I'm done," he said.'

Someone else who saw him was the painter William Orpen, currently engaged on what had been planned as the portrait of the victor of the Dardanelles. Churchill arrived as usual for his sitting at the painter's studio. 'All he did,' said Orpen, 'was sit in a chair before the fire with his head buried in his hands, uttering no word'. Orpen went to lunch without disturbing him, and found

Winston in the same position when he returned. At four o'clock Winston got up, asked Orpen to call a taxi, and departed without further speech.

Churchill speechless was a frightening phenomenon, and there is no disputing the misery and shock dismissal brought him. It was his greatest setback since his father had died, and it began a period of depression even worse than the Home Office years. He was nearly forty-one, older than his father when he fell, but the parallel between their situations could not be avoided. In the words of Lord Randolph's biographer, Churchill 'found himself – like Lord Randolph in December 1886, – completely isolated'.

All was not lost. Churchill had his family to turn to, and they united loyally round him, forming the embattled 'citadel of the heart' he needed. For several weeks, Jennie had been walking across the Park each morning to see him at the Admiralty and 'impart something of her own vitality to sustain him'. She was maternally outraged at his treatment by his former colleagues.

So was Clementine, who had pleaded with the Prime Minister to keep her husband at his post. He alone possessed 'the power, the imagination, the deadliness' to fight Germany, she insisted. Asquith, never an admirer of Clementine, described her letter as 'the letter of a maniac'.

She, too, fell into a depression. 'She was so sweet but so miserable, crying all the time,' wrote Edwin Montagu. 'Poor Clemmie looks very sad, poor thing,' added Cynthia Asquith. 'She said she had always known it would happen from the day Fisher was appointed.' However, anger overcame Clementine's misery, and soon she was saying that her dying wish would be 'to dance on Asquith's grave'.

The disaster meant the loss of her home at the Admiralty, a drop in salary, and a husband in a deep depression. But all the family continued to provide the stricken leader with support – including the adored Randolph and seven-year-old Diana. Later Randolph would recall ending his bedtime prayers with 'God bless Mummy and Papa. God bless the Dardanelles. And make me a good boy. Amen.' Even the members of the family who found themselves serving in Gallipoli were united in their loyalty to Churchill. Jack was attached to the staff of the commander-in-chief, Churchill's friend and comrade from South

Africa, that amiable but uninspiring general, Sir Ian Hamilton. His letters give a vivid picture of the chaos and the sufferings of the troops; but, loyal brother and subordinate that he was, there is not a hint of criticism of Churchill's strategy for the Dardanelles – nor of General Sir Ian Hamilton.

In the circumstances, this was particularly noble; for, while Jack was suffering the flies and bullets of the Dardanelles, his brother and family had moved in with Goonie and the children, and were sharing his comfortable house in the Cromwell Road. Clementine's brother, Bill Hozier, a lieutenant aboard his Majesty's destroyer *Edgar*, was also strong for Churchill. He complained bitterly of 'inactivity', and the lack of 'ginger' in the Government since his brother-in-law's demotion. As late as September he was writing loyally to Churchill saying that the straits could still be forced provided all available warships and destroyers 'blazed away like hell'.

Throughout that second summer of the war, Churchill was sustained by one great hope – a crushing military victory over the Turkish army in Gallipoli which would lead to the capture of Constantinople and vindicate his strategy. And, although still suffering withdrawal symptoms after four exhilarating years at the Admiralty, he was at least being miserable in style, having rented a small country house for all the family some thirty miles from London. This was Hoe Farm, near Godalming in Surrey. With Hoe Farm, three young children, a devoted and attractive wife barely in her thirties, and a new hobby in painting, life cannot have been all bad. 'We live vy simply – but with all the essentials of life well understood & well provided for,' he wrote to Jack. 'Hot baths, cold champagne, new peas and old brandy.'

At this stage, Churchill still had hopes of regaining what he called 'a fuller measure of control before the end of the year'. In the mean time he was on the verge of visiting Gallipoli in person.

It was an adventure he had set his heart on, but his enemies had no intention of letting Churchill back into the limelight. On the eve of his departure, Bonar Law and Curzon blocked the journey. It was yet another disappointment. But by then he had written Clementine a letter to be opened in the event of his demise on the field of battle. It was most revealing.

'Randolph', he wrote, 'will carry the lamp', and Clementine was not to grieve:

Death is only an incident, not the most important wh happens to us in this state of being. On the whole, especially since I met you my darling one I have been happy & you have taught me how noble a woman's heart can be. If there is anywhere else I shall be on the lookout for you. Meanwhile look forward, feel free, rejoice in life, cherish the children, guard my memory. God bless you.

Not only did he never reach Gallipoli, but also the victory which he hoped would prove him right and bring those glittering strategic prizes he had dreamed of never came. Instead the generals bungled a surprise assault in early August with hideous casualties. 'The golden opportunity has gone, and positions that might have been won with a little perspiration will only be gained now with blood,' Jack reported.

During this crisis in his fortunes, Churchill still found time to deal with the problems of another member of his all-important family – his gloomy cousin Sunny.

Now completely separated from independent elegant Consuelo, Sunny had become a bitter, somewhat scandalous recluse, shunned at Court, unpopular with former friends in politics, and thoroughly disliked among his county neighbours. But with the country at war Sunny had felt the patriotic urge to 'do his bit'. An admirable proportion of the Marlborough acres was ploughed up to grow potatoes for the war effort; but potatoes were not enough. He had therefore called on cousin Winston, asking him to find him 'something suitable' at the centre of affairs. Churchill had obliged. Through the good offices of Field Marshal Kitchener, the Duke of Marlborough was appointed a War Office messenger – a humble role, but one which gave him the right to wear a major's uniform and have an office in Whitehall. Then, as the fighting raged in Gallipoli, Sunny once again appealed to cousin Winston in his troubles. He was in danger of being passed over for the Lord Lieutenancy of Oxfordshire.

Churchill, obsessed as always with his close relations, solemnly agreed that this would be unthinkable – a 'terrible reproach to my family'. He used all his powers of persuasion with the Lord Chamberlain (Sunny's uncle by marriage, Lord Lansdowne) to ensure that Sunny got the post. Sunny had already seen his uncle, who had found him 'so violent and abusive . . . that anyone listening to his language would have doubted whether he was fit for any appointment requiring the possession of good manners and an even temper'. But, for Churchill, blood was thicker than bad manners – and using all his influence, including raising the support of the future Lord Birkenhead, he ensured that Sunny was appointed.

For Churchill it was a small triumph in the midst of great disasters, but for Sunny it spelt victory over all his enemies. As he wrote to cousin Winston, 'the dirty dogs have been downed and may they now come and lick their chops in rage and annoyance'. Churchill's enemies were not so easily put down. That October, when the Government accepted that Gallipoli was unwinnable, Churchill was ousted from the Dardanelles Committee, thereby losing his last scrap of influence upon the war effort. For him this was the ultimate disgrace, the end of any hope of vindication by events. Nothing was left but resignation from the Government.

There was one option still available to bring him out of depression and despair. Field Marshal French, the British commander in France, had already offered him the rank which he had so desired at Antwerp – that of a general commanding a brigade.

Warfare had never failed to produce an upswing of his spirits. Battle had always been his favourite way of testing destiny; 'The tuning fork of death' would show if fate was with him any longer. He would forget political disgrace by once more seeking military glory.

Belloc and Scawen-Blunt toasted him with words which once celebrated Marlborough's departure: 'Malbruck s'en v'a-t-en guerre' – 'Marlborough goes off to war'. Violet Asquith sent him a copy of Kipling's 'If'. And the newly ennobled Canadian newspaper millionaire Lord Beaverbrook described the scene as the warrior departed for the front:

. . . the whole household [was] upside down while the soldier statesman was buckling on his sword. Downstairs, Mr Eddie Marsh, his faithful secretary, was in tears. . . . Upstairs, Lady Randolph was in a state of despair at the idea of her brilliant son being relegated to the trenches. Mrs Churchill seemed to be the only person who remained calm, collected and efficient.

In this crisis, Clementine was more admirable than Beaverbrook suspected. To save her sanity, she had already taken on war work of her own – organising YWCA canteens for munitions workers in North-East London – and she made no attempt to stop her husband going. The dangers for him at the Front can have seemed no worse than the horrors he had lived through in the last six months in government.

Even in Flanders, the disgrace of the Dardanelles pursued him. Although one of his early letters home to Clementine contained detailed orders for his general's uniform, it would not be needed. Faced with the anger of the Tory faithful, Asquith would not risk confirming French's offer of a generalship to Churchill. Had he done so – and had Churchill had the chance to play the general's role he longed for – he might well have passed the rest of the war happily in high command (how successfully is another matter). Instead he was merely appointed to the rank of lieutenant-colonel, saw service with the Guards, and was finally consigned to the lowlier Royal Scots Fusiliers in charge of nothing larger than a battalion.

During his brief period as a front-line infantry commander, Churchill was once again a happy man and an undeniable success – tough, resourceful, charismatic and courageous. With absolute assurance he lectured on the art of laying sandbags, bridging trenches or destroying lice. Obsessed as ever with ballistics, he enjoyed few things more than calling up a barrage of artillery at the slightest provocation – Margot Asquith always said he had 'a noisy mind'. This was the boyhood world of high adventure which he loved. 'War is a game to be played with a smiling face,' he told his dour Lowland Scots – and did his best to show them how to do it.

The adventure of war – its danger and hardship – proved an instant therapy for the Dardanelles. At forty-two, he noted proudly that 'many years of luxury have not impaired the tone of my system'. Of course, private luxuries of a certain sort were sent by a motherly Clementine in answer to his regular requests – a folding bath, Jaeger underwear, brandy and a stock of very large cigars.

Soon he could write to her that 'amid these surroundings, aided by wet and cold and every minor discomfort, I have found happiness and contentment such as I have not known for many months'. In his letters he would sometimes use Marlborough's method of address to Sarah, calling her 'My Dearest Soul'.

*

Battle and aggression revived his confidence and gusto. Fate even left its reassuring calling-card when a chance visit to a general saved his life as his billet was destroyed by shellfire.

By December 1915 it seems that service at the Front had saved him from depression and fully restored the self-appointed man of destiny. He could now tell Clementine: 'I am superior to anything that can happen to me out here. My conviction that the greatest of my work is still to be done is strong within me.' Churchill was hungry to return to power. The rank of a general might have kept him happily in France, but beyond the day-to-day excitements there was little long-term satisfaction in the duties of an infantry commander.

Clementine, however, was in two minds over her husband's desperation to return from soldiering to politics. 'My darling,' she wrote, 'these grave public anxieties are very wearing — When next I see you I hope there will be a little time for us both alone — We are still young, but Time flies stealing love away and leaving only friendship which is v. peaceful, but not stimulating or warming.'

Infected by her mood he made a most extraordinary reply, confessing to his desire for 'tranquillity'. 'Sometimes also I think I would not mind stopping living very much – I am so devoured by egoism that I wd like to have another world & meet you in a nobler setting, & pay you all the love and honour of the great romances.'

Just before Christmas, William Sheridan, recently married to Churchill's cousin Clare Frewen, was killed in action. Responding to this, Clementine wrote to her husband: 'My Darling, I don't know how one bears such things. I fear I could not bear such a blow. . . . You must come back to me my dear one.' But she knew the full extent of feeling ranged against him at Westminster. In his absence she had kept in touch with political life in London, even dining quite politely with the Asquiths. She knew he might well be safer in Flanders than staging a comeback in Westminster.

In May 1916, Clementine's doubts notwithstanding, Churchill relinquished what he called 'the rough fierce life under the Hammer of Thor' in France. But Clementine was right. The stigma of the Dardanelles persisted, and he found himself a political untouchable, suspected (correctly) of designs on Asquith's faltering government, unemployable, untrusted and unhappy.

For more than a year he hung in limbo, witnessing the terrible attrition of a war he no longer had a part in. When the grim disaster of the Somme was added to the old disaster of the Dardanelles and Asquith's government was ousted at the end of 1916, it was not the scion of warlike Marlborough who succeeded, but the humbly born ex-pacifist and Little Englander, Lloyd George, who now received the chance of making history.

According to Lord Beaverbrook, throughout this period Churchill remained 'a character depressed beyond the limits of description'. Eddie Marsh described him as being 'like Beethoven deaf'.

The one who saw the full extent of his misery was naturally Clementine. Many years later, talking to Birkenhead's son, Freddie, she admitted, 'the worst part of our life together was the failure of the Dardanelles expedition. W. was filled with such a black depression that I felt that he would never recover from it, and even feared at one time that he might commit suicide.'

One would like to think that he was troubled by the death-toll of the Dardanelles, but there is little evidence that he was seriously haunted by the loss of so many lives pursuing his strategic dream. It was war, and he had taught himself to close his mind to death in battle. During this period he visited no hospitals to see the wounded, made no contact with the widows, and remained majestically apart from the misery of others. Except in that painful period as Home Secretary, when the anguish of murderers got through to him, his lonely insulation from the lives of ordinary people was total. So was the great aristocrat's aloofness, and H. G. Wells was not unfair to Churchill when he described him as believing 'quite naïvely, that he belongs to a peculiarly gifted and privileged class of beings to whom the lives and affairs of common men are given over, the raw material of brilliant ideas'.

Still less does Churchill seem to have been troubled by the thought that his great idea to force the straits was less than 'brilliant'. During the years ahead, much time and energy would flow in demonstrating his intense conviction that he had been right about the Dardanelles. Others could be blamed, and were: his old enemy, slow-moving unimaginative Kitchener; drunken Asquith – 'Supine, sodden but supreme' as he privately described him; and of course the origin of all his troubles, Admiral Fisher, whom he would call 'the dark angel of the Service'. Only one crucial actor in this gruesome tragedy could he never bring himself to blame – himself. And it is this that makes his state of suicidal misery so revealing.

It is Beaverbrook who gives the clue to what was happening. 'His thoughts', he wrote, 'turned inwards as if he was anatomising his own soul.'

Remembering the course of Churchill's life ever since his father died, it is not hard to appreciate his soul's torment. Political power, military glory, a place in history – all protected him against the deep depressive misery which any setback unfailingly produced. Churchill's essential attitude to life had been summed up in a chance remark he made to Violet Asquith. 'We are all worms,' he said resignedly, 'but I intend to be a glow-worm.'

As a glow-worm, high above the worm-like mass of dull humanity, Churchill had been happy: hence his unabashed delight in power, his joy in battle, and his exultation at the prospect of his place in history. Hence, too, his lonely misery when all this vanished in the debris of the Dardanelles.

Power with its splendid consolations was denied him; so was military glory, and the chance of shaping history. Hope was lost. The glow-worm lost its light. Black Dog in all its awfulness descended.

Churchill himself described something of the pain of his inactivity. 'Like a sea-beast fished up from the depths, or a diver too suddenly hoisted, my veins threatened to burst from the lack of pressure.' And in the small book from which this is taken he also described the antidote he used to save his sanity.

He called his book *Painting as a Pastime*; but, once adopted as a pastime, Churchill's painting rapidly became a source of true salvation. Quoting an American psychologist, he described himself as suffering from chronic worry: '. . . a spasm of the emotion; the mind catches hold of something and will not let it go.' Painting proved the one activity to divert his mind from what he called worry's 'convulsive grasp', and he described how a painter's wife, the glamorous Hazel Lavery, gave him his first true lesson in the art, by teaching him not to fear his canvas.

'Painting! But what are you hesitating about?' she said. 'Let me have a brush – the big one.' Splash into the turpentine, wallop into the blue and white, frantic flourish on the palette – clean no longer – and then several large, fierce strokes and slashes of blue on the absolutely cowering canvas. Anyone could see that it could not hit back. No evil fate avenged the jaunty violence. The canvas grinned in helplessness before me. The spell was broken. The sickly inhibitions rolled away. I seized the largest brush and fell upon my victim with berserk fury. I have never felt any awe of a canvas since.

Ever since childhood, Churchill had been turning to aggression to dispel depression, and now he had found the ideal method of directing it. By painting he coped with Black Dog as best he could, and waited. Then in the early summer of 1917 patience and painting were rewarded, and the new Prime Minister, Lloyd George, summoned his old colleague from misery and exile. On 12 July 1917, Churchill was re-admitted to the Cabinet, with a task suited to his energies – if not to his original ambitions. The 'man of war', as Baldwin called him, was made Minister of Munitions.

16

Lullenden

On a perfect summer afternoon in 1918, a group of Royal Flying Corps mechanics waited by a staff car on the perimeter of a former meadow – now officially a 'flying station' – just outside the Surrey village of Godstone. Less than a hundred miles away across the English Channel, the last throw of the German High Command was about to be bloodily repulsed by the Allied armies on the Western Front, but none of this disturbed the rural calm of Southern England.

The aircraft the men were waiting for was late, but finally they heard the staccato buzzing of an aero-engine, and a biplane came in low across the trees, circled the airstrip, then made a bumpy landing on the freshly mown grass. Before the propeller had stopped, a bulky figure in a sheepskin coat had heaved himself out of the passenger cockpit. The car to pick him up had already started off; the driver knew from experience that Churchill was invariably in a hurry.

Forty minutes earlier, Churchill had been driven in a very large Rolls-Royce to the aircraft from his headquarters at the Château Fouquienberg, just behind the Allied lines near Amiens. He referred to the place as 'Château Fuck and Bugger', and the Rolls had been specially lent him for his spell in France by his great friend Bendor, Duke of Westminster. 'You might tell Winston, in answer to his wire, that I only have a shut Rolls at present, if that is any use to him,' Westminster told Churchill's secretary after he had asked if he could lend him a Rolls tourer on his appointment as Minister of Munitions in Lloyd George's government in July 1917.

It seemed a typically casual arrangement, but the use of this personal Rolls-Royce exemplified the optimistic and flamboyant mood with which Churchill undertook his duties as the war was ending. After the personal disaster of Gallipoli and the months of deep depression following his active service at the Front, he was back where he knew that he belonged – in power. His task, as Lloyd George also knew when he appointed him, was one that matched his ingenuity and boundless energy. Present at every major battle to ensure that the guns had their munitions, he was a war-lord once again, bullying the generals and thriving on the breath of battle. Half-seriously Clementine called him 'a Mustard Gas fiend, a Tank juggernaut and a Flying terror', but at least he was no longer the grey-faced husband she remembered, with the doom of the Dardanelles across his brow.

A few days before he flew to Godstone he had spent a day at the Front with the seventy-two-year-old French premier, the white-mustachioed 'Tiger' Clemenceau. (This indefatigable old statesman was a man after Churchill's own heart who insisted on getting as close as possible to the fighting and clearly relished all the risks of war.) Now Churchill was back to make his personal report to the Prime Minister on Monday morning. In the meantime there was the weekend to enjoy at his new country house where the whole family was awaiting the returning hero, descending like Mars, the god of war, in time for a very good dinner.

Clementine had always wanted what she called 'a country basket' where her three 'kittens' would be safe and healthy in the middle of the war. Although essentially an urban being who tended to get bored with country pleasures, she felt Jack's house in the Cromwell Road was no place to bring up the children, particularly now that the German zeppelins had started bombing London. Diana was eight, Randolph six and Sarah three. Jack's two boys, Johnny and Peregrine, were eight and four, so there was nothing to prevent them all living happily together if she could find a 'basket' big enough for the two families to share, which was also close enough to London for Winston's politics and friends, and for Jack when he was home on leave from France.

Churchill loved the English countryside for short periods and provided the sun was shining. When the chance came up to buy a farmhouse of their own in the Sussex farming country near East Grinstead they took it. The house was called Lullenden and seemed as peaceful and romantic as its name.

It is hard to reconcile the family's accounts of Lullenden with the house as it exists today. During the two years Churchill actually owned it it was still very much 'Lullenden Farm', and

Sarah simply called it 'a small farm outside East Grinstead'. But small it was not, and today it is emphatically 'Lullenden Manor', a very beautiful, distinctly grand, late-Tudor stone and timbered Sussex country mansion, with some sixty acres of fields and woodland. (In 1990 it was sold for £2 million.)

When Churchill bought it, Lullenden was still very much a working farm. It was managed by a bailiff but it was clearly more elaborate than he and Clementine had bargained for. Soon it proved to be one more example of the boring problems of extravagance which Churchill's demanding way of life would always land them in; he could ignore them, but Clementine worried as she always did when the farming failed to pay, the bills piled up, and his decreased salary since leaving the Admiralty failed to cover them.

This apart, Lullenden appeared ideal, a country haven in the middle of the war and a place where the grown-ups could lead the sort of comfortable country-house existence they still took for granted. There was no problem finding local girls to cook, to clean and to act as nursery-maids for the children. There were seven bedrooms, a dining room to seat eighteen, and a galleried seventeenth-century drawing room. Lloyd George, Sir Ernest Cassel, the press proprietor Lord Riddell and the American lawyer, diplomat and businessman Bernard Baruch were among the weekend visitors.

But, for the Churchill children, this period at Lullenden was anything but gracious living, and it was here that patterns for their future were established and the collective character of the family itself took shape. Everyday life at Lullenden was primitive. A barn had been converted to provide them all with communal sleeping-quarters, well away from the adults. They drank water from the pond, untreated milk from the local cows, and their only weekday supervision came from the Sussex nursery-maids, who were even less effective than the Admiralty House domestics had been at quelling Randolph and Diana. One of the few events they all remembered was the arrest of a German prisoner-of-war, working on the farm, for poisoning the water after they had all been infected by a mystery illness. Local diversions of this sort were rare, and in effect the children at Lullenden were living two quite separate lives. For most of the time they were simple little savages, uncontrolled and rather undernourished, playing their games, attending the village school and wandering at will

around the farm. Throughout the week the grown-up members
of the family would be away in London: Lady Goonie had her
social life, which continued much as usual with friends like the
Asquiths and the Horners; and Clementine, who was following
a sterner line of wartime duty to match her husband's, continued
her work organising her YWCA canteens.

Only at weekends did adult life impinge on Lullenden; then
and only then would the children be spruced up and brought
together for contact and conversation with their elders in the
drawing room before their bedtime. This apart, they were left to
their own devices in a world already largely ruled by Randolph. It
was a very different world from Clementine's sentimental dream
of country kittens.

At five Randolph was already showing signs of the emergent
monster who would terrorise his enemies – and friends – in the
future. Peregrine, who was a somewhat gentle child, remembers
his cousin as 'a powerful ally who would defend the others to the
death against the village children. But life in the nursery with
Randolph could never be exactly comfortable.'

Randolph was tough and confident, already showing a total
disregard for any sort of criticism or punishment from outsiders.
He is remembered taking dares to confess to frightful misde-
meanours he had not committed for the sheer pleasure of
showing he could take any punishment his nurse could give him.
One of the Lullenden domestics, presumably goaded beyond
endurance, filled his mouth with mustard. Randolph screamed
but swallowed it.

Johnny also still has memories of this diabolical small boy and
the terrible behaviour he engaged them in. On one occasion
Randolph egged Johnny on to tip the contents of his chamberpot
out of his bedroom window. He did not tell him that sitting underneath was the Prime Minister, Lloyd George. (Lloyd George,
according to Johnny's recollection, was used to the rain of his
beloved Wales, and took no notice of the extra drops of moisture
in the air.) On another occasion Randolph had the bright idea of
shutting the infant Peregrine and Sarah inside a model caravan,
presented to the children by rich Lord Riddell, and letting it run
off down a hill. The children emerged more or less undamaged.

If none of the hired help at Lullenden was any match for
Randolph, how could the children be? Johnny, an artistic easy-
going child, had found his role as the joker of the family, and

red-haired Sarah was an elfin, rather sickly infant who by 1918 had most probably picked up the glandular tuberculosis which would dog her childhood. As for Diana she was already showing signs of retreating into herself in the midst of this rumbustious family. She was a doll-like pretty child; but, whereas Randolph seemed to have been born with one skin too many, Diana had one too few and quietly resented Randolph's domination.

Churchill's lightning appearances made a deep impression on all the children. Neither Johnny nor Peregrine had any particular recollection of their unassuming father when he returned on leave from France, but with 'Uncle Winston' it was different.

He was always marvellous with very young children – one of those adults who loves them in theory, plays great games with them, over-excites them, and then abruptly has had enough. But to them he was glamorous and fun. Peregrine remembers playing 'bears' with him and being chased by a growling Churchill through a tunnel made of piled-up picture-canvases. Another game he played at Lullenden was called 'gorilla' in which he would jump down on the unsuspecting children from the trees.

Churchill's presence served to liven up the humdrum life at Lullenden in other ways. His arrival would invariably spell important guests for the weekend, together with the chauffeurs, guards and extra servants who accompany the great in time of war. Lullenden would come to life as a proper country house and, however briefly, all the children had a glimpse of the status and excitement Churchill would always generate around himself. No one was more impressed by his effect than Randolph. Clementine's influence on Randolph at this time was minimal. Wisely, she tended to ignore what she could not control. But between Winston and Randolph there was growing mutual adoration which nothing could shake, as when Randolph learned of his father's role at the Dardanelles.

At the local school there was one village boy who would not play with Randolph because, the boy explained, he was Winston Churchill's son, and Winston Churchill was responsible for his father's death at the Dardanelles. Puzzled by this, Randolph asked his mother what the boy had meant. When she told him, he was completely unabashed. Instead, as he would relate the story later, he felt extremely proud to have a father who 'was a boss man who could order other fathers about' so easily. This echoes Lord Randolph Churchill's remark to Lord Rosebery that the only position worth having in life was 'the boss man's'. A true Churchill, Randolph was already thinking much the same.

If Randolph's admiration for his father was straightforward, Churchill's feelings for his son and heir were more involved. It was as if the infant Randolph was already filling a mysterious vacuum in his complex nature.

Randolph was a beautiful child, and Churchill must have been extremely proud of the press photographs of his son dressed as a page at the St Margaret's, Westminster, wedding of Venetia Stanley and Asquith's former secretary, Edwin Montagu. With fair hair and angelic countenance, Randolph could have been a young medieval prince.

He was also very bright and, like his father, never at a loss for words. The combination of looks, intelligence and precocious confidence struck chords in the sentimental side of Churchill's nature. They also appealed to his pride and passion for his family, for Churchill always had the old-fashioned aristocrat's firm conviction of the primacy of the Churchills, an eighteenth-century sense of dynasty and breeding, setting the members of the family high above ordinary humanity.

This sense of dynasty found full expression at the end of 1918. Peace came in mid-November, and a few weeks later the whole tribe of Spencer-Churchills enjoyed the first Christmas of the peace together in fine old feudal style at Blenheim Palace.

For the first time since before the war, Jack and Winston with their wives and children joined Sunny Marlborough and his sons, 'Bert' Lord Blandford and Lord Ivor Churchill, to bring that sombre house alive in a burst of unaccustomed celebration.

The festivities that year were on a truly ducal scale: a great bonfire close to the Column of Victory with its brooding statue of the omnipresent 1st Duke of Marlborough; an effigy of one of Blenheim's most honoured former guests, the German Kaiser, thrown to the flames; and a whole ox roasted in the courtyard for family and friends and favoured members of the tenantry. Bert was now twenty-one, and everyone had much to celebrate.

Churchill was at his ebullient best – or worst – having ended the war with his reputation more or less patched up after the horrors of the Dardanelles. At forty-three he had begun to put on weight, which suited him, and he had just received the finest Christmas

present anyone could give him – the knowledge that his political
star was still ascending. Cashing in on the nation's gratitude for
victory, the Prime Minister, Lloyd George, had smartly called a
snap election in early December which his coalition government
had won. Churchill himself had been elected for the constituency
of Dundee with his majority increased, and Lloyd George had
promised him promotion in the Government.

After his success as Minister for Munitions, Churchill had
dreamed of returning to his old position at the Admiralty. It
would have laid the ghost of the Dardanelles for good, and besides
he loved the Navy. Admiralty House would have been an invaluable London base for his growing family. He and Clementine now
possessed no settled London home, and she had just presented
him with one more kitten to be taken care of – yet another
daughter, which was probably just as well. A son might have
complicated his relationship with Randolph, who was there to
carry on the line, and Churchill enjoyed the easy devotion of
his daughters. This latest one was pretty, equable and red-haired.
She would be christened Marigold, but in accordance with the
code of private whimsy in the family was already known as 'the
Duckadilly'.

Unfortunately for them, the family were not able to make their
home at the Admiralty, but the alternative was almost as good.
By the time Churchill reached Blenheim, he had exciting news
for Clementine. Lloyd George was offering a more important
role, tailor-made to suit his talents: combined responsibility for
War and Air within the new administration. Churchill had heard
rumours that certain generals were 'horrified' by the prospect,
which must have pleased him; the War Office would offer him
continued scope for his martial instincts and immense capacity
for work, while the official salary of £5,000 a year would be
useful with his ever-growing family commitments.

The future settled, Churchill was able to relax happily for a
few nostalgic days in the splendour of the only place on earth
he looked on as his true ancestral home, with his precious
family around him. Clementine was less entranced. She had
never forgotten or forgiven Sunny for the way he had once
insulted her at Blenheim; and little she had heard about his
private life can have particularly endeared him to her. Nor was
she at ease amid these great tribal gatherings of Churchills. She

knew the sentimental importance Churchill himself attached to them, and for his sake endured them – as she endured so many other things within their marriage – but she had never felt at home at Blenheim, and she profoundly disapproved of the rumours of loose living which had grown up around the house. Since Sunny and the Duchess had parted, Blenheim had become the sort of place mothers advised their daughters to beware of.

Luckily for Clementine's peace of mind, there was one noted absentee from this year's party – her particular family *bête noire*, and another of her husband's favourite relations – the extremely rich and lecherous Ivor Guest, 2nd Baron Wimborne. The eldest son of the steel magnate the 1st Lord Wimborne – husband of Sunny's devoted sister, Cornelia – Ivor had inherited his father's fortune, with few of the family's redeeming qualities. This Christmas he was enjoying a brief period of unaccustomed splendour holding court in Dublin Castle as last Viceroy in Ireland.

Only the year before, he had been ill-advised enough to attempt nocturnal rape on another of Blenheim's Christmas visitors, the beautiful and unassailable Lady Diana Manners (afterwards Cooper). Forewarned of Blenheim's reputation – not to mention what she already knew about Lord Wimborne – Lady Diana had gone to bed with a loaded service revolver. This proved sufficient to calm his lordship's ardour when he burst into her room on his midnight foray. Never one to place discretion before the chance of a thoroughly good story, Lady Diana afterwards made sure that everybody heard about the incident. This year the Wimbornes had not been invited (nor had Lady D).

The rest of the family was there in force, including Sunny's mother, the ill-used but indestructible 'Goosey', Lady Blandford, now in her seventy-eighth year, and his indomitable old aunt, Lady Sarah Wilson, who had been at Mafeking. Several grand local families like the Duffs and Birkenheads were also invited, so that together with their personal maids and valets more than a hundred extra faces thronged the palace, bringing a resurgence of its prewar splendour. The nurseries and corridors were loud with children. Something like forty indoor servants were on hand to guarantee the stately running of this stateliest of homes; and Christmas dinner, though it might be cold (the kitchens being far away from the dining room), was eaten off the Marlborough gold plate, and served by footmen wearing powdered wigs and the red and silver-braided Marlborough livery.

There were good cigars and very good champagne, and the family appeared united with all the living generations in their legendary habitat. This was what Churchill really loved. After his own experience at the centre of a European war, the 1st Duke had become more of a source of inspiration to him than ever. What greater pleasure than to be returning to his palace at the conclusion of the conflict with the sort of power Marlborough himself had once enjoyed?

Churchill's nephew Johnny has described a particular 'Blenheim smell' remembered from his childhood visits, 'like the weighty smell of locked-in history'. The past was re-created in this enormous house with its dusty tapestries and old brocade, its hordes of silent, deeply deferential servants, and the footmen and the gamekeepers in their eighteenth-century velvet coats.

With his old green top-coat and awareness of the dignity of his position, Sunny might easily have been an eccentric eighteenth-century nobleman; so might his most unlikely friend, Lord Birkenhead, wildest, wittiest and most bibulous of politicians.

Birkenhead was one of Churchill's oldest friends in politics, co-founder of the 'Other Club', and one of the few men capable of standing up to him in argument. With Birkenhead as his verbal sparring partner, Churchill was guaranteed the sort of political talk late into the night that he enjoyed; while with his brother Jack, recently returned from France, he could relive the memories of boyhood, organising the children in the games of their own youth, the most popular of which was 'French and English'. This was played in the great hall, with the children lining up as rival armies. Churchill commanded the English, and Jack (as he always had in the past) the French. Battles were fought, prisoners taken and released, and according to Birkenhead's daughter, Eleanor, the two grown men 'took such a passionate interest in the game, and played so roughly that they soon scattered the children, conducting some violent struggle of their own that resembled nothing so much as American football'.

As with the games he played at Lullenden, Churchill appears as one of those disturbing adults who enter a little too exuberantly into the remembered joys of childhood. Of all the children, only Randolph seems to have truly enjoyed such rough play; but, then,

Randolph was always inventing dangerous games of his own. The other children tired much more easily, and then they would sprawl together on the bear-skin rugs in the Long Library, listening to the Duke's organist, Mr Perkins, playing on Blenheim's mighty Willis organ.

This first Blenheim Christmas of the peace was a time everyone remembered as a last glimpse of a world now gone for good. But while the guests were eating, drinking and enjoying this most pagan festival, there was one melancholy stranger in their midst, a small man in his late forties, 'slight, and frail looking, with beautiful manners' as Lady Eleanor remembered him – the Duke himself. He was a lonely isolated figure now; and, in contrast with his cousin Winston, one sees how unenviable was the fate he had inherited at Blenheim, how badly he had fared in the genetic lottery, and how the curse of his unhappy house was still pursuing him.

Sunny had irrevocably sold himself for his inheritance when he had married Consuelo Vanderbilt. The Vanderbilt money – and the regular annual 4 per cent he still received from the original marriage settlement – had enabled him to do what he conceived to be his duty to his ancestor's voracious palace. Acres of leaking roof had been repaired, two of the state rooms sumptuously restored with gilt French *boiseries*, and even now he was embarking on ambitious plans to make the exterior of the palace grander still. A series of elaborate formal terraces, à la Versailles, were to be built to connect the palace with the lakes.

It had become something of an obsession with his locked-in nature to enhance the setting of the dukedom, and to maintain the dignity and splendour of his great position. Lord Birkenhead was one of his few friends with the wit to try to make him occasionally unbend – but Sunny was too far gone in dukedom to appreciate everyday reality.

One gets a clear impression of Sunny's Blenheim in the twenties from one of its visitors, the French Duchess of Clermont-Tonnerre:

. . . I heard the fire crackling in my room without having seen it lighted, the curtains were drawn in my room without my being wakened, and . . . by eight o'clock in the morning the lawn was rolled, the dead leaves removed and the flowerstands filled with fresh flowers.

After a day or two of this, the Duchess found 'the majestic silence of those great mute corridors' getting on her nerves, and she was not the only one. In her otherwise nostalgic memories of Blenheim Christmases, Lady Eleanor Smith includes one episode which reveals a touch of nightmare, barely concealed behind the dignity and splendour:

One day, at Blenheim, a housemaid went mad. She ran through the state rooms, screaming, stalked by grim, powder-headed footmen. It was just before dinner. Her screams rang through the vast rooms, and they were so terrible that I will never forget them. They reminded me of a hare's screams. Finally, she ran to the furthest state room, and there, in the darkness, she was cornered. Four footmen carried her away; she attacked them furiously, and the powder flew from their hair like clouds of snow. They bore her across the huge hall through green baize doors, behind which her anguished cries were no longer heard. That same night she was removed to a lunatic asylum.

This was the world the Duke had made it his life's mission to preserve and which had brought him little but that private bitterness reflected in the down-turned mouth and set expression on his pallid features. As Winston had told Clementine when Sunny separated from Consuelo before the war, his cousin was 'absolutely dependent upon feminine influence of some kind for the peace and harmony of his soul' – but his situation had made it all but impossible for him to find it.

There was a sort of grim poetic justice over what had happened to him since he sold himself to Mrs Vanderbilt and saved Blenheim by marrying her daughter Consuelo. Twenty years later he was as much the victim of his house as ever, and the cost of maintaining and improving it made him still dependent on the income from his marriage settlement. Any attempt to end the marriage by divorce, without Consuelo's co-operation and assent, could have forfeited, not just the income, but the capital as well. It was a risk he could not take. And beautiful rich Consuelo had not the faintest intention of doing anything to make life easier – let alone more pleasurable – for her husband.

She had a splendid house in London, and would soon begin to build another, even more beautiful still at Eze sur Mer, near Monte Carlo, in the South of France. Like the Duke she had her lovers, but unlike him, was remarkably discreet. She still enjoyed her title, and she undoubtedly enjoyed annoying Sunny. After those early indignities of marriage, it was understandable.

Sunny had some consolations. One of the most attractive of them was still Consuelo's former friend, the beautiful sophisticated Gladys Deacon from Boston, friend of Rilke, Proust and Charles de Montesquieu. Since well before the war, Sunny had shared her favours with many other lovers who had included the successful but dubious aesthetic pundit Bernard Berenson, the great sculptor Auguste Rodin and the President of France. But, as beautiful as ever, by 1918 she was secretly approaching forty, and was as eager to become a duchess as Sunny was to make her one. This did not suit Consuelo. The 'peace and harmony of his soul' that Sunny thought that he would find by marrying Miss Deacon sadly eluded him.

Nor did he find it in either of his sons, both of whom were adding to his Christmas cup of bitterness. At twenty-one, his heir, the egregious Bert Lord Blandford, gave every sign of being vastly stupid, which Sunny was not. Bert was immensely tall, largely incoherent, and generally irresponsible. Sunny blamed his deficiencies upon the Vanderbilt strain, which was probably unfair. Having just left the Life Guards, Bert was having an affair with an actress called Miss Barnes, to considerable speculation in the press that he would either marry her or be heavily sued for breach of promise. Neither prospect can have added greatly to the Christmas spirit.

Sunny's other son, Lord Ivor Churchill, could not have been more different from his brother – but he presented the Duke with other problems. As short as Bert was tall, as intelligent as he was stupid, he was very much Consuelo's favourite, and spent more time with her than he ever did at Blenheim. He was highly civilised, already something of a connoisseur of furniture and modern painting, and as precious and refined as brother Bert was insensitive and boorish. (Bert's character, it was often said, derived largely from the fact that Consuelo had rejected him for Ivor.) Cynthia Asquith, who had a motherly crush on Ivor at around this time, described him as 'a mannikin', as delicate as a porcelain 'figure de Limoges'; while his Oxford contemporary Chips Channon, who admired his style and cleverness, detected a fatal touch of melancholy and lack of purpose in his life.

Shortly after leaving Oxford, he seems to have had some sort of breakdown, and for many years Ivor was psycho-analysed by Freud's biographer Dr Ernest Jones. The leading Freudian in Britain must have found the young nobleman a fascinating

subject. Freud would have made much of Lord Ivor's close
relationship with the powerfully appealing figure of Consuelo,
and his difficulty relating to Sunny.

Perhaps the only person who appreciated what Sunny had done
and sacrificed for Blenheim was his cousin Winston. Churchill
was the only one who really shared Sunny's obsession with the
ancestral palace, for the family traditions it enshrined, and for
the dukedom. He always demonstrated unfeigned respect for
the reigning duke as head of the family and maintainer of its
honours.

But whereas Sunny's devotion to Blenheim had helped to ruin
his life, making him a bitter introverted character, Blenheim's
influence had had an opposite effect on his cousin Winston, who
might almost have been the 1st Duke reincarnate.

17

To Russia with Love

Not long before the Armistice, Siegfried Sassoon, the war-hero turned pacifist and poet, had a bizarre encounter with Churchill at the time when he was still Minister for Munitions. While recovering from service at the Front, Sassoon had become an overnight celebrity with his book *Counter-Attack*, and Churchill himself seems to have been disturbed by the power of Sassoon's anti-war poetry – and by its potential danger to national morale. Somewhat cynically he had already tried to compromise him by offering him a desk job in his own ministry. When this failed Churchill decided to employ his powers of personal persuasion on the sensitive young officer.

He knew all about Sassoon from his secretary Eddie Marsh: he was a member of a prominent Anglo-Jewish family and kinsman to Lloyd George's private secretary, the wealthy Liberal politician Sir Philip Sassoon; he was also a great country-lover, horseman, patriot, and manifestly not a coward. Through Marsh, Churchill arranged a meeting so that he could 'have it out with him' on a subject still engaging all his energies and passionate excitement.

The meeting started comfortably enough. Churchill seemed 'almost boyish' as he talked about the war, and Sassoon began to feel that he 'would have liked to have had him as my company commander in the front line'.

But then, as so often with Churchill, what began as a discussion soon became a monologue. Sassoon felt tongue-tied as, 'pacing the room, with a big cigar in the corner of his mouth, he gave me an emphatic vindication of militarism as an instrument of policy and stimulator of glorious individual achievements and social progress'.

'Head thrust well forward and hands clasped behind his back', Churchill the orator had taken over, leaving the poet more or less forgotten. 'Transfixed and submissive in my chair, I realised that what had begun as a persuasive confutation of my anti-war convictions, was now addressed, in pauseful and perorating prose, to no one in particular.'

Other visitors and business now forgotten, the rhetoric flowed on. When it finished, Sassoon emerged from the great man's presence shaken, and baffled. Had Churchill been entirely serious? he asked himself. Could he have meant it when he insisted that 'war is the normal occupation of man'?

Having experienced modern war in all its horror, he found it inconceivable that anyone could honestly believe this after four long years of conflict. But Churchill had been plain, and Sassoon concluded: 'It had been unmistakable that for him war was the finest activity on earth.'

To set such a man in charge of the War Office when the war was over was the sort of joke to be expected of Lloyd George, but he should have known Churchill better than take such a risk. Just as it seemed that he would be Secretary of State for War without a war, he promptly found one.

The Russian Revolution of 1917 had left the victorious Western Allies in an awkward situation. The Bolsheviks had initially been abetted by the German High Command, and the revolution swiftly led, as the Germans had hoped, to Russia's withdrawal from the war. The Russian royal family was killed, and civil war had broken out between the Bolsheviks and groups from the old Imperial Army ranged against them. French and British forces, which had been fighting the Germans with their former Russian allies, remained on Russian soil to help the White Army.

Among the Western powers, the general feeling was to disengage and leave the Russians to get on with it. Europe was sick of bloodshed, and few wanted yet another war. But Lenin and the Bolsheviks were proclaiming worldwide revolution against capitalist oppression. The communist Béla Kun had established his government in Budapest. Even in Britain there was widespread discontent following the war, and the red flag threatened postwar Europe. There were arguments for supporting the anti-Bolsheviks in Russia and crushing the revolution in its infancy.

Most of the Western statesmen hedged their bets. America opted for withdrawal, but France favoured intervention, and

Lloyd George seemed to waver. Not so his Secretary of State for War.

From the beginning of the Russian Revolution, Churchill had felt passionately about the Bolsheviks; it is clear that they offended the profoundest elements within his nature. Since his aggression was aroused, he saw Tsar Nicholas as a tragic hero, and Lenin as beneath the range of civilised contempt – 'A plague bacillus' which had infected Russia with 'the foul baboonery' of communism, 'a monster crawling down from his pyramid of skulls', as he described him.

Lenin, he remarked, almost converted him to Christianity – only the most atrocious depths of hell were fit to receive so terrible a man.

Although he felt strongly about the revolution, in fact Churchill knew very little about the aims and characters of those involved. He would fulminate against the revolution as the work of 'a group of international semitic conspirators', despite the fact that Trotsky was the only Jew among the Soviet leaders and that of all the causes of the Russian Revolution a conspiracy of evil Jewish gentlemen was even then the least convincing.

'Before all things, he desires a dramatic world with villains – and one hero,' H. G. Wells once wrote, and Lord Beaverbrook described him at the War Office in the spring of 1919, striding up and down the room on little feet, 'tingling with vitality. Bold and imaginative in the sweep of his conceptions, prolific of new ideas, like a machinegun of bullets and expelling his notions in much the same manner.'

Until now, the Germans had been the hated enemy who raised this sort of energy: now that peace had broken out, the Bolsheviks were there to take their place. When Violet Bonham Carter enquired about his latest policy, Churchill answered: 'Kiss the Hun and kill the Bolshie.'

Throughout the spring of 1919, Churchill set out to do just that. Lloyd George's preoccupation with the peace conference in Paris left Churchill a free hand at the War Office, and he was clearly on a high as he mounted his machine-gun-like campaign in Cabinet, Parliament and press against the monsters he so vividly created with his powerful imagination.

It was good theatre, and a vintage Churchill one-man show as usual. On the pretext of covering their ultimate withdrawal, he was soon ordering the British forces in Archangel to advance. He

kept the White Russian General Denikin supplied with money
and 'surplus' British war material, and proposed the annexation
of the Caspian Sea by the Royal Navy and the use of poison
gas against the enemy. When it looked as if the communists
were crumbling, he even talked of 'going out there to ride a
white charger' into Moscow at the head of the Tsarist forces.
His friend Lord Riddell said half-jokingly that Winston dreamed
of being Tsar himself.

Perhaps he did, or possibly he dreamed of beating his old hero
Napoleon to the gates of Moscow. Whatever he dreamed, by late
spring of 1919 Britain was on the brink of war. Or, as Lloyd
George put it, Britain was in 'a state of war' with the Soviets,
but had no intention of actually 'making war' upon them.
    Churchill had no such reservations. 'If we don't put our foot
on the egg, we shall have to chase the chicken round the world's
farmyard,' he remarked. But mutiny was already breaking out
among British forces in Murmansk, the White Russians were in
chaos, and Churchill's scant support at home was fading. Long
before the winter of 1920 started he was having to admit the
failure of his great campaign as the 'intervention' against the
Soviets collapsed.
    The star was eager, but the show was ending. He would not
be riding into Moscow, or making Europe safe from communism.
It was an ignominious failure, which ended with Lloyd George
demoting him from the War Office to the Colonies early in 1921.
By then the Bolshevik revolution was haunting Churchill, even
in his home. It was at a weekend gathering of Churchills at
Templeton, the Roehampton mansion of his rich cousin, Freddie
Guest (second son of Aunt Cordelia) early in September 1920
that Churchill's nephew, Johnny, heard the beginning of a scandal
which suddenly shook the family.

I was a child, just home from school, and I was fascinated to
hear a terrific commotion from the drawing room. There was my
Uncle Winston, beside himself with rage, and Lord Birkenhead
who seemed to be trying to calm him down. But Uncle Winston
went on shouting, 'Clare's in Russia. Clare's in Russia with those
filthy Communists. She's mad, I tell you. Mad! It's absolutely typical
of Clare, but this time she's really gone too far. I'll not forgive her.'

For the rest of the weekend, chaos reigned as the gathered Churchills tried to decide what on earth to do about their cousin, who at that very moment was in Moscow with the 'hairiest Bolshevik baboon' of all, Vladimir Ilyich Lenin.

Clare Sheridan, then aged thirty-five, was the widowed daughter of Jennie's younger sister, Clara, and her handsome husband, Moreton 'Mortal Ruin' Frewen. Churchill's Aunt Clara was a true Jerome, with much of her sister Jennie's extravagance and energetic charm. Racily romantic, she had managed to combine marriage with her long affair with the most improbable of lovers, Milan Obrenovich, the dispossessed King of Serbia. Her husband, Churchill's Uncle Moreton, seems to have been more than a match for her. Inventor, speculator, spendthrift and philanderer – 'every woman I have ever enjoyed has been completely paralysed by the vigour of my performance' – he was probably the most unreliable man in England, as Churchill had discovered years before when Uncle Moreton edited the proofs of *The Malakand Field Force*.

Golden-haired dramatic Clare inherited her parents' beauty and most of their other qualities as well. Her marriage to William Sheridan, a descendant of the playwright, had ended with his death in action. Since then she had indulged her artistic temperament as a sculptress and achieved considerable success.

Much of this was due to the support of her cousin Winston, who was fond of her and helped promote her work. She had sculpted him, and several of his friends had also sat for her, including Lord Birkenhead, Lord Reading and the egregious Freddie Guest.

By the summer of 1920, Churchill and his friends had been seeing much of cousin Clare. She had started an affair with the fifty-two-year-old Lord Birkenhead, who was now Lord Chancellor of England and happily infatuated. When Jennie heard of what was going on, she laughed and told her that, although Birkenhead was married, he was just the sort of man Clare needed to 'perk her up'.

According to Clare's grandmother, Mrs Frewen, who also knew of the affair, Churchill was equally complacent:

He adores Clare, thinks she can do no wrong after all she has suffered and he is devoted to Lord B. – you know how he always stands by his friends. So whatever scandal these two create together is in Winston's view no scandal – they are 'splendid', and whatever they feel like doing is 'perfect'. So there it is. . . .

At weekends, Lord Birkenhead collected Mrs Sheridan from her studio in his Rolls and brought her back to Templeton, where she also had a studio, so that love and sculpture could continue their idyllic course among the Churchills. Clementine's views of what was going on were not recorded.

Clare was industrious as well as romantic, and Agnew's Gallery in Bond Street had promised her a one-woman exhibition before Christmas if she produced portraits of enough celebrities to make a show. Since the failure of Churchill's intervention policy in Russia, Lloyd George had invited a Russian trade delegation to visit London; and, although her cousin indignantly refused to have anything to do with them, Clare remarked casually: 'What fun to add a Bolshevik to my Agnew exhibition!'

This chance remark was reported to Kamenev, the leader of the Russian delegation, who was smart enough to see the publicity potential of a close relation of the dreaded Winston Churchill doing portrait busts of Russian leaders for a Bond Street show. He met Clare, flattered her (which was not difficult) and promised her that if she came to Moscow, he would guarantee her introductions to the leading members of his government.

She must have known that Kamenev was brother-in-law to Trotsky, the creator of the Red Army, who was second only to Lenin as arch-enemy of her cousin Winston. She had also recently agreed to join Churchill and the Lord Chancellor for a cruise aboard her lover's yacht. But she was not Moreton Frewen's daughter for nothing. An adventure such as this was irresistible. So was the thought of adding the notorious face of Lenin to her other portraits – it would make her famous. Secretly she took the train to Stockholm, then journeyed on to Moscow, leaving her cousin and the jilted Birkenhead aboard their yacht wondering what could possibly have happened. When they returned to Templeton they discovered – and Johnny was there to witness the result.

Clare, in the meantime, was blithely unconcerned with the furore she had roused at home. Thanks to Kamenev's influence, she was lodged – in considerable discomfort – in the official guest-house on the Sofiskaya Embankment (now the British embassy), and various leading Bolsheviks were produced to sit for her. The notorious Grigoriy Zinoviev, President of the Third Communist International, was succeeded by the most feared man in Moscow, Felix Edmundovich Dzerzhinsky, a leading organiser of the original Bolshevik *coup d'état* and head of the Soviet secret police, the Cheka. (Clare found him pale, undersized and sickly, and he explained that eleven years in prison had destroyed his health – a compliment he was busily repaying his ancient enemies in spades.)

Then it was Lenin's turn. The sittings took place in his office in the Kremlin, and were curiously peaceful and relaxed. While Lenin worked away in silence at his desk – 'I have no interest in art, but you can work here as long as you don't disturb me' – the indomitable sculptress tried doing justice to the head of the most powerful man in Russia. Although Lenin spoke English, it was not until the bust was nearly finished that she coaxed a little conversation from him.

'Your cousin, Winston Churchill, he must be pleased with you!' he said, with what could just have been a touch of unexpected wit.

'Is he hated in Russia?' she enquired.

To which Lenin answered that Churchill was the Russian people's greatest enemy, since 'all the force of your Court and your army lie behind him'.

She replied that, although Churchill was Minister for War, the Court had little actual power in England; but Lenin, who seemed very conscious of King George's hatred of the Bolsheviks for murdering his Russian royal cousins, would not accept this.

'It is a pose to say the King does not count. He counts very much. He is the head of the army, and he is the bourgeois figurehead. Churchill is backed by him.'

With which, apparently, this singular conversation ended. Asked for an opinion of the finished bust, Lenin's secretary dutifully pronounced it 'good'.

'I like a fast worker,' Lenin said. And that, after shaking hands, was that.

But, before leaving Russia, Clare was determined to complete her gallery of leading Bolsheviks with a portrait bust of Trotsky – and it was this that brought a romantic grand finale to her visit. From the start she found Leon Trotsky a more responsive subject than Comrade Lenin. The scholarly-looking figure with the pince-nez spectacles was commander-in-chief of an army of five million men which was in the process of mopping up the remnants of the White Russians Churchill was supporting in the Crimea. Yet he found the time to meet her in the white-pillared ballroom of the Soviet Ministry of War.

Clare would not forget the sessions that ensued each evening as she worked on the 'magnetic' features of her favourite Bolshevik. Did he really kiss her frozen hands and warm them by the fire? Did he tell her 'even when your teeth are clenched and you are fighting with your work *vous êtes encore femme*'? And, when the bust was finished, was she unable to resist him amid the damask-covered walls of her lonely bedroom, when he murmured that 'a woman like you could be a whole world to a man'?

This was the story as she recounted it to her niece, Anita Leslie, many years later; and according to this version it was touch and go whether she should accompany her latest lover on campaign in the Crimea. 'C'est à vous de décider,' he told her with his arms around her. Luckily for Churchill back in London, cousin Clare placed art and duty over the promptings of her heart, and headed homewards with her sculptures and her memories.

As it was, it was embarrassing enough. Through its secret agents, the British government was kept informed of what went on in Moscow, and the doings of this close relation of the Secretary of State for War were naturally reported back to London. 'Poor Winston. Lloyd George chaffs him terribly in the Cabinet about you,' Clare's cousin, the literary Shane Leslie, informed her. Lloyd George was not remarkable for delicacy in sentimental matters. He would not have missed so obvious a chance to embarrass the strongest critic of his reconciliation policy with Russia. And Churchill was notoriously touchy over any scandal which involved his family.

For a while he was extremely angry. According to Shane Leslie, he seriously proposed having his cousin placed in quarantine on her return and, not unnaturally, refused to meet her. So did her father, who complained that, thanks to Clare, he was now unable to show his face in White's Club bar. The royal family were reported 'scandalised' and, according to Clare's own account, the only Churchill to support her was 'Aunt Jennie' who supposedly told her: 'You're so like me really – I would have loved to do it in your place.'

Perhaps she would, and certainly her niece's escapades were very much in character with the headstrong and romantic Jennie. Churchill's mother had recently remarried for the third and final time – to a lonely colonial official called Montagu Porch, who was three years younger than her eldest son. (Although apparently delighted with her gentle husband, Jennie had no intention of being Mrs Monty Porch, and made it known that she was to be addressed as Lady Randolph Churchill. 'My boys asked me to,' she said.)

Clare soon discovered that life in London was impossible. Far from making her fortune as she hoped, her sculptures of the Bolsheviks were little more than competent and did nothing to advance her artistic reputation. With her family and most of her former friends – including, not surprisingly, Lord Birkenhead – giving her the coldest of cold shoulders, she wisely headed for the lecture circuits of America, where her tales and talents were appreciated. In Hollywood she sculpted Charlie Chaplin.

When she had safely left the shores of England, Churchill sent her off a letter. Given the circumstances, it was one of the most tolerant he ever wrote. But he was not a man for bearing grudges, particularly not with women he was fond of, and he was genuinely fond of cousin Clare.

It had been, he said, impossible for him to meet her on her return from Russia, 'fresh from the society of those I regard as fiendish criminals'. But that did not mean that he had ceased to regard her with affection, and he earnestly wished her 'success and happiness in a right way'. She could always count upon his friendship and – more important still – his kinship, and he trusted they would meet again when there was 'a healthy gap between you and an episode which may then have faded and to which we need neither of us ever refer'.

Clare's departure for America coincided with Churchill's from the War Office early in 1921 – and with this vanished any further serious concern for what went on in Russia. Having brought Britain to the brink of war to indulge his dreams of conflict with his 'hairy' Bolsheviks, he washed his hands of them. Never one for lingering on the field of failure, he had found himself fresh enemies closer to home to keep him happily involved in politics and 'man's normal occupation'.

The new ministry to which Lloyd George had shifted him was one he had already occupied, earlier in his ministerial career – Secretary for the Colonies. Although it was seen as a demotion, the workaholic Churchill soon immersed himself in complex new responsibilities which were a welcome contrast to the snows and gloom of Russia.

Almost his first task was to impose the British government's proposed settlement on Palestine, which he accomplished at the Cairo Conference in 1921 with a speed and firmness much applauded at the time – and commemorated in unceasing Arab–Jewish conflict ever since.

Time would be no kinder to him over his solution to another problem awaiting him at the Colonial Office – the transformation of Turkish Mesopotamia, conquered by the British in 1918, into the modern Arab kingdom of Iraq. Anxious to safeguard British oil interests at minimum expense, Churchill selected malleable King Feisal for the newly created Iraqi throne backed by British arms and influence. Rather than rely on large expensive troop detachments, Churchill devised a policy of swift retaliation by British armoured cars and RAF bombers against troublesome Iraqi villages as 'a deterrent to the unruly tribesmen', most of them members of the harshly treated Kurdish minority, who opposed Baghdad.

It was a policy which set a chilling precedent for the future of this unhappy country. His old Harrow contemporary, Richard Meinertzhagen, now British military adviser on Middle East Affairs, wrote to him anxiously of rumours he had heard of the use of poison gas against rebellious tribesmen. But Churchill had never been sentimental about rebellious tribesmen. Far from condemning the use of poison gas against them, his reaction was to authorise 'the construction of such bombs at once. . . . In my view they are a scientific expedient for sparing life wh shd not be prevented by the prejudices of those who do not think clearly.' Luckily, the rest of the Cabinet failed to share the 'unprejudiced' views of the Colonial Secretary on chemical warfare, and, despite his enthusiasm for poison gas, Churchill did not become the first to use it to suppress the Kurds.

Besides, Churchill's main preoccupation during 1921 was not Baghdad but Dublin. Here, too, as a warrior-politician he had already had his chance to make a contribution to the miseries of Ireland. While Secretary for War he personally devised the plan for what he called a 'Special Emergency Gendarmerie' of a thousand former servicemen to give backbone to the harassed Royal Irish Constabulary, in the face of growing violence and disorder. Swiftly drafted into Ireland, in khaki uniforms and black military belts, his thousand troops acquired the nickname of the 'Black and Tans' and rapidly became a byword for organised brutality and British government-backed terror in retaliation for the murderous activities of the IRA.

Just as with the Bolsheviks (with whom he compared them), Churchill was strongly urging ruthless war against the equally ruthless Irish revolutionaries – which included retaliatory murder, the destruction of much of the city of Cork, and the proposed bombing and machine-gunning from the air of the revolutionary Sinn Fein meetings. Only when it became crystal clear that such a policy was pushing Ireland to the verge of anarchy did he suddenly change course, opting for the granting of dominion status to a new Irish Free State, with only Protestant Ulster in the north remaining part of mainland Britain.

These proposals were neither simple nor particularly popular in Dublin or in London. Their final acceptance owed much to Churchill's vigorous espousal, in particular to the ruthless way he faced the Irish delegates with the alternatives of settling or facing all-out bloodshed. The Irish Treaty, signed at the end of 1921, was hailed as a triumph for the conciliatory powers of Lloyd George and the skilled advocacy of Lord Birkenhead. It was also a considerable success for Churchill, whose ministerial responsibility it was, and whose ruthlessness and energy, particularly in the House of Commons, had also helped to bring it to fruition.

The settlement, however temporary, of Palestine, Iraq and Ireland, helped restore Churchill's tattered credibility after the failure of his Russian policy. This made 1921 a year of spectacular recovery for him – indeed, he judged it one of the most successful of his whole career. His only serious regret was that it had not been crowned with that 'great office of state' he had always set his heart on: his father's old position at the Treasury. Churchill's rage on hearing that Lloyd George had entrusted it to pedestrian Sir Robert Horne in succession to Austen Chamberlain widened the rift between the two of them, and was proof of the extent to which his powerful ambitions were reviving.

What was particularly remarkable about Churchill's political recovery in 1921 was that he achieved it in the face of a succession of family disasters and private tragedies. All were unforeseen and might have been expected to divert if not prostrate a man of Churchill's naturally depressive temperament; but the reverse occurred. Aggression and political success sustained him, so that the tragedies which now befell him and his family barely appeared to interrupt the brisk momentum of his days.

The first sign that Churchill's private life was threatened came from Clementine, who by the last months of 1920 was clearly heading for a nervous breakdown.

Behind the cool and carefully controlled exterior, Clementine was always nervously at risk. Even before her marriage there had been a long period of prostration after she ended her engagement with her older suitor, and throughout her life she was afflicted by dramatic outbursts of hysteria which could be followed by lethargy, depression and a sudden inability to cope with life. Much of her trouble lay in chronic insecurity, which seems to have had its origins in her fatherless and insecure girlhood.

Although not the easiest of husbands, Churchill the confident, ambitious older man had offered her the reassurance that she needed, and she determined early on to place him and his great career before family and children. She had stuck to this with all the dedication of her own romantic nature, sharing his triumphs and seeing him through times of deep depression. When it suited Churchill they could enjoy their family together, and there had been carefree sentimental times with all their 'kittens' when she had played the temperamental 'Mrs Kat' to his adoring 'Mr Pig'. (It was around this time that 'Pug' mysteriously changed to 'Pig'.) But for Clementine the most important moments came when just the two of them were united in Mr Pig's advance to greatness, and he relied upon her for encouragement and advice. She must have known that clever people like the Asquiths and even the vivacious Goonie sometimes mocked her earnestness behind her back, but at times like this it barely mattered. Her lack of learning and sophistication could become a virtue. 'Just becos' I am ordinary & love you I know what is right for you & good for you in the end,' she wrote to Churchill on one occasion. Convinced of this, she could be reassured of her importance as the handmaid of the superman, guiding his destiny with simple intuition and helping him against his enemies.

But supermen can be erratic husbands. Churchill 'up' was egotistical and self-absorbed. Once on the warpath he had little need of anyone – apart from enemies and allies.

This was the side of Churchill that Clementine distrusted. One of her constant plaints towards the end of his time as Minister of Munitions had been that he should turn from 'Hunnish' violence towards the paths of peace. 'Can't the men munition workers build lovely garden cities?' she had asked him with a touching faith in Churchill's own pacific nature. But, while he was smiting the Bolshevik baboon and scourging the disaffected Irish, Clementine's vision of 'lovely garden cities' faded. So did her favourite role of guardian and guide of her aggressive husband.

It was unfortunate that this had had to coincide with a period when they were homeless and Clementine was having to accept the hospitality of cousin Freddie Guest at Templeton. Young Randolph had just gone off to boarding school and, lacking any close maternal feeling for Sarah or Diana, Clementine must have felt vulnerable and lonely in the midst of Churchill's rich relations and overpowering friends like Birkenhead and Beaverbrook, whose influence she never trusted.

It was then that Clementine's troubles started. Lassitude and hysterical outbursts were followed by attacks of hopelessness. These may have been a cry for help, or a way of attracting Churchill's sympathy. If so, they seemed to work, and in the summer of 1920 Churchill took her on an unusually lengthy holiday, first to the obliging Duke of Westminster's palatial house in Normandy which Churchill loved, then on to Italy. It was an unusual concession to Clementine for Churchill to tear himself away from hunting boar with Bendor to stump around the sights of Florence.

On their return they were due to leave resplendent Templeton for the London house which Clementine so badly wanted. Number 2 Sussex Square was a comfortably capacious mid-Victorian cream-stucco house near Marble Arch which Jennie had discovered. It seemed ideal, and Clementine's troubles should have been over in her own home near the park. There were servants, the sort of drawing room she wanted, a proper nursery where a nursery-maid could tend the baby Marigold, and Churchill had his study and his library and could entertain his friends and ride down Rotten Row for exercise.

But at Sussex Square the troubles of the Churchills were far from over. The girls were sickly, and Clementine's depression and listlessness persisted. At eight years of age, the once 'bonny' Sarah had changed into what she herself described as a 'listless little old lady', and after Christmas she and Diana were packed off to a boarding-house at Broadstairs, accompanied by a maid called Annie. Marigold was left in London with the nursery-maid; and Churchill, more concerned than ever for his wife, took her to the South of France to stay with rich Sir Ernest Cassel at his luxurious villa outside Nice.

Clementine's illness was becoming increasingly mysterious. It was certainly serious enough to rouse her husband's deep concern, and he urged her to observe her doctor's advice to the letter, avoid undue exertion, stay in bed and 'subordinate everything in yr life to regathering yr nervous energy and recharging yr batteries'. But in mid-January, as soon as he returned to London, Clementine achieved a startling recovery. Moving on from good but dull Sir Ernest to younger friends with a villa nearer Cannes, she was soon lunching out, enjoying a most untypical flutter at the casino at Monte Carlo, and all but winning the local tennis championship.

From London, Churchill, now on the death-list of the IRA and guarded by a Scotland Yard detective, was writing anxious letters. 'I do hope you will soon see sunshine & preen yr poor feathers in it.' But Clementine, no longer moulting, had spread her wings and was thoroughly enjoying life – suggesting that her troubles were essentially bound up with Churchill and the family, and that the surest cure was a period apart.

This was something she was able to enjoy, as she went on energetically recharging accumulators in the warmth of the Riviera, while Churchill and the children, back in London, soldiered on as best they could. She had further treats in store. In early March, Churchill collected her from Nice and took her on to Cairo, with Eddie Marsh and fascinating Colonel Lawrence (of Arabia), for the signing of the Palestine Treaty. This was followed by a visit to Jerusalem, much enjoyed by Clementine, before returning to the girls in rainy Sussex Square after almost three months' absence.

But, although she appeared recovered, Clementine was far from cured, and at intervals for many years to come that winter's strange neurotic pattern would be repeated, with hysterical attacks accompanied by lowered vitality and deep depression, leaving the doctors baffled and only able to suggest yet another holiday. Since this became part of Clementine's existence, Churchill and the family accepted it and learned to live with it.

In fact they learned to cope rather well without her for long periods, thanks to the servants and to Churchill's self-reliance, but this meant that Clementine's relations with the children, tenuous already, became still more distant. Churchill himself always seemed extremely sympathetic to his wife's neurosis – perhaps his own experience of depression helped him understand what she was suffering – and he rarely complained about her absences. They may have suited him. Anything was better than a weepy and neurotic wife as a companion, and he made sure nothing interfered with life as he wished to live it. Impregnably involved in politics, and girded round with valet, secretaries and detective, he was happy in his own unshakeable routine. Whenever Clementine was absent, he would write her loving sentimental letters signed by Mr Pig. Then, magnificently undeflected from his work – and from his pleasures – Mr Pig would cheerfully continue life as usual.

Clementine, while certainly not feigning attacks, seems to have increasingly relied upon them to escape the strains of life with Churchill. All who knew her were impressed by her sense of duty and her dedication to her home and to her husband. But it was also clear that the very dedication and involvement she had always had in Churchill's life and political career placed a growing burden on her rigid nature.

Clementine was not a weak-willed woman. 'Had she been a man', insists her secretary, Grace Hamblin, 'you would have called her the strong silent type.' But such a type is always liable to collapse rather than complain, and in the midst of her troubles no one seemed to notice that Randolph was becoming a young monster, Diana was introverted and neurotic, Sarah was suffering from tuberculosis and that even baby Marigold, the treasured 'Duckadilly', who had been suffering from bronchial infections all winter, was at risk.

Whatever the nature of Clementine's illness, it can hardly have been helped by the tragedy that greeted her on her return in April 1921 from Cairo and Jerusalem. At thirty-two, her only brother, profligate and handsome Bill Hozier, formerly of the Royal Navy, had blown his brains out in a hotel room in Paris, and Clementine was badly needed in Dieppe to help her scatty sister Nellie cope with a grief-stricken Lady Blanche and make arrangements for the funeral.

For Clementine, so recently the victim of nervous illness herself, the irrational suicide of such a close relation must have been particularly harrowing. She was apparently convinced that Bill, like Nellie and their mother, had inherited a 'gambling gene' which ruined their lives, but what else was there in her own heredity? Knowing her mother as she did, she must have had her doubts about her own paternity – along with fears that she, too, had inherited whatever streak of instability had brought her brother to a suicide's grave.

One thing the whole miserable episode emphasised was her own dependence on her husband during times of crisis. In the small expatriate community of Dieppe, a suicide like this created a considerable scandal, and the normally rumbustious Lady Blanche was incapable of coping with it. She struck Clementine as 'shrunk and small' sitting in her chair, consumed with grief, and at first it seemed as if the local chaplain would deny her son a proper funeral. Churchill, deeply involved with Parliament and the Irish situation, had left Clementine to cope alone, but she begged him to find the time to come across to France. 'Oh Winston my Dear do come tomorrow & dignify by your presence Bill's poor suicide's funeral,' she implored him. He promised that he would, and the funeral was specially delayed for him.

The arrival at Dieppe of the cabinet minister in black top-coat aboard the afternoon ferry helped ensure that his brother-in-law at least received a dignified and Christian burial.

Soon after, it was Churchill's turn to face bereavement, which was as unexpected as Bill Hozier's death. Since her remarriage Jennie seemed to have taken on a fresh lease of life, making her appear a great survivor from a richer age. 'She was still a handsome woman, her dark eyes had lost none of their sparkle with the passing of the years, and the shape of her face was always admirable,' wrote her friend the Duchess of Sermoneta, with whom she spent part of that spring in Rome. And, while the self-effacing Mr Porch had vanished on a business trip to Africa, the sixty-seven-year-old Jennie, her white hair à la Pompadour, enjoyed herself with all her old vivacity.

She still made money out of property. Only a year before she had sold a house in Berkeley Square for £35,000 – 'a clear profit of £15,000' – and she spent as lavishly as ever. After her trip to

Rome she went to stay with another *grande dame* from an earlier age, Lady Frances Horner, at her house at Mells in Somerset, and while wearing a pair of highly fashionable shoes bought in Rome slipped on the stairs and broke her ankle. Gangrene set in. Churchill was summoned to the hospital as next of kin, and the leg was amputated. 'Please make sure you have cut high enough,' she told the surgeon.

She soon seemed to be recovering. 'My poor departed leg served me well for 67 years & led me into some very pleasant walks,' she wrote philosophically to her old admirer Lord Curzon. But on the morning of 29 June she called her nurse. 'I think my hot water bottle's burst,' she said. In fact the main artery had haemorrhaged, and late that afternoon the placards for the London evening papers were announcing the sad death of Lady Randolph Churchill.

With Mr Porch still out of sight and out of mind – he was reported to be 'heartbroken' and hurrying back to London in a ship from Lagos – her two sons set about making funeral arrangements. On 3 July, thirty-five years after Lord Randolph's death, Jennie was buried beside him in Bladon churchyard, with the name 'her boys' had wanted, Lady Randolph Churchill, on her tomb. Her second husband, George Cornwallis-West, had sent a wreath 'for auld lang's syne', nobody mentioned Mr Porch, and Shane Leslie described Jack and Winston standing 'like widowers' beside the grave.

Both were in tears, and Churchill threw a spray of crimson roses on the tomb. 'I do not feel a sense of tragedy but only of loss,' he wrote to Curzon.

Tragedy remained in store for him and Clementine. The beginning of August saw their family split up again, with Churchill staying on in London, Clementine up at Eaton Hall with the Duke and Duchess of Westminster for a tennis tournament, and all four children – including two-and-a-half-year-old Marigold – packed off to Broadstairs in the charge of a solitary and inexperienced young French nursery governess. Churchill was not the man to waste his precious weeks away from politics on seaside holidays 'bunged up with brats'; and the deeply unmaternal Clementine seems to have felt much the same.

Presumably no one noticed that Marigold was suffering from a throat infection. By 2 August it was serious enough for Randolph to comment on it in a letter to his mother, but it was nearly two weeks later before anything was done. Only when Marigold lay in bed with septicaemia was Clementine summoned by the anxious governess.

Finally some action was taken. Churchill arrived after Clementine, together with a London specialist, but in the days before antibiotics there was little available in the way of treatment. In this dramatic situation Clementine was assiduous in bedside duties, sitting up all night beside her stricken daughter. But it was too late; and on 23 August, with both her parents by her bedside, Marigold died.

According to what Churchill told his daughter, Mary Soames, 'Clementine in her agony gave a succession of wild shrieks, like an animal in pain'. But nothing was permitted to deflect the Churchills from their plans. They had already arranged to go with the children to another ducal home, Westminster's house at Loch More in Sutherland, and afterwards Churchill was due to spend a fortnight on his own with the Duke of Sutherland at Dunrobin Castle. Dukes could not be disappointed, and stoically they made the best of things. Marigold was buried at Kensal Green Cemetery, the family had their holiday at Loch More, and then, barely a fortnight after Clementine had lost her youngest daughter, Churchill left her, as arranged, for the pleasures of Dunrobin Castle.

While Clementine was back at Sussex Square arranging for the children to return to school, Churchill found time from his painting to write another deeply sentimental letter, expressing tender thoughts about their 'sweet kittens' and the hurt that he was feeling for the Duckadilly. Hardly surprisingly, Clementine was soon exhibiting symptoms of lassitude again. But Churchill was buoyed up by political success throughout that autumn, and immediately after Christmas arranged to accompany Lloyd George – with whom relations were more or less restored – on yet another trip to the Riviera.

Clementine was to be permitted to join her husband in the South of France a few days later. She was, in fact, delayed by yet more illness in the family. There was an influenza epidemic, and Marigold's demise had taught her the danger of entrusting sick children to the servants. She did not succeed in joining him in Cannes until the end of January, when he was almost ready to return to London for the start of the new parliamentary session. As Clementine planned staying on in France for a little more 'recharging', this meant that they had just a few brief days together – but it was time enough to create a replacement for their lost and much lamented kitten.

18

The Chartwell Dream

Priced at £5,500, the property had hung on the market for more than a year, although it was something of a bargain – even for 1922 when house prices this close to London were at their lowest since the war. It comprised some sixty unkempt hillside acres on high ground close to the village of Westerham in Kent, a once grand but decidedly derelict high-Victorian villa built around the inner core of an earlier small farmhouse, and a spring at the bottom of the hill – the Chartwell – from which the house inherited the name of Chartwell Manor.

It needed an optimistic buyer, for it was not a cheerful-looking place. Dry rot had rampaged through the woodwork, damp from the overhanging trees had 'slimed the walls with green' and, according to its future architect, the unloved house had 'grown weary of its own ugliness so that the walls ran with moisture and creeping fungus tracked down the cracks and crevices'.

Its greatest feature was the view. On a clear day one could see for miles across the profoundly boring but romantic-sounding stretch of southern England known as the Weald of Kent. It was the sort of view a commanding general would appreciate: so, from the moment he clapped eyes on it, did Winston Churchill.

He would be forty-eight that November and was at the start of another period of upheaval for himself and for his family. There was also dry rot in the Liberal government in which he had been Colonial Secretary since February 1921. He was in angry disagreement with the Prime Minister, Lloyd George, whose current intention was to offer not just recognition but a £4 million trading loan to the very men he had tried so desperately to topple, those 'semitic conspirators', the Bolshevik leaders of the Soviet Union. And from his cousin, the former Liberal Chief Whip, the wealthy Captain Freddie Guest (known in political circles as 'the Paying Guest'), he unquestionably knew more than enough about Lloyd George's involvement in the widespread scandal of the sale of honours to break him had he felt inclined.

In fact, of course, he didn't feel inclined, although it must have been a strong temptation for he strongly disapproved of the blatant sale of titles in return for contributions to Lloyd George's party funds. But he did not denounce his chief in public. He and the old 'Welsh Wizard' had been through too much together for this to have been a possibility. However, by that all-important autumn of 1922, both Churchill and the electorate at large were tiring of Lloyd George and the Liberal Party. Churchill's attentions had been increasingly – and lucratively – involved in authorship as he prepared to write the first volume of his war memoirs. He had already garnered a useful £5,000 publisher's advance, together with a further offer of £3,000 for serial rights from *The Times*.

In addition, Churchill had also just enjoyed one of those strokes of sudden luck which traditionally light up the lives of hard-pressed members of our aristocracy. That spring his childless Londonderry cousin, Lord Vane Tempest, had perished in a railway accident in Wales. As something of a sweetener to the loss it transpired that the victim owned an Irish castle which, for want of any closer heirs, descended somewhat casually to cousin Winston, who in turn, having little use for Irish castles, had sensibly disposed of it for £20,000. His friend and patron, good Sir Ernest Cassel, the Jewish multi-millionaire and one-time crony and financial aide of Edward VII, had been advising him on his investments. (Unlike 'semitic conspirators', semitic bankers had their uses.)

Now, for the first time in his life, Churchill possessed a private income of some £4,000 a year, and more than £20,000 in the bank, spelling independence on a scale that he had never known before. Should the Government crumble, and Churchill's ministerial salary go with it, he and Clementine and the family could live in the style and comfort to which they had grown accustomed – provided, just provided, they were sensible.

Such was Clementine's dream and her intention, and she pleaded anxiously for tranquillity and common sense. 'Now that the sharp edge of financial anxiety has been removed, if only we could get a little country home within our means, and live there within our means, it would add great happiness and peace to our lives,' she wrote to her husband in September 1922. By then, however, Churchill had a very different dream.

The Churchills had already been to Chartwell Manor the year before, and had turned it down. They had done so partly on the grounds of cost – Lord Vane Tempest's railway accident was still some months away, and for Clementine nothing could have been further from her simple dream of the 'little country home within our means' than this mouldering semi-ruin which instantly appalled her. But Churchill had not dismissed it from his mind, and as the summer of 1922 faded he was being carried forward on a dangerously optimistic mood-swing in his private life – as so often happened when he found himself apart from Clementine.

At thirty-seven, Clementine was pregnant for the sixth and final time, as something of a consolation and replacement for poor Marigold. Churchill was, as always, profoundly sentimental at the *idea* of childbirth and children – 'I think a great deal of the coming kitten – it will enrich your life' – but he was not one for the realities of pregnancy and parturition, and took elaborately selfish steps to ensure that neither impinged upon his pleasures or his peace of mind. The child was due in mid-September. Clementine spent July in Barnstaple in Devon with her sister-in-law, Lady Goonie, and then went on to Frinton, before coming back to London for the birth. Churchill, his 'monstrous ego' free and unencumbered, floated happily away to be with those he most enjoyed: the powerful and very rich.

First he visited Lloyd George at his newly purchased country house at Churt in Surrey, then spent some golden days at his favourite 'hotel' on the Riviera: Maxine Elliott's ever-open villa, Château de l'Horizon, on the doorstep of his beloved casino in Monte Carlo. Even he could not avoid returning for a few days to Britain for the birth, but almost immediately afterwards he intended to go back to France to 'Benny' Westminster's Château Mimizan in Normandy for the wild-boar hunting – 'where you can join me as soon as you are fit', he wrote generously to Clementine.

However, *en route* to London he spent a night with yet another very wealthy friend amid his very grand surroundings. The exotic Jewish politician, Lloyd George's Parliamentary Private Secretary, Sir Philip Sassoon had built himself an extraordinary red-brick palace with a moorish courtyard at Port Lympne just inland from the coast of Kent.

During his visit there, Churchill met Port Lympne's architect, a fashionable neo-Georgian revivalist called Philip Tilden. Tilden specialised in homes for wealthy politicians and had, by a coincidence, just been working on Lloyd George's house at Churt.

With his £20,000 in the bank and that view from Chartwell in his memory, Churchill's ambitions ballooned far beyond that boring 'little country home within our means' that Clementine desired. The passion for grand houses is notoriously contagious, and without his wife's restraining presence, he was seeing more grand houses than were good for him. If Lloyd George could have a country mansion, he the grandson of a duke could go one better. If Sassoon could entertain the great in style, think how much better Churchill could do so if he only had the sort of country place he needed.

Churchill's imagination, boosted as it always could be by a surge of confident good living, was already picturing the Port Lympne style of dream house he could so splendidly create at Chartwell: the lakes he could construct like those at Blenheim; a study and a generous dining room to entertain his friends, a setting for the near-ducal luxury his happiness required, and of course a studio for his painting; a heated swimming pool for exercise, a private cinema like Sassoon's in which he could relax, a library, a garden for Clementine, and the chance for all and sundry to enjoy those views across the Weald of Kent.

Churchill discussed much of this with Philip Tilden but said nothing of his plans when, next day, back in London, he was reunited with his decidedly neglected wife, who was entering the last few days of pregnancy. She also knew nothing of his trip to Chartwell two days later when the architect confirmed that the house would need virtually rebuilding. Nor did she know that, shortly afterwards, he summoned a Mr Marshall from the estate agents, Knight Frank & Rutley, to the Colonial Office in Whitehall and against the awesome background of his study, used all the Churchillian powers of rhetoric to persuade him to accept an offer of £4,500 for the house. But Mr Marshall evidently knew his trade, and Churchill finally agreed to pay £5,000 for Chartwell Manor.

'Let us beware of risking our newly come fortune on operations which we do not understand,' Clementine had warned him, but with her baby imminent she could be kept safely in the dark about the mystery tour her now elated husband organised for

Randolph, Sarah and Diana. Inevitably it ended up at Chartwell. Swearing them all to secrecy, he made them excited conspirators in his latest venture as they rambled through the dank deserted house and overgrown shrubberies.

'Do you like it?' he enquired.

Later, Sarah would remember having felt 'delirious' about the place. 'Oh, do buy it! Do buy it!' she exclaimed.

'Well, I'm not sure,' he said, not admitting that everything was settled.

By the time Clementine was gratefully delivered of yet another daughter, to be christened Mary, on 14 September, the contract for Chartwell Manor was irrevocably signed. As Clementine recovered she was apparently still unaware of the cross she would have to bear in the shape of Churchill's dream of Chartwell Manor.

According to her secretary, Grace Hamblin, Clementine never entirely forgave her husband for the 'underhand' way in which he purchased Chartwell, but by the time she did find out about the *fait accompli* there was not a great deal she could do about it. More than anyone, she knew the power of her husband's sheer determination, and no sooner had he signed the deeds than he was conveniently involved in yet another crisis, making any anger that she felt more or less irrelevant.

For some time Churchill had been suffering chronic indigestion. Serious eater, steady drinker, and something of a hypochondriac to boot, he had often complained of indigestion in the past. With the workload he was bearing – and with worries for his political future as a general election loomed – it would have been surprising if his harshly treated stomach had not started to rebel.

Since summer he had also been complaining of acute pains in his side; and that October, three days before Lloyd George's government collapsed, his doctor diagnosed appendicitis. Churchill's appendix was removed on 23 October, at the King Edward VII Hospital for Officers.

Although recuperating from what was still a major operation, Churchill could not postpone his fight to save his parliamentary seat for the Scottish city of Dundee. Gamely and very bravely, everything considered, Clementine largely fought it for him.

It was a situation that showed her at her best. However intolerable he could be to live with, and whatever the strains and disappointments in their private life, in one thing she would never waver: her loyalty towards her husband and his great political career. Although as a lifelong Liberal she was by no means personally convinced of the rightness of his recent warlike policies, particularly against the Turks, she went as his champion and proxy to the cold unwelcoming election.

It was a forlorn endeavour. Dundee, like the rest of the country, had swung decisively against the Liberal Lloyd George government of which Churchill was a member, and Clementine had a tough time justifying him. But this tall shy woman with her tweed coat and her English accent did her best, as she later told her husband, to present him to the Scottish voters in the unlikely guise of 'a Cherub Peace Maker with little fluffy wings around your chubby face', at a number of profoundly hostile meetings.

Just before polling day he arrived in person and, as always, stole the show. Even in illness he was still the old accomplished actor; a wan and weakened figure in overcoat and large black hat, he was carried to the meetings in a special chair. This wife and husband, freshly risen – she from childbed, he from sick-bed – made a gallant picture for the press photographers, but it failed to work. When the results of the election were announced on 23 November, Churchill was out by 10,000 votes to his Conservative opponent; and Lloyd George's government was out as well. For the first time since 1904, Britain had a Conservative government led by a new Prime Minister, the Canadian Bonar Law. 'In the twinkling of an eye', said Churchill ruefully, 'I found myself without an office, without a seat, without a party and even without an appendix.'

The defeat at Dundee was not entirely a joke. For almost the next two years Churchill would be out of Parliament and power, and for his career it was a setback second only to the disaster of the Dardanelles. Stranded by his failed allegiance to the Liberals, his only hope was to 're-rat' as he put it, back to the Conservatives where his instincts, as well as his interests, increasingly resided. Even for him this would be a difficult manoeuvre, as he knew he had to overcome the deep distrust and fear that he aroused among the old-guard Tories. But he did not repine.

There was no evidence of Black Dog now, still less of failing confidence. Instead, with Clementine beside him, he departed for the South of France where he rented a villa called appropriately Le Rêve d'Or, the dream of gold. While Clementine played tennis (she was a good, enthusiastic player), he engaged a secretary and proceeded to dictate the first volume of his memoirs, *The World Crisis*, in three months flat.

With its sweep of narrative, its powerful romantic rhetoric and Churchill's personality on every page, *The World Crisis* is in a class apart from any other memoir of the First World War. He made no pretence that this was calm unbiased history. 'It is my case,' he growled, and his 'case' included a passionate defence of his actions over the Dardanelles.

He was not over-scrupulous in rearranging facts and misrepresenting his opponents – so much so that the conclusion of modern historians (in particular of Robin Prior, the young Australian historian who has written a full-length study of *The World Crisis*) is that its value is literary rather than historical. But at the time *The World Crisis* was most effective in its primary purpose: that of rehabilitating Churchill's wartime reputation. There was another fascinating point about the book which Maynard Keynes would shrewdly notice. Churchill's essential criticism of the conduct of the war was the absence of what Keynes called 'that supreme combination of the Warrior–King–Statesman who is apparent in the persons of the great conquerors of history'.

For Churchill the blunders of the war had stemmed from blunders of leadership, a constant failure to engage politics and strategy under a unified decisive command. Churchill's two greatest heroes, John, Duke of Marlborough and Napoleon, were examples of the sort of ideal wartime leadership he had in mind; and the Churchillian concept of the warrior–king–statesman leading an undivided nation in time of war would not be left to moulder in his memoirs.

Churchill seems to have enjoyed the bouts of long dictation that produced his book. He once said that he looked on any book he was writing as 'a companion'. It was the ideal friend who could not answer back as, large cigar in hand and brandy and soda on his desk, he walked back and forth, long into the night, regaling his attentive secretary with his own uninterrupted version of events from his extraordinary memory.

Certainly the composition and the great success on publication of *The World Crisis*, when it appeared that autumn, did much for Churchill's private happiness. He was still out of Parliament, but he had firm plans for the future. The next volume of his memoirs was waiting to be written, and that overgrown hillside outside Westerham was claiming his attention.

The view apart, to Churchill the most exciting feature of dilapidated Chartwell Manor was the very thing that most appalled the careful Clementine – its ruinous condition. He could respond to architectural splendour but, as Tilden put it, he 'would not allow the sentimental appreciation of beauty to obscure practical essentials'. The existing house with its high-pitched gables and long windows facing out towards the shrubbery was simply one more enemy to be demolished.

The core of the oak-beamed farmhouse could remain; oak beams appealed to him. Around them he was planning the extraordinary red-brick fortress of a house one sees today. It was a fairly massive undertaking, for the house was effectively turned round to take advantage of the view, and a new four-storey wing constructed. There were to be long french windows facing out on to the garden, a brick-built terrace which he called his 'palanquin', and the centre of the house would be his high-beamed study, with his bedroom conveniently leading from it. Chartwell was to be a centre for his work, his friends, and all the members of his family. Such was, at any rate, the plan.

Relations between Churchill and his architect were doomed to be fraught. Tilden, a fussy man, was not the sort of character to appeal to Churchill; and, as he soon discovered, the new Lord of Chartwell Manor was hardly the sort of client he was used to. Most of the busy wealthy men Tilden had worked for were grateful to entrust the details of their future home to his expertise; not so Churchill, who rarely met an expert without fairly swiftly knowing more than he did on his chosen subject.

Once Churchill was safely back from France, Tilden would be summoned at a moment's notice out to Chartwell. The great man, invariably late, would roar up in his big black Wolseley, chauffeur at the wheel. Then, in the heavy boots he had worn on the Western Front, Churchill would plod around his property with Tilden trying to keep up with him.

As in everything he set his mind to, Churchill was deeply, often maddeningly involved with what was going on, 'laying bricks, trying experiments with baths, and theorising about matters which most men have taken for granted all their lives, but to which in some miraculous fashion, he managed to give a new turn of thought'.

As a result of this, Chartwell started to emerge as a decidedly eccentric house. It was very much its owner's personal creation. Although he made a show of trying to include a reluctant Clementine in the operation, keeping her painstakingly informed of what was happening, it was not in her nature to disguise her disapproval of the whole endeavour.

The purchase of Chartwell, coinciding as it did with the birth of their final child, conclusively changed the set-up of the family and altered much within the Churchills' marriage.

Had Clementine had the sort of house she wanted, the story might have turned out differently. Life would have been quite undemanding, money would not have been a constant worry, and there might have been a chance of the sort of order and perfection she enjoyed in her surroundings. It would have been emphatically her house as well as his, and at this crucial period in her life the planning and creation of a country home could have been a bond between them. Instead the reverse was happening, and her husband's 'Chartwell Dream' was emphasising something of a rift within their lives.

Clementine was alone in her disapproval. Churchill kept the children closely involved in all he did at Chartwell, and one of his earliest activities was to build them all a tree house in the garden. A nearby house called Bosey Rigg (inevitably rechristened 'Rosy Pig') was rented for the summer, and for the three children all the excitement centred inevitably around their father and his fascinating playground. Clementine tended to become the odd one out, as the children joined an exuberant Churchill laying bricks, levelling the terrace, and damming the waters of the stream at the bottom of the hill to make a lake.

It was just after Mary's birth, and the purchase of Chartwell, that the Churchills hit upon their own solution to Clementine's continuing depression and the complexities of Chartwell. Clementine's spinster cousin, Maryott Whyte, was poor, practical and good, and fresh out of that academy of well-adjusted upper-class British babyhood, the Norland School of Nursing. A fully qualified Norland Nanny, 'Cousin Moppett' was looking for a job.

In effect she took the baby over, nursing and mothering the infant Mary with the devotion and expertise that Clementine could never manage. Maybe it was heartless, but it was eminently practical. Clementine had never been particularly maternal. As

Churchill's cousin Anita Leslie said, 'Clementine was more deeply tied to her husband than to her offspring, and she herself said that she did not have sufficient energy to support them all.'

Cousin Moppett and the two-month-old baby moved into Bosey Rigg; Clementine was given a period of respite in which she could try to cope with life and with her husband; and Mary, most fortunate of all the Churchill children, was to enjoy what all the rest disastrously lacked – a stable ordered childhood, more or less insulated from the dangerous emanations of her father's genius.

Somewhat surprisingly, considering the scale of the work and Churchill's constant interference, Chartwell was ready to move into by early 1924.

It had been a busy spring for all the family, with Churchill's political fortunes dramatically reviving. The Conservatives were defeated in 1923, and there had been a minority Labour government in power, supported by the Liberals. Although theoretically still a Liberal himself, Churchill considered the behaviour of his old party in abetting socialists a national disgrace 'not dissimilar from missionaries assisting cannibals'. This confirmed his strengthening conviction that his future lay on the right in politics, and he prepared himself for a fresh crusade against an enemy at home – socialism.

For him Ramsay MacDonald's Labour Party was little different from 'those bloodstained Bolsheviks who killed the Tsar'. Worse still, they were totally 'un-English' with 'not the slightest idea of fair-play or sportsmanship'. Accordingly, in February 1924, Churchill placed himself firmly in the role of the great opponent of the Left, by standing as an independent anti-socialist in a parliamentary by-election at Westminster.

It was the sort of knockabout political extravaganza Churchill thrived on. Undeterred by an official Conservative candidate against him, he organised Conservative celebrities like Balfour and Birkenhead to speak in his support, together with a stand-up cast of jockeys, dukes and chorus-girls. On polling day, Churchill drove around the constituency with all his family in a coach and four. There was much noise, immense publicity; and, although he lost by a whisker, this memorable by-election returned him firmly to the map of politics.

Clementine, as always when it came to politics, was with him

throughout the ten days of the campaign. However, when, within
a few weeks of the Westminster by-election, her excited husband
was ready to take charge of his splendid new domain, Clementine
left him to get on with it alone. She chose this moment to visit
her aged mother in Dieppe.

After a lifetime of strained relations it cannot have been
a particularly exhilarating holiday for Clementine. The once
beautiful Lady Blanche had lost her looks and was obviously
ill, after years of gambling and drink and crazy living. Even so,
for Clemetine Dieppe could offer a release from the tensions of
the Churchill family. 'I am enormously and unbelievably tired
and the strong air makes me drunk with sleep,' she wrote to
Churchill.

Her husband's state of mind could not have been more different
as moving-in day dawned; and by the evening of 17 April 1924,
tired but triumphant, he sat down in the absent Clementine's
bedroom to write her a battlefield report.

He had commanded the troops in person – the three elder
children, his bodyguard Sergeant Thompson, a gardener and six
labourers from Westerham. Two van-loads of furniture arrived
from the house in Sussex Place, 'the weather was delicious', and
they were out 'toiling all day like blacks in dirty clothes and only
bathing before dinner'.

Apart from installing the furniture, they had also started turfing
what he called 'the plateau' and the bank beneath the house,
and he sounded an extremely happy man, 'drinking champagne
at all meals and buckets of claret and soda in between'. As he
concluded in his letter: 'Only one thing lack these banks of green,
The Pussy Cat who is their Queen.'

19

'Paradise on Earth'

On 5 November, Guy Fawkes Day, 1924, Churchill was summoned from his London house in Sussex Square to Downing Street by the new Prime Minister, Stanley Baldwin. He came punctually for once, clad in top-hat and the astrakhan-collared top-coat he had worn at Sidney Street, knowing the importance of the interview to his career.

Two days earlier the minority Labour government had fallen in a landslide election to the Tories, and Baldwin was back at the head of a Conservative administration with an absolute majority.

After his busy two-year absence, Churchill was also back as member for the highly convenient Conservative constituency of Epping on the suburban north-east fringe of London. He was still not officially a Conservative, having fought the election as an anti-socialist 'constitutionalist', but Baldwin had ensured that his party had not opposed him. The long march from the Liberals to the rewarding foothills of the Right was all but over.

'I am what I have always been – a Tory Radical,' Churchill insisted. In fact he was poised to return to the party where he started, and where power with all its pleasures now resided.

Seven years Churchill's senior, Baldwin, the former iron-manufacturer from Worcestershire, was his political antithesis; ruminant where Churchill was flamboyant, soberly shrewd where Churchill tended to be brilliantly erratic, he was to give Britain fourteen years of soporific leadership. By the end of it, Baldwin, 'the quiet man at the top', would embody much that Churchill politically detested. But for the moment Baldwin alone could offer Churchill what he wanted.

Churchill knew the strength of his position. In two weeks he would be fifty, but he possessed more experience of government than Baldwin and the rest of the Conservative leadership put together. The Westminster by-election had reconfirmed his status as a national celebrity, while the force of his anti-socialist invective during the campaign had convinced his enemies, inside as well as outside the Conservative Party, that he was still the most dangerous, and the most eloquent, single presence on the uninspiring scene of British politics.

'Unique, wayward and exciting, a man with a particular glamour of his own,' Harold Macmillan described him at this time. Baldwin could not afford to leave so powerful a figure outside the folds of the faithful much longer.

Churchill also knew. 'I have no intention of joining the government except in some great position,' he assured Clementine, and when ushered into Baldwin's presence made himself very much at ease. While the two men chatted, he produced a large cigar.

'Do you mind the smoke of a cigar?'

'No,' said Baldwin; and, as Churchill ignited his Havana, Baldwin pulled out the stubby pipe which was *his* trademark. Through a cloud of retaliatory pipe-smoke he posed his all-important question.

'Are you willing to help us?'

'Yes. If you really want me.'

There was a pause, more puffing at his pipe, then Baldwin said: 'Will you be Chancellor of the Exchequer?'

It was a genuine surprise. This was a 'greater position' than even Churchill had been hoping for. (In fact Baldwin offered it because Neville Chamberlain had just refused it. Chamberlain would become Minister of Health instead, and in 1937 would succeed Baldwin as prime minister.)

'Will the bloody duck swim?' Churchill later said he felt like answering. Instead, recalling the formality of the occasion, he replied, like the politician that he was: 'This fulfils my ambition. I still have my father's robes as Chancellor. I shall be proud to serve you in this splendid office.'

According to varying accounts, Churchill's eyes then may or may not have filled with tears. Probably they did. He had a lachrymose tendency when moved emotionally, and this must have been one of the most emotional moments of his whole political career.

There was the joy of power again, a great state office, the house next door to Baldwin's house in Downing Street as his official residence, and a salary of £5,000 a year. No lover pining for the return of his beloved can have felt a keener satisfaction than Churchill at the prospect of this 'great position', at the head of the Treasury, with responsibility for the nation's economy.

But, as his reply made clear, there was more to it than this. Nearly forty years earlier Lord Randolph's appointment to the Chancellorship had marked the pinnacle of his doomed career – just as his resignation from it five months later spelled the start of the disaster which had dominated Churchill's adolescence. Now the strange drama which tormented and inspired him through his long political career seemed to have run its course.

He would speak piously of his delight at being able to 'vindicate' Lord Randolph by his appointment to his former office, but it is hard to see what vindication he was offering his father's memory. It was himself he was vindicating – rather late in life – from those never-forgotten moments when the sick Lord Randolph had ignored him, cast him in the role of failure, consigned him to the infantry and issued such dire warnings for his future.

Churchill had proved him wrong, and in the most effective way he could. What better answer could he give his unforgiving father than to reach that self-same 'splendid office' which had once distinguished him?

Churchill had also justified his mother's faith all those years ago when she carefully preserved Lord Randolph's robes of office after his resignation, as if intent on showing even then that her son had a duty to succeed where her husband had failed.

With great skill – and unfaltering determination – he had somersaulted back to power. And as he entered the Treasury and set himself to master the intricacies of his forthcoming Budget he was already standing out, as Asquith said of him, 'like some Chimborazo or Everest among the sandhills of the Baldwin cabinet'.

But the Treasury was really not the place for Churchill. Finance was not his *forte* – either publicly or privately – any more than it had been for his father, who was equally extravagant, and who once admitted that he never understood 'those damned dots' in the Treasury accounts. But in April 1925 an exuberant Churchill had the private satisfaction of achieving the one important act Lord Randolph had signally failed to accomplish during his time as Chancellor: the presentation of his Budget. Top-hatted and with large cigar he drove from Downing Street holding

Gladstone's original Chancellor's despatch-box to present *his* Budget in the House of Commons.

The Churchill succession was continuing. As a boy of twelve, Churchill had watched his father's speeches from the gallery. Now fifteen-year-old Randolph sat in the front row of the gallery with Clementine beside him.

As a sheer performance, this first Budget speech of Churchill's must have made them very proud. This was Churchill witty, Churchill lucid, Churchill dominating the House as no other politician could have done. Baldwin told King George V that he had 'risen magnificently to the occasion', showing 'not only consummate ability as a parliamentarian, but also all the versatility of an actor'.

But, although this first Budget speech was hailed as a triumph, confirming Churchill's dominant position in the Government, it also managed to enshrine what he himself would come to think the greatest blunder of his whole career, which would dog him and the nation for the rest of his five years in office. Again like his father, Churchill had little time for the 'dismal science' of economic theory; despite this, he rashly decided to return the pound sterling to the old-fashioned gold standard at prewar parity against the US dollar.

The result, which Churchill does not seem to have foreseen, despite loud warnings from economists like Maynard Keynes, was a prolonged deflation of the whole economy. The high rate of the pound priced British goods out of world markets. Unemployment rose, wages fell, and hardship and widespread working-class bitterness led directly to the catastrophic General Strike of 1926.

Churchill was not given to self-recrimination, but years later, over dinner, he remarked: '. . . everyone said that I was the worst Chancellor of the Exchequer that ever was. And now I'm inclined to agree with them. So now the world's unanimous.'

A less self-confident and self-obsessed statesman would have resigned in the face of the disaster he had created. But Churchill, being Churchill, rose cheerfully above the nation's troubles, and thoroughly enjoyed his tenure of his 'splendid office'. He could dominate his grey colleagues in the Cabinet with his cleverness and wit, while his eloquence and personality made him a star performer in the House of Commons.

In the light of what happened later, it is ironic that in this period he was keen to cut spending on defence in order to lower taxation. The Air Force suffered badly, and only determined opposition by a group of admirals saved the Navy. But Churchill had not turned pacifist, and the General Strike brought forth his warlike zeal against the strikers. Natural journalist and propagandist that he was, he jumped at the chance which Baldwin gave him to create his own official newspaper – the sensational and tendentious *British Gazette*, which he edited and master-minded for the Government throughout the strike, and which enjoyed a circulation of 2 million by the time it finished.

Throughout his time as Chancellor, Churchill showed constant ingenuity in the fine print of his Budgets, and was said to have worked out his best schemes in his bath. While lying there he must have mused upon the whole extent of government, for during these years in office he would blithely range across the jealously protected interests and responsibilities of all the other ministers, the Premier included. This quietly infuriated Baldwin, who was not as somnolent and stolid as he seemed. As his government neared its end in 1929, Baldwin swore that he would not be including Churchill in any future administration.

But Churchill had the thickest skin in politics, and was largely unaware of the antagonism he aroused by his suggestions. He loved power and he loved Parliament, and he enjoyed the chance to wear his father's robes of office on ceremonial occasions. All the photographs taken of him in this period show the round and smiling face of a satisfied and happy man whose life was working out exactly as he wanted.

While the Chancellorship of the Exchequer marked the fulfilment of a dream which had haunted him since adolescence, Chartwell seemed to fulfil a dream with origins in the ducal world he had known as a boy. Once he had built his two lakes at the bottom of the hill, the vista from his long french windows would match the not dissimilar view across the lakes at Blenheim – the one his father boasted of to Jennie as 'the finest view in England'. And, whatever the expense, Churchill demanded many of the features of a substantial country mansion: stabling for his ponies, a home farm for the animals he loved, spacious rooms where he could dine happily with men of influence and power, cottages for his retainers, pools for his pet fish, and grounds laid out with terraces and walks and gardens where the grandson of a duke could feel at ease.

Chartwell was becoming a sort of tiny principality where Churchill could truly be himself. Reverting to his Spencer-Churchill ancestry, he was like some energetically eccentric eighteenth-century Whig grandee, with everything he wanted round him. When the lakes and terraces were finished, there was the long brick wall around the kitchen garden to be built, keeping him busy for the next three years. Then came a cottage for the gardener and an original heating system for his outside swimming pool to think about. He had his painting studio, his oak-beamed study and his library. Boredom would never be a problem – nor should 'Black Dog' return in such surroundings.

During the blazing August of 1925, Churchill went to visit Blenheim; but Blenheim had lost its magic, and he found cousin Sunny almost as miserable as ever. He should not have been, for he was now entirely free from Consuelo. Four years earlier she had fallen in love with the romantic Jacques Balsan, a French wartime flying ace, and in order to marry him had agreed to an amicable settlement with Sunny. Since Sunny had now become a Catholic, and the Balsan family was Catholic, too, the marriage was dissolved by the Vatican, on the grounds that Consuelo had been coerced to marry Sunny.

Nothing now prevented Sunny from making the beautiful Miss Deacon his Duchess, which he did in Paris in the spring of 1921. 'We are both awfully poor,' he told reporters. 'Just say I gave the bride a motor-car as a wedding present.'

To start with the new couple was happy. Sunny completed his precious terraces, and Gladys tried to bring a touch of European art and culture back to Blenheim. Among her guests was Lytton Strachey, who coveted the place: 'I wish it were mine. It is enormous, but one would not feel it too big. The grounds are beautiful too, and there is a bridge over a lake that positively gives one an erection.' H. G. Wells arrived one Saturday and danced with the Duchess – 'a most comic business' according to Professor Lindemann, who was present. She also invited Marcel Proust to stay. (When the great novelist replied that he was too ill, Sunny said he wouldn't mind at all if he stayed in bed.)

But none of this social life had lasted. The marriage, like most things in Sunny's life, soon went sour. Gladys had three miscarriages in swift succession, the last allegedly brought on when Sunny, 'in an ungovernable rage', had struck her in a hotel in Brighton.

Then, with a final touch of the grotesque, his Duchess's face had started to collapse before his eyes. Some years before, desperate to preserve her beauty, and perfect the shape of her nose, Gladys had had paraffin wax injected underneath the skin. Now the wax was slipping inexorably towards her jaw.

By the summer of 1925, Sunny and Gladys were living separate angry lives, which must have suited Churchill, who had never liked her any more than she liked him. (The Churchills had always preferred Consuelo, and had wisely kept in touch with her. They often stayed with the Balsans at their glamorous new house at Eze, or at the château they had bought in Normandy.) Sunny was devoting all his energies to building fountains and yet further terraces to enhance the only thing he really loved – his palace. Cousin Winston, fresh from similar construction work at Chartwell, could advise him.

So could the ingenious Professor Lindemann, who loved dukes and great houses, and who was returning to Chartwell after the weekend. The writer and politician Harold Nicolson made up the trio, and the three of them drove back to Chartwell, with Churchill at the wheel. According to Nicolson, Churchill was thrilled to return to Chartwell after Blenheim. Far from envying Sunny any longer, 'Winston was so delighted with his house, that it was a pleasure to witness his enthusiasm,' he wrote. 'He considered it his paradise on earth.'

It was an expensive paradise, for, perpetually busy, Churchill needed servants to maintain momentum. At one point there were eighteen on the Chartwell payroll, and when Clementine became alarmed at the expense Churchill told her 'servants exist to save one trouble, and should never be allowed to disturb one's inner peace'.

It was a very ducal definition of the role of a domestic, and once again there seems something deeply nostalgic in Churchill's need to have servants perpetually on hand to do his bidding. His valet, Inches, had to call him punctually at eight each morning, bring him his breakfast in bed with all the morning papers, run and prepare his bath and dry him afterwards, help him dress and even tie his tie and lace his shoes. Churchill's demands upon this faithful man did not cease there – he was on call seven days a week – and besides his valet Churchill required the services of at least two full-time secretaries and a research assistant, together with housemaids, footmen, gardeners, and associated building labourers who also had to be on hand.

Churchill was immensely organised, but he would always need such people round him who would act as obedient extensions of his will. It was a pattern he would steadily develop, so that by the time the war broke out in 1939 he had perfected the routines of work and relaxation which he had devised for himself at Chartwell, together with the personnel and friends required to make them function.

The friends were as important as the servants, for Churchill was a social animal whose ideas of entertaining were very similar to those of his parents: extremely good food, excellent champagne, vivid personalities and conversation fundamentally concerned with politics.

His greatest friend, apart from Sunny Marlborough, remained Lord Birkenhead, the Lord Chancellor. But with Chartwell a new sort of follower appeared upon the Churchill scene. Churchill had always had people he relied on and who appeared dependent on him, showing all the signs of unquestioning loyalty. Eddie Marsh, *littérateur* and civil servant, who had been his official secretary before the war, was the first of them. He was devoted to his master, finding in Churchill an excitement and affection lacking in his highly social life. In return Churchill invited him frequently to Chartwell, picked his highly cultivated brains, and used him as a sort of resident literary adviser.

A very different figure, who was adopting a similar role in matters scientific, was the rich tennis-playing polymath from Oxford, Professor Lindemann. Snobbish and remote, this Alsatian teetotaller hardly seemed the sort of character whose company Churchill would enjoy; but they became devoted, and 'the Prof' with his famous slide-rule and academic manner was soon something of a fixture during long weekends at Chartwell.

So was the even more improbable self-made financier and newspaperman Brendan Bracken, who arrived at Chartwell one summer afternoon in 1924, introduced himself to Churchill, and for the remainder of his life would be devoted to him, acting as stimulant, factotum, clown and faithful friend.

These three men would all be of immense importance to the efficient running of Churchill's life. All unmarried, highly talented outsiders, they were lonely men who seemed to find a purpose in the strange regime Churchill was building round himself. They would be joined by others in the years to come, acting as courtiers, advisers, ministers in exile to the potentate of Chartwell.

Such were the important elements of Churchill's Chartwell Dream; but there was an impossible side to it as well. When it came to the details of everyday existence he could be extra-ordinarily impractical. This led to problems.

As at Lullenden, Churchill's attempts at farming were fore-doomed to failure. His herd of handsome belted Friesian cows would never pay, the pigs contracted lice, the chickens fowl-pest, and the swans he had carefully imported for his lakes were killed by foxes.

More serious, as Clementine foresaw from the beginning, was the expense. Churchill had overspent wildly on the project. The building costs alone were £19,000 – this on top of the original purchase price, so that around the time of his appoint-ment as Chancellor he had all but bankrupted himself. The Chancellorship saved both him and Chartwell, for in addition to the ministerial salary of £5,000 a year it meant that he and Clementine were able to move into the Chancellor's official London residence in Downing Street and sell the house in Sussex Square for £10,750. This gave them both a breathing-space, although the never-ending costs of Chartwell were still draining their resources as the Gold Standard produced similar effects on the national economy.

Churchill refused to be depressed on either score. As Chan-cellor he continued to devise ingenious new taxes which did little for the nation's underlying malady; and he was equally resourceful as he began to grapple with his personal finances. Here he was more successful, as he turned to journalism to pay for Chartwell and ensure, as he put it, that he 'would never be unable to drink a bottle of champagne and offer another to a friend'.

Churchill's reliance on popular journalism as a way to pay the bills would prove of great importance, for it meant that he in-creasingly treated politics and journalism as complementary activi-ties. Knowing everyone, and having an opinion on absolutely everything, he was a natural journalist who could dictate an effort-less two thousand words on almost any subject without so much as getting out of bed.

As a political celebrity, anything he wrote was news, and at half a crown a word he became one of the highest-paid journalists of his day. It was a crucial source of power, as well as income, as it ensured that his views stayed at the centre of debate whatever his relations with the Government. Popular journalism also developed Churchill's flair for mass communication: like his father, this most insulated aristocrat was adept at sensing the feelings of the common people he almost never met – or really cared about.

On the other hand, knowing where his bread and butter came from, Churchill took considerable care to cultivate the leading press proprietors. Since the war he had had a close if turbulent relationship with the Canadian proprietor of the *Express*, Max Lord Beaverbrook. ('Some take drugs. I take Max,' Churchill muttered, explaining the uneasy friendship.) In some respects the two men were similar: both bullies when the need arose, both nonconformists in the inside world of politics, and both obsessed with the pursuit and exercise of power. As high-powered egomaniacs they tended to distrust each other, much as they generally enjoyed each other's company. For Churchill, simpler and more lucrative journalistic friendships were those which he carefully pursued with Lord Rothermere of the *Daily Mail*, and the future Lord Camrose of the *Daily Telegraph*.

All were entertained at Chartwell, where dinners graced by barons of the press had a habit of resulting in ideas for articles. Churchill never missed a deadline, and in a good year managed to augment his income by up to £20,000 from his journalism.

But, for Churchill, money earned was money to be spent. Wage bills and maintenance costs at Chartwell were heavy, while in food and drink, both for himself and for his many guests, Churchill was more prepared than ever to 'be satisfied with the very best'.

At Chartwell the result was a life of intermittent luxury, unpaid tradesmen's bills, and periodic family discussions on economy. Within months of moving in, Churchill was already contemplating letting the whole house for £80 a week. This came to nothing, but he could always manage to dismiss his money problems as airily as his spendthrift Marlborough ancestors. Clementine, so different from him in this as in so many other things, never managed to forget them.

'A full-blown Victorian prig.' John Winston, 7th Duke of Marlborough, with his second son, Lord Randolph Spencer Churchill.

The man Disraeli called 'a thorough-going blackguard'. Winston Churchill's uncle George Charles, 8th Duke of Marlborough, more commonly known as 'the Bad Duke'.

Blenheim Palace, begun in 1705 as both home and monument for the triumphant 1st Duke of Marlborough – 'an uncomfortably ill-omened house, hated or admired, but rarely loved, the scene of much noble misery and gloom.'

'A mourner at his own funeral.' Lord Randolph Churchill, aged forty-four, affected by encroaching madness.

'A dark lithe figure, a diamond star in her hair . . . its lustre dimmed by the flashing glory of her eyes, more of the panther than the woman in her looks.' Lady Randolph in her prime.

'Links in the chain.' The Vanderbilt heiress, Consuelo, as Duchess of Marlborough with her two sons, John Albert Edward William, Lord Blandford, future 10th Duke of Marlborough (commonly known as 'Bert') and her favourite, the future connoisseur-perfectionist, Lord Ivor Churchill.

Was this Winston Churchill's true father-in-law? Captain W. G. (Bay) Middleton, great horseman, 'rampant womaniser' and, according to strong evidence, the father of Clementine Hozier, future wife of Winston Churchill.

'An aboriginal desire to kill several of these odious Dervishes.' Winston Churchill, a lieutenant in the 4th Hussars, at the time of the Charge at Omdurman.

'Christ!' Churchill said when seeing himself in the Glengarry cap he should have worn as Lieutenant Colonel with the Royal Scots Fusiliers in France in 1916. Instead he adopted the French *poilu*'s steel helmet which flattered his bulldog features.

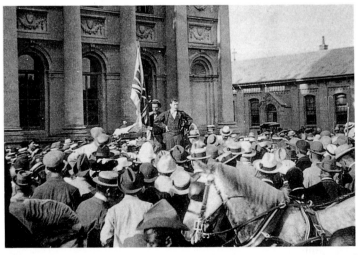

'Hero of five wars, author of six books, and the future prime minister of England' – Winston is given a hero's welcome at Durban after his escape from Boer captivity.

Winston's 'oldest dearest friend', Sunny, 9th Duke of Marlborough.

Churchill and Clementine on Armistice Day, 1923. 'In the midst of arms what vile and wicked folly and barbarism it all is,' he told her.

20

The Happy Family

While Churchill was supremely happy with his role as Chancellor of the Exchequer and his earthly paradise at Chartwell, it is clear that Clementine was not. What is less clear is the source of her dissatisfactions, for her troubles obviously ran deeper than mere pique at the way her husband had ignored her wishes when he purchased Chartwell or their financial worries.

At this period she frequently appears a remote unhappy figure. Although she had all the domestic help she needed, she remained unnaturally aloof from her baby daughter, Mary, and was quite prepared to leave the admirable Miss Whyte as virtual foster-mother in her place. As for the three elder children, her unconcern could verge on positive neglect. In her relations with the teenage Randolph there was no hint of the rapport which wayward Jennie had maintained with the youthful Winston. Aged thirteen Randolph had gone off to Eton in September 1924; but it was Churchill, not Clementine, who took charge of everything to do with this event.

Far from putting any pressure on him to go to his old school, Harrow, Churchill simply left the choice of school to Randolph, who chose Eton. And Churchill remained the most tolerant, concerned of fathers where Randolph was concerned. He even asked Birkenhead's son Freddie to make sure that Randolph did not suffer corporal punishment at Eton. This did not prevent him being swiftly beaten for being 'bloody awful all round' – 'the kind of comprehensive verdict', as his friend Michael Foot would put it, 'which others who had dealings with him were always searching for'.

Clementine's relations with Sarah and Diana were little better. Sarah described her mother as 'formidable', and both girls seemed in awe of her and kept their distance. Diana, plump, vulnerable and painfully shy behind a garrulous exterior, appears to have suffered badly from the way her elegant mother seemed to freeze her off. In many ways she was more like Clementine than any of the other children, introverted and emotional, but this only exacerbated mother-and-daughter antagonism.

Contact with Sarah was easier, thanks to her sunnier nature, but they were far from close. On the edge of adolescence, Sarah was only just recovering from the illnesses which had dogged her childhood, and changing from a red-haired waif into quite a beauty. She had her father's toughness and a streak of independence which enabled her to cope better than Diana with her distant temperamental mother.

People who knew Clementine well explained the situation by saying that Clementine was 'far more wife than mother'. But throughout this period she was frequently apart from Churchill too, staying with her mother in Dieppe or with Consuelo in the South of France.

When Lady Blanche died suddenly in March 1925, Churchill was preparing for his next Budget, and Clementine was forced to go to the funeral in Dieppe alone. To make up for his absence, he wrote Clementine one of his cheering letters, saying 'what a true mother, and grand woman' Lady Blanche had been. He was, he added, 'proud to think her blood flows in the veins of her children.'

It is hard to think that Clementine agreed, having spent so much of her life steeling herself against those weaknesses which had helped destroy her mother. More than ever, Clementine appeared the total opposite of Lady Blanche – painfully self-controlled, a perfectionist in food and dress and her surroundings, and always vulnerable to those elements of chaos and excess which were inseparable from life with Winston.

Cruelly tested as it often was, her self-control would sometimes crumble; then she would suddenly erupt in such a rage that, as Jock Colville, Churchill's future secretary, noted, 'the tallest of trees would bend'. 'When her nerves were stretched,' he added, 'she sometimes turned on Winston with vitriol in her voice and the flashing eyes of fury.'

On one of these occasions she made family history by hurling a dish of spinach at him. (It missed.) But her anger was not confined to members of the family, and her verbal lash could unexpectedly flash out at any of her husband's friends. The effect was awesome. 'You know, Clemmie dropped upon him like a jaguar out of a tree,' said Churchill after one such occasion.

According to his niece Clarissa, Churchill's reaction to these outbursts was to 'take no notice, keep his head down and carry on with whatever he was doing'. But tantrums invariably left Clementine weakened and depressed, for just as she could not control them, so they contravened the sense of order and decorum she believed in. She was at heart a kindly puritan, and away from all the strain and tension in her family the kindness showed.

Bertrand Russell's cousin Conrad met her on holiday in Wales during the summer of 1924 when Churchill was once more hunting the Duke of Westminster's wild boar in Normandy. Accompanied by ten-year-old Sarah, she was spending a few days in a small hotel beside the sea. Russell, an intimate of the Asquiths and reputedly the lover of Diana Cooper, was the only other guest – and his summing-up of Clementine to his sister, Flora, catches something of her loneliness, as well as the condescension with which the Asquith circle still regarded her.

'Mrs C', he wrote, 'is highly friendly, and quite incredibly chatty. I'm afraid I find her a bore and she has a common sort (but an amicable sort) of mind.'

When Russell met her, Clementine was at something of a crisis of her life. She was approaching forty. Had 'Time' stolen love away, as she had once predicted, leaving only friendship in its place, which she had described as 'very peaceful but not stimulating or warming'?

For Clementine it seems as if it had. Hers was a passionate romantic nature, and from the moment she first fell in love with him, she had given Churchill all the love she possessed. But it must have been a struggle to maintain the great illusion of romantic love with such a total egotist.

For him there was no problem. He had a simple view of marriage: that, as he put it, one 'married and lived happily ever after'. This was another of his saving myths; and by believing this, the sentimental section of his life was taken care of, leaving him free to dedicate himself to the countless other things demanding his attention.

It had been different in the past, when Clementine had sacrificed her friendships and her role as mother to his great career. Now her dream of their shared political adventure was threatened. As a Conservative, Churchill had beliefs which, as a

Liberal, she could not endorse, and plutocratic friends she did not like. He also had the precocious Randolph to confide in now, and a bond was forming between the two of them from which she was more or less excluded. She resented this, as she resented much within her family, but there was little more to be done about it except put up with it or angrily explode when things became too much for her.

Selfish and blithely sentimental, 'Mr Pig' continued much as usual. He needed the assurance of her love and her affection, but she must have known that he would never cease to lead that self-absorbing driven life he wanted. She had her own allotted part in it, rather like Mrs Everest in Churchill's childhood, for there were times when he depended on her still. 'I feel far safer from worry and depression when you are with me and I can confide in your sweet soul,' he wrote when trying to convince her of the joys and pleasures of their 'new abode'. 'You are a rock and I depend on you and rest on you.'

He had a gift for words, and what he wrote was true and touching. But to be a husband's 'rock' in moments of his depression was neither 'stimulating or warming' for a romantic nature. Being needed could be terribly exhausting. He was so often like a wayward child himself, petulant, demanding and so moody that he frequently became impossible to live with.

The Exchequer had rejuvenated him. So had Chartwell. Here in this workaholic's playground, 'the darling old schoolboy', as Diana Cooper used to call him, had all his hobbies to absorb him – ever more bricks to lay, lakes to dam, pictures to be painted. He had his growing court of carefully selected cronies – audience, supporters, intellectual stimulants – and the affection of his fascinated children. He had his fame and his intense activity. Even his life-long driving force, ambition, was requited for the moment, leaving him content with his world around him. It was up to Clementine to accept it, too.

He was firm with her over Chartwell, telling her that he intended it to be their home for many years to come. As Blenheim descended to the Marlboroughs, so Chartwell would be handed on to Randolph and his heirs. That was his intention. Should she thwart him over this, 'If you set yourself against Chartwell or lose heart or bite your bread and butter or your Pig,' he told her, 'then it only means further instability, recasting of plans and further worry and expense'.

So Clementine had accepted, as she had had to. She took charge of the furnishing and decoration of the house, aiming to make it 'charming' as he knew she would.

She had ladylike good taste and could make the house comfortable with patterned curtains, rush matting on the floors, and colour washes on the walls, against which she dutifully hung her husband's pictures. Yet, despite her efforts, several visitors remarked on the 'strongly masculine' character of the house. Churchill's aura was too strong to be subdued: the set-up reminded Harold Macmillan of a government department and for A. L. Rowse, Chartwell possessed 'something of a collegiate atmosphere, a hive of masculine activity mitigated by family life'.

Where her perfectionism showed was in the way she managed to impose a sense of order on the running of the house, which, given Churchill's habits, was no mean achievement. By 1926, Churchill was approaching thirteen stone, and the assurance of good food to soothe and satisfy his inner man was not achieved by chance. His nephew Johnny Spencer-Churchill described Clementine's role at Chartwell as 'that of ADC extraordinary and Super Quartermaster to the greatest Captain General' – and he still waxes eloquent over the Chartwell meals he remembers.

The hospitality which my uncle and aunt offered at table was quite out of this world. In addition to special dishes to suit the idiosyncrasies of the most demanding guests – Professor Lindemann for instance was a vegetarian which meant arranging two separate menus – there was always champagne, superb port and brandy for lunch, followed by more port, brandy and cigars when the ladies had withdrawn.

But where Clementine's nature really showed itself was in the Chartwell gardens, where she could plant her roses and wisteria and colourful herbaceous borders – calming activity for a highly strung perfectionist.

She could always be relied on to cope with tribal gatherings of the family, particularly at Christmas-time, which according to the childhood recollections of her daughter Mary was 'always a glorious feast' at prewar Chartwell. With Sunny married to the disapproving Gladys, the shared Christmases of the past were over. Chartwell took the place of Blenheim as the place where the Churchills gathered for their celebrations.

Only close family were invited. First on the list would always be faithful brother Jack with Lady Goonie, the two boys Johnny and Peregrine, and their precocious baby sister, Clarissa, who was born in 1920. Usually there would also be Clementine's sister, the now widowed Nellie Romilly, with her two 'little lambs', the tiny monsters Esmond and Giles. The one regular outsider at these Chartwell Christmases was indispensable Professor Lindemann – who, Eddie Marsh apart, was the only member of Churchill's inner circle Clementine could tolerate for long. He had the additional advantage of being both single and extremely rich, and he provided splendid Christmas presents. Churchill particularly enjoyed these. 'The Prof' could be relied on to provide the very best cigars and a case of the great man's favourite champagne.

Good champagne inevitably played its own important part in any Churchill Christmas, and Jack would propose his regular – and somewhat typical – Christmas toast: 'Good champagne for our real friends – and real pain for our ex-friends!'

As a non-believer, wedded as ever to his unshakeable routine, Churchill would stay in bed on Christmas morning while Clementine shepherded the children to the morning service at Westerham parish church. For the evening she would organise a Christmas tree with real candles, followed by the inevitable amateur dramatics in which all the children had to perform. But Churchill was, as always, at the centre of these family affairs, and after Christmas dinner he would tell his stories of the past, recite his favourite poems, and sing the music-hall songs that he remembered word-perfect from his youth.

Chartwell was always a centre for all the family, together with their friends and their relations during school holidays. The result could be exciting – especially for Randolph, who was soon being treated by his father as honorary crown prince of Chartwell. Remembering his own unhappy time at public school, and the anguish he had suffered from Lord Randolph's anger at his own unsatisfactory school reports, Churchill was determined not to make the same mistake with Randolph. Randolph's reports from Eton were not dissimilar from his father's when he was at Harrow – 'lack of concentration', 'failure to understand the importance of his work'.

But at Chartwell, and in close proximity to Churchill, a different Randolph seemed to be emerging. Like all the Churchills, he was extraordinarily precocious, already fascinated by politics and politicians, well informed, and with a fluency in argument that delighted Churchill. Totally without shyness, he could expound his views with a youthful eloquence his father actually envied.

Randolph, of course, was picking all this up from Churchill and his circle, just as Churchill himself had done from Lord Randolph and the politicians round him in his youth, and Churchill never saw the dangers for his golden boy. Clementine did, but had little influence against her husband. Randolph was soon permitted to stay up for dinner with the great man's 'great contemporaries'. Birkenhead, Lloyd George, Beaverbrook and Bracken – the great political talkers of the day – would come; and after dinner, when Clementine and the ladies had retired, Randolph would be permitted to stay on to join the conversation.

His father 'like a potentate' at the head of the table would sometimes raise his large cigar to interrupt the flow of talk, and thus ensure that sixteen-year-old Randolph had his say – which Randolph, being Randolph and a Churchill, duly did.

There were never-to-be-forgotten moments during these early years at Chartwell – Lawrence of Arabia upstaging everyone at dinner (even Churchill) by appearing in the robes of a desert prince, 'the Prof' bringing out his slide-rule to calculate how much champagne Churchill had drunk in his lifetime (it was enough to fill a railway carriage), and Chaplin at dinner rousing Churchill's wrath by arguing for socialism, then making everybody laugh by slipping into his routine as Charlot.

It seemed idyllic, and many visitors' memories of Churchill's paradise were of golden days, basking in the sunlight of the great man's pleasure. But for some it proved a dangerous paradise. Nephew Johnny can remember driving back to London with Aunt Clementine after what had seemed a lively if tempestuous weekend, and hearing her wearily exclaim: 'I just can't stand it any longer.'

Johnny was a carefree soul, and something of a joker in the family. Unambitious and totally uninterested in politics (he would become a painter), he enjoyed Chartwell and his Uncle Winston, learned to imitate him (a useful party trick), but otherwise remained quite unaffected by his contact with the great.

Not so his younger brother, Peregrine, who reacted differently to Uncle Winston and the atmosphere at Chartwell. He was a serious child: when asked by a friend what he wished to be when he grew up, he replied, 'A retired banker'. (In fact he became a successful engineer.) But Churchill's world was not the place for retiring natures. Peregrine insists that at times life at Chartwell was 'remarkably invigorating' and he enjoyed his holidays there. But politics and politicians already bored him.

By her late teens, his cousin Diana seems to have felt the same; she would soon gratefully depart for the peace and freedom of a family in Paris, to learn French, before returning for the London season. Her parents, and the society around them, seem to have overwhelmed her, and the memories people have of her at Chartwell are of a self-conscious little figure, worried about her plumpness, easily upset, often walking off alone, singing tunelessly.

Patterns formed in childhood persist, and for much of her life Diana would be a lonely figure in a world in which she tried to find her private happiness.

Another member of the family on whom Churchill and the 'Chartwell Dream' would have a permanent effect was his favourite daughter, Sarah. Unlike Diana, she enjoyed the rough and tumble of discussion: she had charm and wit, and was at ease with her father's famous friends. At heart she says she was 'a father's girl', dominated by him, half in love with him, and fascinated by the fame and power around him. Throughout her life Sarah would be ruled by an unceasing quest for fame – and for other father-figures.

But, among those who were affected by the spell of Chartwell, the most unusual fate of all concerns the elegant fifteen-year-old blonde girl Randolph became enamoured with during his last year at Eton. This was his cousin, Diana Mitford, daughter of the 2nd Lord Redesdale (who in turn was cousin once removed of Lady Blanche), and sister of an extraordinary group of female siblings, of whom Nancy Mitford would become the famous novelist, Jessica the left-wing journalist, Unity the devotee and friend of Adolf Hitler, and Deborah the Duchess of Devonshire. Diana's brother, Tom, was at school with Randolph, hence the introduction; and Randolph invited her to Chartwell during the summer holidays of 1928. She had seen nothing like Chartwell in her somewhat sheltered life before, and fell in love with it at once.

Coming from a spartan section of the aristocracy, Diana found in Chartwell something of a revelation of the earthly pleasures life could offer – a bathroom of her own, delicious food and château-bottled claret. She was dazzled by clever

Professor Lindemann, and fascinated by Eddie Marsh's stories of famous writers and artists he knew. She was also captivated by Clementine's kindness and good taste. 'I used to think that if I could grow up to be as beautiful and elegant as Cousin Clementine and Lady Goonie, I should be totally happy.'

But her favourite experience was to listen to Winston, who struck her instantly as 'the cleverest, and most original and most forceful person I had ever met. To sit next to Winston was my *ideal*, even if he paid little attention to me. He would hold forth, always about politics, and I drank in his words.' He was the first live politician she had ever met and he clearly overwhelmed her.

'If Winston doesn't talk to you, just pull his sleeve and start him off,' said Clementine. Diana never dared to, but her hero-worship of great men and power-figures seems to have started at the Chartwell dinner-table. It would dominate her life – and involve her with cousin Winston in a very different guise during the years ahead.

21

Wilderness

As the 1920s drew towards their close, life for Churchill changed abruptly.

There was a general election in the spring of 1929. Unlike Premier Stanley Baldwin, who went to the country with the slogan 'Safety First', Churchill campaigned full-bloodedly against the prospect of a second Labour government. He claimed that Labour, 'the Party of Plunder', having once condoned the 'constitutional outrage' of a General Strike, were utterly unfit to govern.

The votes were cast on 30 May, and that night Churchill was at Downing Street, whisky-glass in hand, to witness the results arrive by ticker-tape. Although he kept his seat at Epping, it was soon clear that there had been a Labour landslide. As the news grew worse, his face grew redder. Shoulders hunched, and fury in his face, he looked like a bull about to charge the ticker-tape machine. One of the civil servants feared that if any more Labour gains came in 'he would smash the whole apparatus'. Apparently his language was 'unprintable'.

As Churchill feared, the result of the election was Ramsay MacDonald's disastrous second Labour government; and for Churchill it was also a disaster. Not merely was he out of office, but his actions as Chancellor were strongly held against him; he had made himself appear an out-of-date reactionary, a figure from the past, who was himself unfit for power. Two years later, when Baldwin joined the faltering Ramsay MacDonald in a National Government, Churchill would not be included. That night at Downing Street was thus the beginning of a grim decade in which Churchill, although still in Parliament, would stay unheeded and alone in what he called the wilderness of politics.

To take his mind off political defeat, and the prospect of a

Labour government, in the summer of 1929 Churchill visited North America as guest of the Canadian Pacific Railway. The invitation included as many of his family as he wished to take but, since Clementine was not enthusiastic and needed another therapeutic break from Churchill and the family, he decided it would be a good occasion to take eighteen-year-old Randolph, brother Jack and nephew Johnny.

The party sailed first-class from Southampton on 3 August. 'What fun it is to get away from England and feel one has no responsibility for her exceedingly tiresome and embarrassing affairs,' he wrote to Beaverbrook.

The fun continued throughout the whirlwind trip across Canada and through the United States. In contrast with his reputation back in England, in North America he found himself a great celebrity. The CPR had placed a luxurious rail-car – he described it as 'a land yacht' – at the Churchills' disposal; and his speeches, emphasising 'the mighty ties, incomprehensible to Europeans', linking the Empire and the English-speaking nations, were received with acclamation. This was the first time he had really witnessed the full potential of the land of his maternal ancestors, and he was mightily impressed.

He was also thrilled with Randolph, who seemed to be justifying the hopes he had for him. 'I think he has made a good impression on everybody,' he wrote to Clementine. 'He was taking a most intelligent interest in everything, and is a remarkable critic and appreciator of the speeches I make and the people we meet.'

Randolph was being treated as a celebrity, too, and was showing signs of that 'bumptiousness' with members of the press which would bring such trouble in the future. A female reporter from the *Toronto Star* reported him saying that he thought women 'simply did not fit in' with British parliamentary life and caused a lamentable 'lack of dignity'. But, for Churchill, gaffes like this were of little importance compared with the growing admiration he was feeling for his son.

Johnny Churchill still recalls an evening when the party camped by the shores of Lake Louise. Twilight was falling and, touched by the beauty of the scene, Churchill fondly said: 'Randolph, recite us something.' Randolph responded with a passage which he must have memorised at Eton from Lecky's *History of European Morals*. It was on prostitution. Randolph, an actor like his father, made the most of this long dramatic passage. By the end of it, Churchill was in tears of admiration.

These feelings seem to have survived their journey on to Hollywood, where the party was lavishly entertained by William Randolph Hearst at his legendary castle at San Simeon. Always thoroughly at home with press proprietors, Churchill made a hit with the megalomaniac publisher and agreed to write for him, while Randolph took advantage of their situation by losing his virginity with some rapidly forgotten female guest of Hearst's.

If Churchill was aware of Randolph's escapades, he tactfully ignored them. Up to this point the trip was a great success and an exercise in family togetherness, with Randolph sharing in his father's fame, and his father rejoicing in the company and friendship of his handsome son. But, for Churchill, this visit to America had a gloomy ending. Throughout the summer he had played the stock market, confident that he would come back with a fortune. Gambler that he was, he was speculating on tips from one of his millionaire admirers, the financier Bernard Baruch, and ignoring Jack's advice to play it safe. After Hollywood, he enjoyed himself, visiting battlefields of the Civil War (on which he was an expert). Then he reached New York in time to witness a ruined speculator throw himself from a window in Wall Street.

The Crash of 1929 had come. Churchill's savings and his rash investments vanished overnight, and he returned to England, not in triumph, but on the edge of ruin. Following the loss of office, the loss of so much money was a bitter blow. During the next few years he kept himself afloat only by prodigious efforts as an author and a journalist, living, as he said, 'from mouth to hand'.

The optimistic years were over and Churchill was badly hit by a mid-life crisis. Harold Nicolson was shocked by his deterioration when he saw him in January 1930: 'very changed from when I last saw him. A white round face like a blister, incredibly aged . . . His spirits have also declined, and he sighs that he has lost his old fighting power.' It was now that he first began to think seriously of Randolph as his ultimate political successor. He seems to have genuinely believed that he was all but finished as a politician and that his mortal end was not far off. It almost was.

At the end of 1931 Churchill returned to New York, to begin a lecture tour across America (thirty-nine lectures for a guaranteed fee of £10,000). Crossing Fifth Avenue, he forgot which way the traffic came and was hit by a taxi. Injured on the head and thighs and badly shocked, he still managed to identify himself in no uncertain terms. 'I am Winston Churchill, a British statesman,' he told doctors before passing out entirely. Later he manfully completed his lecture tour, but the accident proved an unexpected blow to his powerful physique. Six weeks later he still described himself as 'very weak and debilitated', and miserably informed his wife that this was the third blow he had suffered in the last two years: first, the loss of his position in the Conservative Party; second, the loss of all his money in the Crash; 'and now this terrible physical injury'. On the verge of yet another deep depression, he told Clementine that he did not think he could 'ever recover completely from the three blows'.

Trouble dogged Churchill after his return to England, and he talked gloomily of being 'finished'. Politics, family, finance were all creating deep anxiety, and his old resilience had not returned.

The parallel between his own life and his father's was not lost on him. Both had been Colonial Secretary and Chancellor. Both had known great political success, dominating Parliament with their oratory. Then in both cases there came the fall from power, political rejection, and the misery of money troubles. Churchill had already lived longer than Lord Randolph; time was closing in on him. His premonitions of an early death returned, and he wrote to Clementine that he was 'entering what will certainly be the last decade of my existence'. The time had come to make his dispositions for the future.

That sacred 'lamp', the all-important gift of power, could soon be safely handed on to brilliant Randolph, just as he had grasped it from the lifeless fingers of his father thirty years before. It was very much with this in mind that Churchill planned the famous birthday-dinner at Claridge's to celebrate his son's majority in June of 1932. It was then that Lord Rothermere called Randolph 'Britain's Young Man of Destiny', and briefly it seemed as if twenty-one-year-old Randolph was truly set to follow in his father's massive footsteps.

During the early summer of 1932, Randolph did behave rather

like Churchill at the start of *his* career. He used many of his
father's early ploys – the pull of family connections, reliance on
the Churchill name, the supercharged ambition, and the flair for
picking an occasion which would bring him instantly to public
attention. And by using these tactics skilfully Randolph made a
striking début as a journalist.

True to his father's early adage, inherited from Jennie, about
'doing business only at the top', Randolph cashed in on Lord
Rothermere's support to get himself appointed special correspondent of the *Sunday Graphic*. He was to report the German
general elections in which the rising Nazi Party was bidding to
control the country's tottering Weimar Republic. It was not lost
on Randolph that both Lord Randolph and his father had written
for the old *Daily Graphic* in their time, and he set off for Berlin
at the tender age of twenty-one, with the aura – and expense
account – of a top reporter.

To the annoyance and surprise of less-privileged journalists
like Bruce Lockhart, the 'rollickingly bumptious' Randolph did
not blunder as expected. He was a natural journalist and he
was also very energetic. Thanks to his father, he was well primed
on the resurgent militarism which was to dominate the voting,
and he somehow used the Churchill name to get himself aboard
the aircraft Hitler himself was using for the campaign trail.

The result was a journalistic scoop, with Randolph actually
observing the future Führer at close quarters. He sent back some
of the earliest accounts of Nazi rallies, describing them as a
mixture of an American football game, a boy scout jamboree and
a revivalist meeting 'conducted with the discipline of the Brigade
of Guards'.

It is hard to know how taken he was by Hitler's personality,
but he was certainly impressed by him. As he predicted, the Nazis
failed to win the elections outright, but emerged as the largest
single party in the Reichstag. Randolph sent Hitler a telegram of
congratulation. But he also understood the danger that Hitler
represented, and his final report from Germany contains one of
the most prophetic of the early warnings on the Nazis. It also gives
some indication of Randolph's political awareness and potential
as a journalist.

Nothing can long delay their arrival in power. Hitler will not betray
them. But let us make no mistake about it. The success of the Nazi party

sooner or later means war. Nearly all of Hitler's principal lieutenants fought in the last war. Most of them have two or three medals on their breasts. They burn for revenge. They are determined once more to have an army. I am sure that once they have achieved it, they will not hesitate to use it.

Later, Randolph would modestly deny that he had 'thought all this out for himself' at twenty-one. As he said, 'I had sat for many years at the feet of my father.' But the words were his, and thanks to his recent close involvement with the Nazi leadership he was closer to Hitler's true significance than his father.

At this point in his political career, Churchill was more pre-occupied with a very different enemy: that 'seditious Middle Temple lawyer, now posing as a fakir of a type well known in the East', as he called him, the leader of the Indian Civil Disobedience Campaign, Mahatma Gandhi. For several years, Churchill thought him far more dangerous than Hitler.

Early in 1931, Gandhi had been released from prison by the British authorities in Delhi. The Labour Prime Minister, Ramsay MacDonald, was promising India dominion status; and Baldwin, for the Conservative opposition, had given his support. Sensing a sellout of the great King Emperor's Indian possessions, Churchill was enraged. 'Gandhi,' he told the Secretary for India, Edwin Montagu, 'ought to be laid, bound hand and foot, at the gates of Delhi, and then trampled on by an enormous elephant with the new Viceroy on his back.'

He was particularly furious with Baldwin, and from this moment Churchill found himself fatally at odds with his party leaders over India. He was to fight a long and self-destructive battle with them which continued after the Conservatives joined the government in 1932. It was a battle which absorbed his energies, confirmed his public status as a double-dyed reactionary, and brought relations with his party leader, Baldwin, virtually to breaking-point. It also deflected his attention from his future enemy, Adolf Hitler.

But Randolph was anxious to alert his father to the aims and the hypnotic influence of the rising German leader, and stayed on in Germany for some weeks after the elections, knowing that his parents and his sister Sarah were due to arrive for a brief stay at the Hotel Continental in Munich in Bavaria. Churchill had started researching his biography of the 1st Duke of Marlborough and was passing through Munich on the way to the battlefield of Blenheim. Randolph decided that, since Hitler would be in Munich at the same time as his father, the two of them should meet.

There was no problem persuading Churchill to agree to this – he was keen to see this leading Nazi for himself. Persuading Hitler was more difficult, and Randolph relied on the good offices of the notorious Putzi Hanfstaengl, the Harvard-educated socialite and close friend of Hitler, whom Randolph had got to know during the election. Hanfstaengl conveyed the invitation to Herr Adolf Hitler to join the Churchill family for dinner at the Hotel Continental.

Hitler's reaction was distinctly odd, almost as if he had some premonition of the role this visitor would play in his terrible career, and he seemed of two minds whether to accept. 'But what would I talk to him about? And in any case, he is a rabid Francophile,' he told his henchman. After some arguing, it was Hanfstaengl who went off to dinner with the Churchills in Hitler's place.

He seems to have had an uncomfortable time of it when the conversation turned to the subject of the Jews. 'Tell your boss that anti-semitism may be a good starter, but it's a bad sticker,' Churchill told him.

There was still a chance of Churchill delivering his message to Hitler personally. As Hanfstaengl left the restaurant, he was surprised to see Hitler talking to someone in the hall outside, and suggested he should meet the Churchills over coffee. Hanfstaengl gives the firm impression that Hitler was not there by chance; but again he refused, this time giving as his excuse the strange reason that he had not shaved. He then hurried from the hotel, and Hanfstaengl saw no more of him until Churchill and his party left for Blenheim.

This was the nearest Churchill ever came to meeting Hitler. Later, when he knew more about him, he would adamantly refuse to have anything to do with him, although a meeting could have been arranged. Perhaps this was as well. When Churchill met Mussolini in Rome in 1927, he had been dangerously impressed by the Italian dictator. The same might all too easily have happened with the German leader, and it was possibly with this in mind that Randolph would say how glad he was that Hitler never did accept the invitation. But he had no reason to reproach himself for having so very nearly staged one of the more intriguing might-have-beens of modern history at the age of twenty-one.

Where Randolph did have reason for reproach was over what happened next. For, having achieved a more successful and precocious début than even his father managed in his early twenties, he cheerfully proceeded to throw almost everything away.

Diana Cooper's fortieth birthday fell at the end of August, and to mark the anniversary the extremely rich and socially obsessed Conservative MP Henry 'Chips' Channon organised a party for a group of fashionable rich friends on the Venetian island of Murano. It was the social highlight of the Venice summer season, and somehow Randolph got himself invited. Channon never quite got over what ensued.

Randolph arrived from Munich in the best of spirits – in both senses. He knew everybody at the party: Lady Cunard and her lover the conductor Sir Thomas Beecham, Robert Boothby, Lady Castlerosse, Brendan Bracken, the art collector Edward James, and his own adored Diana Mitford, who was now married to the gentle Bryan Guinness but actually in love with Sir Oswald Mosley, who was also present. Encouraged by so many friendly faces, Randolph drank copiously and, becoming even happier, intervened in a lovers' argument between the heiress Doris Duke and the baronet Sir Richard Sykes. Randolph's intervention was misunderstood by Sykes, who hit him. Randolph hit him back, Doris Duke joined in, and Diana Cooper's birthday rapidly became one of the smartest public brawls of the early thirties. What Randolph had started rapidly became a rough-house with broken bottles, broken jaws and considerable outrage from the general public, which was faithfully reflected in the morrow's British press.

While this was going on, Churchill, accompanied by Sarah and Clementine and his 'military adviser', the military historian Colonel Pakenham-Walsh, was stumping the far-off battlefield of Blenheim; but even there he managed to maintain his lifelong habit of reading the London morning papers, the more sensational of which graphically recounted Randolph's participation in the fight. More followed. Blithely unperturbed by the scandal he was causing, Randolph embarked on three weeks of riotous relaxation with half the gossip columnists of Europe in pursuit.

Randolph rarely failed an audience. Drunk, pugnacious, lecherous and loud, he was the scourge of Venice. At the Lido he called Brendan Bracken 'Brother' (a tactless reference to the unfounded but persistent rumour that Bracken was Churchill's

bastard son), and when the myopic Bracken chased him down
the beach he grabbed his spectacles and threw them in the water,
leaving the half-blind financier 'standing in the shallow sea and
roaring like a bull'.

There were more rows, more drunken evenings and, more
seriously, an affair with the shapely Doris Lady Castlerosse. This
was improvident on two accounts. In the first place the lady's husband, Viscount Castlerosse, a former friend of Randolph's, was
a famous gossip columnist himself, and a notoriously aggressive
enemy. (When Castlerosse rang him up and said, 'I hear you're
living with my wife,' Randolph replied: 'Yes, I am; and it's more
than you have the courtesy to do.') And, in the second place,
there was another rumour – which many happened to believe
was true – that several years before, in the Ritz Hotel in Paris,
Doris had gone to bed with Winston Churchill.

As with so many rumours of this sort, it is unprovable either
way (as is the veracity of the great man's reputed compliment to
Lady Castlerosse after the event, 'Doris, you could make a corpse
come!'). But in such circumstances it was thoughtless of Randolph
to appear to follow where his father trod, and Churchill cannot
have been amused to read in another London paper that Lady
Castlerosse's pet name for his son was 'Fuzzy-Wuzzy', and that
the two of them were constantly together.

Back in London, Randolph continued to enjoy his princely
role, taking a well-paid staff job with the *Sunday Dispatch* and
then renting an enormous chauffeur-driven limousine and the
best suite in the Mayfair Hotel. He was installed there when
his father returned to England after a spell in a sanatorium,
having contracted paratyphoid on the Continent. Illness had
not improved his temper, and that autumn father–son relations
plummeted.

Gone were the inflated hopes with which Churchill had planned
Randolph's birthday-dinner barely six months earlier; gone, too,
was the idea of 'handing on the torch' to an inspired successor.
Venice had changed all that, and angry rows began.

'What are you doing?' Churchill asked him. 'When I was your
age I was reading five hours a day. You spend most of your time
in night-clubs, staving off a vast army of debtors by eking out a
precarious living as a hack journalist.'

After another bitter row, Randolph stormed from the room
(as he would do on numerous occasions in the years ahead),

and Churchill turned as he often did to 'the Prof', Professor Lindemann, for solace and advice.

'Lindemann,' he said. 'You are a professor of biology and experimental philosophy. Tell me, am I, as a parent, responsible for all the biological and chemical reactions of my son?'

Lindemann's reply is not recorded, but it was an interesting question, for the truth was that, with womanising as the one exception, all the essential weaknesses and vices which afflicted Randolph were shared with his father, having been inherited or learned from him or from his friends and cronies. Indeed, their similarities were rather startling.

A love of gambling, an undiscriminating passion for rich friends and luxury, snobbery and bumptiousness applied equally to Churchill; so did the gluttony, the bullying, the almost pathological self-assurance and that rarefied upper-class sense of unreality over the humdrum facts of life. Apart from a touch of snobbery, none of these weaknesses afflicted Clementine. Randolph and his father were both utter egomaniacs who, again unlike Clementine, were uncomfortably accustomed to getting their own way about anything they wanted. Both were heavy drinkers with a taste for racy company and very large cigars. They were both nocturnal, both obsessed with politics, and both great talkers with capacious memories. They were so similar, in fact, that Randolph increasingly appeared a carbon copy – or caricature – of his father.

So what was going wrong with Randolph? Why should those very characteristics, each of which appeared an inherent part of Churchill's nature, be proving so disastrous in his son?

The answer surely lies with Churchill's situation and achievements. Both father and son were similar over-size personalities, but Churchill had been driven since his early twenties by the constant need to beat the dreaded possibility of failure; Randolph instead possessed the inner confidence of effortless success. Churchill had learned to keep Black Dog at bay through rigorous self-discipline and concentrated work; talented Randolph, with a happier temperament, saw the need for neither.

But the greatest – and, for Randolph, the most disastrous – difference between their situations was a very simple one. Churchill had lost his disapproving father-figure in unforgettable circumstances at the age of twenty. Randolph, with his dominating father always present, would never have a hope of taking on his father's role. Churchill might talk of 'handing on the lamp', but as long as there was breath in Churchill's body he was not relinquishing his hopes of power to anyone – not even Randolph.

But at the end of this depressing year there was excitement from an unexpected quarter: at twenty-three, Diana, his eldest, shyest daughter, had found some belated limelight for herself at last as the chosen bride of a rich and handsome husband.

She needed it, for it had not been easy for this elfin redhead to maintain her confidence in a family of such overwhelming egos. Clementine, preoccupied as ever with her husband and her own uncertain health, had less patience than ever with her now. Sarah described a painful visit to the dressmaker together with Diana and the 'beautiful and elegant' Clementine, during which their mother airily remarked that 'Sarah is so easy to dress', not realising that this was a 'near mortal blow to Diana'.

Diana's obsession with her mother's disapproval never left her, and would always tend to sap her confidence. Her cousin, Anita Leslie, remembered finding her in tears at the end of her dreaded first London season 'because Mummy is horrid to me and I haven't been a success'.

Anita asked her why she thought she had been a failure.

'Because I have sandy-coloured eyelashes,' she sobbed.

With Sarah soon due to begin her own London season, Diana had felt it a disgrace not to have found herself a husband, and her insecurities increased at the thought of people comparing her unfavourably with her prettier, more popular younger sister.

Her father was kinder to Diana than her mother, but he had neither time nor temperament to understand her problems; nor could he hide the fact that Sarah was his real favourite. The result was predictable, with Diana anxious to escape from home and find her own success, pursuing fame and glamour where they seemed most instantly available – on the stage.

Sarah would do the same a few years later; but, unlike her, Diana had little acting talent. Her greatest asset was her name, but even this was not the help it might have been; on joining the Royal Academy of Dramatic Art, she had found a talented student there already named Diana Churchill (who would, in fact, enjoy a long and successful theatrical career).

During the disastrous lecture tour of America, as a favour to Churchill, Warner Brothers had offered Diana a screen test; following which Lord Beaverbrook's *Express* ran an article about

her with a headline asking the question 'Mr Churchill's daughter
a film star?'

'No,' came the answer from the tests; and back in England
a disconsolate Diana spent time addressing envelopes in
Churchill's constituency office, then took a summer holiday at
Chartwell.

She would later tell her daughter that it was then that she finally
decided to get married 'to escape from all the endless talk around
the Chartwell dinner table'; and that autumn came news of her
engagement – to thirty-two-year-old John Milner Bailey, son of
South African mine-owner Sir Abe Bailey.

She was reported to have known him 'for several years', and
Churchill was said to be delighted. Diana clearly needed to get
married, and the colourful Abe Bailey was an old ally and admirer
of Winston Churchill. He was also very rich. Diana seemed to
have found herself an ideal husband, and on 12 December 1932,
at St Margaret's, Westminster, they married.

The *Telegraph* reported large crowds of embattled women
breaking through police cordons when the bride arrived. The
scenes were a reminder of the excitement Churchill's name could
still inspire. This must have pleased him, coming as it did at such
a low point in his political fortune and personal morale.

He had been determined that his daughter's wedding would
be a demonstration of family solidarity and his own political
importance.

It was a very grand occasion, with the aristocracy and leading politicians on parade. The present-list was headed by the
King and Queen (who sent a blue enamel dressing-table set); the
bride 'in shimmering ivory-coloured silk' wore pearls and orange
blossom; Churchill gave the bride away, and cousin Sunny lent
his London house in Carlton Terrace for the reception.

There in the ballroom, lit by quantities of real candles in
the enormous Marlborough chandelier, several hundred guests
toasted Diana with extremely good champagne. All agreed that
she had never looked prettier, and her husband was described
'bearing himself manfully' through the considerable ordeal of a
full-scale society wedding. Afterwards he took Diana off for a
peaceful bridal night at the Ritz Hotel, then on to a honeymoon
in Venice.

But Diana had not known her husband as well as she pretended: in her anxiety to escape from Chartwell and marry

somebody her parents would approve of, she had accepted his proposal in a hurry. She did not know, for instance, that he had recently been in love with a young novelist called Barbara Cartland, who had found him 'sweet and perfectly charming', but who had also rapidly discovered that he drank so much that he frequently became 'utterly impossible'.

It was a lesson Diana learned for herself on her honeymoon; and after her return to London the lessons would continue.

Lending his cousin Winston his splendid London residence for Diana's wedding was not the only favour Sunny Marlborough did him during this fallow period in Churchill's life. For years the two of them had taken it for granted that one day Churchill would commence the great work they had frequently discussed – the monumental life of their greatest ancestor, John, 1st Duke of Marlborough.

Churchill had always been convinced that their ancestral hero had been unjustly treated by the historians, in particular by Lord Macaulay. With his exaggerated feelings for his family, and his habit of identifying with his heroes, he had taken particular offence at Macaulay's accusations of the great Duke's avarice, disloyalty and greed, seeing them as slurs upon himself and on his family. As early as 1924 there had been talk about the book that he would write to reinstate his hero's reputation. But with his history of the First World War unfinished, and his five-year stint as Chancellor to come, it was a project that had had to be postponed. However, in 1929, when Churchill fell from office, Sunny had been able to offer practical assistance for Churchill to begin the book.

A large proportion of the great Duke's papers were at Blenheim, and Sunny had jealously preserved them for his cousin. He seems to have taken particular pleasure in denying access to them to the greatest historian of the day, G. M. Trevelyan, who was working on his massive history of Queen Anne: Sunny was not one to overlook the fact that Trevelyan was the great-nephew of Macaulay.

Thus Sunny had been able to offer Churchill what amounted to an authorised exclusive for his book, and the writing of the 1st Duke's life began as something of a sacred trust. This did nothing to prevent its author demanding and receiving a record publisher's advance of £10,000, having promised to complete a full two-volume life in two years flat.

It would be one rare occasion when Churchill failed to meet a deadline. Politics and crises in his private life diverted him, and his subject-matter steadily expanded, so that by the time he finished, his life of Marlborough had taken up four large volumes and nine years of its author's life. Since it rapidly developed wider implications both for Churchill and for those around him than an ordinary biography, it is important to understand the nature of this long, involved and most unusual book.

Even his way of writing it was entirely his own and, as with much that Churchill undertook, the life of Marlborough was seen and planned like a military campaign. 'He is happiest with a battle on his hands,' H. G. Wells had said of him, and from the start Churchill had an aggressive purpose to inspire him – the championing of his hero, and the destruction of his enemy Macaulay.

He organised the work accordingly, enlisting the support of expert allies for his task. Along with his universal adviser, Professor Lindemann, and his military expert, Colonel R. Pakenham-Walsh, he also relied upon a naval historian and Professor Feiling, the leading historian of late-seventeenth-century politics at Oxford. Through Feiling he was also able to enrol a promising young Oxford graduate student, Maurice Ashley, for the donkeywork of the research.

Ashley – who was middle-class, left-wing and serious – has described the extraordinary charm Churchill could always summon up for those he liked or needed, and which rapidly reduced the young historian to the status of devoted slave. He also described his employer's working habits: how after an admirable dinner in the Chartwell dining room they would retire to Churchill's oak-beamed study at around 11 p.m., where a secretary would be waiting for dictation and the day's real work would start.

He liked particularly to try out ideas or arguments to see if he could make them work. At about two he would express well-feigned surprise at the time and his secretary would be sent home in a hired car. An hour or so later he would reluctantly allow me to go to bed. Then he himself retired to do some serious reading, going to sleep around four. Next morning he would be reading his newspapers and his correspondence in bed about eight. Like Napoleon he was able to manage on four hours' sleep. He rarely seemed to be in a hurry.

As a scholar, Ashley was particularly surprised by the way Churchill started to dictate the beginning of his book before any of the detailed reading or research had started. What Ashley did not know was that the Duke had been Churchill's hero for so long that he already knew the case that he would be making for him. Churchill would rarely bother with the documents himself, lacking the time and training to decipher them; that was Ashley's task.

'Give me the facts, Ashley,' he would mutter, 'and I will twist them the way I want to suit my argument.'

It was very much the way he worked in politics, and he employed his other experts similarly, using the facts which they provided to create the essential scenery around the character and exploits of the Duke, which he would then recount. The result is a most unusual work of the imagination, and less a conventional biography than the work of a great romantic actor creating and interpreting a favourite role. The Duke who emerges from these pages bears an unmistakable resemblance to Winston Churchill.

There were more than sufficient similarities between them for Churchill to feel totally at home in Marlborough's world and Marlborough's character. They shared the same blood and the same heroic name. Marlborough was fifty-two when fate selected him to be what Churchill called 'the Saviour of Europe', with his great campaigns against the French. Like Churchill he had been opposed by insular and petty politicians, like him he gloried in warlike enterprises upon the broadest stage, and like him was indomitably ambitious in his search for honour.

In Churchill's account, dull Queen Anne becomes 'a great Queen championed by a great Constable'; his wife, the tetchy Duchess Sarah, emerges as a noble heroine. Marlborough himself, his meannesses and double-dealing barely noticed or flamboyantly overlooked, becomes the noblest of warriors, selflessly defending both his country's honour and the integrity of Europe against the King of France.

At the beginning of his political career Churchill had constructed his own political scenario by telling the story of his father's life. Now there was something even more prophetic in the way that he described the role of this more distant ancestor, a 'warrior, king, statesman' who 'was for six years, not only Commander in Chief of the Allies, but, although a subject, virtually master of England'.

Work on the life of Marlborough strengthened Churchill's links with Blenheim, and soon after starting on the book he took Ashley there to meet the Duke and show him round the archives.

The contrast between the two devoted cousins had grown with the years. Even in adversity, Churchill remained outgoing, confident and full of zest for life, but most of whatever charm Sunny had once possessed had gone. Ashley took against him instantly, and described him later as 'an inspissated little man' (the *Oxford Dictionary* defines 'inspissate' as 'condensed, dried up', as in the phrase 'inspissate gloom', which seems to have summed him up). The great cause of his life had been to save and to enhance what still remained of the 1st Duke's patrimony; but, whereas Churchill was romantically inspired by Marlborough's great example, his cousin had been driven to the edge of desperation by his task.

All Sunny could now see was the threat the outside world presented to his mausoleum of a house and the feudal way of life that still survived within it. He was convinced that almost everyone was a potential thief. When Ashley gained access to the archives, the Duke insisted that a servant watch him as he worked to ensure that nothing disappeared. Apparently, Churchill's friend, Hilaire Belloc, unlike Trevelyan, had been let into the archives some years earlier, and Sunny was convinced that he *had* stolen something.

More obsessive still was Sunny's hatred of the lower orders. Sharing his cousin Winston's pathological dislike of socialists and communists, he envisaged armies of embattled workers as part of some socialist plot drawn up beyond the gates of Blenheim waiting for the moment to invade it. He became apoplectic when he spotted some unauthorised old woman from the village gathering firewood in his park, and during Ashley's first visit, when Churchill mentioned the current unemployment figures, Sunny said he hoped the figures would reach 2 million as rapidly as possible. (Afterwards, Churchill assured Ashley that Sunny had, of course, been joking.)

As he had grown older, Sunny had reverted uncannily to Marlborough type, increasingly resembling those misanthropic late-eighteenth-century hermit Dukes of Marlborough. But, although he had come to hate the modern world as a threat to everything he stood for, his greatest enemy was now his wife. Blenheim was the perfect setting for their mutual loathing and bizarre hostilities. Slightly mad herself, her beauty ravaged and her life in ruins, Duchess Gladys turned to breeding dogs to satisfy her maternal instincts. She employed them in persecuting her husband, encouraging them to foul the carpets. It was war by spaniel.

Anita Leslie offers a front-line account of the progress of hostilities; she was at Blenheim with her cousin Randolph in the early thirties. Randolph knew the form already, for as they were waiting for the Duchess to make her appearance before dinner he whispered to Anita: 'Watch Sunny, he hates her guts. Great sport!'

Shortly afterwards, with what Anita calls 'the claw-clutter of many little dogs', Gladys made her stately entrance into the great *salon* surrounded by a 'moving carpet' of King Charles spaniels. She was 'extraordinary to look at – absolutely hideous and yet exotic, with golden hair swept back in a bun and strange blue eyes staring out of the ruin of the stretched face. She advanced in her dirty old clothes, shook hands and waved us gracefully to chairs.'

During dinner the conversation turned to the subject of marriage, and in her loudest voice the Duchess firmly advised Anita not to marry in a hurry. Then, as if Sunny were not present, she continued: 'I didn't marry until I'd been to bed with every prime minister in Europe – and most of the kings.'

Everybody laughed, except the Duke, who attempted to remain impassive as his grimy duchess continued to torment him. But that night in the splendour of the famous Blenheim dining room Anita thought its owner bore a marked resemblance to a rat caught in a trap.

22

Psychic Dynamite

'My dear Maxine!' Churchill exclaimed, smiling, as he descended from the limousine which had brought him and a mountain of luggage from the station. Despite considerable losses on the stock market, his old friend, vast Miss Elliot, the rich and famous American ex-actress, was still maintaining open house at the Château de l'Horizon near Cannes.

It was early August 1933. Parliament was safely in recess, and for a few weeks truce reigned in the increasingly bitter battle Churchill was still waging against change in India, despite the hostility of Stanley Baldwin and Churchill's growing isolation from his party.

As he began his holiday in this most luxurious of villas, with its scented gardens and its view across the bay, he could also briefly forget the threat of German rearmament which was concerning him as well. He had brought his paints and the final proofs of the first volume of his life of Marlborough to keep him occupied.

With no ministerial income for the last four years, and having long since spent the Marlborough advance, he was short of money, but staying with Miss Elliot cost those fortunate enough to be invited very little. Several of his family would soon be joining him, and as a personal sacrifice to their current economy campaign he had boldly decided not to bring his valet – a hazardous experiment but, rather to his surprise, it seemed to work.

'You have no idea how easy it is to travel without a servant,' he told his hostess. 'I came away from London alone, and it was quite simple.'

'Winston, how brave of you,' replied Miss Elliot.

Miss Elliot was a lion-hunter and a considerable snob. 'Always remember, dear,' she told her niece, 'that a lord is that much better than anybody else.' That year her house was full of gilded lions – including the Duke of Sutherland, Viscount Ratendone, Lady Castlerosse and other representatives of the international smart set. Less gilded but more decorative was a promising young actor called Peter Willes, whom Miss Elliot had recently befriended.

Willes was just nineteen, and it is interesting to note that this member of the younger generation, who had grown up since the war, had little real idea who Churchill was. It is also interesting that, unlike serious young Maurice Ashley, he instantly disliked him. Instead of the Churchill charm, he found him 'bullying and overbearing' when he met him.

At meals he just banged on and on, regardless of anybody else's interests or desire to talk; and if you weren't deeply involved in politics – and I wasn't – he really was a most dreadful bore. All he seemed to do was smoke cigars, eat, drink and talk far more than anybody else, and never give a damn what anybody thought about him.

But, for Willes, this uncomfortable experience was not the end of his contact with the Churchills. Randolph arrived, and Willes found him even more objectionable than his father – especially when he threw his considerable weight about and attempted (unsuccessfully) to bully Miss Elliot into giving him Willes's bedroom. Then Clementine arrived with Sarah, and Willes was captivated – particularly by Clementine. 'She was enchanting, but you could see at once that she was unhappy in that world of the super-rich which her husband obviously adored and felt at home in.'

Clementine had hated the French Riviera all her life. 'God, it's a ghastly place!' she once remarked, conceding as an after-thought: 'I expect it's all right if you're a flower-shop owner or a waiter.' Being neither, Clementine had to suffer the additional discomfort at the Château de l'Horizon of feeling at a personal disadvantage in the fast and glossy company.

For, as Willes discovered, 'the Churchills simply hadn't a bean'. Churchill, of course, never let this trouble him in the least, 'but Clementine worried dreadfully, and used to feel that the others were laughing at her behind her back because of her clothes, which weren't particularly *chic* by the standards of the South of France'.

A further source of irritation must have been the presence there of Lady Castlerosse, but Clementine had never been particularly concerned with idle gossip and, with his mother present, Randolph was briefly on his best behaviour. The trouble came from his sister Sarah.

Willes describes her at this period as 'a Bolshie Deb' – not on account of her political beliefs (she had none) but from her undisguised dislike of the pampered 'smarts' and the snobbish lives she saw them leading. This attitude, which Sarah seems to have originally picked up from Clementine, would stay with her for life; but that summer at the Château de l'Horizon its chief effect was deep antipathy towards hospitable title-worshipping Miss Elliot. Sarah thought her vulgar, old and ugly, and took so little pains to hide her feelings that her father noticed and reproved her.

'My dear,' he muttered when she tried to justify herself, 'I feel that you are still too young to appreciate the rich and mellow vintage.'

His words made little difference. Few things did when Sarah made up her mind, and she and Clementine departed earlier than expected.

Randolph stayed on, having none of his sister's scruples against the undeserving rich. Like his father, he was always ready 'to be satisfied with the best', and perfectly prepared to eat their food and drink their excellent champagne. He had just been back to Oxford, and had made a valiant showing in debate at the Union Society to reverse the now notorious motion that 'This House is not prepared to fight for King and Country'. He had lost, but Churchill felt that he had acted 'bravely and courageously'. With good father–son relations restored, he could happily enjoy the company of Lady Castlerosse or sample the delights of Monte Carlo.

Churchill appeared entirely oblivious of both. Much of the day he painted in the hot Riviera sun, and after dinner laboured through the small hours on the page proofs of his book about his favourite ancestor.

The first volume of *Marlborough: His Life and Times* appeared in the autumn of 1933 to long and generally enthusiastic reviews. Granted the author's fame and carefully promoted friendships with so many press proprietors, this was not entirely surprising. Despite his exclusion from the Blenheim archives and the attacks upon his ancestor, Lord Macaulay, G. M. Trevelyan generously hailed it as 'a major work upon a major figure of the period'.

Arnold Bennett in the *Express* said that it was 'destined to become one of the great biographies in English literature'. It is interesting that one of the very few dissenting voices came from the great expert on the eighteenth century, Sir Lewis Namier. He thought that Churchill's obsession with attacking Macaulay was excessive, and he objected to a key ingredient in the author's literary method: his habit of placing himself in Marlborough's place and then describing what he would have thought or done himself. The result, said Namier, was 'too much supposition' – and, he might have added, too much Winston Churchill mixed up with the life and the achievements of his ancestor.

Not that this diminished the success or readability of the book, which sold 7,500 copies within a month of publication. But *Marlborough* was not the moneyspinner Churchill hoped for. It did not earn out the large advance his publishers had paid him, yet he was saddled with a mammoth project which would take him years to finish.

Churchill sent presentation copies to his friends – and several of his enemies – in politics. All, of course, were polite in their replies. The Prince of Wales – who was never known to read a book – wrote that he had been unable to put it down, and Stanley Baldwin said how much he envied Winston his 'unrivalled style and command of English'. Baldwin was Prime Minister again, but his admiration for his former Chancellor's literary style did not include rewarding him with the only gift he really wanted – a position in his government.

Churchill was still angrily adding to his enemies by continuing to fight against reform in India. He would not change his attitude to Gandhi and found it 'nauseating' to think of this over-educated Indian 'striding half-naked up the steps of the Viceregal palace . . . to parley on equal terms with the representative of the King Emperor'.

Since Baldwin was irrevocably set on granting India a measure of self-government, this sealed Churchill's fate; the bulldog spirit kept him resolute against Indian reform until 1935, when even he admitted he was beaten. By then he had of course totally destroyed all hopes of Baldwin giving him a post in government. As Lord Salisbury said when asked if he would ever have Lord Randolph Churchill back: 'When you have just got rid of one boil on your neck, why get yourself another?'

Thus 1934 began a dismal period for Churchill. He was out of office, short of money, and increasingly regarded as a played-out figure from the past. That spring he also had a grim reminder of his own mortality. His 'oldest dearest friend', his cousin Sunny, was seriously ill.

Gladys and the spaniels had briefly driven him from Blenheim, but she had finally been persuaded to depart, and both began collecting evidence for their divorce. He set detectives on to her, hoping to prove that she was mad and taking drugs. She set detectives on to him, hoping to prove that he was habitually committing adultery. Hers was the easier task.

By the beginning of 1934, Gladys and her lawyers had a cast-iron case against the Duke, with evidence of Sunny's various affairs, ranging from weekends with Edith Sitwell's sister-in-law, the actress Bunny Doble, to intercourse with call-girls in the backs of taxis. Everything was set for the crowning scandal of poor Sunny's life: a bitter society divorce, with Gladys almost guaranteed to win with heavy damages. Then, in the spring of 1934, Sunny discovered he had cancer and only weeks to live.

For those of the family who knew of the impending divorce, the illness must have seemed a blessing. Sunny's death was now the only way of warding off a further scandal for the Marlboroughs. But Winston was distraught. When his friend Birkenhead had died in 1930, he told Clementine: 'I feel so lonely.' With Sunny gone, he would be lonelier than ever.

Sunny, as expected, died with dignity, spiritually consoled by his confessor Father Martindale, shunning morphine to the last, and even holding a bedside party for his closest friends – including Winston – the day before. A Catholic funeral at Farm Street Church, Mayfair, followed, with the family – Protestant to a man – attending.

As expected, neither Consuelo nor Gladys came. Consuelo was happily at Eze with husband Jacques; Gladys, her plans for a highly profitable divorce frustrated, was facing a straitened future as an ageing duchess. Dreading being seen – except by her dogs – she embarked upon the life of a penurious recluse, which ended forty-three years later in the public ward of an old people's home in Northampton, where she died, still a duchess, aged ninety-six in 1977.

After the Mayfair funeral, Sunny was interred at Blenheim; and following the burial Churchill intoned the formula traditionally used at the death of kings. 'Le duc est mort. Vive le duc!' he shouted. This was typically Churchillian, but a touch excessive as a way of welcoming Sunny's successor, the obtuse and elongated Bert, formerly Lord Blandford and suddenly 10th Duke of Marlborough.

With his meanness and general boorishness, the 10th Duke has his place in the social history of the thirties as *noblesse disoblige* incarnate. He also stands as an example of the Spencer-Churchills at their worst – philistine, bullying and with that extraordinary armadillo skin which could protect them from an everyday awareness of their actions.

In his day, his neighbours vied in collecting 'Bert Marlborough stories', most of which convey the stunning rudeness of the Duke, generally to those beneath him.

There was, for instance, the occasion when an American female guest at Blenheim innocently lit up a cigarette between courses.

'Why are you doing that?' barked His Grace.

'Because I enjoy it,' came the not entirely nonsensical reply.

'Madam,' Bert replied, 'I enjoy fucking, but I don't do it at the dinner-table.'

In 1920 he had married Lord Cadogan's daughter, Mary. A large lady with a pronounced military bearing, she was descended from a Cadogan who had fought with Marlborough at Blenheim; taking after her ancestor, during the Second World War she commanded the women's army forces and was once mistaken for a male general. However, despite her mannish looks, the Duchess gave her husband five children, including the requisite son and heir, Lord Blandford. (Known confusingly as 'Sunny', he was born in 1926.)

She did her best to make Blenheim a happy home for all the children, but with Bert she had her problems. As with his parents, the marriage had effectively been an arranged one and it was no more satisfactory. Bert bullied his well-meaning duchess, was openly unfaithful to her, and had nothing of his father's feeling for the palace.

Churchill liked Mary, and treated Bert with the respect due to a Duke of Marlborough, but when cousin Sunny died, the Blenheim he had known died as well. Churchill was sixty that November, and it must have seemed as if the best of life was over. If only he had been in government, he might have still been happy. Power was the element in which he flourished, and in government he could have acted – but out of government he brooded. Black Dog began to trouble him again; and the more he thought about the future, the more he envisaged an appalling fate before humanity.

Since 1932, German rearmament had troubled him acutely, for with resurgent German militarism he could foresee a repetition of the steps that brought the First World War. The first time this had happened, he had been at the Admiralty with power to create a modern navy. Now he was all too conscious of his impotence – and of the unwillingness of Western governments, especially his own, to halt what he believed to be the march to war. The result for Churchill was a grim depressive's vision of the future.

As former Minister of Munitions, none knew better the awful power of modern mass destruction, and he foresaw another war as a cataclysm for humanity, with massive civilian casualties, horrendous destruction from the air, and the probable collapse, not only of Britain and the Empire, but also of Western civilisation.

In previous spells of prolonged depression, Churchill had always found relief through action and aggression and it is not fanciful to see his furious attacks upon proponents of Indian self-government as a form of therapy against the melancholy afflicting him. Certainly there was little logic in his self-destructive battles over India – or in the grotesque bogy-figure he created from the hated Gandhi. Nor could his India campaign bring a solution to his troubles, still less alleviate the nightmares that obsessed him.

Luckily he still possessed a surer method of escape: diversion into the life and times of the great warrior–statesman with whom he was consorting every night as he laboured on at his biography. More than ever, Marlborough obsessed him. 'I am sick and tired of politics; my heart is in the 18th century,' he told his publisher; and one can feel his envy of the Duke in the dedication which he penned in the luxuriously bound first volume of the biography which he sent George V:

This is the story of how a wise Princess and Queen gave her trust and friendship to an invincible commander, and thereby raised the power and fame of England to a height never before known and never since lost . . . and is submitted in loyal duty to a sovereign, under whom our country has come through perils even more grievous with no less honour.

Had Churchill but possessed the power and position of a modern Marlborough, he was confident that he, too, could conduct his country through its latest 'perils'. Lacking such power entirely, Churchill was forced to adopt a very different role from Marlborough's.

Among the countless articles he wrote around this time were a number of profiles of great men who intrigued him. Most were modern statesmen, but among them stood one very different figure from the past: the prophet Moses. Here, like Marlborough, was another warrior–king–statesman who, late in life, became the saviour of his nation, leading Judaea to greatness in its hour of need. But the emphasis in Churchill's article was not on Moses's victories, but on his afflictions as a prophet.

'Every prophet', Churchill wrote with feeling, 'has to come from civilisation, but every prophet has to go to the wilderness. He must have a strong impression of a complex society and all that it has to give, and then he must serve periods of isolation and meditation. This is the process by which psychic dynamite is made.'

For the prophet Churchill it was uphill work to warn the nation of the nightmare which obsessed him. His party was against him – so was his reputation – as he began to preach the danger of resurgent Germany, the need for toughness in his nation's foreign policy, and his desperate message of rearmament. This was the 'psychic dynamite' that he was brewing; but the prophet's role did not sit easily on his shoulders.

On the surface, life in the Chartwell 'wilderness' could still appear as happy and as enviable as ever. One of the prewar Chartwell secretaries, Grace Hamblin, recalls the deceptively easy-going atmosphere: 'the front-door was rarely locked, even at night, and in the holidays the house was usually full of animals and children'. When feeling particularly relaxed, Churchill would sometimes amble out towards the gates, spot a passer-by, and ask him in to see the fish and chat about the world in general.

But as he wrote, 'When a politician dwells upon the fact that he is rid of public cares and finds serene contentment in private life, it may usually be concluded that he is extremely unhappy.' And when the holidays were over, Churchill could exhibit very different moods at Chartwell. There were times when Miss Hamblin remembers that 'a black cloud seemed to hover round him, and it was best to keep your distance'. In moods like this, he could spend an entire meal sunk in heavy silence.

When visiting Chartwell, his nephew Johnny often found that

lunch was devoted to unrelieved gloom about the international situation. My uncle was convinced that war was inevitable . . . and the depressing conversation used to make William Nicholson [the painter] quite sick. More than once he repeated to me: 'Johnny, I'm going to leave the table on an excuse. I cannot stand it any more.'

To make his gloomy situation worse, Churchill can have found little consolation in the closest members of his family. There was the worry of Diana's marriage, which had finally collapsed: after an unsuccessful spell in an alcoholics' clinic, her husband had agreed to a divorce, with the hearing scheduled for January 1935.

Randolph had become an even greater source of worry, and Churchill was finally admitting to his wife that he could not control him. Randolph had started losing heavily at gambling, and during 1934 Churchill felt obliged to find him £1,500 for gaming debts.

Even his beloved Sarah seemed more the 'Bolshie débutante' than ever. She had come out with her Mitford cousin Unity (recently expelled from several girls' schools in succession), and this maverick Mitford had a disturbing influence upon her cousin. Sarah described how she and Unity used to go to débutante dances, 'but spent much of the time together in the ladies loo, gossiping and playing cards'.

This was emphatically not what Churchill and Clementine desired for their daughter, but there was little they could do about it, especially as Clementine herself was withdrawing more than ever from the family.

She and her husband owed an increasing debt of gratitude to rock-like Moppett Whyte, who continued to perform the practical maternal duties of the family which Clementine continued to reject. Thanks to Miss Whyte, Mary was developing quite differently from the older children – a sunny, uncomplicated, well-behaved small girl who loved her pony, learned her lessons and adored her parents (when she saw them). Thanks also to Miss Whyte, Clementine could spend increasing periods at Morpeth Mansions, the Churchills' London flat, seeing a few close women friends, and keeping clear for days on end from her demanding

Citadel of the Heart

and disruptive family. Her problems were now aggravated by the menopause, and family tensions, like Churchill's moods, could so easily spark off another of her nervous crises.

It became an established pattern that Clementine would come to Chartwell mainly at weekends, and that she and her husband spent longer periods apart. Churchill did not object. As long as he knew that he could count upon her, he could fill every moment of his day – and a large proportion of the night. Separation from her only seemed to make his sentimental heart grow fonder.

23

Distant Friends

In a number of respects Churchill and Adolf Hitler were uncomfortably alike. Both were ruthless men, obsessed with military power and a driving sense of private destiny. Both were self-educated, self-absorbed, intensely nationalistic, and powerfully aggressive in the face of opposition. Both, too, were strongly egocentric characters, overwhelming orators, natural actors and mesmeric talkers, more than capable of dominating those who fell beneath their spell.

In contrast with the ranting demagogue of his public speeches, Hitler in private was reportedly something of a mimic who could amuse his guests and arouse undoubted loyalty from those around him by force of personality. Both he and Churchill were obsessive workers who enjoyed luxurious surroundings, finding their relaxation in painting, speculative monologue and nocturnal screenings of their favourite films. There was even an uncanny similarity in the way the two men both sketched out strongly autobiographical fantasies of their intended paths to power, Churchill in *Savrola* and Hitler in *Mein Kampf*.

In the early years of Hitler's rise to power, there is a sense that this is how Churchill, too, might well have acted had he been a German politician in a similar chaotic situation. Although utterly opposed to fascism in Britain, Churchill was not against dictatorship *per se*. In 1927 after his visit to Italy, he had told Mussolini, 'If I had been an Italian I am sure that I would have been wholeheartedly with you from start to finish in your triumphant struggle against the bestial appetites and passions of Leninism.' As late as October 1937 he was praising Mussolini as 'the Roman genius' and 'the greatest lawgiver among living men'. And in 1935, in an article he wrote on Hitler, he had expressed admiration for 'the courage, the perseverance, and the vital force which enabled him to challenge, defy, conciliate, or overcome all the authorities or resistances which barred his path' in what he called 'his long wearing battle for the German heart'.

Churchill was not over-troubled by the nature of the power that Hitler wielded when he wrote these words; nor even, at this stage, by Hitler's anti-semitism. Both were still matters for the German people.

But, as with the Kaiser at the time of Agadir, what concerned him were the Führer's military ambitions – whether, as he put it in his article, Hitler intended to 'let loose upon the world another war in which civilisation will irretrievably succumb', or instead would choose to restore 'the honour and peace of mind of the great Germanic nation' through the ways of peace.

In his role of prophet, Churchill feared the former. Frustrated by his lack of power, and periodically depressed, it was natural for him to be profoundly pessimistic for the future and to take the gloomiest of views of a resurgent Germany. But this alone fails to explain Churchill's uncanny insight into Hitler's motives and the danger he presented in the years ahead. Churchill was not noted as a judge of character. On the contrary, he was easily impressed by bogus or flamboyant personalities, and often blundered in his personal assessment of people round him.

Yet over Hitler he was unerringly perceptive; and, without sharing Hitler's capacity for evil, Churchill had enough in common with him to appreciate the nature of his power and the scale of his ambitions. Almost alone among major Western politicians, Churchill seemed to understand that, if unchecked, Hitler would lead this new aggressive Germany to war.

He also must have realised the way his own career was rapidly becoming linked with Hitler's. For, however genuine his nightmares of another European conflict, war or the threat of war was almost certainly the only issue likely to bring him back to a place in government.

Even before his anger over Gandhi and India subsided, Churchill's private information service was reporting what was happening in Nazi Germany. This secret information came from various sympathetic sources – including highly placed officials in the Foreign Office, like the young Ralph Wigram and Colonel Desmond Morton, head of the Government's industrial information service. The mysterious colonel – an unmarried former Guards officer and spy – lived in a cottage close to Chartwell, and provided his distinguished neighbour with much of his inside knowledge of Germany's industrial potential and growing power in the air.

There were also other links between Chartwell and Berlin, as relations between certain members of the Churchill family and the higher reaches of the Nazi establishment – Hitler included – suddenly became extremely close.

In 1932, Sarah's cousin and reluctant fellow-débutante, Unity Mitford, had decided that the London social scene was not for her, and made a passionate conversion to Sir Oswald Mosley's newly founded British Union of Fascists. The following year this led her to attend the Nazi Rally in Nuremberg as a dedicated British fascist, and her fate was sealed.

There was a family precedent for Unity's infatuation with all things German. Her grandfather, Lord Redesdale (Lady Blanche's brother-in-law and lover), was a great admirer of Wagner and the racial theories of the anti-semitic Stewart Houston Chamberlain, whose collected works he edited. But Unity, who was barely literate and slightly mad, was not influenced by Lord Redesdale's theories so much as by the whole exciting counter-culture offered by the Nazis. A large, blonde, overgrown schoolgirl, she managed to combine deep hatred for the Jews with a late-adolescent crush on Adolf Hitler. What particularly distinguished Unity was a combination of fanaticism with the sort of dewy-eyed devotion to the Nazis which English maidens traditionally lavish on their ponies or their Labradors. When at the end of 1933 she rented a small flat in Munich to be near 'the darling Führer', the most hardened Nazis were impressed, for none had seen anything quite like this hoydenish relation of Winston Churchill with her gushing dedication to the cause.

She set her heart on meeting Hitler, and sat for days on end in his favourite restaurant, the Osteria Bavaria, at around the time the vegetarian dictator arrived for lunch. With long legs and intent blue eyes, framed by impeccably Aryan blonde hair, Unity was not a presence to be missed. Interest aroused, the Führer enquired who she was and, being told that she was the daughter of a member of the House of Lords, the founder of the Reich invited her for lunch and conversation.

It is unlikely that (as widely rumoured) the Führer ever slept with her. He generally steered clear of physical relationships with the women round him, but he enjoyed her company and found her sufficiently amusing to provoke the jealousy of his one accredited mistress, Eva Braun.

On her side, Unity remained devoted to 'the darling leader', religiously wearing the gold Nazi badge engraved with his signature which he gave her, loyally proclaiming her hatred of the Jews wherever possible and, as some believed, even dreaming of the day when she might marry Hitler and become Empress of a newer, greater Germany.

Churchill had no direct contact at this time with Unity, and seems to have regarded her as one more embarrassing member of his wife's family, of whom the less said the better. (What he would have done had Unity become Frau Hitler remains one of the quainter might-have-beens of history.)

But Unity's close connections with Hitler and the Nazi court helped promote a more serious relationship between the Nazi hierarchy and a close habitué of Chartwell, which would bring considerable embarrassment in years to come. For Unity was accompanied on many of her early trips to Munich by Churchill's favourite Mitford and object of his son Randolph's Etonian infatuation, Unity's sister, the beautiful Diana.

Since the unforgotten days at Chartwell, when she had hung devotedly upon the words of cousin Winston holding forth across the dining table, Diana had developed a growing passion for politics – and in particular a vulnerability for men of power. Her love-affair with Oswald Mosley, the most dominating British politician after Churchill, had ended her marriage with the rich and gentle Bryan Guinness.

Her involvement with her lover coincided with the fateful period of Mosley's life when, impatient with parliamentary politics and strongly influenced by Mussolini and Italian fascism, the former Labour cabinet minister staked his future on the leadership of the British Union of Fascists.

For Diana, love for Mosley naturally involved acceptance of the fascist cause, which in turn brought her closer to Unity. (At the same time it started a lifelong alienation from her sister Jessica, who had decided, with the Mitford taste for passionate extremes, that she was a dedicated communist.)

In Germany, Diana's situation was different from Unity's. She was older than her sister, more intelligent, financially independent, and a well-known figure in society on her own account. She did not live with Mosley until well after the death of his first wife, Cimmie, in 1933; and thus, on her visits to Unity in Munich, she was independent, encountering her sister's friends and the excitements of the Nazi scene on her own terms. Mosley, meanwhile, was fully occupied with organising his own fascist movement back in England, complete with its military-style Blackshirt rallies.

Had she not been who she was, it is unlikely that Hitler would have troubled with Diana as he did. But well-connected twenty-four-year-old aristocratic English beauties sympathetic to the Nazi cause were not exactly common in Munich in 1935, and her links with Churchill and with the influential leader of the British Union of Fascists, clearly made it worth the Führer's while to cultivate her friendship.

The friendship also flourished because Diana found in Hitler something rather similar to what had so impressed her while listening to her cousin Winston. Here was also the same mesmerising flow of talk, the same concern with power, and what she describes as 'that surprising frankness often found in men at the top in contrast with mystery-making nonentities'.

It is hard to tell how much she was being consciously outrageous and how much she secretly enjoyed the dangerous notoriety around the Nazi leader. Hitler could offer those he liked many of the flattering and very tempting benefits of power. There were select luncheon-parties in his flat in Munich, places of honour at the Nazi rallies, and invitations to his private box at gala performances of Wagner at Bayreuth. (When Diana told Hitler that *Parsifal* was her least favourite of all the Wagner operas, he paternally assured her: 'You will find as you get older that you love *Parsifal* more and more.')

When she visited Berlin she would make sure to inform the Führer's secretariat in advance – and soon after her arrival an evening call would follow from Hitler's adjutant, Bruckner. 'Gnädige Frau, wollen Sie zu uns hierüber kommen?' At this, she would stroll from the Kaiserhof Hotel across the Wilhelmplatz to the Reichskanzlei where she would find Hitler sitting, waiting for her by an open fire. She had taught herself fluent German, and she enjoyed listening to him, much as she enjoyed listening to Churchill. She insists that Hitler could be every bit as charming, and sometimes – just like Churchill – he would end the evening with a film-show in his private cinema.

It was very much the off-duty Hitler she was seeing;

and, however improbable, she still insists she found him solicitous, knowledgeable about painting and architecture, and an accomplished raconteur who made her laugh. She was impressed by his peculiarly mesmeric blue eyes, and found no difficulty closing her own to other elements in Nazi Germany. The horrors of the Second World War lay in the future. The treatment of the Jews, the early labour-camps, Hitler's slaughter of his various opponents on the path to power – these were German problems it would have been impolite for a favoured foreign guest to mention, particularly when so many leading Nazis were so exceedingly polite and kind to her. Herr Doctor Goebbels was particularly hospitable, and she found a close friend in his homely and much put-upon wife, Magda.

Befriended by these leading Nazis, Diana felt so confident among them that in the autumn of 1936 she asked a favour which would ultimately appear the crowning blunder in the German adventures of this Mitford cousin of the Churchills.

By 1936 she had set up home with Mosley, and they wished to marry; but with the threats he was receiving from the communists, Mosley feared for Diana's safety if it were known she was his wife. A secret marriage was impossible in Britain, and even in an embassy abroad, news of the ceremony was bound to reach the press. So Diana asked her friend the Führer for assistance.

On 5 October, Sir Oswald Mosley led his Blackshirt followers through the East End of London to be confronted by the anti-fascists in what is still remembered as 'the battle of Cable Street'. In romantic contrast, he then travelled that same night to Germany, and next day was secretly married to Diana by the Berlin registrar. Hitler had personally ensured that no news of the ceremony leaked out to the press. Even energetic Randolph, who suspected what had happened, proved unable to discover any facts.

Magda Goebbels gave the wedding lunch in her home close to the Reichschancellery. The bride wore yellow silk, and her sister Unity was the only member of her family present. Dr Goebbels gave the happy pair a twenty-four-volume set of the works of Goethe. And that evening, at a private dinner, Hitler also gave them both his wedding gift – a signed portrait of himself.

This was the second and the last occasion Hitler and Mosley met, and on the following day the bridegroom returned to London. According to Mosley's son, Nicholas, Diana much later admitted that it had been this contact with Hitler which had ruined his life. In later years, Mosley himself was known to refer to Hitler as 'that dreadful little man'.

But what is so extraordinary about Diana's friendship with the Führer is that it continued right up to the outbreak of the war and in no way seems to have affected her friendship and admiration for her cousin Winston and his family. They remained on close terms, Randolph was still extremely fond of her, and shortly before her marriage Churchill had even given her lunch at his flat in Morpeth Mansions.

The food was simpler than at the luncheon-parties she was used to in the Führer's flat in Munich, but there were guests she knew and whose company she enjoyed. Apart from Clementine, there was Lord Ivor Churchill, and her cousin Sarah who 'dashed in from a dancing lesson'.

One might have thought Diana's fascism and her friendship with Hitler and the leading Nazis would have been one subject which was totally taboo among them all. Instead, as lunch proceeded, she soon discovered 'that simply everyone from Winston down, longed to hear any detail I could give them about Hitler'.

From Churchill there was no suggestion that it might be ill-considered – let alone dangerous – to have Hitler as a friend. On the contrary, 'Winston only wanted to hear about Hitler', recalls Diana, but while telling him all she knew, she says she had a strong impression that he was 'already looking on him as a personal rival'.

Finally she told him they should meet. She could easily arrange it. 'You would be captivated by him if you knew him,' she assured him.

'Oh, no. *No!*' the great man growled.

For Churchill, the rise to power of Hitler marked a time of growing tension in politics and in his private life, and the bull-like figure and the brooding features seemed to be reflecting his powerful preoccupations. He was increasingly concerned with danger from the air. Most experts, Professor Lindemann included, believed that 'the bomber would get through'. Studying what proved to be exaggerated estimates of German airpower from Colonel Morton, Churchill was convinced that war with

Germany would spell the death of at least a million civilians in London alone from aerial bombardment.

At the same time, lacking a ministerial salary, and with the costs of Chartwell to be met, he was working as even he had never worked before to make ends meet. On top of his weekly journalism, there was his never-ending life of Marlborough, which had now expanded into its third volume with no appreciable end in sight.

His best hope of solving his financial problems seemed to lie in the cinema. The film magnate Alexander Korda had offered him £10,000 to prepare a film biography of George V to be shown at his Jubilee in 1935. Churchill had gratefully accepted.

One might have thought a man with such a load of work and worry was a man who needed all the support and sympathy of a devoted spouse – particularly one like Clementine, who once formed her life around his great career. But this was not entirely the case. As he explained in *Painting as a Pastime* two years earlier, he had evolved what he believed to be the perfect method of avoiding mental strain and psychological fatigue. The secret lay in giving the brain fresh interest and activities through constant change. The more variety the better for the overburdened brain cells – a private recipe he increasingly adhered to as his workload grew. With his determined powers of concentration, he could fill his days – and much of his nights – with obsessive and obsessional activity: writing, talking, painting, building the interminable wall around his garden, and planning further drastic alterations to the Chartwell landscape.

All were pursued with total self-absorption, keeping him happy and productive. They also made him largely self-reliant – and very boring to his wife. The ministrations of a valet and the close attention of a stenographer were all he really needed (apart from the regular productions of his cook) for days on end of preoccupied contentment.

That left Clementine in a superfluous position, like the wives of many chronic workaholics. He undoubtedly loved her, as he always sentimentally assured her in the letters which he wrote when they were parted. But much of her life with him was unromantic and distinctly unrewarding.

Whatever he might write about each day being like a holiday, it was very much a solitary vacation. His painting was a private pleasure; so were his enthusiastic plans for Chartwell. Clementine continued to dislike the house and she was not the sort of wife to share the joys of laying bricks.

Nor was politics the absorbing interest they had shared in the past. She was growing tired of the ceaseless battles which unfailingly aroused her husband's energies. Still a Liberal at heart, she showed little solidarity for his last-ditch stand on India – nor did she want to get deeply involved with Germany or the unthinkable prospect of another war in Europe.

Despite his glaring faults, Randolph remained his father's faithful ally in politics. He shared his angriest and most reactionary beliefs and was always desperate to be his public champion. Clementine was not.

In 1934, Clementine was forty-nine, an attractive woman with a distinctly limited interest in her family and a sense that youth was running out. To keep her happy, an overburdened Churchill agreed to the 'enforced interruption' of a month's holiday with her aboard Lord Moyne's luxurious motor-yacht *Rosaura* in the eastern Mediterranean, visiting the beauty-spots of Syria and Egypt.

This holiday proved a considerable success – not least because Churchill was able to start work on the script for Alexander Korda – and Clementine conceived a taste for more ambitious foreign travel. This owed a great deal to the amenities of *Rosaura*, and also to the charm and interests of their extremely wealthy host.

Moyne was an old friend of Churchill. Chips Channon described him as 'an extraordinary man, colossally rich, well-meaning, intelligent, scrupulous, yet a viveur, and the only modern Guinness to play a social or political role'.

He could be a generous if eccentric host, who spent large amounts of money on long sea-voyages, and who was planning a four-month winter voyage to the Pacific to bring back specimens of the Sumatran giant lizard for the London Zoo. The Churchills were invited.

A four-month absence from work and politics was unthinkable for Churchill, but Clementine was keen to go. According to Sarah, she had been ill again – but was well enough to travel. Solicitous as ever, Churchill agreed, and two days after Christmas the family waved her off aboard the boat train from Victoria. *En route* to Messina where she was due to embark aboard *Rosaura*, she wrote tenderly to Churchill, saying how much she loved her 'sweet and darling Winston' and telling him not to be vexed with his vagabond Kat. 'She has gone off to the jungle with her tail in the air, but she will return presently to her basket and curl down comfortably.'

Busy as ever, Churchill was a more devoted correspondent than his wife during the five months they were parted. Lengthy news-bulletins were conscientiously dictated and despatched from Chartwell, giving a detailed picture of both Mr Pig's activities and what was happening to members of the family – particularly to Randolph.

But, reading them on deck aboard Lord Moyne's luxurious motor-yacht as it cruised its way through warm seas and enchanted islands, the 'vagabond Kat', all signs of illness rapidly forgotten, can have felt little but relief at being so far away from the turmoil of her distant family. Her own replies were sparse – on several occasions Churchill felt obliged to cable her for news – and, when she did write, hers were very much the letters of a wayward wife: hurried, detached and with those flashes of solicitude guilty wives so often use with absent husbands.

Clementine had found another interest on her voyage apart from the temples of Bali and the Sumatran giant lizard, whose capture remained the ostensible objective of the trip.

Moyne had his current mistress on the voyage; his son, Kenelm, had his wife; and Moyne, the perfect host, had also provided Clementine with a companion for the journey. He was a forty-two-year-old bachelor called Terence Philip, who was director of the London branch of Knoedlers, the New York art dealers. Born in Russia, Philip was a handsome cosmopolitan, charming, witty, and a friend of Lord Ivor Churchill. Living in the close familiarity of the ship, it is not surprising that Clementine fell romantically in love.

Clementine had always had a strong romantic streak, and she had reached what Balzac called 'that dangerous time of life when women realise that it is possible to grow old'. It must have been reassuring to receive the close attention of a handsome younger man, particularly one like Philip who could offer her those very things which Churchill had so little time for – trivia and gossip and some light relief from the doom that hung so heavily upon mankind. She would have been less than human had she not hankered after a simpler, happier way of life, freed from the tensions and the constant worries of an ageing superhuman husband and a largely unrewarding family.

What she cannot have known is that her love for the attractive Terence Philip posed no danger to her marriage. For the charming Terence Philip was what was known in prewar social parlance as a 'society tame cat'. Rumoured to be discreetly homosexual, he enjoyed the company of women, particularly of slightly older women, and like many of his sort fulfilled a most important social role. Very much a gentleman, he could be invited anywhere – and as a spare man safely entrusted with anybody's wife or daughter. Women might fall in love with him, but he would never fall in love with them. This seems to have been what happened during Clementine's brief romantic interlude.

Interestingly in his letters Churchill showed no sign of jealousy or concern at the presence aboard *Rosaura* of handsome Mr Philip. This suggests that the worldly Moyne had made the situation clear to him in advance, as one would with a friend in such circumstances. On the other hand, Mr Pig did miss his Kat. He had been, he told her, 'sometimes a little depressed about politics and would have liked to have been comforted by you'. He had not grudged her her 'long excursion', as he called it, 'but now I do want you back', he wrote at the beginning of April 1935.

She responded as she knew she had to, telling him how much she loved him, 'and that I long to be folded in your arms'.

Doubtless by now she did, for there must have been a sense of comfortable relief to be returning to the familiar, if turbulent, world of Mr Pig.

In fact many of his present troubles seemed to be coming from Clementine's side of the family. 'Bad blood,' the Churchills would mutter knowingly among themselves, recalling Lady Blanche with her promiscuity and drink and compulsive gambling, and Clementine's brother, Bill, who had killed himself. Now they had her sister Nellie and her children to contend with.

It is a moot point how much Churchill's influence and example were unwittingly to blame for what occurred to one of the Romilly children. He had always been extremely kind to his sister-in-law, welcoming her and the boys for their holidays at Chartwell, and taking a particular interest in her tough and argumentative younger son, Esmond. When Esmond declared himself a Jacobite, and a passionate believer in the Stuart cause, Churchill was amused and started referring to him at Chartwell as 'the White Rose'. Esmond enjoyed his uncle's company: indeed,

his biographer believes that he came to adopt him as a sort of
father-figure in place of the ailing Colonel Romilly. Certainly,
before long the fifteen-year-old schoolboy was displaying a suspicious number of Churchillian qualities in a most precocious and
uncomfortable form. So much so that his cousin Nancy Mitford
(who dismissed him as 'a giggling little anarchist') could not resist
spreading the rumour that the Romilly boys had been fathered by
their uncle Winston. Like the similar rumour involving Brendan
Bracken, this was totally untrue. (Apart from anything else, the
dates of possible conception fail to coincide with the movements
of Churchill and his sister-in-law.) Nevertheless, Esmond conducted himself like a left-wing version of his cousin Randolph,
with the same unsquashable temperament and much the same
uncaring toughness. Like Randolph at the same age, Esmond
was exceptionally full of himself and something of a bully. During
one Christmas holiday at Chartwell, he had attempted to cure
his cousin Mary of her faith in Jesus by holding her head in a
bowl of water until she provisionally agreed that she was not a
Christian. (Having developed something of a masochistic streak,
she later admitted she 'had been rather in love with him'.) Then,
at his public school, his reaction against established values took
a more dramatic turn.

Rejecting the strict regime of Wellington College, Esmond
suddenly decided he was a communist and founded a schoolboy's
revolutionary magazine called *Out of Bounds*, extolling Soviet
Russia, pacifism and teenage masturbation in roughly that order.
Esmond possessed his uncle's ability to shock and make a nui-
sance of himself for any cause that he believed in. He also had a
marked flair for publicity. Copies of *Out of Bounds* soon reached
the press, and the *Daily Mail* erupted with headlines denouncing
the 'Red Menace in Public Schools!' and 'Moscow's Attempts to
Corrupt Our Public Schoolboys'. According to the *Daily Mail*,
Scotland Yard was just about to swoop on the subversives at
Wellington.

But, before this could happen, Esmond Romilly decamped –
again with maximum publicity, much of which inevitably centred
on the fact that it was 'Mr Churchill's 15-year-old nephew' who
had vanished.

In fact 'Winston's Red Nephew', as the press henceforth
referred to him, was acting much as a teenage Churchill might
have done in similar circumstances. Like his uncle, Esmond was

'A modern prince, taking his inheritance for granted.' The twenty-first birthday portrait of Randolph Churchill by Sir Philip László.

Diana with her first husband, John Bailey. Later she told her daughter that she married chiefly to escape the endless talk at the Chartwell dinner table. The marriage lasted barely a year.

'A woman like you could be worth a whole world to a man,' said Trotsky of Churchill's romantic cousin, Clare Sheridan. Here she is seen with her children.

Churchill's least favourite son-in-law – the Austro-American comedian Vic Oliver, with his wife Sarah (*right*) and Phyllis Luckett, the young actress whom the Svengali-like comedian wished them to adopt.

The Cecil Beaton picture which brought Clementine to a state of 'near hysteria', when a friend told her that it made her look 'like a hard-bitten virago who takes drugs'.

Pamela Churchill with Winston Churchill junior in 1943 when her marriage was already under strain. When she reminded Randolph that Winston was her son, her husband bellowed, 'No! My son. I'm a Churchill.'

The US President's personal representative, Averell Harriman, the British Foreign Secretary, Anthony Eden, and the US Ambassador to Britain, John 'Gil' Winant. All three would be romantically involved with members of the Churchill family.

Churchill and Clementine may have been hoping that their daughter Mary would wed a prince, but her marriage to Captain Christopher Soames in 1947 brought a key new personality into the family.

Sarah with her second husband Anthony Beauchamp shortly after their marriage at Sea Island, Georgia, in 1949. 'If you think that by insulting him you can change by one jot the opinion I hold of him, you are most sorely mistaken,' she had told her father.

Churchill, 'at peace within his habitation', in the Chartwell garden surrounded by three generations of his family. (*From left to right*) Duncan Sandys with his wife Diana and their son Julian, the two eldest Soames children Emma and Nicholas, then Winston Churchill junior and Clementine with his sister Arabella, and their father, Randolph.

Onassis drives Sir Winston. The Greek multi-millionaire became Churchill's favourite host when he was in his eighties, and for Onassis Churchill was 'the big fish' who added immensely to his prestige.

'I'm not an alcoholic. I'm a dipsomaniac. I love the stuff,' said Sarah, seen here outside her favourite bar in Rome in the 1960s.

In adversity the dynasty continues. Shortly before his dismissal from his post as Opposition spokesman on defence in 1979, young Winston Churchill and his wife Minnie stand with their son Randolph before the Parliament Square statue of Winston Churchill.

immensely tough and obsessed by politics and action. Predictably, he and his friend Philip Toynbee (who described him as 'a short, square, dirty figure with a square white face and sweaty hair') soon decided they must join the fight against fascism.

This took various youthful forms. In June 1934 they armed themselves with knuckledusters and were forcibly ejected from Sir Oswald Mosley's first mass rally of the British Union of Fascists at Olympia. For much of the summer, Esmond was writing a book to spread his revolutionary message to other schoolboys, which he entitled, like his magazine, *Out of Bounds*. And just before Christmas he was once more in the news.

Nellie Romilly, shocked and horrified by her lamb's behaviour, had panicked and decided to disown him. Esmond was not merely out of bounds but out of all control, and after a drunken late-night foray to his mother's house in Pimlico he and Toynbee were arrested. The following day, both boys appeared before the West End magistrate.

Toynbee's father, the historian Arnold Toynbee, spoke up for Philip and offered sureties for good behaviour, thus securing his release. But no one was there to speak for Esmond. Churchill could have done so but refused. By now he had had more than enough of his communist nephew – who on Christmas Eve received a fortnight's sentence to a home for juvenile delinquents. While there, his cousin Diana Churchill was the only member of the family to visit him.

24

Two Love-Affairs

Despite the behaviour of his wife's young relations, one might have thought that Churchill could find harmony and peace within the bosom of his own devoted family. Sadly, this was not the case. However much he needed a united family at this time of setback and frustration, on the whole he failed to get it.

After her long cruise and her unsatisfactory romance with Terence Philip, Clementine had no alternative but to return to Churchill. Yet she was soon longing to get away again. 'It's very nice being back but, oh dear, I want to start out again,' she told a friend. She would never manage another four-month foreign voyage away, but with Moppett Whyte still looking after fourteen-year-old Mary and the day-to-day running of Chartwell, she could at least resume her independent life in London and continue to insist upon the breaks she needed from her marriage.

Diana was little help to her father, either. Finally divorced from her alcoholic husband, her own miserable marriage had left her feeling guilty and unsettled. And Randolph's hero-worship of his father did not prevent him causing Churchill much anxiety and occasionally acute embarrassment.

Even before Clementine returned from Indonesia, early in 1935, Randolph was embroiled in a typical adventure which had added to his father's problems. He had been sent to report a by-election in the Liverpool constituency of Wavertree. Until his arrival, Wavertree had been the safest of safe Tory seats, with the official candidate certain to defeat his Labour challenger. But Randolph changed all that. Profoundly disagreeing with the official Conservative, he instantly decided to stand against him as a rival Tory, and enjoyed himself immensely, trumpeting his father's policies and winning the press support of Beaverbrook and Rothermere. As a result, the right-wing vote was split so neatly that Conservative Wavertree returned a Labour member for the first time in its history.

Randolph remained undaunted, but the Conservative high command in London was enraged, blaming Churchill for his son's behaviour. This was hardly fair, since Churchill had attempted to dissuade him from standing, and had then supported him only from paternal loyalty. But few believed this, and Randolph had seriously added to his father's troubles with his party, at a time when he was not in need of further troubles.

Randolph was now in his stride politically. Undeterred – and unrepentant – he proceeded to sponsor another independent Tory candidate in another safe Conservative constituency, at Norwood in Surrey. This proved even more ill-judged than Wavertree. Randolph's candidate was a notorious ex-fascist; Churchill was so infuriated with his son's behaviour that he temporarily banned him from the house; and Randolph's candidate, despite support from rich eccentric Lady Houston, duly came bottom of the poll.

However, for the Churchill family, the Norwood by-election did bring one unexpected bonus. Randolph had taken Diana to help with the campaign and, although he lost the by-election, Diana found herself a husband – none other than the winner, a tall red-headed young ex-diplomat called Duncan Sandys. They married late that summer, and Churchill was particularly pleased – for he had got not only a son-in-law, but also what he had hoped to find in Randolph, a young and vigorous supporter in the House of Commons. Then, as Diana's life seemed sorted out at last, came trouble from an unexpected quarter: Sarah.

Despite her début as a 'Bolshie débutante' and the influence of her cousin Unity, by the age of twenty-one Sarah had given every sign of contentedly accepting life with her parents' blessing. She once described herself as 'stage-struck since I was in socks'; and her parents, indulging her passion for the theatre, had allowed her to start professional dancing lessons in London with a friend called Jenny Nicholson.

Miss Nicholson was grand-daughter of Churchill's friend, the painter Sir William Nicholson, a frequent visitor to Chartwell. Sir William was not just an artist, but also a gentleman; and, if he felt it safe for Jenny to study dancing, it must be safe for Sarah, too – particularly as Jenny said that she could share her flat and had promised to keep an eye on her in London.

Churchill was in certain ways the most innocent of men, particularly where his beloved family was involved. Great events concerned him, but the small change of the social scene had always bored him.

In contrast with the 'rollickingly bumptious' Randolph, Sarah had always seemed predictable. She had escaped the awkwardness and shyness of Diana, and was exuberant and full of fun. With bright red hair and fine complexion, she was almost beautiful. She was very conscious that her nose, inherited from Clementine, was just a shade too long (later she would have it fixed), but this had done nothing to scare off a succession of extremely nice young men who duly fell in love with her.

One of the nicest was the young Harry Llewellyn, who had just come down from Cambridge. Son of a landowning Welsh baronet, he was already a splendid horseman. (As Sir Harry Llewellyn with his super-equine Foxhunter, he would become an Olympic gold medallist and the most celebrated show-jumper of his generation.) Sarah visited the Llewellyn home in Wales, and Sir Harry still has sentimental memories of her. 'With her beautiful red hair tied up in a bun under a bowler hat, she was a nice horsewoman, and she would really have a go out hunting.'

Sarah appeared virginal, safely unintellectual, and devoted to her famous father. There seemed every reason to believe that in a year or two she would behave as a gently born young ex-débutante was expected to behave, and marry, if not young Llewellyn, then some other suitable young man, preferably with a title and certainly with money. In the meantime those simple dancing lessons with Miss Nicholson kept her occupied and out of trouble.

But Sarah was not as placid or predictable as she seemed, and beneath her agreeable exterior lurked the teenager who was so put out by rich old Maxine Elliot at her villa in the South of France. Sarah preferred the unconventional, the free and the artistic. Above all, she loved the theatrical people she was meeting now through Jenny Nicholson and her dancing teacher.

In a sense, it was Churchill's fault that things turned out the way they did – although to be fair, he had weightier matters on his mind than Sarah's future when, in October 1935, she applied for an audition with the West End impresario C. B. Cochran for a part in his current theatrical revue, *Follow the Sun*.

Mussolini's war in Abyssinia was threatening to spread to Europe. German rearmament, particularly in the air, was obsessing Churchill, and in less than three weeks' time there would be a British general election. There was always the chance that, if the Conservatives won their expected victory, Stanley Baldwin might decide to offer Winston office. (They did, but he did not.)

Had Churchill been a little less preoccupied and a little more informed about theatrical society, he might have sensed the possible effect of C. B. Cochran and the world around him on his daughter.

For Sarah was secretly more ambitious than she seemed. Like Randolph, she longed for a success that would impress her father. She was fame-struck from an early age, and the stage appeared the shortest route to stardom.

Cochran was an old-style theatrical survivor, a producer–impresario who had tried everything from rodeo and roller-skating to representing the queen of the French music-hall, Mistinguett, and producing Noël Coward. Coward's musicals had saved him from bankruptcy, since when he had been shrewd enough to spot the potential of a certain social cachet in his shows.

A thoroughgoing snob, he had invented a new-style chorus girl of class and breeding and renamed his chorus line 'Mr Cochran's Young Ladies'. Some were, some emphatically were not, but Sarah wished to join them.

To have Winston Churchill's daughter in his show would be a coup, but Cochran was a realist who knew the dangers that ensue when nice young ladies come in contact with the manifold temptations of the stage. Cochran also knew Churchill rather well, having been general manager of a show of Jennie's at Earls Court just before the war called *Shakespeare's England*. The show had flopped, but Cochran's friendship with the great man's mother had survived until her death. So he wrote to Churchill, saying that Sarah had asked for an audition and requesting his consent.

I pointed out to her that she can only learn the necessary experience to become a star by learning her job in the smallest capacity which, as she fancies light musical shows rather than straight plays without music, means chorus, with perhaps a tiny part or so.

Churchill replied with equal courtesy, saying – somewhat surprisingly – that he had no objection to his daughter pursuing a career as a professional dancer 'at this period of her life', but there were two interesting discrepancies in the correspondence. Churchill made a definite point of saying that Sarah should 'play under a stage name'. Cochran never mentioned this, and in fact she never did; her theatrical career would always have the full publicity that went with being Winston Churchill's daughter. More important was Cochran's reference to Sarah's ambition to become a star. This was very different from her father's view of her dancing as something that would simply occupy her 'at this period of her life'.

Sarah duly had her audition – and Cochran offered her the 'tiny part' he promised. *Follow the Sun* included a short up-market ballet sequence choreographed by Frederick Ashton and based on Osbert Sitwell's parody of an Edwardian shooting party 'The First Shoot'. The music was by William Walton, the scenery and costumes by Cecil Beaton; and Sarah, suitably attired by Beaton, had to imitate a wounded pheasant.

Follow the Sun was an uncertain step on Sarah's road to stardom. The true star of the show was the comedian Vic Oliver, for whom it proved a most successful London début. Born in Vienna thirty-eight years before, son of Baron von Samek, a Jewish clothing manufacturer from Brünn, young von Samek had trained at the Vienna Conservatoire of Music under Gustav Mahler before leaving for the States to seek his fortune as a concert pianist. He dropped the 'von', while touring the States with dance-bands, but it was not until he renamed himself Vic Oliver that he found success in the last role he really wanted – that of a stand-up comic cracking jokes in fractured Brooklyn Viennese at the Old Palace Theater in New York.

Vic Oliver was profoundly serious, a workaholic and, like many professional comedians, entirely devoid of humour. He was also a womaniser, twice married, with a relinquished but still legal second wife in Austria and a devoted mistress in New York.

His taste in women was unusual. Seeing himself as a theatrical Svengali, he was attracted to beautiful but serious young women whose potential he alone could spot, and whose career as artists he alone could foster. When he met Sarah in her nightly struggles as a wounded pheasant, the outcome was inevitable – a suave Svengali had met an all too eager Trilby.

Sarah described herself in this period as 'a father-girl' (which with Churchill's influence is not surprising), and confessed to a taste for older, wiser men. Vic Oliver, eighteen years her senior, was both father-figure and a star – an elegant Central European with the sophisticated knowledge of the world that sheltered Sarah lacked. He was also undoubtedly impressed by everything that Churchill represented and always held him in immense respect. Whether the social and professional advantages of marrying the great man's daughter attracted him as well is debatable. If they did, the illusion cannot have lasted long.

It was a swift passionate romance, with the awakened Sarah showing all the ardour of a young girl in her first real love-affair. *Follow the Sun* opened in London in November, and by December she and Vic were sufficiently in love to talk of marriage. By now they were together all the time, and within the theatrical world their secret could not stay concealed for long.

The actress Ellen Pollock remembers lunching with Vic Oliver at the Carlton Grill where he confided that he 'could be marrying into a most unusual family before too long'. She had already heard rumours about Sarah, so asked him outright if she was the girl. When he admitted it, she asked if he was in love with her. 'I *think* I am,' he said. Later, Sarah joined them, and Miss Pollock knew that nothing would stop Sarah marrying the man she loved – not even Winston Churchill.

At the start of 1936, Churchill was under increasing pressure from almost every quarter. Hitler, now firmly in power in Germany, had reoccupied the Rhineland; Churchill, totally convinced that a European war was inevitable, had got over Gandhi, and was stepping up his own campaign to tell the nation of the Nazi danger and the need for serious rearmament. A majority of his fellow-Conservatives distrusted and disliked him, but his influence was growing. Impressive as ever in Parliament, he still hoped that Baldwin, who had invited him to join a secret official committee on defence, would appoint him to the one post in the Government he wanted – that of minister for overall defence co-ordination.

As well as keeping up his parliamentary duties, speeches, meetings and committees, he was working almost every night until two and three in the morning on his biography of Marlborough – this on top of his weekly journalism, by which he 'laid the golden eggs' which paid the bills for Chartwell, more or less. It was a workload to floor any man, but Churchill seemed to thrive on it. ('The well flows freely,' he told Clementine. 'Only the time is needed to draw water from it.')

It was those around him who tended to collapse. That summer his secretary, Violet Pearman, suffered a stroke brought on by years of overwork. This workload did not help the Churchill marriage, either. Clementine was once more feeling the urge to get away from the tensions of her married life, and that February found her enjoying an extended holiday in Austria with Mary and with Jack and Goonie's daughter, Clarissa. Clementine enjoyed skiing, and after years of opting out of her maternal role discovered a closeness with her youngest daughter which she had never had with any of her other children.

Clementine's absence meant that when Sarah broached the news that she was in love with Vic Oliver and wished to marry him, Churchill had to cope with it alone. Even today there cannot be that many overburdened politicians who would respond with sympathy to the news that their favourite daughter wished to wed a twice-married foreign comedian eighteen years her senior. For Churchill it was quite unthinkable, and he responded as he always did when anything he loved was threatened: his aggression roused, he fought, with every means that lay within his power.

There was more bullying than subtlety from him in the days that followed. Vic Oliver was summoned to Morpeth Mansions. Churchill refused to shake hands with him. That evening he wrote to Clementine that Oliver was 'common as dirt', with a 'horrible mouth and foul Austro-Yankee drawl'. Churchill had treated him accordingly, telling him that should he dare persist with the engagement he would issue 'an immediate public statement which would be painful to them both'.

Vic Oliver seems to have acted rather well in this awkward situation. Summoning what dignity he could, he agreed to Churchill's terms: a year apart, after which there would be no further family opposition to the marriage if they still wanted it.

As a man of honour, the son of Baron Samek gave his word; and, as a man unusually accustomed to getting his way where *his* honour was concerned, the grandson of the Duke of Marlborough must have felt the worst was over.

But Churchill still had to deal with Sarah, which he did a few days later in his study at Chartwell. He tried to bully her as he did her lover. According to her own account, she was 'addressed like a public meeting' on the perils of marriage with this 'itinerant vagabond'. Then with a fine dramatic touch he produced his British passport. 'In three or four years,' he said prophetically, 'you may be married to the enemy, and I shall not be able to protect you once you have lost this.'

Sarah saw his point, and the interview ended with her promising that she would not marry Vic Oliver until he had American citizenship. Churchill thought that he had won.

'I think I have put her off,' he said afterwards, smiling at Diana.

'On the contrary,' his eldest daughter said. 'I think you have chased her away.'

Not for nothing was Sarah known in the family as 'the Mule', having inherited all the Churchill obstinacy behind her carefree manner. She was in no way party to the gentlemanly agreement between her father and her lover, and had not the faintest intention of abiding by it – even though Vic Oliver, keeping to his word, swiftly departed for a fresh theatrical engagement in New York.

By now, Clementine, refreshed and rested from her winter holiday, was on the scene and able to take over Sarah's problems. Clementine's tactics were subtler than her husband's.

Both Sarah and her mother were early risers, and often breakfasted together, enjoying the view across the Chartwell gardens to the woods beyond. Clementine had always found it hard to break through her emotional reserve with Sarah and Diana, and since her return had kept off any serious discussion of Vic Oliver. But finally, at breakfast, Clementine brought herself to make what Sarah later called 'an extraordinary suggestion'. After saying that the marriage was bound to end in disaster, Clementine proposed that if Sarah promised to abandon Vic for ever she could have the total freedom her 'strong personality' needed – her own flat in London, and no questions asked.

Sarah was deeply shocked by what struck her as the 'immorality' of what her strait-laced mother was suggesting, and refused to discuss the subject any further.

During the weeks that followed, Clementine invited several presentable young men as weekend guests at Chartwell but Sarah made it clear she was not interested. The subject of her love for Vic was no longer mentioned in the family. By August, when Churchill departed for his painting holiday in

France, he and Clementine believed their daughter's infatuation
was forgotten.

Had it been left to Vic Oliver, it probably would have been. His
career in vaudeville was booming in the States, and he was now
rehearsing for the starring role in a new revue, opening in Boston
and then moving on to Loew's State Theater on Broadway. He
was deeply preoccupied, as he always was before a show; and,
although his previous affair had ended when he met Sarah, there
was no shortage of pretty girls in Boston.

But Churchill's daughter was not a girl to be discarded.
Throughout that summer she had been in constant touch with
Vic Oliver in America, begging him to let her join him in
New York.

As she pointed out, she had made no promises not to see *him*,
and he finally relented, sending her a ticket to New York aboard
SS *Bremen*.

Had Churchill been at Chartwell that September day in 1936,
events could not have happened as they did. Sarah found it hard
to lie to him, and he would have guessed what she was up to.
But once again he was holidaying apart from Clementine in the
South of France, painting, enjoying an occasional flutter at the
tables in Monte Carlo, and basking in the familiar comforts of the
Château de l'Horizon. He then planned to head north, as guest of
the French High Command, for a brisk tour of inspection round
the Maginot Line at Metz.

Clementine, who remained at Chartwell, was less perceptive
than her husband over Sarah and did not realise that she
had visited the bank and withdrawn all her worldly wealth
– which amounted to a little over £4. When Sarah told her
she would be spending the night in London at the flat in
Morpeth Mansions, and visiting her hairdresser next morning,
she suspected nothing.

Sarah caught an evening train from Westerham to London,
then stayed at Morpeth Mansions. But next morning, instead of
going to the hairdresser, she took a cab to Waterloo. Photographs
taken of her later that morning show her looking very young and
pretty and distinctly flustered as she tried to cope with suitcase,
passport and the enormity of what she was about to do.

At Waterloo station she was met by Jenny Nicholson, who was
now in the cabaret at the Dorchester Hotel. They had little time
together as the boat train for Southampton left at nine-thirty. As

she boarded it and kissed her friend goodbye, Sarah handed her a letter.

'Be sure to give this to my mother.'

'Certainly,' said Miss Nicholson.

However, as the train pulled out with Sarah waving from the window, Miss Nicholson decided otherwise. Instead of facing Clementine in person, she had Sarah's letter sent by train to Westerham, then telephoned a reporter friend on the *Daily Express*. This explains the presence of a press photographer by the gang-plank of SS *Bremen* at Southampton later that morning as Sarah embarked in the German liner for New York. It also explains how the *Express* for Wednesday, 16 September carried an exclusive interview with Miss Nicholson about Sarah's love-affair under the front-page headline 'Miss Sarah Churchill Elopes to the USA'.

It was romantic and exciting, but the lovers underestimated Churchill's wrath. Even now things might just have turned out differently, had it not been for Jenny Nicholson's passion for publicity.

The letter Sarah had written Clementine had been carefully worded to appeal to her heart. 'Please don't be worried – please don't be sad. I will keep you fully informed of my whereabouts and plans. . . . My love to you, darling Mummy.' She even added a postscript begging Clementine to use her calming influence upon her father. 'Please make Papa understand.' Once the elopement was splashed across the papers, any chance of 'making Papa understand' was over. Battle started.

Events now took a fascinating turn, revealing just how contradictory Churchill could be in a human crisis. By a strange coincidence, these autumn weeks of 1936 saw him suddenly involved with two romantic muddles, both concerning people he was deeply fond of.

Just as Sarah was steaming off aboard the SS *Bremen* with the scandal in the daily papers, a far greater scandal was about to break. The love-affair between Edward VIII and his married mistress, Mrs Ernest Simpson from Baltimore, was on the point of turning from an open secret in society into the gravest crisis to afflict the monarchy since the far-off days of George IV. The foreign press, particularly in America, was full of it, and although the British press proprietors had been loyally shielding the British public from the dreadful news, Churchill had known from early 1936 that his monarch, like his daughter, was passionately in love.

Churchill had long been an admirer and friend of Edward's. During his years as Prince of Wales, the King's youthful glamour and apparent deep concern for his empire had convinced the statesman that in his future monarch he had something of a fellow-spirit. They often met, and earlier that year Churchill had been introduced to Mrs Simpson at Fort Belvedere. He had subsequently had several opportunities of observing them together.

There were in fact some striking similarities between the royal love-affair and Sarah's: both involved unmarried adults bent on union with twice-married foreigners who themselves were in the throes of a divorce; both marriages, in different ways, appeared 'unsuitable'; and in both Churchill felt impelled to intervene. What is fascinating is the extraordinary difference in his behaviour towards his daughter and his King.

With Sarah he reacted like the heaviest of high-Victorian fathers; as she complained bitterly in a letter to her mother, no allowances at all were made for her feelings or for the man she loved. He was simply 'treated as a low adventurer'.

When the story broke in the *Express*, Churchill was still in France, but he promptly ordered Randolph, of all people, to Southampton in his place, sent him a first-class ticket for the *Queen Mary*, and told him to bring his sister safely home and to her senses. Churchill the man of action was in fact creating a new drama which Randolph and the press would make the most of.

Queen Mary was twenty-two hours behind the *Bremen*, and with Randolph now in hot pursuit the elopement instantly became a front-page story as well as a patriotic race between the German and the British transatlantic liners. A mid-Atlantic hurricane heightened the suspense; but *Bremen* kept her lead, and by the time she docked more than fifty newsmen were in readiness to interview 'Winston Churchill's daughter, the runaway débutante' in person.

It was a good example of how to turn a private crisis into a very public spectacle, which Churchill, with a lifetime's experience of dealing with the press, should have avoided. Sarah, actress that she was, handled the reporters rather well. On the unlikely advice of one of her fellow-passengers, Randolph's *bête noire*,

Lady Astor, she called an impromptu press conference aboard the ship. Flustered but very pretty with her red hair and a pale blue dress, she dispensed much English charm but little in the way of her intentions.

Nor did Vic Oliver, who had already been given the full treatment by the press. He had been most correct, denying any plans of instant marriage – which was true, since his previous marriage was still in the final stage of its dissolution. Randolph, however, showed up rather badly as he usually did when confronted by reporters. As *Queen Mary* docked, he was met by his anxious-looking sister and half the press corps of New York.

'I'm here to take Sarah home. It simply won't do,' he blustered.

'But does she want to go?' somebody enquired.

'*That* makes no difference. Sarah's too young to know her own mind.'

But Sarah emphatically did know her mind – and Randolph departed with his mission unaccomplished. This did little to affect the resolution of his father, who had now returned to Chartwell from the fortresses of France. The light of battle in his eye, Churchill was set to fight this home-grown skirmish to its bitter end.

Through his old New York friend, the financier Bernard Baruch, who had been in touch with Sarah, highly paid lawyers were secretly engaged to set legal barriers against the marriage. Meanwhile private detectives started dredging up anything unpleasant they could find in Vic Oliver's past. Sarah's appeals by telephone to Clementine – and to her father's deeply sentimental nature – made no difference.

But Churchill *could* be sentimental and extraordinarily romantic over a love-affair in different circumstances; and those circumstances were rapidly approaching in the relationship between his King and Mrs Ernest Simpson. From the beginning Churchill had seen the dangers in Edward marrying his mistress. When informally consulted by the royal lawyer, Walter Monckton, in July 1936, he had firmly advised against Mrs Simpson seeking a divorce from her husband. But her divorce proceeded, and by the end of October Mrs Simpson had her freedom. When discussion of the royal romance was finally permitted in the British press, it was clear that the King was bent on marriage. To those in

the know, it was also clear that the Prime Minister, stolid
Stanley Baldwin, and his obedient supporters were never going
to permit the King, who was also head of the established Church
of England, to commit the scandal of marrying a divorcée.

On 2 December, Baldwin spelled this out clearly to the King;
Edward answered that he was set irrevocably on marriage.
Impasse ensued, and the King requested leave to seek advice
from his friend Winston Churchill. Baldwin raised no objection,
and Churchill was invited for dinner at Fort Belvedere, the King's
own private residence, two evenings later.

Had Churchill been consistent, and taken the same stern
attitude towards his King's romance as he was taking with his
daughter's, he would have saved himself a lot of trouble – and
one of the most humiliating setbacks of his political career. His
political antennae should have warned him that down-to-earth
public feeling was hardening against this royal marriage. As Edith
Sitwell put it, 'She has been divorced twice to often for a queen,
and I don't think Queen Wally would sound well.' He should have
seen that his king's romance was far more 'unsuitable' than his
daughter Sarah's, and that the issue was a dangerous diversion
from his mission to persuade a lethargic government to rearm
against the growing might of Germany. But Churchill was rarely
particularly consistent once an issue truly stirred the depths of his
imagination; and few things in life could stir it more dramatically
than royalty.

Clementine knew all the symptoms in advance. She once
described him as 'the last believer in the divine right of kings',
and warned him against becoming irretrievably involved. She
might as well have advised him not to have joined the charge
at Omdurman.

Once in the presence of his still-to-be-anointed king, a lifetime
of devotion to his sovereign made the decision for him. His
monarch was in love and was personally appealing for assistance.
How could a Churchill not become his champion?

The dinner between Churchill and King Edward must have
been an emotional occasion. Haggard from the strains of love
and statecraft, Edward apparently 'blacked out' twice at the table.
Churchill solicitously suggested he retire to Windsor Castle to
recover his composure while two royal doctors manned the gates
against the politicians.

It was in fact too late for such ludicrous delaying tactics, as

Baldwin, coolly judging the hostility of the nation now to Mrs Simpson, pressed the King to choose between his mistress and his crown. As events would prove, unromantic Stanley Baldwin was for once completely right; while royalist romantic Churchill made one of the worst blunders of his whole political career.

Immersed in his trusted role in this royalist scenario, he pleaded in Parliament on the King's behalf for 'time and patience' to devise a way for him to keep his crown and the woman he loved. As so often in Churchill's life, Churchill the romantic was taking over from Churchill the realist and man of destiny. The result was deep humiliation; on the two occasions he attempted to plead the King's case in the House of Commons he was howled down from all sides. Faced with an unprecedented constitutional crisis, everyone but Churchill knew that the King would have to make an irrevocable decision – which he did by his official act of abdication in December. But Churchill was shocked and bitterly shaken by his own reception in the Commons, muttering darkly (as he did after the Dardanelles) that he was 'finished'.

His own supporters were bitterly disappointed, feeling that he had sacrificed his growing reputation as the prophet of rearmament for the sake of an ill-judged royal fiasco. Not so Churchill. Devoted to Edward to the last, he lunched with him on the very day he made his abdication broadcast. He had actually written every word of the speech for him, as the King was all but incoherent.

It was one of Churchill's finest efforts, straight from the pages of a romantic novel (Savrola, too, once gave up power for the woman he had loved) and full of phrases which would catch the heart-strings of the nation. Most effective was the line in which the King expressed his deep regret at not possessing 'one matchless blessing, enjoyed by so many of you and not bestowed on me – a happy home with wife and children'. Churchill might have felt the same and, according to Edward's own account, when he said goodbye, he paused on the steps of Fort Belvedere, 'hat in one hand, stick in the other', with tears in his eyes. Later, at Chartwell when he listened to the broadcast he had written, he wept copiously. Afterwards he dictated a personal memorandum, which remained unpublished until his death, revealing the full extent to which the novelist had taken charge of his emotions at the climax of this deeply sentimental business.

He began by speaking of King Edward's 'deep attachment for Mrs Simpson'.

He delighted in her company, and found her qualities as necessary to his happiness as the air he breathed. Those who knew him well and watched him closely noticed that many little tricks and fidgetings of nervousness fell away from him. He was a completed being instead of a sick and harassed soul. This experience which happens to a great many people in the flower of their youth, came late in life for him, and was all the more precious and compulsive for that fact. The association was psychical rather than sexual, and certainly not sensual except incidentally. Although branded with the stigma of a guilty love, no companionship could have appeared more natural. . . . One must have something real somewhere. Otherwise far better die.

Most of these deeply sentimental words applied equally to that other 'harassed soul', his daughter Sarah; but, even while dictating them at Chartwell, Churchill was still refusing to concede an inch in his opposition. Meanwhile, unhappy and rejected by her family, Sarah naturally relied increasingly upon the surrogate father-figure of her lover – and grew more and more attached to him.

There would always be a side of her that craved publicity, and she was getting it by dancing in Vic Oliver's show on tour in Boston. When *Follow the Stars* reached Broadway, Sarah had what any stagestruck girl would dream of – her name in lights on Broadway, and a billing as 'Britain's runaway dancing débutante in person, the guest of Vic Oliver'.

Through his detectives, Churchill kept in touch with what was happening, and was unflagging in his desperate attempts to stop the marriage. His lawyers had discovered there was still a period to go before Vic Oliver's Austrian divorce was finalised. Game to the last, Churchill tried everything he knew to persuade the lady in Vienna to delay things further. She refused, and finally on Christmas Eve, at New York City Hall, Vic Oliver changed Sarah from his 'guest' into his wife.

In fact it was a simple unromantic ceremony, with only a lawyer and a cleaning lady as witnesses. *Follow the Stars* was over, and shortly afterwards they sailed for England in *Aquitania*. Then, and only then, did Churchill see the necessity for simultaneous surrender – over the love affairs of both his daughter and the King.

Stanley Baldwin's reputation had been strengthened, the case for Britain's rearmament was weakened, and the former king of England was in exile. Churchill's own marriage had suffered, too. Exhausted by the tensions and the drama of these frantic weeks, and upset by her husband's treatment of Sarah, Clementine had had enough and left wearily for Austria to think things over.

It was then that Churchill understood the full extent of his defeat and realised that as a result of these disastrous weeks he might well lose Clementine as well as Sarah.

He tried to make the best of things, and if this meant forgiving Sarah, and accepting an 'itinerant vagabond' as his son-in-law, then so be it. Sarah was invited to a reconciliation lunch at Chartwell together with her husband – 'I suppose we must call him Vic,' he wrote to Clementine. But all he could bring himself to tell Clementine about his new son-in-law was that he was making £200 a week in his current show. Sarah he found 'serious and gentle'. 'Like the ill-starred Duke of Windsor,' he concluded, 'she has done what she liked, and now has to like what she has done.'

25

The Return of the Prophet

Early in July 1939, on the eve of what Cyril Connolly called 'closing time in the gardens of the West', Winston Churchill came to Blenheim for the last and most spectacular prewar party ever witnessed in his great ancestral home.

The sense of an impending war made this a vintage year for balls and parties, and money-conscious Bert decided just for once to spare no expense in celebrating the coming-out of his daughter, Lady Sarah Spencer-Churchill.

A thousand guests had been invited, including the handsome Duke of Kent, the sister of the future American President, Eunice Kennedy, and the Duke's distinguished-looking mother – now plain Mme Jacques Balsan – who made a rare return to the scene of so much former misery and splendour.

The terraces lovingly created by her ex-husband with the Vanderbilt money were festooned with coloured lights and Chinese lanterns, and the footmen wore the Marlborough livery and powdered their hair for the occasion. (It was the last time they would do so as they complained that the powder made the scalp itch and their hair fall out.) Searchlights lit up the trees across the lake, and an orchestra played the waltzes of Vienna in the Duke's Long Library.

Not everyone, however, was impressed. Randolph, who disliked his cousin Bert and hated Blenheim, had come only to be near the woman he was now in love with. This was Laura, the beautiful and discontented wife of Lord Long. Formerly Laura Charteris, a grand-daughter of the Earl of Wemyss and younger sister of the future wife of Ian Fleming, this wilful beauty had a taste for Randolph's company but was not in love with him. But Randolph, as obstinate in love as over politics, refused to be deterred.

'Randolph, you've been drinking,' she accused him (hardly an original remark).

'Who hasn't?' he replied. 'Anyhow, the food is ghastly and the whole performance at a time like this is a disgrace.'

He left her, and shortly afterwards was engaged in one of his all too frequent heated arguments with a fellow-guest. Most of his arguments were now about his father, who was still detested by most loyal Tories, as well as by fascists, pacifists and pro-German members of the aristocracy. There was a scene and, as Laura recollects, someone had to take him home.

Churchill, oblivious for once of his son's behaviour, was dining quietly beneath the Chinese lanterns with his old friend Consuelo and the ever-youthful former Foreign Secretary, Anthony Eden. At forty-two, Eden was almost fourteen years older than Randolph but did not look it, which may explain why Randolph, who had put on weight and was looking old beyond his years, had taken so strongly against him. He may also have been jealous of his father's closeness with Eden ever since Eden's resignation from the Chamberlain government over Mussolini's seizure of Abyssinia the year before. Churchill later described Eden at this time as 'one strong young figure standing up against long, dismal drawling tides of drift and surrender'.

Soon after the seizure of Abyssinia, Neville Chamberlain, who succeeded Baldwin as prime minister in 1937, had made his disastrous attempt to appease Hitler over Czechoslovakia by meeting him in Munich in September 1938. This had not stopped the European war, which Churchill had so long and so unpopularly predicted, advancing step by step towards them.

Despite his promises at Munich, Hitler had marched his armies into Prague. He was threatening the port of Danzig, and his emissaries would soon arrive in Moscow to arrange a pact with Stalin which would include the dismemberment of Poland. War would start in nine weeks' time, sweeping away so much of the world that Blenheim represented.

The novelist Daphne Fielding, who was present at the party, compared it with the great ball thrown by the Duchess of Richmond on the eve of Waterloo. It was the last fling of a social order which war would change for ever, and the end of the old Blenheim Churchill knew and loved; but, for Churchill and his family, the Blenheim ball also marked the end of ten long years of isolation and frustration in the wilderness of politics.

That very week, as the crisis deepened on the Continent, the newspaper placards were proclaiming 'Churchill must come back!' Neville Chamberlain, obstinate as ever, still believed that by including the anti-German Churchill in his government he would be making war with Germany inevitable. But in truth, with Hitler and his new-found Russian allies planning to dismember Poland, nothing Chamberlain did would make the slightest difference.

Most of the Churchills were in London when war with Germany was officially declared on 3 September 1939. Sarah and Vic Oliver listened in to Chamberlain's solemn radio announcement at eleven in the morning in their flat in Westminster Gardens; Randolph, nursing a hangover in his apartment in the same block, indignantly refused to listen.

It was a sombre moment, with Chamberlain admitting that this war meant that 'everything that I have worked for, everything that I have hoped for, everything that I have believed in during my public life has crashed into ruins'. But, for Churchill, war meant something very different.

It was the vindication of all the warnings he had been making for so many years. It also brought a personal and long-awaited triumph. Earlier that day, before he broadcast to the nation, Chamberlain had ended Churchill's ten-year exile. Party differences were over. A wartime government was formed, and Churchill was offered his old position at the Admiralty and a seat in the Cabinet.

As First Lord of the Admiralty, Churchill was back where he had been that August day, a quarter of a century before, when war began with Kaiser William's Germany. 'It was a strange experience,' he wrote, 'like suddenly assuming a previous incarnation.'

Over lunch the family discussed their plans. Churchill and Clementine would be moving back to their old home in the Admiralty, which would soon mean closing Chartwell. As a territorial officer attached to the artillery, Diana's husband, Duncan Sandys, would be joining his anti-aircraft regiment; his wife, not to be outdone, planned to enlist in the Women's Royal Naval Service as soon as someone could be found to look after their three-year-old son Julian and new-born baby

Edwina. (Since seventeen-year-old Mary was now in London with her parents, the invaluable Moppett Whyte obliged, making a temporary home for Diana's children in one of the Chartwell cottages.) Sarah was just as anxious as Diana to go to war, but there was a problem no one liked to mention. Vic Oliver's new American citizenship meant, in theory, that it was his duty to return to America. Sarah emphatically refused to join him if he did. This was not the time to press the point, but war placed a question-mark over the couple's future.

The one member of the family for whom war appeared to pose no problems was Randolph. He had already enrolled as a reserve officer with his father's regiment, the 4th Hussars, and was keen to fight the foe. So was Churchill as he raised his glass and made a toast.

'To victory!'

'To victory!' all of them repeated.

From the beginning, Churchill's return to the Admiralty placed him in a unique position for a politician. The prophet's prophecies had come to pass, the seer so long rejected was recalled to power. Even if he found himself required to wait to lead the nation while sick discredited Neville Chamberlain tottered on as premier, he was at once the dominating presence in the wartime government.

For somebody of Churchill's temperament, this position was no happening of chance or simple justice: more was involved than that. Here was a role which his especial destiny appointed him to play. There could be no more thought of failure and rejection, no further struggles with his secret enemy Black Dog, still less with those recurrent fears of being doomed to follow his father's fate in politics – outcast, increasingly ignored with age, and mocked by friends as well as foes as impotence advanced. Approaching sixty-five, Churchill had won the greatest gamble of his life. When he proposed the toast 'to victory', it could have been his own.

The first message to the Fleet on his appointment was 'Winston is back!' – and he was soon displaying much the same energy with which he had transformed the Royal Navy in his youth. These months at the Admiralty coincided with the strange lull of the so-called 'phoney war' before Hitler launched his big offensive

against western Europe. But Churchill swiftly placed his imprint
on the naval high command. He was soon feuding with his
admirals, planning his hare-brained expeditions, and generally
invigorating everything he touched and working wonders for
morale. Both in Parliament and from his seat in Cabinet, he was
establishing credentials once again for what he was – the nation's
greatest and unrivalled man of war. This was in painful contrast
with the man of peace, sick and dispirited Neville Chamberlain,
whose days as Prime Minister were clearly numbered.

Throughout the first months at the Admiralty, Churchill's
staunchest ally and admirer was his son. Unlike Clementine,
Randolph's faith in Churchill had never wavered through the
thirties; nor had their fights and disappointments touched the
bonds which linked them.

'Randolph's adoration of his father is truly touching,' wrote
Harold Nicolson, and while Churchill's love of Randolph stopped
somewhere short of adoration, Randolph was still of deep importance to him. As his precious heir, Randolph was his lifeline to
the future and the extension of his destiny.

Now that destiny had brought his father back to office,
Randolph was in a situation which few outside the family quite
appreciated. As Churchill's son he had privileges and responsibilities for which he was painfully unfitted. But his worship of
Churchill knew no bounds, and like some over-eager schoolboy
he would do anything to please him – as he showed in no uncertain
manner a few weeks after war broke out and he found himself in
London on a weekend's leave.

He was sleeping, when he could, with the vaudeville star
Clare Luce, while still romantically in love with Laura; but that
Saturday neither was available. Miss Luce was out of town, and
Laura had decided she was suddenly in love with an older man,
forty-five-year-old Eric, Earl of Dudley.

Meeting an old friend, Lady Mary Dunn, in the doorway
of the Ritz, Randolph asked her out to dine. She, too, was
unable to oblige, but suggested that he telephone her home
and invite instead a friend who was staying with her. This was a
pretty girl called Pamela, the nineteen-year-old daughter of the
backwoods Dorset peer Lord Digby (a former President of the
Royal Horticultural Society, known to his intimates as 'Carnation
Digby').

Randolph took the number.

'What do you look like?' he is said to have enquired with customary bluntness when Miss Digby answered. Legend has it she replied: 'Red-headed and rather fat, but Mummy says the puppy fat will disappear.' No sylph himself, Randolph accordingly asked her to dinner.

One of the most unlikely characters to enter the orbit of the Churchills thus made her début. And few were to be more totally transformed by contact with the Churchills than this friendly, pony-loving virgin from the shires.

Randolph's intentions were, for once, impetuously honourable, and nothing as frivolous as love was serving to distort his judgement. As he told the American journalist John Gunther shortly afterwards, he was determined to embark on active service and believed he would probably be killed. As heir apparent to the Churchills, it was his duty to his line – and, more important, to his father – to ensure a legitimate successor lest this happened. Pamela was obviously healthy, and as a family the Digbys were perfectly acceptable, even to a Churchill. Three days after meeting her, Randolph proposed and was accepted.

Clementine disapproved; but as she disapproved of almost everything that Randolph did, this carried little weight, especially as Churchill was delighted. He had married swiftly himself and, practical as ever, told his son: 'All you need to be married are champagne, a box of cigars and a double bed!'

He also approved of Randolph's motives. As he wrote to his multi-married friend Bendor Westminster, 'I expect he will be in action in the early spring, and therefore I am very glad that he should be married before he goes. She is a charming girl and they both seemed very pleased about it.'

Three weeks later, at St John's, Smith Square, the ceremony took place, with Churchill present. The bride wore blue, and Randolph donned his sword and full cavalryman's regalia.

However unromantic Randolph's overall approach, Pamela at least believed herself decidedly in love. As she explains:

I had had no experience of life or men, and was entirely unformed. I had been to Paris and to Germany to learn the languages, but I had certainly never met anyone like Randolph. What most appealed to me about him was his absolute certainty about everything – particularly about the war, which he believed was going to be extremely long and bloody, and that we should therefore enjoy life to the last bottle of champagne.

As she soon discovered, Randolph had a dangerous knack of always finding one more bottle.

Almost everything in Randolph's nature unfitted him for matrimony. He was wayward, spoiled, pig-headed, drunken, lecherous and disastrously naïve. Thus the matrimonial scales were weighted heavily against him from the start. What weighted them further still was the way his family, while all too well aware of Randolph's failings, warmed to his unspoiled, very charming child-b.ide. As one of Randolph's friends remembers, 'Pam was not particularly beautiful or witty, but she already had an extraordinary talent for making gentlemen of all ages happy.' This was certainly true for Churchill. She played bezique with him, called him Papa, laughed at his jokes, and listened to his stories.

Randolph meanwhile went off to join his regiment. But, instead of being sent abroad, he stayed in camp in northern England, where Pamela joined him. Life as Randolph's wife on a captain's pay soon proved a sobering experience. But the newlyweds spent Christmas back in London with the Churchills; Randolph did his duty to the dynasty, and when Pamela found that she was pregnant everyone was thrilled, Churchill especially. This was the precious grandchild who would bear the Churchill name, and during the months before its birth Churchill would seize that final chance which he had longed for all his life to inscribe the Churchill name in history.

Britain's failure to prevent Hitler invading Norway early in May 1940 sealed the political fate of Neville Chamberlain. Churchill attempted to defend him in debate, but it was Leo Amery (once Churchill's victim in the school swimming pool at Harrow) who repeated Cromwell's dramatic words against their leader in the House of Commons: 'In the name of God, go!'

Knowing he had lost all credibility, Chamberlain took Amery's advice and resigned, recommending that the King appoint Churchill his successor. On the morning of 10 May, Hitler's armies invaded France and Belgium. That same evening Churchill was prime minister and began to form the coalition government which he would lead until war with Germany was over.

What did it mean to this power-haunted doom-obsessed old orator, who for ten long years had nursed his dreadful vision of his nation's fate, to be summoned by events to that 'supreme office of State'?

He made no bones about the sense of exaltation which swept over him, despite the gloom and grimness of the situation. This was the position his father had failed to achieve, the culmination of a lifetime's unyielding ambition. As he put it, 'I felt as if I were walking with destiny and that all my past life had been a preparation for this hour and this trial'.

As so often in the past, the prospect of waging full-scale war aroused his remarkable powers of aggression, and banished any lingering anxieties. Before the First World War he had asked Clementine, 'Is it not terrible to be thus constituted?', when telling her of his longing to 'direct great formations' of men in battle. But since this second war had come, despite his constant warnings, he was relieved of all such feelings of compunction. Someone had to lead the nation, and it was plainly better that the someone was a man who gloried in the challenge and excitement of the task, whose whole character exhaled a warlike spirit and who could make his judgements after a sound night's sleep, than by some admirable pacific human being who could be torn apart by an awareness of the pain and suffering he dealt in as a wartime leader.

'Savrola' was now in his middle sixties, but Churchill had not changed from the romantic hero of the novel which he wrote at twenty-five. He had always relished awesome situations where he could play the warlike saviour. At Antwerp he had thrust himself into the role of defender of the stricken city; at Gallipoli his master-plan was meant to alleviate the hideous bloodshed of the Somme; and almost single-handedly he had tried to overturn the Russian Revolution. All had failed, and he had sought consolation in history with his military heroes. Napoleon's bust was still before him on his desk, but it was Marlborough who had offered him his greatest inspiration as he had laboured at his vast biography. He could exaggerate the tenuous blood relationship into a mystic bond between them, and Marlborough's life was crammed with those 'tremendous situations' which so excited him.

Now, as France was falling, and Britain stood alone against another European tyrant, Churchill, like Marlborough, was presented with the greatest role within the repertoire.

Even his age was in his favour, making him seem a sort of martial father of the people as he made his famous wartime speeches to the nation. Here he was in his element, offering beleaguered Britain a nostalgic vision of itself from his own embattled view of history. At the climax of his greatest speech as France was falling, and he offered the population 'blood, toil, tears and sweat', he was in fact echoing the rallying-call of another of his military heroes, whose biography, like Napoleon's, he had once considered writing.

This was the father of united Italy (a country with which in a few days Britain would find itself at war), the indomitable nationalist and general Garibaldi, who had told the gallant remnants of his own defeated army: 'I offer neither pay nor quarters nor provisions; I offer hunger, thirst, forced marches, battles, death.'

Not everyone responded. 'Rallied the nation indeed!' wrote Evelyn Waugh. 'I was a serving soldier in 1940. How we despised his orations!'

But for the majority, particularly for those at home, Churchill's heroic vision of the moment seemed to work. The remnants of Britain's army limped back from Dunkirk. The Battle of Britain started, and invasion threatened. Britain was weak and isolated now against an overwhelming enemy. But throughout these awful weeks Churchill's was the voice which offered courage to the people, refusing Hitler's overtures of peace, and making a national disaster appear as one of the great heroic moments in the nation's history.

Thus did an eccentric aristocrat/historian, who never travelled on a bus and who was lost without the daily ministrations of his valet, briefly unite all classes against an evil enemy. Thus did he also make himself the symbol of their will to fight.

But Churchill's wartime leadership did not rest entirely on speeches and the projection of his personality. It was his human limitations almost as much as his superhuman strengths which had conspired to fit him for the warlike power he wielded.

The strengths were obvious: great physical endurance, sustained capacity of will, and powers of total concentration even in his late sixties made him unique among the politicians of his day. So did his less admirable qualities. There was that driving egotism, for instance, which endowed him with a massive certainty about himself and a refusal to endure any who opposed him. As he put it, 'All I wanted was compliance with my wishes after reasonable discussion.' There was the aggression in his make-up, which would emerge whenever he was 'up' or thwarted. There was the simple schoolboy love of battle. And there remained the iron in his soul, forged to withstand those periods of despair when misery and deep depression had assailed him.

He was perfectly prepared to charm or bully to maintain ascendancy over all around him, and could arouse great loyalty even from those he treated badly. When this failed he could still out-argue anyone who dared to go against him.

It was Lady Goonie who had first described him as 'a pasha' from the way he imposed his will upon his underlings. 'A secretary is as essential to him as a fountain pen,' one of his former private secretaries remarked, and he treated them accordingly. More than ever, he was both workaholic and intensely organised. Only with such qualities was he able to assume the role of effortless dictator.

But there would always be one crucial difference between Churchill and the Marlboroughs, Napoleons and Nelsons who inspired him. All were commanders in the field whose power and fame had come, in the words of Chairman Mao, 'through the barrel of a gun'. Churchill's had not. However powerfully he roused himself to the dreadful drama of the clash of arms, his power resided in the written and the spoken word.

He was essentially an *amateur* of battle, but such was the force with which he acted out the part of great war leader, such the conviction he conveyed, that he virtually became the role which he created, and was swiftly in an unassailable position. His leadership appeared the only credible alternative to domination by 'that doom-laden, haunted, evil man', Adolf Hitler. No general or politician could gainsay him the ultimate authority for waging war.

In theory Churchill was the loyalest, most deferential of King George's subjects – 'the last believer in the Divine Right of Kings', as Clementine had called him in the abdication crisis. He knew that both the King and Queen would have preferred tame Lord Halifax as premier and once in power he deployed his impressive battery of charm and courtliness to woo the royal couple and finally efface their lingering distrust of this former champion and ally of the Duke of Windsor.

It was a task which brought out all his reverence for the monarchy, and few prime ministers were more scrupulous than Churchill in attendance on the sovereign. But the truth was that it was Churchill, rather than uninspiring nervous George VI, who became the essential royal presence during this time of war. George did his duty, but Churchill ruled – with the unselfconscious power of a medieval monarch, directing armies, dismissing and promoting generals, relying on a carefully selected group of favourites to do his bidding, and jealously preventing any over-mighty subject from eclipsing him.

He had the presence and the dignity of royalty in his person. While paradoxically the King exhibited all the sober virtues of a conscientious citizen, 'doing his bit' for the war effort with his middle-class family around him, Churchill was increasingly displaying the traditional habits and activities of an autocratic monarch.

George tried to make himself and his family subsist on the food rations of an ordinary subject, but Churchill had no time for such pretence. 'This war will be won by carnivores,' he growled; and, thanks to extra 'diplomatic' rations, Clementine was able to ensure that her cook, Mrs Landemare, was always able to provide the leader of the nation with the provender he needed.

George personally painted a line around the royal bathtub at Windsor to ensure that precious fuel was saved by having a mere five inches of hot water. Churchill was so insistent on having his all-important hot relaxing baths that a heat accumulator was specially installed in the system so that there would be hot water even in a power cut.

If his appetites for food and drink were regal, so was his love of uniforms and fancy headgear. His journeys through the kingdom in his special train could become like royal progresses, his foreign trips had many of the trappings of the voyages of potentates, and even his everyday routines had echoes of the way great kings had once conducted the affairs of state.

As a subaltern in India, one of the seminal books he studied, along with Gibbon and Macaulay, was the duc de St-Simon's memoirs of life at the court of Louis XIV. Now, like the King of France, he developed the habit of despatching much of the day's business by dictating every morning to his secretaries as he sat in bed. Like Louis, he would arise around midday, then meet generals, ministers and visiting celebrities at table with members of his family. He also used, to great effect, that haughty king's technique of making those he disapproved of wait upon his favour, often very late at night.

When Clementine referred to Churchill's belief in the divine right of kings she spoke truer than she probably suspected. For, as effective wartime king of England, Churchill certainly believed that he possessed some supernatural backing to the power he wielded.

This lay in the philosophy of life which this agnostic pessimist had carefully constructed to convince himself that he was super-naturally 'chosen' for the exercise of power. Natural gambler that he was, he based this valuable belief upon the enormous odds that had always seemed so firmly stacked against him. In the past, whenever he survived a bullet or a bomb, this faith had been strengthened. Now that he had also managed to survive the even greater odds against political disaster to be called upon to lead the nation at its greatest crisis, what further proof was needed?

'There has to be a purpose to it all,' he told his secretary, Jock Colville. And when the war was almost over he assured Lord Moran: 'I believe that I was chosen for a purpose far beyond our simple reasoning.'

A regal sense of power with supernatural sanction is a potent combination, and Churchill as a warlike leader was formidable – to friends and allies almost as much as to his enemies.

26

Family at War

In the autumn of 1940, *Picture Post* commissioned Cecil Beaton to take some photographs of Clementine to accompany an article and shortly after taking them he also photographed the Prime Minister himself, enthroned in solitary majesty in the Cabinet Room, looking, as he wrote, 'immaculately distinguishedly porcine, with pink bladder wax complexion and a vast cigar freshly affixed to his chin'.

Beaton promised to let Churchill see the proofs for his approval, and by the time he brought them to Downing Street, *Picture Post* had published his photographs of Clementine. They were not particularly flattering, and a candid friend had told her that they made her look 'like a hard-bitten virago who takes drugs'.

Clementine was painfully upset, and no sooner was the favourite photographer of royalty inside Number 10 than he found himself assailed by the wife of the Prime Minister at the epicentre of one of her celebrated rages. Accusing Beaton of all manner of deception and betrayal, she was soon in a state of near-hysteria, face flushed and eyes awash with tears.

But her rage went as swiftly as it came, and Beaton was left with a pathetic middle-aged woman on his hands.

'Really it's too damnable,' she wailed. 'It isn't as if my life has been too easy. It hasn't – but when I married Winston, he loved me.'

Beaton took her hand, insisting, 'But he *still* does. We all know that!' – but she wept more uncontrollably than ever. The photographer, unaccustomed to consoling great men's wives, felt obliged to kiss her on the forehead and held on grimly to her hand. This still had no effect, and instead of 'coming round' she proceeded to sob out an extraordinary confession.

I don't know why it is, but I suppose my friends are not exactly jealous but they think that other people could do the job better and that I shouldn't have been married to Winston. After all, he is one of the most important people in the world. In fact he and Hitler and President Roosevelt are the most important people in the world today.

Beaton felt the situation getting out of hand and that the time had come to make Churchill's wife 'behave with more dignity', rather than offering any more disclosures. He swiftly changed the subject to his pictures of her husband. She recovered her composure, said she liked them, and Beaton managed to effect his exit.

He tactfully sent a bouquet of orchids and roses of Beatonesque proportions to Downing Street, and received an 'affectionate telegram' from Clementine in return. His pictures of Churchill were published in the press in time for Christmas, and proved a considerable success.

But Beaton's strange encounter with Clementine lingers in the mind like a candid camera shot of one of the few occasions when the public image slipped, revealing the anxieties which afflicted her relations with her husband in his 'finest hour'.

With his attention focused on the war, Churchill can have had little time to demonstrate affection, but one wonders if he was ever seriously interested in the sort of deep romantic love Clementine evidently wanted. He had consistently written her romantic sentimental letters when they were parted; but letters, like his speeches, were his stock in trade, and literary love is not necessarily the real thing. Nor was the loving dependence he had always shown for Clementine in times when he was 'down' – he had shown the same for Mrs Everest and Jennie.

He had been frequently 'down' throughout the thirties, and Clementine had not always given him the support and constancy he needed. There had been her nervous absences, her separate life in London, her love for Terence Philip, and her permanent dislike of Chartwell. Unlike Randolph, she had not maintained blind faith that Churchill's hour would come: on the contrary, she had often tried to make him face reality, dispose of Chartwell, accept the fact that he would almost certainly not return to power so late in life, and settle for writing books in benign old age instead.

Now this had changed abruptly. History – and Hitler – had dramatically disproved all Clementine's sensible advice and wifely doubts. Her husband, against all odds, had scaled that 'great and commanding position in this country' which she had once predicted for him – but much had happened to their marriage in the interim. Now that he was challenged by his 'walk with destiny', there was loneliness in Clementine's position.

Having achieved the greatness he had always dreamed of, Churchill had little need of wifely consolation. What he required was a semi-regal consort, able to act a public role beside his own and ensure that his private life proceeded with the 'pasha-like' efficiency he wanted. Neither task was easy for her. Nervous and insecure as ever, she was haunted by those feelings of inadequacy and guilt which she had blurted out to Beaton. Apart from Mary, she still had little closeness with her children. Earnest and overwhelmed by a realisation of her husband's extraordinary importance, this lonely woman did her best to act the great man's wife – and did it with immense determination.

There were some bumpy moments at the beginning since she could be rough with underlings when she felt her dignity impugned. For example, Churchill's private secretary, Jock Colville, found her 'abusive' when he took the liberty of giving instructions to her secretary, the admirable Grace Hamblin, brought over from Chartwell.

'Mrs C considers it one of her missions in life to put people in their place and prides herself on being outspoken,' he recorded grimly in his diary. (Later, it is only fair to add, he became one of her great admirers.)

Nor was it only private secretaries she put in their place. Her daughter Mary has described the luncheon-party at Downing Street shortly after the collapse of France, when she turned upon no less a figure than General Charles de Gaulle.

The British, acting on Churchill's orders, feared that the large French battle-fleet in North Africa might be taken over by the Germans. On 3 July, the British fleet, having failed to persuade the French ships in the harbour at Oran to join them, had arrived there in force and, failing to persuade the French to join them, had attacked, sinking three French battleships and killing more than a thousand Frenchmen. During the lunch which took place at Downing Street shortly after, someone tactlessly asked de Gaulle whether the remainder of the French fleet would join the Allies – bringing the swift rejoinder from the General that what the

French navy would probably like to do would be to turn their guns upon the British.

It was a remark to be diplomatically ignored, which Churchill did; but Clementine turned on the General, and in the French she had picked up as a schoolgirl in Dieppe – and liked to show off when she had the chance – treated him much as she treated Colville, saying that his words 'ill became either an ally or a guest'.

The General, who must have realised he had met his match in Clementine, apologised profusely, and next morning Clementine received an even larger bunch of flowers than she had had from Beaton.

Around this time, she also felt obliged to lecture Churchill in writing on what she called his 'rough, sarcastic and overbearing manner' to colleagues and subordinates, suggesting that with 'the terrific power' he possessed he should 'combine urbanity, kindness and if possible Olympic [sic] calm'. This was valuable advice, which only Clementine could give her husband (how much effect it had on Churchill is another matter). But it is an interesting reflection on the marriage, that even such wifely counsel had to be entrusted to a letter.

What is clear is that, whatever fears she may have had about her husband's love and her own abilities, this vulnerable woman was learning to adopt a regal role to match his own.

Despite Beaton's photographs, her looks were perfect for the part. So was her manner. Unlike Churchill, she maintained genuine rapport with ordinary people, taking much trouble to visit working-class Londoners when German air-raids started at the end of 1940. It was partly thanks to her visits to Londoners sheltering nightly from the Blitz, in extreme discomfort in the London Underground, that their crowded conditions were improved. She launched aircraft-carriers, sponsored homes for nursing mothers, acted as patron for important wartime charities, and performed her self-imposed duties with exhausting dedication.

She was particularly concerned with the regal burden of example. Her own was admirable. Pursuing what she saw to be her duty, she really was the most selfless of patriotic figureheads. The same could not be said of all the members of her family, and since she felt a moral obligation to correct them, this caused problems.

The most glaring case of all was one that not even Clementine could do anything about. Within weeks of taking power, Churchill himself had had to face an uncomfortable conundrum: what to do about his wife's fascist relatives, the Mosleys.

In strictly practical terms, it was hard to think that Diana Mosley or her husband posed a real threat to the safety of the realm. Diana was nursing a four-week-old baby, and was preoccupied with her sister Unity.

When war broke out, conflict between Britain and her beloved Germany had been more than Unity could bear. She had tried to shoot herself but bungled the attempt. On Hitler's orders, she was returned to Britain via Switzerland and was now surviving, brain-damaged and with nothing left to live for, a pathetic victim of the war created by the leader she had worshipped. Diana helped look after her.

Oswald Mosley was even less of a menace than his wife. Once a close associate of Churchill and member of the 'Other Club', he had been a guest at Randolph's famous twenty-first-birthday dinner at Claridge's, and had supported Churchill's calls for British rearmament. His true hero had been Mussolini – 'the most interesting man in Europe' he once called him – and his brief involvement with Hitler had been solely through his wife. Now in his late forties, and in uncertain health, he had attempted, unsuccessfully but with total seriousness, to re-enlist in his old regiment to defend the Empire.

All of this was, however, totally beside the point – particularly for a new Prime Minister rallying his country in a struggle for existence. As Mosley's biographer writes, 'an extraordinary and typically British feature of the situation was that the Mosleys, Churchills, and other leading personalities in this drama, all came from a tiny social and political class', who 'knew each other well, had stayed in each other's houses and shared the same life-style'.

This could have made Churchill – and this 'tiny social and political class' – highly vulnerable, had there been a hint of favoured treatment for his relatives and friends. There was also the uncomfortable fact that, at that very moment, the swift collapse of western Europe to the Germans was being helped by a 'Fifth Column' of fascist and pro-German elements within each country.

The Mosleys might protest their patriotism: fascists like Pierre Laval and Quisling did the same. But the fact remained that Sir Oswald Mosley was notoriously the leader of the principal fascist organisation in Britain, and that his wife was known, not merely as an old admirer of Nazi Germany, but as a close and valued friend of the arch-fiend Adolf Hitler. She had actually met him for the last time at Bayreuth on the very eve of war in August 1939, when he told her he was perfectly convinced that Britain would honour its treaty obligations and go to war if he invaded Poland.

But there did remain a human problem for the Churchills. Whatever motives lay behind her close relationship with many of the leading Nazis, Diana Mosley had been perfectly within her rights to visit Hitler in Berlin in time of peace – just as Churchill's other cousin, Clare Sheridan, had been when she got to know the leading Bolsheviks in Moscow back in 1922. And, as with cousin Clare, Churchill had had a particularly soft spot for his adoring 'Dynamite' as he called Diana in the days when she had been a favoured guest at Chartwell.

Her shadowy portrait, in a large half-finished painting by Churchill himself of the family at dinner, was still at Chartwell. Randolph had never ceased to love her, even after she married Mosley. And Churchill, though perfectly aware of the full extent of her contacts with the leading Nazis, had felt no need to warn her of the potential consequences. (Indeed, as we have seen, he used her as a source of information on the Führer when she lunched with the Churchill family in 1936.)

But, if Churchill felt pity or responsibility for someone who had been so close to him and to his family, he could not show it. The Mosleys were passionately hated, not only among the parties of the Left, on whom Churchill was relying for the unity of his coalition government, but also by many on the Right, who had envied them their looks and wealth and past success in Germany and Italy, and saw them as useful scapegoats for their own pro-Nazi or pro-fascist sympathies. In Diana's own words, she and her husband had become 'untouchable', and within a month of Churchill taking power, both were arrested on his ultimate authority.

No charges could be brought against them, for they had done nothing illegal. Despite this, both were imprisoned under the Emergency Regulations in conditions of considerable hardship, and among convicted criminals – Mosley at Brixton and his wife in a lice-infested and insanitary basement cell in the women's gaol at Holloway. She was also parted from her four-week-old son, Alexander.

This treatment of the Mosleys caused a split within the family. According to Colville's diaries, news of their plight produced 'much merriment' between Sarah and Diana, who presumably felt their fascist relatives had received their just deserts. But faithful Randolph almost instantly attempted to obtain improved conditions for them. According to Colville, family-loving Churchill, too, was 'piqued' to hear of the state that they were in, but any change was certain to be picked up in the press and could have been politically disastrous.

With hindsight, Lady Mosley herself makes an interesting point about her situation. 'Of course it was extremely difficult for him', she says of Churchill, 'and without trying to be at all conceited, the closest parallel I can think of was with the way that George V felt obliged to cut off totally from Lord Mountbatten's father, the German Prince Louis of Battenberg, because of the anti-German outcry at the beginning of the First World War.'

There was one concession Randolph was able to obtain for Diana through his father. What had thoroughly disturbed him was the news that a female member of the upper classes was unable to take her daily bath, and an order came to Holloway that Lady Mosley was to have this privilege. It was, she says, 'a kindly thought of Winston's', but as there was insufficient water and only two 'degraded bathrooms' in the entire prison wing, this was one wartime order Churchill issued which could not be observed.

Clementine seems to have remained implacable about the Mosleys' fate – even as late as 1943 when her cousin, Lady Redesdale (who had been her bridesmaid when she married Churchill), asked for her help in securing the release of her daughter and her son-in-law, whose health was causing some anxiety. Lady Redesdale was the original of the eccentric 'Muv' in her daughter Nancy Mitford's novels, and the meeting of the two extremely strong-willed cousins was distinctly frosty, with Clementine apparently 'irritating' Muv 'beyond measure' by assuring her that 'Winston has always been so fond of Diana' and adding that the Mosleys were probably better off in prison than they would have been facing anti-German patriots outside.

In 1940 there may have been some truth in this, but by 1943 feeling against the Mosleys had subsided, along with the threat of enemy invasion, and in fact the Mosleys were released shortly after. Whether or not Clementine played any part in this remains unclear, but is most improbable.

The Mosleys spent the rest of the war quietly in the country. They then departed for a house they bought not far from Paris called the Temple of Glory. Neither Clementine nor Churchill saw either of them again, but Randolph and Diana both picked up the friendship when the war was over.

The best example of Clementine's sharp concern that her family set a good example – not to speak of the queenly way with which she managed to enforce it – came at the beginning of the invasion scare in 1940. Many children had already been sent to Canada in an attempt to save them from the war, and someone suggested that the two princesses, Elizabeth and Margaret Rose, should go as well. This brought the famous retort from Queen Elizabeth 'The children can't go without me. I can't leave the King and of course the King won't go.'

Simultaneously came the news that, despite the royal example, a Churchill child – nephew Johnny's five-year-old daughter Sally – was on the point of being shipped to friends in Canada. This would never do. With the royal children bravely staying put how could a Churchill, even a five-year-old, think of quitting?

Through Clemetine's direct intervention with the Foreign Office, Sally's passport was cancelled and, just as the child was about to leave, an official was especially despatched, on Clementine's authority, to stop her boarding the boat-train to Southampton. There were tears and inevitable publicity – the gist of which was that the Churchill children, like the royal family, were staying put before the enemy.

There was a curious postscript to this incident. Churchill had emphatically agreed with Clementine, and was deeply touched by the publication in *The Times* of an anonymous letter from an eleven-year-old schoolboy, begging his parents not to send him off to Canada. The patriotic child insisted he would rather run the risk of death in Britain than miss the chance of witnessing his country's finest hour.

Here was a true Churchillian, and Churchill was so moved that an eleven-year-old should pen such noble sentiments that he insisted the child be found. After considerable efforts by his secretariat he was, and Churchill personally inscribed one of his own books and sent it by special messenger to David Wedgwood Benn, son of former Labour Secretary of State for

India, William Wedgewood Benn (later Lord Stansgate), and brother of the future Labour cabinet minister and left-wing activist Tony Benn.

Happily for Churchill, his own son and heir was just as patriotic. Despite their bitter fights and Randolph's drunkenness, gambling debts, sexual escapades, social and electoral disasters, arrogance and sloth, he remained the loyalest of sons to his embattled father. A devoted heir is a boon to any monarch – especially to one with a sense of dynasty as strong as Churchill's – so that when the old man came into his kingdom in 1940 Randolph was in a strong position. From the beginning this caused problems.

Clementine, for one, could not abide her son's influence upon her husband; still less could others in the entourage. The difficulties Jock Colville first encountered with Clementine were as nothing compared with the outright shock and horror this natural courtier experienced on coming face to face with her son.

'One of the most objectionable people I have ever met; noisy, self-assertive, whining, and frankly unpleasant,' was how Churchill's private secretary wrote about Randolph in his diary after the first encounter. There was more to follow during the heroic summer months of 1940, including Randolph's behaviour at a celebrated dinner held at Downing Street in June for members of the general staff. Randolph shared his father's visceral contempt for the generals of the First World War and, well primed with parental whisky, was soon holding forth on the inefficiency, complacency and lack of warlike spirit in high places. During another uproar with the military this freshly enlisted young officer was heard bellowing: 'But, General, I was not accusing you *personally* of cowardice. . . .'

Such incidents explain why Randolph never had a hope of playing Pitt the Younger to the great wartime prime minister or of even enjoying the preferment which his father could so easily have given him. Churchill had nothing against nepotism. (Quite the contrary: old allies like the Prof and Brendan Bracken would be promoted to the House of Lords.) But Randolph continued in his strange position near the throne, unemployable, unpromotable, but somehow necessary to his father's peace of mind.

One thing that Churchill's vast new reputation won for

Randolph was that seat in Parliament which he had struggled to secure on his own merits. A vacancy occurred for the constituency of Preston, and since elections had been discontinued with the war Randolph was nominated by the local Tories. This was done solely as a loyal tribute to his father, and he took his seat for Preston unopposed in September 1940.

It was an emotional moment for them both – particularly for Churchill. He had once dreamed of taking his seat in Parliament beside Lord Randolph; now the succession was continuing in the flesh. When Randolph made his maiden speech, Churchill made a point of being present, but he kept his back to Randolph throughout, for fear of showing his emotion.

Soon afterwards, Churchill was able to enjoy an even more important moment for his precious dynasty for which Randolph *was* responsible. At Chequers, on 10 October 1940, Pamela was safely delivered of a boy.

During her pregnancy, as bearer of the great white hope of the Churchills, Pamela had been accepted as a total member of the family in a way that neither Duncan Sandys nor the unfortunate Vic Oliver had ever been. While Randolph was training with his regiment, Pamela lived with the family at Downing Street, was often included in official dinner-parties and became a real favourite of her new 'Papa'. When the air-raids started, she even slept in the bunk bed beneath him in the former wine-cellar in nearby Storeys Gate, which had been converted into a shelter for the Churchill family. This meant that poor Pamela was regularly awakened by him when he rolled into his bunk around 1.30 – and kept awake by heavy snoring through the night. Clementine, as always, had insisted on an adjacent single-bedded room.

Pamela makes the point that, during this period before her child was born, she still regarded Churchill, not as a great world figure, but as a very busy but devoted paterfamilias. 'As far as I was concerned,' she says, 'he was primarily someone who loved his family, and who was very kind to me, so that it seemed quite natural to be living in his house. It was only gradually I realised I was also living in the presence of history.'

One thing she did see was a glimpse of Churchill's aggressiveness and private relish for the threat of battle, during the invasion scare that autumn. In the presence of Clementine, she asked him what they could do if the Germans came.

'Well, you can both take one dead German with you,' he replied.

'But how could we do that without a gun?' said Pamela.

'My dear,' said Churchill with total seriousness, 'you would both go into the kitchen and arm yourselves with carving-knives.'

(At that very moment Churchill had devised the motto 'Take one with you!' to inspire his countrymen in the event of an invasion.)

Almost simultaneously Pamela also received her first hint of the importance Churchill was now giving to his place in history and to the continuation of his name within the Churchill dynasty. Somewhat late in life, Bert Marlborough's long-suffering Duchess, Mary, had just produced a second son. With grown-up children (Lady Sarah was working in a factory in Oxford; and the heir, Lord Blandford, was at Eton), Bert professed to be both shocked and baffled by this late-term pregnancy, but the Duchess was delighted. Despite the fact that the Battle of Britain was occurring in the skies of southern Britain, she was determined this latest child should have a traditional christening at Blenheim.

One of the guests, Diana Cooper, wrote in her diary of 'champagne and tenantry on the lawns and nannies and cousins and healths drunk, all to the deafening accompaniment of aeroplanes skirmishing, diving, looping and spinning' in the sky above. She also described the baby as being 'godmothered by Clemmie Churchill looking most radiant and gay'. But the most interesting entry in her diary is the name this 'Ducal Marlborough baby' was given at its christening. To go with the splendid christening, the Duchess had proudly picked the name of the most celebrated member of the family: Winston Spencer Churchill. It must have caused a fearful upset when Clementine relayed the news to her husband on her return to Downing Street. According to Pamela, Churchill had already set his heart on passing on his name to her unborn baby. He had been taking it for granted that his grandchild would be a boy – and was determined it should bear the name of Winston Churchill. Pamela had agreed, not anticipating the strain she might one day be placing on her son to live up to the greatest name in Britain. (Had she realised, she says that she would almost certainly not have given her assent.)

Churchill was incensed at the thwarting of his plans, and was instantly on the telephone to Blenheim. The name Winston Churchill, he insisted to the Duchess, belonged to him, and he was determined to pass it on to his grandson.

'But how d'you know it's going to be a boy?' she asked.

'Of course it will be. And, if it isn't, there'll be others.'

'But we've already registered him as Winston.'

'Then you'll have to change it.'

Only Churchill could have made a duchess change her child's name after it had been officially registered and christened. But it was obviously so important to him that the Duchess finally agreed. 'Winston' became Lord Charles Spencer-Churchill, and when Pamela duly produced the son the family was counting on, the greatest name in British politics was awaiting it.

The christening, held in the nearby church at Chequers, made clear the depth of feeling Churchill was attaching to the dynasty, the family, and to this child who would bear his name after he was dead. He sat throughout the ceremony with tears streaming down his cheeks.

'Poor infant,' he said finally, 'to have been born into such a world as this.'

27

'Poor Randolph!'

For eighteen-year-old Mary Churchill, 1940 ended with what she recorded in her diary as 'the happiest Christmas I can remember'.

She had recently left school, and her tomboy pony-loving phase was over, leaving her a credit to the secure and straightforward upbringing given her by cousin Moppett Whyte. She was fresh-faced, blue-eyed, serious and good, with none of those hang-ups for one or other of their parents which plagued her siblings. She loved them both with total and uncomplicated dedication. 'She has', wrote Colville of her now, 'a naïve and rather charming adoration for everything connected with her family' – 'except Randolph', as he added in discreet parenthesis.

In this she was evidently echoing her mother's feelings about Randolph as a source of worry and disruption to the family. But that Christmas even Randolph was basking in the family's approval as he brought his pretty wife and eight-week-old Winston to Chequers for the Christmastide reunion.

It was an entirely family occasion like the Chartwell Christmases of yore, the only outsider being the duty clerk, John Martin, and that sere Chartwell regular, the Prof. Sarah had brought her husband, suave Vic Oliver, who had decided to stay on in England, and who was finding fame and fortune as a highly popular wartime stage comedian. ('Much the most courteous member of the family,' Lady Goonie once remarked about him, 'and the only one you could count on always to open a door for a lady.')

Diana, still working in London with the WRNS, also arrived, with the two young children, Julian and Edwina, and her husband, Duncan Sandys, who, while remaining an MP, was now on active service with the Royal Artillery. Moppett Whyte, the linchpin of the family, was also present.

But the happiness which marked that second Christmas of the war exuded from the very centre of the family. During the years before the war, Christmases had brought brief moments of relief from the frustration and bitterness which never ceased tormenting Churchill while he was out of office. But now, unchallenged in supreme authority, with a great war on his hands, Churchill was a happy man. During the 1940 summer, when he had been one of those who knew how little stood between invasion and defeat, he had awakened every morning with a sense of imminent disaster – but Britain had survived, and so had he.

His only cares were now heroic ones, and he greeted each fresh morning feeling, as he said, 'as if he had a bottle of champagne inside him and was glad that another day had come'. With an official salary of £10,750, and Downing Street and Chequers both staffed and provided by the State, he had no money worries, no problems with the servants, no sense of encroaching doom which he was powerless to fight. None could gainsay him, the country was united round him, and he was fully in command against the powers of evil which he felt threatening the nation.

In the air the Battle of Britain had been fought and won. Hitler had missed his opportunity to invade across the English Channel, and the first stage of war in North Africa had ended with the Italian army in mass surrender.

Although the German Blitz against London was reaching its peak, his prewar nightmare of widespread panic following a million casualties from German bombs had not occurred. 'London could take it' and already the RAF was beginning to retaliate against German cities. But neither side had sent its bombers out on Christmas Eve. Before leaving London, Churchill had chosen and despatched his personal presents to George VI and Queen Elizabeth. The King received one of the famous 'siren suits' which Churchill had devised himself – a sort of one-piece romper-suit for adults in dark blue velvet. For Elizabeth he chose that invaluable guide to sound English, Fowler's *English Usage*. His staff made do with his greetings for 'a busy Christmas and a frantic new year', and a suggestion that they went to church on Christmas Day.

He did not go himself, but worked all morning. In the evening the Churchills dined off a gigantic turkey, sent on behalf of his old benefactor Lord Rothermere, who had died a few weeks earlier and had asked from his deathbed for this gift to go to Churchill.

There were also Cox's Orange Pippins, an offering from another leader in an earlier war, the ailing Lloyd George, who sent them from his home at Churt.

Dinner over, it was time for the traditional Churchill Christmas sing-song. The Christmas truce extended to Vic Oliver, who accompanied on the piano. According to Martin, 'the PM sang lustily, if not always in tune, and when Vic played Viennese waltzes, he danced a remarkably frisky measure in the middle of the room'.

'I have never seen the family look so happy or so united,' wrote Mary as she closed her diary.

But the war which united them would soon be driving them apart. All three married Churchill children who were there that night would be hit by it; and first to suffer was the couple who should have been happiest of all.

Proud of having done his duty by continuing the Churchill line, Randolph sailed off to war in February 1941, with the small No. 8 Commando group which he had joined some months earlier. His destination was Cairo, and he was keen to fight. But, for Randolph, war, like peace, had to be conducted like a party; and No. 8 Commando, a distinctive group of flamboyant misfits, alcoholics and idle rich, including one novelist of genius called Evelyn Waugh, was the sort of party he enjoyed. He felt very much at home among them.

Pamela was equally at home with baby Winston in a rented rectory in the country which they had found for £30 a week. 'Oh Randy . . . oh my darling, isn't it rather thrilling. Our home, yours and mine and baby Winston's – our own family life – no more living in other people's houses,' she had written. But, as his ship continued round the coast of Africa, Randolph's memories of family togetherness faded.

The gambling gene, which Clementine believed had helped destroy her mother and her brother Bill, was doing much the same for Randolph. It certainly brought him little profit. Aboard ship, Waugh recorded in his diary, 'there was very high gambling, poker, roulette, *chemin de fer* every night. Randolph lost £850 in two evenings.'

By the time the ship reached Cape Town he was seriously broke, and after lunching with the South African Prime Minister, his father's old friend General Smuts, he was obliged to cable home for money.

Until now, despite increasing evidence to the contrary, Pamela had been able to convince herself that life with 'Randy' could turn out to have a happy ending. Now this conviction left her. In a flash she saw that 'if there was going to be any security for baby Winston and me it was going to be on our own'.

Some jewellery was sold, and the rectory closed up. Baby Winston was parked on a most unlikely baby-minder, his god-father and Randolph's erstwhile employer, Lord Beaverbrook (who was continuing to pay Randolph his prewar journalist's salary); and Pamela, undaunted and alone, set out for wartime London and a £12-a-week job in a ministry. The sheltered English rosebud was about to flower.

Early in 1941, with Britain still beleaguered but America considering joining in the war, the President of the United States despatched two envoys who would both play crucial roles in the Grand Alliance Churchill had set his heart on forging between Britain and the United States. They would also have an intimate effect upon his family.

One was the former Democratic Governor of Massachusetts, the bushy-browed and idealistic Lincoln-lookalike, John 'Gil' Winant. The other was a very different character appointed by Roosevelt as his personal representative to expedite the flow of arms to Britain and her allies – including Russia. This was his old friend and political associate, the coolly patrician Averell Harriman, son of the immensely wealthy railway king, E. H. Harriman, creator of the Union Pacific. 'I want you to go over to London and recommend everything that we can do, short of war, to keep the British Isles afloat,' Roosevelt had told him.

At fifty, and with all the money and possessions even a very rich American could want, this twice-married, power-loving sports-man saw in the task the sort of challenge he was looking for.

Both Americans were naturally received with open arms by Churchill and his entourage. Withdrawn Gil Winant, who, as Hugh Dalton soon discovered, 'improved considerably after a shot or two of good Scotch Whisky', swiftly made himself a close and trusted member of the family. He got on particularly well with Clementine, who warmed to the manner and beliefs of this shy and idealistic American Liberal. Unhappily married, and with a wife deposited in far-off Concord, Massachusetts, Winant was soon discovering among the Churchills the sort of surrogate wartime family he needed. Scarcely a week went by without the trusty Gil invited as a weekend guest to Chequers or to Ditchley Park in Oxfordshire, that perfect eighteenth-century house belonging to the rich Anglo-Americans, Ronald and Nancy Tree. Churchill used Ditchley Park as a retreat from the periodic threat of German bombers, for like some eighteenth-century grandee the Prime Minister would always spend his weekends in the country, continuing his work far from the pressures and destruction of the capital.

Harriman was also fêted by the family, and particularly by Churchill, who was doing everything he could to woo America. Here was a sympathetic presence who was in close and trusted contact with the President, and on Harriman depended much of the detail and extent of American aid for Britain. But in his case there was neither time nor inclination for Winant's sort of friendship with the Churchills to develop. Harriman was far too rich and smart to arouse much sympathy in Clementine, which made the friendship which he did strike up with one of the family particularly important.

On 7 April 1941, just a few weeks after Harriman's arrival, Jock Colville was up early. Strolling after breakfast in the morning sun down Horse Guards Parade, he was intrigued to see 'Pamela Churchill and Averell Harriman also examining the devastation' at such an early hour.

Harriman was more than old enough to have been father to twenty-year-old Pamela, and she would soon be sharing a flat with his daughter, Kathleen, who was studying in London. The girls were of an age, and got on famously. But it was tall dark Averell who really interested 'the auburn, alluring Pam Churchill', as people were suddenly beginning to call her.

'He was the most beautiful man I ever met,' she would say nearly forty years later when recalling that far-off London springtime. 'He was marvellous, absolutely marvellous-looking with his raven-black hair. He was really stunning.' And, according to Lord Drogheda, Averell, too, 'was mightily smitten by Randolph Churchill's glamorous young wife'.

After the *Sturm und Drang* of life with Randolph, who could blame Pamela for enjoying the company of a handsome and devoted older man? Certainly Churchill and senior members of his government, like Lord Beaverbrook and Brendan Bracken, were delighted that the influential Harriman and his daughter were so well looked after by this charming member of the Churchill family. When Harriman departed on a brisk fact-finding visit to the Middle East, it was natural to suggest that good old Randolph entertain this distinguished American just as his little wife was doing back in London.

Since arriving in Cairo, Randolph had failed to find the heroic military life which he had set his heart on from the outbreak of war. Once, in the Oxford Union, he had gallantly proclaimed his eagerness to 'fight for King and Country', but nobody would let him.

It was another problem which he had to face as part of his inheritance as son of the most important living Englishman. The precious 'Rabbit' had to be protected, for Churchill felt himself unequal to the sacrifice he was prepared to ask of the family of every serviceman or woman in the country. According to Colville, 'when Randolph had asked to be allowed some more active part in the war' Churchill remarked that 'if R were killed he would not be able to carry on his work'.

So it was that, despite his genuine eagerness to fight, something always kept Randolph from the battle-zone. Commanding officers were shy of using him and, in early May, when most of his former comrades from No. 8 Commando were despatched to Crete after Greece surrendered, something mysteriously stopped him going. It was just as well, as most of them were either killed or captured.

Instead, Randolph was promoted to major, and placed in charge of press relations as Staff Officer at GHQ where he swiftly made himself unpopular. Deprived of his chance to prove himself in battle, he returned to his customary diversions of gambling, drunken rows and fornication. His unpopularity increased with the knowledge that he regularly exploited his privileged contacts with his father.

His criticisms of the Commander-in-Chief (which he sent to Churchill in the diplomatic bag) seem to have played a part in General Wavell's swift departure to become Viceroy of India after the Greek débâcle. Similarly, his suggestions for a resident British minister in the Middle East led to Churchill sending out Oliver Lyttleton to the post which he created. When Harriman arrived in Cairo to discover how American supplies could be increased, Randolph joined his mission on his father's orders.

The mission was a marked success, and Randolph was soon sharing the enthusiasm of his wife and his father for the handsome East Coast millionaire.

'I have been tremendously impressed by Harriman,' he told his father. 'In ten very full and active days he has definitely become my favourite American.'

'I found him absolutely charming, & it was lovely to be able to hear so much news of you & all my friends,' he wrote simultaneously to Pamela. 'He spoke delightfully about you and I fear that I have a serious rival!'

Just as Harriman was leaving for the Middle East, Churchill was upset to hear that his son-in-law, Duncan Sandys, had had 'a frightful accident'. Now a colonel, he was working as liaison officer between the Defence Secretariat and Anti-Aircraft Command. On a night-time drive to Wales, his driver fell asleep, his staff-car hit a bridge, and Sandys, who had been snoozing with his shoes off, had both feet crushed and suffered injuries to his back.

Diana, still working with the WRNS, arrived from London just in time to stop the surgeons amputating both her husband's feet. But he was badly crippled, which marked the end of his military career and Diana's naval one. He required looking after, and it pleased the devoted Diana to have her husband dependent on her for a change; a third child, Celia, was conceived. As for the broken military career of Colonel Sandys, there was, as Churchill wrote to Randolph, 'always the House of Commons'.

Churchill was now powerful enough to indulge in more regal nepotism. Since Randolph had his unearned seat in Parliament, and the Prof was basking in the splendour of a peerage as Lord Cherwell, why not make his deserving son-in-law a minister? As soon as Sandys was able to hobble around Westminster with a walking-stick, his father-in-law appointed him Under-Secretary at the Ministry of Defence, thus starting an important political career.

'What about Vic Oliver for Minister of Information?' somebody shouted in the House when the appointment was announced. But that ministry was occupied already by another of Churchill's faithful friends, Duff Cooper, and by now the comedian's days within the Churchill family were numbered.

On the surface, Sarah's marriage was a success. She and Vic had bought a large house in the country, and both had been appearing on the London stage. The problems of her husband's nationality had been sorted out, and as well as his stage appearances, Vic had become a popular radio celebrity. With success and prosperity around her, Sarah's marriage and career seemed unaffected by the war. Then in October 1941, during a weekend at Chequers with her parents, Sarah asked her father a most unexpected favour. It was, she always claimed, the one occasion when she asked him to use his influence on her behalf.

It must have come as a surprise to Churchill when she suddenly announced that relations with her husband had reached 'breaking point'. But, far from being particularly upset, Churchill's first concern seemed to be with keeping up appearances.

'I hope he is going to be a gentleman and give you a divorce.'

'Of course not, Papa,' she said. 'I'm leaving him.'

This amused him.

'Cheeky bitch!' he said. 'I wouldn't let you leave me.'

'And I'm not asking you for your advice. But you can do me a favour.'

It was then that Sarah asked her father to arrange for her to join the ranks of the Women's Auxiliary Air Force as soon as possible.

Within twenty-four hours all was settled. Sarah became Aircraftwoman Second Class Oliver, leaving her marriage and her stage career effectively behind her.

For the time being there was no question of divorce. There was no one else she wished to marry, and her relations with Vic were amicable. The rest of the family professed to be puzzled and upset to hear the news – romantic Mary was actually in tears.

Sarah later liked to claim that even her father 'had become rather fond of Vic by now', but this was not the case. Far from being 'fond' of his son-in-law, Churchill himself bore part of the responsibility for the sudden break-up of his daughter Sarah's most unusual marriage.

Churchills can be magnanimous to those they defeat – but not to those who have defeated them. Churchill had never really forgiven Vic Oliver for having once defied him by stealing his beloved Sarah. This apart, there was also much about his son-in-law that grated on his nerves: his looks, his wisecracks, the outrage he inflicted on the sacred English language, and even his success as a comedian which was bringing him more than twice Churchill's salary as Prime Minister.

Churchill's dislike of Vic did not help the marriage; and, although its breakdown had much deeper roots than this, most of them traced back to his influence within the family – particularly over Sarah.

She was always said to be the child who was most like him. She was certainly the only one to have inherited enough of his spirit to have stood up against him to marry the man she loved against his wishes. But despite this she had firmly remained 'a father-girl' and had obviously attempted to exchange one father figure for another when she opted for her middle-aged comedian. As a dominating father, Churchill had undoubtedly influenced her choice of husband in another way as well.

Like Randolph – and, to a point, Diana too – Sarah had always been obsessed with fame and with achieving some glittering success which would impress him. Success on her own terms would also let her face him without being either swamped or bullied.

Hence her obsessional longing to become a star existed even before going on the stage. Vic had genuinely done his best to make her one. She had come to love the theatre, she also loved her fellow-actors and would clearly never want for work. But at twenty-six she was not a star, and it was all too obvious she never would become one.

It was this, more than anything, that broke the marriage. She and Vic had both failed – she to become a great actress, and he to make her one. Then came the ultimate indignity. Vic found himself another protégée with whom to act Svengali. Her name was Phyllis Lucket and Vic was convinced that she had the makings of success which Sarah lacked. There was no question of him having an affair with her. He was simply and straightforwardly obsessed with the hidden passion of his life – the creation of a great star from an unknown actress. So single-minded was he that he failed to see why Sarah was upset when he suggested that, since they had no children of their own, they should jointly adopt Phyllis.

It was shortly after this that Sarah decided that her marriage – like her quest for stardom – had no future. It left her in a vacuum, with little idea of what could take their place. As she told her father, she was in no hurry for a divorce, and by joining the WAAF she intended to postpone making a decision until the war was over.

When Sarah and Randolph weren't arousing Churchill's parental anxieties, trouble came from the furthest reaches of his extended family. In early 1940, Clementine's nephew, the erratic Giles Romilly, had been captured in Norway while working as a war correspondent for the *Express*.

The Germans failed at first to realise who he was, but when they did discover he was put in isolation as a potential hostage, and then transferred to the top-security camp for very special prisoners-of-war in the notorious castle of Colditz where he spent the remainder of the war.

Meanwhile Giles's brother, Esmond, since fighting with the International Brigade in the Spanish Civil War, had migrated to America and married his cousin Jessica Mitford, and settled in Washington. As a dedicated anti-fascist, he decided to enlist.

Esmond saw no other way to go about this than to go directly, accompanied by his wife, to the British ambassador in Washington to volunteer for flying service with the Canadian Air Force.

'Are you a communist?' the ambassador, Lord Lothian, enquired of Churchill's notorious 'Red Nephew'.

'Are *you*?' Decca answered for him, one member of the British upper classes to another.

By summer 1941, Esmond was on active service as navigator with a light bomber squadron stationed in Lincolnshire; at the end of November his aircraft failed to return from a raid on Hamburg. Jessica was still in America, but just about to bring their daughter, Constancia, back to join Esmond in England, when she heard that he was missing.

With Malaya threatened by the Japanese, and Singapore about to fall, Churchill had greater claims on his attention than the fate of a nephew who had aroused his deepest disapproval in the past. In the Soviet Union, Stalin's armies were fighting for survival, and in just a few days' time, on 7 December 1941, Japanese aircraft were to launch their surprise attack on the American

base at Pearl Harbor which would finally bring America into
the Second World War.

It was a crucial moment for the Western Alliance. Churchill
decided that the time had come to confer with his most important
ally on the joint conduct of the war, and he sailed aboard the
flagship *Duke of York* through the submarine-infested North
Atlantic to meet the President in Washington.

Jessica was away from Washington when he arrived. Returning
shortly after, she was told a posse of secret-servicemen had come
to take her to a service at Arlington church – where Churchill
and Roosevelt, comrades-in-arms at last, would be singing their
favourite martial hymns together – so that she could meet her
famous relative.

'I told them it would have taken more than a car-load of cops
to get Decca into a church, even with the Prime Minister and the
President of the United States,' her host remarked. But Jessica
was desperate for any news of Esmond. So she telephoned the
White House, and getting through to Mrs Roosevelt fixed an
appointment to see Churchill there next morning.

Clutching eight-month-old Constancia, swaddled in a white
wool suit, she was conducted to the great man's presence. As
usual, he was doing his morning's work in bed, 'and looking
absolutely marvellous, like some extravagant peacock in his
bright silk dressing-gown'.

The troubles of the past forgotten, he greeted her affection-
ately. 'He was extremely sympathetic from the start, and it
turned out that he had made his own enquiries about Esmond.
But the worst had happened. He had to tell me that there was
not the slightest chance that Esmond had been taken prisoner.
His aircraft had come down in the North Sea and there were no
survivors. Winston seemed deeply moved.'

He was so moved, in fact, that to cover his emotions he changed
the subject and proceeded to give Jessica news of other members
of her family. This included an update on her sister Diana, who
was still in prison but who had recently been united with her
husband.

Completely unaware of Jessica's feelings on the subject, he
assured her that he was doing all he could to make the Mosleys
comfortable, even arranging for some of the other prisoners to
do their prison chores for them.

'I went into a total rage at this,' says Jessica – 'servants for the Mosleys when Esmond had just been killed by my sister's precious friends! I told him they should both be put against a wall and shot.'

If Churchill was startled by the reaction of Clementine's embattled niece, he did not show it; instead he returned to the subject of Esmond Romilly, speaking of his admiration for his hero's death. As she was leaving, his secretary discreetly handed Jessica an envelope. Inside were five hundred dollars.

'Later the rumour went round London that I threw the money back at him,' Jessica recalls. 'Of course I didn't. Five hundred dollars was a small fortune in those days. But I did feel there was a flavour of blood-money about it, although I'm sure that it was kindly meant. So I gave some of it to my host's daughter to buy a horse, and the rest went to a political campaign.'

Before flying back to England, Churchill had a five-day holiday in Florida with one of his oldest friends, Sunny Marlborough's former duchess. The elegantly ageing Consuelo was seeing out the war with her husband Jacques Balsan in considerable luxury in Palm Beach.

Churchill needed the break to recharge his own 'accumulators' after the strain of his visit to the Roosevelts with so much at stake. He was sixty-seven. During this historic visit to North America he had made his famous address to the joint session of Congress, playing up his own American ancestry and proudly promising that the two great English-speaking peoples would 'walk together side by side in majesty, in justice and in peace'. He had addressed the Canadian parliament, and signed both the new Grand Alliance against the Axis powers and the pact that led directly to the United Nations Organisation. He had also secretly sustained a minor heart-attack, which left him tired and weakened.

He flew back to London knowing that, despite this, he would be called to account for some of the worst disasters of the war. In Malaya, Singapore was just about to fall, as Britain's Far Eastern empire crumbled to the Japanese. Stalin's armies seemed unable to withstand the Germans on the Eastern Front, and in North Africa victory had switched abruptly to defeat as Rommel's Afrika Korps prepared to retake Benghazi and threaten Cairo. When Churchill returned to face these setbacks in London, Randolph was there to greet him, having flown from Cairo on three weeks' leave.

Happily for one and all, Averell Harriman was currently

back in the United States, after his historic Moscow visit. He had arranged supplies of American war materials to his country's latest ally, Joseph Stalin. Baby Winston was still gurgling contentedly with his Nanny Hills at Cherkley, kind Lord Beaverbrook's country house in Surrey; and Pamela seemed resigned to reunion with the returning warrior.

She soon had a chance to witness him in action – not in battle but in the House of Commons, in the role which he had always dreamed of. He was defending his hard-pressed father in a full-scale parliamentary debate on a vote of confidence.

The loss of Singapore had produced the first real signs of discontent at home with Churchill's leadership, and there were criticisms of 'the central direction of the war' from both sides of the House. There was a bitter personal attack on Churchill from the socialist Emanuel Shinwell, who claimed that he was out of touch and had fatally misjudged events. (More effective was a later taunt from his other main parliamentary critic, Aneurin Bevan, that 'the Right Honourable Member wins every debate but loses every battle'.)

Randolph, resplendent in his major's uniform, rose to defend his father – and, as always, overdid it.

Misjudging the mood of the House, his florid oratory fell flat as he bitterly attacked that great majority of members who had supported Chamberlain at Munich, then tried to flaunt his military knowledge as a serving soldier.

Predictably this brought trouble and noisy interjections.

'Will the Honourable and Gallant Member – I call him that because of the uniform he wears – please tell me on what occasion he has been, as a soldier, in a battle where he has been shot at by the enemy at 1500 yards?' enquired Commander Archibald Southby from the Conservative backbenches.

From his nearby seat, Harold Nicolson saw Churchill 'looking embarrassed and shy' at this. Directly after the debate, the commander had the misfortune to encounter Churchill in the corridor. He tried to excuse himself, but Churchill was beside himself with rage.

He shook his fist in Southby's face. 'Do not speak to me,' he shouted. 'You called my son a coward. You are my enemy. Do not speak to me.'

Randolph's loyalty to his father had once again backfired, and making an exhibition of himself in Parliament can have done little to enhance him in Pamela's less than star-struck eyes. Nicolson had not missed the sight of 'Randolph's little wife squirming in the Gallery throughout his speech'.

Once again it was left to Churchill to assert his kingly powers in one of his most powerful parliamentary speeches. The next day, on 29 January he pulled out all the stops and, tired as he was, convinced the House of his unfailing confidence, 'never stronger than at this moment, that we shall bring this conflict to an end in a manner agreeable to the interests of this country, and in a manner agreeable to the future of the world'.

In spite of Randolph's ill-judged intermission, Churchill won his vote of confidence by 464 to 1, and after the vote was taken, Nicolson observed him 'arm-in-arm and beaming' with Clementine as 'they pushed through the crowds in the Central Lobby'.

At this grim moment of the war, Clementine was unassailable. Gone were the feelings of inadequacy which she had blurted out to Cecil Beaton two years earlier. Dignified and conscientiously aware of where her duty lay, she had taught herself the queenly role that suited her. Gone, too, was the memory of that period before the war when she had doubted Churchill's sense of destiny. Pressed at this crisis of the war, he increasingly relied upon her to ensure the smooth running of his private world that meant so much to him. Nor had she grown averse herself to the pleasurable accompaniments of power – the chauffeurs, secretaries, bodyguards, and the sense of being at the hub of things.

So there was some significance in the fact that it was Clementine rather than her son who was side by side with Churchill in the Central Lobby after his successful peroration. It should have been Randolph. He, after all, was the precious heir briefly back from active service, and he had done his best to plead his father's cause as so often in the past. But he had failed – and it was Clementine who inevitably gained.

Clementine had never made a secret of her original decision to place husband before children to promote his great career. Then, largely thanks to Randolph, it had seemed that she had failed. The bond between the father and the son appeared to have displaced her from her position as Churchill's prime supporter. Even the worst excesses of the heir apparent's private life had been unable to dislodge the old king's faith in him – and the illogical deep love he bore him.

But now that Clementine had made herself so indispensable it was Randolph who began to find himself displaced.

'The cause of all the trouble between Randolph and his mother was simple jealousy for Winston's affection and attention,' one of his closest friends remarked. 'Originally she couldn't forgive Randolph for taking Winston from her, but now the boot was on the other foot and it was Randolph who envied Clementine her place beside his father.'

In this potentially explosive situation, Randolph, true to form, continued to place himself firmly in the wrong, often from the very best of motives. One of the greatest sources of contention between Randolph and his parents proved to be his marriage, which was already showing classic signs of being past repair. According to Bruce Lockhart, Pamela soon reached the stage where she could hardly bear the sight of Randolph, who physically 'repelled her with his spotted face and gross figure'. Heavy drinking and the Cairo flesh-pots had done little for his personal appeal, and the contrast between this khaki-clad Silenus and the elegant Averell was unfortunate. So was the state of Randolph's temper.

According to reports Bruce Lockhart had from Kathleen Harriman, Randolph attempted much the same 'pasha-like' behaviour towards his wife that he had seen his father use – but with less success. He objected strongly to the way young Winston was still parked out on Beaverbrook with a nanny.

'I want you to be with my son,' he told her.

'He also happens to be *my* son,' Pamela replied.

'No!' bellowed Randolph. 'My son. I'm a Churchill.'

But Pamela now had war work of her own which was engaging much of her attention. Impressed by the way she made visiting Americans feel at home in wartime London, Brendan Bracken had suggested that her talents be employed more systematically. He proposed the creation of a select club with official backing where top-ranking American servicemen, journalists and diplomats would find themselves welcome, hear lectures, and generally mingle with the cream of political and polite society.

Thanks to Bracken's influence, money and premises were found. Pamela moved into a flat in Grosvenor Square, and the club was established in the shadow of Westminster Abbey in the evocative surroundings of Westminster School (the boys having been evacuated).

As head of London's Churchill Club, the younger Mrs Churchill was a great success. Her credentials as the wife of Churchill's dauphin were impeccable. So were her personality and her appearance. Gone for ever were the shyness and the puppy fat.

'She is quite a dish,' wrote Evelyn Waugh to Nancy Mitford. And Carnation Digby's daughter was becoming an accomplished hostess – svelte, attentive, immaculately dressed and projecting something of the authentic aura of Churchillian regality on her own account.

This was something she would never lose, and which would launch her on one of the most colourful society careers of her generation. She would be much admired by the American celebrities who visited the Churchill Club, and several beside Harriman fell in love with her. These included another multi-millionaire, Jock Whitney, and the famous war-correspondent and hard-bitten broadcaster from wartime London, Ed Murrow, who, despite the existence of Randolph, Averell Harriman, and a Mrs Murrow back in the United States, tried hard to marry her.

Such success inevitably caused jealousy and gossip among the more feline members of society. But Clementine and Churchill remained devoted to their daughter-in-law. From her own marital experiences, Clementine could sympathise with Pamela's problems with Randolph; and Churchill, who loved her as a daughter, was impressed by the efforts she was making to improve Anglo-American relations.

'Pamela seems very well, and is a great treasure and blessing to us all,' he assured Randolph in a letter which he wrote him in May 1942.

But Randolph, back in Cairo after two months' unrewarding leave, was beginning to think otherwise. Always attuned to the gossip which emanated supersonically from White's Club bar even at the height of war, he had heard gossip – probably misleading – of the relationship between his wife and the man who had once been 'definitely my favourite American'. He was not jealous. Sexual jealousy was almost unique among the deadly sins in not being found in Randolph's nature. But he was angry that Harriman had apparently taken advantage of his friendship after being recommended by his father. He was also most upset that his parents – and particularly his mother – refused to see the slightest wrong in Pamela, but could be so critical of him.

Once again his worthiest intentions had misfired, and there was more trouble from one of his genuine efforts to redeem himself. Sick of his protected life, and galled by the jeers which he endured in Parliament, he had volunteered for parachute training and attachment to an embryonic unit of the Special Air Service.

It was the sort of military adventure his father would once have been unable to resist, but when Clementine heard about it she was furious. How typical of Randolph to be trying to do something 'sensational' again, without a thought of his responsibilities! Not only had he a 'very young wife and baby', but also his father was carrying the burden of the war. How could he think of adding to his worries?

So incensed was Clementine that she felt impelled to write her husband one of her wifely missives on the subject. Bearing in mind what Colville wrote of Churchill's fears about being unable to continue 'should anything happen to Randolph', it makes interesting reading. For Clementine, consciously or unconsciously, was clearly undermining Randolph by playing on her husband's fears.

After the scene in the corridor with Commander Southby, Churchill's natural instincts must have been to admire Randolph for disproving the slur of cowardice by his dangerous decision. Not so Clementine. Instead of praising their son for his courage, all she could bring herself to say was: 'I grieve that he has done this because I know it will cause you harrowing anxiety, indeed, even agony of mind.' She ended by suggesting that she should send Randolph an 'affectionate' telegram, begging him simply to rejoin his regiment for his father's sake, and give up further thoughts about the SAS.

Wisely she had second thoughts about sending this letter to her husband, and Randolph was permitted to begin his life of long-delayed adventure with his father's blessing. But, while he gained with Churchill, Randolph only made worse his very poor relationship with his mother.

As usual, nothing he could do was right.

'Poor Randolph!' said Miss Hamblin. 'I don't know quite why, but I always used to say, "Poor Randolph."'

28

Master of Alliances

By the end of 1942 the heroic phase of Churchill's wartime leadership at home was ending. He was no longer heading an embattled nation in a lonely struggle for survival. The true test of his leadership now lay in guiding Britain in her new position with her two great allies, America and the Soviet Union, in a world-wide struggle with Japan as well as with Nazi Germany.

America and the Soviet Union were infinitely larger and more powerful than Britain, with interests and war-aims of their own, but Churchill was determined to maintain his own position in this massive coalition. Inspired by his sense of history and his dreams of destiny, he deployed the whole armoury of his complex nature to achieve this. It was a masterly performance. Marlborough had 'ridden to victory with the alliances of Europe in his hand'. The time had come to follow his example.

As head of his 'Grand Coalition' against the French, Marlborough's most important ally had been faithful Prince Eugene of Austria, who placed the essential troops and resources of the Austrian Empire alongside Britain's at Marlborough's disposal.

Inevitably Churchill cast the President of the United States in the role of his trusty Prince Eugene. As such he courted, lectured, and attempted to inspire him like a warrior monarch with a richer, less experienced ally in a common cause.

Thanks largely to the understanding Churchill established with Franklin Roosevelt in their early correspondence, Britain had been able to rely on the United States as the all-important 'arsenal of democracy' when Britain fought alone. At the end of 1942, Churchill still appeared the dominant partner in their close relationship, and when the statesmen met – as meet they did on ten occasions – the Premier never failed to impress the President with the rhetoric and trappings of a great occasion.

Up to a point, the President had gone along with this, but the more America became involved in the war, and the greater her contribution in material and men, the clearer it became that Eugene would not accept Marlborough's supremacy for ever. At the Casablanca conference with Roosevelt early in 1943, Churchill was able to persuade the President to accept his plans to advance through Sicily and Italy; but General Eisenhower commanded the Allied forces when they invaded northern France, and Churchill agreed to American demands that war with Germany would end only with its 'Unconditional Surrender'. Even then America faced the prospect of a long hard war in Asia, where its interests would be very different from those of Britain and her precious empire.

Despite these differences, there still appeared to be no greater contrast than between Churchill's statesmanlike devotion to Franklin Roosevelt and the obvious distrust with which he treated Joseph Stalin. Stalin, after all, had been one of the original 'hairy Bolshevik baboons' whose crimes in the purges of the thirties far exceeded those of the 'fiendish criminals' Churchill attempted to destroy in 1920.

But with Stalin's armies having just achieved their greatest victory of the war before the city now named after him co-operation was essential, and Churchill needed to establish a relationship with the Soviet leader which, if not as close as with Roosevelt, would permit at least an element of trust and understanding for the future.

'If the Germans invaded Hell, I'd put in a good word for the Devil,' he remarked, and when he had flown to Moscow in August 1942, personal contact modified his attitude towards the 'Ogre' and he found in Stalin less the Bolshevik baboon than a tough hard-drinking warrior–statesman, and something of an actor on his own account.

Churchill had always had a taste for coarse hard-drinking men of power, and in their late-night sessions in the Kremlin (Roosevelt, an early-nighter, had tended to drop off in Churchill's late-night perorations) Churchill and Stalin formed a natural, if unlikely, twosome.

This did not stop them having bitter disagreements, with only little Pavlov, the interpreter, in attendance. Churchill was anxious not to launch the 'second front' in northern France which Stalin was demanding before all preparations were complete – and there were arguments about the form and scale of Western aid to the

Soviet Union. Crucial questions over future Soviet spheres of influence, particularly in eastern Europe, stayed unresolved.

But, while arguing over these enormous questions, the two superstars seemed to enjoy each other's company – and delight in outdoing one another when they had an audience. Acting up to Churchill's publicised (but carefully controlled) capacity for alcohol, Stalin arranged a table set with uncorked bottles for their delectation. And, upstaging the old warrior with his well-known love of meat, Stalin ostentatiously consumed a pig's head before him.

He was also shrewd enough to leave the older man with the impression that he could still outdrink him and stay sober – as all the evidence suggests that Churchill could.

As far as Churchill was concerned, the result was a sense of considerable rapport enabling him to overlook the crimes of Stalin's earlier existence.

'Call me Winston. I call you Joe behind your back,' said Churchill.

'No, I want to call you my friend,' replied the genial mass-murderer.

Although it could not last, this friendship was important in these early days of the wartime coalition, but the true test of Churchill's role as the 'Master of Alliances' came on the threshold of his seventies, when all three leaders met together for the first time to confer in Tehran in November 1943.

Two weeks earlier, on 12 November, he had sailed from Southampton aboard the battleship *Renown*, accompanied by Randolph and Sarah, and a retinue of statesmen, generals, ambassadors and personal advisers, to confer once more with the President of the United States in Cairo.

He had been far from well, with a heavy cold, a bad sore throat – which almost stopped the flow of words – and the after-effects of various injections. When the ship stopped off at Malta he had had to spend two days in bed.

But in Cairo, in the presence of the President, he rapidly revived. 'It really is wonderful how they both get on – they really like and understand each other . . . ,' wrote Sarah to her mother. Even his Foreign Secretary, Anthony Eden, who was present at their meetings, was 'amazed' at the patience with which Churchill 'played the role of courtier' to Roosevelt as they discussed the fraught strategic issues of the disposition of their massive forces.

(It would have been more amazing had Churchill not treated the President with patience, remembering how much richer, greater, stronger his resources were, and how much victory depended on the United States.)

On 28 November the two leaders journeyed separately to meet Stalin in Tehran, the furthest point outside the Soviet Union they could tempt the suspicious leader.

November 30 was Churchill's sixty-ninth birthday, and clearly an emotional occasion. There were tears in his eyes when he received the presents and congratulations from the British residents of Tehran. That evening, with Sarah and Randolph to support him, he gave a formal birthday-dinner in honour of Roosevelt and Stalin at the British legation. Amid the caviare, the endless toasts, the heavy humour and the large cigars, neither the historical nor the personal significance of the occasion was lost upon him.

From his earliest days his one unwavering ambition had concerned the active exercise of power. Now, as he reminded the two other leaders, they jointly represented probably 'the greatest concentration of worldly power that has ever been seen in the history of mankind'.

There is no mistaking the pride behind his own description of that birthday-dinner in the Persian capital.

On my right sat the President of the United States, on my left the master of Russia. Together we controlled a large preponderance of the naval and three-quarters of all the air forces of the world, and could direct armies of nearly twenty millions of men in the most terrible of wars that had yet occurred in human history.

In Tehran, Churchill did his best to impose his historical– romantic concept of the war on the principal performers. One of his first acts was to present courageous Marshal Stalin with a sword of chivalry. Stalin, uncomfortably decked out in a mustard-yellow Russian marshal's uniform which was hurriedly produced for the occasion, received the famous 'Sword of Stalingrad' – symbolic gift of the distant King of England – from Winston Churchill, who was similarly attired in the uniform of a commodore of the RAF, complete with pilot's wings. Stalin kissed the hilt; but Roosevelt, unimpressed by Churchill's gestures, brandished it around him from his position in his wheel-chair.

As the conference proceeded, it was Roosevelt who made it

clear that his role as Churchill's Prince Eugene was definitely over. Despite their carefully nurtured friendship – and Churchill's past romantic but implausible declarations of brotherhood and unity between the two great English-speaking nations – Roosevelt was tiring of Churchill playing Marlborough at their meetings. There were also signs that he was impatient with Churchill's imperial view of history and the whole grand manner of this extremely clever, dominating actor–statesman, who could be seen as taking him and the massive efforts of the great United States for granted. He was particularly worried that Churchill might be attempting to divert the power of the United States to Britain's interests – and in particular to supporting and recovering something no decent Democrat could countenance, the old outdated British Empire.

When Churchill was not present, Roosevelt could not resist the chance of making deals direct with Stalin – thereby causing trouble for the future and fuelling suspicion that the English-speaking allies were not immutably united.

Despite this, in Tehran at least, Churchill's rhetoric and sense of history offered the conference a unifying theme and even brought a measure of agreement on a concerted strategy in Europe before dealing with Japan. Stalin was reconciled to the delay of the Anglo-American second front until midsummer 1944; it was agreed that the Soviet Union would enter the Far Eastern war after victory in the West, and the pattern of the war in Italy and the Mediterranean was broadly if pragmatically decided, with the Allies even agreeing to Churchill's pet plan for a daring amphibious landing at Anzio eight weeks later. In the circumstances, it is doubtful whether Marlborough, the master of alliances, could have done much better.

But, for Churchill, the exalted role that he adopted also served a private purpose. One of the mysteries about this phenomenal old statesman is how he sustained the energy and passion of his wartime leadership, continuing to dominate his generals and domestic politicians and playing his impressive part in Tehran despite the weakness of his own position.

Ever since his time in India in his early twenties he had been learning to transform himself, by concentrated bouts of will, to act the great dramatic roles his strange imagination could create to overcome his dread of fear or failure. The mechanism rarely seemed to fail, and the most effective roles were still the old aggressive ones. It was aggression that sparked off the formidable afflatus of the 'Churchill up' syndrome. That 'great talent for show-off exaggeration and make-believe' his father once complained of had produced something akin to what is seen with legendary actors in their greatest roles. Imagination and reality converged as he embraced the part that he created. Power was his theme, history his stage, and in looks, speech, gesture he became the warrior–statesman locked in battle for the future of the world above the dross of commonplace existence.

Even his conversation to his doctor sounded like something out of Shakespeare. 'Stupendous issues', he remarked before dropping off to sleep, 'are unfolding before our eyes, and we are only specks of dust which have settled for a night on the map of the world.'

In the past, this sort of rhetoric had been a source of inspiration and of great disasters. But now, at the very centre of 'the most terrible of wars in human history', he seemed able to sustain it, marshal his power within it, concentrate his energy and intellect upon it – then diffuse it like some force of nature on to those around him, including the members of his family who had to cope with it.

Sarah enjoyed herself in Tehran. She used to say she chose the WAAF because of the colour of the uniform: air-force blue set off her auburn hair and pale complexion. At twenty-seven she still possessed a dancer's figure, animated features and considerable feminine allure. She certainly remained enough the actress to play the part of her father's favourite princess, employing all her charm upon the Allied leaders.

Roosevelt, who flirted mildly with her, she 'simply loved', and she even acted up to Stalin. Seeing him simply as genial 'Uncle Joe', she was much taken by the avuncular Georgian. He was, she wrote, 'a great man, of that there can be no doubt', and she detected that his sense of humour was every bit 'as darting and swift as Papa's'.

But her real interests were beginning to turn towards the American ambassador, John Gil Winant, who had fallen seriously in love with her. He was very much her type – another older man, assured, good-looking and something of a loner at the centre of the diplomatic world. However, she needed no reminder of the trouble her love-affairs could cause within the family. Winant was married, and she could not risk a scandal. She had seen the trouble Randolph's marital disasters caused. She knew how jealously her father viewed her. She was very cautious.

In Papa's reflected glory, she was safely back where part of her had always longed to be, the perfect 'father girl' with no Vic Oliver to come between them.

For all her 'mulish' obstinacy in the past, it was impossible for her not to fall beneath her father's dominating spell. At his birthday-banquet, when all the toasts were being drunk, it was only her 'old restraint' which stopped her proposing 'Papa's health' and telling everyone that he was not only a great statesman, but 'a nice father too – and more'.

As far as the family was concerned, Sarah's natural warmth was working to offset the tensions and the jealousies within it. She was that rarity in families, a natural peacemaker, who genuinely wanted those around her to like each other. During her time in Tehran she took much trouble writing her mother long newsy letters to make her feel included in what was happening. In the course of them she even did her best to put in a good word for Randolph.

She described his exemplary behaviour at the birthday-banquet – no arguments, and only a moderate amount to drink. 'He is trying you know – there is a big change in him,' she added. And it was partly thanks to Sarah that the close relationship between Churchill and his son seemed to have been restored. She was certainly a loyal ally to her brother, but the balance between Churchill and his son was as delicate as ever.

Randolph remained important to his father. They had so much in common – similarities of character, memories and anecdotes and shared ambitions from the past. There was no one else Churchill could confide in as he did with Randolph, and on the voyage to Cairo they had been inseparable.

During the conference this trust continued. Randolph scored something of a coup with a long after-dinner *tête-à-tête* with Stalin. He was really 'trying', and in Churchill's eyes this must have made a satisfying contrast to the behaviour of Roosevelt's son, Elliot, who had infuriated Churchill by taking seriously one of Stalin's 'jokes' on the need to exterminate the entire German high command when the war was over. (Churchill stumped from the table in disgust.)

As evidence of the confidence between them, it was in Tehran that Churchill entrusted Randolph with the sort of task by which he could have made himself indispensable. It had been decided to woo Turkey to the Allied cause, and Randolph was despatched to the Turkish city of Adana, in his father's personal aircraft, to meet the Turkish President Inonu on his behalf. In fact, he made two visits to Turkey in swift succession, and it was largely thanks to them that a very worried Inonu was persuaded to meet Churchill when he returned to Cairo. (Here the courtship of Turkey ceased as its anxious President, despite kissing Churchill on both cheeks, wisely made it clear how much he cherished his neutrality.) Randolph was excited to have been of use. Then, as so often in his life, success was followed by catastrophe.

When the Tehran conference ended, Churchill's great performance ended with it. The act was over, the willpower which had been sustaining him relaxed, and the next few days spent back in Cairo finishing his discussions with Roosevelt were dogged by diarrhoea and a reappearance of his earlier ailments. One of the three most powerful men on earth admitted he was now so weak that he could no longer dry himself after his evening bath, but 'lay on the bed wrapped in my towel until I dried naturally' – something he could not remember ever having done before.

His doctor – Dr Charles Wilson, soon to be ennobled for services to Churchill as Baron Moran – feared that his master had been 'profligate of his resources' in Tehran. He noted a worrying lack of concentration as the great man spent a lunchtime meeting swatting flies, then rambling on in a disjointed after-dinner monologue without realising that some of his distinguished guests were fast asleep. But the chief victim of his change of mood was Randolph.

Randolph confided what occurred in a note to his beloved Laura. She, despite all his baffled efforts to the contrary, was now indubitably married to the Earl of Dudley; but Randolph had made a way of life of refusing to acknowledge facts that did not suit him, and firmly refused to think about her as a married woman, or to consider the existence of the earl. As much in love as ever, he insisted on writing to her as he always had – and unrequited passion played its part in his current troubles with his parents.

It was a letter written on 8 December 1943 which gave the news. After describing the excitement of his trips to Tehran and

Turkey, he added gloomily: '. . . my pleasure in all this has been greatly spoiled by the fact that W and I still don't get on. It is the same old trouble in the back of his mind, reinforced by his belief (so true in political affairs) that he can get his way by bullying and obstinacy.'

Another of the 'blood rows' which battered their relationship had suddenly erupted. After the high of Tehran, Churchill was suffering stomach pains, and was in far from the best of tempers. Randolph had drunk too much as usual, and a reference to his marriage brought an immediate explosion.

Churchill was obsessed about the breakdown of this marriage at the centre of his sacred family. 'R's marriage is going wonky and W is terribly distressed,' wrote Harold Nicolson. 'The old boy is tremendously domestic and adores his family.' This was 'the same old trouble in the back of his mind' to which Randolph had referred, and the situation between them had become intolerable. Tehran had provided a diversion, but now the subject could not be avoided.

Churchill and Clementine still insisted on regarding Pamela as the harshly treated mother of the scion of the Churchills and had even been helping her with money. To Randolph's chagrin they were paying her £500 a year tax-free on a seven-year covenant.

Churchill had not objected to divorce in Sarah's case; but, then, he had thoroughly disliked Vic Oliver. ('I find myself rather envying Il Duce,' he supposedly remarked, on hearing how Mussolini had executed his son-in-law, Count Ciano.)

In contrast, he and Clementine remained fond of Pamela, who treated them with kindness and concern. Besides, young Winston was involved. Churchill doted on his grandson; and, once embarked upon this whole emotive subject, it was a short step on to Randolph's failings – his extravagance, his irresponsibility, his lack of feeling for his family and his father. Clementine was absolutely right about him.

Randolph saw things differently. He, after all, had rushed into marriage at the start of war, largely to please his father and provide an heir and namesake for his precious dynasty. He had acted from the best of motives and had done his duty. Now he was getting all the blame because the marriage had not worked.

The family had encouraged Pamela's friendship with Harriman, and she had other smart American admirers. What hypocrisy to say that Pamela was wholly innocent and he was totally to blame.

Having just faced Roosevelt and Stalin, it was not surprising that Churchill was in a mood to be 'obstinate and bullying' to Randolph on the subject of his marriage. Harsh words were spoken, and Randolph stormed off in tears, swearing that everything was finished between them. Relations were still strained when Churchill flew to Tunis three days later.

He had a crowded schedule, as he was planning to confer with American and British leaders in Tunis and Algiers before visiting his favourite general, General Alexander, in southern Italy. Churchill's excitement was building up for the forthcoming landing at Anzio, south of Rome, despite ominous similarities with the landings at Gallipoli.

Churchill envied Alexander his command in the field, and could not keep away from action. But by the time his plane touched down in Tunis the strains of the last few frantic weeks caught up with him.

On 11 December he collapsed. Pneumonia set in. He had a minor heart-attack – his second after the undisclosed attack which Moran knew he had suffered two years earlier in Washington. By 15 December the 'Lord Doctor' – as Diana Cooper christened him – was seriously worried for his patient's life.

Churchill was not. With his star performance in Tehran behind him, he seems to have regarded the descent of life's great drop-curtain with equanimity. Death had never worried him particularly: 'an event so natural and indispensable to mankind', as he had once described it.

He and his party were occupying a villa outside Tunis, close to the ruins of an empire which had been suddenly destroyed for ever. The parallel was not lost upon him.

'I suppose it is fitting I should die beside Carthage,' he remarked. 'If I die, don't worry,' he told Sarah, who had remained beside him. 'The war is won.'

Others regarded his departure less philosophically. Back in England, news of his illness caused alarm, and it was by prescribing the new wonder-drug, M & B, and organising specialists and nurses for his patient that Moran earned his barony. Sarah read him *Pride and Prejudice*.

Until now, Churchill had never found the time for anything as frivolous as English literature; but he enjoyed Miss Austen, and she seems to have assisted his recovery. So, to a point, did the arrival at the villa of other members of his family – first Randolph, who had departed in agitated circumstances some days earlier, then Clementine, who was rushed from England in considerable discomfort together with the secretaries Miss Hamblin and Jock Colville.

By Christmas Day he was back on whisky and cigars, and after conferring with General Eisenhower – newly appointed Allied supreme commander for the forthcoming invasion of northern France – he was able to enjoy what his secretary, John Martin, called 'a soporific Christmas lunch of turkey and plum pudding' with his wife, his daughter and his son. It seemed like a united family, with its members offering affection and support around the convalescent statesman. Of course, beneath the surface it was not that simple.

Clementine made an odd remark on her arrival. Welcoming her, Lord Moran spoke of the emotion Churchill showed when told that she was coming. At this she 'smiled whimsically', remarking: 'Oh yes, he's very glad I've come, but in five minutes he'll forget I'm here.'

Her first attempt to accompany her husband to a major wartime conference – to Quebec in 1942 – had proved a singular ordeal. Eleanor Roosevelt, most fluent and engaged of political wives, with her obvious intellect and awesome self-assurance, made her feel at a disadvantage. This in turn had made her irritable – even with Roosevelt when he indulged in the *lèse-majesté* of calling her 'Clemmie' to her face. Only her husband and oldest friends and family were permitted that. 'Intimately as both my wife and I knew Lady Churchill,' wrote Colville, 'we never called her Clemmie to her dying day.'

She was upset and angry; and then, as so often in the past after one of her nervous outbursts, prostration followed. When she recovered it was decided she would not accompany her husband on any future major trips abroad. Instead, Sarah and Mary would take turns in acting as what they called 'family ADCs' to give their father familiar support upon these great occasions.

This left Clementine with the role of queen in residence at Downing Street and Chequers, consort and consolation in his moments of infrequent relaxation, and gracious hostess when the need arose. She was far from idle. She took the charities she ran extremely seriously – especially the chairmanship of the YWCA and of the nationwide Red Cross 'Aid to Russia' campaign she headed after 1941.

But, despite so much activity, there remained an element of discontent in her position which could erupt with unexpected passion, particularly when jealousy became involved.

She was not given to forgiveness and could be as venomous as ever against any she believed to have usurped her rightful place in her husband's confidence. Lord Beaverbrook was one of Churchill's oldest surviving friends. He had also been one of the very few he trusted in the bleakest days of 1940. By February 1942, when Beaverbrook had just finished his heroic stint as Minister of Aircraft Production – and also providing a home for several months to baby Winston – Clementine wrote about him to her husband thus: 'My Darling – Try ridding yourself of this microbe which some people fear is in your blood – Exorcise this bottle imp and see if the air is not clearer & purer.'

Within the family she could act rather similarly. Diana got on particularly well with her father, who enjoyed her sense of humour. During a period when she worked as a voluntary helper in a West End hospital, Diana made a point of collecting remarks people made about him which she thought would amuse him. They invariably did. But Clementine's relations with her eldest daughter were as difficult as ever. Diana was dotingly in love with her cold and dominating husband, and fully occupied with her three young children and her house in Chester Square. Clementine seemed to resent this, and her relations with this segment of the family were not improved by the fact that she seemed to find her son-in-law a bore.

But within the family circle of the most powerful man in Britain the fire-power of its presiding matriarch tended to be drawn most frequently to the son and heir. Randolph's friend, the cartoonist Osbert Lancaster, exaggerated when he said 'his mother hated him, absolutely loathed his guts'. But it was fair to say that the old antipathy between mother and son found further aggravation from the war and from the jealousies and strains that came from Churchill's position. Once these strains were eased – as they were now with Churchill's illness – relations between Randolph and his mother temporarily improved.

Although he was rapidly recovering, Churchill accepted Lord Moran's firm advice that he should go somewhere warm to convalesce, and not join General Alexander's troops in Italy. So, Christmas over – and cheered by the news of the sinking of the German warship *Scharnhorst* – Churchill and his rapidly expanding court flew from Tunis to one spot which he would always love: the French Moroccan holiday-resort of Marrakesh.

Although it was January, there was sunlight and luxury amid what Clementine described as a 'mixture of the Arabian nights and Hollywood'. And there to greet him was one of the few women from the past whose company he genuinely enjoyed – the still beautiful Diana Cooper, whose husband Duff was now Churchill's representative with the Free French in Algiers.

The warlord of Tehran was suddenly transformed – as he always could be when his aggression was switched off – into someone gentler and touchingly eccentric, whom Diana Cooper recognised from the Chartwell of before the war.

'There was our old baby in his rompers, ten-gallon cowboy hat and very ragged oriental dressing-gown,' she wrote; and for the next fortnight the convalescent 'schoolboy' cheerfully enjoyed his unexpected holiday in 'a millionairess's pleasure dome, all marble and orange-trees, fountains and tiles in the richest Mahomedan style'. The potentate was at his ease. Neither the war nor a visit from de Gaulle could mar his pleasure.

He slept, he drank, he picnicked and he painted. Even Clementine's enemy, the 'bottle imp' Lord Beaverbrook, turned up to keep her husband happy; since Churchill obviously loved his company, there was little Clementine could do but graciously accept him.

Gracious acceptance was the order of the day, and with Sarah still present to keep an eye on father, Clementine could gratefully depart for bed each night at 9.30, leaving her husband talking the night away as usual.

Diana Cooper described how Churchill finished an elaborate picnic by insisting on clambering up a massive boulder, and how members of his entourage hauled him up, puffing like a grampus, with a table-cloth around his middle. In the Moroccan heat, and after a recent heart-attack, this must have been alarming; but according to Diana, 'Clemmie said nothing, but watched him like a lenient mother who does not wish to spoil her child's fun, nor yet his daring'.

The person who particularly benefited from this happy atmosphere was Randolph, whose defects as a husband and a son were temporarily forgiven – if not entirely forgotten. Since seeing action briefly with the SAS in Sicily and southern Italy, he had been pushing hard to get more active service. Thanks to one of the decisions made by the Western powers in Tehran, he seemed to have finally succeeded.

In Tehran it was agreed to give full support to the Yugoslav partisan leader, Tito, in his fight against the Germans; and a British military mission, headed by the Tory MP Brigadier Fitzroy Maclean, was being sent to his assistance. Maclean was still in Cairo. Randolph knew him, and the courageous brigadier did something few commanding officers would have contemplated. He said he was perfectly prepared to take Randolph with him.

(Explaining his decision, Maclean insisted that not only was Randolph 'thoroughly dependable, possessing both endurance and determination', but also he 'felt he would get on well with the Jugoslavs, for his enthusiastic and at times explosive attitude to life was not unlike their own'.)

Randolph was genuinely overjoyed. After four long years of waiting, this was the sort of important active-service mission he had always wanted – and which his father might have undertaken in his own heroic youth. But first it was essential to obtain Papa's consent and arrange the final details with him. With the sort of princely gesture he could still summon when the need arose, Randolph personally conducted Brigadier Maclean from Cairo to Marrakesh aboard the aircraft which had been consigned for General Alexander.

Author and man of action, Maclean was the sort of man to appeal to Churchill. 'No gentler pirate ever cut a throat or robbed a ship,' he wrote about him later, quoting Byron's description of a character in *Don Juan*. In the happy atmosphere of Marrakesh, the 'gentle pirate's' plans and optimistic attitude to Randolph proved contagious. Not only was Churchill totally convinced by Maclean of the need to back the communist Tito against his royalist partisan opponent, Mihailovich; he was also excited by the prospect of his son, Randolph, joining his military mission.

Although it would obviously be hazardous to join the partisans behind the German lines, no more was heard about the dire effect on Churchill should anything happen to his son. Great kings traditionally entrusted their sons to their allies as sign of earnest intent in time of war. And Randolph, now promoted to major, flew off to Yugoslavia with his father's blessing. Maclean bore a fulsome letter from Churchill to Tito, promising him 'all the aid in human power', and setting out Maclean's credentials. 'With him at your headquarters', Churchill proudly added, 'will be serving my son, Major Randolph Churchill, who is also a Member of Parliament.'

Since Churchill had sanctioned Randolph's mission, Clementine could only go along with it. In a letter to Mary she said she thought the work would suit him.

29

'The Shadows of Victory'

Clementine's most revealing remark about what the war meant to her husband came in a conversation with Diana Cooper shortly after Randolph's departure for Yugoslavia. With victory in Europe now in sight, Diana drew the inevitable parallel between Churchill and Marlborough, but suggested that 'when the war was over, instead of building Winston another Blenheim', his grateful country ought to give him 'an endowed manor house with acres for a farm and gardens to build and paint in'. Clementine shook her head. 'I never think of after the war,' she said. 'I think Winston will die when it's over. You see, he's seventy and I'm sixty and we're putting all we've got into this and it will take all we've got.'

When she said this, Winston and Clementine were in their seventieth and sixtieth years respectively but there were several times during the last eighteen months of the war in Europe when it looked as if Clementine would be proved right. Nevertheless this final chapter of the war was a triumph for Churchill's powers of survival, as age and circumstances turned increasingly against him. Despite them he was able to sustain the legend he had now created, and it is fascinating to see the legend growing as both his health and his grasp upon the world-wide conduct of the war began to fail him.

His great plan for an amphibious attack on Anzio to the north of Naples was a grievous disappointment, like so many of his flights of strategy. Strongly resisted by the Germans, the landing was not that sudden 'wildcat' blow which he believed would lead to the rapid liberation of the whole Italian peninsula. Italy became the scene of a bitter war of slow attrition, instead of that lightning strike at what he called 'the armpit' of the Reich by which he had hoped to bring a swift conclusion to the conflict.

This ended Churchill's dream of forestalling the Soviet advance through eastern Europe and striking a crucial blow against the Germans in the Mediterranean and the Balkans before the 'Second Front' began in northern France. It also underlined the way that overall direction of the war was passing to America and the Soviet Union. Nothing could disguise his subordinate position to the American command, once the Allies finally invaded northern France with their Operation Overlord in June 1944. With the Red Army rolling back the enemy in eastern Europe it was also clear that Stalin would impose his will on all he conquered.

As Clementine feared, pneumonia and the heart-attack in North Africa had hit her husband harder than generally appreciated – and at times he felt weakened and depressed.

'I'm through,' he told Beaverbrook in the spring of 1944. 'I just can't carry the burdens any longer.'

Having said this, and being Churchill, he almost instantly revived; but the strains were showing, not on him alone, but on those around him. His official – and largely ignored – Deputy Prime Minister, the Labour leader Clement Attlee, was driven to complain by letter of the unbusinesslike conduct of affairs in Cabinet. Churchill reacted like an insulted monarch, took to his bed, and then decided to ignore the letter. More serious, his acknowledged successor in the party, the deeply diplomatic Eden, while continuing his courtier-like submission to his master, secretly agreed with the complaints.

But such was the Premier's prestige and kingly power that none of these difficulties seriously affected his authority. Objections and murmurs of revolt within the House of Commons made little difference, either. He knew how to handle *them* – just as he also knew from long experience how to keep his generals on the tightest rein.

In the process he almost drove his Chief of Imperial General Staff, the down-to-earth Ulsterman General Brooke, insane with his late-night outbursts and the frequency with which he changed his mind. Only the force of Churchill's personality – and Brooke's loyalty – kept this essential general at his post.

As if to offset what was happening within his government, Churchill seemed more immersed than ever in his public role as great war leader, and a frequent reaction now from those meeting him for the first time was that he appeared not only more formidable, but also physically larger than expected. Remarks about his regality were frequent. 'No one dared pursue a topic

of conversation that did not meet with his approval,' wrote a
friend of Randolph's after lunching at Downing Street. 'Many
guests would have found royalty easier to deal with.'

What few noticed – or, if they did, felt it politic to mention –
was the way contact with the war could still revive him. Conflict
had never failed to excite him: once excited, his energies were
unabating.

To witness the fighting at first hand, and keep himself occupied
with fresh activities, he was travelling more than ever. Flying
was still a personal adventure, and as the war expanded he
was continually on the move, with the accoutrements of earthly
power around him. Roosevelt's gift of a luxurious four-engined
Skymaster aircraft for his personal use made this possible. The
large aircraft was equipped with dining room, private bathroom,
bedroom with comfortable single bed from which he could work
as usual, and an office for his staff and secretaries.

In June 1944 the King personally deprived him of the great
event he had been anticipating – his presence at the D-Day
landings. This was one occasion when the gentle George was
known to have overruled the wishes of his mighty subject,
arguing with what appears suspiciously like pique that, if the
King of England was not permitted to be present, neither was his
irreplaceable Prime Minister. It was a test of Churchill's loyalty
towards his monarch, and a dreadful disappointment.

Churchill's Private Secretary, Sir Leslie Rowan, told Colville
that it was at this point he detected that his chief began
'losing interest in the war, because he no longer has control
of military affairs. Up till Overlord he saw himself as Marlborough, the supreme authority to whom all military decisions
were referred, Now, in all but questions of wide or long-term
strategy, he is by force of circumstances, little more than a
spectator.'

Churchill's spectator status did not keep him out of France for
long, and a few weeks later he was being photographed giving
his famous V-sign to the troops in Normandy. Then he was
off to Italy, in the uniform of a colonel of the 4th Hussars,
visiting his front-line troops, and telling General Alexander: 'I
envy you your command of armies in the field. That's what I
should have liked.'

Once more it was his old ambition to have been a fighting general. Instead he was a statesman, and an international celebrity,

vastly famous, universally respected, but with little real power to affect the final outcome of the war.

Despite this, war remained 'man's natural occupation' – for him at any rate – and he refused to be concerned with any other while it lasted, certainly not with growing aspirations in the country for better education, health and housing and a fairer social order when the war was over. Concern with such things struck him as irrelevant and probably unpatriotic, for he was an autocratic ruler, and was growing more reactionary with little tolerance of criticism. There was in fact surprisingly little sign of discontent at home (in the armed forces, things were different), and the press was under strict control. But Churchill was absurdly touchy over the occasional criticism of his government which did reach the press – and touchier still about his personal reputation.

The satirical treatment of aged leadership in the Powell–Pressburger film *The Life and Times of Colonel Blimp* seriously upset him. On the other hand, he could never have enough of the romantic patriotic film *Lady Hamilton* with Olivier starring as his hero Admiral Nelson. He is reputed to have seen it in his private cinema on seventeen occasions, always with extreme emotion.

After his return from Italy, Churchill suffered the indignity of being stricken with pneumonia again. 'If you go on playing the fool like this you're certain to die,' said Brendan Bracken. But, instead of dying, willpower, and Lord Moran helped him rapidly recover to attend another mammoth conference – his second in Quebec – with the President of the United States in August 1944.

This conference involved the most impressive voyage of Churchill's whole career. With a larger retinue than ever and both Mary and Clementine in attendance, it took Britain's greatest liner, *Queen Mary*, to accommodate his party in extraordinary luxury. Colville described the meals aboard as 'gargantuan in scale and epicurean in quality, rather shamingly so'.

Here was the grand opera of wartime leadership which Churchill loved – the infinite accompaniments of power, advisers, press photographers, the drama of the meetings – and the long discussions with the President upon the progress of the war, conducted 'in a blaze of friendship'. It was a blaze which now included Clementine – who finally accepted Roosevelt calling her 'Clemmie'.

But friendship, however heartfelt, failed to convince Roosevelt of the growing threat of Stalin's armies to a future Europe; nor did it make him sympathetic to Churchill's fears for his cherished British Empire. Still less was Churchill able to convince the President and his military advisers of his latest great strategic plan to pre-empt the Soviet advance in Europe by a sudden strike towards Vienna (reminiscent yet again of the strategy which Marlborough followed in the great campaign which led to Blenheim).

But, whatever the limitations on his power which were revealed in Quebec, Churchill himself had rarely seemed more comfortably majestic as he stood before the newsreel cameras like the god of battles in a sailor's hat. Nor did he permit news of the annihilation of the 1st Airborne Division at Arnhem with 7,000 casualties to oppress him unduly. 'I have not sustained any feeling of disappointment over this, and am glad our commanders are capable of running these sort of risks,' he cabled Field Marshal Smuts, who had sent commiserations.

Back in London, other great events were calling him to fresh adventures – first, by aeroplane to Moscow. Since Roosevelt was refusing to stand up to Stalin over Polish independence – the forgotten reason Britain went to war – Churchill would go himself to plead the cause of Polish liberation.

This flying visit was another personal triumph: banquets, a hero's welcome, and an unprecedented public appearance with Stalin at his side at a tumultuous state performance of *Giselle* at the Bolshoi Ballet. (Churchill preferred the singing of the Red Army choir that followed.) No one could question his extraordinary prestige, although the visit finally made little difference to the lost cause of the Polish nation.

There was another demonstration of his international prestige a few weeks later, when he flew with Clementine and Mary to newly liberated Paris. According to General Brooke, enthusiastic crowds along the Champs Élysées 'went quite mad over him', chanting 'Churcheel! Churcheel!' as he drove to the Arc de Triomphe with his ancient sparring partner, General de Gaulle, now head of the provisional French government. (How things had changed since those days in 1941 when Churchill remarked apropos of the General that the heaviest cross he had to bear 'was the Cross of Lorraine'.)

Just before Christmas 1944 he was even able to enjoy a final old-style personal adventure, which Macmillan rightly called 'a sort of super Sidney Street'.

One concession which he had obtained from 'Uncle Joe' in Moscow was an understanding that postwar Greece should stay within the British sphere of influence. However, this was not preventing Greek communist guerrillas from seizing power in the wake of the retreating Germans. Since the communists had fought gallantly against them it was a delicate situation, which Foreign Secretary Eden was prepared to settle with his well-known diplomatic caution. Churchill wanted other methods.

That Christmas Eve at Chequers, he strapped on his large revolver and, leaving a tearful Clementine behind him, boarded his Skymaster for Athens, and personally took charge of operations.

He was a very old Savrola as he drove through Athens with his generals in an armoured car, calling up air support to blast what he called 'the rebels', conferring with the different factions, and personally urging the discredited King of Greece to surrender power to a regency. Flying home, a happy man, a few days later, Churchill could congratulate himself that, thanks to his decisive action, the red tide had been halted in one European country and Greece at least was safe for Greek democracy. (Others did not see it quite that way, and Churchill was strongly criticised, particularly in the US, for interfering in the internal politics of Greece and for attacking Greek patriots who fought the Nazis.)

His trip marked a brief resurgence of the sort of high adventure he had longed for in his twenties, and virtually his last effective exercise of power as an international war leader. When the German counter-attack in the Ardennes was defeated, his urgent pleas to Washington failed to result in the Anglo-American forces taking Berlin before the Russians reached it. Similarly the 'Big Three' conference in Yalta in the Crimea in February 1945 confirmed his fears that the Soviet Union would swamp postwar eastern Europe, but he found himself unable to prevent Stalin from out-manoeuvring Roosevelt. In fact Roosevelt was dying. In Yalta, Colville described him looking 'old and ill . . . a hopelessly incompetent chairman', having lost all powers of concentration. Despite Churchill's presence, Stalin had little difficulty getting all he wanted. On the point of victory the 'Grand Coalition' Churchill had romantically believed in effectively collapsed.

On 12 April he heard Roosevelt was dead. He mourned him

in Parliament as 'the greatest champion of freedom who has ever
brought help and comfort from the new world to the old; but
he failed to attend his funeral on the grounds of pressure of
events in Europe. He was represented by Eden, and later said
how much he regretted not going to the funeral and meeting
the new US president, Harry Truman, at the ceremony. On
the day after Roosevelt died the Red Army entered Vienna.
It was a solemn moment, leaving Churchill with what he called
'the shadows of victory' on the edge of the greatest triumph of
his life as German opposition crumbled. And victory, however
sweet would bring a crisis to his private life as unforseen as he
was unprepared to meet it. The same applied to all the members
of his family, Clementine included.

During this final chapter of the war in Europe, she had been
sharing in her husband's fame – and success had been working
wonders for her brittle confidence.

Since recovering from the nervous crisis which prostrated her
in 1943, she had made a comeback as hostess both at Downing
Street and at Chequers. When roused, she could be as formidable
as ever. Colville remarked upon her 'caustic' interjections in
the conversation, and she was quick to put down any signs of
lèse-majesté towards her husband. She was particularly hard on
the victor of Alamein, Field Marshal Montgomery; she thought
him bumptious and was quick to slap him down for signs of
impertinence which Churchill never seemed to notice. Later she
got to like him.

Her appearance beside Churchill at the second Quebec conference in August 1944 had formed a striking contrast with her
miserable time in Canada in 1942. She had even followed
a public speech of Eleanor Roosevelt's with a short one of
her own.

It was a transformation from the unhappy woman sobbing out
her feelings of inadequacy to Cecil Beaton three years earlier.
But as well as awareness of her popularity there was a subtler
reason for this growth of confidence.

As often happens in such situations, she was becoming stronger
in relation to a considerably older husband whose powers she
felt to be declining. When she confided to Diana Cooper that
she thought that he would not survive the war, she was not
exaggerating. Lord Moran thought the same. He confided to
his diary that 'Churchill was not the man he had been' after

he nearly died in Carthage at the end of 1943, adding that 'he could easily go at any moment'.

Knowing this, Clementine saw it as her duty to protect and comfort him as much as possible. This was not easy, with the manic rate of his activities as the European war was ending, although she had done her tearful best that Christmas Eve before he flew to Athens. Nor could she make him change the habits of a lifetime. He was still eating and drinking on a scale few men of his age could equal, still taking his sacrosanct siesta in the afternoon, conferring until 2 a.m. or 3 a.m. and, after a substantial solitary breakfast, working through the morning from his bed.

Sleeping apart as they always had, this meant that her actual contact with him was largely confined to meal-times, almost invariably in the presence of official guests. (According to her appointments-diary, the two of them dined à deux on weekdays on only four occasions during the whole of 1944.)

All she could really do was offer him her presence and support, be there when needed, and conscientiously perform her own activities aided by Miss Hamblin. In April 1945 she was in Russia with Miss Hamblin on a six-week visit in her role as official head of the Red Cross 'Aid to Russia' campaign. She was there when Germany surrendered.

But there remained one self-appointed task which increasingly obsessed Clementine – as guardian of her husband's greatness. Throughout the tribulations of their marriage, she had always been concerned with this, and now it was of great importance. Nothing must be permitted to detract from the aura which surrounded him – neither troubles in the family nor weaknesses or failings of his own. This was no easy task, but she was lucky to possess one single-minded ally in the family: her youngest daughter, the devoted Mary.

More than ever, Clementine had reason to be grateful for the work of cousin Moppett Whyte. Thanks to her influence on Mary, there was one child of the Churchills who was modest, dutiful and undemanding – and whose love for both her parents was simple and unfeigned. So was Mary's love of God, of country, and the common cause behind the fighting. Still in her early twenties, she worshipped Churchill, both as the hero of the nation and as an aged father-figure bearing the burdens of the war upon his sturdy shoulders.

She was intensely proud of him but, unlike brother Randolph, did not exploit this pride to personal advantage. She had enjoyed no favours as an anti-aircraft battery commander in the London Blitz – apart from occasional informal visits from her beaming father to her Hyde Park gun-site – and had risen, very much on merit, to the equivalent rank of major. When Hitler's final secret weapon, the V1 flying bomb, was launched at southern England, her battery was moved to Kent in the first line of defence.

Most of her weekend leaves were spent at Chequers with her parents, but she was unaffected by the presence of the mighty. In his diaries Colville frequently remarked upon her gaiety and energy. Laura Charteris remembered Mary as 'extraordinarily wholesome, and always so beautifully turned out in her uniform that she would have made a perfect model for an ATS recruiting poster'.

She was inclined to fall in love impulsively. For a few days she was unofficially 'engaged' to Lord Duncannon, and throughout the Quebec Conference was nursing a hopeless passion for 'a handsome young French parachutist'. But, unlike the equally impulsive Sarah, love did not lead her to rebel against her parents. The lord and the parachutist were both discarded on Clementine's advice, and she turned her attention to more serious matters. As her mother's favourite, she shared her sense of personal responsibility towards her father; when Clementine departed on her six-week tour of Russia, it was to Mary that she entrusted him. 'Darling,' she wrote, 'supposing anything happened to me (e.g. air crash) do you think you could be released from the ATS on compassionate grounds to look after Papa? Because he would need it. . . .'

There could be no question of entrusting such a task to Diana. Quite apart from Clementine's antipathy towards her eldest daughter, Diana had her own life to live with three young children, a large house in London, and an ambitious and demanding husband whose political career was flourishing on its own account.

Sandys himself was not anxious for too much contact with his parents-in-law, being sensitive to suggestions that he had married for the sake of his career and owed his position entirely to Churchill. In fact, as Minister for Works, with responsibility for a large department, he succeeded less from family connections than from a driving energy which earned him more admirers than friends. (Brendan Bracken had recently accused him of 'relying too much on the *Führerprinzip*'.)

Although strongly influenced by Churchill as a young MP, Sandys had little of the bonhomie and gusto Churchill liked from those around him. A son-in-law whose company he enjoyed might have drawn Diana back into the family, but Sandys had a tendency to do the opposite. 'There is good stuff in this fellow – great industry and guts – and it makes me sad that Winston is only bored with his son-in-law,' wrote Moran.

But Diana was devoted to him, and photographs reveal a worried-looking wife whose looks were going, with a debonair politician entering his prime. He was handsome and attractive to other women, who offered him a certain independence from Diana's overwhelming family. She was becoming insecure and jealous. He was learning to remain aloof from her unhappiness. And Clementine was not the sort of mother Diana could confide in, any more than she could bother her great father with her problems.

There were also complications in Sarah's relationship with her father which, just as with Diana, would have prevented Clementine envisaging her as his guardian-angel in her absence.

On the surface Sarah had simplified her life when she joined the WAAF and left Vic Oliver. Friends insist there really was no bitterness between them, and in Oliver's extraordinarily discreet short book of memoirs there is not a hint of the indignities he endured from Churchill; he describes the break-up of his marriage as 'a case of two people who had loved each other and had grown apart'. He remained a highly popular radio comedian and apparently continued to be the old Svengali, soon discovering another young actress to adopt, and masterminding her career.

Sarah meanwhile possessed a small income of her own, a bachelor flat in a modern block in Park Lane; and according to Paul Medlicott, who helped write her autobiography, the two important trips she made as 'family ADC' to Churchill in Tehran and Yalta 'brought her closer to her father than she had ever been before, leaving her almost stage-struck with her love and admiration'.

Therein lay the problem which was to afflict Sarah for years to come. The more she fell beneath her father's spell, the more wary she became of forfeiting her precious independence, for she had learned how ruthless he could be at asserting his dominion

over those he loved. It was because of this that she refused
his offer to influence Air Chief Marshal Sholto Douglas to get
her a comfortable job in the operations room of RAF Fighter
Command – which would have meant a promotion and 'being
stationed half-way between Chequers and London'. Instead she
opted for a course in aerial photographic interpretation, then
spent the rest of the war at Medmenham in Berkshire, working
on reconnaissance pictures taken by the RAF over Germany.

This was high-pressure work requiring precision and long
hours. She was popular, proud of her skill, and the job provided
something of the independence she required. But it also meant
she had to live two separate lives – one at weekends in the
all-important world around her father, and the other in her
working life at Medmenham.

One of her fellow-WAAFs, Pauline Bretherton, remembers
'how careful Sarah always was to keep these two existences apart'.
She soon saw the strain this put upon her. 'Sarah was desperately
conscientious, and determined not to ask for favours, but she was
very much aware of being the PM's daughter, and of having to
live up to her position.'

'You've no idea how tough it is, having a famous husband
and a famous father,' Sarah once remarked, and Mrs Bretherton
remembers her acute anxiety about 'letting Papa down'. 'For
Sarah it was crucial to maintain face at whatever cost – which
made her a terrible bottler-up of the emotions.'

'She was always very nice about her mother. "Poor Mummy,"
she would say. "It really gets too much for her at times." But
she was totally and utterly obsessed with her father, going to
Chequers most weekends to see him, and telephoning him
whenever she had the opportunity.'

Mrs Bretherton believes this double life placed an extraordinary strain on Sarah. 'She could be almost hyper-active, and
I've seen her too exhausted when she went to bed to take her
face off.'

She also had a feeling that Sarah was somehow disappointed
in herself. 'It was as if she'd set herself such aims to live by, and
blamed herself for failing to achieve them.'

Against this background Sarah's love-affair with the now
besotted American ambassador, Gil Winant, only added to her
problems. Had he not been already married, he would have been
ideal for her – another older man, idealistic, handsome, lonely

and clearly needing her. Clementine had grown extremely fond of him; and here in wartime Britain, and in close proximity with the Churchills, Winant had found something he had never known before – intimacy with supreme power, a sense of belonging at the centre of great events, and the undoubted spell of Churchill's presence.

'Gil was in love with all the Churchills,' says a diplomat who knew him well – and at the centre of this most glamorous of families was the enchanted vulnerable princess, the great man's daughter. Sarah would meet Gil Winant during his regular weekend visits to Chequers, as well as at the two major conferences they attended. Her Park Lane flat was five minutes' walk from the American embassy in Grosvenor Square.

She found that Winant's love was all-involving. According to Mrs Bretherton, 'Sarah showed not the slightest interest in any of the men around throughout her time at Medmenham.' But she and Winant had to be painfully discreet. Had news leaked out that the United States ambassador was conducting a liaison with Winston Churchill's daughter in the middle of the war, the scandal would have broken John Gil Winant. It would probably have broken Sarah, too.

The agony which followed her elopement with Vic Oliver eight years earlier had been hideous enough. Now it was impossible to contemplate the effect of another scandal on her father at a time when he was bearing such responsibilities.

The result, like so many of Sarah's love-affairs, was a doomed, unhappy, tense relationship. Despite heroic efforts at discretion, it proved impossible to keep it absolutely secret. Colville, for one, knew all about it, and Sarah was convinced her father knew as well. Many years later she would wistfully refer to this 'old love affair which my father suspected but about which we did not speak'.

Now, with the war moving to its close, Winant sensed the pressures there would be from his wife and family in Massachusetts, and an air of tragedy started to infect his love for Sarah Churchill.

Randolph meanwhile had been fully occupied with his private war in Yugoslavia – but even this had proved another anticlimax. Despite his father's fulsome letter, Tito had virtually ignored him, leaving Randolph to soldier on as part of a British military mission to the communist partisans.

His contribution to the partisans is hard to gauge – he spoke no Serbo-Croat, hated communism, and had little interest in the country. He was brave when harried by the Germans, and uncomplaining when injured in an aircrash. But there is a firm impression that the true reason Randolph stayed so long in Yugoslavia was to keep him out of trouble and prevent him bothering his father back in Britain. During one short leave in London there was a dinner at Downing Street, which ended with Randolph shouting down Churchill, striking Sarah and being ejected by the Marines. It was after this that, as something of an incentive to remain in Yugoslavia, Randolph was actually allowed to pick some friends to keep him company; these included Evelyn Waugh and Freddie Birkenhead. But neither friend could cope with weeks on end of undiluted Randolph in the mountain villages of Croatia.

Life with Randolph soon became so tense – and boring – that to keep him occupied Waugh bet him £10 to read right through the Bible. Randolph gave up after the Old Testament, with the verdict 'God! Wasn't God a shit!'

By October 1944, Randolph and Evelyn Waugh had ceased to be on speaking terms. 'He is not a good companion for a long period,' wrote Waugh in his diary, 'but the conclusion is always the same – that no one else would have chosen me, nor would anyone else have accepted him. We are both at the end of the tether as far as work is concerned and must make what we can of it.'

Waugh had in fact spent part of the time with Randolph correcting the proofs of his most successful novel, *Brideshead Revisited*, which he had just completed, but Randolph had accomplished nothing. Even the military glory he hoped for had eluded him; his recommendation for the Military Cross was downgraded to the humbler Member of the British Empire medal to avoid suggestions of favouring Churchill's son. Waugh left Yugoslavia in November at his own request. Birkenhead followed him a few weeks later.

By the new year the mission to Yugoslavia was over and Randolph was in Rome, where he underwent surgery for a damaged leg. He was back in London late that spring as war in Europe drew towards its close. By mid-April 1945 the Allies had reached northern Italy, the American and Soviet armies met in Germany, Mussolini had perished in Turin, and as April ended the Red Army took Berlin.

On the evening of 1 May, Churchill was dining with Lord Beaverbrook when Colville brought a report from Hamburg radio announcing Hitler's death. 'He died', according to the broadcast, 'fighting with his last breath against Bolshevism.'

'Well, I must say I think he was perfectly right to die like that,' said Churchill.

Beaverbrook remarked that he 'obviously' hadn't died like that – and later news confirmed that Hitler had committed suicide in his bunker in Berlin. The European war was over.

Churchill had a brief period to enjoy his victory. Hostilities in Europe officially ceased on 8 May, Victory in Europe Day. Clementine, still in Moscow with Miss Hamblin, cabled: 'All my thoughts are with you on this supreme day my darling. It could not have happened without you.'

At three o'clock he broadcast to the nation. Afterwards he visited the King, and that evening, in his siren suit, he was on a balcony above Whitehall addressing the vast crowd beneath.

'This is your victory,' he told them.

'No, yours!' they roared back, and he led them singing 'Land of Hope and Glory'.

It was a time of triumph and extraordinary emotion, and few suspected how rapidly his reign would end. Churchill had promised a general election immediately the European war was over. It took place on 8 July, but because of delays in counting the votes of servicemen abroad the result was not known until 26 July.

30
Opposition

There are few more potent demonstrations of the fickleness of political power than a change of government after a British general election. And few such changes have been more dramatic than that which summarily dismissed Winston Churchill from the premiership on 6 July 1945, some seven weeks after the greatest triumph of his life.

The day before he had been the victorious war leader and had specially flown home for the election results from Potsdam in defeated Germany where he had been conferring with Stalin and the new American President, Harry Truman. He had discussed the terms to be imposed on Germany, American plans for waging war against Japan, and the President's decision to drop the atom bomb on Nagasaki on 6 August. But after his party's overwhelming electoral defeat he was Premier no longer, and although he kept his parliamentary seat for Woodford (previously known as Epping), he was now effectively a private citizen.

The Labour Party, previously the minority partner in his wartime coalition in the Commons, had won 393 seats, an overall majority of 146 over all other parties in the House; and 585 Conservative seats (relics from the last general election of 1935) were now reduced to 213. In the débâcle, both Randolph and Duncan Sandys had lost their seats. And Clement Attlee, the self-effacing socialist with the moustache, who had been his official (but largely ignored) Deputy Prime Minister throughout the war, now held that 'great position' which had been Churchill's during five of the most exciting years in Britain's history.

Churchill did his best to treat this earthquake philosophically. 'It's absolutely monstrous how ungrateful the nation has been,' the wife of Leslie Rowan told him when she heard the news; but he smiled at her and shook his head. 'That's politics, my dear. That's politics,' he said. In fact the election results came as an appalling shock, and Mary describes lunching with him on the day they were announced, and how they sat 'in Stygian gloom' as 'Papa struggled to accept this terrible blow'.

There was much discussion among the Conservative faithful over whom to blame. For Lord Beaverbrook the culprit was the Conservative Party – and for a large part of the Conservative Party it was Lord Beaverbrook. For others it was Churchill – largely on account of a notorious pre-election speech he had made equating the Labour Party with the Gestapo. Some blamed defeat on the armed forces' vote – others on the women's. But the fact was that the war had brought an overwhelming shift of social aspiration which was reflected through the whole of British society. Churchill and the Conservatives were seen as figures from the past, Attlee and the Labour Party as part of a brave tomorrow, and a sea-change in British politics was occurring. But, for Churchill, it remained a very personal defeat, which hit him even more profoundly than all but his closest friends appreciated.

A few days after the results, Churchill had an early-morning caller in the shape of good Lord Moran. The tradition of British politics that a defeated premier instantly vacates his official residence had deprived the Churchills of their home in Downing Street, and he was 'pigging it' in the penthouse suite at Claridge's.

As usual at this hour, Churchill was sitting up in bed with the newspapers. It was a sunny morning, and he appeared quite cheerful, but when Moran happened to remark upon the room's amenities Churchill replied: 'I don't like sleeping near a precipice like that.' Pointing to the balcony, he added; 'I've no desire to quit the world, but thoughts, desperate thoughts come into the head.'

This extraordinary remark has lain unremarked in the pages of Lord Moran's bulky diaries, but if Churchill was serious – and there is little reason to imagine he was joking – it helps explain much that is otherwise inexplicable in his behaviour at this time and throughout what remained of his extraordinary political career.

The words echo the description, which he also gave to Moran, of the way that deep depression hit him in his late thirties when he was Home Secretary in Asquith's government, and 'the light had faded from the picture'. When those earlier attacks of

Black Dog were at their worst, he had felt a similar urge to violent self-destruction. This political defeat had evidently caused another bout of harrowing depression as bad as any in the past.

This in itself was strange. He was nearly seventy-one, and logically he should have felt at least some relief at being freed at last from all those 'burdens' he had frequently complained of in the war. Logically, too, he must have known his place in history was secure. He had surpassed even his extraordinary ambitions, and all the honours his once honour-hungry spirit could desire were there for the asking. He still had his 'earthly paradise' at Chartwell to look forward to. There were his wartime memoirs to compose, the four volumes of his *History of the English-Speaking Peoples* waiting to be finished. He had his favourite friends to entertain, warm climes to visit, his growing family to enjoy.

With so much awaiting him, it seems incredible that this man who had led his country through the bleakest moments of its recent history was feeling tempted to hurl himself from the sixth-floor balcony of Claridge's Hotel on account of an electoral defeat – and yet, apparently, he was.

Churchill often liked to quote from Maeterlinck's *Life of the Bee* on the way one tiny grub, when fed the magical royal jelly in the hive, became transformed into a queen. It was the same, he said, with power, which was another sort of royal jelly; and he would quote the story to account for the undeniable success which Clement Attlee was enjoying as Prime Minister.

In fact the parable applied equally to Churchill, whose entire life had been a glowing testimonial to the transforming qualities of power. Power and the feeling of omnipotence that goes with it had enabled him to overcome those hidden fears of failure which Lord Randolph had cruelly predicted. With this, his deepest cravings for success had been satisfied; and for the last five years he had played the most exalted role of all, matching the exploits of his greatest heroes.

Now, suddenly deprived of power, he was a monarch toppled from his throne. He who had slept soundly through the grimmest crises of the war found himself needing sleeping pills. 'What is there to stay up for after midnight?' he asked sadly. Potentate no longer, he was at the mercy of the 'unabsorbed residuum of pure emptiness' which had threatened him and driven him since adolescence.

There were simpler deprivations, too, which also rankled: the loss of official cars and residences, the departure of the ministerial secretaries, and the abrupt ending of the special 'diplomatic' rations which so richly sustained him through the darkest moments of the war. He was genuinely shocked when confronted with the weekly rations a normal citizen received in 1945; foremost of the symptoms of despondency Clementine remarked on was the fact that this life-long 'carnivore' was suddenly 'hating his food' with its largely meatless diet.

The abrupt change in life-style hit Clementine, too; for, however wearying at times, the war had given her an unequalled role to play, and undoubtedly revived her marriage. Lonely she may have been, with a husband so preoccupied, but she had been admired and respected on her own account; and she was always there to help him when required, the dignified, supportive and only occasionally complaining consort of the great war leader. This, too, had gone, and suddenly it must have seemed as if her life and her marriage were collapsing round her.

Now her presence only seemed to make her husband's humour worse. Exhausted and depressed herself, she craved the peace and quiet of retirement, the very thought of which filled Churchill with unmitigated gloom. She was wretchedly unhappy, and there seemed no alleviation. 'In our misery', she wrote to Mary, 'we seem, instead of clinging to each other, to be always having scenes.'

At this sudden crisis in their parents' marriage, all three daughters rallied in support. Diana and Duncan lent their flat in Westminster Gardens. Mary secured a compassionate posting back to London. And, since it was clear that her parents needed a period apart, Sarah decided to accompany Papa on a painting holiday to a villa on Lake Como being used by Field Marshal Alexander. With Churchill out of power, even this was complicated. During the war, Churchill had simply ordered Sarah or Mary to accompany him on foreign journeys without a moment's hesitation, but now Sarah needed Winant's intercession to obtain leave of absence from the WAAF.

Once at his easel and away from London the change in the fallen leader was spectacular. A few weeks earlier, Moran had still been witnessing 'constant outbursts of childish petulance', but suddenly it seemed that nothing could upset 'the even serenity of these autumnal days beside the lake'.

As usual, he enjoyed Sarah's company. He also suddenly enjoyed his food, the perfect autumn weather, and the marble and gilt-mirrored luxury of the villa. In fact, as he told Moran, he was finding 'the solution to his troubles in his paintbox', just as he had thirty years before when thrown out of the Cabinet over the Dardanelles. 'Even the sudden appearance of a hernia failed to shake his equanimity.' (Moran despatched an emissary to Milan with the unlikely task of buying a surgical truss for Winston Churchill.)

What everyone was witnessing was a recurrence of that crucial Churchillian phenomenon which Beaverbrook had noticed in the First World War – the baffling switch between the two quite separate personalities which lay at the heart of Churchill's complex nature.

'When successful,' Moran wrote, 'Churchill's arrogance, intolerance and cocksureness assume alarming proportions.' But in adversity he found him 'gentle, patient and brave'.

As usual, absence also made him sentimental over Clementine; and as usual the diplomatic Sarah, trying to repair the rift between her parents, was careful to report this to her mother. 'We never see a lovely sight that he doesn't say – "I wish your mother were here." '

But he also said, gazing out across the lake: 'I'm damned glad to be out of it. I shall paint for the rest of my days. I've never painted so well before.'

In fact he needed to decide about his future. Those who felt he should retire from politics for good included not only Clementine but also his deputy within the party, his 'Princess Elizabeth' as he called him, forty-eight-year-old Anthony Eden. Eden was deeply in awe of Churchill, but privately could not wait for 'the old boy' to go, leaving him free to lead the party. And Clementine, according to Miss Hamblin, was still nourishing her prewar dream of that graceful Georgian country house set in its lawns in perfect English countryside.

But now that Churchill's spirits were reviving he was thinking otherwise. His brush with Black Dog must have reminded him how much he still required the 'royal jelly' of politics and power to keep depressive misery at bay, and he returned from Como with his mind made up. Not only would he lead the party, but he would efface the stigma of defeat and win the next election.

One of the first signs of Churchill's resolution was his decision to purchase an extensive new headquarters in the heart of London. He bought two adjacent houses, close to the park at Hyde Park Gate, which would provide offices for his secretariat and a London residence for the Churchills for the remainder of his life.

A further sign of his recovery was the famous speech he gave in January 1946 at Fulton in Missouri during an early-winter visit to the United States. A few days of preparatory painting and extremely hearty eating with Consuelo Balsan in Palm Beach had added to his strength, and his grim prediction of the growing threat of Russia to the West was a clear return to his prewar role of embattled prophet preaching his testament of doom which once more hung above humanity.

When he warned that an 'Iron Curtain' had descended across Europe 'from Stettin in the Baltic to Trieste in the Adriatic', he was speaking words which few in his audience were prepared for. When he reached Washington, President Truman avoided any reference to his speech. But this time round the seer was not to languish in the wilderness for long. With his former friend and ally 'Uncle Joe' rapidly fulfilling his prophecies, Churchill's reputation for omniscience increased – as did his appetite for life and politics.

Back in London a Conservative MP who lunched with him was surprised to see his aged leader down a dozen oysters, two good helpings of roast beef, steamed pudding and the statutory bottle of champagne.

With Churchill's appetite restored, Eden would have a long wait to succeed him, but many in the party seem to have believed that Churchill could still be tactfully deposed. Instead the excitement of the House of Commons was reviving Churchill's formidable powers of aggression, and the adrenalin was rising.

'I get the impression that the Tory party are most embarrassed by Winston's presence,' wrote Harold Nicolson in May 1946. 'They cannot edge him aside. They can only throw him out and that they do not wish to do.'

Churchill was too important to be 'thrown out', and Attlee's government had become the latest enemy he was itching to attack. R. A. Butler described him now as 'gloomy, grouchy, sullen in his retirement, bursting with vigour and vengeance'. 'A short time ago I was ready to retire and die gracefully,' he muttered. 'Now, I'm going to stay and have them out. I'll tear their bleeding entrails out of them.'

During 1946, as Churchill was girding himself for battle at Westminster, he also had to face the unpleasantness of two divorces in the family.

The first was Sarah's, which occurred, practically unnoticed, early that spring.

Although he generally disapproved of divorce – 'Why can't they forget their troubles and just get on with it?' was his usual attitude to marital problems, his own included – he was clearly delighted to be rid of Oliver as his son-in-law. In a letter to her father, Sarah later reminded him of how, 'when he knew it was all finished finally and legally with Vic, you called me across the room and whispered in my ear: "Free!" ' She added that she had not really been free at all, as she had been in love. What she did not tell her father was that her lover had been Winant.

However, the ending of the war had already brought a crisis to this love-affair. Winant and Sarah had been forced to come to a decision about the future. It was clear that Winant was depending more on her than she on him, and both were still petrified of scandal – Sarah in particular. Deeply concerned at the effect that this could have on relations with her father, and fearful of 'letting the side down', she was still as tense as ever.

From the beginning, the affair had been curiously unreal. There had been too much secrecy and guilt, and too little time for everyday love to grow between them. Now she felt the need to reassert her independence in the only way she knew – by pursuing stardom and success upon the stage. Acting was her one escape from what she called the 'cage of affection' in which she felt herself imprisoned.

As for Winant, since Roosevelt's death he had felt himself increasingly out of touch and out of favour with the new administration in Washington. Unhappy with what was happening in the world, he became hopeless and depressed and begged Sarah to wait for him to get divorced and marry him.

But there were twenty years between them, and this vulnerable man had all the problems of a wife and family in Massachusetts, while Sarah was ambitious for the future. One friend of Sarah's who occasionally saw the two of them together says they reminded him of the old obsessed Emil Jannings and the young Marlene Dietrich in the film *The Blue Angel.*

Their unhappiness increased throughout that summer of 1946. She was still fond of him and very sorry for him, but refused to talk of marriage. He could talk of little else.

For Sarah, what seemed like a solution came when her agent, Al Parker, found her a part as the heroine of a film version of Antonio Fogazzaro's melancholy classic, *Daniele Cortis,* being shot in Rome. Here was her starring role at last, and a perfect excuse to make a break with Winant.

The film's director, Mario Soldati – better known today as a distinguished novelist – had chosen Sarah from film tests she had made in London. 'She was absolutely perfect for the part of the unhappy Elena,' he says. 'I wanted a tortured woman, a tragic woman, a desperate, aristocratic foreign woman – and here she was.'

Acting opposite the Italian matinée idol Vittorio Gassman, Sarah could believe herself a star at last – and in Rome she was to find a place of refuge for the years ahead.

But Winant refused to accept the end of the affair. By now he had resigned his ambassadorship, but instead of returning to America had rented a house in Mayfair, close to his old embassy, to wait for Sarah. He was miserable and lonely. When Colville called, he found him 'only happy talking about old times'. A few months later, with Sarah still in Rome and still refusing to marry him, he finally returned to Concord, Massachusetts, with what friends describe as a broken heart.

By a coincidence, Randolph's marriage ended almost simultaneously with Sarah's – and with just as little fuss. Even Churchill had finally accepted that the marriage was beyond repair; and Randolph was anxious to pick up the threads of the bachelor existence he had led so happily before the war.

Lunatic optimism, personal extravagance, social outrage and the thickest skin in London were helping him not only to survive, but prosper. His greatest asset was the Churchill name. Coupled with the fact that, like his father, he possessed an instant opinion on every subject, this guaranteed a lucrative career in journalism, and he was always on the move, often to America, where his exploits kept him firmly in the news.

Early in 1946, Evelyn Waugh encountered him in Hollywood, and described him as 'Britishly drunk all the time, soliciting respectable women at luncheon parties etc.'. But, although Waugh pretended to be shocked, there was something about Randolph, even at his most outrageous, which made him irresistible – particularly to Americans. He was becoming that old-world speciality, a character; and, as Churchill's son, was something of a draw on the small-town lecture-circuits.

'Do you think that I should use THE NAME?' his friend Alastair Forbes remembers Randolph asking him at a Washington party, as if it were some secret weapon. He could be boorish but he was rarely malicious, and there was a certain democratic gusto even to his famous rudeness. As Alan Whicker put it, 'at least Randolph was always as offensive to ambassadors as he was to waiters'.

'Dear Randolph, utterly unspoiled by failure!' exclaimed Noël Coward as the unmistakable bulk of Churchill's princeling made its majestic entry into the Ivy Restaurant at about this time – a remark which had more truth than Coward probably intended. For Randolph was still convinced of his predestined status as his father's son and heir. He still believed that he would magically inherit the seamless mantle of paternal power and one day still become prime minister himself.

Setbacks ignored, his confidence remained mysteriously unshaken. He still assumed a style he could ill afford. He rented a house in Belgravia. Blackballed from the Beefsteak Club, he unashamedly applied again and was elected. Even relations with his father were stronger than their rows suggested. Before delivering his Fulton speech, Churchill checked it through with Randolph.

In a way divorce from Pamela improved relations between Randolph and his parents, by ending their temptation to take sides against him. Pamela had also made things easier by leaving London for the South of France when war in Europe ended. She felt that once the Churchill Club had closed its doors there was little to keep her tied to London. The rich and powerful Americans she loved had also flown. Averell Harriman had made it clear he could not marry her; nor could Ed Murrow, whose wife had just had his baby.

She says she found English women at this time 'insipid and rather silly'; but she was not a woman's woman, and the social skills which made her such a draw in wartime London had their uses in peacetime France. So did the Churchill name, and in Paris lay a new society for her to conquer.

She found herself a spectacular apartment at 4 Avenue de New York beside the Seine, and with considerable style began to do what best became her, forming a fresh circle of rich admirers around her. Explaining Pamela's success, Diana Cooper – whose husband, Duff, was now ambassador in Paris – used to call her 'The Universal Aunt', because of the trouble that she took with people.

These included such deserving cases as Aly Khan and Elie de Rothschild, who became devoted to her. Throughout this time little Winston spent a lot of time in England with the Digbys and the Churchills, who loved him dearly. He saw little of his father.

Meanwhile Sarah had arrived in Rome, but almost immediately fell ill with a suspected kidney infection. Fortunately the shooting of the film had not begun, but the illness was serious enough to worry Clementine, who despatched Mary to the Holy City 'to keep Sarah company and to see that she was taking proper care of herself'.

In fact she arrived on this errand of mercy in what she describes as 'a state of high emotion with a good-looking young man in tow'. This was twenty-six-year-old Captain Christopher Soames, a very tall young man, who was currently assistant military attaché with the British embassy in Paris. The news of his surprise arrival with the Churchills' delicately nurtured youngest daughter caused much consternation back at Chartwell.

It was not simply their daughter's unexplained and headlong conduct that upset Winston and Clementine. After all, she was twenty-six, and it was high time she thought of marriage. But Clementine liked to think that she and her daughter had no secrets from each other, and the fact was that the Churchills had considerably higher hopes for Mary than an unknown captain in the Guards.

During a recent visit to Brussels they had been warmly entertained by Prince Charles of Belgium, newly elected Belgian Regent in place of his disgraced brother, Leopold, who had been accused of collaboration with the Germans. Mary accompanied her parents on the visit, and Churchill's profound reverence for royalty was aroused by this unassuming patriotic Prince. Churchill had several late-night conversations in the palace, during which Charles evidently bared his soul to the aged monarchist – who now responded with considerable emotion.

'I was painfully affected by all you told me about your brother's singular attitude and behaviour to you in those long tragic years,' Churchill wrote to the prince later. 'I have a brother who is five years younger than me and whom I dearly love and have always cherished. I grieve indeed that you have never found the same kindness and protection which Nature decrees.'

It was not entirely surprising that the Churchills felt that they possessed the answer to this lonely prince's problems. Who better than their daughter Mary to provide him with that 'kindness and protection which Nature decrees'? Who better fitted to support him in his hour of need?

According to Diana Cooper, this was very much what both the Churchill parents had in mind when they arrived with Mary at the Paris embassy *en route* for home after visiting the Belgian Regent. And it was then that, unbeknown to them, their daughter rapidly forgot the forty-three-year-old royal Belgian bachelor for the more robust attractions of Captain Soames.

Soames was not the man to miss the opportunity of a lifetime – nor did he waste the few romantic days he spent with Mary by the bedside of her convalescent sister. Before returning to his duties back in Paris, he and Mary had become engaged.

He must have seemed a most unlikely candidate for the hand of the Churchills' treasured daughter. Descended from a family of brewers, and known at Eton by the nickname 'Soapy Soames', he was not a popular young officer and had emerged from wartime service with the Guards with a somewhat patchy reputation. But, brash and pushy though he may have been, Christopher was the man Mary loved. And, although Clementine was less than pleased to hear of the engagement – having presumably been envisaging herself the mother of a princess – the Churchills had found in Captain Soames the son-in-law they needed.

Almost from the start he got on famously with Churchill. 'The great thing about Christopher', says Julian Amery, 'is that he wasn't in the least frightened by the old gentleman.'

In fact he was too much of a bully himself to let Churchill bully him; and unlike Duncan Sandys, who, as Moran says, 'couldn't follow Churchill's moods', he had a natural instinct for the things that pleased him. He would play cards with him, drink with him, listen to his reminiscences and make him laugh. By the time of the marriage, in February 1947, Soames was firmly and irreplaceably ensconced within the Churchill family. Backed with the power

and influence of Churchill's name, another important political
career was just beginning.

Mary's marriage to 'the Chimp', as Clementine had christened
Soames, took place at St Margaret's, Westminster, and was a
happy family event. Churchill had by now totally recovered from
the shock of his defeat in 1945. He had re-established undisputed
power over his party, and despite his age was proving an effective
leader of the opposition in the House of Commons. Far from
declining gracefully into that impotent old age he dreaded, he
seemed to be defying time itself, and remained the most active
of political volcanoes, spewing the fire of rhetoric upon the Attlee
government in some of the most effective speeches of his whole
career.

In the meantime life in opposition seemed to suit him. During
the worst of the London winter, he was able to depart for the
warmth of Marrakesh or the South of France. He was revered
throughout the world, his words commanded vast respect, and
he was even freed at last from worries over Chartwell. Knowing
his problems of maintaining it, a group of rich businessmen had
bought it from him and presented it to the National Trust as a
future Churchill shrine – with the stipulation that he lived there
undisturbed until he died.

Clementine had also come to terms with her husband's firm
refusal to retire; here Mary's marriage proved an unexpected
blessing. Shortly before the wedding, Christopher developed
symptoms of a duodenal ulcer so that he had to leave the Army.
Since the newlyweds had nowhere to live, the Churchills offered
them the farm at Chartwell, which Christopher could manage.

This started a new era for the house and the estate, with the
Soameses taking over from the aged and increasingly cantanker-
ous Moppett Whyte, running the place efficiently and taking care
of the frequently exhausted Clementine. This left Churchill free
to immerse himself again in all his old activities, and the wartime
memoirs he was now beginning.

But just as it seemed that everything was comfortably arranged
Churchill's equilibrium received another jolt – followed by a most
disturbing episode.

Three weeks after Mary's marriage, he was abruptly summoned
to his brother's deathbed. After Goonie's death in 1942, Jack
had made his home at 10 Downing Street with the Churchills.
He had his own room at the top of the house, and everybody

had loved the Prime Minister's gentlemanly, unassuming brother. He was immensely proud of Winston – and his daughter, Clarissa, believes that this was probably the happiest period of his life. But recently Jack had been ailing for some time with a weakened heart. This had not prevented him enjoying his status as Winston Churchill's brother, a distinction which, not long before he died, had helped him to achieve his final great ambition – election to Lord Randolph's favourite London club, the Turf.

Thus Jack had died a happy man, but his deathbed was an emotional occasion, with his children, Johnny, Peregrine and Clarissa, present. Churchill was in tears when his brother said farewell, and Johnny says that 'when my father began the death agony we left my uncle alone with him in meditation.' According to Churchill his brother 'had no fear & little pain. . . . The only thing Jack worried about was England. I told him it wd be all right.'

But this peaceful patriotic death seems to have sent Churchill into another bout of deep depression. 'Do you think we shall be allowed to sleep a long time? I hope so,' Churchill wrote when replying to a letter of condolence from his old friend Lord Hugh Cecil. He also told him how lonely he was feeling, 'after 67 years of brotherly love', and how he still remembered 'my father coming in to my bedroom at the Vice Regal Lodge in Dublin and telling me (aged 5) "You have a little brother" '.

In fact it was not so much memories of Jack as of Lord Randolph which seem to have now struck Churchill with unusual force. At around this time, Sarah told Peregrine that her father was complaining of recurrent nightmares of his father; and Johnny describes an emotional meeting with his uncle at the time of the funeral in which Churchill, self-obsessed as ever, talked not of Jack but about his own 'prostration' when Lord Randolph died. In an extraordinary scene, Churchill finally mastered his emotion by taking a copy of his book *The River War* from the bookshelf and reading aloud from it for half an hour. 'That's pretty good writing, you know,' he told his somewhat puzzled nephew. 'I wish I could write like that today.'

Some months later, during a weekend at Chartwell, Churchill read Sarah and Randolph something else which he had written. Entitled simply 'Private Article', it was a factual down-to-earth account of how he had recently met his father's ghost.

The 'article' was emphatically not some piece of old man's

whimsy, but a serious treatment calmly describing how Lord Randolph suddenly appeared in the studio at Chartwell, 'looking just as I had seen him in his prime. . . . A small slim jaunty figure with a large moustache.' He was 'filling his amber cigarette holder with a little pad of cotton-wool before putting in a cigarette', just as he remembered.

During the conversation which ensued, Churchill proceeded to fill his father in on some of the key events since his death – two horrifying European wars, the decline of the Empire, and Europe threatened by a Marxist Russia. The ghost said how glad he was not to have had to witness such disasters; and then and only then did Lord Randolph show any genuine emotion towards Winston. It was not benevolent. Suddenly Lord Randolph was repeating all those bitter and dismissive accusations that had haunted Churchill all his life.

Winston remarked to Lord Randolph how he had brought him up 'in the tradition of democracy', producing the stinging rejoinder: 'I never brought you up to anything.' Lord Randolph then proceeded to enumerate all his son's bitterly remembered failings: 'Bottom of the school! Never passed any examination, except into the cavalry. Wrote me stilted letters. I could not see how you would make your living on the little I could leave you and Jack, and that only after your mother. I once thought of the bar for you, but you were not clever enough.'

Here in black and white at last was Churchill's version of Lord Randolph's condemnation, which had been hanging over him for fifty years. Here was the source of those anxieties which had fuelled his intense ambition and brought him to the verge of suicide and bleak despair. And here was that grim prediction of failure which Churchill's whole career had sought to alter.

What is amazing is that at seventy-two the most famous man in Britain was still haunted by such judgements from a sick and long-dead father – and that he felt obliged to write them out in detail, then read them to his family.

But Churchill had his reasons. The 'Private Article' was presumably based upon the recurrent nightmares he had been having of his father, and shows all the signs of careful and attentive composition. It is in fact a very skilful piece of writing whose deadpan style conceals its author's all-important purpose until it is partially revealed at the end. Throughout the account of what has happened to Britain since Lord Randolph's death, it is noticeable that Churchill ventures nothing of his own achievements; when he finishes, it is Lord Randolph who rather condescendingly compliments him on the knowledge he has been displaying.

'Of course you are too old now to think about such things, but when I hear you talk I really wonder you didn't go into politics. You might have done a lot to help. You might even have made a name for yourself.' With which Lord Randolph gives his son a 'benignant' smile – and with 'a tiny flash' vanishes for good.

It is of course Churchill himself who is really having the last laugh on his father and the whole story, far from being the sentimental old man's reminiscence of a much-loved father which it might have seemed at first, is really nothing of the kind. Its author is doing what he must have longed to do on countless occasions since his father died – meet Lord Randolph's ghost on equal terms and prove his predictions wrong.

It is very cleverly and neatly done. There is no argument and no recrimination from Churchill. Instead, very lightly and wittily he lets Lord Randolph demonstrate that the dead can be completely wrong about the living, and that the judgements which he passed on twenty-year-old Winston have been utterly negated. Winston has won. He has become a greater figure than his father ever was, and the fact that his father is so ignorant about his son's achievements actually provides the punch-line of the story.

Churchill was evidently satisfied once he had written out this curious account and had read it to his children. He made no attempt to publish it. Instead, he locked it in a box and never referred to it again. Randolph discovered it after his death, and published it. He called it 'The Dream'. A better title might have been 'The Exorcism', for by writing this 'Private Article' Churchill does appear to have disarmed Lord Randolph's ghost; and with that 'tiny flash' which he described, his father took his leave of him and seems to have troubled him no further.

This left Churchill free to devote his energies to the wartime memoirs. These were his real answer to Lord Randolph's in-difference to his achievements. Although he relied as usual on assistants and advisers – principally Bill Deakin, the Oxford don who had first helped him on his life of Marlborough – this massive work was essentially his personal version of the war that he had waged. In his customary manner, Churchill dictated the book in its entirety to his secretaries, with the result that one hears his voice on almost every page.

But just as *The World Crisis* had presented his own case for Gallipoli, so the six long volumes of the memoirs represent the version of himself as a great war leader which he wished posterity to remember.

Failures are very much glossed over, as are such controversial events as the disastrous commando raid on Dieppe in 1942 or the mass destruction of the City of Dresden by British bombers with vast civilian casualities in January 1945. For as with all his major works, *The Second World War* appears to have one fundamental underlying purpose: to establish that in everything that matters Churchill had been absolutely right from the beginning.

Translated and serialised throughout the world, the memoirs, the first volume of which appeared in June 1948, were an indubitable success, ultimately leading as they did to the award of the Nobel Prize for Literature in 1953. And during their composition Churchill appears to have enjoyed reliving the great events which he described. Certainly he spent more time on writing than on politics and, completely cured of the gloom following his brother's death, he began enjoying all his postwar splendour and prosperity. For the memoirs had also made him rich; and, although to minimise taxation much of the royalties were placed in trust to benefit his children, Churchill was able to enjoy a proportion of his money.

Chartwell was flourishing, and with the Soameses living in the Chartwell farm a new generation was appearing on the premises. Along with the goldfish and the butterflies, the chickens and the geese, there were now three Soames grandchildren for Churchill to enjoy – Nicholas, Emma and Jeremy (two more, Rupert and Charlotte, would arrive in the 1950s). Mary could look after Clementine, and while Soames continued to get on so splendidly with Churchill, the former captain had much to learn from the former lieutenant of hussars – not least on how to turn from soldiering to politics.

But while the Soameses basked in the sunlight of the great man's favour some of his other children were less fortunate. Sarah in particular had a harrowing few months towards the end of 1947.

Since his return to Concord, Winant had been suffering acute depression. Short of money and out of favour in Washington, he was convinced he had no future. His marriage had not recovered from the war, and he still missed Sarah. He had telephoned her frequently in Italy, begging her to have him back. 'If you won't, I'll shoot myself,' he told her. And on the night of 10 October 1947, in an upstairs room of his house in Massachusetts, John Gilbert Winant, former ambassador to London and close friend of the Churchills, carried out his threat.

Sarah was mentioned neither in the press nor at the inquest; but Winant had been talking to her shortly before he killed himself. According to Soldati, the effect of his suicide on her was shattering. She had no reason to blame herself for what had occurred – their old affair had long been over, and Winant had been a congenital depressive – but she inevitably reproached herself, feeling that she brought nothing but unhappiness to those who loved her. To make things worse, *Daniele Cortis* flopped and the critics panned her. As Soldati put it, 'her talents as an actress were not equal to the star she wished to be – and the Churchill name was too big for her to live with'. It was then that friends noticed she was drinking heavily.

Clementine made a point of insisting that she and Churchill attended Winant's memorial service in London. And Churchill, who must have known what Winant meant to Sarah, took her with him when he went to Marrakesh that winter to finish the first volume of his memoirs, expenses paid by his American publisher.

During this period, Randolph, too, was more troubled than he seemed; and as usual relations with his father lay at the root of the trouble. Churchill was getting bored with him. 'We have a deep animal love for one another,' he admitted, 'but every time we meet we seem to have a bloody row.' Worse still, Randolph's role as Churchill's heir seemed under threat. Chartwell had been intended as his patrimony, but it would now pass to the National Trust on Churchill's death.

Mary said that, with age, Churchill could no longer bear the strain of endless arguments with Randolph, but a more serious reason for his dropping out of favour was her husband, Christopher, who, as Colville put it, 'without malice or intrigue or any ostentation on his own part, stepped into the shoes so long predestined for Randolph'.

Christopher would henceforth be a problem for Randolph, but one source of jealousy he no longer needed to contend with was his ex-wife, Pamela. Since she had gone to Paris, his parents saw little of her, and Churchill was heard remarking: 'What's this I hear about Pamela taking up with an Italian motor mechanic?'

This improbable remark was a reference to one of the richest men in Italy, the playboy, sportsman and heir to the Fiat Motor Company of Turin, Avvocato Gianni Agnelli. Still unmarried in his early forties, Agnelli was enjoying wine, women and Ferraris in the South of France before shouldering his great inheritance.

Having spent the war at the court of Winston Churchill, Pamela was inevitably attracted to this future uncrowned king of Italy, just as Agnelli was impressed to know a Churchill. Adaptable as ever, she was soon holidaying at Agnelli's villa in the South of France, talking with a noticeable Italian accent, and even considering converting to Catholicism and having her marriage to Randolph annulled by the Vatican. Marriage to Agnelli would complement her life with the Churchills and provide young Winston with the settled background which he needed. Although he would soon be attending smart Le Rosay school in Switzerland, Pamela was worried at his tendency to eczema and asthma.

Like Pamela, Randolph also felt the urge to settle down, and once more did his best to marry Laura. Since her marriage to Lord Dudley had collapsed – 'insane jealousy, hideous temper, quite impossible' – Randolph tried to take his place. Laura's reasons for refusing him are interesting. 'Fond as I was of Randolph I was never in love with him. Perhaps his father's influence stopped him ever growing up, so that as a lover one could never take him seriously.'

Laura did take the youthful publisher Michael Canfield seriously. As well as being handsome, rich and charming, Canfield was also reputedly the secret offspring of the late Duke of Kent. (His adoptive father Cass Cornfield was head of the New York publishers, Harper and Row.) When in 1948 he graduated to become Laura's third husband, Randolph ignored the marriage, as he had her others, and remained in love with her. But this did not prevent him looking for a wife.

Randolph already knew the beautiful June Osborne. A colonel's daughter, she was nearly thirty, dressed well, spoke impeccably, but remained unmarried, having gravitated to the upper reaches of literary Bohemia where husbands were difficult to find. For a period she was mistress to Randolph's handsome

friend, the journalist Alastair Forbes. Concurrently she shared a
house with the biographer Peter Quennell. And in 1947 the talk
in White's club bar was that Cyril Connolly was in love with her
and contemplating marriage.

Since they had been boys together at Eton, Randolph had
treated this fat distinguished man of letters as a joke; and it was
possibly to annoy him that he proposed to June himself. To his
surprise June accepted.

Neurotic, vulnerable and deeply conventional at heart, June
was even more unsuited to the role of Mrs Randolph Churchill
than Pamela had been. But Randolph was that awkward phenomenon, an unmarriageable man who knew that he required a
wife, and once accepted he was not letting go.

Evelyn Waugh, who understood this, assured June in what
must have been a tongue-in-cheek letter of congratulation, that
Randolph was 'essentially a domestic and home-loving character
who has never had a home'. Waugh also spoke of Randolph's
'unique natural capacity for happiness which, one way or other,
has never been fully developed. I am sure', he added hopefully,
'that you will be able to do this for him.'

The Churchills duly met the Osbornes for lunch at the Savoy,
and a three-month engagement followed. This included never-
ending arguments, a suicide-attempt by June, and a fight between
the lovers on the Thames Embankment after which June seriously
considered charging Randolph with assault.

The engagement would have scared almost anyone but
Randolph from the altar. 'You can't seriously think of going
through with it,' said Laura.

'Of course I am,' said Randolph. 'It's a scientific fact that
couples who fight before marriage live happily ever after.'

This was one more of Randolph's optimistic fallacies; but,
undeterred, he married June in the presence of the Churchill
family at Caxton Hall on 2 November 1948. His father, anxious to
see him settled, and to compensate him for losing the inheritance
to Chartwell, had arranged for the trust fund to buy him a house
in Westminster for £14,000. And, although the marriage was even
stormier than Laura predicted, June rapidly produced a daughter.
She was a pretty baby, and to placate his father, in November
1949, Randolph had her christened Arabella, after the Duke of
Marlborough's sister, Arabella Churchill, who had been mistress
to James II.

Churchill was delighted, and the birth of Arabella seemed to complete the revival of his fortunes. Attlee's Labour government had outlived its popularity, and survived the general election of February 1950 by a mere six votes.

Churchill could afford to wait. He had his memoirs to complete before taking his revenge against the Socialists, and by the summer of 1951 they were all but finished. That August he was at Annecy in the Haute Savoie working on the final volume. When he travelled it was now upon the grandest scale. French rail transported 55 trunks and 65 smaller articles out for him, but finding the weather disappointing he decided to go on to Venice.

His secretary told him that as the train did not stop at Annecy, they would have to drive to Geneva.

'Kindly remember I am Winston Churchill,' he replied. 'Tell the station master to stop the train.'

Eight weeks later, in October 1951, a general election stopped the Labour government for him as well, returning the Conservatives to power with a majority of seventeen. Just a month short of his seventy-seventh birthday, Churchill had reversed the defeat of 1945, and for the first time in his life became Prime Minister by vote of the British people.

31
'The Secret Battle': 1950–55

Had Churchill not become Prime Minister again in October 1951, it is hard to think of any other position in the country which could have been safely entrusted to this elderly and ailing Englishman. He was going deaf and losing his once formidable powers of memory and concentration. He smoked and ate and drank too much. The arteries which fed the brain were closing up, the nerves in his back had been affected, and according to Lord Moran he had never fully recovered from a stroke which he had sustained some eighteen months earlier while staying with Lord Beaverbrook in the South of France. As with most of Churchill's illnesses, this had been effectively hushed up, but Moran thought a recurrence virtually inevitable.

'Very, very old, tragically old,' replied Bob Boothby when Harold Nicolson asked how he found the new Prime Minister, the day after taking office; and Oliver Lyttelton described him as possessing 'the tired look of a trawler captain who had reached harbour after a buffeting'. Not even Clementine believed this storm-tossed skipper of the ship of state could stay much longer on the bridge.

Not that she wished him to. She understood how desperately he had wanted this final spell in office to efface the humiliation of defeat in 1945. But, now that he had it, she urged him to retire gracefully before too long – and he agreed to do so, certainly within a year. This was greeted with relief by his colleagues, and in particular by his Premier-in-waiting, Anthony Eden. Back in his old job of Foreign Secretary, this diplomat's diplomat had been happy to return to his allies and admirers in the Foreign Office – but he was happier still at the prospect of the longest wait in politics soon ending.

However, no one quite appreciated the effect on Churchill of a further taste of that mystical royal jelly, power, and his final ministry provides a signal demonstration of its properties. Once revived by 'the great elixir', almost all the qualities which once made him great – rhetoric, aggressiveness, courage, rock-like obstinacy – were marshalled in one grand endeavour to fight off age and stay in office. Like some ancient general on a long retreat, he soon relied on every subterfuge he knew to dodge the moment of surrender.

To begin with, almost everybody wished him well. 'You and I derive great pleasure from the fact that the old boy is back in power which he revels in, and that the last lustre of his life should be spent in place and power which is health to him,' wrote Lord Bracken to Lord Beaverbrook. Bracken also wrote to Churchill urging him to 'be a lazy premier'.

This seemed sound advice even if there was, as someone said, a strong whiff of 'Auld Lang Syne in the corridors of power', as he assembled his 'cronies cabinet' around him. Although Bracken and Beaverbrook declined to re-enlist, he had R. A. Butler at the Treasury and Harold Macmillan in charge of housing. His son-in-law Duncan Sandys became his Minister for Air; his 'favourite soldier', Field Marshal Alexander, his Minister for Defence; and the newly elected member for Bedford, Captain Soames, was his all-important Parliamentary Private Secretary. His policy, he said, was simple: 'houses and meat and not getting scuppered'. In fact he changed little of Attlee's legislation, and it was still generally assumed that he would 'soon be handing on to Anthony', when the first of an unexpected series of events offered him his chance to play things very differently.

Early in February 1952, Miss Hamblin was working on letters with Clementine in her room in Downing Street, when a grim-faced Churchill entered. 'Go!' he shouted at Miss Hamblin. 'Go!'

Miss Hamblin went – and when Clementine later apologised for his behaviour she explained that he had just received the news that George VI had died in the night at Sandringham. Churchill was deeply – indeed, painfully – affected, and as usual all the romantic feeling in his nature was aroused at a poignant royal occasion. He spent a whole day locked in composition of the epitaph which he broadcast to the nation and which, in terms of rhetoric, rivalled the abdication speech he wrote for George's predecessor back in 1936. 'The King walked with death as if death were a companion, an acquaintance, whom he recognised and did not fear. In the end death came as a friend,' he said.

Churchill did this sort of thing so well that nobody remarked that this simply was not true. Far from treating death as a 'companion', George VI had been kept in ignorance of the seriousness of his illness by his doctors to the last, and had died quite unexpectedly, unaware that he was suffering from cancer.

Churchill was profoundly stirred, but his sorrow at King George's death was sweetened by the succession of Elizabeth II. 'I whose youth was passed in the august, unchallenged and tranquil glare of the Victorian era, may feel a thrill in invoking once again the prayer and anthem, "God Save the Queen!"' his epitaph had ended.

Well might he feel a thrill; for, as he knew quite well, it would take at least a year to complete the arrangements for the coronation (finally set for 2 June 1953) and, as Moran wrote, Churchill instantly 'set his heart on seeing the young Queen crowned before he gave up office'. Nothing would stop him being present as Prime Minister – not even the scare a few weeks later, when a cerebral disturbance affected his powers of speech, making him fear the onset of a further stroke.

It proved a false alarm, and relations between this aged Premier and his impatient Foreign Secretary began to fray, as Eden became increasingly exasperated by Churchill's presence and by the way he ran the Government. Then in August 1952 harmony seemed suddenly restored, thanks to an unlikely member of the Churchill family. Early that August Churchill's niece Clarissa announced her engagement to Anthony Eden.

Clarissa was a most untypical Churchill. From the moment her mother, Goonie, chose her name from the Richardson novel *Clarissa*, she seemed destined for something different from the world of politics and international affairs which so obsessed the other Churchills. Clarissa was as bright as she was pretty; and, although she got on well with her famous aunt and uncle, politics bored her. After a year at the Sorbonne, just before the war, she settled in Oxford, making friends with such Oxford luminaries as Maurice Bowra, Isaiah Berlin and David Cecil. She spent the war doing factory work, then working on cyphers at the Foreign Office. Afterwards she looked after publicity for Alexander Korda and the publisher George Weidenfeld.

Eden, whose first marriage had ended in divorce some five

years earlier, met her outside the orbit of the Churchills at a London dinner-party in 1947. Until then she had not known him, for despite his close political association with his leader, Eden and the Churchill family had little social contact. News of the engagement caught the Churchills rather by surprise.

Churchill himself appeared delighted, and gave Clarissa £500 as an engagement present. He told Colville that he 'felt avuncular towards his orphaned niece' and added that he thought she had 'a most unusual personality'. Colville himself wondered how much marriage would change this 'strange and bewildering' young woman, and whether she would 'help to calm the vain and occasionally hysterical Eden'.

For a while it looked as if she might. After a register-office wedding at the end of August, Churchill gave the reception at 10 Downing Street and seemed untroubled by the thought that before too long he and Clementine would be surrendering their home to the bridal couple. On the contrary, it was generally assumed that the marriage would make Churchill's resignation easier by keeping the succession in the family. Indeed, now that his political heir apparent had married the daughter of his beloved brother, Jack, this should have been the moment for the family to become more united. But with the Churchills things rarely happened quite like that, and the strains within the family, especially among the elder children, were actually increased.

Randolph was particularly torn by his cousin's marriage. He and Clarissa were good friends, and when Evelyn Waugh had publicly criticised Clarissa as a natal Catholic for becoming engaged to a divorcée he had defended her, promptly putting his former comrade firmly in his place. 'What business is it of yours? You are not the Cardinal Archbishop or the editor of *The Tablet* or even like me, a cousin.'

But in fact Randolph disliked the marriage even more than Waugh did – not on religious grounds, but because of his almost pathological resentment of his father's heir apparent. In Randolph's eyes, by marrying 'Jerk' Eden, as he now always referred to him, Clarissa was aiding and abetting the principal usurper of his own predestined place beside his father.

Churchill's victory had left Randolph in a miserable situation. While Soames and Sandys by their re-election to Parliament were both able to enjoy the great man's governmental bounty,

Randolph had once more ignominiously failed to get elected. He had been firmly beaten at Devonport by his friend and fellow Beaverbrook journalist, the Labour politician Michael Foot.

Randolph's old ambition to become Prime Minister was, amazingly, unshaken; but he felt that his father's return to office had spoiled his chances. 'I can do nothing while he is there,' he used to say, and instead of being able to count on Churchill's political support, he watched jealously as it was diverted – initially to Soames and Duncan Sandys, and now to his sworn enemy Eden.

Randolph's misery boiled up a few weeks after the marriage when Churchill failed to take him with him to the Tory Party Conference in Scarborough. Churchill travelled in his special train with Soames and Clementine, and seems to have wanted nothing more sinister than a peaceful journey, but Randolph reacted like a jilted lover. In a long and anguished letter to his father, he complained *inter alia* of the agony of being 'repeatedly disregarded, rejected & snubbed by the person one loves most in the world'. Churchill did his best to reassure him, but as Prime Minister he had more important matters on his plate than a forty-year-old son who drank too much, who embarrassed him in public, and whose second marriage was already showing signs of collapsing just as his first had done. Not even the birth of Arabella had made Randolph change his habits, and he and June were feuding more than ever.

During this early period back in power, Churchill did not enjoy particularly close relations with his favourite daughter, Sarah, either. After the unhappy period following Winant's suicide Sarah had pulled herself together and, cashing in on the Churchill name, had started getting parts as a celebrity actress on American television. Then she fell in love again – with Anthony Beauchamp, a British society photographer currently working in America. (Born Entwhistle, he had changed his name to the aristocratic Beauchamp for professional and social reasons.) Early in 1949, while holidaying in the South of France, Sarah had taken her lover to meet her parents in Monte Carlo. The visit started well enough, with Beauchamp even spending an evening with Churchill in the casino, where he introduced the great man to his special system at roulette. Then something went embarrassingly wrong. Beauchamp, though handsome, smooth and very charming, did not measure up to Churchillian concepts of a gentleman. And Churchill began treating him rather as he had Vic Oliver, whom he had also thought 'common as dirt' at their first meeting. Hurt and insulted, Beauchamp left abruptly. Sarah was very angry, and expressed her feelings in the sharpest letter she ever wrote her father, making it all too plain whose side she was taking.

If you think that by insulting him you can change by one jot the opinion I hold of him – you are most sorely mistaken. . . . I love you very much – nothing can ever change that – but I see now how right I have been to build a life for myself, and arm myself with four good hoofs & a crusty carapace, for the slings & arrows of family life are sharp indeed.

Never again, she swore, would she 'subject any of her friends' to Churchill's contempt and, as good as her word, she failed to inform her parents when she duly married Beauchamp at Sea Island, Georgia, in October 1949. Once she heard about the marriage, Clementine did her best to restore relations with her daughter, but as far as Churchill was concerned Sarah's second marriage was a repetition of her first – bringing yet another son-in-law he could not tolerate. Largely because of this, the Beauchamps had continued living in America.

Sarah was perfectly capable of creating a separate existence away from the family, but her sister Diana was less resilient. During this period she caused Churchill and the family increasing concern. Most of her troubles lay with her feelings of inadequacy, particularly now that her husband was becoming such a success as a minister in her father's government. Sandys was reasonably discreet about his affairs with other women, and she still loved him dearly, but he was not the sort of husband a dependent and insecure wife like Diana needed. Nor was Clementine much help. Diana's neurosis was still bound up with childhood feelings that her mother had no time for her and disapproved of her, and Clementine continued to show little understanding and less sympathy.

Early in 1953, Diana had a severe nervous breakdown. Although its immediate cause was marital unhappiness, it was not her husband who bore the brunt of her neurotic anger. When she lost control, and ran hysterically out of her London house, Randolph was called to find her and finally discovered her close to home, hiding in some bushes and armed with a carving-knife.

Later he told Laura that Diana was threatening to kill her mother. He calmed her down, and brought her home, but said that she was so pathetic that taking the knife away was 'like disarming a butterfly'.

Diana's nervous breakdown was the start of a wretched period spent in clinics undergoing treatment, none of which could change her underlying problems. And while her husband maintained the appearances of the marriage, and her mother tried to get on better terms with her, the only member of the family who always had a calming influence was her father. It was during this period that he told her of his own near nervous breakdown when 'the light faded from the picture' during his time as Home Secretary. Mary writes that Churchill always found 'psychological troubles and their explanation quite beyond his ken', but the fact that they shared a similar depressive tendency must have helped him understand her. Certainly, unlike Clementine, Churchill was always gentle and supportive with Diana, but during this Coronation Year of 1953 he had other family problems to contend with – in particular his own relations with his nephew-in-law and political heir apparent.

Eden's marriage to Clarissa was apparently extremely happy, but by the beginning of 1953 this handsome, highly strung politician was becoming seriously depressed about his future. 'He doesn't think the Old Man will ever go,' wrote his principal private secretary, Evelyn Shuckburgh. He added that Eden was so disheartened that he was listening to Clarissa's advice to quit politics for good at the Coronation and opt for the House of Lords with the title of Lord Baltimore ('after an ancestor of AE's who was Governor of Baltimore').

His defeatist mood was partly due to the sniping against him – particularly in Beaverbrook's *Express* – and partly to his health. Even before his marriage he had suffered recurrent bouts of jaundice which were traced to a gall-bladder infection, and in April 1953 he was persuaded to undergo routine gall-bladder surgery.

This operation was to have far-reaching implications, not only for Eden, but also for British politics and the whole extraordinary conclusion of Churchill's time in office.

Had the operation worked, Churchill could hardly have avoided retiring at the Coronation. On the edge of his ninth decade, even he would have found it hard not to honour his long-term understanding with his successor and relinquish power to Eden as Stanley Baldwin had to Neville Chamberlain after George VI's coronation in 1937.

But the operation did not work. The surgeon's knife slipped, partially severing the bile-duct, and although a second operation did save Eden's life, he was left dangerously ill, with the leaking bile-duct slowly poisoning his system. His only hope lay in a new and risky operation to install an artificial bile-duct, which was being pioneered at the Lahey Clinic in Boston. The doctors gave mid-June – well after the Coronation – as the earliest possible date for this third operation.

With Eden far too sick to act as Foreign Secretary, Churchill insisted on shouldering his responsibilities in addition to his own. Far from being worried by the extra work, he seemed all too eager at the prospect. Suddenly it seemed as if his old friend, destiny, was extending him a golden opportunity to achieve an irresistible finale to his whole career.

Just a few weeks earlier, on 15 March, Stalin had died, and had been succeeded by his virtually unknown fifty-year-old deputy premier, Georgi Malenkov. With Stalin gone, and Eisenhower just elected President of the United States, there seemed an opportunity at last for a fresh start in the West's relations with the Soviets. By making an appeal direct to Malenkov for an informal summit conference with himself and Eisenhower, Churchill saw a chance to be instrumental in 'unfreezing' the Cold War, settle the dangerous disagreements between East and West, and banish the threat of nuclear annihilation for ever. As he put it to Parliament, the leaders of the world 'might feel that they might do something better than tear the human race, including themselves, to bits. At worst they might have established more intimate contacts. At best we might have a generation of peace.'

It is not difficult to guess the way Churchill's mind was working. Here was another great dramatic opportunity on the stage of history, and a summit meeting might provide a repetition of his tripartite meeting with Stalin and Roosevelt in Tehran in 1943. Then he had been a god of war, but now he could make a final contribution to the human race as god of peace.

It would be particularly appropriate in this year of the young queen's coronation. After a historic breakthrough in the cause of peace, Churchill could then stand proudly with his sovereign at her crowning before departing, like the Duke of Marlborough

in Rysbrack's altarpiece at Blenheim, on a cloud of universal
gratitude and glory.

Impotently watching from his sickbed, Eden hated the whole
idea of Churchill's summit, on the grounds that such idealistic
interventions rarely worked. (He vividly remembered Chamberlain's attempt to bring 'peace in our time' with an earlier summit
meeting of his own with Hitler in Munich in 1938.) But there
was little he could do, with his leader thoroughly aroused and
with an enthusiastic press behind him. And, although the mutual
suspicion between the Soviet Union and America soon aborted
the old man's dreams of hopeful summitry, this coronation
springtime was an optimistic period for Churchill. In April he
accepted the Order of the Garter from the Queen (the highest
personal honour in the royal gift). He had glumly turned it down
when offered it after electoral defeat in 1945, but as *Sir* Winston
Churchill he was now at one with history and envisaging the
Coronation as the signal for a national revival to equal the
renaissance of the young queen's namesake, Elizabeth I.

Such was his enthusiasm for the youthful Queen that Colville
genuinely believed that Churchill fell in love with her, although
'he was an old man whose passions were spent'. The palace
audiences lengthened, Churchill placed the Queen's photograph
by his bedside, and was soon reverently hailing her as 'wife and
mother . . . heir to all our traditions and all our glories'.

Churchill's enthusiasm for the Coronation as a source of
national revival may have aroused the feelings of the country,
but did not extend to permitting ordinary people to watch the
ceremony on television. When BBC Television approached the
Government for permission to place their cameras in the Abbey,
Churchill the aristocrat was indignantly against the idea as a
vulgar intrusion which would place too big a burden on the
Queen. (Privately he said: 'I don't see why the BBC should have
a better view of my monarch being crowned than me.') And it was
only the decision of the Queen herself, following angry comment
in the press, that permitted television coverage.

Despite this, his arrival at the Coronation complete with
decorations, bottle-green Trinity House uniform, and dark-blue
Garter robes and hat was one of the great appearances of his
career. All three generations of male Churchills were in the
ceremony: young Winston was a page ('Boy, tell your mother to
get your hair cut,' barked Field Marshal Montgomery at the dress

rehearsal); Randolph had the Alice-in-Wonderland title of 'Gold Staff Officer'; and for Cecil Beaton one of the supreme moments came when, descending from his carriage to the acclamation of the crowd outside the Abbey, 'that great old relic, Winston Churchill, lurched forward on unsteady feet, a fluttering mass of white ribbons at his shoulder and white feathers in the hat in his hand'.

A few days later Churchill and Clementine saw Eden and Clarissa off from Heathrow Airport for the crucial operation in Boston. It was successfully performed on the morning of Tuesday, 20 June. That same evening Churchill, with blue Garter sash worn proudly across his chest, seemed on better form than ever as he welcomed the premier of Italy to dinner at Downing Street. He gave a witty speech about the British visit of an earlier Roman statesman, Julius Caesar, but as the meal ended found himself incapable of rising from his chair. Some thought him drunk; but others, like Soames and Colville, realised the truth. This was the stroke which Moran had predicted. One of the most singular episodes in British postwar politics had started.

To begin with, the effect of Churchill's stroke seemed slight. Tough as ever, he insisted on chairing Wednesday morning's Cabinet, and only Macmillan seemed to notice his unusual silence. But the stroke was what doctors call 'a slow leak', which gradually affected his speech then paralysed his whole left side. He could barely stand when he left by road for Chartwell on Wednesday afternoon, and by Thursday morning Moran was telling Colville that the Premier was unlikely to survive the weekend.

With Churchill on the verge of death, Sarah was summoned from New York. Reaching Chartwell, she was shocked by what she saw; and when she gave her father her old greeting – 'Darling, wow!' – he feebly squeezed her hand but could not answer. Yet her arrival must have helped him; although remaining weak and paralysed over the weekend, he showed little sign of dying. Slowly his speech returned, and he managed to complain to Moran: 'I am a hulk – only breathing and excreting.' Grateful for even this evidence of life, Clementine began 'vehemently asserting' that, whatever else he did, he must definitely retire.

Even now, Churchill was determined not to go, and as on many earlier occasions his strength of will seemed capable of conquering his ailing body. What Moran called his 'Secret Battle' to survive had started.

'There are moments', Moran wrote, 'when he does not want to do anything, when a dreadful apathy settles on him, and he nearly loses heart. But he always sets his jaw and hangs on.'

What was remarkable – and typical – of Churchill was his instinctive grasp of power even *in extremis*. As the effects of the stroke were growing worse during the drive to Chartwell on Wednesday afternoon, he was already instructing Moran that on no account should the press be informed of his condition. And during the days that followed he insisted on a total news-blackout on the truth.

Just as with Moran, he gave Colville 'strict orders not to let it be known that he was temporarily incapacitated and to continue to ensure that the administration continued to function as if he were in full control'. This involved considerable deception of Parliament and press, but his orders were faithfully observed by all around him. Not since the bizarre conspiracy that kept the moribund Woodrow Wilson on as President of the United States had there been anything quite like it.

When the Queen heard that he was ill and thoughtfully suggested visiting him at Chartwell, she was hurriedly put off on the grounds that 'people would think that he was dying and he was not'. A more compelling reason was that the Queen, with her sense of constitutional propriety, would certainly have been alarmed to see her Premier, like his deputy, completely incapacitated, and would have had to insist on a legitimate substitute. 'Tell her we'll meet at the St Leger,' Her Majesty was told.

More of a worry was what Colville cheerfully described as 'gagging' the British press. But this proved all too easy. Three press lords, all close friends of Churchill – Beaverbrook, Bracken and Camrose – were summoned to Chartwell where Colville explained the situation. He describes them 'pacing the lawn in earnest conversation' – the upshot of which was that, out of respect for Churchill's wishes, the three peers used their influence with their editors and other press proprietors to ensure total silence over Churchill's illness. This was extended to the BBC, so that to flatter and placate a sick old man neither Queen nor Parliament nor people was allowed to know that Britain was without an effective legally constituted leader.

During this crucial period much depended on the family at Chartwell. Instead of returning to America, Sarah stayed on and played her part in her father's recovery by reading to him, as she had after his wartime heart-attack in Carthage. (This time it was Trollope, not Jane Austen.) Randolph, on the other hand, was hardly the calming influence his father needed, and Diana had barely recovered from her breakdown. But there was one member of the family more than capable of doing what was needed. Aided by the ever tactful Colville, Christopher Soames effectively took over and assumed a role which Randolph might have dreamed of. Although Colville was possibly overstating things when he wrote that Christopher 'now held the place in Churchill's heart so long reserved for Randolph, who had been incapable of filling it', it is certain that Randolph could not possibly have done what Christopher did for Churchill during five long weeks of incapacity following his stroke.

During this period, R. A. Butler chaired meetings of the Cabinet. Like all the ministers, he knew that Churchill was unwell. (How much more he knew will always be debatable.) But the official line was simply that the Premier was suffering from overwork and resting at Chartwell. Immediately after the stroke, Lord Moran had issued a deliberately misleading bulletin to this effect. It was a fiction which Christopher played a crucial part in loyally maintaining.

For government business to continue, ministers and heads of department needed regular decisions which only the Prime Minister could give. According to Colville, these ministers 'were entirely ignorant of the Prime Minister's incapacity', but as Churchill from the beginning of his stroke refused to delegate his powers to anyone, someone had to deal with these papers. That someone was Christopher.

Theoretically he was forbidden to see cabinet papers or secret documents, but clearly he had to do so; and since he was considered closer to Churchill's thoughts than anybody else, it was left to Christopher's discretion how to deal with the Prime Minister's business until he could deal with it himself. For Churchill this was 'lazy premiership' with a vengeance, and it was largely thanks to his large, bluff, very canny son-in-law that his absence seemed to make so little difference.

Soon a race for recovery was developing between the seventy-eight-year-old Prime Minister and his fifty-four-year-old successor – with Churchill pulling rapidly ahead. After a stroke of such severity, his improvement was spectacular. His friend and American publisher Walter Graebner of Time-Life Inc., seeing him in late July, told him he was looking much as he remembered him before the stroke. Churchill was delighted. 'This decaying carcass can still bring fame to anything, so long as it is not overworked,' he told him.

A convalescent Anthony returned from Boston with Clarissa, then departed on a cruise round the Mediterranean. 'Circumstances', muttered Churchill to his doctor, 'convince me of my indispensability.'

By August he was well enough to resume his governmental business; but, although Eden was now restored to health, there was no talk from Churchill of retiring. Instead he was carefully conserving all his energies for the crucial test which lay ahead if he was to stay in office: the leader's speech to the party conference in October.

With Eden waiting in the wings, Churchill knew that, should he fail or blunder, he would have to yield to him. But Churchill did not fail or blunder. Less than four months after a major stroke, he delivered a prime ministerial speech to the conference which brought a great ovation from the hall and guaranteed his future. A sun-tanned Eden seated prominently on the platform had no alternative but to smile and applaud the leader. After the conference there was no more speculation on the Premier's retirement.

For Eden the situation was becoming ludicrous; but, although his wife was a member of the family, there was little she could do to help him. Under her uncle's premiership, the Government was placidly successful, and feelings in the family had changed. At the time of his stroke, most of them agreed with Clementine that he should 'definitely retire'. But soon afterwards even Clementine believed that for his own sake he should be left to 'enjoy' the premiership as long as possible. To be forced from office now, she thought, would kill him. Even if it didn't, it would spell the start of what she called his 'life in death, his death in life'.

So, as the months ticked by, there was always some compelling reason for Churchill to stay on in power. During 1954 it was the fact that this was the year of his eightieth birthday, and that in November the House of Commons was planning a full-scale presentation in Westminster Hall. Graham Sutherland had been specially commissioned to paint his portrait, and Churchill was determined to enjoy his birthday as Prime Minister. In November both the birthday and the presentation came and went with still no mention of retirement.

By early 1955, Eden, never the most phlegmatic of men, was close to desperation. For over four years this eighty-year-old Prime Minister had excluded him from power. But the fact was that even now Churchill could rise to a great occasion like no one else in Parliament. In his last great speech on 1 March he announced the British production of the H-bomb. Age had not changed his voice or dimmed his rhetoric. 'It may well be that we shall, by a process of sublime irony, have reached a stage where safety will be the sturdy shield of terror, and survival the twin brother of annihilation,' he concluded.

Yet there were times when lethargy descended and 'more time was given to bezique and less to public business'. At one of these moments, Churchill agreed to hand over to Anthony in early April.

Having done this, all his old man's bitterness and rage erupted at the thought of what he would be losing. Cornered and unhappy, he managed to convince himself, and others, that he was being 'hounded out of office'; Colville writes of the 'cold hatred' he began to feel for Eden.

Back in his father's favour, Randolph did nothing to discourage such emotions, and there were signs of Churchill's final days in office ending with the bitterest of battles. That they did not was largely due again to Christopher, who persuaded Churchill to depart with dignity. It was one of the most important services he did him.

Colville was present when the Churchills gave a farewell dinner at Downing Street on 4 April. It was a great political occasion, attended by political grandees, all the family, the Edens, Prince Philip and the Queen. Randolph, true to form, got drunk, 'and insisted on pursuing Clarissa with a derogatory article about Anthony Eden'. Otherwise it was an elegiac evening.

Churchill seemed reconciled at last to his surrender, and on the following day would drive to the Palace where he would give the Queen his resignation. (He would also refuse the formal offer

of a dukedom, thinking that it would do no good to Randolph
and 'might ruin little Winston's political career'.)

However, when the dinner ended, Colville helped him upstairs
to his bedroom, and for a while he sat silently on the bed, still
wearing his knee-breeches, Order of Merit and Order of the
Garter. Colville imagined he was having thoughts of fond regret
at leaving Downing Street – but nothing of the sort.

In a final letter to the Queen, Churchill had told her, 'I feel
that yr Majesty is right to put complete confidence in Anthony
Eden, who has given proof of his character and capacity over so
many years.'

But now Churchill turned to Colville, stared at him, then said
with vehemence: 'I don't believe Anthony can do it.'

32

Pausaland

Back in 1928, when Churchill was enjoying the Riviera sunshine at Maxine Elliot's villa in the South of France, the mistress of his great friend, Bendor, Duke of Westminster, was building a villa of her own a few miles away on a pretty hillside overlooking Menton.

Bendor's mistress was Chanel, the most influential French couturier of her day. The Duke never made her Duchess of Westminster, as she had dreamed of being, but throughout the thirties Coco Chanel continued to regard her villa, which she called La Pausa, as a place of secret refuge and delight. By a coincidence, La Pausa came to serve much the same unexpected purpose for Churchill some twenty-five years later during his early eighties.

He had begun the new year of 1956 in a state of all-too-familiar misery. Hating the English winter, he was unoccupied and bored and more or less intolerable to all around him. He detested being old. 'I feel like an aeroplane at the end of its flight, in the dusk, with petrol running out, in search of a safe landing,' he told R. A. Butler, and even the Lord Doctor, Moran, was writing in his diary of Churchill's wish to die, since 'he no longer finds any fun in life'.

The family had little idea how to cope with him, as he talked gloomily of 'waiting about for death'. Clementine, worn out and miserable herself, began the year in hospital, being treated for neuritis, a painful inflammation of the nerves. Then she departed, as she had often departed from him before, on a convalescent cruise to faraway Sri Lanka, with her old friend Sylvia Henley.

In former days he would probably have spent a month or two in Morocco in her absence – or, failing that, with Max Beaverbrook at Cap d'Ail. But he was now too old and too demanding to entrust himself to a North African hotel, however splendid; and

Beaverbrook was old and ailing, too – certainly too old to offer him the attention and amenities he needed.

None of his other rich Riviera friends could help him, either. Miss Elliot was dead; and Somerset Maugham, in his famous Villa Mauresque at Cap Jean St-Ferrat, was more or less insane. (When Maugham had suggested that Churchill share the rejuvenating therapy of the famous Swiss longevitist Professor Niehans, Churchill refused on the grounds that giving up whisky for six months was a bad exchange for prolonging his existence.)

The one enticing invitation Churchill did receive now came from the very rich Hungarian who had managed his pre-war foreign literary affairs. Jewish millionaire, connoisseur and businessman Emery Reves was living in the South of France at La Pausa, which he had bought in 1953 from Chanel.

In 1946 Reves had enriched himself – and Churchill – still further by selling the foreign rights to the leader's wartime memoirs to great advantage. The deals Reves had made for Churchill had included $1,150,000 from Henry Luce for the first US serial rights to the memoirs on behalf of *Life* magazine. With Churchill now engaged on finishing his *History of the English-Speaking Peoples*, agent and author had further business to discuss.

His current secretary, Miss Pugh, and his daughter Diana were more than willing to accompany him on a winter break, and what began as a business trip for Churchill almost instantly became considerably more.

There was much at La Pausa to appeal to him. The villa was one of Chanel's most stylish creations, a place of light and elegance and casual luxury set amid olives on its hillside high above the sea. Since buying it, Reves had steadily embellished it with his choicest treasures. These included nine Renoirs, four Cézannes, three Degases and his mistress, a lavender-eyed former model from New York named Wendy Russell. There was also a dedicated staff, and a cellar few could equal in the South of France.

For Churchill, it was the perfect house in his favourite spot on earth, and he was treated like the great celebrity he was. The staff included one of the finest chefs in France; Emery was a fluent cosmopolitan who could talk on anything; and Wendy was not only very pretty, but had also learned the knack of flattering the elderly and great.

Visitors to La Pausa were requested to put on slippers to

protect the highly polished floors. Churchill was given slippers
of his own, and scarcely had he put them on his elegant small feet
than he felt remarkably at home. England with its miseries was
forgotten, and so was his oft-expressed desire for easeful death.
Miss Pugh told Moran that 'he had seemed twenty years younger'
with the Reveses. His idyll in what he came to call 'Pausaland'
had started.

For some time, much to Clementine's 'dismay', he had been
talking of purchasing his own abode in the South of France. She
refused to have anything to do with it, but a few months after he
returned from Pausaland he was back there once again, determinedly looking for a house.

But where could he find a home as comfortable and perfect
as La Pausa? Where else a couple as devoted to his every whim
as Emery and Wendy? To this old Victorian 'the charm and
seclusion of "private life" in private houses, with private service,
was very powerful', says his daughter.

Honoured and delighted by his presence (who else on the Côte
d'Azur could boast a guest of such enviable distinction?), the
Reveses insisted that he treat La Pausa as his own. Churchill
duly did.

His visits lengthened, and over his next four years at least
twelve months would be spent at La Pausa. According to Wendy:

I'd have a message through from London saying he was coming, and
often adding he was in a deep depression. But from the moment he
arrived, there'd be no sign of it. He was always happy here. He loved
the weather and the views which he could paint, and he'd say, 'In
England when I look out of the window it's usually raining and it's
really *bloody*.'

'The sun is Churchill's greatest life-maintainer,' said Brendan
Bracken; and as well as the winter sunlight of the South of
France there were other things in Pausaland which England and
rainswept Chartwell could not guarantee: a chance to work in
peace, and freedom from the outside world. 'He was so *soft*, so
very sweet and charming, like a baby. He was no longer leader
of the government, or fighting a war, and he could relax and be
himself with those who loved him.'

The Reveses played him records of Mozart, which he had never
listened to before, and Emery lectured him about Cézanne. They

also spoiled him unashamedly. When he finished his last volume of his *History* there was an engraved gold cigar-case from Van Cleef & Arpels, and on his eighty-second birthday there were eighty-two magnums of Dom Pérignon champagne.

One of the further joys of Pausaland was that everything was free, and that all the members of the family were welcome, too. During the next few years almost all of them descended and enjoyed its splendid hospitality – Sarah and Mary and Diana, and their children – so that at times it seemed as if the Churchills actually owned their villa in the South of France.

Almost the only Churchill who failed to enjoy herself in Pausaland was Clementine. Her ancient phobia against the rich life of the South of France as strong as ever, she found life at La Pausa 'claustrophobic'. And while Churchill thoroughly enjoyed 'pasha-like treatment', as he always had, Mary tells us 'he was not companionable' to his equally demanding wife.

Clementine abruptly found she had 'very little' in common with her hosts; and was less than entranced by the devotion Churchill was arousing in a younger, very pretty woman. Clearly embarrassed by Clementine's behaviour to Wendy, Churchill did his best to smooth things over. After one uncomfortable joint visit, he even wrote to Wendy in an attempt to put her mind at rest: 'Clemmie was astonished that you thought her manner to you had hardened during the last few days of her visit. She was concerned that you should have imagined this. Do put it out of your mind, my dear.'

But, whatever Churchill wrote to the contrary, his wife's attitude was clear. She was determined to have as little as possible to do with the adoring Reveses – and he was equally determined to enjoy their company and the pampered life of Pausaland.

Thus it was that, even in his eighties, much of Churchill's married life continued to be lived apart from Clementine. Outwardly they seemed the most devoted ancient couple in the country, living 'happily ever after' as Churchill had insisted that they should. But their devotion could not bear too much proximity, and thanks to the Reveses and La Pausa their discreetly separated lives continued.

But, while Churchill loved La Pausa, his insistence on these lengthy absences was inevitably a source of tension in the marriage. As Colville put it, 'Clementine thought her husband's least admirable characteristic was a yearning for luxury so pronounced that he would accept hospitality from anyone able to offer the surroundings and amenities he enjoyed.'

Selfishly – or wisely – he refused to change his habits; but, like the practised journalist he was, would write her loving letters of propitiation 'in his own paw' when they parted.

But, if Clementine liked to keep away when Churchill was in residence at La Pausa, others visited him there in splendour – including President Coty of France, Adenauer, de Gaulle, the Rainiers, and even his one-time king, the Duke of Windsor and his duchess. The old monarchist, who knew of the Duke's Nazi contacts in the war, nevertheless greeted him with the respect due to his former sovereign. It was noticeable that he avoided calling the Duchess 'Royal Highness'.

At La Pausa, Churchill was treated much like royalty himself. The Reveses dressed for dinner in his honour, and the great man's guests – however numerous or grand – were welcome at a moment's notice.

On his arrival, Emery would meet him at the airport in his Rolls; and Wendy, combining great respect with girlish adoration, addressed him as 'Darling Sir' or 'Pumpkin Pie' depending on his mood or the occasion.

Churchill glowed visibly in her affection, prompting Noël Coward's sour observation that 'this great man, historically one of the greatest our country has produced, and domestically one of the silliest, is absolutely obsessed with a senile passion for Wendy Russell'.

Perhaps he was, although it seems unlikely. Wendy describes Coward's remark as 'Hogwash', while a willingness to make the most of the pleasures of La Pausa is hardly evidence of silliness, still less of galloping senility.

In his way, Churchill was as resolute during these years of his decline as in the years of his ascendancy, and his enjoyment of La Pausa is only one example of his strength of willpower and remarkable physique. There is no question that he was failing. The arteries to his brain were closing up; in 1956 alone he had two small strokes, producing a condition which Moran called progressive 'bleaching of the seat of reason'. But none of this prevented him from staging constant Sarah Bernhardt-like comebacks from the very jaws of death. Seeing him this year, Cecil

Beaton noted that at eighty-one Churchill actually looked very fit, 'like a very healthy baby'.

In fact he had more to enjoy than a reading of Moran's diaries suggests, and even in London there were certain treats that never failed to cheer him up.

He still enjoyed his visits to the House of Commons where, although he spoke no longer, he was still treated as its most distinguished member. Much as he had hated Harrow, his old school had now attained a golden glow in ancient memory, and every year he loved to go there for the annual 'Songs', joining in the tunes which he assured the school 'have inspired my actions and my life'. (Not, alas, his favourite Edwardian music-hall songs, which were not considered suitable.)

Another source of swift rejuvenation was the bonhomie and conversation of the 'Other Club'. Here he could still hold forth in convivial male company – and still stay up as late as ever with his friends and cronies. This was one of many London clubs of which Randolph was emphatically not a member. When Beaverbrook proposed him, Churchill swiftly blackballed the suggestion.

The death of several of his oldest friends left gaps in the membership which nothing could repair: Lindemann, 'the Prof', had died in 1957, followed by Bracken a year later. It was some measure of what Malcolm Muggeridge once called 'the vast wash of Churchillian influence' that both these strange outsiders also died as members of the House of Lords. Bracken was only fifty-eight, young enough to have once been rumoured to have been his son. 'Poor dear Brendan,' Churchill murmured when he heard the news; and when he arrived for the Prof's funeral at Christ Church, Oxford, the congregation to a man had risen in his honour. Churchill was as ever vain enough to relish all such regal gestures and the majestic status now accorded him. On their first meeting, Aristotle Onassis kissed his hand, and Churchill was delighted when a woman in the Hôtel de Paris in Monte Carlo curtsied as he passed.

He also had more serviceable admirers, like Antonio Giraudier, a rich Cuban living in New York, who sent him free cigars and brandy, and Mme Pol Roger, who, learning of his deep affection for her eponymous champagne, ensured that he would be unfailingly provided with as much of it as he could manage to consume.

During this period Churchill finished his *History of the English-Speaking Peoples*, which he had been writing when interrupted by the outbreak of the war. 'I still like work,' he told A. L. Rowse, who was one of several professional historians helping him complete his labours. Thanks also to Emery Reves's efforts, the history helped to make him rich, the four volumes earning something over a million dollars within a year of publication.

Although extremely well preserved and barely seventy, Clementine was not enjoying life with anything like the relish of her ageing husband; but, then, he had been able to arrange his life entirely to suit himself. She had not.

She was the one who would have to bear the brunt of Churchill's moods of boredom, mounting irritation with the world, and blank despair when he returned from La Pausa back to cold grey England. Chartwell had ceased to be his 'playground'. He could no longer lay his bricks, philosophise about his pigs, or swim in his patent outdoor swimming pool. The farm was sold – the Soameses had moved to a country house near Sevenoaks – and paradoxically, now that Chartwell itself belonged to the National Trust, and was destined to become his personal memorial, Churchill was losing interest in it. Clementine, on the other hand, appeared delighted at the thought of Chartwell, which she had hated, ending as their mutual monument. She began to plan accordingly, but in the meantime there was the living Churchill to be taken care of.

Luckily his most detailed personal requirements were catered for by the saintly Sawyers, his eccentric but devoted valet (on duty fourteen hours a day, seven days a week). Graebner describes how he 'woke him, brought him his breakfast, handed him his newspapers, let his dog in, took his dog out for a walk, ran his bath, dried him, took out his clothes, inserted his cufflinks, helped dress him, tied his tie, handed him his hairbrushes, helped him on with his shoes, tied his laces . . .' There was also his new private secretary, a former diplomat named Anthony Montague Browne; a pillar of discretion and resourcefulness, he would be increasingly relied on by the family – and Churchill – during the difficult years that lay ahead.

But no one could take the place of Clementine entirely, and there were times when the burdens of the marriage were intolerable. One of her friends wrote that 'Clementine's almost pitiful perfectionism and qualms of conscience would always have made happiness less accessible to her than to other people'.

Nervous stress caused the neuritis which plagued her – along with fresh attacks of lethargy. And at the heart of all her problems lay the situation which had dogged her married life from the beginning.

However difficult Churchill was to live with, Clementine had rarely doubted her husband's greatness. This had been the surest bond between them, and she had seen her faith confirmed in his great role as his country's saviour. Now, in the evening of their days, she believed it was her mission to maintain his dignity and the legend of his greatness which had inspired them both and given point and purpose to her married life for nearly half a century.

One sees this most dramatically in Clementine's behaviour over Graham Sutherland's notorious eightieth-birthday portrait of her husband.

Great men are always at the mercy of the portrait-painter, which is why dictators keep official artists under the tightest possible control. During the war, Churchill, too, had taken pains to see that his official portrait photographs expressed the qualities he needed to project: toughness, resolution and the famous bulldog look which matched his speeches.

But, as Sutherland was commissioned for the birthday portrait by Parliament, Churchill had no say over the result. One cannot have a veto on one's birthday present, and Sutherland was far too famous to accept censorship of anything he painted. His portraits of such celebrities as Helena Rubinstein, Lord Beaverbrook and Somerset Maugham had made this former abstract painter the most talked about – and controversial – British portrait-painter of the fifties.

In person he was the least Bohemian of artists – conservatively dressed, a natural charmer and a very handsome man. 'Mr Sutherland is a wow!' was Clementine's first reaction when she met him; and Churchill had responded rather similarly to dark-haired Mrs Sutherland on the occasions when they came to Chartwell.

Knowing how sitters can react, Sutherland had taken care not to allow Churchill to see the finished painting until shortly before the presentation in Westminster Hall. And Churchill, moved and flattered by the great occasion, had been careful to control his

feelings, briefly thanking his fellow-parliamentarians for 'this
remarkable example of modern art, which combines force with
candour'.

Although Churchill was depicted, not as the bulldog who had
defied the Nazis, but as a powerful but haunted elder statesman,
most of the audience felt that the great man had accepted the
unflattering but striking portrait of his aged self with 'typical'
good humour. But those who knew him understood his real
feelings from that giveaway reference to 'modern art'. As a highly
traditional amateur painter, Churchill held strong views on that
controversial subject. 'Alfred,' he once remarked to his friend,
Sir Alfred Munnings, the President of the Royal Academy, as
they strolled down Piccadilly, 'if I saw Picasso walking down the
street ahead of us, do you know what I would do? I'd kick him
up the arse.'

Since Picasso never came to London, there was no danger of
this curious assault occurring; but, stuck with this 'vile' public
portrait which he hated, Churchill felt similarly inclined towards
its 'modern' painter. According to Mary the portrait had 'quite
ruined' his birthday. 'Filthy,' he spluttered to Lord Moran. 'I
think it is malignant.' And Cecil Beaton overheard him talking
angrily with Diana Cooper. 'These modern chaps. You're in their
power. They make some drawings, then they go away and do their
damnedest. They like to make a fool of you.'

Since then, Churchill had been brooding on about the portrait
– which was consigned to the shameful depths of the cellar of his
house at Hyde Park Gate.

His feelings about it were somewhat different from an old
man's brief offended vanity. He, after all, for almost sixty
years had been the butt of political cartoonists taking the most
extraordinary liberties with his appearance, so why was he so
mortified by Graham Sutherland?

Moran gives an interesting explanation. 'Since the end of
the war', he writes, Churchill had spent much time and effort
'arranging and editing the part he will play in history', and
would not submit to anything which undermined it. His whole
life, of course, had been a sustained attempt to gain a place
beside Marlborough and Napoleon where his father's criticisms
could no longer reach him. He had succeeded phenomenally;
but, as Moran noticed, he was now intent upon enhancing and
preserving the legendary afflatus round his person. (The historian

Piers Brendon points out that even his final work, *The History of the English-Speaking Peoples*, is one long heroic epic 'whose unwritten climax and conclusion is his own career'.

His physical appearance, too, was part and parcel of the legacy intended for the history-books, and once more Moran was intrigued by the old man's satisfaction when a bust by a sculptor he approved of – the flattering but fifth-rate Oscar Nemon – was placed between the Guildhall statues of Nelson and the Duke of Wellington.

Churchill the embattled bulldog, Churchill in his siren suit, or Churchill resplendent in his Garter robes – these were the images by which he intended he would be remembered. Graham Sutherland's was not. The fact that the unfortunate artist had genuinely attempted to express his own deep admiration for the ancient statesman, and had produced a work of great originality, hardly mattered. This was not how Churchill saw himself – or intended eternity to see him, either.

Outraged at the personal 'betrayal' by a painter he and Clementine had befriended, Churchill had no intention of permitting Sutherland's subversive image to survive. 'I shouldn't be surprised if no one got the opportunity of looking at it after my day,' he told Diana Cooper.

But, much as he loathed the painting, it is hard to think of Churchill destroying it himself. As a painter he had a respect for any work of art, and the Sutherland had been the unanimous gift of that all but sacred gathering, the British House of Commons.

Clementine, however, was immune to all such qualms. She was not a member of the House of Commons, and some twenty years before had shown her mettle by putting her foot through a Sickert drawing of her husband which she felt had done him less than justice.

It is not difficult to kill a painting, and there is no reason to believe that anybody helped her. The canvas can easily be cut out of the frame and burned; and this, it seems, is what she did, some time in 1956, probably while her husband was abroad.

Ironically, it seems that she had originally liked the picture – certainly she did when given a special preview of it by Sutherland's great friend and patron, the courtly Kenneth Clark. But since Churchill hated it, and it offended the enduring legend of his greatness, Clementine felt that she had no alternative – and did her duty. (Later, when she told Mary and her son-in-law what had happened, she was puzzled by their shocked reaction, and agreed to keep the picture's fate a secret.)

But during the last fraught period of Churchill's life there was a more dangerous threat to his legend – and his equanimity – which Clementine could never cope with. Like some aged monarch at the sad conclusion of his reign, Churchill discovered that the citadel of his heart, his precious family, had started to collapse around him.

This entry in Evelyn Waugh's diary for July 1955 (based on a letter from June herself) gives some idea of what the greatest man in Britain was having to put up with in the bosom of his family:

. . . a gruesome evening at Chartwell. Randolph getting drunk and calling Soames a shit, enraging Winston with diatribes against Jerk Eden. Winston so shaken with fury that June and Clemmie feared another seizure. Randolph stormed up saying he would never see his father again, June already in bed, forced to dress and start packing. Then at 1 a.m. Sir Winston padding down the passage in pyjamas, saying, 'I am going to die soon. I cannot go to bed without composing a quarrel', and kissing them both. Randolph next day sober and obsequious at luncheon.

Hardly surprisingly, Randolph's marriage to his amiable, neurotic and much put-upon second wife ended soon afterwards, with June departing with their infant daughter Arabella.

This did not produce the dramas which had followed Pamela's departure. Churchill was not devoted to June, as he had been to Pamela; nor was the precious grandson, heir and namesake now involved. But, as with the previous divorce, Clementine unwisely took the side of Randolph's injured wife, thus aggravating her customary tense relations with her son.

Most reports of Randolph at this time read like despatches from a battlefield. Not long after the row at Chartwell he was throwing a pot of coffee over Ian Fleming's wife (Laura's sister, Ann), then heaving R. A. Butler into his own fire – quite an achievement, granted Butler's bulk and Randolph's unathleticism. The singed statesman was extracted by Randolph's old friend Julian Amery, who retained patrician calm throughout the fracas.

He also brought a stunned conclusion to a West End dinner-party after quarrelling raucously with the stately Lady Pamela

Berry, wife of Michael Berry (later Lord Hartwell), proprietor of the *Daily Telegraph*. A dark and hirsute beauty, daughter of Lord Birkenhead, Lady Pamela had known Randolph since childhood, giving him what he felt to be the right to the last word in an argument. 'Look here, my girl,' he shouted out as he departed, 'you'd better go home and have a shave. You've not been using that electric razor given you for Christmas.' Later he was puzzled that the Berrys banned him from their home. 'Don't come if you value your life,' Lady Pamela replied, when he suggested himself for dinner.

The catalogue of Randolph's victims at this time included politicians, press lords, television interviewers, society hostesses. And each occasion is distinguished, if not entirely excused, by the fact that most recipients of Randolph's misbehaviour, faintly – if not so painfully – deserved it.

The lapsed puritan Malcolm Muggeridge saw Randolph as a necessary social scourge, Mayfair's own privileged purveyor of the wrath of God to the repellent rich. 'Like the sirens in the blitz, his arrival at any social gathering sends everybody scampering for cover,' he wrote.

Randolph the morning after was less indulgent to his own behaviour. 'I should never be let out in private,' he admitted in a rare moment of repentance.

Some thought that Randolph was unhinged, some saw him as a coarse, insensitive and drunken boor; but there were many who, despite his failings, stayed surprisingly devoted. These included Laura, happily married at last to Michael Canfield, but still the object of Randolph's unrequited love. And he had finally made peace with Pamela. They lunched occasionally, and found they got on surprisingly well together. 'All he really needed', says Pamela, 'was a spot of genuine success to give him something to be proud of', but this was something that continued to elude him.

As a political journalist, he was lively and had all the right connections, but his social reputation made him far too many enemies. His bold attempt at war reporting in Korea ended with an early flesh-wound in the leg. His short book on an ancient enemy, *The Rise and Fall of Sir Anthony Eden*, was too embittered to be taken very seriously (except by his parents, who were said to be deeply embarrassed). His greatest triumphs came in court on the two occasions when he sued successfully for the sort of libel he was inevitably attracting. He received £5,000 damages from the *People*, which had described him as 'a paid hack . . . the slightly comic son of our greatest statesman, who poses as a political expert but whose offer to serve as an MP was rejected time and again'.

Randolph's wit and flow of words made him a notable litigant, and revealed the memorable barrister he might have been. But there were too many might-have-beens about him now, and friends were worried that the habits of a misused lifetime had finally caught up with him.

According to the author and journalist Alan Brien, who in his youth was one of the faithful 'young gentlemen' who worked for Randolph as research assistants, he 'always drank treble whiskies in a tumbler topped to the brim with water – a mixture guaranteed to mainline direct into the bloodstream'. (He believed that neat whisky acted more slowly.) From shortly after breakfast this was Randolph's life-line; but, although drink was blamed for his excesses, some suspected that the causes ran much deeper.

It was Cecil Beaton who suggested that at heart Randolph was 'emotionally upset, and carrying on a feud against the world. One's heart went out to him in his suffering,' he added. And as usual the deepest cause of Randolph's sufferings seems to have lain with his father; relations between them both remained as ambivalent and uncomfortable as ever.

'Winston was the only person Randolph truly loved,' insisted Laura, but like most of Randolph's friends she could never satisfactorily account for the battles which ensued between them. 'Drink,' she used to say. 'Randolph always fought when he was drunk. But he could never tell me why.'

Perhaps it was simpler than she suspected, and Randolph understood the problems that his father's influence had brought him. 'Beneath the mighty oak no saplings grow,' he used to say when asked why he was as he was. But how exactly had 'the mighty oak' destroyed him?

It is at this stage in his life that one discerns Randolph's fate in all its strange complexity, and how the pattern of his life completes the tortuous relationship between his father and Lord Randolph. Randolph's infancy had been ruled by Churchill's obvious desire to re-create an ideal childhood in his close relations with his son. Not only did he spoil him, but he seems to have identified with him as well, casting the golden

Randolph in the part of the perfect son he wished that he had been himself.

Father and son became inseparable in mutual hero-worship. From childhood, Randolph modelled himself upon his father; and Churchill had encouraged this, determined that this eager, powerful small boy should be endowed with all the qualities which he valued for political success: brilliance, skill with words, and knowledge of the powerful and rich and worldly.

In his obsession to placate Lord Randolph's ghost, Churchill's own early life had been ruled by guilt and a passion to succeed his father. Now he was passing on the same exaggerated passion to his son.

After the trauma of Lord Randolph's death, he and his son would jointly re-create the grand succession of the Churchills. Randolph would enter Parliament at his side, as Churchill had dreamed of entering it beside Lord Randolph. And with this child, so lavishly endowed with all the gifts that he could offer, Churchill could finally rebuild his dream of the perfect father–son relationship he had lost for ever at Lord Randolph's death. When his own death came, as come it would, Randolph would be there to 'carry the lamp'.

Out of this perilous – and curious – relationship two things had happened, one predictable, the other almost inconceivable. Predictably, Randolph had remained emotionally a spoiled child, with all the virtues and the vices of his father merged in a sort of complex caricature of Winston Churchill. Precociously possessed of all the skills of politics, society and journalism, Randolph lacked the one essential which had brought his father triumph and success – his unrelenting drive to self-redemption, goaded forward by the memory of a demented and disapproving father.

What was unpredictable in Randolph's situation was what had happened, late in life, to Churchill. He had once believed that, like Lord Randolph, he would 'burn out young', leaving his precious son to take his place. Instead, at the age of seventy, Churchill had started to achieve such greatness as to make an heir superfluous – and particularly an heir like Randolph. Now it was interesting to see how Churchill was effectively disinheriting him. When he first refused a dukedom, one of his reasons was the absurdity of making Randolph 'Marquess of Toodle-do' – and finally successor to the title 'Duke of Chartwell'. Later, the ownership of Chartwell, which he had once regarded as

Randolph's birthright, had passed to the National Trust. And then had come the painful lesion from his son – the constant arguments, the patronage which went to others, and the undisguised preference for Soames's company.

Much of this, of course, was Randolph's fault. But equally one can see how bitter Randolph must have been, and how, in a sense, Churchill was to blame. Randolph had originally been his sole creation: he, more than anyone, had made him what he was. Not only had he spoiled and encouraged him, but he had also thoroughly imbued him with those dreams of the ideal father–son relationship which he had longed for with Lord Randolph.

Now, in his eighties, Churchill had all but solved the strange conundrum of his life. By making himself the saviour of the nation, like Savrola, he had settled accounts with his father – and with himself. He had achieved the place in history he had dreamed of, and had no need of dynasties to keep alive his name. Too great for a successor, he was the culmination of the line, whose myth would guarantee him immortality. Randolph, once the precious 'Chumbolly', the only son and heir, was now superfluous. Churchill no longer needed him, and the true cause of Randolph's 'feud against the world', and so much drunken suffering, was that Randolph knew it too.

Randolph was not the only member of the family to whom the Churchill legacy was bringing problems. On 12 January 1958, while he was in the final stages of divorce from June, a woman calling herself Jane Doe was arrested for drunken and abusive behaviour outside a seaside bungalow at Malibu beach near Los Angeles. The police had been summoned to the house by a telephone operator reporting obscene and abusive language on the line. Miss Doe was even more abusive to the law, and it needed several burly Los Angeles policemen to hold her down and drag her into a police car. At the police station petite Miss Doe became so violent that she required a strait-jacket, and was left to cool off overnight in custody.

Next day, charged with being 'drunk in a public place', Miss Doe admitted that her real name was Sarah Churchill. This was an occasion Sarah found the Churchill name a disadvantage, for the case attracted maximum publicity. After a fifty-dollar fine, she was reported suffering 'exhaustion and emotional strain', but two days later managed to appear in a live television play called 'Love out of Town'.

On sobering up, her first thought was as usual the reaction of her father, who had inevitably seen the widespread press reports. But luckily Churchill was mellowly installed at La Pausa, for once with Clementine, and Wendy was a calming influence on them both, insisting that Sarah come as soon as possible to join them all in Pausaland. Randolph was despatched to Malibu to arrange for her return to Europe.

It was his second mission of this sort, and it was more successful than his attempt to free her from the clutches of Vic Oliver twenty years before. But once again he showed up badly when confronting journalists; interviewed by John Wingate on WABD's *Night Beat* show, an affronted and well-fuelled Randolph gave his most famous public exhibition of the Churchill wrath in action. Questioned about Sarah's antics, he suddenly erupted: 'I never discuss matters affecting members of my family with total strangers. . . . I wouldn't think of asking you about your sisters . . . or your father. I don't even know if you had a father or if you know who your father was.' Wingate kept his cool, but the ensuing uproar was considerable, raising further questions of exactly what was going wrong with Churchill's children.

Clementine was secretly convinced that Sarah, like Randolph, had inherited – probably from Lady Blanche – 'a drink gene' which had helped destroy her mother and her brother Bill. But Churchill was more positive. He, after all, was a lifelong heavy drinker, who had always rigorously controlled his intake.

'Alcohol', he apparently told Sarah, 'must be your servant, never your master.' He might have reminded her of one of his mother's favourite remarks. 'No one with Jerome blood should ever touch spirits. We're born intoxicated,' she used to say. But Churchill, with his love of liquor, had always been a bad example to his offspring, who lacked his massive self-control – and equally massive capacity; but, as with Randolph, Sarah's 'tendencies' had roots which went much deeper into real unhappiness than most suspected.

The immediate cause of her collapse was yet another private tragedy, which had left her lonelier and more vulnerable than ever. Since marrying Beauchamp, Sarah had known little contentment. Obsessed as ever with the stage, she had continued her regular appearances on American television where the Churchill name had proved a substitute for stardom. But her second marriage worked no better than her first. Just as

Sarah had fallen in love with Oliver because she thought that
he possessed the magic key to stardom, so she had genuinely
thought that Beauchamp's photographs of her could still repeat
the process.

'She absolutely *loved* to be photographed,' says her theatrical
agent, Maggie Parker. 'I wished she wouldn't bother so much with
looking at her photographs and concentrated on her acting, but
she adored seeing pictures of herself as a star.' When Beauchamp,
tired of photographing Sarah, turned to television production
back in England, the marriage more or less expired. His career
began to fail, he was involved in several disastrous affairs; then,
early in 1957, Sarah's embittered second husband resolved his
troubles by consuming a massive overdose of sleeping pills.

The residue of suicide is always guilt – but this was worse for
Sarah than when Winant had killed himself. It was the second
suicide of someone she had loved – and this time it was very
public. Recriminations started – with rumours, accusations from
relatives and ex-girl-friends, and considerable press publicity
concentrating on the fact that this was Churchill's son-in-law.

Childless and menopausal, Sarah was haunted by a sense of
failure – first her marriage to Vic Oliver, then Winant's suicide,
and now 'my Tony', as she called him, dead as well. She was
convinced that she brought misery to all who loved her but,
according to several friends who knew her, Sarah's greatest fear
was still her father's disapproval. 'He remained the only man
who really counted in her life,' says her old friend, the actress
Judy Campbell, 'but she was petrified before his greatness,
and felt she had to keep her independence. That was why she
longed to be a star and when she failed, everything collapsed
around her.'

Maggie Parker says the same:

She had been so dedicated, so all-absorbingly ambitious, but she had
never accepted the fact that she lacked the qualities that make a great
actress. She was forced to accept it now, and a light went out for her.
It was then that Sarah really started drinking.

After a fortnight at La Pausa, Churchill paid for her to spend
several months drying out in a clinic near Zurich. This was the
first of many cures and clinics Sarah would endure, but they all
possessed one thing in common. They made no difference to her
drinking. Like Randolph, Sarah was now hooked on alcohol for

life. 'I'm not an alcoholic,' she used to say. 'I'm a dipsomaniac.
I love the stuff.'

Gamely she struggled on with her career. Early 1959 saw her
in the role of a neurotic spinster with Anthony Quayle and Cliff
Richard in a Terence Young film called *Serious Charge*. It was
a part that rather suited her, but soon she was facing a serious
charge in real life.

She was arrested, drunk, in Liverpool, where she was playing
Peter Pan, and four policemen were needed to get her into court.
'Like many real drunks,' says the devoted Ellen Pollock, 'Sarah
was two quite separate people. Sober, she was a golden girl, but
drunk she was a fiend, and very, very strong.'

On conviction – a £2 fine and a year's probation – it was
once again her father she was most concerned with. He was in
Pausaland as usual. 'Love, love, love. Don't bite me!' she cabled
him pathetically. But with Sarah he could be more understanding
than he was with Randolph; and he wrote to Clementine, urging
her support: 'I think they treated her very roughly at Liverpool
& aroused her fiery spirit. I hope she will convince you that her
affliction is part of the periodic difficulties which are common to
women at the change of life, & above all that she will persevere
at her profession.'

Persevere she did, with Churchillian resolution; if she had
finally accepted that she would never be a star, she needed the
sense of purpose and security which the stage could offer more
than ever. Its members, with their gossip and their friendship,
had become her family.

The one member of her actual family on whom Sarah did
rely was now Diana. The two sisters were as much opposites
as ever – Sarah the extrovert, Diana the anxious introvert. But
they had more in common than in the past: disappointment,
loneliness, and the shared strains of being Churchill's daughters.
It was Diana, more than anyone, who saw Sarah through the
aftermath of Beauchamp's suicide. Diana, with her private
sense of humour, could always make her laugh, and seemed
to understand her perfectly. Despite this, in her own withdrawn,
self-effacing way, it was Diana rather than Sarah who was most
at risk.

According to her daughter, Celia, 'she never really recovered
from her nervous breakdown'. A neighbour describes her in her
early fifties as 'a white-faced, tense, little woman, worried about

her looks'. She had had several periods of electric-shock therapy, but it is doubtful how much good they did her.

One of her few close friends, Nuala Allason, says that as well as being 'desperately shy'

Diana was completely lacking in self-esteem. She would occasionally arrange small dinner parties, and take enormous trouble. Like Clementine's, her food was always excellent. 'This is how things were done at Chartwell,' she would say. But then she would add: 'Do you think anyone will want to come?'

She drank – but on nothing like the scale of Sarah and Randolph, and during spells of deep depression sometimes said that she would kill herself. The strains within her marriage troubled her acutely. 'She loved my father to the day she died,' says Celia; and, apart from loving him, she missed the strength and the protection he once offered her against the world outside. For, as Diana Mosley says, being 'quite unlike Randolph and her sisters', Diana 'lacked robustness'.

This was something Duncan Sandys possessed. Efficient, ruthless, debonair, he had continued his ascent up the ladder of political success. Churchill had launched him, but he was now continuing unaided, first as Minister for Overseas Development and then as Commonwealth Secretary. 'A cold fish, but a mightily determined one,' was how one journalist described him. As attractive as ever to women, he never complained that loneliness was his problem.

Nuala Allason discovered that 'one thing never to discuss with Diana was religion. It was somehow mixed up with her breakdown, and she became terribly distressed.' In fact she was deeply religious, and part of that 'desperate lack of self-esteem' was the feeling that even God was rejecting her.

In a very different way, Churchill's favourite niece, Clarissa, also became victim of the fate which seemed to strike the younger members of the family. By marrying her uncle's political heir apparent, she seemingly ensured a glittering future for herself. And, despite her husband's endless wait to succeed her uncle as Prime Minister, it was as if the Edens were inheriting the family business once they took up residence in Downing Street.

But there would be no great succession and in November 1956 her husband's position as prime minister was threatened by a sudden crisis over the Suez Canal. Defying existing treaties, the Egyptian nationalist leader, General Nasser, took over the canal. Supported by France and Israel, Eden replied by sending troops to Egypt, but when widespread international condemnation followed, he withdrew them. Bitter controversy ensued at home and Anthony Eden, by now in failing health, resigned the premiership in January 1957, to be succeeded by Harold Macmillan.

From retirement Churchill gave his attitude to Suez in answer to a question by his grandson Winston. 'I do not know that I should have had the courage to start it in the first place – I certainly would never have dared to stop half way!' And in retrospect, the whole forlorn campaign against Egyptian nationalism and the seizure of the Canal seems like a final curtain-call for Churchill's Empire. With it also vanished the career of Churchill's chosen political heir for ever.

Before her marriage, Clarissa always had a deep antipathy to politics. With a sick and deeply disappointed husband on her hands, she had felt increasingly that it was 'a beastly profession'. Now they were effectively freed from it for good. He was made Earl of Avon, and they settled at their farm in Wiltshire, where Clarissa saw him through his further bouts of illness, and gratefully resumed the country life she loved. She had no regrets for Downing Street; nor finally had he. But in the words of his biographer 'Anthony Eden's greatest source of ill luck had been Winston Churchill.'

The real winners in the family continued to be the Soameses, who, apart from Duncan Sandys, were its only members seriously benefiting from that 'vast wash of influence' which Churchill had dispensed around him.

Marriage to Mary had transformed the captain; and, while the love of this Churchillian princess had not exactly turned the frog into a prince, Soames was rapidly becoming an extremely successful, old-style High Tory politician.

Possibly the key to his remarkable success was summed up in a brief note by a diplomat who knew him well: 'Plays bridge with a lot of flair, and makes money out of it at White's by staying sober.'

As a member of the holy family of British politics, Soames had that all-important aura which would guarantee his almost automatic rise from Churchill's parliamentary private secretary, to a junior ministry in Eden's government and then his appointment as Minister of Agriculture at the age of thirty-nine.

If the Reveses offered Churchill his greatest happiness abroad, the Soameses did the same in England. At the centre of a happy marriage, Mary stayed the ideal daughter to her parents in adversity – and in contrast with all her siblings she remained the optimistic balanced human being Moppett Whyte had brought her up to be.

There would finally be five Soames grandchildren, and even after the family moved from the farm at Chartwell to their larger house in Kent they continued to come to Chartwell whenever Churchill was in residence.

'The older he got the younger he seemed to like young people around him,' says his granddaughter Emma Soames. 'For us he was simply grandpapa, an extremely sweet old man at the centre of the universe, who used to watch us children in the pool at Chartwell or sit in the garden in a sort of reverie. He seemed to glow with a sort of wonderful old age.'

One of Christopher's most successful moves with Churchill was to encourage him to become a racehorse-owner. His horse, Colonist II, carried Lord Randolph's racing colours and delighted Churchill with various successes, including winning the Winston Churchill Stakes. But, for Randolph, even this was unforgivable. 'You mean the Master of the Horse,' he would scathingly reply to anyone unwise enough to mention Christopher.

Randolph's relations with his own two children were predictably stormy. One result of the two divorces was that both children made their homes with their respective mothers – which was just as well since Randolph was a most alarming and erratic father.

He was jealously devoted to his pretty daughter, Arabella, and as if to contrast her with the Soames children did his best to present her as a sort of Churchillian crown princess. 'Arabella will not come out – she will emerge, like a flower,' he said proudly. In fact she had a most disordered childhood, torn between her mother's straitened circumstances (June had not remarried) and the chaos and excitement which was Randolph's element. Sometimes there would be holidays at Chartwell, or briefly in the South of France with Grandpapa. The result, as Arabella puts it, was that 'I grew up to adore my father, but Grandpapa was God'.

Her brother, Winston, was in a different situation. He was still theoretically the favourite grandchild, the natural heir and bearer of the greatest name in British politics. But by now there was little sign of the great succession Churchill had once attempted to create.

Randolph must have been the most undesirable of fathers for a sensitive and conventional small boy. There was much bullying and embarrassment for young Winston, who has memories of waiting endlessly at White's while Randolph finished yet another drink.

On the other hand he hero-worshipped Grandpapa and says: 'I still honestly believe he was the greatest Englishman who ever lived.'

Unlike Randolph, his mother tended to indulge him and, for young Winston, Pamela would always represent the world of rich cosmopolitan society which she inhabited.

As for Pamela herself, she was as ever at the centre of the international social scene – still glamorous, still with the splendid flat beside the Seine, and still as popular as ever with the super-rich with whom she felt increasingly at ease. Agnelli had gone to take control of the family car business, the Fiat empire in Turin, and marry the bride his family desired for him – the beautiful and very grand Neopolitan Princess Marella Caracciolo di Castagneto. But there were others – Elie de Rothschild, Jock Hay Whitney, even Frank Sinatra – whose names would regularly appear with hers in the social columns, along with the inevitable speculation.

Socially the name Churchill meant much the same to Pamela as it did politically to Christopher. It was the password to the super-rich, an international certificate of total social approval, which had brought her almost everything she wanted out of life – except a husband.

As for more distant relations, Sunny's son, Bert, was still bad-temperedly installed as 10th Duke of Marlborough. Like Churchill, Bert had become a legend, but not a particularly appealing one. Evelyn Waugh's son, Auberon, described him as 'One of the stupidest and most richly absurd characters the English aristocracy has ever produced', famous for his 'appalling rudeness, amazing tactlessness, and quite extraordinary greed'.

Many anecdotes support this. One tells of Bert throwing away his toothbrush shouting, 'Bloody thing doesn't work!' when his valet had simply forgotten to put toothpaste on it for him in advance. Another describes Bert arriving in a snowstorm in New York and trying to argue with the recorded message on his daughter's answering machine: 'You stupid woman, don't you realise I'm the Duke of Marlborough?' And there was the time when Bert, a famous shot, went shooting with the film-star David Niven and downed a carrier pigeon by mistake. 'Anything for me Bert?' enquired Niven, and later claimed it took the Duke a week to see the joke.

None of this affected Churchill's affectionate attitude to Bert, whom he treated with the deference due to the head of his distinguished family. Randolph, on the other hand, despised Bert unreservedly. Perhaps the most unattractive of Bert's many unattractive failings was the bullying and public ridicule of his large and long-suffering Duchess, Mary – who, more than anyone, actually made Blenheim work.

But he is said to have been good with children – his own loved him – and when talking to the working classes was rarely at a loss for an appropriate dirty joke. Just before the war, he had a short affair with Laura, which was probably the origin of Randolph's hatred. According to Laura, the Duchess herself used to urge her to go out with him. She said "it kept him happy".' Since then they had remained good friends. Laura discovered that the Duke possessed a closet passion for horticulture, together with an unexpected skill at naming plants, which appealed to her.

But, according to Laura, Blenheim itself depressed him, as so many things did – as he had inherited the Churchill melancholy in full measure. She believed he would have willingly given over his palace and its worries to the National Trust, but for a superstitious dread of being known as the duke who lost his birthright.

One of the many ironies about the Marlborough saga is the fact that now, although nearly sixty years had passed since Sunny married Consuelo, the Vanderbilt inheritance remained as crucial to the family as ever. Consuelo, a great survivor, and the grandest dame of all, was in her eighties, but her fortune continued to be regarded as the one great hope of 'enriching the noble family' (as Sunny's lawyers put it when drawing up the marriage contract back in 1896).

'That must wait until Mummy dies,' was Bert's habitual answer to any major problem in the palace. True Vanderbilt that she was, that powerful old lady with the swanlike neck was hanging

on to her enormous fortune. However, there were hopeful signs
that the bounty of the Vanderbilts would still work wonders for
the Dukes of Marlborough. Although attached to America and
her houses in Palm Beach and Long Island, Consuelo in old age
seemed increasingly attracted to the house – and to the family –
that had caused her so much trouble in the past.

On her frequent trips to visit Bert at Blenheim, Consuelo
was increasingly regarding the mansion as her own ancestral
home. She had started to restore parts of the palace at her
own expense, and had bequeathed several favourite portraits of
herself to hang there. More important still, she had decided to
be buried at Bladon churchyard close to Blenheim where Sunny
was entombed. In life she had loathed him, and found happiness
as Mme Jacques Balsan, but death was different.

For Bert, now pinning all his hopes on the Vanderbilt inheritance, this boded well; but there had been a blow to his
testamentary expectations. His younger brother Ivor – 'the
Mannikin', that 'Créature de Limoges', and Consuelo's favourite
son – had for years been continuing his bachelor existence,
playing competition-standard bridge at the Portland Club, seeing
his analyst each week and still searching for perfection.

Buying a farm in Hampshire, he had spent some happy years
trying to produce the perfect eating apple. As a cattle-breeder,
he had raised an unsurpassed dairy herd. For a period he bred
splendid horses; then aged forty-nine he married. His young wife
Elizabeth was, of course, extremely beautiful. Then in 1956 Lord
Ivor died.

Unfortunately (for Bert) he did this after fathering the perfect
heir, a most appealing child called Robert. Worse still, Grannie
Consuelo had become devoted to the orphaned offspring of her
favourite son, who was now destined to inherit Lord Ivor's portion of the great inheritance. Bert took this badly, as his seeming
stupidity did not extend to money. Nevertheless, determined to
save Blenheim from the taxman on his death, and guided by
his indispensable accountant, he had made over all his great
possessions (apart from the casual million) to his eldest son and
heir, John George Vanderbilt Henry – who had inherited the
inevitable title of Lord Blandford, and who was also known as
Sunny.

Sunny Blandford was a tall and nervous youth, overshadowed
by his dominating father, but he was a successful peacetime

soldier. In 1951, instead of marrying Princess Margaret as the Duchess fondly hoped, he had married Susan Hornby, the spirited daughter of the chairman of W. H. Smith, the newsagents; but the new Lady Blandford, having presented Sunny with a son called James and a daughter, Henrietta, had, after many dramas, left him for another.

So pretty Lady Blandford was not at Blenheim that September day in 1958 when the Marlboroughs gave a special dinner for Clementine and Winston Churchill to commemorate their engagement by the lake at Blenheim half a century before. As well as the family, the guests included A. L. Rowse, who described Clementine as 'all billowing gown and broadened out with age'; but he was shocked to see how much Churchill had aged in the three years since he had seen him last – 'much more feeble . . . unsteady on his feet, the embers of a great fire, all the force,' and with advancing deafness, 'rather impenetrable'. At first, says Rowse, 'we were reduced, as with the very old, to treating him like a child'. He found it touching to observe him now, after another minor stroke, 'all contentment and old-world courtesy' and described how he sat through much of dinner with the Duchess's miniature dachshund on his lap, trying, to the animal's disgust, to feed it delicious lobster mousse.

But Churchill was not as senile as he seemed. After dinner he won £21 off the Duchess at bezique, and when someone asked the old agnostic if he would be attending church next morning he offered him the perfect answer: 'At my age I think my devotions may be attended in private.' Even more private were the old man's secret reasons which had made this sentimental return to Blenheim more significant than any of those weekend guests appreciated.

33

The Dark Angel Beckons

'To die in the sunlight and be spaded under before the dark.' This was how Churchill once described the perfect way to meet one's maker. In fact he had long been taking it for granted that he would be buried in the grounds of Chartwell, preferably in a spot with a view across the Weald.

But, just as he had schooled himself against the threat of death, so he pretended not to be at all concerned about his funeral. During discussions on the disposal of Chartwell to the National Trust, he had casually offered to 'Throw in the corpse as well for £50,000'.

But this was bravado. With his demise approaching, the subject of his funeral and burial became a matter of concern – especially after a brush with death at La Pausa early in 1958. A late lunch, much to drink, and *chemin de fer* until 7 p.m. brought on broncho-pneumonia. Summoned from England, Lord Moran once again preserved him.

Churchill was only faintly grateful. It was, he told Moran, 'a comfort to know that I shall not lurch into the next world without warning'.

Others – Her Majesty the Queen included – took the warning more seriously. On hearing of her greatest subject's latest illness, Moran says that 'it entered her head that he was very old and frail and might die'. Royalty must be professionally concerned about such matters, and with regal common sense the Queen decided that 'her people' would wish Sir Winston to be awarded the supreme post-mortuary honour of a royal-style lying-in-state in Westminster Hall.

But when she questioned the Prime Minister, Harold Macmillan, it transpired that nothing had been arranged. A decision was needed in a hurry; but Supermac, unflappable as ever, reacted with his own distinctly casual brand of old-style practicality.

A few days later Lord Moran was invited down to Birch Grove, the Macmillan country mansion. As the two men strolled together through the daffodils, the Prime Minister enquired: 'How d'you think Winston is? What's likely to happen?'

The doctor was not rating his patient's chances highly, and Macmillan answered with a touch of that weariness he tended to assume when puzzled: 'One doesn't like to talk about it, but I suppose we should do something.' As Moran offered no suggestions, the Prime Minister continued: 'I wonder what *he* would like done? Wellington was buried in St Paul's. Yes, and Nelson, too. Winston likes bands – I think.' With which the conversation ended.

Macmillan's attitude that a gentleman had a duty to consult a friend about his funeral resulted in a telephone call to that effect shortly afterwards. It was, as Montague Browne admitted, somewhat 'macabre', but Churchill was delighted. Nelson and Wellington apart, the only commoner given a state funeral in the last century and a half had been Gladstone; and for someone as concerned as Churchill with his place in history this was the final accolade, the greatest of concluding ceremonies, in which he would effortlessly play the central role himself.

The rarity of such honours meant that there were few precedents to follow. 'What actually is a state funeral?' Randolph enquired of the royal master of ceremonies, the Duke of Norfolk. 'Why, you bloody fool, a funeral paid for by the state,' His Grace, practical as ever, answered.

Churchill also had to approach the matter practically. The first decision to be made was where he wanted to be buried – a question which was on his mind during the weekend spent with Clementine at Blenheim. It was then that he seems to have decided not to spend eternity in the grounds of his 'Earthly Paradise' of Chartwell after all.

Since Chartwell would pass to the National Trust on his death, and be managed by strangers and visited by tourists in their thousands, it would no longer be the seat of the dynasty as he had once intended. Blenheim, however, would always be the tribal centre of the family. It was his birthplace, haven of his youth, and remained an incomparable setting for a hero. In nearby Bladon churchyard lay his parents, and after his sentimental journey back to Blenheim he decided he would join them there for ever.

Once he had picked on Bladon churchyard for the burial,
Churchill's imagination inevitably became hooked on questions
of logistics. He approved of matching Wellington's funeral with
the full-scale service in St Paul's, but how to convey what he
now referred to as 'the Body' afterwards from central London
to far-off Bladon churchyard?

With his perpetual landsman's fascination with water, Churchill
hit on a solution. Since the Thames was navigable as far as
Oxford, it should be feasible to take the bier upstream by barge.
Detachments of the fighting services – together with their bands
– could line the banks, and the population join them to salute
his passing on the bosom of the great historic river.

It was a splendid notion but, alas, as someone pointed out,
the barge would need to pass through countless river-locks *en
route* to Oxford, making the journey impossible in under two
whole days. A further problem was that service cutbacks had left
insufficient personnel in Britain for even the skimpiest attempt to
line the river.

Churchill was disappointed. As Macmillan guessed, he requested 'as many brass bands as possible', but otherwise appeared
content to leave further details of his funeral to a small committee
code-named 'Operation Hope Not'. However, the invaluable
Montague Browne, who was a member, kept him informed of
what was being planned to honour him.

Meanwhile Clementine, watching her eighty-five-year-old
husband's health fluctuate from day to day, was convinced that
his death was imminent. During a car journey from Chartwell up
to London he had had a seizure which had robbed him of all power
of speech. Although it rapidly returned, it left him in the depths
of hideous depression. Even Clementine had never seen him so
bereft. 'It was never like this in the past,' she told Lord Moran.
In the past he had always had a hundred things to do: now all
he had was reading, 'but he does not enjoy what he reads. He
cannot paint. . . . He simply wants to stay in bed.'

Moran diagnosed another minor stroke but, knowing Churchill's
strength of will and powers of recovery, believed that he would
probably survive. Sure enough, within a week Churchill was on his
feet and determined to deliver a promised speech to his constituents
at Woodford, where he was still MP.

As usual, Churchill got his way, and for those who saw it, this
all but final public speech was an unforgettable performance.

Mary and Christopher Soames were there to give support, and Clementine was beside him on the platform, but he appeared immensely old and utterly exhausted. During the introductory speeches he remained slumped and lifeless, bald head nodding, pale grey suit appearing over-large for his old man's body. However, when the moment came for him to speak, there was a transformation. It was as if breath had suddenly been pumped into the deflated statesman, and as he slowly staggered to his feet the skills of the old orator he was sustained him.

He spoke for twenty minutes, somewhat shakily to begin with, then gathering momentum as if that extraordinary voice were emerging somehow out of history. He urged courage in the face of all the perils currently confronting 'this beloved island race', and finished quite abruptly when whatever strength had been supporting him appeared to leave him.

Once more he seemed immensely weary, and only the practised strength of his son-in-law beside him got him safely from the platform.

What his audience saw was the famous willpower once again in action. For periods he could still summon it up, and he did again a few weeks later to make a final trip to Washington where President Eisenhower somehow entertained him. Then, that summer (accompanied by his secretary but not by Clementine), it was time for Pausaland again.

Even now the Reveses' hospitality and the Riviera sunlight did their work, and despite the heat of August he was briefly rejuvenated, relishing the food and the attention, painting once again, and staying up at night as late as ever.

In fact it was his host who was under strain. Late that August, Churchill decided on a brief return to London to attend an official banquet for the American President. Emery Reves saw him safely off from Nice airport, planning to meet him back there in a few days' time. But, returning home, Reves had what proved to be a heart-attack. Thus, instead of rapidly returning to La Pausa as intended, Churchill was compelled to spend the remainder of that summer with Clementine at Chartwell.

He did not know it, but he had seen the last of happy Pausaland. For, although Reves soon recovered from his heart-attack, and he and Wendy were both anxious to have Churchill stay with them again, they were up against an unbeatable opponent. None other than Aristotle Socrates Onassis stood against them in what had now become a battle to play host to the world's most famous house-guest.

It was in 1956 that Randolph first brought Onassis to dinner at La Pausa especially to meet his father. Reputedly the richest man in the world, Onassis had set his heart on meeting Churchill, and had been courting Randolph, hoping for an introduction. Randolph was actually a guest aboard his yacht, *Christina*, on the night of the dinner.

It was an uncomfortable evening. Reves, as a highly cultured Jew, looked down on Onassis as a serious vulgarian, anxious to exploit their treasured guest for publicity or something worse; and Onassis, who was clearly vastly nervous, did behave a little oddly, sweating profusely, talking compulsively, and treating Churchill like some sort of Eastern potentate.

Wendy felt embarrassed by the whole performance, but Churchill was clearly taken with Onassis. 'He made a good impression on me,' he wrote afterwards to Clementine. 'He is a vy able and masterful man & told me a lot about whales. He kissed my hand.'

Churchill had always had a taste for flamboyant buccaneers, particularly if very rich, and even more so if possessing large, luxuriously appointed motor-yachts. Sir Ernest Cassel, Lord Moyne, the Duke of Westminster – those golden ghosts from Churchill's past had all owned sumptuous vessels which he had unashamedly enjoyed. But none could have equalled what Churchill called 'the monster-yacht' belonging to the Reveses' dinner-guest.

Moored in the harbour at Monaco – much of which Onassis also owned – *Christina*, a converted former naval frigate, was the most luxurious example of the genus in existence. There was an impressive El Greco in the stateroom, a two-thousand-year-old Cretan mosaic as a dance-floor, and the bar-stools were covered with the foreskins of whales his whaling-fleet had slaughtered. (Only Reves noticed that the El Greco was a fake.)

'Oh, my dear, dear friend, welcome, welcome aboard!' said the beaming multi-millionaire, while mysteriously invited press photographers snapped the statesman as he staggered up *Christina*'s gang-plank. Churchill seemed delighted with the yacht, ignored the photographers, and made himself agreeable as its nervous owner kneeled at his feet to spoon-feed him with caviare. Churchill's last – and most unlikely – friendship started.

For Onassis, Churchill was 'the big fish' for whom nothing in the world was too much trouble. And, for Churchill, Onassis was a rich man with a very large yacht which he seemed perfectly prepared to place at his disposal. (Later, when asked why he deserted old friends for this dubious Greek, he answered: 'Which of my old friends offers me his yacht?') At times, Onassis undoubtedly bored him; but, then, almost everybody bored him now, and he could always turn his hearing-aid off when he was bored. He was, however, perfectly prepared to invite Onassis back for lunch at Hyde Park Gate, and even propose him as a member of the 'Other Club'.

In return, Onassis was immensely generous, not just in terms of money (which presumably meant little to this multi-millionaire), but with the care and time he personally lavished on Churchill and on almost every member of the family. In all he acted as his host on eight extended cruises, including the West Indies, the Canaries, and the eastern Mediterranean (where *Christina* tactfully sailed through the Dardanelles at dead of night to avoid reminding Churchill of Gallipoli). One of the rules aboard the *Christina* was that anyone playing cards with Sir Winston always lost.

Onassis treated him like royalty – and like royalty Churchill and the family took his hospitality more or less for granted.

'What would you like to be in another existence, Sir Winston?' Onassis asked him.

'A tiger,' said Churchill. 'And what about you, Ari?'

'Your budgerigar, Toby,' said Onassis.

Why he was so obsessed with Churchill is debatable. Onassis was not a sentimental man, but with his wealth he seems to have indulged a passion for acquiring worldly greatness. He had the greatest opera singer in the world as his mistress, would one day have the American President's widow as his wife, and was happy to boast of having the world's greatest living statesman as his friend. Less romantically, friendship with Churchill would certainly impress the smartest international society – and, more important still, his elegant and socially sophisticated wife, Athina. Although the daughter of another Greek shipping magnate, Livanos, 'Tina', as she was known, had been largely educated and brought up in England; and, while Ari was the father of her two children, she could still treat him on occasions as an uncouth peasant.

Also, as Emery Reves had long discovered, friendship with the
Churchills was extremely good for business. In the aftermath of
Suez, when the Canal was blocked, Onassis had the chance to
make vast profits with his supertankers bringing oil to the West
around the coast of Africa. But, according to Nigel Neilson, who
was in charge of his public relations, Onassis required acceptance
from the still-suspicious British oil establishment. Once he was
known as the friend and host of Winston Churchill, Onassis had
the *entrée* that he needed – and was quick to use it. During
the period of his friendship with Churchill, Onassis increased
his fortune impressively.

In return Onassis carefully watched over his guest, and would
even risk interfering with his family if he felt this necessary. Even
aboard *Christina*, trouble could still erupt with Randolph. On one
occasion there was such an argument between him and his father
that Onassis decided Randolph had to leave. This was easier said
than done, as the ship was somewhere off the coast of Greece.
But arrangements were made via radio-telephone to Athens for
an invitation to be sent to Mr Randolph Churchill to interview the
King of Greece. It was a scoop which, as a journalist, Randolph
could not refuse – but how to get to Athens? For Ari, nothing
was too much trouble to protect the peace of mind of his
treasured guest. *Christina* abruptly changed course for a nearby
island, where a seaplane was already waiting in the harbour
from Onassis's Olympic Airways. Randolph embarked – and a
few hours later was in Athens, enjoying an exclusive interview
with King Constantine, while Churchill was enjoying freedom
from the aggravation only Randolph could create around him.

Thus did Onassis keep the great man happy – and for a period
Churchill managed to combine these cruises, on which he was
always accompanied by Clementine, with his bachelor holidays
at La Pausa. But early in 1960, after Reves's heart-attack and
a voyage with Onassis to Antigua, all this ended.

This time, when *Christina* docked at Monaco, Churchill made
no attempt to contact the Reveses or go for his customary stay at
La Pausa. Instead, he and Clementine spent some days as guests
of Onassis at his Hôtel de Paris in Monte Carlo, then returned
to London in his private aircraft.

The Riviera is a small and unforgiving place, and the
Reveses had inevitably aroused resentment from the way they
had jealously guarded and protected Churchill in the past. There

was, for instance, no love lost between them and the Rainiers of Monaco on the subject. For Churchill to be seen so publicly deserting what for years had been his favourite Riviera family in favour of Onassis was the sort of snub to set the gossip-mongers busy.

Majesty is fickle, and Churchill was extremely old and tired – certainly too ancient to resist Clementine's dislike of Pausaland any longer – and the Reveses took considerable offence.

He had, of course, used and dropped people whenever it suited him throughout his life – most politicians do – but, when later that summer he tried returning to La Pausa, Reves refused him in a bitter letter, starting 'Dear Sir Winston' and complaining of the way he had deserted them.

Wendy was ill from the 'intrigues' which followed and would soon be returning to America. Reves was equally upset. 'There is a certain way of disregarding other people's feelings which drives sensitive human beings to the borders of insanity,' he told him.

Churchill apologised to Wendy, assuring her that 'the months I spent at your charming house were among the brightest in my life'. But he had forfeited Pausaland for ever, and subsequent visits which he made as Onassis's guest to the Hôtel de Paris were no substitute for the comfort and attention he had known with the once devoted Reveses.

A year later he was back at the Hôtel de Paris, and Montague Browne was telling Lord Beaverbrook of Churchill's boredom there with 'nobody about at all'. He explained how, for want of somewhere suitable to go, he and Churchill had 'taken the liberty' of sitting in the sun in the deserted garden of Beaverbrook's villa at Cap d'Ail. It was a melancholy picture.

For Clementine, too, the end of her husband's trips to Pausaland was more of a loss than she expected. Without them there was little to alleviate the strain on her as the final stage of Churchill's sad decline began in earnest, and several of the closest members of the family started to decline as well.

Randolph still drank as much as ever, although by now it might have seemed that he had come to terms with the fate which life – and his father – had dealt him. He was too old to change his character, but he had at least changed his habitat, having left London and his favourite perch in White's Club bar for an unassuming pale pink country house at East Bergholt in Suffolk.

As something of a consolation for not inheriting Chartwell, this was paid for from the trust which Churchill had set up from his literary earnings for his children and grandchildren; and here, following the recipe for happiness which Voltaire gives at the conclusion of *Candide*, Randolph had settled down to cultivate his garden.

He was proud of the fact that Constable had once lived and painted in East Bergholt, and as a sort of motto fixed a plaque on the terrace with a neat quotation from the painter's letters: 'I am come to a determination to make no idle visits this summer nor give up any time to commonplace people. I shall return to Bergholt.' There were in fact few 'idle visits' now, for apart from his garden, which he loved, Randolph had discovered certain consolations which kept him safely anchored to East Bergholt. The first of these was Natalie, wife to his nearest neighbour, Robert Bevan, an elderly and highly successful advertising executive. Natalie was fair-haired, beautiful and charming. Randolph, now separated totally from June, and lonely in the country, predictably fell in love. They became lovers, but Natalie was wise as well as beautiful. 'I was in love with Randolph but I knew we could never possibly survive at too close quarters in that house of his.'

She was also very fond of Mr Bevan. The result was that most hazardous of civilised arrangements, which seems to have suited everybody admirably, Randolph in particular. Randolph had always been devoid of sexual jealousy and, while deeply sentimental and susceptible to women, could never cope with all the incidentals of a married situation. Now he had what he had always needed: romance without restrictions, devotion without drudgery, and passion without responsibility. In this one department of his life at least, Randolph appeared a happy and contented human being.

At times he begged Natalie to marry him; but, as she says, 'he was not really marriageable. He loved his friends, he loved to drink and stay up far too late, so I would simply leave him and go home to bed. In the end he never really minded.' At the same time Natalie looked after him, holidayed with him (including trips to the South of France and in *Christina*), and seems to have delighted all his friends, including the ever-loved Laura. (She was still happily married to handsome Michael Canfield, and Randolph spent his Christmases with them. 'Frankly I was delighted to see the old boy so happy. Natalie was a saint,' said Laura.)

One effect of Randolph's move to Suffolk was that he saw considerably less of both his parents. Time had not eased the mutual antipathy between him and his mother, nor had Clementine's support for poor unhappy June improved the situation. Inflexible as ever, Clementine could see few redeeming features in her son, and according to one friend 'there were times when she could hardly bear to be in the same room with him'.

According to Laura, 'Even now Randolph blamed his mother for the trouble there had been between him and his father – and with both his wives. And beneath it all he found it hard to forgive her for never having loved him.' Hardly surprisingly, he felt that she supported Christopher against him. More superficially, he used to say that her stupidity annoyed him, and he became infuriated when he felt that she was showing off her 'schoolgirl' skills at foreign languages. 'What can you do with a woman who pronounces "menu" as "may-nyew" in English?' he exploded.

One of his assistants at East Bergholt has memories of a rare occasion when Clementine actually arrived for lunch. This ended so prematurely that Clementine spent forty minutes at the local station waiting for her train to London rather than endure Randolph a moment longer.

Between Randolph and his father, things were different. Emotionally he was as much bound up with him as ever; even their bitterest rows were never final, and early in 1960 it was Churchill who agreed to the arrangement which, along with the love-affair with Natalie, seems to have given Randolph his most lasting happiness. Even before the war, Randolph had been anxious to write the story of his father's life. Churchill was always wary of revelations by those who knew him at close quarters. 'You're not *writing* anything?' he regularly enquired of Grace Hamblin, during the days when she was working as a Chartwell secretary – and he seems to have been just as wary of anything that Randolph might commit to paper. But, while refusing to allow the youthful Randolph to write about him, he did say that he would one day have the chance, and promised that the book would make his fortune.

Since then the whole subject of Churchill's official biography had been shelved. Throughout his life, Churchill had taken such immense pains to explain and justify himself in print that his literary memorial clearly had to be exactly as he wanted. In his official 'life' the legend he had built around himself should be enshrined for ever, and the literary equivalent of a Graham Sutherland was too terrible to contemplate. Churchill, who never threw a thing away, had hoarded an immense archive for the great biography; but as the years ticked by he seemed unable to decide upon the great biographer. Randolph stayed in the running, and he had set his heart on doing it.

It would redeem the failure of his life and guarantee financial resurrection in the process. Like his father in his heyday, Randolph had chronic troubles with his cash-flow. But Churchill, not entirely surprisingly, still had doubts about his son's fitness for the monumental task. To prove himself to his father, Randolph embarked upon a long political biography of the noble, rich (and, truth to be told, tedious) 17th Earl of Derby. Thanks largely to his highly literate literary assistant, Alan Brien, the book was finished and received polite reviews. And finally, in July 1960, Natalie was greeted at the house by an exultant Randolph, waving a telegram. 'He's asked me! He's asked me at last!' he shouted.

His daughter, Arabella, also remembers the excitement. 'Millions!' he whispered to her as she went to bed. 'It will make us millions!'

'Dearest Papa,' he wrote to Churchill, 'your letter has made me proud and happy. Since I first read your life of your father, 35 years ago when I was a boy of 14 at Eton, it has always been my greatest ambition to write your life.'

While Randolph was euphoric in his new role as the great biographer, his ex-wife Pamela was also happy. Rising forty, and with twelve years as a divorcée behind her, she had married the rich, glamorous and already thrice married New York theatrical producer Leland Hayward. Since the departure of Agnelli, her years in Paris had not been easy. True, she had known the friendship and affection of very rich admirers, and had lived in considerable luxury in her elegant apartment by the Seine. Her furniture was Louis Seize, her Rolls was ever at the service of her friends, and she was rumoured to spend $10,000 annually on flowers. But, as Somerset Maugham had once reminded her, it was time she married.

Hayward, famous as the producer of *The Sound of Music*, and previously married to the actress Margaret Sullavan, was still very much wedded to his third wife Nancy when Pamela met him in New York during a visit to the Whitneys in 1959. Hayward apparently had a prejudice against Englishwomen ('They all have bad teeth and talk through their noses, and they're all amoral'). He also had a formidable young family by Margaret Sullavan, including the budding actress Brooke. But from those formative years with the Churchill Club in wartime London, Pamela had learned the art of capturing the hearts of high-powered, eminent Americans. She also had the aura of Paris and the great brand-image of the Churchill name.

Hayward was spellbound. According to Brooke, 'it was as if he was entering a kind of golden circle through his association with her', and despite the problems of children and divorce, Pamela became the fourth, and final, Mrs Leland Hayward in the spring of 1960.

The Churchills sent congratulations and a cheque; and, while Randolph gave the standard ex-husband's reaction – 'with that round face and those legs how ever did she manage it?' – Pamela proved the perfect wife for Leland Hayward, taking a close interest in his work, nursing him when he was sick, and adapting with extraordinary success to the world of the theatre and smart New York society. 'Mamma is a chameleon,' young Winston is said to have remarked.

Marriage came too late for Pamela to give young Winston what she had long been seeking for him – a reliable step-father and the settled home she knew he needed – but there were still some compensations. Winston got on well with Leland; there was a base for him in America whenever he required it, and on his twenty-first birthday Pamela was able to replace his ancient Fiat with a brand-new Jaguar, while Leland paid for him to take flying lessons. Winston was still at Christ Church, Oxford, at the time, and it is interesting to compare him with his father on the eve of that fateful birthday-party at Claridge's thirty years earlier. Randolph at twenty-one had worshipped Churchill, modelled himself slavishly upon him and, although rebelling hard against authority, believed in his destiny to follow Churchill to the heights of power and glory.

In 1961 his twenty-one-year-old son Winston could not have been more different. Far from worshipping his father, he was extremely wary of him; and, instead of seeing Randolph as a model to be copied, Winston on the whole regarded him as a notable example to be avoided. (To this day, he is a passionate non-smoker, virtually a non-drinker, a non-gambler, and the least gluttonous of men.)

Photographs reveal a physical resemblance between them at the age of twenty-one, although young Winston lacks the slightly suspect beauty of Randolph's László portrait. In temperament, however, Winston seemed much closer to his mother, being equable, agreeable and a late bloomer.

What he appeared to lack entirely were those appalling but distinctive qualities which Randolph had absorbed in childhood from his father: the arrogance, the extra layer of skin, the sense of supercharged superiority – all of which had made young Randolph so difficult to cope with, but which had also marked him out as a distinct phenomenon.

Young Winston, to the probable relief of all around him, was not a phenomenon. Nor was he particularly 'Churchillian'. Although brought up mainly by his mother – and his devoted Nanny Martin – he had remained surprisingly unspoiled by the rich society around her, and was not the playboy he might well have been. He was an earnest, active, otherwise unremarkable young man with one unavoidable distinction. He had been landed with the greatest name in Britain, and his problem was what on earth to do with it.

As cherished heir and namesake, he had always held a special place in his grandfather's affections; but, although he had often stayed with his Churchill grandparents, there had been nothing of that almost superstitious sense of intimate succession which had dominated Randolph's early manhood.

During young Winston's childhood, Churchill was too busy, and later on too old, to get to know his grandson all that well. On one occasion he gave him a cigar-case and two boxes of cigars, not realising his grandson's deep dislike of nicotine; on another, when young Winston had driven up from Oxford to lunch with his grandfather, the old Victorian remarked: 'You did not drive yourself, did you? I trust you had your man drive you. With the provision I have been able to make you, you should certainly be able to afford that.'

It was all extremely touching, and Winston revered his 'Grandpapa Churchill'. For him, as he wrote in his autobiography, Churchill was quite simply 'the greatest Briton in the history of our country'. But the young Winston's sense of awe before this stupendous predecessor who had given him his name was very different from his father's early role as future 'carrier of the lamp'.

Although, as a boy at Eton, Winston had sometimes found his name a burden ('Take this for being a shit! Take this for being a bastard! And take this for being Winston-bloody-Churchill!' his schoolfellows chanted as they beat his bare behind with rubber-soled slippers), there were also tangible advantages to be derived from 'the name'.

As Randolph pointed out, his son possessed 'the greatest by-line in journalism', and after leaving Oxford young Winston made the most of it. World leaders like de Gaulle, the Kennedys and King Hussein were delighted to be interviewed by Winston Churchill (Hussein insisted on calling him 'Sir') – and, as he proudly claims, by twenty-three he was already 'one of the highest paid journalists in Fleet St'.

But for the youthful Winston this was not enough. In 1964, shortly before Churchill died, he married Minnie d'Erlanger, daughter of Sir Gerard d'Erlanger, founder of prewar British Airways and member of an Anglo-French banking family. Churchill gave Winston a generous cheque, and in his thank-you letter Winston promised his grandfather to 'carry the name Churchill, which you made great, with honour into the future'. For young Winston, this meant one thing only: politics. Randolph, speaking from long and sad experience, counselled his son to become an engineer like his cousin Peregrine. But Winston had made up his mind.

While young Winston prepared for his political career, his father took up his role as Churchill's biographer. One of Randolph's earliest tasks was to examine the Blenheim archives. Despite the fact that they heartily disliked each other, Bert grudgingly invited him over for a night, and he arrived in time for dinner, bringing Winston and a young research assistant with him. Bert was living in the palace on his own, his unhappy duchess having died in 1961. Dinner was served in a small unheated room which, although devoid of books, Bert still referred to as 'the library'. The food was uninviting; and Bert, instead of bothering with his guests, sat viewing television at table.

A lesser man than Randolph might have felt annoyed, and after several drinks his rage exploded. 'Bert,' shouted Randolph, 'your bloody library's not a library, your food's disgusting, and television's not a substitute for conversation over dinner.' Bert disagreed as strongly; at which point Randolph arose, summoned his party, and left Blenheim abruptly.

'Never mind,' he said, consoling his research assistant as they drove away. 'I'll get everything sent over. Bert is so ignorant he doesn't even know he's got archives.'

The truth was that, since the Duchess died in 1961, Bert had started missing her and had increasingly retreated into himself. While she was alive, he had bullied and made fun of her, but now he was miserable and bored. One ray of light which did strike Blenheim came from the glamorous remarriage of the heir to the dukedom, which indirectly brought together two quite separate worlds in Churchill's life.

Onassis's attempt to employ his intimacy with Churchill to win over his anglophile wife, Athina, better known as Tina, could not prevent the inevitable divorce in 1958 – but it had produced an unexpected sequel. Athina was not particularly impressed by her husband's friendship with the great man and his family, but she was very taken with a key member of the Churchill circle: the future head of the whole family, Sunny Blandford.

Tina was beautiful, very rich in her own right – and tired of life with Ari. Sunny was vulnerable and lonely – and would one day be a duke. Early in 1961, in a chaotic Greek marriage ceremony in Paris with more journalists than guests, Tina Onassis somewhat improbably became the second Lady Blandford. 'So, Ari, we are related at last,' said Churchill to Onassis when he heard the news.

But even these Churchill relatives, with title, wealth and everything that life could offer, seemed cursed with the family unhappiness. The new Lady Blandford was popular at Blenheim, not least for her generosity towards the servants (something few members of the family could be accused of). But she and Sunny were patently unsuited. There were no children. She and Sunny lived increasingly apart, and in 1970 she summoned her servants, offered them double pay to accompany her to Paris, then swept out of Blenheim taking her Impressionist paintings and her most valuable possessions, never to return. After an amicable divorce from Sunny in 1971, she married her brother-in-law, Stavros Niarchos, and died in mysterious circumstances three years later.

In her own way, Sarah was also becoming a tragic figure, and during 1960 the family had to come to terms with the fact that Churchill's favourite daughter was an incurable alcoholic. She was also a very public one, as her court appearances – and sentences – increased; in February 1960, she was fined £2 for assaulting a taxi-driver in Lucan Place; in July £2 10s (£2.50) for being drunk and disorderly in Ebury Street; and in November given a year's probation following a brawl at the Riverside Club, Westminster. A few months later she broke her probation, and spent ten days in Holloway Prison.

Her father's eminence made little difference. He was too old, and too fond of alcohol himself, to have had the remotest influence against what had now become an illness. Clementine was terrified of scandal, and worry over Sarah must have added to the 'nervous fatigue, depression, and anxiety state' which her doctors diagnosed as requiring hospital treatment in February 1961.

Sarah was concerned about her mother – and had learned to dread her steely disapproval just as she pitied her pathetic states of deep anxiety. But nothing Clementine could do could make her daughter change her habits; neither could clinics, psychiatrists or doctors.

Somehow Sarah managed to continue with her acting in the part of Peter Pan – thanks to extraordinary powers of recovery, and her popularity among other members of the cast. '*Was* there an incident last night?' she would ask her stage director, Ellen Pollock, when arriving late and very hung over for a rehearsal. According to Miss Pollock, she had the usual alcoholic's lack of recollection of her drinking, and refused to think about the consequences.

But by the end of 1961 even Sarah had to realise the trouble she was bringing to the family. It was in order to escape from her psychiatrists, her sense of guilt about her parents, and what she referred to as 'the attentions of the boys in blue' that she decided to decamp to a villa in the South of Spain.

The sun shone, whisky was thirty shillings (£1.50) a bottle, and against remarkable odds Sarah found herself another husband.

Henry, Baron Audley, had ended up in southern Spain after a lifetime of considerable futility. He was drunken and all but penniless, and had just recovered from a massive stroke. But he was good company and extremely charming, and these two unlikely, lonely people fell in love. For a while they lived and drank together. Then in April 1962, at the register office in Gibraltar, Henry made Sarah Lady Audley.

Diana, who flew out from England, was the only member of the family present at the ceremony. As Churchill and Clementine were cruising with Onassis at the time, their attitude was not recorded; but Randolph was delighted. His first, entirely predictable reaction was to look up Henry in *Debrett's Guide to the Peerage* where, on discovering that he was 23rd Baron of the fourth-oldest dynasty in England, he remarked: 'Well, *that* puts the Marlboroughs in their place!' But not, alas, for long.

The Audleys remained contentedly in Spain for fourteen months. Then, in July 1963, Lord Audley died – quite suddenly, of a cerebral haemorrhage, while Sarah was with him.

Clementine, still suffering from nervous stress, was too ill and too fatigued to offer her freshly widowed daughter much assistance; instead she gave Diana £1,000 to fly to Spain to comfort her. This was a role Diana was adept at, and her sister was grateful for her help at the funeral in Malaga. When Sarah finally returned to Chartwell, her father met her at the door. 'We stared silently at each other; then he took my hand and said simply, "We must close ranks and march on." '

Closing ranks became increasingly important for the Churchills during 1963. Clementine was finding it impossible to cope with Churchill. Just as she had never been maternal with her children, so, as Montague Browne says, 'she was not prepared to become a mother to her husband'.

The acute fatigue and depression which had been plaguing her for months grew worse, and in October she was admitted to Westminster Hospital for the same electrotherapy Diana had endured. Not that Diana's many courses of psychiatric treatment had resolved her problems and her deep unhappiness. She remained absurdly insecure, and her sense of religious persecution was as bad as ever. There were periods when she and Clementine attempted to forget the past, but whatever wounds Clementine had once inflicted on her daughter went too deep to be forgotten.

Diana's greatest source of misery was still the break-up of her marriage and the loss of her beloved husband. In April 1962 he had married thirty-three-year-old French-born Marie-Claire, the recently divorced wife of the son of a former colleague, the Tory Agriculture Minister, Lord Hudson. On the day he married,

Diana officially reverted to her maiden name. Typically she tried to make a joke of it by apologising to her former friend and namesake from her days at RADA: 'I am sure that Diana Churchill, the actress, will agree that there is room for two of a good thing,' she told reporters.

Sadly there was little to joke about in Diana's situation. Like Clementine, she remained acutely and dangerously depressed, and sometimes talked of suicide. But she was courageous in the way she fought against her mental misery. By forcing herself to work as a voluntary counsellor with the Samaritans, she involved herself in the lives of others as desperate as herself. Her doctor hoped that this would help her face her problems and for a while it did; but her depressions and loneliness grew worse and were soon insupportable. By the autumn of 1963 she was desperate.

It was on a Saturday evening in mid-October that neighbours saw Diana returning to her house in Chester Row, alone. During that afternoon she had been with her daughter Edwina, and had told her that on Sunday she would be visiting Clementine in hospital, then dining with her father at the house in Hyde Park Gate. Diana never visited her parents. Instead, next morning she was found dead on the bedroom floor when her housekeeper came to call her. An inquest a few days later gave a verdict of suicide from an 'overwhelming' dose of sleeping tablets.

Since Sarah had now returned to Spain, Mary had the task of breaking the news to both her parents. Clementine was under deep sedation, and it took some while for the news to filter through to her, thus cushioning the shock. With Churchill, age and the blunting of his sensibilities had much the same effect. Mary describes how, when he finally understood what had happened, he 'withdrew into a great and distant silence'. 'As he grew older,' she added, 'he seemed to acquire a degree of insulation from sad or unpleasant news about those he loved.'

This was just as well; for, to complete the Churchills' load of misery, there were further worries over Randolph, as the accumulated years of manifold indulgence finally caught up with him. Earlier that year he had proudly visited America together with young Winston to receive the Honorary Citizenship of the United States which President Kennedy conferred on Churchill. At eighty-seven, there could be no question of him going in person and it seemed that Randolph's greatest moment was to stand as Churchill's proxy.

He had always been able to imitate him: at the presidential ceremony in the White House rose garden, he sounded strangely like him as he read the letter of acceptance which Churchill – with Montague Browne's assistance – had composed for the occasion.

Randolph was greatly enamoured of the Kennedys, who represented everything he felt that he had wanted out of life: glamour, youth, vitality, and that greatest prize of all, the political power which had cruelly eluded him. Like the Churchills, the Kennedys appeared as a great political family, but they were still in the ascendant. Randolph was all too well aware by now of his own family's decline, and of the chances he had lost for ever.

He was visiting the Kennedys again when Diana died, and soon after his return to England caught pneumonia. He only partially recovered, and at fifty-two suddenly looked old beyond his years. The fat rumbustious man had turned thin and anxious. He ate little, drank as heavily as ever, and was smoking eighty cigarettes a day. He was losing weight and, when X-rays revealed a patch on his lung, cancer was suspected.

Randolph treated his operation, early in 1964, much as he had treated waiters, women and events he disapproved of all his life. As a snob he had always found something intolerably common about hospitals, and did not permit medical routines to get him down. He charmed the nurses, bullied the matron, and when the surgeon tried to stop him going home Randolph told him: 'Doctor. I pay you to cut me up, not to dictate my whereabouts.'

Lord Lambton visited with some bottles of very good champagne. 'Just put them in a bucket for me, Nurse,' said Randolph, thinking that they needed chilling. He was upset when the nurse tipped three bottles of vintage Bollinger into his plastic slop-pail.

To everyone's surprise, his own included, the excised portion of his lung was not cancerous – prompting Evelyn Waugh's celebrated *mot*: 'A typical triumph of modern science to find the only part of Randolph that was not malignant and remove it!'

Randolph relished the remark when someone told him and irreverently cabled back to the Catholic novelist in time for Easter Sunday: 'Have a Happy Resurrection!'

Randolph convalesced with Natalie in Biarritz and Capri, then returned to East Bergholt to continue work on the biography.

She remembers him 'trying to act as if nothing untoward had happened'. But she thought it ominous that he was now drinking beer instead of whisky. 'After that operation I am fairly sure he knew his days were numbered.'

Randolph still managed to take Laura to visit his father in his room at Hyde Park Gate in the summer of 1964, not long before the great man died. There was an unsmoked cigar between Churchill's lips, and for much of the time they sat in silence – but Laura felt that even now he was still battling determinedly against extinction. As she was leaving, he summoned up his energy and smiled. 'The Dark Angel beckons – but I still say NO!' he muttered.

At the end of Goethe's *Faust* the Devil renders his account; and as Faust is made to pay him back the price of his ambitions those he has loved are sacrificed as well. Churchill might well have been the aged Faust, with the contrast between so much worldly glory and the hopelessness and gloom engulfing him and those around him.

Almost since adolescence, he had lived life as an unrelenting war against depression and a primal dread of failure. To defeat these enemies, he had deployed prodigious energies, had never risked the boredom of an idle moment, and had been ruthlessly and unbelievably ambitious. In the process he had built a legend of indubitable greatness; but now that his active life was over this legend stood as no defence against the self-destructive gloom so basic to his nature. 'My life is over but it is not yet ended,' he had told Diana just before she killed herself.

As an unbeliever he was haunted by the finality of oblivion, which left him no recourse against his old obsessions. Montague Browne, who had the unenviable task of keeping him company through many of his darkest moments, says he was deeply troubled by a bitter sense of failure. 'He felt that everything that he had done had ended in disaster. He had won the war but lost the Empire, Communism had swallowed up half Europe, and Socialism was threatening the world he loved at home.'

Lord Moran, witnessing the same obsession, had told him to forget posterity. But Churchill, in his old man's misery, would not be placated. 'I ought not, I must not, be held to account for what has gone wrong,' he answered sadly. Medically, Moran believed that the atrophying of the senses would slowly blunt the edge of his anxieties. But as a friend he pitied him at Chartwell, 'as he sits there in the great house through the interminable days, often alone, waiting for the end'.

Some years before, Churchill in a sombre after-dinner mood had been gazing at the fire. 'Curious to imagine oneself a log,' he remarked. 'Reluctant to be consumed – yet obliged *eventually* to give way.' Now that the fire of his life was burning low, he was waiting patiently to be consumed.

He found his daughter Sarah his greatest comfort, and she would sit with him for hours, willing the time to pass. 'What time is it, Sas?' he would ask. 'Twelve o'clock, Papa,' she would answer. Five minutes later he would repeat the question. And Sarah would give the answer. In an earlier period of depression, Diana had tried to cheer him up by reminding him of everything that he had done in life. 'I have achieved a great deal to achieve nothing in the end,' he muttered, and refused to listen to her efforts to convince him otherwise.

Perhaps it all seemed like a dream to him by now. Just as he had made the daydreams of his youth reality, and acted out imagined roles in great achievements, were the achievements turning back into a dream?

On 30 November 1964, Churchill turned ninety. He had to spend the day in bed, but he managed to stagger to the window for the small crowd waiting patiently outside, and in the evening had a birthday-dinner by candlelight with all the family around him. Four weeks later came the stroke that was to kill him.

Everybody knew that this was one occasion when not even Lord Moran's skills could save him, and even he seemed finally prepared for those 'smooth black curtains' he had so long avoided. Throughout his life, as Britain's greatest man of war since Wellington, Churchill had borne responsibility for innumerable violent deaths of others. Now, in extreme old age, in comfort and in peace, he waited for his own. It was a fine dramatic deathbed, with no pain – Clementine and young Winston by each side of the bed, Sarah drunk, Mary tactfully shepherding grandchildren in to see him. Randolph was there to kiss his hand, and the Lord Doctor to ease his passing. There was even a priest to give the blessing of a God he never managed to believe in. The Queen was kept informed, and silent crowds attended patiently outside the house. It was in character that his last words were uttered, not to Randolph, but to Christopher when he tried to offer him champagne. 'I'm so bored with it all,' he sighed, then sank into a peaceful coma, so that he never knew that as he lay dying another generation had been added to the line. On 22 January, Winston's wife, Minnie, had a son. Continuing the tradition of alternate names, they called him Randolph.

'In the midst of death we are in life,' the baby's namesake and grandfather wrote to Clementine, telling her the news.

It was very different from that other deathbed, seventy years earlier, when Churchill had witnessed the agonies of his dying father, with the family assembled in his grandmother's house in Grosvenor Square. But as the days continued and he lingered on in coma he must have had some memory of his father. Early in 1950, Jock Colville remembered seeing him one morning, and hearing him remark: 'Today is the 24th of January. It is the day my father died. It is the day that I shall die too.'

For nine days after the stroke, he lay unconscious, as if sleeping gently. Then, on 24 January, Churchill died.

All followed as he knew it would, and in death the worn-out, sad old figure of his final years was re-created into the sort of legendary being he had dreamed of all his life. For three days he lay like a medieval king in Westminster Hall, and despite the cold nearly 200,000 people filed past the coffin. Some wept. All passed in silence. His grand-daughter, Emma Soames, who was fourteen at the time remembers being 'overwhelmed by the beauty and the sheer theatricality of the whole occasion'.

The funeral on 30 January was, as one commentator wrote, 'one of those rare and memorable occasions when television's multiple insect-eye makes us all partakers in a great ritual of race'. It was certainly a unique event – the great cathedral filled with presidents and foreign royalty, the one occasion when the Queen herself attended as a mourner at a commoner's funeral.

More even than with the lying-in, the funeral was inspired theatre, with the bands that he had wanted, the hymns that he had loved and the great religious celebration for this stalwart non-believer. Broadcast on television, with Laurence Olivier reading excerpts from his speeches, each part of this state funeral had enormous impact on the nation – although it was hard to be precise about the essence of this mass emotion.

Some saw it as the funeral of the British Empire, some as a requiem for the heroism of the war, others as the burial of a mighty subject and the nation's final hero. What is certain is that it could have happened for no one else, and that the legend Churchill built around himself was at the centre of an unforgettable media event.

His old enemy, Attlee, who just survived him, nearly fainted, and had to be provided with a chair. One of the few who sobbed emotionally throughout the service was Onassis. The family were dry-eyed, stoical, befitting the occasion. Randolph, as principal mourner, though mortally ill himself, had followed the cortège on foot with his son Winston at his side. Clementine, with Sarah and Mary beside her, rode in a carriage lent for the occasion by the Queen. Grandchildren rode in other carriages behind her.

It was only when the service ended, and the coffin was embarked at Westminster Pier for the symbolic crossing of the Thames which Churchill wanted, that the solemn front adopted by the family was briefly threatened. Sarah had somehow stayed erect throughout the service. In fact she was very drunk, having been barely sober since her father died. Knowing this, Clementine had passed a message on to the attendants, asking them to stop her daughter Sarah as she left the cathedral.

So it was that Sarah did not see her father's body cross the river, or the dockside cranes that dipped in homage at his passing. (According to Sarah, this had been one of Churchill's own suggestions.)

Nor did Sarah travel with the family on the special train – pulled by the locomotive named *Sir Winston Churchill* – which took her father on his final journey back to Blenheim. There, in Bladon churchyard, after so much misery and so much glory, Churchill was reunited with his father.

34

Aftermath

Clementine was seventy-nine when Churchill died and still had twelve more years to live. The National Trust duly took possession of Chartwell for the nation, the house in Hyde Park Gate was sold, and Clementine moved into a small flat just around the corner in Prince's Gate. Here she could relax at last, cherish her memories, and see her friends and family.

Her classic looks refined with age, and there was a serenity about her now which was not evident when Churchill was alive. The nervous symptoms which had once plagued her ended. So did the troubles with her children.

As Churchill's widow, Clementine was much revered and, although she was made a baroness in her own right by the Queen, within the family she seemed increasingly dependent and endearing. Frailer and deafer with the years, she remained as much the perfectionist as ever, still changing for dinner and insisting on the standards at table which she maintained when Churchill was alive. Even when her mind was going at the end, there were glimpses of the strength which enabled her to hold her own with Churchill for more than half a century. She survived to the age of ninety-two before joining him in Bladon churchyard in December 1977.

Other close members of the family were less resilient, and Churchill had left an uneasy legacy for some of the members of his precious citadel who survived him.

Randolph was now beyond repair, a sad successor to that 'rollickingly bumptious' youth whose father had once seen him as his political successor and proudly given him that twenty-first-birthday party at Claridge's thirty-three years earlier.

Cecil Beaton met him shortly after his father's funeral and was shocked at his appearance, 'old and grey like a haggard hawk'. But Randolph, being Randolph, tried convincing him that he was happier than he'd ever been. 'At last I'm doing something to justify my life. The biography of my father will be the best thing I've ever done, my contribution to the world,' he muttered huskily. Beaton was not convinced. 'His eyes looked so abysmally sad,' he wrote.

True to his word, Randolph was hard at work upon the great biography as if to snatch the embers of success from the bonfire of a lifetime. But, not for the first time, he had underestimated the scale of his father's vast career, which would require eight large volumes – and twenty years' hard labour by Randolph's biographical successor, Martin Gilbert – to complete. Randolph saw only the first two volumes published.

He still enjoyed his garden and had Natalie to care for him. His research assistants – 'the young gentlemen' as he called them – kept him company. But he ate next to nothing, and his body was collapsing. He was fifty-seven, eleven years younger than his father had been on becoming Prime Minister in 1940, when he died in his sleep on 7 June 1968. It was one of the few things in his life that he did peacefully.

Like Randolph, Sarah's fate was also inextricably linked with her father. While he was alive, she had loved him deeply, and reacted powerfully against him, feeling the need to keep her independence. After he died the pattern continued – so did her drinking. During her early fifties, Sarah's favourite escape-route was into the life of a Bohemian semi-intellectual on the fringe of Rome's *dolce vita*. She painted, wrote poetry, and chose her lovers as if still needing to proclaim her independence from paternal criticism. For some reason men with aliases attracted her. After Vic Oliver and Anthony Beauchamp, she found another lover who had changed his name. This was Ernest Leroy Jackson, a black painter and entertainer, formerly of Philadelphia, who called himself Lobo Nocho when he came to Rome. He was a flamboyant gentle character, and while they lived together he did his best to cope with Sarah's drinking. For a period in the mid-sixties they were officially engaged.

But Sarah found it hard to maintain any close relationship for long, and when the affair ended she returned to her chaotic ground-floor flat in Belgravia. London was not an easy place for Sarah with her acting career virtually over, but some of her theatrical friends stayed faithful, and helped her devise her own one-woman show of song and recitation called *An Evening with Sarah Churchill*. The vision of an ageing actress with her memories was embarrassing, but she enjoyed the sense of being still the centre of the stage. Among the songs she sang was one her father wrote for his children called 'Mr Puggy Wug'.

Her relations, like her friends, were wary of inviting her to stay, and the only member of the family she saw regularly was Clementine. Until well into her eighties, she would arrive once a week at Sarah's flat in a chauffeur-driven car and take her out for lunch. Sarah's friends discovered this was one day they could count on Sarah staying sober. When her mother died, Sarah was sixty-three, and her looks had gone. At the memorial service in Westminster Abbey, she seemed a tragic figure as she and Mary laid a wreath together on the slab which bears the words 'Remember Winston Churchill'.

During her last years Sarah became notorious in various Chelsea pubs as 'Duchess Sarah'. She sold what jewellery she had, and moved from pub to pub according to the credit they could offer. She was frequently alone, and when drunk was sometimes violent. But even now the Churchill name protected her. The neighbourhood police, knowing who she was, took care of her and often brought her home at night without asking questions.

Like her father, she was inordinately tough, but by 1982 she knew her days were numbered. 'Nothing would induce me to live my life again,' she told a journalist not long before she died; but on her deathbed that September she confided to a friend: 'I don't mind going, because I know Papa is waiting.' She was sixty-seven when she departed.

Mary continued as the one exception to the doom which seemed predestined for all Churchill's children. She was forty-two when he died, and living happily in the country, with Christopher and their five exuberant children, had remained healthy, balanced and pre-eminently sane. According to her daughter Emma, 'she firmly slapped us children down if we showed the slightest sign of getting above ourselves as grandchildren of the Greatest Englishman. She also firmly kept all publicity away from us throughout our childhood.'

When Christopher lost his parliamentary seat at Bedford, after the Labour victory in 1964, something of the old dynastic element still helped him. He was rich, having inherited his share of the family brewing fortune, and in 1968 the socialist Prime Minister Harold Wilson decided that a wealthy Tory married to a Churchill was the perfect representative for a Labour government in France.

In fact he made an excellent ambassador, speaking good French, being tall enough not to be overshadowed by President de Gaulle, and appearing every inch the sort of caricature upper-class Englishman that Frenchmen relish. The banquet years of *la famille Soames* had started, and during their four years in the magnificent embassy building on the Faubourg St-Honoré it was as if the afterglow of Churchill's power was surviving in his youngest daughter and his son-in-law. It was an important time in Franco-British relations, and Christopher had a crucial role in his country's entry into the European Economic Community. Mary was popular in France; so, increasingly, was Christopher, who was mellowing into the distinguished figure who went on to Brussels as one of the first Commissioners of the EEC. By his mid-fifties, he had transmuted from party politician into elder statesman, member of the House of Lords and Conservative grandee. As such he performed his last important task in government, as Governor of Rhodesia presiding .over the changing of this last great British colony into independent Zimbabwe. He did this well, retaining the affection of many African politicians, including the new prime minister, Mugabe, who said he ended by 'fondly loving him'; but there was something strange in the fact that it was Churchill's favourite son-in-law who was winding up this last great remnant of the British Empire. Returning to England, Soames spent a period as leader of the House of Lords, but there was little real sympathy between this old-style Tory and the very new-style Conservative premier, Mrs Thatcher. After angry disagreement over plans for the civil service, he resigned from her government in 1981 and died of cancer six years later.

He had not achieved that central role in politics for which he had once seemed destined as Churchill's son-in-law. Still less has his eldest son, Nicholas, who entered the House of Commons in 1983. A successful businessman and friend and one-time equerry of the Prince of Wales, the young Soames is physically very like his father, but he has lacked the priceless benefit of having Winston Churchill as a father-in-law. His family connections may even have impeded him in the changed political climate of the 1980s, and he has not enjoyed that place in government which members of the Churchill family once almost automatically expected.

Churchill's other son-in-law, Duncan Sandys, continued his ascent through the upper echelons of power after 1965. He had seemed unscathed by Diana's tragedy and, like Soames, having lost his parliamentary seat in 1964, continued as a European statesman and founded the so-called European Movement. With his successful second marriage, his peerage (he was created Baron Duncan-Sandys in 1974) and a rich career in business, he seemed an enviable figure. The Churchill years had served him well, and it was not until his later years that his reputation faltered. His use of offshore trusts to avoid personal taxation was widely criticised – as was the company of which he was chairman, the massive Lonrho Corporation which Prime Minister Edward Heath described as 'the unacceptable face of capitalism'. He died, aged seventy-nine, in 1988. But his personal contact with the Churchills had ended before Diana died, and their children – Julian, Edwina and Celia – have seemed even more removed, living determinedly private lives and benefiting little from what remained of the Churchill connection.

But this connection still had power to affect the lives of certain members of the family, as one sees in the very different fate of Randolph's two ex-wives, Pamela and June. Pamela had always made the most of the Churchill contacts; and in 1971, when the death of her second husband, Leland Hayward, left her suddenly alone and rather badly off, the wartime years with Churchill provided her salvation. Quite by chance she met her old admirer, Averell Harriman. Once the source of such bitterness between Randolph and his parents, he was now in his early eighties, widowed, richer than ever and splendidly preserved – so well preserved that, despite his age, Pamela agreed to marry him. They had ten happy years together, uniting two political families, the Churchills and the Harrimans. He died in 1983 leaving his widow $75 million and the *ex officio* position of Washington's leading hostess of the Democratic Party. In 1993 President Clinton rewarded her with the post of Ambassador to Paris.

When the Gorbachevs came to Washington in 1989, it was Pamela Churchill Harriman that Raisa Gorbachev called on before paying her respects to Nancy Reagan. And, had the

Democrats won the Presidency, Pamela might well have rounded off the career which started in the Churchill Club in wartime London by returning as American ambassador.

But, whereas Pamela owed so much to her contact with the Churchills, June seemed to have been finally defeated by them. Shell-shocked from her years with Randolph, and lacking the panache and bounce of Pamela, she wilted. Sad and unsure of herself, she was too proud, or too impractical, to exploit her situation. Clementine kept in touch with her, largely for the sake of Arabella, but even this made June nervous that she might be criticised about how she was bringing up her daughter. Short of money, she found life immensely difficult, and after a mastectomy in 1968 decided she could not remarry. Instead she had a number of devoted gay admirers, none of whom realised that she was terminally ill with cancer. Early in 1980, rather than end her days in hospital, June, discreet as ever, took a massive overdose of sleeping pills and joined the group of suicides around the Churchill family.

As a very old man, Churchill had always had a soft spot for June's and Randolph's blue-eyed daughter, Arabella. At his golden wedding celebration in Monte Carlo, Arabella had recited Greek poetry (in translation) in his honour; and Nancy Mitford predicted she would marry a duke (conveniently offering to introduce her to her teenage nephew, who was heir to the Duke of Devonshire). But Arabella was afflicted by her mother's insecurity about the Churchills. Grand life depressed her, and instead of marrying her duke, Arabella opted out. For a while she worked for Biafran relief, then for a leprosy charity, then in a vegetarian restaurant. Later she became a hippie in a Welsh hillside commune, married a schoolteacher, had a son called Jake, divorced, and is now married to a juggler and living happily with him and their three-year-old daughter Jessica in a small, extremely simple house in Glastonbury. She runs Children's World, a charity she started in 1981 to provide drama and creative play for handicapped children.

But the most intriguing fate of all the Churchills was that in store for Randolph's other child, her half-brother Winston, whose whole future had seemed so assured when his grandfather argued the Duchess of Marlborough into letting him bestow his all-important name on him in 1940.

True to his eve-of-marriage promise to his grandfather to

'maintain his name with honour', Winston had duly entered politics, and at twenty-nine had duly won the Labour-held seat of Stretford in Lancashire for the Conservatives. (In 1983 the constituency was redesignated Davyhulme.) He was subsequently appointed opposition spokesman on defence, with the likelihood of holding office when the Conservatives returned to power. But politics can be a bitter business, and ironically Winston's name and great political inheritance helped destroy his chances of political advancement.

First came the fraught question of Rhodesian independence, which had yet to be sorted out by his uncle Christopher. During 1979, policy towards that troubled British colony was giving many Conservatives a genuine crisis of conscience. The leadership, mindful of Third World members of the Commonwealth, decided to abstain over the continued use of sanctions against the traditional (but illegal) white-settler regime in Salisbury led by Ian Smith. But Winston absolutely disagreed and, following his conscience, decided to vote against them. Churchill had never feared to vote against his party; but when young Winston did so he received little sympathy from the Conservative chief whip, and was summarily dismissed as an opposition spokesman as he walked out of the division lobby.

All was not lost, however, and it seemed that Winston's lapse might be forgiven. Mrs Thatcher liked him personally, and shortly after, when Ronald Reagan called on her in London, one of the few politicians he wished to meet was Winston Churchill. Mrs T. duly invited Winston for a meeting with the future president in her office. (One story has it that Reagan was surprised that Winston Churchill was so young). And Winston's prospects seemed considerably brighter. Margaret Thatcher was an ardent admirer of his grandfather, and when she became prime minister herself soon after, she was said to be warming to the idea of a Winston Churchill in her government.

But then came another blow to Winston's prospects involving the ultimate political banana-skin, a sexual scandal; and here it was undoubtedly his name that made him vulnerable and magnified the whole disaster. Like many happily married men before him, Winston had been having an affair. Few knew about his relationship with Soraya, ex-wife of the Arab millionaire arms-dealer Adnan Khashoggi. It was appalling luck that during an entirely unrelated Old Bailey blackmail case Soraya was compelled to reveal to the judge the identity of her current lover. The connection between a former spokesman on defence with an ex-wife of a notorious arms-dealer was imprudent, to say the least, but it was the name of Winston Churchill which guaranteed the story front-page banner headlines in the daily papers. The publicity destroyed Winston's fondly nourished hopes of power for ever.

All this may have been a blessing for Winston. Since then he has become an admirable backbench constituency MP and, thanks to his devoted wife, his marriage rapidly recovered and has been happy. He has four children (the eldest son called Randolph), many friends, a chalet in Switzerland, and a Georgian house near Chartwell.

But the good life and the career of a satisfied backbencher are somewhat different from the great political career which his grandfather had envisaged, first for Randolph, then, when that failed, for his grandson Winston. For Churchill had not merely loved his family. He had seen it as a dynasty in the sense in which the dictionary defines it – as 'a line of hereditary rulers'. Churchill himself had carried on the line which stretched back through his father to the Dukes of Marlborough. But Randolph had bungled it, and now young Winston, too, had lost his golden opportunity.

There is, however, one place where a Churchill dynasty of sorts continues – at Churchill's birthplace close by the spot where he is buried, Blenheim Palace. Winston's cousin, Sunny, the 9th Duke and his son Bert may have lived unsatisfactory lives compared with his, but as dynasts they succeeded where he failed. Against considerable odds the Dukes of Marlborough have maintained their right to rule their palace and inherited possessions with remarkable success.

Bert survived as 10th Duke of Marlborough until 1972, and just before the end he even scored off his departed cousin Randolph by persuading Laura, the love of Randolph's life, to marry him. Laura was now a widow, Michael Canfield having died some three years earlier. Bert had offered her the Marlborough pearls, which once belonged to Catherine the Great, and she said that he appeared so lonely, and Blenheim itself was such a challenge, that she finally accepted him. ('Randolph would have turned incandescent had he known what I was doing.')

Laura took her role as Duchess seriously, and was planning to transform and modernise the interior of Blenheim, but never got the chance. The marriage lasted barely forty days. In February 1972 after a wet day's shooting, Bert suffered sudden intestinal failure, and on 11 March his previously overshadowed son, Sunny Blandford, entered into his inheritance as 11th Duke of Marlborough.

But by the time he died Bert had not only beaten Randolph over Laura; in terms of the dynasty, he had also done surprisingly well by Blenheim and the dukedom. Like all provident modern British noblemen, he had been paying close attention to his tax accountants and had already passed on to Sunny the bulk of the inheritance more than seven years earlier. This meant that on his death Blenheim and its land and treasures stayed largely unmolested by the taxman.

The new Duke, too, had staged an early-middle-age recovery himself by finally marrying his ideal modern duchess: Rosita Douglas, a strong-willed former Swedish fashion designer of Scots descent, by whom he had two further children, Edward and Alexandra. Simultaneously he proved to have inherited enough of the Vanderbilt genes – and Consuelo Vanderbilt's money – to make a fortune out of shrewd investments in the boom years of the seventies and early eighties.

Thus his new duchess was able to accomplish what Laura of the Forty Days had dreamed of doing, redecorating, refurnishing and generally updating Blenheim. Thanks to her taste and her husband's business acumen, Blenheim was ideally suited to exploit the growing tourist interest in historic houses, rapidly becoming one of the most popular and profitable stately homes on the British tourist circuit. (In 1990 it rated number three in popularity, with half a million visitors, the adults paying £5.50 a head.)

Sunny was something of a showman, and his new duchess, unlike almost all her predecessors, actually loved living in the palace with her children. This was a further tourist attraction, but just as it seemed as if Sunny had solved the problems which had bedevilled Blenheim since long before his grandfather married Consuelo, trouble started at the point at which all dynasties are vulnerable: the heir apparent.

With a chaotic childhood, and all those melancholy Marlborough ancestors, it was not entirely surprising that Sunny's eldest son, James Blandford, had problems. His lack of intellect hardly mattered: intelligence is not required to inherit a dukedom. But when, following his Harrow education, the Brigade of Guards refused him a commission, trouble started.

As a titled, rich trainee insurance-broker in New York, the young Lord Blandford turned as easily to drugs as Randolph and Sarah had to drink; and rapidly progressed from marijuana and cocaine to heroin. Someone described him as 'born with a silver spoon under his nose', and by his return to England in 1982, the twenty-five-year-old marquess was addicted.

His step-sister, Christina Onassis, was so alarmed at his condition that she tried to save him by having him kidnapped on a trip to France and forcibly detained at the Château Gage clinic outside Paris. He inevitably escaped, and his next three years form a melancholy tale of failed cures and dramatic press reports as the heir to Blenheim spun out of all control. A policeman was assaulted, a chemist's shop was ransacked for drugs, and finally a judge sentenced Blandford as 'a common criminal' to three months' imprisonment, two of which he served in Pentonville.

All this was bad publicity for the upper classes. More to the point, Blandford's addiction posed a real threat to Blenheim and the Marlborough dynasty. Nothing could dispossess James Blandford of his title and his rights to the dukedom when his father died, but it was impossible for Sunny to follow Bert's example and make over palace and possessions to an heir who was an addict. For a period Sunny cut off completely from his son, and Blenheim itself was highly vulnerable. For, had Sunny died, the Marlborough estate would have been hit by such heavy death duties that Blenheim would almost certainly have been sold.

With so much at stake, it was particularly important to secure a happy ending to the troubled story of James Blandford. And luckily for him, and for the future of the Marlboroughs at Blenheim, his life as an addict had reached a crisis in the summer of 1986, when he was discovered by the police in a cellar off the Edgware Road in London. He was three stone under weight, and barely surviving on a mixture of cocaine and vodka. Faced with a choice between life as a marquess and death as a junkie, Lord Blandford chose the former.

It was a choice he has adhered to. A clinic practising the so-called Minnesota Method helped him kick the habit, and he was reunited with his family. For a while he studied at an agricultural college, and lived in a house on the Blenheim estate. Recently he married twenty-six-year-old Rebecca Few-Brown, an extremely pretty girl who could one day make a charming duchess. Whether the marriage lasts that long, however, already seems in doubt.

The current Duke sees himself as 'virtually a trustee and custodian of Blenheim – not only for Britain, but for those, throughout the world, who cherish the historic and artistic tradition that Blenheim represents'. He and the trustees have been taking steps to protect the future of the palace and the park by vesting them in a heavily endowed Blenheim Foundation to guarantee them in perpetuity – whatever, perhaps, the vagaries of any future heir inheriting the title.

It is appropriate that 'Blenheim's greatest son' is also helping to maintain the Marlborough dynasty in residence in this house which meant so much to him. For Churchill's legend now forms Blenheim's principal attraction for the tourists, who flock to see the place where he was born, the grounds which he enjoyed with his cousin Sunny, and the family plot where he is buried in Bladon churchyard.

Once a year, on 24 January, his daughter Mary comes to place flowers on his grave, and throughout the tourist season Churchill's voice echoes through the palace which he loved – on tape-recordings of his wartime speeches which are played in the small museum filled with relics from his life, close by the room where he was born.

'We shall fight on the beaches, we shall fight on the landing grounds, we shall fight in the fields and in the streets, we shall fight in the hills, we will *never* surrender.'

Notes

In the Notes I use the abbreviation CB, followed by the volume number, for references to the invaluable eight-volume official Churchill biography by Randolph Churchill and Martin Gilbert, *Winston S. Churchill* (Heinemann, 1966–88); CV for the five-volume companion of letters and documents, *Winston S. Churchill: Companion 1874–1939* (Heinemann, 1967–82); and WSC for Winston Spencer Churchill. Full details of all the works referred to in the Notes will be found in the Select Bibliography.

1. Fathers, Sons and Others

2   'What an amazing thing'. Bruce Lockhart, vol. 1, p. 219.
3   'Gentlemen, let us only hope'. *Evening Standard*, 17 June 1932.
    'Had anyone told me.' Randolph Churchill, *Twenty-one Years*, p. 117.
6   'Like a fairy'. Sarah Churchill, *Keep on Dancing*, p. 15.
7   'My oldest dearest friend'. Colville, *The Churchillians*, p. 22.

2. The Ancestor

9   'A private monument'. Sitwell, p. 162.
    'A poor Cavalier knight'. Macaulay, vol. 1, p. 162.
    He cuckolded his king. *Ibid.* p. 225.
11   'That wild, unmerciful house.' Martin, vol. I, p. 54.
    'An auctioneer'. Horace Walpole to G. Montague, July 1760, *Letters of Horace Walpole*, vol. IV, (Bentley, 1840).
    'His greatest weakness'. Montgomery-Massingberd, p. 51.
12   'A physical monument'. WSC, *Marlborough*, vol. III, p. 370.
    'What about God?' Green, p. 146.
13   At least five subsequent dukes. Moran, p. 745.

14   'The latter years of his life . . . ' *The Annual Register*, 1840.
15   'A full-blown Victorian prig.' Rowse, *The Later Churchills*, p. 215.
     Close friends of Disraeli. Montgomery Hyde, p. 29.

3. Two Brothers

16   'I cannot be grateful enough'. Rowse, *The Later Churchills*, p. 217.
     'My dearest, dearest friends'. Martin, *Lady Randolph Churchill*,
     p. 89.
17   'Prepared to share'. Montgomery-Massingberd, p. 104.
19   'I don't like ladies at all'. Martin, vol. I, p. 64.
     'Until his tongue was sore'. Rhodes James, *Lord Randolph
     Churchill*, p. 33.
     Jeanette Jerome. Anita Leslie, *Jennie*, p. 16.

4. The Jeromes

21   'Poppy' Marlborough eyes. Rhodes James, *Lord Randolph
     Churchill*, p. 48.
     'From what I have heard'. Martin, vol. I, p. 58.
     'Under any circumstances'. *Ibid*. p. 60.
22   Brought his family back. Anita Leslie, *Jennie*, p. 2.
     'That Wall Street Jungle'. Anita Leslie, *Leonard Jerome*, p. 57.
23   A many-sided hedonist. *Ibid*. p. 91.
24   'I have found the Court I want'. *Ibid*. p. 81.
     'Little Mondays'. Martin, vol. I, p. 10.
     'But gentlemen'. Anita Leslie, *Jennie*, p. 22.
25   The Emperor's dinner service. *Ibid*. p. 20.

5. 'A Victorian Tragedy'

26   'The test of time'. Martin, vol. I, p. 34.
     A settlement of $50,000. *Ibid*. p. 36.
27   A mountainous trousseau. Anita Leslie, *Jennie*, p. 56.
28   'I loathe living here'. *Ibid*. p. 77.
     'The most tragic career.' Rowse, *The Later Churchills*, p. 285.
     'Very little money'. WSC, *Lord Randolph Churchill*, p. 70.
29   Sporting Joe had been in India. Anita Leslie, *Edwardians in
     Love*, p. 85.
30   Proclaimed her son illegitimate. Proceedings of the House of
     Lords (November 1877).
31   'Powerful enemies'. WSC, *Lord Randolph Churchill*, p. 74.
     'A dark lithe figure'. WSC, *My Early Life*, p. 12.

32   'The speech of a foolish young man'. Rhodes James, *Lord Randolph Churchill*, p. 54.

33   'From tip-cat to tiger-shooting'. *Ibid.* p. 255.

34   Two hundred of her lovers. Asquith, p. 444.

36   'I like to be the boss'. Rosebery, p. 34.
    'He is so mad and odd.' Martin, *Lady Randolph Churchill*, p. 180.

37   He suddenly objected. Foster, p. 314.
    'When I came down to breakfast'. Lady Randolph Churchill, p. 141.

6. Family Troubles

39   His grand-daughter, Mary Soames. Soames, *A Churchill Family Album*, p. 14.

40   'One long yellow tooth'. Harris, vol. II, p. 532–3.
    A mistress he was keeping in Paris. Anita Leslie, *Edwardians in Love*, p. 195.

41   Treated by a Dr Robson Roose. Foster, p. 218.

42   'How long will your leadership last?' Rosebery, p. 47.
    He departed hurriedly. Martin, vol. I, p. 186.
    An affair with another woman. Churchill and Mitchell, p. 160.

44   'Strangers took off their hats'. Cowles, p. 33.
    'Winston was taken to a pantomime'. Churchill and Mitchell, p. 160.
    'A violent, uncontrollable small boy'. CB, vol. I, p. 53.
    'The naughtiest little boy in the world'. Cowles, p. 30.

45   'Dearest Winnie'. CV, vol. I, p. 221.
    'Gave Winston his lessons'. Lady Randolph Churchill's diary for 1882. Churchill College Collection.
    'One day these will be needed'. Martin, vol. I, p. 192.

46   The terrifying 'Boneless Wonder'. CB, vol. V, p. 389n.
    'You never came to see me'. CB. vol I, p. 83.

47   'Chief mourner'. Rosebery, p. 181.

48   'Inclined to abuse his wife'. Anita Leslie, *Jennie*, p. 83.

7. Death in the Family

50   'He was his own worst enemy'. *The Times*, 12 November 1892.

51   'Charming and joyous'. Montgomery-Massingberd, p. 113.
    'Given no kindness'. Anita Leslie, *Jennie*, p. 85.
    'The construction of an English sentence.' WSC, *My Early Life*, p. 25.

52   'This astonishing gift for writing'. CB, VIII, p. 343.

52   'With some resentment'. Sir Oswald Mosley, p. 29.
      'I mistook you for a fourth form boy'. WSC, *My Early Life*, p. 26.
53   'Precocious, bumptious and talkative'. Meinertzhagen, p. 175.
      'I cannoned'. *Ibid*. p. 177.
54   'Plenty of tin'. Anita Leslie, *Leonard Jerome*, p. 280.
55   'They say'. Balsan, p. 84.
      Looking 'very peaceful'. Churchill College Collection, November 1982.
57   'Cursed with so feeble a body'. CB, vol. I, p. 211.
58   'Show-off exaggeration and make-believe'. CV, vol. I, p. 386.
      'Harum scarum style of work'. CB, vol. I, p. 189.
      Someone has neatly snipped. Churchill College Collection, 5 October 1883.
59   'Such information about Lord R's condition'. CV, vol. I, p. 544.
      'I know instinctively'. Churchill College Collection, 8 June 1894.
60   According to Dr Buzzard's notes. Buzzard Collection, Royal College of Physicians.
      'My Darling's Last Letter'. Churchill College Collection, 22 November 1894.
61   'Physically he is better'. Anita Leslie, *Jennie*, p. 173.
      'I am not *quite* the meek creature'. *Ibid*.
62   'Masses of Churchills'. CV, vol. I, p. 546.
      'Lord Randolph had a quiet night'. Buzzard Collection, Royal College of Physicians.

8. Ambition

63   'All my dreams of comradeship'. WSC, *My Early Life*, p. 70.
      'Like an Aladdin's Cave'. *Ibid*. p. 74.
64   'A freak – always that'. CB, vol. VIII, p. 562.
65   'This is a pushing age . . . ' CV, vol. I, p. 856.
66   'He reported'. *Daily Graphic*, 15 July 1895.
      'Slough of despond'. CB, vol. I, p. 260.
67   'The natural catharsis of accompanying grief.' Styron, p. 79.
68   'Many depressives deny themselves rest'. Storr, p. 16.
69   'Many of which I know already by heart'. CB, vol. I, p. 260.
      'I took my politics unquestioningly from him'. WSC, *My Early Life*, p. 54.
      'Beat my sabre into an iron despatch box'. CB, vol. I, p. 288.
70   'All the influential friends that you possess'. CB, vol. I, p. 288.
      'My stay here might be of value'. CB, vol. I, p. 297.
      He seemed to be 'of endomorphic structure'. Storr, p. 11.
71   Bartlett's *Familiar Quotations*. Sir Oswald Mosley, p. 105.

72   'A good knowledge of the *Annual Register*'. CB, vol. I, p. 333.
73   'All along the front of the skirmish line'. CB, vol. I, p. 359.
74   'Vehement, high and daring'. WSC, *Savrola*, p. 43.
75   'The struggle, the labour'. *Ibid*. p. 42.

9. 'Faithful but Unfortunate'

77   'Neither pretty nor ugly'. Churchill College Collection, 25 August 1892.
78   Mrs Willie sensed victory. Vanderbilt, p. 32.
79   Her mother set about her with a riding crop. Balsan, p. 6.
     The coming-out ball at the Breakers. Vanderbilt, p. 78.
80   'In tears and alone'. Balsan, p. 53.
81   'The roof of the Marlborough Castle'. *Washington Post*, 12 November 1896.
     'How strange that in so great a house'. Balsan, p. 84.
     'Pushed his plate away'. *Ibid*. p. 79.
     'Your first duty'. *Ibid*. p. 72.

10. Power and Glory

83   'The rogue elements'. Martin Green, p. 82.
84   'One more example of your slovenly shiftless habits'. CB, vol. I, p. 378.
85   'If there is anything', WSC, *My Early Life*, p.170.
86   'Life is very cheap'. CV, vol. I, p. 962.
87   'Like a dream'. *Ibid*. p. 973.
     'A Ripper'. *Ibid*. p. 957.
     'The consolations of philosophy'. *Ibid*. p. 969.
88   'Christian or any other form of religious belief'. CB, vol. I, p. 407.
     'A great general he may be'. CB, vol. I, p. 407.
90   'The most beautiful girl I have ever seen'. CB, vol. I, p. 296.
91   'He was slim, slightly reddish-haired'. Atkins, p. 57.
94   'Bronzed by African sunshine'. WSC, *Marlborough*, vol. I, p. 58.

11. Politics

96   'Dry hair like a wax-work'. Buckle, p. 270.
     'A little, square-headed fellow'. Blunt, p. 16.
     'What was difficult to see'. Rhodes James, *Churchill: A Study in Failure*, p. 34.

96   'Easy for the Boers to surrender'. *Hansard*, 18 February 1901.
97   But Jennie's marriage. Anita Leslie, *Jennie*, p. 253.
      'A broad writing-table'. WSC, *Savrola*, p. 40.
99   'The passions of the multitude'. CV, vol. I, p. 818.
      'Of all the talents'. *Ibid*. p. 816.
100   'I loved to hear Lord Rosebery talk'. WSC, *My Early Life*, p. 56.
101   'Startling' resemblances. *Pall Mall Gazette*, September 1903.
      'When the young member for Oldham addresses the House'.
      Punch, 8 June 1904.
102   'He gave himself entirely to work'. Atkins, p. 135.
103   'Inclined to leave the Conservative leadership to Mr Balfour'.
      Warwick, p. 138.

12. Love and the Pursuit of Power

106   A liberated and cosmopolitan lady. Vickers, p. 51.
      'He is quite different from me'. CV, vol. I, p. 800.
      'Nothing could exceed the tranquil *banalité* of my relations with
      M'. CV, vol. II, p. 587.
107   'Went into dinner with Winston Churchill'. Webb, p. 269.
108   'The simplicity of a child'. Beaverbrook, *Politicians and the
      War*, p. 284.
      'His approach to women'. Bonham Carter, p. 148.
110   'Please don't become converted to Islam'. CV, vol. II, p. 672.
      'It is positively cruel of Fate'. CV, vol. II, p. 672.
111   'Dear Mr Winston'. CV, vol. II, p. 674.
      'She would sacrifice'. CV, vol. II, p. 696.
      'The vitality of these brutes'. CV, vol. II, p. 693.
115   'We all swooped down in motor-cars'. *Ibid*. p. 798.
      'Her last laundered and starched dress'. Soames, *Clementine
      Churchill*, p. 40.
      'I want so much to show you that beautiful place'. CV,
      vol. I, p. 806.
116   'People of the better sort'. *The Times*, 13 September 1908.
      The bride wore ivory coloured silk. *Ibid*.
117   The father of the two elder girls was 'the gallant Bay Middleton'.
      Longford, p. 386.
118   The horse-mad Empress Elizabeth. Haslip, pp. 286–9.

13. Light Fades from the Picture

119   'To her simple and rather austere taste'. Soames, *Clementine Churchill*, p. 50.
      'Vain and frivolous'. *Ibid.*
120   Lord Esher discovered Kat and Pug. Esher, vol. II, p. 462.
      'I am a solitary creature'. CV, vol. II, p. 787.
      Is she a pretty child?' *Daily Mail*, 21 October 1965.
122   'Winston swept me off'. Masterman, p. 122.
      'I would rather sweep the streets'. Brendon, p. 42.
      'I would like to see him and Lloyd George'. Frank Owen, *Lloyd George*, p. 179 (Hutchinson, 1954).
123   'I confess that I am often struck'. Edel, vol. I, p. 500.
      'The light faded from the picture'. Moran, p. 167.
124   'I have no good opinion of myself'. Soames, *Clementine Churchill*, p. 64.
      'Thought that he might trip up'. Moran, p. 181.
125   'He is his own superman'. A. G. Gardiner.
      'I would greatly like to have some practice'. CV, vol. II, p. 893.
127   'What the hell have you been doing now, Winston?' Brendon, p. 58.
      'The Club'. Colville, *The Churchillians*, p. 12.

14. Admiralty

129   'Small emotions'. Soames, *Clementine Churchill*, p. 63.
      'Churchill's delight was to dine with F. E. Smith'. Colville, *The Churchillians*, p. 7.
130   Rolling together down the steps of the Admiralty. Randolph Churchill, *Twenty-one Years*, p. 12.
131   Predicted the course events would follow. From 'Military aspect of the Continental Problem', Cowles, p. 154.
      'War castles foaming to their stations'. Brendon, p. 62.
132   'Churchill suddenly become so melancholy'. Morgan, p. 338.
133   'Sweetest of the sweets of office'. Bonham Carter, p. 261.
      'A kind of floating hotel'. Searle, p. 123.
      'Dearest Mama, it would do you a great deal of good'. CV, vol. II, p. 1639.
      'He is like no one else'. Bonham Carter, p. 18.
      'Those Greeks and Romans'. *Ibid.* p. 262.
134   'Side by side against the taffrail'. *Ibid.*
      'How much coal?' *National Review*, August 1912.
      'Winston is for 4 ships'. Young, p. 32.
      'Excursions to the beach'. John S. Churchill, p. 27.

15. God Bless the Dardanelles

136   According to Nellie. Moran, p. 601.
       'Upon this grave assembly'. Stevenson, p. 38.

137   'Everything tends towards catastrophe'. CB, vol. II, p. 710.

138   'I ought to have remained in London'. WSC, *Thoughts and Adventures*, p. 16.
       'Frère aîné de la Trinité'. Brendon, p. 62.

139   'His mouth waters'. Brock, p. 266.
       'Rather disgusted with Winston'. Stevenson, p. 251.
       'Like sheep to the shambles'. Brock, p. 275.

140   'Chewing barbed wire'. Bonham Carter, p. 351.
       'This is living history'. CV, vol. III, p.400.
       'Conducting warfare on the grand scale'. Keynes, *Essays in Biography*, p. 169.

141   'An *idea* enters his head'. Rhodes James, *Churchill*, p. 29.
       'One of the great events of history'. Bonham Carter, 377.

144   'Melodrama to megalomania'. Wilson, p. 40.
       'You don't care'. Stevenson, p. 275.
       'Silent, despairing'. Bonham Carter, p. 402.
       'His head buried in his hands'. Stevenson, p. 253.

145   'Found himself – like Lord Randolph in December 1886'. Rhodes James, *Churchill*, p. 78.
       Jennie had been walking. Anita Leslie, *Cousin Clare*, p. 69.
       He alone possessed 'the power'. Soames, *Clementine Churchill*, p. 123.
       'Dance on Asquith's grave'. *Ibid*. p. 124.
       'God bless the Dardanelles'. Randolph S. Churchill, *Twenty-one Years*, p. 14.

146   'Blazed away like hell'. Hozier to WSC, CV, vol. III, p. 1098.
       'We live vy simply'. CB, vol. III, p. 494.
       'Randolph will carry the lamp'. CV, vol. III, p. 1098.

147   'The golden opportunity has gone'. *Ibid*. p. 1071.
       Potatoes were not enough. *Ibid*. p. 1078.
       'A terrible reproach to my family'. CV, vol. III, p. 1078.
       'So violent and abusive'. CV, vol. III, p. 1078.

148   'The dirty dogs'. *Ibid*. p. 1080.
       'Malbruck s'en va'. Blunt, p. 132.
       'Household upside down'. Beaverbrook, *Politicians and the War*, p. 276.

149   A noisy mind. Bonham Carter, p. 20.
       'War is a game'. Cowles, p. 211.
       'Many years of luxury'. CV, vol. III, p. 1286.

150   'I am superior to arything'. *Ibid* p. 1317.

150 'When next I see you'. Soames, *Clementine Churchill*, p. 266.
'I don't know how one hears such things'. Anita Leslie, *Cousin Clare*, p. 78.
'The hammer of Thor'. *Ibid*. p. 180.
151 'Depressed beyond the limits of description'. Beaverbrook, *Politicians and the War*, p. 282.
'Like Beethoven deaf'. Hassall, p. 340.
'Worst part of our life together'. Birkenhead, p. 392.
'The raw material of brilliant ideas'. *Ibid*. p. 250.
152 'His thoughts turned inwards'. Beaverbrook, *Politicians and the War*, p. 282.
'We are all worms'. Bonham Carter.
'Like a sea-beast'. WSC, *Painting as a Pastime*, p. 16.
'A spasm of the emotion'. *Ibid*. p. 8.

16. Lullenden

154 'A shut Rolls at present'. CV, vol. IV, p. 397.
155 'A Mustard Gas fiend'. Soames, *Clementine Churchill*, p. 187.
'Country basket'. *Ibid*. p. 185.
156 'A small farm outside East Grinstead'. Sarah Churchill, *Keep on Dancing*, p. 2.
157 Everyday life at Lullenden. Peregrine Churchill to the author.
'A most dreadful bully'. *Ibid*.
Contents of his chamberpot. John S. Churchill to the author.
158 Proud to have a father who 'was a boss man'. Randolph Churchill, *Twenty-one Years*, p. 17.
162 'Weighty smell of locked-in history'. John S. Churchill, p. 24.
'Passionate interest in the game'. Smith, p. 83.
163 'Slight and frail looking'. *Ibid*. p. 126.
'I heard the fire crackling.' Montgomery-Massingberd, p. 161.
164 'One day, at Blenheim'. Smith, p. 163.
'Dependent on feminine influence'. WSC to Clementine, CV, vol. II, p. 800.
165 She was secretly approaching forty. Vickers, p. 165.
'A mannikin'. Asquith, p. 313.
A fatal touch of melancholy. Rhodes James, *Chips*, p. 22.

17. To Russia with Love

167 A bizarre encounter with Churchill. Sassoon, p. 77.
'Head thrust well forward'. *Ibid*. p. 79.
169 'A plague bacillus'. Rhodes James, *Churchill*, p. 117.

169 'Tingling with vitality'. Beaverbrook, *Men and Power*, p. 142.
'Kiss the Hun and kill the Bolshie'. Brendon, p. 92.
170 'Ride a white charger'. Brendon, p. 93.
'Put our foot on the egg'. Mosley, p. 108.
'Just home from school'. John S. Churchill to the author.
171 'Every woman I have ever enjoyed'. Anita Leslie, *Cousin Clare*, p. 82.
'He adores Clare'. *Ibid.* p. 118.
173 'I have no interest in art'. *Ibid.* p. 120.
174 'Even when your teeth are clenched'. *Ibid.* p. 128.
'You're so like me really'. *Ibid.* p. 132.
175 'My boys asked me to'. Martin, vol. II, p. 301.
'Those I regard as fiendish criminals'. Anita Leslie, *Cousin Clare*, p. 138.
176 Poison gas ' . . . a scientific expedient for sparing life'. CV, vol. IV, p. 1695.
178 'Just becos' I am ordinary'. Soames, *Clementine Churchill*, p. 194.
179 'Build lovely garden cities'. *Ibid.* p. 187.
'Listless little old lady'. Sarah Churchill, *Keep on Dancing*, p. 3.
180 'Subordinate everything in yr life'. Soames, *Clementine Churchill*, p. 194.
181 'Had she been a man'. Grace Hamblin to the author.
182 'Shrunk and small, sitting in her chair'. Soames, *Clementine Churchill*, p. 199.
'Oh Winston my Dear do come tomorrow'. *Ibid.* p. 199.
'She was still a handsome woman'. Sermoneta, p. 243.
'A clear profit of £15,000'. CV, vol. IV, p. 521.
183 'Make sure you have cut high enough'. Martin, vol. II, p. 305.
'I do not feel a sense of tragedy'. WSC to Curzon, CV, vol. IV, p. 1524.
184 'Clementine in her agony'. Soames, *Clementine Churchill*, p. 202.

18. The Chartwell Dream

186 'Slimed the walls with green'. Tilden, p. 115.
187 Perished in a railway accident. Soames, *Clementine Churchill*, p. 288.
'Now that the sharp edge of financial anxiety has been removed'. CB, vol. V, p. 793.
188 'I think a great deal of the coming kitten'. Soames, *Clementine Churchill*, p. 206.

188 'Join me as soon as you are fit'. CV, vol. IV, p. 1934.
189 'Let us beware.' Soames, *Clementine Churchill*, p. 217.
190 'Do you like it?' Sarah Churchill, *A Thread in the Tapestry*, p. 22.
191 'A Cherub Peace Maker'. Soames, *Clementine Churchill*, p. 208.
    'In the twinkling of an eye'. Cowles, p. 243.
192 The conclusion of modern historians. Prior, p. 23.
    'A Warrior–King–Statesman'. Keynes, *Essays and Sketches in Biography*, p. 168.
193 'The sentimental appreciation of beauty'. Tilden, p. 118.
    'Trying experiments with baths'. Tilden, p. 120.
195 'Clementine was more deeply tied to her husband than to her offspring'. Anita Leslie, *Cousin Randolph*, p. 2.
196 'I am enormously and unbelievably tired'. Soames, *Clementine Churchill*, p. 326.
    'The Pussy Cat who is their Queen'. CV, vol. V, p. 144.

19. 'Paradise on Earth'

197 'I am what I have always been'. CB, vol. V, p. 57.
198 'Except in some great position'. CB, vol. V, p. 56.
    'Do you mind the smoke of a cigar?' CB, vol. V, p. 59.
199 'Like some Chimborazo'. CB, vol. V, p. 91.
200 'But also all the versatility of an actor'. CV, vol. V, p. 473.
    'From economists like Maynard Keynes'. Keynes, *The Economic Consequences of Mr Churchill*.
    'I was the worst Chancellor of the Exchequer that ever was.' Rowse, *The Later Churchills*, p. 439.
202 'We are both awfully poor'. Vickers, p. 179.
    Lytton Strachey who coveted the place. Vickers, *Gladys*, p. 200.
    H. G. Wells danced with the Duchess. Birkenhead, *The Professor in Two Worlds*, p. 128.
    'In an ungovernable rage'. Vickers, *Gladys*, p. 206.
203 His Duchess's face started to collapse before his eyes. *Ibid.* p. 123.
    'Winston was so delighted with his house'. Lees-Milne, vol. I, p. 235.
204 The rich tennis-playing polymath from Oxford. Birkenhead, *The Prof in Two Worlds*, p. 127.
    'Improbable self-made financier and newspaperman Brendan Bracken'. Boyle, p. 99–100.

20. The Happy Family

207   Left the choice of school to Randolph. Randolph Churchill,
      Twenty-one Years, p. 27.
      'Bloody awful all round'. Brendon, p. 109.
      'Formidable'. Sarah Churchill, *Keep on Dancing*, p. 17.
208   'What a true mother, and grand woman'. CB, vol. V, p. 445.
      'The tallest of trees would bend'. Colville, *The Churchillians*,
      p. 21.
      'Like a jaguar from a tree'. Soames, *Clementine Churchill*, p. 231.
209   'Take no notice, keep his head down'. Lady Avon to the author.
      'Mrs C is highly friendly'. Blakiston, p. 71.
      'I feel far safer from worry'. CV, vol. V, p. 434.
210   'The darling old schoolboy'. Cooper, *The Light of Common
      Day*, p. 155.
      'If you set yourself against Chartwell'. Soames, *Clementine
      Churchill*, p. 223.
211   'Something of a collegiate atmosphere'. Rowse, *The Later
      Churchills*, p. 451.
      'ADC extraordinary and Super Quartermaster'. John S. Churchill,
      p. 143.
      'Always a glorious feast'. Soames, *Clementine Churchill*, p. 246.
213   'I just can't stand it any longer'. John S. Churchill to the author.
215   'I could grow up to be as beautiful and elegant as Cousin
      Clementine'. Lady Diana Mosley to the author.

21. Wilderness

217   'What fun it is to get away from England'. Young, p. 110.
      'I think he has made a good impression'. CV, vol. V, p. 342.
      'Randolph, recite us something'. John S. Churchill to the author.
218   'A white round face like a blister'. Nicolson, vol. I, p. 41.
219   'I am Winston Churchill, a British statesman.' Gilbert, *The
      Wilderness Years*, p. 41.
      'The last decade of my existence'. CV, vol. V, p. 394.
220   A boy scout jamboree and a revivalist meeting. *Sunday Graphic*,
      3 March 1932.
221   'Nothing can long delay their arrival'. *Ibid*.
      'Seditious Middle Temple lawyer'. CV, vol. V, p. 357.
222   'But what would I talk to him about?' Hanfstaegl, p. 184.
      'Anti-semitism may be a good starter but it's bad sticker'.
      Ibid. p. 184.

224   'Roaring like a bull'. Lady Diana Mosley, p. 92.
      Lady Castlerosse's pet name for his son was 'Fuzzy-Wuzzy'.
      Leonard Mosley, p. 113.
225   'Lindemann, you are a professor of biology'. Bruce Lockhart,
      vol. I, p. 229.
226   'Beautiful and elegant' Clementine. Sarah Churchill, *Keep on
      Dancing*, p. 15.
      'Because Mummy is horrid to me.' Anita Leslie, *The Gilt
      on the Gingerbread*, p. 83.
227   'Mr Churchill's daughter a film star?' *Daily Express*, 5 March 1932.
      'To escape from all the endless talk'. Celia Perkins to the author.
      Embattled women. *Daily Telegraph*, 13 December 1932.
228   Discovered that he drank so much. Dame Barbara Cartland
      to the author.
229   'He liked particularly to try out ideas'. Ashley, p. 32.
232   'Watch Sunny, he hates her guts'. Anita Leslie, *The Gilt on
      the Gingerbread*, p. 57.

22. Psychic Dynamite

233   'My dear Maxine!' Forbes-Robertson.
      'Winston, how brave of you!' *Ibid*.
234   'At meals he just banged on and on'. P. Willes to author.
236   Stanley Baldwin said how much he envied. CB, vol. V, p. 496.
237   'I feel so lonely'. Soames, *Clementine Churchill*, p. 251.
239   'My heart is in the 18th century'. CV, vol. V, p. 660.
240   'Every prophet'. WSC, *Thoughts and Adventures*, p. 283.
      'The front-door was rarely locked'. Grace Hamblin to the author.
      'When a politician dwells'. WSC, *Thoughts and Adventures*.
241   'Lunch was devoted to unrelieved gloom'. John S. Churchill,
      p. 101.
      'Spent much of the time together in the ladies loo'. Pryce-
      Jones, p. 24.

23. Distant Friends

243   'If I had been an Italian'. CB, vol. V, p. 226.
      'The Roman genius'. CB, vol. V, p. 457.
244   Hitler's 'long wearing battle for the German heart'. WSC,
      Great Contemporaries, p. 265.
      The mysterious Colonel. Thompson, p. 21.
245   Unity's infatuation with all things German. Pryce-Jones, p. 159.

246 'The darling leader'. *Ibid*. p. 159.
247 'That surprising frankness often found in men at the top'. Lady Mosley, p. 149
   'You will love Parsifal more and more'. *Ibid*. p. 142.
249 This contact with Hitler which had ruined his life. Nicholas Mosley, p. 170.
   'simply everyone from Winston down.' Lady Mosley to the author.
   'Winston only wanted to hear about Hitler'. Lady Mosley to the author.
251 'An extraordinary man, colossally rich'. Rhodes James, *Chips*, p. 396.
   'Sweet and darling Winston'. CV, vol. V, p. 396.
252 Clementine fell romantically in love. Soames, *Clementine Churchill*, p. 266.
253 'A little depressed about politics'. CV, vol. V, p. 1136.
254 A sort of father-figure. Ingram, p. 18.
   'A giggling little anarchist'. *Ibid*. p. 156.
   'Had been rather in love'. Ingram, p. 16
   'Red Menace in Public Schools'. *Daily Mail*, 2 February 1934.
255 'A short, square, dirty figure . . . '. *Ibid*. p. 84.

24. Two Love-Affairs

256 'Oh dear, I want to start out'. Soames, *Clementine Churchill*, p. 269.
258 'With her beautiful red hair'. Sir Harry Llewellyn to the author.
259 Cochran was an old-style theatrical survivor. Harling, p. 64.
   'I pointed out to her'. CV, vol. V, p. 1295.
260 'At this period of her life'. CV, vol. V, p. 1295.
   Born in Vienna thirty-eight years before. Oliver, p. 12.
261 He 'could be marrying into a most unusual family'. Ellen Pollock to the author.
262 'The well flows freely.' CB, vol. V, p. 735.
   Oliver was 'common as dirt'. CV, vol. V, p. 52.
   'Addressed like a public meeting'. Sarah Churchill, *Keep on Dancing*, p. 36.
263 'I think I have put her off'. *Ibid*. p. 36.
267 'I'm here to take Sarah home'. *New York Times*, 17 September 1936.
268 'Queen Wally would not sound well'. Pearson, *Façades*, p. 316.
269 He had written every word of the speech for him. Bradford, p. 202–3.
   'Hat in one hand, stick in the other'. Windsor, p. 409.

270   'He delighted in her company'. CB, vol. V, p. 810.

25. The Return of the Prophet

273   'Randolph, you've been drinking'. Laura, Duchess of Marl-
      borough, to the author.
      'One strong young figure'. WSC, *The Gathering Storm*, p. 231.
      'The great ball thrown by the Duchess of Richmond on the
      eve of Waterloo'. Fielding, p. 187.
274   'It was a strange experience'. CB, vol. VII, p. 32.
276   'Randolph's adoration of his father'. Nicolson, vol. I, p. 339.
      Meeting an old friend in the doorway of the Ritz. Lady Mary
      Dunn to the author.
277   'Red-headed and rather fat, but Mummy says the puppy fat
      will disappear'. Anita Leslie, *Cousin Randolph*, p. 47.
      'In action in the early spring'. CB, vol. VII, p. 167.
      'I had had no experience of life or men.' Mrs Averell Harriman
      to the author.
278   'Pam was not particularly beautiful'. Alastair Forbes to the author.
279   'A preparation for this hour'. WSC, *The Gathering Storm*, p. 527.
280   'I offer neither pay nor quarters nor provisions'. Trevelyan, p. 231.
      'How we despised his orations'. Amory, *Letters of Ann
      Fleming*, p. 364n.
      'All I wanted was'. WSC, *The Second World War*, vol. IV, p. 78.
281   'A secretary is as essential'. Nel.
282   'This war will be won'. Brendon, p. 165.
      Extra 'diplomatic' rations. Soames, *Clementine Churchill*, p. 391.
283   'There has to be a purpose to it all'. Colville, *The Fringes of Power*.
      'A purpose far beyond our simple reasoning'. Moran.

26. Family at War

284   'Immaculately distinguishedly porcine'. Vickers, *Cecil Beaton*,
      p. 244.
      'A hard-bitten virago who takes drugs'. *Ibid*. p. 245.
286   Found her 'abusive'. Colville, *The Fringes of Power*, p. 273.
      The swift rejoinder from the General. Soames, *Clementine
      Churchill*, p. 290.
287   'Rough, sarcastic and overbearing manner'. *Ibid*. p. 291.
288   She had tried to shoot herself. Pryce-Jones, p. 232.
      'Typically British feature of the situation'. Skidelsky, p. 458.

289 She and her husband had become 'untouchable'. Lady Diana Mosley, p. 177.

290 'Of course, it was extremely difficult for him'. Lady Diana Mosley to the author.
'A kindly thought of Winston's'. Lady Diana Mosley, p. 188.

291 'The children can't go'. Bradford, *George VI*, p. 321.

292 'One of the most objectionable people I have ever met'. Colville, *The Fringes of Power*, p. 177.

293 'He was primarily someone who loved his family'. Mrs Averell Harriman to the author.

294 'Champagne and tenantry on the lawns'. Cooper, *Trumpets from the Steep*, p. 62.

295 'How d'you know it's going to be a boy?' Winston S. Churchill Jr, p. 12.
'Poor infant'. Cowles, p. 326.

27. 'Poor Randolph!'

296 'The happiest Christmas I can remember'. Soames, *Clementine Churchill*, p. 300.
'Naïve and rather charming adoration'. Colville, *The Fringes of Power*, p. 201.
'Much the most courteous member of the family'. Peregrine Churchill to the author.

298 'The PM sang lustily'. CB, vol. VI, p. 962.
'Oh, Randy . . . oh my darling'. Winston S. Churchill Jr, p. 14.
'There was very high gambling'. Amory, *Letters of Evelyn Waugh*, p. 149.

299 'To keep the British Isles afloat'. Harriman and Abel, p. 3.
'Improved considerably after a shot or two of good Scotch Whisky'. Pimlott, p. 199.

300 'Pamela Churchill and Averell Harriman examining the devastation'. Colville, *The Fringes of Power*.
'The most beautiful man I ever met'. Isaacson and Thomas, p. 329.
'Mightily smitten by Randolph Churchill's glamorous young wife'. Drogheda, p. 98.

301 'If R were killed'. Colville, *The Fringes of Power*, p. 178.

302 'I found him absolutely charming'. Winston S. Churchill Jr, p. 20.

303 'I hope he is going to be a gentleman'. Sarah Churchill, *Keep on Dancing*, p. 58.

305 'Are you a communist?' Ingram, p. 205.

306 'More than a car-load of cops to get Decca into a church'. Jessica Mitford to the author.

308   'Looking embarrassed and shy'. Nicolson, vol. III, p. 208.
       'You called my son a coward'. *Ibid.* p. 209.
309   'Arm in arm and beaming'. *Ibid.*
310   'The trouble between Randolph and his mother'. Laura, Duchess
       of Marlborough, to the author.
       'Repelled her with his spotted face'. Bruce Lockhart, vol.
       II, p. 158.
311   'She is quite a dish'. Amory, *The Letters of Evelyn Waugh*, p. 349.
       'Pamela seems very well'. CB, vol. VII, p. 101.
312   How typical of Randolph. Soames, *Clementine Churchill*, p. 315.
       'It will cause you harrowing anxiety'. *Ibid.* p. 315.
       'Poor Randolph!' Grace Hamblin to the author.

28. Master of Alliances

316   'On my right sat the President of the United States'. CB,
       vol. VII, p. 570.
       'Roosevelt, unimpressed by Churchill's gestures'. Roosevelt,
       p. 182.
318   'Stupendous issues are unfolding before our eyes'. Moran, p. 140.
319   Not only a great statesman, 'but a nice father'. Sarah Churchill,
       Keep on Dancing, p. 71.
320   'Wrapped in my towel'. CB, vol. VII, p. 602.
       'Profligate of his resources'. Moran, p. 144.
321   'The fact that W and I still don't get on'. Letter to Laura,
       Lady Dudley, from Randolph Churchill, undated 1942.
       'R's marriage is going wonky'. Nicolson, vol. III, p. 397.
322   'An event so natural and indispensable'. WSC, *Great Contem-
       poraries*, p. 256.
       'If I die, don't worry'. CB, vol. VII, p. 845.
323   'A soporific Christmas lunch'. CB, vol. VI, p. 606.
       She 'smiled whimsically'. Moran, p. 152.
       'Intimately as both my wife and I knew Lady Churchill'.
       Colville, *The Fringes of Power*.
324   'Try ridding yourself of this microbe'. Soames, *Clementine
       Churchill*, p. 314.
       'His mother hated him'. *The Times*, 11 October 1982.
325   'There was our old baby in his rompers'. Cooper, *Trumpets
       from the Steep*, p. 178.
       'Clemmie said nothing'. *Ibid.* p. 182.
326   'Felt he would get on well'. Roberts, p. 253.
       'All the aid in human power'. Roberts p. 255.

29. 'The Shadows of Victory'

328 'I think Winston will die when it's over.' Cooper, *Trumpets from the Steep*, p. 182.
329 'I'm through'. Brendon, p. 187.
     'No one dared pursue a topic'. Cowles, p. 325.
330 'Losing interest in the war.' Colville, *The Fringes of Power*, p. 574.
     'I envy you'. *Ibid*. p. 190.
331 'If you go on playing the fool like this'. Boyle.
332 'Glad our commanders are capable of running these sort of risks'. CB, vol. VII, p. 975.
333 'Old and ill'. Colville, *The Fringes of Power*, p. 560.
334 'Churchill was not the man'. Moran, p. 181.
335 Dined *à deux* on weekdays on only four occasions. Soames, *Clementine Churchill*, p. 355.
336 'Extraordinarily wholesome'. Laura, Duchess of Marlborough, to the author.
     'Supposing anything happened to me'. Soames, *Clementine Churchill*, p. 367.
337 'Good stuff in this fellow'. Moran, p. 539.
     'A case of two people who had loved each other'. Oliver, p. 146.
     'Brought her closer to her father'. Paul Medlicott to the author.
338 'Half-way between Chequers and London'. Sarah Churchill, *Keep on Dancing*, p. 60.
     'How careful Sarah always was'. Pauline Bretherton to the author.
339 'Old love affair which'. Sarah Churchill, *Keep on Dancing*, p. 187.
340 'God! Wasn't God a shit!' Davie, p. 587.
     'He is not a good companion'. *Ibid*.
341 'Fighting with his last breath against Bolshevism'. CB, vol. VII, p. 1325.

30. Opposition

342 'It's absolutely monstrous'. CB, vol. VIII, p. 119.
343 Sat 'in Stygian gloom'. Soames, *Clementine Churchill*, p. 386.
     'I don't like sleeping near a precipice'. Moran, p. 288.
344 The way one tiny grub, when fed the magical royal jelly. Moran, p. 757.
     'What is there to stay up for?' Soames, *Clementine Churchill*, p. 391.
345 'In our misery'. *Ibid*. p. 391.
     'Constant outbursts of childish petulance'. Moran, p. 299.
346 'The sudden appearance of a hernia'. *Ibid*. p. 297.

346 'I wish your mother were here'. Sarah Churchill, *Keep on Dancing*, p. 78.

347 A dozen oysters, two good helpings of roast beef. Brendon, p. 202.
'Cannot edge him aside'. Nicolson, vol. III, p. 63.
'Gloomy, grouchy, sullen'. *Ibid.* vol. III, p. 79.

348 'I'll tear their bleeding entrails out.' Moran, p. 313.
'Finished finally and legally with Vic'. Sarah Churchill, *Keep on Dancing*, p. 95.

349 'Perfect for the part of the unhappy Elena'. Mario Soldati to the author.
'Only happy talking about old times'. Colville, *The Fringes of Power*, p. 773.
'Britishly drunk all the time'. Amory, *The Letters of Evelyn Waugh*, p. 248.

350 'I should use THE NAME'. Alastair Forbes to the author.
'At least Randolph'. Anita Leslie, *Cousin Randolph*, p. 118.
'Dear Randolph'. Roberts, p. 294.
'Insipid and rather silly'. Pamela Harriman to the Author.

351 'To keep Sarah company'. Soames, *Clementine Churchill*, p. 414.

352 'I was painfully affected'. CB, vol. VIII, p. 267.
'The great thing about Christopher'. Julian Amery to the author.

354 'When my father began the death agony'. John S. Churchill, p. 180.
'Do you think we shall be allowed to sleep?' CB, vol. VIII, p. 317.
Her father was complaining of recurrent nightmares. Peregrine Churchill to the author.
'That's pretty good writing you know'. John S. Churchill, p. 181.

355 'Just as I had seen him in his prime'. CB, vol. VIII, p. 308.

358 'Her talents as an actress'. Mario Soldati to the author.
'We have a deep animal love for one another'. CB, vol. VIII, p. 308.
'Without malice or intrigue'. Colville, *The Churchillians*, p. 28.

359 'What's this I . . . '. Private source to the author.
'Fond as I was of Randolph'. Laura, Duchess of Marlborough, to the author.

360 'A domestic and home-loving character'. Amory, *The Letters of Evelyn Waugh*, p. 285.
'You can't seriously think of going through with it'. Laura, Duchess of Marlborough to the author.

31. 'The Secret Battle': 1950–5

362 'Very, very old, tragically old'. Nicolson, vol. III, p. 212.
'The tired look of a trawler captain'. Rhodes James, *Eden*, p. 345.

363 'You and I derive great pleasure'. Boyle, p. 313.

363   'Go!' he shouted at Miss Hamblin. 'Go!' Grace Hamblin to
      the author.
364   George VI had been kept in ignorance. Bradford, p. 456.
      'Set his heart on seeing the young Queen crowned'. Moran, p. 374.
365   'Felt avuncular towards his orphaned niece'. Colville, *The
      Fringes of Power*, p. 653.
      'What business is it of'. Anita Leslie, *Cousin Randolph*, p. 121.
366   'Snubbed by the person one loves most in the world'. CB,
      vol. VIII, p. 766.
367   'If you think that by insulting him'. CB, vol. VIII, p. 451.
368   'Like disarming a butterfly'. Laura, Duchess of Marlborough,
      to the author.
      'Psychological troubles and their explanation quite beyond his
      ken'. Soames, *Clementine Churchill*, p. 443.
      'He doesn't think the Old Man will ever go'. Shuckburgh, p. 74.
369   The surgeon's knife slipped, partially severing the bile-duct.
      Rhodes James, *Anthony Eden*, p. 362.
370   Genuinely believed that Churchill was in love with her. Colville,
      The Churchillians, p. 121.
      'Wife and mother'. CB, vol. VIII, p. 700.
      'Why the BBC should have a better view of my monarch
      being crowned than me'. Pearson, *The Ultimate Family*, p. 72.
      'Boy, tell your mother to get your hair cut'. Winston S.
      Churchill Jr, p. 76.
371   'That great old relic, Winston Churchill'. Buckle, p. 256.
      'Darling, wow!' Sarah Churchill, p. 147.
      'I am a hulk'. Moran, p. 415.
372   'There are moments'. *Ibid*. p. 426.
      He gave Colville 'strict orders'. Colville, *The Fringes of
      Power*, p. 669.
      'Pacing the lawn in earnest conversation'. *Ibid*. p. 669.
373   'The place in Churchill's heart so long reserved for Randolph'.
      Ibid. p. 669.
374   'This decaying carcass'. Graebner, p. 18.
      'Circumstances'. *Ibid*. p. 433.
375   'Safety will be the sturdy shield of terror'. *Hansard*. 1 March
      1955.
      'More time was given'. Colville, *Fringes of Power*, p. 704.
      The 'cold hatred' he began to feel for Eden. Colville, *The
      Fringes of Power*, p. 706.
      'Insisted on pursuing Clarissa with a derogatory article on
      Anthony Eden'. *Ibid*. p. 708.
376   'Might ruin little Winston'. *Ibid*. p. 709.
      'I feel that yr Majesty is right'. CB, vol. VIII, p. 1128.

32. Pausaland

377   A place of secret refuge and delight. Charles-Roux, p. 63.
      'I feel like an aeroplane'. Brendon, p. 220.
      'He no longer finds'. Moran, p. 688.
      'Waiting about for death'. *Ibid*. p. 688.

378   Nine Renoirs, four Cézannes, three Degases, and his mistress.
      Evans, p. 156.

379   'He had seemed twenty years younger'. Moran, p. 693.
      Purchasing his own abode in the S of France. CB, vol.
      VIII, p. 1215.
      'The charm and seclusion of "private life" in private houses'.
      Soames, *Clementine Churchill*, p. 460.
      'I'd have a message though'. Wendy Reves to the author.
      'The sun is Churchill's'. Boyle, p. 289.
      'He was so soft, so very sweet'. Wendy Reves to the author.

380   'Very little' in common with her hosts. Soames, *Clementine
      Churchill*, p. 462.
      'Clemmie was astonished'. CB, vol. VIII.
      'Clementine thought her husband's least admirable characteristic'.
      Colville, *The Churchillians*, p. 215.

381   'Absolutely obsessed with a senile passion for Wendy Russell'.
      Payn and Morley, p. 323.

382   Churchill looked 'like a very healthy baby'. Buckle, p. 285.
      'Poor dear Brendan'. CB, vol. VIII, p. 1274.

383   'I still like work'. Rowse, *Memories of Men and Women*, p. 6.
      'Woke him, brought him his breakfast'. Graebner, p. 39.

384   'Mr Sutherland is a wow!' Soames, *Clementine Churchill*, p. 445.

385   'This remarkable example'. *Ibid*. p. 446.
      'I'd kick him up the arse'. Brendon, p. 220.
      'Quite ruined' his birthday. Soames, *Clementine Churchill*, p. 446.
      'Filthy,' he spluttered to Lord Moran. Moran, p. 620.
      'These modern chaps. You're in their power'. Buckle, p. 288.

386   One long heroic epic. Brendon, p. 222.

387   'A gruesome evening at Chartwell'. Davie, p. 732.

388   'Look here, my girl, you'd better go home and have a shave'.
      Anita Leslie, *Cousin Randolph*, p. 126.
      'All he really needed was a spot of genuine success'. Mrs
      Averell Harriman to the author.

389   'Always drank treble whiskies'. Alan Brien to the author.
      'Carrying on a feud against the world'. Buckle, p. 288.
      'Winston was the only person Randolph truly loved'. Laura,
      Duchess of Marlborough to the author.

390   Making Randolph 'Marquess of Toodle-do'. Moran, p. 376.

391 Jane Doe was arrested for drunken and abusive behaviour. *The Times*, 12 January 1958.

392 'Never discuss matters affecting members of the family with total strangers'. *Time* magazine, 28 January 1958.
'Alcohol'. Sarah Churchill, *Keep on Dancing*, p. 169.
'No one with Jerome blood should ever touch spirits'. Anita Leslie, *Cousin Clare*, p. 91.

393 'She absolutely *loved* to be photographed'. Mrs Al Parker to the author.
'Petrified before his greatness'. Mrs David Birkin to the author.

394 'Sober, she was a golden girl'. Ellen Pollock to the author.
'Love, love, love. Don't bite'. CB, vol. VIII, p. 1233.
'Treated her very roughly at Liverpool'. CB, vol. VIII, p. 1286.
'She never really recovered'. Celia Perkins to the author.

395 'Diana was completely'. Nuala Allason to the author.
'Diana lacked robustness'. Lady Diana Mosley, p. 239.

396 'I do not know what I should have'. Winston Churchill Jr, p. 90.
'The courage to start it in the first place'. Winston Churchill Jr, p. 90.
Politics 'a beastly profession'. Rhodes James, *Anthony Eden*, p. 600.
'Greatest source of ill luck had been Winston Churchill'. *Ibid*. p. 621.
'Plays bridge with'. Private source to the author.

397 'Young people round him'. Emma Soames to the author.
'Arabella will not come out'. Anita Leslie, *Cousin Randolph*, p. 180.
'I grew up to adore'. Arabella Churchill to the author.

398 'I still honestly believe'. Winston Churchill to the author.
'One of the stupidest'. *Daily Mail*, 11 March 1972.
'Bloody thing'. Michael Tree to the author.

399 'You stupid woman'. Michael Tree to the author.
'Anything for me, Bert?' Laura, Duchess of Marlborough, to the author.
To go out with him. *Ibid*.

401 Clementine 'all billowing gown and broadened out with age'. Rowse, *Memories of Men and Women*, p. 22.

33. The Dark Angel Beckons

402 'To die in the sunlight'. WSC, *The River War*.
'Throw in the corpse as well'. CB, vol. VIII, p. 256.
'A comfort to know'. Moran, p. 733.

402 'He was very old and frail'. *Ibid*. p. 739.
403 'How d'you think Winston is?' *Ibid*. p. 739.
     'A funeral paid for by the State'. Winston Churchill Jr, p. 183.
404 Take the bier upstream by barge. Private source.
     'Operation Hope Not'. CB, vol. VIII, p. 1347.
     'It was never like this in the past'. Moran, p. 762.
406 It was an uncomfortable evening. Evans, p. 156.
     'He made a good impression on me'. CB, vol. VIII, p. 1174.
     'Oh, my dear, dear friend'. Evans, p. 158.
408 Onassis required acceptance. Nigel Neilson to the author.
409 'Dear Sir Winston'. CB, vol. VIII, p. 1315.
     'The months I spent at your charming house'. *Ibid*. p. 1315.
410 'I was in love with Randolph'. Mrs Natalie Barclay to the author.
     'Frankly, I was delighted to see the old boy so happy'. Laura,
     Duchess of Marlborough to the author.
411 'What can you do with a woman who pronounces "menu"
     as "may-nyew"?' Alan Brien to the author.
     'You're not *writing* anything?' Grace Hamblin to the author.
412 'He's asked me at last!' Anita Leslie, *Cousin Randolph*, p. 150.
     'Dearest Papa'. CB, vol. VIII, p. 1313.
     Rumoured to spend $10,000 annually on flowers. *Vanity Fair*,
     July 1988.
413 They all have bad teeth'. Brooke Hayward, *Haywire* (Knopf,
     1977).
     'With that round face'. Laura, Duchess of Marlborough, to the
     author.
414 'You did not drive yourself, did you?' Winston S. Churchill
     Jr, p. 183.
415 'Take this for being a shit'. *Ibid*. p. 80.
     'Carry the name Churchill with honour into the future'.
     Ibid. p. 175.
     'Your bloody library's not a library'. Laura, Duchess of
     Marlborough, to the author.
416 'So, Ari, we are related at last'. CB, vol. VIII, p. 1339.
417 'Nervous fatigue, depression, and anxiety state'. Soames,
     Clementine Churchill, p. 480.
     '*Was* there an incident last night?' Ellen Pollock to the author.
418 'Well, *that* puts the Marlboroughs in their place'. Sarah Churchill,
     Keep on Dancing, p. 194.
     'We stared silently at each other'. *Ibid*. p. 204.
     'She was not prepared to become a mother to her husband'.
     Anthony Montague Browne to the author.
419 'Room for two of a good thing'. *Daily Express*, 18 April 1962.
     Verdict of suicide. *Daily Telegraph*, 25 October 1963.

419 'As he grew older'. Soames, *Clementine Churchill*, p. 481.

420 'Doctor, I pay you'. Roberts, p. 353.
'Just put them in a bucket for me, Nurse'. Lord Lambton to the author.
'The only part of Randolph that was not malignant'. Davie, p. 792.

421 'Trying to act as if nothing untoward had happened'. Natalie Barclay to the author.
'The Dark Angel beckons'. Laura, Duchess of Marlborough, to the author.
'My life is over but it is not yet ended'. CB, vol. VIII, p. 1317.
'Everything that he had done had ended in disaster'. Montague Browne to the author.
'I ought not, I must not, be held to account'. Moran, p. 753.

422 'Curious to imagine'. CB, vol. VIII, p. 1269.
'A great deal to achieve nothing in the end'. Sarah Churchill, *A Thread in the Tapestry*, p. 17.
'I'm so bored'. Soames, *Clementine Churchill*, p. 489.

423 'In the midst of death'. *Ibid*. p. 492.
'It is the day that I shall die'. Colville, *The Churchillians*, p. 19.
'Overwhelmed by the beauty'. Emma Soames to the author.
'Television's multiple insect eye'. Maurice Wiggin, *Sunday Times*, 3 February 1965.

34. Aftermath

425 'Old and grey like a haggard hawk'. Buckle, p. 387.

427 She and Mary laid a wreath together. Soames, *Clementine Churchill*, p. 524.
'I don't mind going'. Idris Evans to the author.
'She firmly slapped us children down'. Emma Soames to the author.

428 'Fondly loving him'. *The Times*, 17 September 1987.

432 'Randolph would have turned incandescent'. Laura, Duchess of Marlborough, to the author.

434 His step-sister, Christina Onassis. Dempster, p. 131.
A policeman was assaulted. *Evening Standard*, 6 November 1986.

Select Bibliography

The literature on Winston Churchill forms an ever-expanding universe of its own, and it would be impossible to list all the sources I have relied on for this book. The following bibliography however may be useful for further reading, and includes full details of all the works mentioned in the chapter notes.

Amory, M. (ed.). *The Letters of Ann Fleming* (Collins, 1985)
    The Letters of Evelyn Waugh (Weidenfeld, 1980)
Asquith, Lady Cynthia. *Diaries 1915–1918* (Hutchinson, 1968)
Ashley, Maurice. *Churchill as Historian* (1966)
Atkins, J. B. *Incidents and Reflections* (Unwin, 1921)
Balsan, Consuelo Vanderbilt. *The Glitter and the Gold* (Harper, 1952)
Beaverbrook, Lord. *Politicians and the War* (Oldbourne, 1959)
    Men and Power (Hutchinson, 1956)
Birkenhead, Earl of. *Churchill 1874–1922* (Harrap, 1990)
    The Prof in Two Worlds (Collins, 1964)
Blakiston, Georgiana. (ed.). *The Letters of Conrad Russell* (John Murray, 1987)
Bonham-Carter, Lady Violet. *Winston Churchill As I Knew Him* (Collins, 1965)
Boyle, Andrew. *Poor Dear Brendan* (Hutchinson, 1974)
Bradford, Sarah. *George VI* (Weidenfeld, 1989)
Brendon, Piers. *Winston Churchill, A Brief Life* (Secker, 1984)
Brock, M. and E. (eds.). *H. H. Asquith: Letters to Venetia Stanley* (Oxford University Press, 1982)
Bruce Lockhart, Sir Robert. *Diaries* (Macmillan, 1973)
Buckle, R. (ed.). *Cecil Beaton: Selected Diaries* (Weidenfeld, 1979)
Charles-Roux, Edmond. *Chanel* (Cape, 1976)
Churchill, John S. *Crowded Canvas* (Odhams, 1961)
Churchill, Peregrine and Julian Mitchell. *Jennie, Lady Churchill. A Portrait with Letters* (Collins, 1974)
Churchill, Lady Randolph. *Reminiscences* (Arnold, 1908)

Churchill, Randolph S. *Twenty-one Years* (Weidenfeld, 1964)
  Winston S. Churchill vols. I and II (Heinemann, 1966, 1967)
Churchill, Sarah. *A Thread in the Tapestry* (Deutsch, 1967)
  Keep on Dancing (Weidenfeld, 1981)
Churchill, Winston S. *Savrola* (Longmans, 1900)
  Lord Randolph Churchill (Macmillan, 1906)
  The World Crisis and the Aftermath (Butterworth, 1923–31)
  My Early Life (Butterworth, 1930)
  Thoughts and Adventures (Butterworth, 1932)
  Marlborough: His Life and Times (Harrap, 1938)
  Great Contemporaries (Butterworth, 1939)
  Painting as a Pastime (Odhams, 1948)
  The Second World War (Cassell, 1948–52)
Churchill, Winston S., Jr. *Memories and Adventures* (Weidenfeld, 1989)
Colville, John. *The Churchillians* (Weidenfeld, 1981)
  The Fringes of Power (Hodder, 1985)
Cooper, Lady Diana. *The Light of Common Day* (Hart-Davies, 1959)
  Trumpets from the Steep (Hart-Davies, 1960)
Cowles, Virginia. *Winston Churchill, the Era and the Man* (Hamish
  Hamilton, 1953)
Davie, M. (ed.). *The Diaries of Evelyn Waugh* (Weidenfeld, 1976)
Dempster, Nigel. *Christina* (Weidenfeld, 1989)
Drogheda, Lord. *Double Harness* (Weidenfeld, 1986)
Edel, Leon. *Life of Henry James* (1962)
Esher, Lord. *Journals and Letters* (Nicholson and Watson, 1934)
Evans, Peter. *Ari: The Life and Times of Onassis* (Cape, 1986)
Fielding, Daphne. *Mercury Rising* (Hamish Hamilton, 1982)
Forbes-Robertson, Diana. *Maxine* (Hamish Hamilton, 1964)
Foster, R. F. *Lord Randolph Churchill. A Political Life* (Oxford, 1981)
Gardiner, A. G. *Prophets, Priests and Kings* (Dent, 1908)
Gilbert, Martin. *Winston S. Churchill* vols. III–VIII (Heinemann,
  1971–88)
  Winston S. Churchill: Companion, 1914–1939 (Heinemann, 1982)
  Winston Churchill. The Wilderness Years (Macmillan 1981)
Graebner, Walter. *My Dear Mr. Churchill* (Collins, 1972)
Green, David. *The Churchills of Blenheim* (Constable, 1984)
Green, Martin. *Children of the Sun* (Deutsch, 1978)
Hanfstaengl, P. *Hitler, the Missing Years* (Collins, 1957)
Harling, James. *Cochran* (W. H. Allen, 1982)
Harriman, W. Averell and Elie Abel. *Special Envoy* (Random House,
  1972)
Harris, Frank. *My Life and Loves* (Richards, 1947)
Harrod, Roy. *The Prof: A Personal Memoir of Lord Cherwell*
  (Macmillan, 1959)
       —

Haslip, Joan. *The Lonely Empress* (Weidenfeld, 1968)

Hassall, Christopher. *Sir Edward Marsh* (Longmans, 1959)

Ingram, Kevin. *Rebel: A Short Life of Esmond Romilly* (Weidenfeld, 1985)

Irving, David. *Churchill's War* (Veritas, 1987)

Isaacson, W. and E. Thomas. *The Wise Men* (Simon & Schuster, 1986)

Keynes, J. M. *The Economic Consequences of Mr Churchill* (Hogarth, 1926)

    Essays and Sketches in Biography (Hart Davies, 1951)

Lees-Milne, J. *Harold Nicolson* (Chatto, 1980)

Leslie, Anita. *The Fabulous Leonard Jerome* (Hutchinson, 1954)

    The Gilt on the Gingerbread (Hutchinson, 1960)

    Cousin Clare (Hutchinson, 1968)

    Jennie (Hutchinson, 1968)

    Edwardians in Love (Hutchinson, 1972)

    Cousin Randolph (Hutchinson, 1985)

Leslie, Seymour. *The Jerome Connection* (Hutchinson, 1964)

Longford, Elizabeth. *A Pilgrimage of Passion. The Life of Wilfred Scawen-Blunt* (Weidenfeld, 1979)

Macaulay, Lord. *The History of England* (Longmans, 1889)

Martin, Ralph. *Lady Randolph Churchill* vols. I and II (Cassell, 1969)

Masterman, Lucy. *C. F. G. Masterman* (Nicolson and Watson, 1939)

Meinertzhagen, Col. R. *Diary of a Black Sheep* (Oliver and Boyd, 1964)

Montgomery Hyde, H. *The Londonderrys: A Family Portrait* (Hamish Hamilton, 1979)

Montgomery-Massingberd, Hugh. *Blenheim Revisited* (Bodley Head, 1985)

Moran, Lord. *Winston Churchill: The Struggle for Survival* (Constable, 1966)

Morgan, Ted. *Churchill: Young Man in a Hurry* (Simon and Schuster, 1982)

Mosley, Diana. *A Life of Contrasts* (Hamish Hamilton, 1977)

Mosley, Leonard. *Castlerosse* (Hodder, 1968)

Mosley, Nicholas. *Beyond the Pale* (Secker, 1983)

Mosley, Sir Oswald. *My Life* (Nelson, 1968)

Nel, Elizabeth. *Mr Churchill's Secretary* (Hodder, 1958)

Nicolson, Nigel (ed.). *Harold Nicolson, Diaries and Letters 1930–1962*, 3 vols (Collins, 1966–68)

Oliver, Vic. *Mr Showbusiness* (Harrap, 1954)

Payn, Graham and Sheridan Morley (eds.). *The Noël Coward Diaries* (Weidenfeld, 1982)

Pearson, John. *Façades* (Macmillan, 1978)

    The Ultimate Family (Michael Joseph, 1986)

Pimlott, Ben (ed.). *The Hugh Dalton Diaries* (Cape, 1986)

Prior, Robin. *Churchill's World Crisis as History* (Croome Helm, 1985)

Pryce-Jones, David. *Unity Mitford: A Quest* (Weidenfeld, 1976)

Rhodes James, Robert. *Chips: The Diaries of Sir Henry Channon* (Weidenfeld, 1967)
  Churchill: A Study in Failure (World Publishing, 1970)
  Anthony Eden (Weidenfeld, 1986)

Riddell, Lord. *Intimate Journal of the Peace Conference and After* (Gollancz, 1933)

Roberts, Brian. *Randolph* (Hamish Hamilton, 1984)

Roosevelt, Elliott. *As He Saw It* (Duell Sloane and Pearce, 1946)

Rosebery, Lord. *Lord Randolph Churchill* (Humphreys, 1906)

Rowse, A. L. *The Early Churchills* (Macmillan, 1956)
  The Later Churchills (Macmillan, 1958)
  Memories of Men and Women (Eyre Methuen, 1980)

Sassoon, Siegfried. *Siegfried's Journey* (Faber, 1946)

Scawen-Blunt, Wilfred. *My Diaries,* (Secker, 1965)

Searle, G. R. *Corruption in British Politics* (Oxford, 1989)

Sermoneta, Duchess of. *Sparkle Distant Worlds* (Macmillan, 1926).

Sheridan, Clare. *To the Four Winds* (Deutsch, 1957)

Shuckburgh, Evelyn. *Descent to Suez* (Weidenfeld, 1986)

Sitwell, Sacheverell. *Great Houses of Europe* (Weidenfeld, 1961)

Skidelsky, Robert. *Oswald Mosley* (Macmillan, 1975)

Smith, Lady Eleanor. *Life's a Circus* (Collins, 1962)

Soames, Mary. *Clementine Churchill* (Cassell, 1979)
  A Churchill Family Album (Penguin, 1982)

Stevenson, F. *Lloyd George: A Diary* (Hutchinson, 1971)

Storr, Anthony. *Churchill's Black Dog* (Collins, 1989)

Styron, William. *Darkness Visible: A Memoir of Madness* (Random House, 1990)

Taylor, A. J. P. *English History 1914–45* (Oxford, 1965)

Thompson, R. W. *Morton and Churchill* (Hodder and Stoughton, 1976)

Tilden, Philip. *True Remembrances of an Architect* (Country Life, 1954)

Trevelyan, G. M. *Garibaldi's Defence of the Roman Republic* (Longman's, 1908)

Vanderbilt, Arthur. *Fortune's Children* (Michael Joseph, 1989)

Vickers, Hugo. *Gladys, Duchess of Marlborough* (Hamish Hamilton, 1979)
  Cecil Beaton (Weidenfeld, 1985)

Warwick, Frances, Lady. *Life's Ebb and Flow* (Collins, 1920)

Webb, Beatrice. *Our Partnership* (Secker, 1938)

Windsor, Duke of. *A King's Story* (Collins, 1962)

Wilson, K. (ed.). *The Rasp of War: The Letters of H. A. Gwynne of the* Morning Post (Sidgwick & Jackson, 1988)

Young, Kenneth. *Churchill and Beaverbrook* (Eyre, 1966)

Index

Abercorn, James Hamilton, 1st Duke of, 18

Abingdon, Montagu Arthur Bertie, 7th Earl of, 109

Adenauer, Konrad, 381

Agnelli, Avvocato Gianni, 359, 398, 412

Airlie, David Graham Drummond Ogilvy, 7th Earl of, 45, 113, 114, 116

Aitken, Max (the younger), 1

Albert Edward, Prince of Wales see Edward VII

Alexander III, Tsar, 19, 60

Alexander, General Harold Rupert Leofric George (later Field-Marshal), 322, 324, 326, 330, 345, 363

Allason, Nuala, 395

Althorp, Earls of, 13

Aly Khan, 351

Amery, Julian, 352, 387

Amery, Leo, 52, 278

Anne, Queen, 9–10, 228, 230

Ashley, Maurice, 229–32, 234

Ashton, Frederick, 260

Asquith family, 157, 178, 209

Asquith, Cynthia, 145, 165

Asquith, Herbert: appoints Winston to Admiralty, 128; collapse of government, 151; Dardanelles disaster, 144; *Enchantress* trip, 133; opinion of Winston, 111, 139, 199; Prime Minister, 111–12, 137, 343; relationship with Clementine, 121, 123, 145, 150, 178, 209; war declared, 136; Winston's maiden speech, 96; Winston's military ambitions, 138–9, 149; Winston's opinion of, 151

Asquith, Margot, 133, 140, 149, 150

Asquith, Violet see Carter, Lady Violet Bonham

Astor, Nancy, Lady, 267

Atkins, J.B., 91–92, 102

Attlee, Clement, 329, 342–4, 347, 361, 363, 424

Audley, Henry Touchet, 23rd Baron, 417–18

Aylesford, Edith, Lady, 29–30

Aylesford, Heneage Finch ('Sporting Joe'), Earl of, 29

Bailey, Sir Abe, 227

Bailey, John Milner, 227, 241

Baldwin, Oliver, 2

Baldwin, Stanley: abdication issue, 268–9, 270; Indian policy, 221, 233, 236; National Government, 2, 216; opinion of Winston, 153, 200, 201; Prime Minister, 197; relationship with Winston, 2, 5, 197–8, 201, 236, 259, 261; successor, 198, 273, 369

Balfour, Arthur, 34, 96, 103–4, 195

Balsan, Jacques, 202–3, 237, 307

Baring family, 115

Baring, Maurice, 44

Barnes, Miss (actress), 165

Barrymore, Ethel, 106

Baruch, Bernard, 156, 218, 267

Battenburg, Admiral Prince Louis Alexander of, 132, 140, 290

Beaton, Cecil: description of Clementine, 284–6, 309, 334; descriptions of Winston, 371, 381–2, 385; *Follow the Sun* costumes, 260; on Randolph, 389, 425–6; photographs of Clementine, 284, 287

Beauchamp, Anthony, 366–7, 392–3, 394, 426

Beaufort, Henry Adelbert Wellington Fitzroy Somerset, 15th Duke of, 122

Beaverbrook, William Maxwell Aitken, 1st Baron: at Chartwell, 213; Clementine's opinion of, 179, 324, 325; descriptions of Winston, 4, 107, 148, 151–2, 169, 346; Express articles, 226, 368; general election (1945), 343; Harriman, 300–1; on Hitler's death, 341; on naval budget, 134; opinion of Clementine, 148; portrait, 384; Randolph's coming-of-age party, 1; relationship with Winston, 206, 324, 325, 329, 363,

377–8, 409; support for Randolph (and son), 3, 256, 299, 308, 310, 324, 382; Winston's illness, 372

Beecham, Sir Thomas, 223

Beerbohm, Max, 96

Belloc, Hilaire, 148, 231

Belmont, August, 22, 23

Belmont, Oliver P., 80

Benn, David Wedgwood, 291

Benn, Tony, 292

Benn, William Wedgwood, 291–2

Bennett, Arnold, 236

Berenson, Bernard, 165

Beresford, Admiral Lord Charles, 56

Berlin, Isaiah, 364

Bernhardt, Sarah, 381

Berry, Michael (*later* Lord Hartfield), 388

Berry, Lady Pamela, 387–8

Berry, Seymour, 1

Bertie, Lady Gwendeline ('Goonie') *see* Churchill, Lady Gwendeline

Bevan, Aneurin, 308

Bevan, Natalie, 410–11, 412, 420–1, 426

Bevan, Robert, 410

Birkenhead, Frederick Edwin Smith, 1st Earl of: affair with Clare Sheridan, 171–2, 175; Blenheim Christmas, 161–2; at Chartwell, 213; daughter, 388; death, 237; friendship with Sunny, 148, 163; friendship with Winston, 127, 129, 162, 170, 195, 204, 237; Irish Treaty, 177; 'The Other Club', 127, 162; Randolph's coming-of-age party, 3; relationship with Clementine, 179

Birkenhead, Frederick Winston Furneaux (Freddie), 2nd Earl of, 3, 151, 207, 340

Blood, General Sir Bindon, 72–3

Boothby, Robert, 1, 223, 362

Bowra, Maurice, 364

Bracken, Brendan: death, 382; friendship with Winston, 204, 213, 292, 331, 363; opinion of Pamela, 300–1, 310; opinion of Sandys, 337; paternity rumours, 223, 254; relationship with Randolph, 213, 223; Winston's illness, 372, 379

Braun, Eva, 246

Brendon, Piers, 386

Breteuil, duc de, 77

Bretherton, Pauline, 338, 339

Bridgeman, Admiral Sir Francis, 132

Brien, Alan, 389, 412

Brooke, General Sir Alan, 329 332

Bruckner, Wilhelm, 247

Buller, Sir Redvers, 91

Butler, R.A., 347, 363, 373, 377, 387

Buzzard, Dr Thomas, 41–2, 58–61

Cadogan, Henry Arthur, Viscount Chelsea, 238

Callas, Maria, 407

Cambridge, George William Frederick Charles, 2nd Duke of, 58, 60, 63

Campbell, Lady Colin, 55

Campbell, Judy, 393

Campbell, Mrs Patrick, 133

Campbell-Bannerman, Sir Henry, 104, 108, 111

Camrose, William Ewert Berry, 1st Baron, 1, 206, 372

Canfield, Michael, 359, 388, 410, 432

Caracciolo di Castagneto, Princess Marella, 398

Carden, Admiral Sackville Hamilton, 143

Carter, Lady Violet Bonham (*née* Asquith): *Enchantress* holiday, 132–4, 141; on Winston's family feelings, 5; on Winston's attitude to Dardanelles, 141, 144; on Winston's attitude to life, 152; on Winston's attitude to women, 108; on Winston's Russian policy, 169; present for Winston, 148; relationship with Winston, 5, 129

Cartland, Barbara, 228

Cassel, Sir Ernest, 34, 84, 134, 156, 180, 187, 406

Castlemain, Countess of, 9

Castlereagh, Charles Stewart, Viscount, 15

Castlerosse, Doris, Lady, 223, 224, 234, 235

Castlerosse, Viscount, 224

Cecil family, 103

Cecil, Lord David, 364

Cecil, Lord Hugh, 101, 116, 354

Chamberlain, Austin, 177

Chamberlain, Joseph, 91, 96, 104

Chamberlain, Neville, 198, 273, 274–6, 278, 308, 369

Chamberlain, Stewart Houston, 245

Chanel, Coco, 377

Channon, Henry ('Chips'), 165, 223, 251

Chaplin, Charlie, 175, 213

Charles I, King, 9

Charles II, King, 9

Charles, Prince of Wales, 428

Charles, Prince Regent of Belgium, 351–2

Charteris, Laura (*later* Lady Long, *then* Countess of Dudley, *then* Mrs Michael Canfield, *then* Duchess of Marlborough): affair with 'Bert', 399; description of Mary, 336; marriages, 272, 320, 359, 388, 432–3; memory of Winston, 421; on Randolph, 389;

relationship with Randolph, 272–3, 276, 320, 359–60, 368, 388, 410–11, 432–3

Cherwell *see* Lindemann

Churchill, Albertha ('Goosey'), Duchess of Marlborough (*but known as* Lady Blandford), 18, 29, 50, 55, 161

Churchill, Lady Alexandra Spencer, 433

Churchill, Lady Anne Spencer, 16, 28

Churchill, Arabella Spencer, 360–1, 366, 387, 397, 412, 430

Churchill, Lord Charles Spencer, 295

Churchill, Charles Richard John Spencer ('Sunny'), 9th Duke of Marlborough: achievements, 432; attitude to Blenheim, 12, 56–7, 76–7, 82, 163–6, 203, 231–2; biography of Marlborough, 228, 231; birth, 18; childhood, 50–1; Christmas (1918), 159, 162; death, 237; Diana's wedding, 227; Jennie's second marriage, 97; Lord Lieutenancy, 147–8; marriage, 77–82, 147, 161, 163–5, 202, 399; mistress, 106, 165; politics, 123; relationship with Clementine, 123, 160; relationship with stepmother, 55; relationship with Winston, 7, 56–7, 116, 123, 147–8; reputation, 147; second marriage, 202–3, 211, 232; South African war, 94; temperament, 7, 51, 76, 147, 202, 231–2

Churchill, Clarissa Spencer *see* Eden

Churchill, Clementine (*née* Hozier): abdication issue, 268; appearance, 112–13, 215, 234, 284, 287, 294, 401, 425; attitude to Mosleys, 290–1; background, 113–115, 117–18; Blenheim battlefield, 223; Blenheim christening, 294; Blenheim party, 401; charity work, 323; Chartwell, 187–90, 193, 196, 203, 210–13, 215, 250–1, 383; concern for Winston's health, 328, 329, 334, 404; death, 425; death of brother, 181–2; death of daughter, 183–4; death of Winston, 422; depression, 418; Diana Mitford lunch, 249; disagreement with Sunny, 123, 160; dislike of La Pausa, 380–1, 409; divorce plans, 271; 'drink gene' anxiety, 392; Dundee election, 190–1; finances, 129–30, 156, 187, 206, 234; French Riviera, 234–5; friendship with Winant, 299, 339, 358; general election (1945), 345; health, 114, 130, 178–81, 377, 385, 418-19; holiday with Mary and Clarissa, 262; last years, 425; love affair, 252–3, 256; Marrakesh visit,

325; marriage, 115–17, 129–30; meets Winston, 112-113; motherhood, 120–1, 130, 158, 178, 183–5, 194–5, 207–8, 286; nervous breakdowns, 114, 178–81, 334; Onassis visits, 408; opinion of Beaverbrook, 324, 325; political views, 121, 123, 191, 209–10; Quebec conferences, 323, 334; relationship with daughters, 207–8, 226, 262, 286, 324, 335, 336–7, 345, 351, 357, 367–8, 418–19; relationship with Jennie, 118, 119; relationship with Pamela, 311, 387; relationship with Roosevelt, 323, 331; relationship with son, 5, 158, 207, 213, 277, 292, 312, 324, 334–5, 327, 387, 411; relationship with Winston, 5–6, 119-21, 124, 129–30, 145, 148–51, 178–81, 190-1, 200, 208–11, 217, 241–2, 250–3, 284–7, 309–310, 323, 325, 328, 334–5, 341, 345, 353, 380–1, 383–4, 418; *Rosaura* cruise, 251–3, 256; Sally's passport, 291; Sarah–Vic Oliver affair, 263–5, 267, 271; Sutherland portrait, 384–7; temperament, 6, 114, 121, 208–9, 284–7, 334, 383–4; wartime food, 282; war work, 148, 157, 287, 323; Winston's funeral, 424; Winston's retirement, 362, 371, 374; withdrawal from family, 241–2

Churchill, Consuelo, Duchess of Marlborough (*née* Vanderbilt, *later* Mme Jacques Balsan): attitude to Blenheim, 400; background, 78–80; Churchills' visit, 203, 208; Gladys Deacon friendship, 106, 165; granddaughter's coming-out, 272, 273; marriage, 80–2, 163–6, 202; old age, 399–400; second marriage, 202, 237; separation, 147, 161, 164; Vanderbilt fortune, 399–400, 433; Winston's visits, 307, 347; Winston's wedding, 116

Churchill, Lady Cornelia Spencer (*later* Lady Wimborne), 16, 28, 161

Churchill, Diana (*first* Mrs John Milner Bailey, *then* Mrs Duncan Sandys): appearance, 6, 120, 226, 337, 394–5; attitude to Mosleys, 290, 291; birth, 120; 'Blenheim' suggestion, 328; Chequers Christmas, 296; childhood, 130, 155–8, 179–80, 181, 190, 194, 214; children, 274–5, 324; divorces, 241, 256, 418–19; husband's accident, 302; London season, 226; marriage, 237–8; nervous breakdowns, 124, 367–8, 373, 395; RADA, 226;

relationship with Duncan Sandys, 324, 336–7, 367–8, 418–19; relationship with father, 124, 145, 226, 345, 395, 421, 422; relationship with mother, 207–8, 226, 263, 324, 336–7, 345, 367–8; relationship with Sarah, 394, 418; religion, 395, 418; school, 179; screen test, 226–7; second marriage, 257; suicide, xv, 419; temperament, 6, 130, 158, 181, 214, 226, 394–5, 418; visits Esmond, 255; visits to La Pausa, 378, 380; WRNS, 274–5, 296, 302

Churchill, Lord Edward Spencer, 433

Churchill, Elizabeth, Lady Ivor, 400

Churchill, Lady Fanny Spencer, 16, 28

Churchill, Frances (Fanny), Duchess of: Irish famine relief fund, 31; leaves Blenheim, 50; marriage, 15; Randolph's illness, 41, 43, 58–9, 63; relationship with Consuelo, 81; relationship with Jennie, 27, 28, 43; relationship with Winston, 51, 53, 81–2, 83

Churchill, George Spencer, 4th Duke of Marlborough, 13–14

Churchill, George Spencer, 5th Duke of Marlborough, 14

Churchill, George Spencer, 6th Duke of Marlborough, 14–15

Churchill, George Charles Spencer (Marquess of Blandford, *later* 'the bad Duke'), 8th Duke of Marlborough, 16–18, 29–30, 50–1, 54–6

Churchill, Lady Georgiana Spencer, 16, 28

Churchill, Gladys, Duchess of Marlborough (*née* Deacon), 106, 165, 202–3, 211, 232, 237

Churchill, Guy Spencer, 30, 55

Churchill, Lady Gwendeline ('Goonie' *née* Bertie): Chartwell Christmas, 212; daughter, 262, 364; death, 353; description of Winston, 281; marriage, 115, 116; opinion of Vic Oliver, 296; relationship with Clementine, 178, 188, 271; relationship with Jack, 109–12; relationship with Winston, 109–12; social life, 157; style, 215; temperament, 109, 121; wartime, 136, 146

Churchill, Henrietta, Duchess of Marlborough, 13

Churchill, Lady Henrietta Spencer, 401

Churchill, Lord Ivor, 82, 159, 165–6, 249, 152, 400

Churchill, James Spencer, Marquess of Blandford, 401, 433–5

Churchill, Jennie, Lady Randolph (*née* Jerome, *afterwards* Mrs George Cornwallis-West): affairs,31–2, 34–5, 45–8, 89, 97, 118; appearance, 21, 182–3; birth of Jack, 32; birth of Winston, 27–8; death, 183; family background, 21–2, 25; finances, 113–14; marriage, 19, 26–9, 34–5, 42–8; Randolph's illness, 40, 41–4, 59–62, 67; relationship with Clementine, 114–15, 118, 119; relationship with Jack, 109, 110; relationship with Winston, 45, 54, 63, 65, 71–2, 84, 89–90, 97, 100, 108, 110–11, 145, 148, 199, 285; second marriage, 97, 105, 133; South Africa hospital-ship, 94; support for Clare, 174–5; third marriage, 174–5, 182; Winston's wedding, 116–17

Churchill, John, 1st Duke of Marlborough: Blenheim, 8–9, 10–12, 328, 369; comparision with Winston, 83, 148, 230; finances, 10–11, 14; heirs, 13; influence on Winston, 12, 15, 49, 139, 141, 149, 192, 279, 281, 313, 317, 330, 332, 369–70, 385; life, 9–11; Macaulay on, 11, 74, 228; temperament, 10, 13; Winston's biography, 221, 228–31

Churchill, John Albert Edward William ('Bert'), 10th Duke of Marlborough (*earlier* Marquess of Blandford): appearance, 165; attitude to Blenheim, 399–400, 433; birth, 82; Blenheim archives, 415–16; Blenheim Christmas, 159; Daughter's coming-out party, 272; death, 433; lifestyle, 415–16; manners, 165, 238, 398–9, 415–16; marriage, 238; second marriage, 432–3; second son's name, 294–5; Vanderbilt inheritance, 399–400; Winston's wedding, 116

Churchill, John George Spencer ('Johnny'): childhood, 134–5, 155, 157–8, 162, 212; daughter's passport, 291; father's death, 354; North American visit, 217; memories of Chartwell, 211, 213, 241; memories of Clementine, 211; memories of Randolph, 157, 217–18; memories of Winston, 134–5, 158, 170, 172; Randolph's coming-of-age party, 6; temperament, 157–8, 213

Churchill, John George Vanderbilt Henry Spencer ('Sunny'), 11th Duke of Marlborough (*earlier* Marquess of Blandford), 238, 294, 400–1, 416, 433

Churchill, John Strange Spencer ('Jack'):
appearance, 105; birth, 32; Blenheim
Christmas, 159, 162; career, 84;
Chartwell Christmas, 212; childhood,
45, 48–9, 51, 53; children, 134, 146,
155, 158; death, 353–4; death of
mother, 183; First World War, 145–6,
155, 158; Gallipoli, 145–6; marriage,
109–12, 115, 116; North American
visit, 217; Randolph's coming-of-age
party, 6; relationship with brother, 6,
48–9, 109–12, 134, 136, 145–6, 218;
relationship with father, 58, 61, 62;
relationship with mother, 97, 183;
South African war, 94; temperament, 6,
45,48
Churchill, John Winston Spencer, 7th
Duke of Marlborough, 15, 16–17, 19,
21–2, 26–8, 30–2, 51
Churchill, June (*née* Osborne), 359–60,
366, 387, 391, 397, 410–11, 430
Churchill, Laura, Duchess of Marlborough
see Charteris, Laura
Churchill, Lilian, Duchess of Marlborough,
54–6
Churchill, Marigold, 160, 179–80, 181,
183–4, 188
Churchill, Mary (Mrs Christopher
Soames): appearance, 296, 336; birth,
190; Chartwell, 353, 357, 397;
Chequers Christmas, 296, 298;
childhood, 6, 194–5, 207, 211, 241,
256; children, 357, 397, 427; *Churchill
Family Album*, 39; death of father, 422,
422; Diana's suicide, 419; family
history, 39, 119, 184; father's grave,
435; lifestyle, xv, 397, 427–8; love
affairs, 336; marriage, 351–3;
memories of Winston, 343; on
Randolph, 358; Quebec conference,
331, 336; relationship with father, 323,
343, 345, 405; relationship with
mother, 262, 335–6, 345, 357;
Sarah–Vic separation, 303; Sutherland
portrait of Winston, 385, 387;
temperament, 296, 335–6; visits to
La Pausa, 380; wartime, 275, 335–6,
345
Churchill, Mary, Duchess of Marlborough,
238, 294–5, 399, 401, 415–16, 430
Churchill, Minnie (Mary Caroline, *née*
d'Erlanger), 415, 423, 432
Churchill, Pamela (*née* Digby, *later* Mrs
Leland Hayward, *then* Mrs Averell
Harriman): appearance, 277, 300, 311;
background, 276; Chequers Christmas,
296; Churchill Club, 310–11, 350;
divorce, 350; friendship with Averell
Harriman, 300–2, 321, 350, 429;
lifestyle, 350–1, 359, 398, 412, 429–30;
marriage, 277–8; memories of Winston,
293–4; naming of son, 294–5;
pregnancy, 278, 293; relationship with
Randolph, 298–9, 308–9, 310–11,
321–2, 388; relationship with son, 299,
310, 351, 398, 413; second marriage,
412–13; third marriage, 429
Churchill, Peregrine Spencer: career, 213,
415; childhood, 155, 157–8, 212;
father's death, 354; memories of
Chartwell, 205, 213-14
Churchill, Lord Randolph: appearance, 21,
93; Aylesford affair, 29–31, 32, 34, 37;
death, 4, 62, 63, 183; education, 18–19;
finances, 42, 44, 47, 54; illness, 39–44,
58–62; marriage, 19–20, 26–9, 34–5,
42–3, 44; plans for Sunny, 77; political
career, 4, 26–7, 28, 32–8, 43–4, 46–7,
199, 219; political views, 101, 158–9;
relationship with brother, 51, 55, 62;
relationship with Winston, 44, 46–7,
53–4, 56, 58–9, 62, 64, 74, 199, 212,
344; temperament, 18–19, 33, 93
Churchill, Randolph: American visit,
415–16; appearance, 1, 159, 273, 310,
425–6; author's encounter with, xv;
biography of father, 39, 411–12,
415–16, 420–1, 426; birth, 127–8; birth
of grandson, 423; Blenheim party,
272–3; Blenheim visit, 232; brawls,
223–4, 387–8; Chequers Christmas,
296; childhood, 130, 155–9, 162–3,
190, 194, 212–13; coming-of-age party,
1–3, 219, 224; coronation title, 371;
death, xv, 426; death of father, 422;
death of sister, 184; divorces, 349–50,
387, 391; drinking, 223–4, 310,
349–50, 366, 375, 389, 392, 409; East
Bergholt, 409–10, 420–1; father's
funeral, 424; father's retirement, 375;
French Riviera, 234–5; gambling debts,
241, 298–9; health, 420–1; Hitler
reporting, 220–2; journalism, 3, 220–2,
224, 349–50, 388, 408; last years,
425–6; lawsuits, 388–9; leg injury, 340;
lifestyle, 349–50; love affairs, 224,
272, 276, 410–11; love for Diana
Mitford, 214, 223, 246, 249, 289, 290,
291; love for Laura, 272, 276, 320, 359,
388, 432; marriage, 277–8; opinions of,
157, 207, 234, 292; 'The Other Club',
382; Oxford Union debate, 235;

political ambitions, 3; political career, 256–7, 293, 302, 308–9, 342, 366; relationship with children, 397-8; relationship with Eden, 365–6, 375, 387, 388; relationship with father, 130, 145, 158–9, 200, 210, 212–13, 217–18, 224–5, 235, 251, 257, 276–7, 292–3, 301, 307–12, 319–22, 340, 350, 358, 366, 373, 375, 389–91, 411–12; relationship with mother, 158, 207, 213, 277, 292, 312, 324, 327, 387, 411; relationship with Onassis, 406, 408; relationship with Pamela, 310–11, 321–2; relationship with sisters, 266–7, 367–8, 392, 418; relationship with Soames, 358, 387, 391, 397, 411; *The Rise and Fall of Sir Anthony Eden*, 388; scandal in Venice, 223–4; school, 179, 207, 212; second marriage, 359–60, 366; Tehran visit, 316, 319–21; temperament, 130, 157, 162–3, 181, 213, 224–5, 278; war declared, 274, war service, 275, 278, 292, 298, 301–2, 307, 312, 325–7, 339-40; Wavertree election, 265–7; Yugoslavia mission, 325–7, 339–40

Churchill, Randolph (son of Winston the younger), 423, 432

Churchill, Rebecca, Marchioness of Blandford (*née* Few-Brown), 435

Churchill, Robert Spencer, 400

Churchill, Lady Rosamond Spencer, 16, 28

Churchill, Rosita, Duchess of Marlborough (*née* Douglas), 433

Churchill, Sally Spencer, 291

Churchill, Lady Sarah Spencer (daughter of 10th Duke), 272, 294

Churchill, Sarah (*later* Mrs Vic Oliver, *then* Mrs Anthony Beauchamp, *then* Lady Audley): appearance, 208, 258, 318; attitude to Mosleys, 290; Beauchamp's suicide, 393, 394; birth, 139; 'Bolshie deb', 235, 241, 257;career, 226, 257–61, 303, 304, 348–9, 351, 358, 366, 392, 394, 417, 426–7; Chartwell, 190; Chequers Christmas, 296; childhood, 155–8, 179–80, 181, 190, 194, 209, 214, 223; dancing lessons, 249, 257; death, 427; divorce, 348–9; drink problem, xv, 358, 391–4, 416–17, 422, 424, 426–7; father's death, 422, father's funeral, 424; father's illness, 322–3, 371, 373; French Riviera, 234–5; German visit, 221; health, 158, 179, 181, 208, 351; last years, 427; lifestyle, 426–7;

London season, 226, 241; lovers, 426; Marrakesh visit, 325; marriage, 270–1, 275, 393; on father's nightmares, 354; relationship with father, 214, 262–3, 270–1, 303–4, 319, 322, 337–8, 345–6, 371, 373, 393–4, 422, 426; relationship with mother, 207–8, 209, 226, 263, 319, 338, 427; relationship with Randolph, 319; school, 179; second marriage, 366–7, 392–3; separation from Vic, 303–5, 337; Tehran visit, 316, 318–19, 337; temperament, 6, 214, 258, 263, 304; third marriage, 417–18; Vic Oliver affair, 260–7, 270–1, 275; visits to La Pausa, 380, 392; WAAF, 303, 305, 318, 337–8, 345; wartime, 274–5; Winant love affair, 338–9, 348–9, 358; Winant's suicide, 357–8, 393; Yalta, 337

Churchill, Sarah, Duchess of Marlborough, 9-11, 139, 149, 230

Churchill, Lady Sarah Spencer (daughter of 8th Duke), 16, 28

Churchill, Susan, Marchioness of Blandford (*née* Hornby), 401

Churchill, Sir Winston (father of 1st Duke), 9

Churchill, Winston Spencer: abdication issue, 267–71; Admiralty, 128, 129, 131–2, 139-44, 160, 274–6; American visit, 306–7; Antwerp, 137–9, 279; Anzio, 328; appearance, 96, 101, 105–6, 325, 386, 401, 405; appendicitis, 190–1; army career, 63–6, 69–73, 85; army plans, 57–8, 60, 63; Arnhem, 332; attitude to Blenheim, 49, 51–2, 57, 115, 162, 166, 201–2; attitude to Labour Party, 195, 216, 343, 347–8; attitude to war, 125, 136–7, 140, 149, 167–8, 279, 330–1; Battle of Britain, 280, 297; belief in destiny, 5, 87–8, 94, 136–7, 150, 275, 283; Bill's funeral, 182; biography of father, 31, 36, 98, 100–1; birth, 27–8; 'Black and Tans', 176–7; 'Black Dog', 13, 66–9, 108, 123, 152, 225, 275, 343–4, 346; Blenheim Christmas, 159, 162; Blenheim engagement anniversary party, 401; Blenheim party, 273; broadcasts, 279–80; Chancellor of the Exchequer, 198–201, 210; Chartwell, 186–90, 193–6, 201–6, 240–1, 344, 353, 383, 390–1; Chequers Christmas, 296–8; childhood, 28–9, 44–7, 51–3, 124; Clare Sheridan in Russia, 170–5; Colonial Secretary, 170, 176–7, 189;

Conservative Party, 101, 103–4, 191, 197–8, 220, 347; coronation of Elizabeth, 364, 368–71; Crete, 301; Cuba, 65–6, 91; D-Day landings, 329, 330; Dardanelles, 140–5, 150, 151–2; death, 422–3; death of daughter, 183–4; death of father, 62, 63–4, 89, 108, 423; death of mother, 182–3; depression, 13, 66–9, 107–8, 123–5, 145, 152–3, 344–5; Diana's wedding, 227; Dublin, 176–7; Duchy of Lancaster, 144; dukedom refusal, 375–6, 390; Dundee elections, 160, 190–1; Dunkirk, 280; education, 44–5, 47, 48, 52–4; *Enchantress*, 132–4; entertaining, 129–30; Epping elections, 197, 216; Esmond Romilly's death, 305–7; finances, 84, 109, 119, 156, 187, 205–6, 218–19, 233, 234, 250, 357; Flanders, 149–50; French Riviera, 233–5; friends, 204; funeral, 402–4, 423–4; Gallipoli, 141, 143, 145–6, 279; games with children, 134–5, 158, 162, 194; general election (1945), 341, 342; general election (1951), 361; General Strike, 200–1; German rearmament, 239, 240; Gold Standard, 200, 205; Goonie affair, 109–12; Grand Alliance, 307; Greece, 333; Harrow School, 47, 48, 52–3, 57, 66, 124–5, 382; health, 190, 219, 224, 307, 315, 320, 322–3, 325, 329, 331, 362, 371–4, 402, 404; *History of the English-Speaking Peoples*, 344, 378, 383, 386; Hitler comparison, 243–4; Hitler interest, 244–5, 249, 341; Home Secretary, 123, 126–7; image, 83–4; India, 221, 233, 236, 239, 251; Iraq, 176; Ireland, 176–7; 'Iron Curtain' speech, 347; journalism, 65–6, 72–3, 86, 91, 94, 205–6, 240, 250; last days, 421–2; leadership, 278–83, 317–18, 329–31, 347–8; Liberal Party, 104, 108, 121–2, 134, 191, 197; liberation of Paris, 332; lisp, 72, 98; love affairs, 90, 106–7; Lullenden, 155–6; maiden speech, 96–7; *The Malakand Field Force*, 73, 84–5, 171; *Marlborough: His Life and Times*, 221, 223, 228–31, 233, 235–6, 239–40, 250, 261; Marlborough influence, 12, 15, 49, 69, 137, 149, 192, 230, 279, 281, 313, 330, 332, 385; Marrakesh, 325–6; marriage, 115–17, 119–21; meets Clementine, 112–13; Mosley embarrassment, 288–91, 306; Munitions Ministry, 153, 154–5, 160,

167, 178–9, 239; Mount Street house, 97–8; *My Early Life*, 63–4; naming of grandson, 294–5; Napoleon influence, 64, 68, 71, 91, 102, 138, 170, 192, 279–80, 281, 385; National Government, 216; North American visit, 217–18; North-West Frontier, 72–3, 84, 91, 124; old age, 362–3; Oldham elections, 90, 94–5, 104; Omdurman, 86–9, 91–2, 102, 124, 137; oratory, 98–9, 375, 405; 'The Other Club', 127, 162, 382; painting, 146, 152–3, 233, 235, 250, 346, 379; Palestine, 176, 177, 180; Poland, 332; political career, 4–5, 72, 90, 94–5, 96–7, 101–4, 108–9, 160, 186–7, 191, 195, 197–201, 216, 278, 342–4, 353; Potsdam, 342; press blackout of illness, 372; Prime Minister (1951), 361, 362–3; 'Private Article', 354–6; racehorse, 397; reading, 71–2; relationship with aunts, 49, relationship with brother, 48–9, 109–12, 134, 352, 354; relationship with Clementine, 5–6, 119–21, 129–30, 145, 148–50, 178–81, 190–1, 200, 208–11, 217, 242, 250–3, 284–7, 309–10, 325, 334–5, 341, 345–6, 380–1, 383–4, 418; relationship with daughters, 214, 262–3, 270–1, 303–4, 319, 322–3, 337–8, 345–6, 366–9, 393–4, 419, 421, 422; relationship with father, 31, 36, 44, 46–7, 53–4, 56, 58–9, 60, 62, 63–4, 67–8, 74, 84, 96–8, 199, 212, 219, 344, 354–6, 385, 389–91; relationship with grandchildren, 397–8; relationship with mother, 45, 54, 63, 65, 71–2, 84, 87–8, 89–90, 97, 100, 108, 145, 148, 183, 199, 285; relationship with Onassis, 406–9; relationship with Pamela, 293–4, 311, 321, 350, 359; relationship with Reveses, 378–81, 392, 405–9; relationship with Roosevelt, 313–17, 330, 331–2; relationship with Soames, 352–3, 357, 358, 371, 373, 375, 391, 405, 422; relationship with son, 1–4, 127–8, 130, 145, 150, 158–9, 210, 212–13, 217–18, 224–5, 235, 251, 257, 276, 277, 292–3, 301, 307–12, 318–22, 339–40, 350, 358, 366, 373, 382, 389–91, 411–12; relationship with Stalin, 314–16, 319; relationship with Sunny, 7, 51, 56–7, 61, 115, 147–8, 204, 227, 237–8; retirement issue, 346, 347, 362, 363, 368–9, 371–6; *The River War*, 88, 141, 354; Russian policy,

168–70, 177, 279; Sandhurst, 54, 56–8;
Sarah–Vic Oliver affair, 260–7, 270–1,
302–4, 321; *Savrola*, 73–5, 89, 90,
97–8, 99, 102, 108, 137, 141, 243, 269,
279, 391; 'The Scaffolding of
Rhetoric', 99; *The Second World War*,
356–7; servants, 203–4, 383; Siege of
Sidney Street, 126–7; South Africa,
90–5, 124, 137; Sudan, 85–6;
Sutherland portrait, 384–7, 412; Tehran
conference, 316–17, 319–20, 326, 369;
Tonypandy massacre, 126; Treasury,
198–201, 210; war declared, 274–5;
War Office, 160, 168–70, 175; wartime
leadership, 278–83, 317–18, 329–31;
Westminster by-election, 195, 198;
working habits, 229–30; *The World
Crisis*, 192, 357; Yalta, 333;
Yugoslavia, 326–7
Churchill, Winston Spencer (junior):
appearance, 414; birth of son, 423;
childhood, 296, 298–9, 308, 310, 321,
351, 398; coronation of Elizabeth, 370;
grandfather's death, 422; grandfather's
funeral, 424; health, 359; journalism,
415; marriage, 415; naming, 294–5,
415, 420; political career, 415, 430–2;
relationship with father, 398, 413–14,
419; relationship with mother, 299,
310, 351, 398, 413–14; relationship
with grandfather, 321, 398, 414–15;
scandal, 431–2; school, 359, 415;
temperament, 414
Ciano, Count, 321
Clark, Kenneth, 386
Clemenceau, Georges, 155
Clermont-Tonnerre, Duchess of, 163–4
Cochran, C. B., 258–60
Cockrane, Bourke, 65
Colville, Sir John ('Jock'): Hitler's death,
341; knowledge of Sarah–Winant
affair, 339; memories of Winston, 283,
330, 331; on Clarissa's engagement,
365; on Clementine, 129, 208, 286,
287, 323, 334, 380; on Mary, 296, 336;
on Mosleys, 290; on Pamela and
Harriman, 300; on Randolph, 292, 358;
on Roosevelt's illness, 333; on Soames,
358, 373; on Winant, 349; on
Winston's attitude to Queen, 370; on
Winston's attitude to Randolph, 301,
312; on Winston's entertaining,
129–30, 331; Tunis, 323; Winston's
death, 423; Winston's illness, 371–3;
Winston's retirement, 375–6
Connolly, Cyril, 272, 360

Constantine, King of Greece, 408
Cooper, Diana: birthday party in Venice,
223; Blenheim christening party, 294;
Blenheim rape attempt, 161;
Clementine confidences, 328, 334; on
Churchill's plans for Mary, 352; on
Moran, 322; on Pamela, 351; on
Winston, 210, 325; relationship with
Conrad Russell, 209; Sutherland's
portrait of Winston, 385, 386
Cooper, Duff, 302, 325, 351
Cornfield, Cass, 359
Cornwallis-West, Jennie *see* Churchill,
Jennie
Cornwallis-West, Patsy, 89
Coty, President René, 381
Coward, Noël, 259, 350, 381
Cromwell, Oliver, 278
Cunard, Emerald, Lady, 223
Curzon, George Nathaniel, Marquess
Curzon of Kedleston, 34, 146, 183

D'Abernon, Sir Edgar Vincent, Viscount,
31
Dalton, Hugh, 299
D'Annunzio, Gabriele, 107
Deacon, Gladys *see* Churchill, Gladys
Deakin, William ('Bill'), 356
Denikin, General Anton Ivanovich, 170
Derby, Edward Henry Stanley, 15th Earl
of, 29
Derby, Edward George Villiers Stanley, 17
Earl of, 412.
D'Erlanger, Sir Gerard, 415
D'Erlanger, Mary Caroline ('Minnie') *see*
Churchill, Minnie
Diana, Princess of Wales, 13
Digby family, 351
Digby, Edward Kenelm ('Carnation'), 11th
Baron, 276, 311
Digby, Pamela *see* Churchill
Dilke, Sir Charles, 64
Disraeli, Benjamin, 15–16, 18, 30, 32,
35–6, 72
Doble, Georgia Louise ('Bunny'), 237
Douglas, Air Chief Marshal Sholto, 338
Drogheda, Henry Charles Ponsonby
Moore, 12th Earl of, 300
Dudley, Eric, 3rd Earl of, 276, 320, 359
Dudley, Laura, Countess of *see* Charteris
Duff family, 161
Duke, Doris, 223
Duncannon, Frederick Edward Neuflize
Ponsonby, Viscount, 336
Dunn, Lady Mary, 276
Dzerzhinsky, Felix Edmundovich, 172

Eden, Anthony (*later* Earl of Avon): Greek policy, 333; health, 386–9, 371, 374, 396; marriage, 364–5; on Winston–Roosevelt relationship, 315; relationship with Randolph, 273; relationship with Winston, 273, 329, 364; Roosevelt's funeral, 334; Suez, 395–6; waiting to succeed Winston, 346, 347, 362, 364, 368, 374–5

Eden, Clarissa (*née* Churchill): Austrian holiday, 262; Chartwell Christmas, 212; on Clementine–Winston relationship, 209; father's death, 354; husband's career, 368, 374–5, 395–6; husband's health, 371, 374, 396; marriage, 364–5, 368

Edward VII, King (*earlier* Albert Edward, Prince of Wales): Aylesford affair, 29–31, 33; friendship with Cassel, 187; relationship with Lady Randolph, 34, 59, 84; relationship with Lady Warwick, 32; relationship with Lord Randolph, 19, 27, 29–31, 34, 59; relationship with Winston, 84, 85

Edward VIII, King (*earlier* Prince of Wales, *later* Duke of Windsor), 236, 265–71, 281, 381

Eisenhower, General Dwight, 314, 323, 369, 405

Elgin, Victor Alexander Bruce, 9th Earl of, 104, 109

Elizabeth, Empress of Austria, 117–18

Elizabeth, Queen, 281, 291, 297

Elizabeth II, Queen (*earlier* Princess Elizabeth), 291, 364, 370, 372, 375–6, 402, 422–5

Elliot, Maxine, 106, 188, 233–5, 258, 377–8

Entwhistle, Anthony *see* Beauchamp

Epstein, Jacob 12

Erleigh, Gerald Rufus Isaacs, Viscount, 1

Esher, Reginald Baliol Brett, 2nd Viscount, 120

Eugene of Austria, Prince, 313, 317

Eugènie, Empress, 24

Everest, Elizabeth, 28, 45, 75, 108, 130, 210, 285

Falmouth, Evelyn ('Star') Boscawen, 7th Viscount, 31

Feiling, Sir Keith, 229

Feisal, King of Iraq, 176

Ferdinand, Archduke, 134

Fielding, Daphne, 273

Fisher, Admiral John Arbuthnot ('Jacky'), 140–2, 143, 144, 145, 151

Fleming, Ann, 387

Fleming, Ian, xv, 272, 387

Fogazzaro, Antonio, 349

Foot, Michael, 207, 366

Forbes, Alastair, 350, 360

Forster, Colonel, 31

French, Field-Marshal Sir John, 148, 149

Freud, Sigmund, 165–6

Frewen, Clara (*née* Jerome), 21–2, 49, 62, 116, 171

Frewen, Clare *see* Sheridan

Frewen, Moreton, 49, 84, 116, 171, 172, 174

Gandhi, Mahatma, 221, 236, 239, 244, 261

Gardiner, A. G., 125

Garibaldi, Giuseppe, 280

Garner, Miss, 77

Gassman, Vittorio, 349

Gaulle, General Charles de, 286–7, 325, 332, 381, 415, 428

George V, King, 139, 173, 200, 227, 239, 250, 290

George VI, King: coronation, 369; death, 363–4; relationship with Winston, 278, 281–2, 297, 330, 341; wartime, 282, 291, 330, 341

George II, King of Greece, 333

Gibbon, Edward, 19, 71–2, 88, 282

Gilbert, Martin, xvi, 426

Giraudier, Antonio, 382

Gladstone, William Ewart, 34–6, 58, 60, 72, 403

Goebbels, Magda, 248

Goebbels, Paul Joseph, 248

Gorbachev, Raisa, 429

Gordon, General Charles George, 85, 86

Graebner, Walter, 374, 383

Guest family, 116, *see also* Wimborne

Guest, Freddie, 170, 171, 179, 186

Guinness, Bryan, 223, 246

Guinness, Diana *see* Mosley

Guinness, Kenelm, 252

Gunther, John, 277

Hailsham, Douglas McGarel Hogg, 1st Viscount, 1

Haldane, Aylmer, 91–3

Halifax, Edward, 1st Earl of, 281

Hall, Admiral Sir Reginald ('Blinker'), 140

Hamblin, Grace: Clementine's war work, 335; Colville relations, 286; death of George VI, 363; Moscow, 341; on Chartwell, 240; on Clementine, 181, 190, 346; on Randolph, 312; on Winston, 240, 411; Tunis, 323

Hamilton, General Sir Ian, 146
Hammersley, Lilian, 54–6
Hanfstaengel, Putzi, 222
Harmsworth, Esmond, 1
Harriman, Averell, 299–302, 307–8, 310, 311, 321, 350, 429
Harriman, E.H., 299
Harriman, Kathleen, 300, 301, 310
Harris, Frank, 40
Hartington, Spencer Compton Cavendish, Marquess of, 30
Hauk, Minnie, 23
Hayward, Brooke, 413
Hayward, Leland, 412–13, 429
Hayward, Nancy, 413
Hearst, William Randolph, 218
Heath, Edward, 429
Henley, Sylvia, 377
Hills, Nanny, 308
Hirsch, Baron Moritz von, 34
Hitler, Adolf: comparison with Winston, 243; death, 341; invasions, 278; invasion plans, 297; Mosleys, 247–9, 289; Munich, 273, 370; nearly meets Winston, 222; Poland, 273–4; Randolph's reporting, 220–1; Rhineland occupation, 261; Unity Mitford affair, 214, 245–7, 288
Hogg, Quintin, 1, 2
Hornby, Susan, 401
Horne, Sir Robert, 177
Horner family, 157
Horner, Lady Frances, 183
Houston, Lucy, Lady, 257;
Hozier, Lady Blanche: appearance, 117, 196; children, 113–14, 117–18; Clementine's wedding, 117; death, 208; drinking, 113, 196, 253, 392; family, 113, 214; gambling, 113, 182, 196, 253, 298; illness, 196; love affairs, 45–6, 113, 117–18; marriage, 113, 114; son's suicide, 181–2
Hozier, Clementine *see* Churchill, Clementine
Hozier, Sir Henry Montagu, 45–6, 113, 114, 117–18
Hozier, Katherine ('Kitty'), 113, 117
Hozier, Nellie *see* Romilly
Hozier, William ('Bill'): Clementine's wedding, 116; drinking, 392; gambling, 182, 298; paternity, 113, 117; suicide, 181, 253; war service, 146
Hudson, Robert Spear Hudson, 1st Viscount, 418
Hunt, Richard Morris, 78
Hussein, King of Jordan, 415

Iddesleigh, Walter Stafford Northcote, 2nd Earl of, 48
Inches (Winston's valet), 203
Inonu, President Ismet, 320
Iznaga, Consuelo, 78

Jackson, Ernest Leroy, 426
James, Edward, 223
James, Henry, 123
James II, King, 360
Jennings, Louis, 39
Jerome, Clara *see* Frewen
Jerome, Clara (Mrs Leonard), 21–5, 26, 77
Jerome, Jennie *see* Churchill
Jerome, Leonard, 21–4, 26, 27, 47, 54
Jerome, Leonie *see* Leslie
Joycelyn, John Strange (*later* 5th Earl of Roden), 32
Jones, Dr Ernest, 165
Jowett, Benjamin, 32

Kamenev, Lev Borisovich, 172
Keith, Dr, 60–2
Kennedy family, 415, 420
Kennedy, Eunice, 272
Kennedy, Jackie, 407
Kennedy, President John, 419
Kent, George Edward Alexander Edmund, Duke of, 272, 359
Keppel, Alice, 121
Keynes, John Maynard, 140, 192, 200
Khashoggi, Adnan, 431–2
Khashoggi, Soraya, 431–2
Kinsky, Count Charles Rudolph Ferdinand Andreas, 46, 48, 54, 59, 61, 98
Kipling, Rudyard, 134, 148
Kitchener, Field-Marshal Sir Horatio Herbert, 85–9, 138, 142–3, 147, 151
Knollys, Francis, 27
Korda, Alexander, 250, 251, 364
Kun, Béla, 168

Lambton, Antony Claud Frederick, Viscount, 39, 420
Lancaster, Osbert, 324
Landemare, Georgina, 282
Lansdowne, Henry Charles Keith Petty-Fitzmaurice, 5th Marquess of, 147
Lansdowne, Maud Evelyn, Lady, 51
László, Sir Philip, 1, 414
Laval, Pierre, 288
Lavery, Hazel, 152
Law, Andrew Bonar, 144, 146, 191
Lawrence, T. E., 180, 213
Lenin, Vladimir Ilyich, 168–9, 171, 172–3
Leopold III, King of Belgium, 351

Leslie, Colonel Alexander, 49, 116
Leslie, Anita, 32, 40, 174, 195, 226, 232
Leslie, Leonie (*née* Jerome), 21, 23, 32, 49, 61–2, 116
Leslie, Shane, 49, 174, 183
Lincoln, Abraham, 67
Lind, Jennie, 23
Lindemann, Frederick Alexander ('the Prof', *later* 1st Viscount Cherwell): advice, 229, 249, 282; Blenheim visit, 202–3; Chartwell visits, 204, 211, 212, 213, 215; Chequers Christmas, 296; death, 382; description, 204; friendship with Winston, 204, 224–5, 282; peerage, 292, 302; Randolph's coming-of-age party, 1
Llewellyn, Sir Harry, 258
Lloyd George, David: at Chartwell, 213; collapse of government, 190–1; Dardanelles crisis, 144; Irish Treaty, 177; Lullenden visits, 156, 157; naval budget, 134; opinion of Winston, 139; oratory, 96; peace conference, 169; Prime Minister, 151, 153, 160; relationship with Winston, 116, 120, 122, 129, 133, 137, 144, 174, 184, 186–9, 298; Russian policy, 169, 170, 172, 175; transport strike, 127
Lockhart, Sir Robert Bruce, 2, 5, 220, 310
Londonderry, Charles William Stewart, 3rd Marquess of, 15
Long, Laura, Lady *see* Charteris
Long, Walter Francis David, 2nd Viscount, 272
Longford, Elizabeth, Lady, 118
Lothian, Philip Henry Kerr, 11th Marquess of, 305
Louis XIV, King, 10, 230, 282
Luce, Clare, 276
Luce, Henry, 378
Lucket, Phyllis, 304
Lugard, Flora, Lady, 112
Lyttelton, Oliver, 301, 362

Macaulay, Thomas Babington, 9, 11, 52, 71–2, 74, 228–9, 235, 282
MacDonald, Ramsay, 2, 195, 216, 221
Maclean, Fitzroy, 326
Macmillan, Harold, 198, 211, 333, 363, 371, 396, 402–4
Mahler, Gustav, 260
Malenkow, Georgi, 369
Manchester, George Victor Drogo Montagu, 8th Duke of, 78
Mao Tse Tung, 281
Margaret Rose, Princess, 291

Marsh, Eddie: Beaverbrook's description, 148; Chartwell visits, 204; description of Winston, 151; East Africa, 110; Egypt, 180; Jack's wedding, 115; Lady St Helier friendship, 112; relationship with Clementine, 212; Sassoon–Winston meeting, 167; storytelling, 215
Marshall, Mr (estate agent), 189
Martin, John, 296, 323
Martin, Nanny, 414
Martindale, Father, 237
Mary, Queen, 227
Masterman, C. F., 122, 127, 141
Maugham, Somerset, 378, 384, 412
Medlicott, Paul, 337
Meinertzhagen, Colonel Richard, 53, 124, 176
Middleton, Captain W. G. ('Bay'), 46, 117–18
Mihailovich, Draza, 326
Milan Obrenovich, King of Serbia, 49, 171
Milner, Sir Alfred, 1st Viscount, 91
Mistinguett, 259
Mitford family, 114, 116, 214, *see also* Redesdale
Mitford, Deborah, 214
Mitford, Diana *see* Mosley
Mitford, Jessica, 214, 246, 305–7
Mitford, Nancy, 214, 254, 311, 430
Mitford, Tom, 214
Mitford, Unity, 214, 241, 245–7, 257, 288
Monckton, Walter, 267
Montagu, Edwin, 143, 145, 159
Montague Browne, Anthony, 383, 403–4, 409, 418, 420, 421
Montesquieu, Charles de, 165
Montgomery of Alamein, Field-Marshal Bernard Law, 1st Viscount, 334, 370
Moore, George, 34
Moran, Charles Wilson, Baron: coronation of Elizabeth, 364; on Clementine, 323; on Sandys, 337, 352; on Winston's clinging to power, 372–3; on Winston's image, 385, 386; on Winston's moods, 123–4, 343, 345–6; opinion of Winston's health, 334–5, 362, 371, 377, 381–2, 403, 404; reassuring Winston, 421; Tehran conference, 320; Winston's belief in destiny, 283; Winston's convalescence, 324; Winston's death, 422; Winston's pneumonia, 331, 402
Morley, John, 137
Morton, Colonel Desmond, 244, 249
Moses, 240

Mosley, Alexander, 289
Mosley, Cimmie, 247
Mosley, Diana (*née* Mitford, *then* Mrs Bryan Guinness): at Chartwell, 214–15, 289; Diana Cooper's party, 223; friendship with Hitler, 247–9, 289; love for Mosley, 223, 246–7; marriage to Mosley, 248; on Diana, 395; wartime experiences, 288–91, 306
Mosley, Nicholas, 248
Mosley, Oswald: British Union of Fascists, 245, 246–8, 255; marriage, 248, 289; meetings with Hitler, 248–9, 288; Randolph's coming-of-age party, 1, 288; Diana love affair, 223, 246–8; relationship with Winston, 52, 71; wartime experiences, 288–91, 306
Mowatt, Sir Francis, 100–1
Moyne, Walter Guinness, 1st Baron, 251–3, 406
Mugabe, Robert, 428
Muggeridge, Malcolm, 382, 388
Munnings, Sir Alfred, 385
Mussolini, Benito, 243, 246, 259, 273, 288, 321, 340

Namier, Sir Lewis, 236
Napoleon Bonaparte, Emperor: influence on Winston, 64, 68–9, 71, 91, 102, 138, 170, 192, 279–80, 281, 385; objectives, 64; Russian campaign, 170; sleep patterns, 230; stance, 91
Napoleon III, Emperor, 24–5
Neilson, Nigel, 408
Nelson, Horatio, Viscount, 71, 281, 331, 386, 403
Nemon, Oscar, 386
Niarchos, Stavros, 416
Nicholas II, Tsar, 19, 169
Nicholson, Jenny, 257–8, 264–5
Nicholson, Sir William, 241, 257
Nicolson, Harold, 203, 218, 276, 309, 321, 347, 363
Niehans, Professor, 378
Niven, David, 399
Nocho, Lobo, 426
Norfolk, Bernard Marmaduke Fitzalan Howard, 16th Duke of, 403
Northcliffe, Alfred Harmsworth, Viscount, 134

Oliver, Vic: background, 260; career, 260, 296, 303–4, 337; Chequers Christmas, 296, 298; Churchills' attitude to, 262–3, 266, 271, 293, 298, 303–4, 321, 367, 392; divorce, 348; love affair with

Sarah, 261–7; manners, 296; marriage, 270, 302–4, 426; memoirs, 337; separation from Sarah, 303–4, 337; wartime, 274–5, 296
Olivier, Laurence, 331, 423
Onassis, Aristotle, 382, 405–9, 416, 424
Onassis, Athina (Tina, *later* Lady Blandford, *then* Mrs Stavros Niarchos), 407–8, 416
Onassis, Christina, 434
Orpen, William, 144–5
Osborne, June *see* Churchill

Paget, Minnie, Lady (*née* Stevens), 79
Pakenham-Walsh, Colonel Ridley, 223, 229
Parker, Al, 349
Parker, Maggie, 393
Patti, Adelina, 23
Pavlov (interpreter), 314
Pearman, Violet, 262
Peel, Sir Robert, 72
Perkins, Mr (Blenheim organist), 163
Philip, Prince, 375
Philip, Terence, 252–3, 256, 285
Picasso, Pablo, 385
Plowden, Pamela (*later* Lady Lytton), 64, 90, 106
Plowden, Sir Trevor, 90
Pollock, Ellen, 261, 394, 417
Pope, Alexander, 11
Porch, Montagu, 174, 182–36
Powell, Michael, 331
Pressburger, Emeric, 331
Prior, Robin, 192
Proust, Marcel, 165, 202
Pugh, Miss (Winston's secretary), 378–9

Quain, Sir Richard, 60
Quayle, Anthony, 394
Quennell, Peter, 360
Quisling, Vidkum Abraham Lauritz, 288

Rainier, Prince, of Monaco, 381, 409
Ratendone, Viscount, 234
Reading, Rufus Isaacs, 1st Marquess of, 1, 171
Reagan, Nancy, 429
Reagan, Ronald, 431
Redesdale *see also* Mitford
Redesdale, Bertram Mitford, 1st Baron, 114, 116–17, 245
Redesdale, Clementine Mitford, Lady, 113
Redesdale, David Bertram Ogilvy Mitford, 2nd Baron, 214
Redesdale, Sydney, Lady ('Muv'), 290

Reves, Emery, 378–81, 383, 397, 405–9
Rhodes, Cecil, 102–3
Richard, Cliff, 394
Richmond and Gordon, Charles Henry
    Gordon Lennox, 6th Duke of, 72
Riddell, George Allardice Riddell, 1st
    Baron, 156, 157, 170, 206
Rilke, Rainer Maria, 165
Roberts, Frederick Sleigh, 1st Earl, 65, 94
Rodin, Auguste, 165
Roger, Madame Pol, 382
Romilly, Constancia, 305–6
Romilly, Esmond, 212, 253–5, 305–7
Romilly, Giles, 212, 305
Romilly, Nellie (*née* Hozier), 113, 117,
    136, 181–2, 212, 253, 255
Rommel, General Erwin, 307
Roose, Dr Robson, 41, 58–9
Roosevelt, Eleanor, 306–7, 323, 334
Roosevelt, Elliot, 319
Roosevelt, President Franklin Delano:
    death, 333–4, 348; envoys to Britain,
    299; Grand Alliance, 299, 307; Poland,
    332; Quebec conferences, 323, 331–2;
    relationship with Clementine, 323, 331;
    relationship with Sarah, 318;
    relationship with Winston, 313–14,
    315–16, 330; Tehran conference,
    316–18, 320, 369; Winston's visit,
    306–7; Yalta, 333
Rosebery, Archibald Philip Primrose, 5th
    Earl, 36, 42, 47, 64, 100, 102, 158
Rothschild, Elie, 351, 398
Rothschild, Lionel, 106
Rothermere, Harold Sidney Harmsworth,
    1st Viscount, 1, 206, 219–20, 256, 297
Rowan, Sir Leslie, 330, 342
Rowntree, Seebohm, 121
Rowse, A. L., 211, 383, 401
Rubens, Peter Paul, 17
Rubinstein, Helena, 384
Russell, Conrad, 209
Russell, Flora, 209
Russell, Wendy, 378–81, 392, 405–6, 409
Rutherfurd, Winthrop, 79
Rysbrack, Michael, 12, 370

St Helier, Mary, Lady, 112, 114
St-Simon, duc de, 71, 282
Salisbury, Robert Arthur Talbot Gascoyne,
    3rd Marquess of: Prime Minister, 36–7,
    41, 85; relationship with Lady
    Randolph, 35, 84; relationship with
    Lord Randolph, 4, 36–7, 41, 43–4, 47,
    58, 103, 236; relationship with
    Winston, 84, 85–6

Samek, Baron von, 260, 262
Sandys, Celia, 302, 394–5, 429
Sandys, Diana *see* Churchill
Sandys, Duncan (*later* Baron Duncan-
    Sandys): affairs, 337, 367, 395; car
    accident, 302; Clementine's opinion of,
    324; death, 429; divorce, 418;
    marriage, 257, 336–7, 367–8, political
    career, 257, 296, 302, 336–7, 342, 363,
    365–6, 367, 395, 396, 429; relationship
    with Winston, 257, 293, 302, 336–7,
    345, 352; second marriage, 418–19,
    429; war service, 274, 296
Sandys, Edwina, 275, 296, 419, 429
Sandys, Julian, 274, 296, 429
Sandys, Marie-Claire (*formerly* Lady
    Hudson), 418–19
Sargent, John Singer, 109
Sassoon, Sir Philip, 167, 188–9
Sassoon, Siegfried, 167–8
Sawyers (Winston's valet), 383
Scawen-Blunt, Wilfred, 96, 117–18, 148
Schopenhauer, Arthur, 71
Sermoneta, Duchess of, 182
Shaw, George Bernard, 133
Sheridan, Clare (*née* Frewen), 49, 150,
    170–5, 289
Sheridan, William, 150, 171
Shinwell, Emmanuel, 308
Shuckburgh, Evelyn, 368
Sickert, Walter, 386
Simpson, Wallis (Mrs Ernest), 265–70,
    381
Sinatra, Frank, 398
Sitwell, Edith, 237, 268
Sitwell, Osbert, 260
Sitwell, Sacheverell, 9
Smith, Lady Eleanor, 162, 164
Smith, F. E. *see* Birkenhead
Smith, Ian, 431
Smuts, General Jan, 298, 332
Soames, Charlotte, 357
Soames, Christopher: marriage, xv, 351–3,
    396; political career, 363, 365–6,
    396–7, 427–8; relationship with
    Randolph, 358, 387, 391, 397;
    relationship with Winston, 352–3, 357,
    358, 366, 371, 373, 375, 391, 397, 405,
    422; Sutherland's portrait of Winston,
    387
Soames, Emma, 357, 397, 423, 427
Soames, Jeremy, 357
Soames, Mary *see* Churchill
Soames, Nicholas, 357, 428–9
Soames, Rachel, 357
Soldati, Mario, 52, 349, 358

Southby, Commander Sir Archibald Richard James, 308, 312
Spencer, Anne, Countess of Sunderland, 13
Spencer, Charles, 3rd Duke of Marlborough and 5th Earl of Sunderland, 13
Spencer-Churchill *see* Churchill
Staël, Madame de, 14
Stalin, Joseph ('Uncle Joe'): American aid, 308; death, 369; Hitler pact, 273; 'Iron Curtain', 347; military position, 305, 307, 329, 332; Potsdam, 342; Tehran conference, 316–19, 369; Winston's Moscow visits, 314–15, 332; Yalta, 333
Stanley family, 116
Stanley, Venetia, 139, 143, 159
Stevenson, Frances, 136, 139
Stoker, Bram, 46
Storr, Anthony, 70
Strachey, Lytton, 202
Styron, William, 67
Sullavan, Margaret, 412–13
Sutherland, George Granville Leveson-Gower, 5th Duke of, 184, 234
Sutherland, Graham, 375, 384–7, 412
Sutherland, Kathleen, 384
Sykes, Sir Richard, 223

Tempest, Lord Herbert Vane, 187, 188
Thatcher, Margaret, 428, 431
Thompson, Sergeant, 196
Tilden, Philip, 189, 193
Tito, 326, 339
Toynbee, Arnold, 255
Toynbee, Philip, 255
Trafford, Tom, 42
Tree, Ronald and Nancy, 300
Trevelyan, G. M., 228, 231, 235
Trotsky, Leon, 169, 172, 173–4
Truman, President Harry S., 334, 342, 347
Twain, Mark, 95
Tweedmouth, Edward Marjoribanks, 2nd Baron, 48, 116

Vanbrugh, John, 9, 10
Vanderbilt, Commodore, 22, 77
Vanderbilt, Consuelo *see* Churchill
Vanderbilt, Mrs Cornelius II, 77, 79, 164
Vanderbilt, Gertrude, 79–80
Vanderbilt, Willie Kissim, 77, 80, 82
Vanderbilt, Mrs Willie Kissim, 77–80
Victoria, Queen, 16, 30, 36–7, 41

Wagner, Richard, 245, 247
Walpole, Horace, 11

Walton, William, 260
Warwick, Anne, Lady, 42–3, 102–3
Waugh, Auberon, 398
Waugh, Evelyn: criticism of Clarissa, 365; friendship with Randolph, 298, 340, 349–50, 360, 420; on Pamela, 311; on Randolph–Winston relationship, 387; on Winston's rhetoric, 280; Yugoslavia, 340
Wavell, General Sir Archibald Percival, 301
Webb, Beatrice, 107
Weidenfeld, George, 364
Wellington, Arthur Wellesley, 1st Duke of, 9, 13, 386, 403–4, 422
Wells, H. G., 107, 151, 169, 202, 229
Wemyss, Hugo, 117
Westminster, Hugh Richard Arthur Grosvenor ('Bendor'), 2nd Duke of: marriages, 277; mistress, 377; Normandy house, 179, 188, 209; Rolls-Royce, 154; tennis tournament, 183; yacht, 406
Westminster, Violet, Duchess of, 183
Whicker, Alan, 350
Whitney, Jock, 311, 398, 413
Whyte, Maryott ('Cousin Moppet'): Chartwell, 256, 275, 353; Mary's upbringing, 194–5, 207, 241, 256. 296, 335, 397; Sandys children, 275
Wigram, Ralph, 244
Wilhelm II, Kaiser, 125, 136, 244, 274
Willes, Peter, 234
Wilson, Dr Charles *see* Moran
Wilson family, 116
Wilson, Harold, 428
Wilson, Muriel, 106
Wilson, Lady Sarah, 161
Wilson, Woodrow, 372
Wimborne, Ivor Guest, 2nd Baron, 161
Winant, John ('Gil'): arrival in Britain, 299–300; love affair with Sarah, 318–19, 337–8, 348–9; relationship with Churchill family, 299–300, 339, 345; suicide, 357–8, 366
Windsor, Duchess of (*earlier* Mrs Ernest Simpson), 265–70, 381
Windsor, Duke of *see* Edward VIII
Wingate, John, 392
Wolfe, Sir Drummond, 65
Wyndham, George, 122

Young, Terence, 394

Zinoviev, Grigoriy Yevseyevich, 172